BIG BOSOMS
AND SQUARE JAWS

Jimmy McDonough is the author of *Shakey: Neil Young's Biography* and *The Ghastly One: The Sex-Gore Netherworld of Filmmaker Andy Milligan*. He lives in the Pacific Northwest.

Jimmy McDonough

Big Bosoms and Square Jaws

The Biography of Russ Meyer, King of the Sex Film

VINTAGE BOOKS
London

Published by Vintage 2006

2 4 6 8 10 9 7 5 3 1

Copyright © James McDonough 2005

James McDonough has asserted his right under the Copyright, Designs
and Patents Act 1988 to be identified as the author of this work

First published in Great Britain in 2005 by Jonathan Cape

Vintage
Random House, 20 Vauxhall Bridge Road,
London SW1V 2SA

Random House Australia (Pty) Limited
20 Alfred Street, Milsons Point, Sydney,
New South Wales 2061, Australia

Random House New Zealand Limited
18 Poland Road, Glenfield, Auckland 10, New Zealand

Random House South Africa (Pty) Limited
Isle of Houghton, Corner of Boundary Road & Carse O'Gowrie,
Houghton 2198, South Africa

Random House Publishers India Private Limited
301 World Trade Tower, Hotel Intercontinental Grand Complex,
Barakhamba Lane, New Delhi 110 001, India

The Random House Group Limited Reg. No. 954009

www.randomhouse.co.uk

A CIP catalogue record for this book is available from
the British Library

ISBN 9780099464648 (from Jan 2007)
ISBN 0099464640

Papers used by Random House are natural,
recyclable products made from wood grown in sustainable forests;
the manufacturing processes conform to the environmental
regulations of the country of origin

Book design by Mauna Eichner

Printed and bound in Great Britain by
Bookmarque Ltd, Croydon, Surrey

For Tempest
Eve
Lorna
Haji
Babette
Alaina
Erica
Uschi
Edy
Shari
Raven
Kitten

But especially for Tura

Contents

Introduction: Bigger than Life   1

1   Mother Meyer and the Poor Dear   21

2   Sgt. Meyer   39

3   Tittyboom or Bust   56

4   Love and Kisses, Eve Meyer   74

5   The Immoral Mr. Meyer   90

6   The Handyman   112

7   Top Lust, Top Hate, Top Heavy   130

8   Klieg Eyes on a Dry Lake Bed   157

9   Shit Floats   180

10 The Look of Love 207

11 The Watusi Gun-Bearer 239

12 Strapping On Fox 250

13 Run Like a Gazelle, Dear 288

14 The Ultra-Vixen 311

15 Mondo Meyer 334

16 Janice and the Handyman 349

Epilogue: Smell of Female 399

Source Notes 401

Filmography 435

Acknowledgments 449

Index 453

Big
Bosoms
and
Square Jaws

Introduction:
Bigger than Life

The memory of a particular image is but regret for a particular moment.
—MARCEL PROUST, Swann's Way

It was one of those colorless, nothing-happening days in downtown Stockton. Russell Albion Meyer, the dutiful son, stood at his mother's grave, ready to detonate. He'd paid that damn florist good money to deliver a Christmas tree to Lydia's grave every year, but this time they'd blown it. *No tree.* The next morning he'd make a beeline straight for their office. Of course they'd be closed for Christmas day, so Meyer would scribble an angry note and shove it through the mail slot in the door.

But on this 1991 Christmas Eve, all he could do was stand there apologizing. "Hi, Mom, sorry about the Christmas tree. I'll get on those people. Merry Christmas, Mom. I'll see you tomorrow." Screenwriter John McCormick, RM's companion on the drive up from Hollywood—Meyer rarely did anything alone—hung in the background, transfixed. "I'd never witnessed anyone speak to a grave before except in John Ford films," he later reported. But then, Meyer didn't do anything by the book. He was no ordinary "high-class pornographer," as he liked to refer to himself. This was Russ Meyer.

"The song is ended, but the beautiful melody lingers on—
Mother, we love you—Russell and Lucinda," read the white marble tombstone before him. Lucinda—or The Poor Dear, as RM
called her—was his half-sister, and she would never see the tribute bearing her name. Lucinda had been institutionalized since
her late teens, her brother picking up the tab for her existence.
She'd routinely go into paranoid fugues, calling RM's office endlessly and in a tremulous voice, whispering of dark plots and dirty
deeds. *Get me out of here, Russ. Save me.* But there was no saving
The Poor Dear. Perhaps not surprisingly, Russ Meyer grew up minus a strong male role model. His father had split before he was
born; his stepfather was a sickly, passive man whom his mother regarded with open contempt. Lydia Meyer was a tough cookie, but
she believed in Russ, even hocking her wedding ring to buy her
son his first camera. She was crazy about him, and more than a little crazy in general. Lydia and Lucinda—the templates for how
Meyer would view the female race.

$ $ $

The picture is midnight black, save for the visible blips of an optical
soundtrack that begin replicating across the screen in a rather ominous, twilight-zone way. An imperious, testosterone-heavy voice intones: "Ladies and gentlemen, welcome to violence, the word and
the act . . . while violence cloaks itself in a plethora of disguises, its
favorite mantle still remains sex . . . let's examine closely then, this
dangerously evil creation, this new breed, encased and contained
within the supple skin of woman—the softness is there, the unmistakable *smell* of female . . . but a word of caution: handle with care
and don't drop your guard. This rapacious new breed prowls both
alone and in packs . . . who are they? One might be your secretary,
your doctor's receptionist . . . or a dancer in a *go-go club!*"

Cut to an eye-popping triad of outrageous, impossibly built
women shimmying with frenzied abandon. A swaggering, bargain-
basement Tom Jones chest-beater belts out a number on the
soundtrack—"She will tease and taunt you and she'll take just
what she wants / You belong to pussycat . . ." Cut! Close-ups of gy-

rating, disembodied breasts and hips. Cut! A shiny, alluring juke-box. Cut! Leering, predatory faces of cigar-chomping manimals impotently cheering the women on: *"Go, baby, go!!! Wail!"* Cut! Cut! Cut! Each new shot seems to add another crazy angle, an-other fabulous detail. The montage makes your head spin.

Cut to raven-haired, black-gloved Varla—one of the dancers—head thrown back and cackling maniacally as she hammers the gas pedal of a gleaming Porsche. Vrrrrooom! Varla's an evil bitch. Half Cherokee, half Japanese, and all woman, this heavy-lidded, sneer-ing, ultra-beautiful creature looks more alien than human. The Porsche screams down a Mojave Desert highway, the head of a menacing trio of bisexual go-go superwomen itching to annihi-late any man who gets in their way. *Faster, Pussycat! Kill! Kill!* screams the title. And this is just the first two minutes of the pic-ture. Yikes!

The delirium this little snatch of drive-in opera induces in this author is hard to describe. It's a visceral, emotional thing, analo-gous perhaps to experiencing Busby Berkeley at his most berserk or the opening charge of some Roxy Music opus like "The Thrill of It All." *Pussycat* knocks you off your feet, the undertow ripping you right out to sea. But beneath all the sneering and leering, there lurks—dare I say it, Russ?—an oddly passionate vision of the world.

Russ Meyer at his best: as instantly recognizable, as exhilarat-ingly American as a ride on a rickety state-fair roller-coaster, Chuck Berry's duck walk, or those addictive little onion slivers on a McDonald's burger. Meyer's got a two-fisted, twin-missile attack, approaching filmmaking the way Buick once did cars: fatter curves, crazier fins, bigger headlights, more, more, more. Emerg-ing from the shadows of both Alfred Kinsey and Hugh Hefner, Russ Meyer, particularly in his sixties/seventies heyday, exerted a huge influence on the common man's sexual psyche. Meyer, a pio-neer who represents what's most seductive *and* most repulsive about the USA. Think Henry Ford, Howard Hughes, Elvis Presley. Meyer: a man who made an empire out of female flesh.

$ $ $

From 1959 to 1979 Russ Meyer made twenty-three theatrical features, all but two of them independently made and largely self-financed. Nearly all were profitable, and a few made him millions. At one point RM had four films in *Variety's* 100 all-time top grossers—not bad for movies in which, as Meyer liked to point out, the only name that mattered was his own. His first smash-eroo was 1959's *The Immoral Mr. Teas,* an unapologetic ode to voyeurism that gave birth to an adult film industry that Meyer ultimately scorned. Then came his black-and-white backwoods melodramas, depraved-go-go-dancer documentaries, oversexed-housewife exposés, and apocalyptic girl-group soap operas. These are strange movies that radiate, as one critic put it, "a directness, an energy, a certain guileless honesty that was not always seen in Hollywood films."

The late, great photographer Helmut Newton, who, like RM, championed big, bad women in his work, once said, "I love vulgarity. I am very attracted to bad taste." Well, HN, there's a truck-load of it to be found in Meyer's work. Expect nothing subtle here: half a dozen or so of RM's titles end in exclamation points.* Meyer presents a garish vision of an oversexed America and demands you wallow in it. "I don't pretend to be some kind of sensitive artist. Give me a movie where a car crashes into a building, and the driver gets stabbed by a bosomy blond, who gets carried away by a dwarf musician. Films should run like express trains!" For those in the audience, this unrestrained bombast is intoxicating, inspiring. It can also sicken, one french fry too many. It is certainly unrelenting. There is something to thrill, amuse, and offend one and all in RM's oeuvre. Wrote Alan Brien, "Meyer is both for and against almost everything—liberated women and macho men, faith healing by radio and gay dentists, petroleum jelly and black socks, race prejudice and free enterprise. Tastelessness on this scale eventually amounts to a kind of style."

Meyer's films are so dynamic, so rife with explosive imagery and conflicting impulses, interpretation often depends on who

---

* Definitively deciphering exactly *which* Meyer titles end in an exclamation point is a bit of a challenge. See my note in the filmography for further explanation.

owns the eyeballs viewing them. Perverts thrive on the abundant flesh. Film fanatics savor the craft, and RM has even earned his own brand of deconstructionist critic. "In Meyer's film world of 'big bosoms and square jaws,' it is clear that women possess the 'big bosoms,'" writes Doyle Green in his 2004 book, *Lips, Hips, Tits, Power.* "It is less clear whether men or women possess the 'square jaws.'" (Green also compares RM to both Douglas Sirk and the Marquis de Sade.) A swarm of less intellectual rockers dig the hallucinogenic quality of Meyer's color-saturated comic-book visuals. "The first time I saw a film of his, I thought, man, this guy is in sync with psychedelia, the psychedelic state," said Redd Kross's Jeff McDonald.

You will find many a reference to scratchy old 45s of a particular era and attitude in this book. Believe me, I can sling cinematic references with the best of the film snobs, but with Meyer I hear music. RM's movies possess a monster beat, and by that I mean his intricate montage-style editing builds a groove that could have a Memphis rhythm section nodding in approval. In 1983, nearly twenty years after *Faster, Pussycat! Kill! Kill!* was released, the Cramps unleashed a scorching version of the theme song on a live EP whose title was copped from the same film's opening monologue: *Smell of Female.* "That movie is so great," said the band's singer (and, in tandem with guitarslinger Ivy Rorshach, songwriter), Lux Interior. "It kinda stands for anything the Cramps stand for."

A highly influential band that mixes sex and violence into the sort of garish cocktail a Russ Meyer could appreciate, the Cramps, also like RM, are defiantly original, funny as hell, and often misunderstood by killjoy critics who dismiss their straight-from-the-heart sincerity as "kitsch" or "camp" (two words you won't find the author using in this book). Interior's own cheesecake photography for the seedy *Smell of Female* album is worthy of RM himself, and sullen, sexy cover girl Rorschach could just as well have escaped from the same girl gang as Meyer bombshell Tura Satana.

This was the first of a legion of bands to pay homage to Russ Meyer, and the fact that the films of an anti-drug, Dixieland-jazz-loving superpatriot could speak so directly to a bunch of misfit reprobates young enough to be RM's offspring underlines the obvious (if old school) notion: Meyer shares a certain energy with untamed youth. His movies burst forth with the sort of crazed abandon one finds in the most primeval rockabilly recordings—for instance, the frenzy of Meyer's *Mondo Topless* brings to mind the wild, pussy-mad shriek by Jimmy Wages known as "Miss Pearl." I see the malevolent Luther in RM's *Lorna* and I hear Lonnie Allen belt out that divine down-home fuck-you "You'll Never Change Me." And so on. Meyer's films crackle with the same swagger, the same urgency, the same I-don't-care. "I'm laughing at the world," said RM.

Love him or hate him, Russ Meyer has left his tainted fingerprints all over American culture. See the sticky evidence on MTV, Howard Stern, big-budget Hollywood, the snobbiest fashion catwalks, and in the work of such comic art illustrators as Daniel Clowes and Chris "Coop" Cooper. He's influenced a legion of filmmakers from John Waters to Quentin Tarantino. Remember the poster for 1999's Oscar winner *American Beauty*—a close-up of a young girl's naked midsection, her hand holding a rose across her belly, with the tease line "Look closer"? Well, Meyer concocted high-concept shocker ad campaigns long before they were a Tinseltown (or Fox News) staple; he just did 'em with a big-boobed broad, a bombastic title, and a "Wow!" phrase: "MUDHONEY . . . leaves a taste of evil!"

Go into any rental store's cult section and you'll find shopworn copies of numerous Meyer films. He has rabid followings in France, Germany, and Italy. Russ Meyer cannot be denied a place in cinema history. "I believe the serious film historians of the future will discuss him with such radical structuralists as Mark Rappaport, Chantal Ackerman, Sergei Eisenstein, and Jean-Luc Godard," states an unlikely player in this story, film critic Roger Ebert. "That's if they can see past the heaving bosoms."

$ $ $

Ah yes, the breasts. Meyer's films are filled with them. Giant, unbelievable, sometimes scary appendages. "I won't become involved with a woman personally or photographically unless she has huge breasts," instructed RM. Female superstructures that simply defied reality were his trademark, and Meyer was downright rabid when it came to tracking them down: "Like an explorer, Marco Polo or Magellan, I'm constantly looking for bigger bosoms." As with many a fetish, it was comical, irrational, and, in the end, grotesque. To dismiss Meyer's films as mere vehicles for a tit obsession, though, is to miss a universe that's as particular and self-contained as any created by David Cronenberg, Sam Peckinpah, or Martin Scorsese.

How to describe the Russ Meyer dynamic? "The pneumatic woman, the stupid man," said RM, whose no-frills recipe for success was "big bosoms and square jaws." Despite the bold and expansive imagery, the reality is that the Meyer universe is so rigid and limited in its construction it could fit inside a thimble. His is a world of weak-willed masochistic twits and monosyllabic alpha-male brutes, all lusting after the overabundant, oversexed bringers of pleasure, chaos, and destruction that Meyer calls women. The dames in Meyer's films are "as distinctive as Hitchcock's icy blondes," writes Kristen Hatch, who goes on to describe them as "viciously bitchy, flouting nearly every rule invented by man . . . no Meyer heroine is faithful to her husband." Who wins in this battle of the sexes? Nobody, really, but "the women are always more powerful than the men," as Hugh Hefner observed. "In retrospect it seems to be empowering rather than exploitive. How much of that was conscious and how much was unconscious? I think it was relatively uncalculated. Quite frankly, most of what Russ did came from the gut."

Was RM a Grandma Moses in crotchless panties or something far less primitive—and far more calculated? One runs into an interesting conflict of opinion when it comes to how much of the humor in Meyer's films is intentional. "It's not a satire," maintains RM superstar Erica Gavin. "It's how Russ sees the world." David K. Frasier agrees. "I'm not sold on the idea that Russ started out making these films to be ironic. He was dead serious." Roger Ebert insists that Meyer knew exactly what he was doing, and RM's longtime editor Richard Brummer agrees. "Even in the earlier films the humor is intended. Russ was very sophisticated. If you think you're laughing at him, you're not. He's laughing at you."

Meyer himself didn't analyze, he just spewed forth. "I have my fantasies. I put them on film," said he. RM sought instant gratification, and it gave his pictures a screaming-from-the-id immediacy. "I get an idea and I say: next Tuesday at 2:45 I will make a movie." Likeably unpretentious, RM didn't try to justify his work with dopey theories or by insisting on their socially redeeming significance—unless it was legally prudent to do so due to the many obscenity prosecutions his pictures faced. When it came to sexual freedom on the silver screen, Meyer fought and won many a battle against the censors, the church, and the squares, but he balked at being declared anyone's hero. "I'm in it for lust and profit," maintained the man the *Wall Street Journal* dubbed King Leer.

When RM was asked what sort of picture he would make with $20 million, he responded, "I'd probably make twenty Russ Meyer films." Longtime secretary Paula Parker chuckled over the memory of filling out and mailing a $1 soap rebate at RM's insistence. The same stingy attitude permeated his productions. "I would hit upon an idea and then impose strict limitations on myself even before considering a budget." Meyer's early financial success—along with his miserly ways—afforded him a freedom most directors never even imagine. He did it his way, which usually meant transporting a gaggle of actors, strippers, and a five-man crew off into the middle of a white-hot desert to somehow crank out a movie.

Although RM would undoubtedly frown on such an arty, highfalutin term, he was the very definition of auteur: writing, shooting, editing, and distributing his films as well as directing them. "It wasn't so much that he operated his own camera as that he also *carried* it," wrote Roger Ebert, who'd contribute scripts for a number of Meyer films, including the now-infamous X-rated outrage for 20th Century Fox, 1970's *Beyond the Valley of the Dolls*. Incredibly, not only would RM thrive after being denied entry to the Hollywood establishment, he'd be the one outlaw invited in and handed keys to the kingdom, however briefly. Not that Meyer detected any big difference between Tinseltown and grindhouse row. "Every film is exploitation. We're all in the same game."

But Meyer belongs neither to the exploitation world nor to mainstream Hollywood. His movies are much too exuberant and far too striking technically and visually to be lumped in with the usual lugubrious drive-in fare. "Meyer films don't produce the oppressive grindhouse sense of shame in their audiences," noted critic David Ansen, yet RM's overtly sexual content, haphazard scripting ("I don't let the story get in the way of the action," he boasted), and gleefully juvenile attitude often preclude his work from being considered alongside that of the big boys. Meyer's a lone wolf, an odd and solitary figure in film history. Said RM, "It's my genre. If you like it, fine. If you don't, it doesn't really matter."

However raw the content, Meyer was a savvy filmmaker. RM was a tremendous cinematographer and editor, equally seasoned by previous careers as both combat and cheesecake photographer. Meyer's early experience and expertise making industrial films not only imbued his own movies with a velour professional gloss sublimely at odds with the raunchy content matter, it inspired a cosmically absurd narration style all RM's own. With a Meyer film, the script may be crap, the acting might have you howling at the moon, but in the middle of it all will be some preposterous, highly charged, not to mention boob-driven image of some chick watusiing away atop an oil rig, and it just takes your breath away.

$ $ $

"I deal with women who are archetypes—in fact, they're *beyond* women." Indeed, the Russ Meyer women are an extraordinary bunch, and this is as much their story as RM's. Even their names are otherworldly—Lorna, Tura, Uschi, Haji, Kitten, Eve—and their lives are as compelling as their measurements. Nearly all were strippers, and many had escaped abusive backgrounds, fending for themselves in a man's, man's, man's world that regarded them as little more than a disposable outlet for sexual frustration. "Women like us have been thrown to the sharks since we were babies," said Raven De La Croix.

Meyer took these already outrageous dames and—instead of downplaying the attributes that by their very nature practically branded them the scarlet women of their day—amplified them to almost Wagnerian extremes. RM let 'em all hang out, and again, when the Meyer movie machine is firing on all eight cylinders, these gals utterly transcend the inherent limitations of his often tawdry and infantile sprocket-holed comic strips. "We're all cartoons—every one of us," insisted De La Croix. " 'Cartoon' doesn't mean 'wrong,' it just means bigger than life."

At times Meyer was not only coldly dismissive but even downright sadistic to his fleshy femmes fatales, yet his women invariably manage to make something positive and noble out of their characters despite the many unspeakable horrors inflicted upon them. I don't think I'm alone when stating there are times when I find Meyer's women heroic. The first thing you notice when you meet any of them is the fierce dignity with which they carry themselves. They're hot stuff, these women, and they don't pussyfoot around. Their alliance with RM had to be uneasy at best—this was a man who boasted his philosophy was that of the "Four F's: find 'em, film 'em, fuck 'em, forget 'em"—but his women remain loyal, even now expressing the sort of bittersweet affection for Meyer one has for a wayward and often exasperating crackpot member of the family. Despite his frequently tasteless antics, Meyer has made their stars shine, given them immortality.

"He portrayed women as a work of art," said Charles Napier. "It's like classic photography on film—there's no mussed hair, smeared lipstick, stuff like that. Almost posed scenes. He'd say things like, 'Get your tits up, honey, they're sagging.' But that wasn't meant to be offensive—Russ just wanted her to look good." Said Haji, star of numerous RM epics, "Russ not only brings out the breast in women, he brings out the best in women."

$ $ $

There are those who even dare to declare Meyer feminist-friendly. "His women had an exuberance and vitality you rarely see in films anymore," writes Camille Paglia, who's alleged to be a big Tura Satana fan. B. Ruby Rich boasts that *Faster, Pussycat! Kill! Kill!* "deals a body-blow to the idea that women are victims" and saw the film as "an unexpected celebration of bad-girl empowerment." Well, trust the art and not the artist. "I've never seen a good-looking feminist," maintained Meyer, who often groused he didn't get enough resistance from the women's movement, despite doing his best to incite its wrath. Sayeth RM, "I don't care to comment about what might be inside a lady's head. Hopefully it's my dick." And yet in a day when such credits weren't exactly plentiful, a woman ran Meyer's distribution company and co-produced his films.

You will find extreme opinions within these pages when it comes to what Meyer really thought of the opposite sex. He worshiped; he hated; he was ambivalent. "I think Russ loved women," said Tura Satana—perhaps his most intense femme fatale, and one of the very few who battled him and won. "He always put women on a pedestal. Even though he exploited the figure part of them, their sexuality, he still adored women. You could tell that from the way he always talked about his mom."

In my mind, the sexual tension in Meyer's movies is not dissimilar to that within such classic Ike and Tina Turner records as "You Got What You Wanted" or "I'm Gonna Find Me a Substitute." Ike Turner—another infamous control freak who worried every detail down to the fringe on the Ikettes costumes—crafted tense, tough, tightly constructed songs for Tina, with melodramatic and often masochistic lyrics that portray a mythical dream woman willing to subjugate herself to Her Man at any expense. At times Ike deliberately puts the number in a key out of Tina's range, and she struggles to stay on top of the number, singing like there's a gun at her head. The song is a cage, built for Tina to bust loose from. Her desperate, impassioned, angry vocals often seem at odds with the words, adding a layer of divine complexity to one very bizarre and moving puzzle.

A similar conflicted dynamic goes on in Meyer's work: he pushes his women to the end of their rope, then another three feet farther. They are constantly in motion, running, dancing, jumping, fucking, all the while spewing forth (often at top volume) Meyer's you-Tarzan/me-Jane manifestos. Yet these she-demons overcome by sheer, sexy brute force. Not unlike Ike and Tina, the best moments in RM's movies come when he's working with a high-voltage dame he can neither vanquish nor drown in his cockamamie philosophies, as we shall see is particularly the case with Tura Satana in *Faster, Pussycat* or Erica Gavin in *Vixen*.

$ $ $

In Meyer's films, men and women enjoy only a momentary truce, and it comes during quick, animalistic copulation that is more wrestling match than any expression of affection. "I love to put sex in outrageous locations," said RM. "Up a tree. In a canoe. Behind a waterfall. Screwing under tremendous odds strikes me as both erotic and funny." Scheming, seducing, and survival of the fittest: in Meyer's world the sexual combat never ends, and if RM's movies are about anything, it is that the cavernous abyss between the sexes just cannot be bridged, except for brief moments of depraved need. "The cleansing of sex—that was his theory," said actor Charles Napier. "When things got really rough, you just went out and got a hooker, got sucked out, and this took care of all your problems. For Meyer, sex is something like a bowel movement."

"Who knows more about sex than Russ Meyer?" he'd challenge, and the answer turns out to be just about everybody. As we will learn, RM was no Don Juan, despite his carefully manufactured reputation. "I portray sex in my movies as I perform sex in bed," he boasted, king of the no-frills motel fuck. "I love to see men and women go at it in a ratty old room like a couple of warthogs. It reflects my own personal tastes—fast and quick."

At the same time, there is something weirdly wholesome about Meyer, particularly if you compare his work to hard-core pornography, which, much to RM's displeasure, is where the unknowing often dump him. Graphic sex appalled Meyer. "He was not a sleazy porn merchant," said Roger Ebert. "He was more of an All-American kind of a guy." Half W. C. Fields, half Sgt. Rock, Meyer could've stepped right out of one of his films—a burly, moustached, and macho former combat cameraman who wore his patriotism on his sleeve and suspected all enemies of commie leanings. The press loved describing his paunchy belly, jug-handle ears, and Clark Gable–gone-to-seed mug. John Simon likened

RM's look to that of a "former prizefighter now operating a successful chain of South American brothels." It all contributed to a persona that was, as Richard Corliss wrote, "genuine, impure, adulterated, no-bullshit working class American."

World War II is the key to Meyer, and his combat life is described in detail in these pages. His war experiences galvanized him in a way he could never transcend. RM's movie productions resembled military operations, and he'd fill cast and crew with beloved combat buddies whose mission was now to document another kind of battle—the one in the bedroom. Meyer spoke loudly to postwar males made both anxious and hungry by the chaos of the sexual revolution. RM was one of them, albeit slightly demented. He had crazy, insane lust for his female ideals, yet he was disinterested and disturbed at what actually lurked inside that flesh. Meyer was all about surface, and anything betraying the fantasy was an enemy.

$ $ $

There is a photo I keep on my desk, an old black-and-white still from *Please Don't Touch Me,* a 1959 no-budget exploitation picture made by the Ormonds, a Nashville-based family who'd cross over from the drive-in pits to the church, making Christian scare films starring the likes of Jerry Falwell (the packaging and particulars from grindhouse to pulpit might have been different, but the product was amusingly the same).

The still shows a scantily clad couple in a room; the harsh lighting's suitable for a crime scene, the forlorn furniture looks like motel resale, and the angle of the photo is slightly askew to suggest (take your pick) art or ineptitude. An amply endowed redhead, her bust barely contained in skimpy black lingerie, leans over a shirtless man—a faint, crude tattoo ("Mirtle") on his arm—to light his cigarette. Across the top of the image a rather suggestive line of dialogue flirts: *"And after the cigarette we'll—."*

Now, fortunes are made, careers ruined, and lives lost over just what's expected after that "we'll," and this tawdry image says much to me about the sheer folly of male-female relations. He looks very appreciative, very excited, a bit desperate; she seems calm, cool, and collected, in utter control of the situation. Despite the crassness, there is something alluring about the image, somewhat akin to your hand discovering a garter affixed to a silk stocking that just happens to be clinging to the leg of someone you'd like to investigate further. It's the game of sex. For its time, Russ Meyer's work offered the most visceral, yet technically refined portrait of this nerve-racking dance, and the choreography of all that sex-wrestling somehow transforms into a bizarre, even epic tango. Which is not to say Meyer's any more aware—quite the contrary—he was just the one who packaged his wet dreams with the kind of commercial sheen acceptable to middle America.

Meyer came along at exactly the right time. Critic D. K. Holm pits RM against Walt Disney: "Like Marlon Brando versus Doris Day or Elvis versus Pat Boone in the 50s, they accounted for the weird and incoherent tension in an America experiencing a difficult transition. And they both made cartoons . . . Meyer unearthed what Disney attempted to bury, the roiling sexual subtext and supertext to everything in the culture." But most of all, RM made people laugh at sex, creating a kooky cartoon universe that touched a chord. "I figure if it's good for RM it's good for the world," he boasted.

In the heady, world-domination affluence of the postwar era, America was bursting at the seams in a way that was not unlike the tortured bodice on one of RM's abundant femme fatales. Everything became supersized, from the Cadillac Coupe de Ville to Jayne Mansfield, and, somewhat symbolically, Meyer was the classic consumer. "He liked big things—big women, big steaks, big Mixmasters, the biggest vacuum cleaner," said longtime editor Richard Brummer.

$ $ $

The kind of man who discovers that slapping a leg of lamb is a perfect sound effect for a breast striking a face has to be somewhat unusual, and RM does not disappoint. "Russ Meyer could have a friendship with God and a friendship with the devil, and at the same time," said childhood friend Lou Filipovitch. Biographer and friend David K. Frasier saw RM as a Dickensian character, Mr. Micawber with a movie camera. Meyer loved language and invented an arcane, hard-boiled vocabulary straight out of a never-made film noir—shoes were "ground grippers," a helmet was a "brain bucket," breasts were (among a thousand other such assignations) "ticket sellers," a toilet "the growler," his own crotch "the grinch." Meyer had a bittersweet style, and it got to you. As Frasier fondly recalled, "When getting dressed he'd say, 'Let me put on my Sy Devore jacket' and shoot the cuffs like Art Carney."

As of 1990, one would find six tubes of Mennen #29 hair dye in RM's bathroom and eighteen identical burgundy V-neck sweaters in his closet. Charles Napier once accompanied RM on a footwear run to Hollywood Boulevard. "He wore a type of shoe that buckled on the side you don't see anymore. The shoe guy says, 'Can I help you?' and RM goes, 'You see these shoes I got on? I want every pair you got.' 'Every pair?' 'All of them.' The guy had about twenty-five pairs. We bought 'em all."

Meyer, a man of often ridiculous extremes, would weep while watching *Casablanca*, yet thought nothing of terrorizing cast and crew with a loaded gun. A sneering iron man, RM was so thin-skinned he'd write voluminous, murderous diatribes to critics who dared to pan his work. Meyer was fanatical about restaurants—with a battle cry of "Let's go cut some meat" he'd charge off for an hours-long drive to some ancient steakhouse, treating his pals to a bacchanalian feast—but God forbid you didn't pick up the tab when RM divined it time. Such a perceived slight could result in a thirty-year banishment.

Different people knew different Meyers. Some insisted he was exactly the image he sold to the world—jolly Mr. Blue-Collar Tit Lover. His combat buddies knew RM as a devoted if controlling friend who'd do anything necessary to keep their group together. Others saw him as an outright monster. You will encounter all these Meyers in the pages that follow.

$ $ $

"Meyer's life is as thoroughly documented as Churchill's," wrote Roger Ebert, and the one with the eye for posterity was Meyer himself.

RM's Hollywood home was a shrine unto himself, packed to the gills with framed memorabilia from his films—posters, pictures, articles, and tributes. Huge nude portraits of the women he'd worked with covered the walls, the ones he'd bedded earning a special inscription affixed to their image—"To the Mutual Exchange of Wondrous Body Fluids." Each film got its own plaque, and attached to each was some symbolic production prop—the straw hat worn by Bill Teas in *The Immoral Mr. Teas*, Tura Satana's black leather glove from *Faster, Pussycat! Kill! Kill!* Every little scrap from his life became a treasured memento, down to his dead mother's car and his late sister's wheelchair. Meyer was one of those guys who longed for the past even while it was still the present. "He was always referring to his old films," said Ebert. "They were things that he had lived."

Intoxicated by his own history, Meyer tried to control any and all interpretations of it. German biographer Rolf Thissen wrote the first in-depth biography of the director in the mid-eighties. After perusing a rough draft, RM insisted on numerous deletions and then went to court to prevent the book from ever being published outside of Germany. Meyer trashed his biographer in the press, and, when contacted by this author, Thissen made it clear he never wanted to discuss Russ Meyer again. Defiant that only *he* could tell the tale, Meyer spent over a decade writing *A Clean Breast*—a massive three-volume autobiography he published himself. "Who'd know more about Meyer than Meyer? My joke is mine."

Despite its very colorful 1,213 pages, there is one thing missing from *A Clean Breast*—Russ Meyer's life. The book, not unlike his movies, is unashamedly skin deep.

$ $ $

A few problems present themselves when writing a biography on a character like Meyer. Brutally honest, he was also a master of disinformation. "Everybody gets a different story," he admitted to biographer David K. Frasier. If myth suited him better than the truth, it had a way of creeping into the record. To this end, RM once recounted a highly amusing anecdote to interviewer Harvey Fenton concerning a fishing trip to Ireland and a pair of cowboy boots. RM noticed the adolescent in charge of rowing him around staring longingly at the boots he was wearing. Meyer asked the kid if he'd ever heard of John Wayne, and the youngster piped up with an emphatic affirmative. RM then told him he'd done some photography for Wayne, that they were close friends, and that the Duke had even given him *the very* cowboy boots he was wearing— boots that Meyer now gave to his boat boy in appreciation for his hard work. Mused RM, "I wonder how many times he got in some bar and said, 'See these boots, they used to belong to John Wayne . . .' Untrue, of course." Quintessential Meyer, this.

RM revealed only what he wanted to reveal, which wasn't much. Meyer never took his game face off, never flinched, never cried for the TV camera or unloaded his innermost to any scribe. "Never let the chink in your armor be exposed," RM advised David K. Frasier. "He was a crude, smart individual," said Arv Miller, who conducted a series of combative, in-depth interviews with Meyer in 1990 for *Fling* magazine. "He'd be a psychoanalyst's dream. Sort of like Tony Soprano going to Dr. Melfi."

When I grilled David F. Friedman on his long friendship with RM, he reflected on how little he really knew about the man. "This is almost like a mystery novel," he mused one cool night in Alabama. "You've got to find the real Russ Meyer. There are so many anomalies there that you can't put it together."

$ $ $

"It's not supposed to progress," said Lux Interior about rock and roll. "It isn't art. It is a simple thing that is supposed to stay simple. When you write a postcard to somebody and do it again next year, it isn't supposed to be better than the last." One could say exactly the same about Meyer's oeuvre. His films were postcards, albeit from a gloriously demented mind. Some refinement occurred over the long haul, but expect no advancement, no progression, no soul-searching relevatory moments. Meyer may have utilized flesh-and-blood actors, but there aren't any real human emotions on display in any of his pictures excepting maybe lust and anger.

When asked about the meaning of Meyer's films, Roger Ebert retorts, "Is there any particular statement that Rauschenberg is making? Kandinsky? His films are abstract as their paintings." Ebert champions the "robust, positive, cheerful" nature of RM's work, and his blanket defense of Meyer is understandable given his close alliance with the man. But there is something else happening in Meyer's movies, an unsettling weirdness that can't be swept away by declaring, "This is only a cartoon." The more movies RM made, the more his anger raged out of control, as did the more unsavory aspects of his sexuality. Meyer's childhood cast a long shadow over his life and his work. There is a palpable madness to be found within. No doubt RM would've killed the messenger carrying that missive, since it's so utterly contrary to everything he stood for.

Meyer was the boss, Meyer knew best, and yet it turns out Meyer might've been too smart for his own good. By the conclusion of this book you might just find yourself wondering who had the last laugh. Sex was RM's reason for being, and sex was his undoing. "In the end [Meyer] is not Vladimir Nabokov but Humbert Humbert, sending his confession from his stew of lust and guilt," writes critic Gordon Burn.

Obsessions rarely end happily. I speak from experience. There's that sublime honeymoon period where you can't get enough of whatever it is you're chasing. You become the all-knowing expert, the absolute master of your subject, or so you con yourself into thinking. Then a certain malaise sets in, and sooner or later your little obsession eats you for lunch. Meyer was fixated on youth and beauty—is there any greater folly? "Russ was a case of arrested development," maintained writer and sometime Meyer crew member Stan Berkowitz. "He was basically a fourteen-year-old. I don't think Russ ever grew up. He stopped. Which is, of course, the reason for his success."

$ $ $

Still, you ask, why a book about Russ Meyer? The reasons, Dear
Reader, get very personal. Come closer and I'll whisper them in
your ear. I came upon the work of RM as a young buck. I'd see a
picture of a Meyer dame or one of his movies at the drive-in and
they hit like a lightning bolt. Over time I recognized it as the work
of one man, and I was hooked. Of *course* I coveted the women. But
this went way beyond the sexual. It was Meyer's way of looking at
the world, a certain lust for life. It influenced my writing and being. For other people it's God, family, politics, or drugs. I'll take
Meyer, with all his myriad faults.

There is a shot Russ Meyer once snapped of girlie mag goddess
June Wilkinson. I believe it's from *Gent*, circa 1959. Wilkinson's
rolling around in the buff, her mystical love rockets barely covered
by a few slinky furs. She's got a wide, inviting smile on her face, and
her mile-long legs are thrusting another animal skin skyward.
Everything about the image screams, "How about it, big boy?"

I want to tell you here and now that this picture has all I personally desire from life. Put Sam and Bill belting out "I Feel Like
Crying" on the stereo,* give me Coke in the small green glass bottle served alongside a big pile of peanut M&Ms, forgive the intake
of a half a Xanax to slide my nervous system out of the way, and I'll
gladly expire right there in my easy chair, soaking up every subtle
detail of Miss Wilkinson's ample charms. What gams, what a figure, what a woman! One tries to savor these visions as long as hu-
manly possible, for in real life the flesh doesn't last, nor does the
high, and even the tune grows old. But this image doesn't fart,
belch, wrinkle, tinkle, cry, or die — it's a freeze-dried fantasy, a
nonexistent forever. That's the glory of it all, as well as the madness and misery. Life is momentary, Sluggo, so grab all the candy
you can while still ambulatory, because it will all turn to dust,

---

* An effete, obscure idea, to be certain, but Meyer's still photographs sure do look
majestic when accompanied by male "deep" soul duos. The author also recom-
mends blasting the Sims Twins' "I Gopher You" or Lonnie and Floyd's "I Pledge"
while perusing RM's work.

along with you and your chintzy dreams. Yep, I get all of this out of a goddamn Russ Meyer photograph. Now if that's too over the top, buddy, you've stuck your nose in the wrong tome. That's the way this book is and that's Russ Meyer.

At the end of an obituary for Meyer, the critic David Thomson noted the fact this biography was coming out and reflected on the meaning of the words "big bosoms and square jaws." "It could be a subtitle to a history of America," Thomson mused. I'll buy that, albeit in a $1.98 way. This is an oversized, overblown story, a map of a cultural universe that no longer exists: an open-all-night, cocktails-on-the-house, ten-pound-steak, nude-truck-stop U. S. of A., a glittery, funhouse-mirrored Vegas where one roll of the fuzzy dice could make a mess of fevered dreams come true. Ultimately it is the story of one man's very crazy vision, the way it changed our landscape forever, and how it inevitably consumed its maker: Russ Meyer.

Mother Meyer and the Poor Dear

The question always arises: did your mother have a big bust? Yes.

—RUSS MEYER*

Manny Diez saw Russ Meyer show fear. A very unique event, and it only happened once. Meyer had just finished his big X-rated outrage for 20th Century Fox, 1970's *Beyond the Valley of the Dolls*, and he was riding high. Diez worked as his round-the-clock assistant. "Russ said, 'Manny, I would like you to come with me today.' We got in his car, just started driving, I guess it was about a forty-minute drive. I had no clue where we were going." There was no conversation. RM seemed to be in a melancholy mood.

They pulled into a large psychiatric hospital. "Russ said, 'My mother has been in residence here for quite some time. If you wouldn't mind, would you please wait out here in the car for me?' I guess he was gone forty-five minutes. He came back, his mood

---

* For the record, it should be noted that most of the time RM did state his mother was generously endowed, but there were others when he maintained he said yes only because the question irritated him and he'd learned to tell reporters whatever they wanted to hear. It is hard to gauge measurements just by looking at the few photos of Meyer's beloved mother Lydia floating around and as far as I know, although RM saved everything, none of her brassieres were archived.

even more somber. We got in the car, left again, pretty much a dead silence. Eventually he said, 'My mom has been here X number of years and my sister's in a similar facility. Manny, I'm really scared that I'm gonna wind up in a place just like this.' He just felt that was his destiny. I just listened. It was never mentioned again."

$ $ $

Meyer could be a paranoid fellow—one crew member from his films told me RM outlawed whispering on the set because he was sure his minions had to be talking about him—and he sure wasn't forthcoming on matters he felt were negative in any way. Even those who knew him well don't know much about RM's early life. "He mostly talked about his war years," said Meyer star Tura Satana. "I think his childhood was very lonely for him." Very rarely would RM volunteer any facts regarding his formative years and nobody felt permitted to pry. "There were certain places you didn't go with Russ," said longtime secretary Paula Parker. "Russ was a very close-mouthed guy," maintained Meyer's film distributor Fred Beiersdorf. "He was not gonna share. But the entire family wasn't happy."

Tight-lipped as he was, Meyer certainly purported to idolize his mother Lydia. He'd mention her constantly during interviews but spew forth nothing more than one-dimensional platitudes. "Mother influence is extremely important and I had a great one. She defended me to the teeth, and everything her son did was right. . . . She was a very God-fearing woman who instilled a desire for success in me. . . . Anything I achieved was because of her." Wherever Meyer went he carried a portrait of his mother in his wallet (sometimes side by side with a nude shot of his current heartthrob). A silver-framed picture of his mother sat next to the Moviola as RM worked. Combat buddy Warren Harding recalled that whenever RM came to visit, the photograph of Lydia was front and center on the nightstand. On one trip Meyer lost the picture and he flipped until it could be located.

Meyer was no slouch when it came to looking after Mom. "Russ was a wonderful son," said family friend Dolores Fox. "You couldn't ask for anyone to take better care of his mother. He was so devoted. He paid for her every need." There was no joking with Meyer about Mom. Editor Richard Brummer came into the cutting room one day absently singing the "Lydia, the Tattooed Lady" song made famous by the Marx Brothers. A stone-faced Russ tersely muttered, "My mother's name is Lydia."

Likewise, in Lydia's eyes, Russ could do no wrong. "She used to adore him, adore him so," said RM's first wife Betty. "If I ever did anything to Russ, she would kill me. He was her idol." Dig a little beneath the surface of the mother-son relationship, though, and things were naturally more complex. "She was a manipulator, his mother," said close friend Charlie Sumners. "She pretty much ran Meyer," maintained RM's right-hand man, Jim Ryan. "He just said, 'Yes, Ma, yes, Ma' to whatever she said."

"We used to call her Mother Meyer—not to Russ's face, of course," said actor Charles Napier, who felt that RM's relationship with his mother "was sad and funny at the same time. Funny in the sense she was about as eccentric as he was. Sad in the sense that he worshiped her, the only human being he probably ever loved. He would say, 'She got me my *first* camera and she *made* me learn how to use it and now it's *paying off.*'"

$ $ $

Russell Albion Meyer was born March 21, 1922. Even here we find conflict: biographer Rolf Thissen discovered two birth certificates filed twenty years apart for RM, and the first lists his name as Russell Elvan Meyer. Early photos show a dazed, chubby baby with a messy mop of hair sitting in the lap of mother Lydia, a rather solid and strong-looking brunette sporting an ornate feathered hat. Both mother and son share luminous, searching eyes. There is a shot of Russ a few years later looking rather delicate, wearing knee socks and grasping an American flag. Although he'd never admit it, RM was something of a mama's boy. "He said he breast-fed til he was three," said Meyer star Tura Satana. "I told him, 'Jeez, Russ, I only breast-fed til I was two.'"

Lydia Lucinda Hauck Howe was born March 30, 1897. In numerous articles it was reported that Lydia had been married six times, although it was nothing her son bragged about (in his autobiography, RM notes three marriage surnames for Lydia, but only in the index). Writer David K. Frasier worked on a 1990 Meyer bibliography with RM's assistance, and Frasier wrote a biographical sketch in which he mentioned Lydia's serial matrimony. A very upset Meyer claimed to have read the draft of the document Frasier had given him while visiting his mother's grave, at which point he promised the dead matriarch the offending information would be excised immediately.

Certainly Lydia's most significant betrothal was to William Arthur Meyer, a Missouri-born East Oakland cop of German heritage possessing a bad gambling habit. Little is known about the relationship other then the fact that Lydia was granted a divorce on April 9, 1923, a little over two weeks after the birth of their son. William was thirty-six, Lydia twenty-five, and RM's birth certificate lists them as both living at 1255 Santa Rosa Street in San Leandro, California. RM claimed to know few details of the breakup, stating his mother always said positive things about his dad. Only when pressed—and only after any attempt for a relationship between father and son had failed—did she tell him that during the court battle over child support for the then-pregnant mother, William had shouted out, "I hope they both die!" In his autobiography, Meyer rather dramatically states that it was in May 1988, while leafing through a baby book in which Lydia had penned a few notes, that he first learned his father had pressured her to get an abortion (in an earlier draft of the manuscript RM says his mother told him directly).

Over the years Meyer related a few terse, varying tales concerning his father, none of them suggesting that William wanted anything to do with his son. In one he gets the door slammed in his face attempting to visit his father; in his autobiography *A Clean Breast*, RM describes a single visit from his dad. Dressed in a swanky camel-hair coat, refusing to come in, William stood at the screen door, inquiring as to how things were going with Lydia and Russ. The visit was so casual Meyer thought it might begin one of many, but William never returned. Lydia prodded her son into attempting a visit with his father at the police station. Told that

William wasn't there, Russ left an ashtray he'd made for his dad in shop class. William never bothered to respond.

"He was a bastard, he was no good, he wasn't worth a damn," said a seventy-seven-year-old RM of his father in 1999. That's as far as you could go on the subject with Meyer. Jean-Pierre Jackson, Meyer's French distributor, first biographer, and friend, recalled RM clammed up when asked about his dad. "I asked him many times about his father—nothing. Not a word." But the shadow of his absentee father looms large in dumb Nazis and stupid cops in Meyer's films, as RM actress and longtime paramour Kitten Natividad explains, "because his father was a German policeman. I go, 'You're gonna put another Nazi in this movie?' 'Yeah, reminds me of the old man.' He got off on that. He said it to me lots of times through the years."

In *A Clean Breast*, Meyer does grant a few kind words for his stepdad, Howard Haywood, an ailing WWI vet whose bout with tuberculosis left him barely able to work as a furniture salesman. Howard and Lydia had one child together, the aforementioned Lucinda. RM's childhood friend Lou Filipovitch said Lydia treated Howard with contempt, and others told me she'd forced her sickly husband to live in the garage. "Howard was a quiet, gentle, pleasant man," said Lou. "She ridiculed Howard Haywood constantly, called him 'whistle britches,' 'eagle beak.' She was brutal, absolutely brutal. She just humiliated and insulted Howard."

$ $ $

It was the Depression, and the Meyers barely got by. Lydia got $50 a month in child support from William Meyer for Russ, which was later knocked down to $35. "When I was young I was poorer than Job's turkey," said RM, who said that his family would frequently have to "shoot the moon"—skip out on unpaid rent. "His mother always had a garden because they didn't have enough money to buy the vegetables," said Kitten Natividad. "Russ couldn't stand onion or celery soup because he had to eat it all the time." RM had to peddle the produce and other items door-to-door. "Lydia was a hustler—I'm not saying that in a derogatory way," said Pete

Filipovitch. "She'd get us into selling perfume, then subscription magazines."

The Filipovitch family lived near the Haywoods when they lived on Birch Street in East Oakland, and Russ was friendly with the children, Lou, Pete, and Martha—or at least as chummy as Lydia would allow. "I don't think his mother allowed Russ to have too many friends when he was a kid," said Tura Satana. "She kept him at home a lot, kept him on a tight leash. But he loved that she was a very strict disciplinarian, kept him on the straight and narrow."

Lydia worked as a cashier at the McMar grocery in Oakland and needed someone to babysit her two children. "My mother was a widow and immigrant and Lydia treated her outwardly nicely, probably because she didn't have anybody else," said Lou Filipovitch. "She was aloof and above the neighborhood." A devoutly religious woman, Pete Filipovitch recalled her carting him off to church. "Oh, she'd drive me crazy. She took me to the Protestants, she took me to the Baptists . . ."

To say the least, times were tough in this Oakland neighborhood—as Pete noted, "unless you were with the civil service or the railroad, you didn't have a steady job." The Haywoods were poor, but the Filipovitchs, who couldn't even afford a phone, thought Russ and Lucinda "were the rich kids" according to Lou, especially due to the way Lydia doted on her son. "Lydia gave him everything that he wanted or needed," Pete agreed. "She pampered him; he was never without." Lou remembered Russ as being very generous with his pocket change. Lou and his sister Martha once walked a mile and a half to the local movie theater to see *A Midsummer's Night Dream*, the excursion funded by Russ. "It was his treat," said Lou. "He had spending money, he bought us candy and popcorn. Russ was one of the nicest guys I ever knew. He was kind and gentle. I don't think there was a mean bone in his body."

Lydia, however, was another story. She was a racist, missing no opportunity to slight blacks, Jews, or Irish. "Lydia didn't like anybody!" said RM's pal Jim Ryan. Pete's brother Lou felt her behavior was rather less than Christian at times. "It seemed she was visiting kindnesses upon people, but she had a malice in her.

Lydia claimed to be many things, including a registered nurse. One time I had a severe case of poison oak and she proclaimed her expertise as an expert nurse. She told me to rub bacon on it, and I almost died with pain. It was a mad, crazy thing to do to a little kid. Lydia was just nasty and mean and a little bit cuckoo."

And she was a very independent woman who took no guff. "Lydia was born at the wrong time—she should've been a rank-and-file 1930 union representative and union organizer, like John L. Lewis," said Pete Filipovitch. "You talk about believing in women's rights! That's what was wrong with Lydia—and that's why her husband left her."

$ $ $

There was something strange about Russ's younger sister, Lucinda. The Filipovitchs rarely saw Russ, but they never saw Lucinda. She just didn't venture outside of their home. It was as if she was imprisoned there.

Pete Filipovitch detected a disturbing sexual undercurrent while in the presence of either Lydia or her daughter. "I never wanted to be alone with Lucinda when she was by herself. It made me very uneasy. Same reason I didn't want to be left alone with Russ's mom as a kid. I felt very uncomfortable—she'd say, 'You're the most handsomest boy alive.' My mother would just shake her head. After I got older I looked back and I thought, 'My God, I could've been in bed with that woman.' " Pete recalled gossip about a scandalous affair involving Lydia and a married man across the street. "Lydia liked men, but she hated men—she liked to have sex with a man," said Lou. "Lydia was not on the short end of doing what comes naturally."

Lucinda started having serious problems with mental illness in her teens, and some say it was schizophrenia. She would be shuttled from institution to institution the rest of her life, the bills paid by her brother, who'd made a promise to Lydia to take care of Lucinda.

"I had seen her a couple of years before she was committed," said Meyer producer Tom McGowan. "Absolutely lovely girl—she could've been a young starlet. Meyer escaped by filmmaking; she was a prisoner of the house. She hooked up with some cabdriver that was a lot older than she was and tried to escape. The mother went after her and took her right back into the torture chamber."

It is hard to glean any concrete details about Lucinda's condition. She's the ghost in Meyer's life. RM's first wife Betty became anxious discussing Russ's half-sister. "Lucinda, she was a beautiful girl. Poor thing, I felt sorry for her. I think she went man-crazy. Got with the wrong people, I guess. I often thought maybe if I had taken her under my wing she might've ended up better. It's a terrible thing. I knew she was gonna have a bad ending. I could just tell. And it was her mother and Russ's fault. I don't think he even paid attention. He was busy, he was busy." When I said Russ had paid for her keep after she was institutionalized, Betty said forcefully, "He should've."

Those who knew the family blamed Lydia for Lucinda's illness—even, at least on one occasion, RM himself. Said associate George Costello, "It came up one time—'Where's your sister?' And he said, 'My mother drove her into a nuthouse.' Lydia rejected all of Lucinda's boyfriends, wouldn't let her go out with guys, and was constantly on her to the point where the poor girl was destroyed. The mother should've been in the nuthouse, not the daughter."

"I don't really think Russ got a good feeling for women from his mother," said Meyer star Erica Gavin. "I think he felt that they were all whores and that his mother was a whore. Was she not sleeping with other men in front of him and bringing home different men all the time? Didn't she have a lot of sailors around? I don't know why, but I get the feeling that she was extremely promiscuous in front of him." More than one of Meyer's intimates hinted at sexual abuse in the family—even farfetched tales concerning boarders taken in by Lydia and given sexual access to Lucinda in exchange for money. Thus far the stories have amounted to nothing more than wild hearsay, but they don't seem completely out of the realm of possibility. Jim Ryan vaguely recalled Lucinda having been molested by a stepfather.

Others got the impression from Meyer that Lucinda had been

the victim of a gang rape while institutionalized. Family friend Dolores Fox said that RM had told her that as adults, Lucinda had asked her brother if he'd have sex with her. "She'd never had sex. He told her, 'No, I'm your brother, I can't do that.'" Curiously, Meyer declared a brother-sister shower sex scene in his 1968 picture *Vixen* as his all-time hottest. "We quit doin' that when you turned twelve," brother Judd protests in vain to sister (and instigator) Vixen.

Meyer tried to be kind to Lucinda, occasionally freeing her from her institution home for hamburgers and ice cream, but invariably there would be some awful scene. "I was always wary of any kind of situation with her along," said RM right-hand man Jim Ryan. "A couple of times she'd lock herself in the toilet in the restaurant and wouldn't come out." They put Lucinda into a residential facility where she could venture into the outside world, but "she got out and was wandering in the street without her clothes on," said Ryan. "The other time she kicked open a door and the glass cut her leg. They finally sent her to full-time confinement in Camarillo. Lucinda was combative towards the other patients. She'd hit somebody first to make them hit her."

"Lucinda got kinda large—and she got mean," said Meyer combat buddy Charlie Sumners. "She talked like a ten-year-old and she wanted Russ to stay there with her. Of course, that was impossible. Later they had to almost put her in a straitjacket." Tom McGowan recalled a foggy drive up to northern California to visit Lucinda. "I'd never been in a madhouse. It was a horrifying experience. It wasn't like a first-class operation—it was state-run, smelled of urine. All these nuts were walking around. They were in these dressing gowns, shells of people. It was like a Boris Karloff insane asylum. She was very docile." McGowan claimed that Lucinda had been subjected to "more electroshock treatments than anybody in the history of California at that time. She was zombied."

Not surprisingly, Lucinda slowly disintegrated over the decades. Kitten Natividad accompanied Meyer on visits to see his sister in the seventies and eighties. "She had had some strokes, so she was in a wheelchair. She couldn't enjoy eating certain foods because she was on medication and she was a diabetic. And sometimes she'd get her schizophrenia really bad, and she'd cuss everybody like you wouldn't believe! And she had been beat up and raped in there. That was no life. It was very, very horrible. Russ used to cry over it." Said Charles Napier, "I've seen him suffer over her. One time on location I had a tent set up and I went in and he was sitting there sobbing. I asked him what was wrong and he mumbled something about his sister. Never got into it, but heaving sobs and whatnot. Never said much about her."

Several close friends and ex-girlfriends independently raised the notion that Meyer himself suffered from some sort of mental illness. "I just felt he was a little crazy, he was just too bizarre," said longtime secretary Paula Parker. "His thinking wasn't normal at times. I had a very hard time communicating with him, quite frankly." Longtime associate George King Carll agreed. "You saw flashes of—I wouldn't say *insanity,* but some mental things. The fact of his sister, it was easy to relate the two."

No wonder Russ was afraid.

$ $ $

Once RM was an adult, he took care of his mother's needs but kept her at a comfortable distance. The older Lydia got, the weirder and more difficult she became. Lou Filipovitch remembered taking his family to visit her around the early sixties, when Lydia was living in Vallejo, California. His wife, Darlene, recalled that Lydia served them all dinner in the dark, "which was a strange experience. One of my little girls went over and turned the lights on. Next day I received a phone call about how terrible we all were. I think I hung up on her."

Meyer associate George Costello visited Lucinda in the midsixties and found her living in "one of these houses where there's pictures of Jesus Christ all over. The mother would treat Russ like he was still fourteen. An old-lady version of Meyer—plump, wearing a 1940s dress." The only positive review anyone can recall Lydia giving to one of her son's raunchy movies came when she saw 1965's *Motorpsycho,* in which Russ has a cameo as a moronic, corrupt, pro-rape cop. "His mother went to see the movie and said, 'Oh, Russ, you were such a wonderful policeman,' " said actor John Furlong. " 'Your father would've been proud of you.' "

It's no shock that Lydia tangled with nearly all of her son's women. "Russ said his mom would always refer to women that she didn't like as an old rip—'Eh, that old rip,' " said biographer and friend David K. Frasier. "Meyer always laughed about that." According to Jim Ryan, Lydia was partial to males but "didn't like women too much. I think she saw them as rivals for Russell. She called his women with big breasts 'cows.' She'd say, 'I don't want you bringin' home any of those cows around my home.' " If Meyer let a few too many days pass before calling Lydia, she'd call the sheriff's office. Said Ryan, "They'd come over and say, 'Why don't you call your mother?' "

And what effect did Lydia have on her son? "I don't think Russ liked women," said George Costello. "They were all no damn good. I think they were all representative of his mother, who failed him or did something to him. Or drove off his father."

"I noticed when Russ talked about his mother he idealized her, but he was very controlled by her," said Meyer actress Raven De La Croix. "But he controlled the last straw. He took care of her minimally—saw her minimally—all at arm's length. I think Russ could never win women's approval, really. He was gonna make all the women pay for how he felt through his films. He made a point of making them the strong characters, but they always had to go through hell and high water."

Pete Filipovitch felt it was one case where the apple didn't fall far from the tree. "Lydia was predominantly controlling; Russ did the same thing." As far as the women in his life, "he'd control them the same way she controlled him. He was definitely his mother's son." While RM put his mother on a pedestal, he would treat the other women in his life—women who were often playing characters in his films who shared more than a thing or two in common with Mother Meyer—as little more than nude doormats. I don't think it's a stretch to suggest that RM was on some level coping with a relationship he could never confront in life by making movies. That's one reason his antiheroines are so compelling—they charge at you like fully formed nightmares from a raging subconscious, the sirens on the rocks whose come-hither whisperings serve only to get your ship crashed.

$ $ $

Unfortunately, it must also be noted Lydia liked to give her son enemas, and this made a lifelong impression on Russell Albion Meyer.

"Shit is very important to Russ's life," said girlfriend Kitten Natividad. "Mr. Poo-Poo! He was obsessed with this enema thing. He'd tell me, 'My mom was a nurse, and whenever I was sick, she'd just put me on her lap, put that in me, and just *hose me out.*'" In later years everybody was subjected to Meyer's infantile interests. "He would talk about it a lot—'a good shit,'" said actress Erica Gavin. "I would think that Russ wouldn't mind taking a shit in front of you. Basically I think he was sexually abused—he was taking it up the ass in an enema from his mother."

"I love farting," admitted Meyer in an interview, and for his 1979 movie, *Beneath the Valley of the Ultra-Vixens,* he'd tape his own gassy emissions, then play them in reverse for use as sexual sound effects. "I get a lot out of a fart, don't you? I'd get the feeling of a fart coming on, and I'd yell, 'Bonus fart' and I'd put the mike to my ass. . . . I'd hate to come across as too . . . *fecal,* you understand, but next to a good fuck give me a good fart any day." Meyer slipped a laxative to at least one pal before he got on a plane, and for years after had a good belly laugh over his friend's "brownout over Denver."

$ $ $

"Sexually I was a late bloomer," said Russ Meyer. As an adolescent he was shy and not adept with the opposite sex. Pete Filipovitch recalled how he bumped into the Meyer family at a nearby lake and snuck off with a neighborhood girl who had come with Russ. "I got acquainted with her, and that kinda upset him," said

Filipovitch, who noticed Meyer had followed them and was spying from the woods. "I thought, 'Jesus Christ, I wonder how long Russ was out there watching us.' " Meyer, already a little voyeur.

Even in his youth a large fantasy world hovered around Meyer, much of it involving Al Capp's satirical comic strip, *Li'l Abner.* It is not hard to recognize a link between the overheated females and dumb hillbilly hunks of Dogpatch and the creatures inhabiting Meyer films. While RM was loath to admit influence, he didn't mind referencing *Li'l Abner,* stating, "I make Al Capp cartoons come to life." The pneumatic Daisy Mae was of specific interest to young Russell, and as an amateur cartoonist himself, he'd try to draw the blonde in the polka-dot halter top and cutoffs. "I'd always make her breasts twice as large, and when my mother came in I had to hide the stuff, because she thought I was doing things that might affect me later in life." No kidding, Russ. Lydia had bought him a drafting set, and he used the compass to make huge round breasts on his cartoon women. Only fourteen, RM was already "obsessed with boobs," said Lou Filipovitch. "He had some kinks and quirks."

Around this same time Meyer and a few of his teenage buddies managed to slip into the President Follies, a San Francisco burlesque house on McAllister Street. A stacked stripper named Margaret Sullivan was on the bill, and when RM laid eyes on her it lit a fire in his crotch. He was transfixed by her top-heavy build. "If she moved too fast she could throw herself right down to the deck— the centrifugal force was enormous," said Meyer, who trekked over and over to the President Follies "just to worship at her shrine." Margie Sullivan functioned as a mammary Rosebud for the rest of RM's life: "From then on, she's been the carbon copy that I've constantly been looking for."

My efforts to find a picture of Meyer's first inspiration came to naught. The other ecdysiasts of RM's time had never even heard of her, save one. Veteran burlesque stripper Dixie Evans chuckled when I asked about Margaret Sullivan. " 'Sully' Sullivan—she was just a tacky old stripper with sandy blond hair. She'd come back in the dressing room and go, 'Get a load of the sax man's basket.'* That's a typical kind of thing that Sully would say. She was strictly what we call house. Didn't travel. Typical straight strip. She would strut right across that stage, she could really move and dance the old-fashioned way, the way those men liked. She got a big hand. She had very big boobs. Sully and her watermelons— they were like two huge cantaloupes."

And thus it was that a life's work was set in motion for Russell Albion Meyer. Or was it a life's curse? "Most people who develop fetishes have lower self-esteem, or they've developed a unique pattern of sexual arousal that doesn't include people," maintained psychologist and fetish expert Dr. Kevin McGovern. "If you're into objects, you don't need to have a personal connection with someone."

$ $ $

There was one escape hatch for Russell Albion Meyer from all the misery and misanthropy of his family, and it came in the form of a cheap 8-mm movie camera he received at age fourteen or so. "$9.95 Movie Camera Makes Memories Live Forever," shouted the ad for the UniveX Cine 8. It was a tiny, no-frills unit with a crude viewfinder and f 5.6 Ilex lens made in 1936 by the New York–based Universal Camera Corporation, a company run by a banker and insurance man that was regarded with disdain by "real" photographic equipment companies such as Kodak. But the UniveX took the relatively new 8 mm format and made it affordable for the poor and unwashed. Thirty feet of orthochromatic black-and-white film cost only sixty cents a roll and a buck to process. As legend goes, Lydia pawned her wedding ring to snag the camera for Russ, who'd been entranced by an ad. "All the other kids had roller skates, Russ got a camera," said Pete Filipovitch, who maintained it "gave him an excuse to get the hell away from her."

---

* One more odd detail about Margaret Sullivan Freud might've taken an interest in: she lived in fear of snakes. "She had big stacks of magazines in the dressing room," said Dixie Evans. "I'd have to go through every magazine, and if there was a snake in it, I had to tear it out of the magazine or throw it away. She was terrified of snake photos."

Up until this time Meyer's chief interest had been model planes, and he daydreamed of being a pilot. But something clicked when he had the UniveX in his hot little hands, just as it had when he saw Margie Sullivan shaking her stuff at the Follies. In the years to come the industrious RM would combine both obsessions and invent a career, but for now Meyer just went nuts with the camera, shooting pets, sporting events, parades, and, if he is to be believed, a few neighborhood girls whose parents weren't happy about it. "He did make a movie with Lucinda," said army buddy Charlie Sumners. "Some fifty years later I saw that. It was in color, just her playing piano and doing girlie things around the house."

In 1969, Meyer would tell the *New York Times* how at age fifteen he earned $66 painting a bakery, enough to fund a trip to Catalina Island to shoot a little film and enter it in an Eastman Kodak contest. En route in Los Angeles, a stranger slipped him a mickey, swiping his hard-earned loot. Meyer said that for four days he lived only on crackers, made it to Catalina anyway, and won the competition. In his autobiography there is no mention of this tale, only that RM won fourth prize in a local Kodak contest. Maybe one of the stories is actually true.

$ $ $

RM had grown into a strapping, handsome kid. He worked as an usher at the Fox Oakland Theater and as a mattress carrier for a department store chain ("It's kind of a curious connection there, my films and the mattresses," said Meyer). He then got a job as an assistant messenger at the U.S. Army Engineers office in San Francisco, where he'd work his way up to accountant. Whatever money didn't go into helping Lydia pay the bills went into new 8 mm movie equipment. At nineteen Meyer registered for the draft, but fate would intervene at the last second, offering a real escape from family life—and entry into a new brotherhood that would last a lifetime.

Meyer subscribed to *Popular Photography*, and there he saw a small ad placed by the Academy of Motion Picture Arts and Sciences looking for men willing to volunteer as combat photographers. "Action . . . Camera!" shouted the headline. "My heart jumped," said RM. "Here was a chance to train in Hollywood at something I had always been interested in. It certainly beat accounting."

He waited forever to hear back, and was heading to the mountains for some fishing when word came in that the Academy requested his presence in Los Angeles. He hopped a Greyhound to Los Angeles, getting off at Hollywood and Vine. After a couple of preliminary interviews—most notably with Eastman Kodak's Emery Huse, a man who'd assist Meyer once the war ended—and an army physical in downtown L.A., RM was inducted into the Signal Corps Reserve. At his side was Paul Fox, another inductee who'd become of one Meyer's closest friends.

For the first time RM was on his own, away from Lydia, living in a little Hollywood rooming house on Las Palmas near Sunset Boulevard with Harry Downard, another Signal Corps volunteer who like many in the troop, already had experience in filmmaking and photography. "He was a young kid then, pure as a drift of snow," said Downard of Meyer. "He was not forward at all, but quiet and demure." Meyer wanted to shoot a short movie on the beach with his 8 mm UniveX, so Harry helped out.

The star of this tiny opus was Paul Fox, who played a husband with a wayward eye. Before taking a nap, his wife ties a string from her toe to his in order to alert her that her mate is attempting to run off after some tramp, which of course he does. When it came to filmmaking, Meyer "was a natural," said Downard. "He took to it like fish to water." But when it came to still photography Harry "could never see his way of doing things. The commercial photographer usually has just one chance to get the picture. Russ worked on a different premise—he shot a hundred pictures, and hoped to Christ he got one that could be used!"

One cloud hung over Meyer's head at Las Palmas. "He mentioned that his mother had problems," said Downard. "She was mentally unbalanced, I guess. As it came across to me, he thought a great deal of his mother and tried to take care of her. It was difficult for him just to know she was goin' the way she was."

Meyer attended classes at both Eastman Kodak and the MGM

School of Motion Picture Photography, where he was taught to thread 35 mm Mitchell cameras, a piece of equipment they'd never even use during the war. Meyer found the studio's involvement dubious at best and felt they were sharing their knowledge only in order to score teaching deferments for their employees.

But RM excelled at the big assignment, which was to utilize a hundred-foot roll of film to shoot a short scene—all under the tutelage of one of MGM's top-notch photographers, who would then grade their footage. RM took his assigned actor out to a set for one of Mickey Rooney's Andy Hardy movies on the MGM lot and shot a sequence involving a window washer that was to culminate in a through-a-window shot of the washer throwing the contents of his bucket at the glass. Unfortunately, the window shattered, drenching Meyer, his teacher (noted studio cinematographer Joseph Ruttenberg), and the camera. But the resulting footage was sharp and the exposure right, allowing RM to place second-highest in his class. Ruttenberg's assessment of Meyer's talents boiled down to one apt word: "aggressive."

Meyer returned home to Oakland to await word on his future. On November 10, 1944, Harry Downard wrote to slip RM some advance good news. He had been appointed staff sergeant with the 166th Signal Photographic Company. At the end of December Meyer boarded a train for Camp Crowder, Missouri. Arriving a week early for training, RM headed straight for the Kansas City burlesque theaters, where his eyes were singed again, this time by a stacked blonde and former Miss St. Louis whom he was to see again after the war under much more personal circumstances.

To say that Meyer connected with the men of the 166th is putting it mildly. They were an extraordinary bunch, among them the gentle Paul Fox, who kept everybody laughing; poker-faced Jim Ryan, who'd physically hold together the intestines of a wounded soldier until help arrived; short, dapper Ken Parker, who, according to fellow serviceman Tom McGowan, "got more snatch than anybody" and later became a police photographer when not shooting pinups alongside Meyer; big, burly Fred Owens, later known for playing cameos in Meyer films, usually some sort of hapless hayseed victim; Don Ornitz, whose father had been one of the Hollywood Ten and who'd become a renowned magazine photographer; goateed William Ellis "Bill" Teas, a brilliant lensman who did as little as possible during the war but somehow managed to take the best pictures in the process. Three of the 166th—Charles Sumners, Ralph Butterfield, and Meyer—would write about their World War II experiences, although only RM's book would alternate shots of tanks and explosions with pictures of busty naked women.

Meyer spent World War II filming and photographing the advances of General Omar Bradley's First Army and General George S. Patton's Third Army as they battled their way from France to Germany. As he would say over and over throughout his career, there was no greater experience in his life. Central to this was the iron-clad bond he felt with the men of the 166th. "If you've never been in combat, it's hard to explain why a lot of guys remain friends," said Joe Longo, head of the International Combat Camera Association. "Combat draws people together." As any crony of Russ Meyer's will tell you, first came the films, then came the combat friends, and last came the women. "His army buddies were the brothers he never had," said Charles Sumners. "They were his family."

For Russell Albion Meyer, World War II meant freedom. "I don't remember him ever telling stories about growing up and doing this or that with his mother—to me, it was like Russ's life started when he was in the army," said Meyer star Erica Gavin. "He was born, he popped out in a uniform. There was no childhood."

Sgt. Meyer

I really didn't want the war to end. It was the best time I ever had.

—RUSS MEYER

"Russ would get so involved in makin' the picture that he would forget about the danger," said Charlie "Slick" Sumners. "He was a perfectionist."

January 1945 — it was a bitter cold day in the Ardennes forest outside of St. Hubert, Belgium. A bloody fight was raging, the one they'd call the Battle of the Bulge. Newsreel Unit 1's Meyer and Sumners had joined the 87th Infantry Division in the pines and snow. Germans were firing on the company from a church steeple. RM saw it as a perfect opportunity to try out his new lens, a Cooke 20-inch telephoto. He grabbed its long wooden case out of the back of the jeep and jumped into the fray. The barrel-shaped lens was so huge that it required a bulky tripod — RM's 35 mm Eyemo camera had to be screwed into it instead of the other way around.

The big black lens made Slick nervous. Some Nazi in the distance might mistake it for an artillery barrel and blow them both to hell. "You're gonna get us killed!" muttered Sumners, who pointed the jeep away from the action to ensure a quick getaway, then waited. There was one advantage the combat photographers had over the other GIs — if the furnace got too hot, they could split. But Meyer wasn't going anywhere. He was fearless, even reck-less. All that mattered was the shot. "The excitement of getting some footage that you knew was good—that really looked like *war*—it overcame any kind of fear, really," he'd say decades later.

Screaming artillery fire flew overhead as Meyer ripped through hundred-foot rolls of Ansco Supreme, stopping only to frantically reload the magazine. The GIs scored a direct hit on the church. The Germans fought back, sending a shell in on the left of Meyer and Sumners about a hundred yards away. Blammo! An-other landed directly in front of them. That was it for Sumners, who was certain they'd been spotted. "You better get in now, or I'll come back and pick up the pieces!" he barked at RM, throwing the jeep into gear. Meyer was fighting mad, cursing a blue streak, but he gave in, diving into the back of the vehicle, the camera still at-tached to the tripod. The jeep had gone about twenty-five yards when a shell exploded smack dab where they'd just been, blowing the area to kingdom come. "It just looked like a sawmill had been through there," said Sumners.

It was there in the Ardennes that Sumners and Meyer would come upon a couple of American tanks under fire in a clearing. They lay on their bellies in the snow, peering out from the relative safety of the woods. One of the tanks took a direct hit, then an-other. It rolled toward them and stopped. The turret clanked open and a wounded soldier climbed out. Slick started off to help, but Meyer held him back. If they ventured out into the clearing, they could be hit next. RM waved the soldier in their direction. He staggered toward them and fell. Sumners and Meyer dragged him into the woods, trailing blood in his wake. The soldier's body was torn apart by shrapnel. He moaned, "No, God, not me. Not me, God, not me." A few minutes later he was dead, a pool of blood spreading across the snow.

For the man who'd admit, "I'm probably the greatest voyeur of all," the war must've held a strange fascination. "Nothing can match the truth of seeing a man die and knowing his terrible secret—that he's dead and that the people who loved him don't know that yet," Meyer later said. When recording casualties—part of the combat photographer's job—RM tried not to include the deceased's face in the frame. The footage might wind up in some newsreel, and Meyer figured it would be a hell of a way for the soldier's family to find out he was no longer alive.

$ $ $

Combat photographers from the 166th Signal Photographic Company stuck with the combat troops like lampreys on a shark, documenting the war with Speed Graphic 4-by-5-inch still cameras and spring-loaded Eyemo 35 mm silent motion picture machines (they were originally equipped with Wall single-system sound units, but the roar of battle rendered soundtracks unusable). The 166th was right in the thick of it, M1 rifles their only means of protection. It is estimated that one of every four combat photographers never made it home. The 166th was comparatively lucky, going on to become one of the most decorated outfits in the European theater of operations: fifty-five Bronze Stars (one going to Russ Meyer), two Silver Stars, thirteen Purple Hearts, one Air Medal, one Legion of Merit, one Croix de Guerre. "They saw a lot of action, and they were in the right places at the right time to get good pictures," said Air Corps combat photographer Joe Longo.

Originally the 166th was made up of six-man teams—a driver, a motion picture photographer, a still photographer, a clerk, and an officer. As the demand for their presence grew, the units were broken into two- and three-man teams that now had to do the work of six. After a full day on the front lines, they'd caption their photos, fill out their exposure reports, and stick the raw film in a press bag.

The footage was gathered up and flown to London (later in the war, France), where the Army Pictorial Service developed it. If a picture was deemed newsworthy (and unclassified) it was radioed to the States. A combat photographer's work could be on the front page of a newspaper within thirty-six to forty-eight hours after turning it in. Motion picture film was flown to the States for use in newsreels. The 166th sent some three hundred thousand photographs to the Army Pictorial Service during the war. Another twenty thousand feet of motion picture footage was shot each week.

Five prints were made of each picture to disseminate among various departments of the military, with one going back to the photographer alongside a terse, one-page critique of his efforts. Known somewhat derisively among the photographers who received them as "good-good-complete," the reports were made up of one-word commentaries for each of six areas: focus, exposure, camera steadiness, composition, coverage, and captioning. Each sheet was signed by one Captain Fred "F.F." Fox, later to be a Hollywood producer and obviously a man not easily pleased. Often the picture was marked with a grease pencil indicating a spot where the photographer could've taken a closer or more dramatic picture. "They say you should've been over *here*," said Sumners. "If you'd have been over there, you'd be dead!"

Now a novice motion picture photographer, Meyer got a similar critique with a Cinex strip of still frames from his footage attached. "Ninety-five percent of his critiques were good," said Sumners. "Russ was that good." Meyer's combat footage wound up in an Oscar-winning 1945 short subject, *Eisenhower: True Glory*, and a pair of 1970 films, *The Rise and Fall of the Third Reich* and *Patton* (two frequently seen Meyer war shots include one of a tank battering its way into a building and another of a terrified young German soldier surrendering as he is kicked in the pants by an American GI).

Already present in his wartime work was a glimmer of Meyer's talent for montage, later to be a hallmark of his filmmaking. On a report concerning footage RM shot of General Patton in June 1945, Captain Fox compliments Meyer's inserts showing Patton's gun and the stars and horn on his jeep. RM was particularly proud of the material he shot documenting the destruction of the French town Maizieres-les-Metz toward the end of a nearly thirty-day battle in 1944. Meyer and Ralph Butterfield crawled through the demolished Hermann Goering Steel Mill, coordinating their coverage like a Hollywood production. The pair even climbed atop a railroad trestle to get better coverage of the fight, fully exposing themselves to enemy fire.

$ $ $

A year before the events in the Ardennes, at boot camp in Camp Crowder in January 1944, Russ Meyer went through technical training with newsreel cameraman Major Gatskill and cinematographer Arthur Lloyd. Lloyd—who'd shot many *Laurel and Hardy* and *Our Gang* comedies—imparted a lesson that would stick with Meyer the rest of his life. "He would always hold up five fingers to us and say, 'If you get a long shot, medium shot, closeup shot, insert and reestablish action, you'll always be able to cut that scene.'" Despite being a low-budget filmmaker, Meyer was a stickler for coverage, often shooting extra inserts to cover flubs or beef up lackluster footage, yet another way his films later outclassed the competition.

Sloughing off his mama's-boy adolescence, Meyer was now becoming Meyer—a brash, take-charge guy who wasn't afraid to tell you just how talented he was. "RM had an attitude that served him very well," said Tom McGowan of the 166th, who'd later coproduce and write Meyer's 1969 feature *Cherry, Harry and Raquel.* "He was a rather egotistical show-off type."

Fellow soldier Warren Harding related a story involving members of the 166th taking a break from technical training in Astoria, New York. A few of the men—Harding and Meyer included—decided to go into Manhattan, where they visited Toots Shor's swanky nightclub. "The waiter came over and asked everybody what they wanted to drink. He got to me and I said, 'Milk.' He said, 'What did you want to drink?' 'Milk.' He said, 'Are you *sure*?' Well, Russ stood up, and Russ is a big guy. And Russ goes, *'The soldier said he wanted milk!'* The guy turned around and I got my glass of milk. That's the way Russ was."*

Away from his crazy, fractured family, Russ grew up in the

---

* Years later, when Meyer came to Philadelphia for a distributor's screening of his 1964 sexploitation picture *Lorna,* he invited a few 166th alumni living in the area to attend, Harding among them. A religious man, uncomfortable with RM's brand of smut, Warren attended the screening to avoid hurting his friend's feelings, but stared at the floor the entire length of the picture. "Anything for Russ," he told me. "He was a real good friend."

166th. "He became a man," said Harry Downard. "It kind of brought out the macho in him. Where before he was a nice, quiet guy, now he had that raise-his-eyebrows look down at you."

$ $ $

At the completion of their training, the 166th boarded the USS *Susan B. Anthony* for the North Atlantic crossing. On March 9, 1944, the ship pulled into Belfast Harbor, the 166th bound for a two-hundred-year-old castle in Groomsport, Northern Ireland, for practice sessions with Master Sergeant Fred "Fritz" Mandl, a newsreel cameraman who would become a lifelong friend to Meyer and would later contribute cinematography to a couple of his movies. On May 6 the group moved on to Mobberly, a small village outside of Manchester, England, for six more weeks of training. By June, the 166th had been together six months and were thick as thieves.

Amid swarms of General Patton's Third Army, gearing up for the invasion of Normandy at Omaha Beach, the 166th boarded a landing ship tank and headed across the English Channel to France, "destiny wonderfully upon us," as Meyer wrote in his autobiography. Assigned to film the troops landing, RM got lost in the ensuing chaos. Meyer, his Eyemo, and his M1 rifle wandered for two days before rejoining the 166th at their Nehou command post.

After another combat photography outfit—the 165th Signal Corps—suffered heavy losses covering Bradley's First Army, five men from Newsreel Unit 1 were sent to assist in covering the 29th Infantry, battling in St. Lô, France, Russ Meyer among them. Not assigned to any particular division, Newsreel Unit #1 hopped from battle to battle, and, according to Charles Sumners, saw "more combat situations than any other unit."

On July 19, 1944, RM shot his first combat footage—an infantry platoon chowing down on their first meal in two days. The next day he photographed medics tending to a soldier's foot, which had nearly been blasted off by a land mine. Meyer even had time to write an editorial for *Stars and Stripes*, declaring, "Until a man has done a dogface's job he doesn't know the score." Typical Meyer—one day in combat and already an expert.

On July 21, Newsreel Unit 1's commanding officer, Lt. Gene Moore, brought bad news. "We were getting ready to go down the hill the next morning into St. Lô with the infantry, and we received word that Lieutenant Shaddon's unit had been wiped out," said Charles Sumners. In the struggle, a German mortar shell had hit a five-man unit of the 166th. Two men had been killed (one beheaded), another two lost a leg each, and the only survivor had gone crackers. "The whole unit, just gone," Sumners recalled. "That solidified the company. We realized a photographer could get killed as easily as a guy with a M1." The hijinks of basic training seemed light-years away—the 166th was now at war.

"It really shook us up," Meyer recalled. "And we were scared." RM mulled over the situation with Charlie Sumners, an Alabama recruit who'd first encountered Meyer back at Camp Crowder. "Russ called me aside and said, 'What are we gonna do?'" said Sumners. "I replied, 'Well, if we don't go down the hill tomorrow, we won't be worth a damn the rest of the war.' We went down into St. Lô the next day, and from that day on we've been very close."

$ $ $

On the surface, Charlie "Slick" Sumners and Russell Albion Meyer were one odd couple. Charlie was a diminutive, laid-back Southern Baptist gentleman, Russ a clumsy, hyperactive bear soon to become a high-class pornographer. And while Meyer would later spend years writing a thousand-page autobiography, Sumners was a man of few words. "Charlie didn't talk about the war," said his wife Floyce. "I would never have known that he saved Russ's life if Russ hadn't come and told me himself."

The two were lifelong friends regardless of their differences. The first image you see in Meyer's massive autobiography is a picture of Charlie Sumners. And while Sumners granted that Meyer's movies "were not the kind that you would show at your PTA," he'd shrug off disparaging comments from his fellow churchgoers in Alabama. "It was a Mutt and Jeff deal," said fellow 166th member Warren Harding. "They were inseparable. Charlie was very devoted to Russ, Russ was very devoted to Charlie." "We never in all the years had a disagreement that amounted to a hill of beans," declared Sumners, laughing. "I'm probably the only one he didn't fight with. Russ was real bullheaded, stubborn. He resented authority. He didn't want people telling him what to do and how to do it."

One person Meyer did routinely clash with was his commanding officer of his unit, Lieutenant Gene Moore. RM would load up on film and disappear into the field for days, only to be chewed out by a frantic Moore on his return. Finally Moore gave up, letting Meyer and Sumners plot their own course. Other GIs were afraid to venture out with them, figuring those two cowboys were bound to get themselves plugged. As future RM film editor Richard Brummer said, "Russ believed once he was looking through the lens that nothing could hurt him."

Initially, Charlie was just the man behind the wheel. "Meyer was a terrible driver," said Sumners. "He'd scare the hell out of me, so I did all the driving." In St. Malo, France, Charlie would drive straight into the thick of battle to save Meyer, Lt. Moore, and another GI from heavy shelling. Although the jeep sustained two bullet holes and a cracked windshield, nobody was hit, and Sumners was awarded a Bronze Star for his bravery. Under RM's tutelage, Charlie quickly became not just a wheel man but a fine photog himself. A shot Sumners took in Oberdorla, Germany, of GIs advancing up an alley while a dead German lies in the foreground landed on the front page of the New York *Daily News* in April 1945 and was chosen as one of the 100 best photos of the European theater by the International Association of Combat Cameramen.

Meyer had found his element in the 166th. He loved the romance of it all—jumping into a jeep with an loaded Eyemo, heading off for God knows what mayhem with his buddy Charlie by his side. Every day was another town, a new adventure. "In the war I felt like Tom Swift and his Electric Underwear," said Meyer. "It was a great and wondrous game." There were also dark laughs to be had amid the more hair-raising events. Outside of Labitz, Germany, Meyer and Sumners came upon two seemingly dead soldiers near their abandoned tank. When they stopped to get it on film, Charlie thought he saw one of the stiffs move, which led to a little expected fun. Sumners cocked his .45 while Meyer announced in broken German, "This soldier is not dead. Shoot him in the head!" Up jumped the former corpse, begging for mercy. Now Russ and Charlie had their very own POW—not to mention a Luger pistol as a souvenir. "We had a lot of good times together," said Sumners.

Sumners even spent a few weeks as RM's nursemaid. Outside of Metz, France, the jeep in which Meyer was riding skidded on an icy road and overturned. "Russ was pinned underneath the jeep, and it knocked him out for a few minutes." Meyer's leg was badly mangled in the accident, but he refused to get into the ambulance with the two other Gis injured in the crash. "Russ discovered they had stolen his watch—he was mad and he wouldn't go to the hospital. He was afraid he'd miss something, I suppose." With Charlie's help, Meyer hobbled back to the old, unheated house the unit had been staying in. Sumners had to take care of RM for the next three weeks while the rest of their group convalesced in a proper hospital. "I burned up every stick of furniture in the house except the bed he was on and one chair tryin' to keep him warm."

The liberation of Paris was a heady time for those of the 166th who were present. When the Second French Armored Division marched into Paris on August 25, 1944, Sumners and Lt. Moore drove right in with the tank division. The streets of the city were mobbed with ecstatic civilians, and when their jeep was overrun by pretty French girls anxious to kiss and squeeze an American soldier, Meyer was on the hood, movie camera in hand, getting it all. In perfect Meyer fashion, and much to Charlie's amusement, RM promptly ripped the seat of his pants open on a windshield knob and spent the next few hours being goosed by the exuberant French women swarming all around them.

$ $ $

When you're talking Russ Meyer, breasts have to poke into the picture sooner or later, even during a world war, and the moment finally came in Rambouillet, France. Meyer, Sumners, Moore, and one other GI were holed up there for a week and a half waiting for the French to orchestrate the August Paris takeover. A number of war correspondents were there as well, including Ernest Hemingway, who was holding court at the Hôtel du Grand Veneur. He'd send a few Free French soldiers out to ferret out stories for him, then everybody would meet back at the hotel for a booze fest with such luminaries as columnist Ernie Pyle and photographer Robert Capa. Charlie Sumners remembers all sorts of weaponry stockpiled at the Grand Veneur, lending credence to rumors that Hemingway was running guns for the French underground. Sumners didn't care for Hemingway—"He was arrogant and just a big blowhard." Perhaps, but this particular blowhard would, believe it or not, get Russ Meyer laid for the first time.

Meyer and three 166th cronies were camped behind the overbooked hotel in a pup tent when Hemingway apparently took pity on them. On the morning of August 23, 1944, the GIs were relaxing in a bistro when one of Hemingway's flunkies—a short Portuguese man—extended a rather generous offer from the eminent scribe. The four were invited to visit the local cathouse that night, on the house, courtesy of Ernest Hemingway, who was pals with the local madam. Meyer no doubt broke into a sweat. The twenty-two-year-old couldn't admit to his comrades that he was still a virgin. It was do-or-die time, like when he was back on that hill above St. Lô.

That night, under a full moon, the men sauntered over to the house of ill repute. A short, heavy-set French woman with her hair pulled back ushered them through a neatly manicured garden and a candlelit vestibule, then into a shadowy bar filled with women in various states of undress. Meyer couldn't believe his eyes. "It was like something out of de Maupassant," he said. "Fifteen girls, their children, a woman with a bun sitting in the back."

With visions of Margie Sullivan dancing in his head, RM picked the dame with the biggest balcony. Little else is known about Babette, but Meyer has said that she seemed to recognize his inexperience and was happy to take the lead. She beckoned him to follow her up the stone staircase, holding aloft a GI-issue Zippo lighter as a torch. A brass bed with Russ in the missionary position followed, sending the novice straight to heaven, albeit a little too quickly: "The quail flew early that night, as the boys from the South used to say." Russ and Babette went at it again—at which point, if RM is to be believed, he heard Lieutenant Moore shouting to his men, "Let's pull out!"

Meyer never grew tired of telling this story, which merits the most purple of prose in his autobiography. "A newfound tingling . . . the emptying of sacks . . . a logjam burst asunder" (alongside stills of a high-heeled foot crushing a cherry). As if there had been any doubt before, RM was now hooked on super-structured women. From here on in, Meyer would insist that when faced with a flat-chested frail, he'd "rather play cards."

Now that RM had popped his cherry, he had to share it with the world. "It was so thrilling, he had to tell somebody about it," said Sumners. "'Course, we went back again. And *again.*"

Decades later, Meyer returned to the scene of this glorious conquest, documenting the visit on film with the solemnity of a trek to Stonehenge for the Discovery Channel. He was happy to find a large marble monument to the Third Army not far from the doorway of the old whorehouse. Tits and war—was there anything better?

$ $ $

Meyer loved to regale listeners with his war tales, and Charlie Sumners is not the first to suggest that a bit of embellishment went on. While in England, Meyer and Sumners were sent to a re-mote area to photograph the inhabitants of a prison stockade. In-side were some ornery-looking creatures—according to Charlie, considerably more than a dozen, and most of whom were African American. They were heavily guarded, not allowed to talk, and bound in leg chains. Once Meyer and Sumners had shot film, the colonel in charge confiscated the footage.

In June 1959, Meyer recounted the visit to E. M. "Mick" Nath-anson, a freelance writer who worked as an editor at *Adam* and *Sir*

Knight, skin magazines RM had been shooting pinups for during his postwar career. Meyer called the inmates "the Dirty Dozen," and Nathanson writes that the group comprised "a black man, an Indian and ten white men of various ethnic backgrounds ... soldiers who had been convicted of capital crimes or major felonies while in the Army, had been sentenced to death or long prison terms, but had been given the choice of ... going on a secret, extremely dangerous mission instead." Nathanson did his best to investigate the matter factually, with Meyer even writing letters of inquiry to Army officials on his behalf, to no avail. Instead, Nathanson wrote a 1965 novel based on the idea, which led to the hugely successful film of the same name. (Meyer got 10 percent of Nathanson's *Dirty Dozen* deal—ten grand—for his trouble).

More curious is a war tale Meyer told more than once concerning an event he said happened while he and Sumners were stationed in Leipzig, Germany, near the end of the war, in April 1945. RM claims he was rousted out of bed in the middle of the night and sent to S2 (intelligence), where he came face-to-face with a Sixth Armored Division colonel—and General Patton. Intelligence had revealed that Hitler and Goebbels were heading for a hideout in Weimar. Patton wanted them both assassinated—not taken alive—and he barked at Meyer, whose "knees had turned to jelly," that he'd better be "damn careful" about what he filmed. The next morning both he and Sumners joined the regiment heading to Weimar, their jeep shielded between a couple of tanks. RM figured that if he could capture this momentous event, he'd be assured of a future career as a newsreel cameraman. The troops arrived only to discover, by "beating the Burgermeister, the Mayor," that Hitler and Goebbels had indeed been there but had decided to return to Berlin. The assassination mission was aborted.

It's a tremendous story and, according to Sumners (whom Meyer placed right in the middle of it), "a fabrication. He made up the story. There's not one ounce of truth in that." When I asked him why Meyer would feel the need to spin such a yarn, he laughed and simply said, "I don't know."

$ $ $

On May 7, 1945, Eisenhower signed for the Allies in Germany's unconditional surrender in Reims, France. Waiting to return to the States, the 166th was sent to Wildbad Kreuth, a former health resort thirty miles from Munich, at the base of the Alps. It was a beautiful location for blowing off steam. A few of the men built their own darkroom, while others went fishing (sometimes with grenades). In June, both Meyer and Sumners received battle stars for each of the five major campaigns they'd been part of.

For a moment, it looked like the 166th wasn't quite through, as word came in that their presence was required for the invasion of Japan. On July 5, the company moved to Camp New Orleans, a ratty tent city in France. There they awaited further instructions until the atomic bomb brought what Meyer called "the last good war" to an end.

RM and Paul Fox, another 166th comrade, then killed time by hawking contraband film to finance more trips to the brothel, but by November 21, Meyer was aboard the *Cody Victory,* sailing home to the States. Leaving Europe was bittersweet. RM wasn't kidding when he said he didn't want the war to end. What was there to go home to—an accounting job?

Charlie Sumners said that during his war duty Meyer told him the same thing over and over again, and it's significant because this is the first time RM had communicated his mission in life: he was gonna make it big in the Hollywood movie business, he was gonna be rich, and he wasn't gonna answer to anyone: "*I'm* going to be the one telling people what to do." Little did Sumners know that RM had big plans for him. "When we said goodbye in France, Russ said, 'Oh, this is not goodbye. I'll see you again.' " Charlie thought he was crazy. After all, the war was over.

$ $ $

But Russ Meyer was crazy like a fox. Back in California, he kept in constant touch with all the members of the 166th. He tracked down their numbers and addresses and organized their reunions, and once his films started earning the big dough, he'd occasionally spring for travel fare when somebody didn't have the funds. He even went as far as to get a couple of old pals suffering in sexless marriages laid. When out on the road, Meyer sought out members of the company he barely knew and sprang for dinner. When it came to the 166th, Meyer was unrelenting. "I love finding and meeting up with these guys again. It's more exciting than finding a broad."

"Russ Meyer was the father of the group. He would make the decisions," said fellow 166er Bill Tomko, laughing. "Nobody else made a suggestion!" Kay Hively, a Missouri reporter who wrote a history of Camp Crowder and helped the 166th organize reunions at their former training ground, remembered Meyer as "the charismatic leader" and mother hen of the group. "He was always worrying that somebody was gonna be left or somebody didn't wake up, that everybody was on the bus, everybody was comfortable."

At the same time, even at these reunions Meyer was "a bull charging ahead." In the eighties, when the 166th had an emotional reunion at their training camp, he had to document the gang's every move on film. As Kay Hively recalled, "RM was directing a movie the whole time we were here—'Don't get off the bus until I get this camera up. And then when I yell, you can start getting off the bus. I'll film you coming off.' When it was time to go, it was, 'Don't get on the bus until I get the camera set up.'"

Of course, even among 166th alumni Meyer would be a source of controversy. He quarreled with nearly all his combat buddies; sometimes the tiffs went on for years. There were spouses in particular who didn't care for RM or his line of work, and the feeling was usually mutual. "By and large if I'm with friends and they're with their wives, the wives are very secondary," he'd tell biographer David K. Frasier. "I really don't embrace them."

$ $ $

Forget breasts—there is no greater key to Russ Meyer than the 166th Signal Photographic Company. Patriotism was now a central component of Meyer's personality, along with a deep hatred of the Red menace—"I am a rabid anti-Communist," Meyer told Roger Ebert in a 1968 interview. RM would use the commie tag to tar any enemy, perhaps most amusingly with ex-166th member Stanley Kramer, producer-director of such "liberal" Hollywood fare as *On the Beach* and *Guess Who's Coming to Dinner,* although Meyer right-hand man Jim Ryan maintains that the real reason RM "didn't like Stanley [was] because they were both successful people—but Stanley was on a real higher level."

In the hands of Meyer, a self-described "vicious capitalist," "patriotism" and "communism" seem to function as vague, comic book concepts at best, white hats versus the black hats in a Technicolor western. "I don't think he was the shrewdest political thinker you're ever going to run across," said David K. Frasier.[*] "He was too busy lusting after tits, making money, spending it on himself, and moving on. RM looked upon America as a place someone from a disadvantaged background could, with hard work, make a fuck of a lot of money." Frasier felt that Meyer's hatred of communism simply boiled down to "the idea that he would work his ass off and then have to share it with someone," someone who he felt couldn't or wouldn't put their nose to the grindstone like our natural-born workaholic RM. The bottom line was the war had freed Meyer from home, taught him a craft, and got him laid. It was just one big bang of big bosoms and square jaws, not unlike the many pictures of nude women mashed together with combat shots in the wartime chapters of his autobiography, and RM would express his love for country in the exuberant jumble of neon signs, car dashboards, and giant knockers that crowd his movie montages.

"Meyer uses his productions, I believe, to recapture the joy he felt during the formative and most enjoyable period of his life—the war," wrote Roger Ebert. During his career, Meyer made

---

[*] Adds Jim Ryan, "Meyer didn't have any really firm views—of anything. Not enough to send anybody a hundred bucks, or buy 'em a placard. Anything Meyer thought that would be better for Meyer he was for, regardless of the party. He didn't like the Kennedys, probably because they were Irish—Meyer never cared much for the Irish. I think his mother taught him all that stuff."

movies with jeeps, cameras, even guns, and certainly a feeling of battle. As RM actor Charles Napier so aptly put it to writer Nathaniel Thompson, "Working with Russ Meyer was like being in the first wave landing in Normandy during World War II, crossed with a weekend in a whorehouse." Members of his Hollywood crew frequently came from the 166th, and they continually pop up in the films as bit players. There are some very amusing stills from Meyer's 1963 film *Heavenly Bodies* that show a bunch of RM's combat cronies with cameras slung around their necks—but instead of clicking away at a burning tank or dead Nazi, they're pointing their cameras at naked women.

In the eighties, when Meyer's movie career had essentially dried up, he'd head back to Europe again and again to retrace each and every step of his war experiences with a movie camera, invariably with Charlie "Slick" Sumners by his side. Thirteen chapters of RM's autobiography deal with the war, and a few are simply titled with the names of 166th men who played influential roles in Meyer's early years.

French distributor (and Meyer's first biographer) Jean-Pierre Jackson maintains that for RM, "women were just pleasure, and that's it. His real interest was remembrance, friendship with his army buddies. He's a very sentimental guy, nostalgic. He cried a lot."

Jackson, also a film buff, was at one point in Los Angeles working on a book about the old cliffhanger serials. While visiting Meyer, he mentioned he was heading off to Arizona to interview William Witney, director of such forgotten epics as *Dick Tracy's G-Men.* "Russ said, 'Oh, that old guy from Republic Studios?' He had tears in his eyes and said, 'It's very good that you are going to see him. Don't let him alone.' "

That was Meyer. A tough guy, but one who wept when somebody gave a shit about a old, forgotten filmmaker. A man who not only covered his walls with cheap, funny little plaques commemorating each and every movie he created, but who also built small shrines in his home to celebrate dear, departed pals. According to actress Alaina Capri, "Russ acted tougher or meaner than he really was—he tried to be tough on the set, but he had a big heart and was really kind to everyone. He was a complete gentleman—always."

And a man desperate to hold on to the one thing that no one can keep: the past. "I have never been able to recapture those moments," he said of his combat duty to a reporter in 1969. "You never can."

3

Tittyboom or Bust

Tits are a means to an end. —RUSS MEYER

Like many servicemen returning home after the war, Russ Meyer
was at a loose end. The great adventure had come to an abrupt
halt, and his comrades were now strewn across the country. No
more Hemingway, whorehouses, or heroics. No action at all. In
December 1945, just after he received his honorable discharge
from Fort MacArthur in southern California, Meyer made the Hollywood rounds looking for motion picture work. A movie camera
hadn't left his hands since he was a kid and surely his experience
as an expert combat photographer gave him an advantage. RM
found nothing but rejection, however, and it stung. Tinseltown
was more interested in protecting its own than hiring outsiders,
and there were plenty of men returning who'd already had industry jobs before they were drafted.

RM moved back into his mother's house at 918 Donovan
Street in San Leandro. Mother, of course, was ecstatic to have her
son back, but Russ sensed a distinct lack of enthusiasm from
stepfather Howard and half-sister Lucinda. To complicate matters, Lydia's husband had taken up with a nurse he'd met while
laid up in the veterans' hospital, and Lucinda, now a very pretty
young woman, was showing more and more signs of having a
screw loose.

Meyer had to figure out a future for himself. With funds he'd socked away from his sergeant's pay, he bought himself a Speed Graphic camera. And he was already on the prowl for women. When RM found out that Evelyn "Treasure Chest" West was scheduled to make an appearance at Don's Cabaret, an Oakland nightspot, he made sure he was front and center. While, as he writes somewhat creepily in his autobiography, Meyer knew he "couldn't begin to possess" such a beauty "on a personal level . . . to photograph her remarkable abundance would certainly suffice." For the time being, anyway.

West, known as the "the Girl with the $50,000 Chest"—she'd had it insured by Lloyd's of London—and infamous for her publicity-generating feuds with other dancers, had a "very good act, very theatrical," as fellow stripper Dixie Evans recalled. "She'd come to the microphone and murmur, 'Oh, my underwear is made of lace / Now, if I remove them before you, would that be a disgrace?' She had a way of strutting like no other—a certain tune would play and just her boobs would bounce. The audience would stomp and stomp and stomp and nothin' else would move but these boobs goin' up and down, up and down."*

Wowed by West's Oakland appearance, Meyer made a pitch to her agent: if Meyer was allowed to photograph the dame, he'd supply them with free eight-by-ten publicity stills. It worked like a charm. There in the club during off hours, West, posing in garter belt, hose, a fur stole, and little else, mimed her act while Meyer snapped away. With his potential distraction safely corralled inside a "sturdy jockstrap," RM's first known attempt to combine his two great passions, big-busted women and photography, went off without a hitch. RM was ecstatic, and although he was nervous as hell, West didn't notice Meyer breaking a sweat. "I thought he was handsome," she said. "And very sincere about his work."

---

* Although West insists the story isn't true, fellow stripper Tura Satana said West once worked with a reptile, which slithered into Satana's dressing room one too many times. "I finally told her, 'If that snake ends up in my dressing room one more time, you're gonna feel sorry for it.' I took it and swung it until it died, broke the snake's back. Evelyn had to go out on stage with the dead snake, trying to make it look like it was still alive. She learned not to screw with me anymore."

And a gentleman with an oddly supportive mother. Lydia's first glimpse of her son's lifelong obsession came as shots of the top-heavy model developed in the family bathtub. If Meyer is to be trusted, her only response was, "What a lovely girl, Russell—and what big, beautiful breasts." Dear old Mom.

Meyer's modus operandi was now in place: give 'em the old "Can I take your picture?" rap first, and a trip into their shorts might even follow. RM couldn't believe how well the deal worked. He kept his camera equipment in the back of his Oldsmobile, combat-photographer ready. In his autobiography there is a shot of Meyer backstage among nude dancers in a Vegas revue that is just incredible. The look on his face as he ogles a topless female is so purposeful and intense—RM's on the hunt for That Certain Female, one in possession of a pair of deadly weapons that just so happen to be made of flesh. "I went at it in a very precise manner," Meyer told writer Dale Ashmun. "Not any broad, just specific broads. And I went through mountains of shit just trying to find those broads . . . nothing would stop me."

While shooting strippers was an immense turn-on, Meyer needed an income. Emery Huse, the Kodak bigwig who'd helped RM get into the 166th, wrote a letter of recommendation that got Meyer in with a San Francisco Kodak honcho named Bob Antz, a man who'd play a small but significant role in RM's early career. Antz sent Meyer to Gene Walker, who ran an industrial film company bearing his name. Gene K. Walker Films churned out 16 mm promotional films for the likes of Southern Pacific Railroad, Standard Oil, and the Western Pine Association. Meyer would work on and off for approximately eight years as one of Walker's chief cinematographers. "Walker was sort of a father figure towards him," said Meyer cohort Jim Ryan.

During the war, RM had merely shot raw footage and turned it in, getting feedback only on his cinematography and coverage. At Walker's, he'd get an education in making a finished product that was edited, had a soundtrack and told a story, however bland. "Industrial films, that's where I learned my craft," said Meyer. "You'd go out with three people and do everything." With an earnest but robotic narrator's ad-copy prose, intricate product montages, picture-postcard landscapes, and duller-than-white-bread content, this mathematical film style was an essential inspiration to Meyer's filmmaking, although he'd warp it into something sexual and strange.

A number of Walker co-workers would assist in RM's early productions, in particular Charles G. "Chuck" Schelling, a balding, bespectacled chap later to function as Meyer's first soundman, editor, and occasional actor. RM's job at Walker also provided an opportunity to travel, enabling him to reconnect with his army buddies while checking out local burlesque houses along the way.

$ $ $

Curiously, the one paramour in Russ Meyer's life who would never step naked before his camera was his first wife. RM met Betty Valdovinos on the bus he'd board at Davis and 14th in San Leandro, bound for Gene Walker's outfit on Commercial Street in San Francisco. A curvaceous, pint-sized Spanish-French hybrid, Betty worked at Mark Hopkins Hospital. Russ "was a wonderful, wonderful man," said Betty, who maintained that Meyer was "shy" and not very experienced. "He was just very kind, very sweet, and very generous. He was a big, strong man, and when he'd run after me I'd cringe, because I'm only about five foot two. It would scare me to death. Russ had a way about him that was real man's man. Macho."

The pair dated for several years before marrying around 1949. Meyer was fond of recounting amorous evenings spent "parking" with Valdovinos in his Oldsmobile, but as far as marriage goes, he suggests in his autobiography that he acquiesced only after Betty made the announcement to friends and family while he was away on a business trip. At any rate, they slipped off to Vegas to tie the knot, with combat buddy Ralph Butterfield and his wife the only friends in attendance.

The newlyweds settled in San Francisco, renting an apartment Betty had found at 801 Pine Street, right down the street from her hospital job. "We kinda shared whatever we had, and it wasn't much," said Betty. Russ bought his wife a yellow Chevy. "We used to gallivant and rush all over at night," she said. Betty remembered Russ as "always up and at 'em, ready to go, busy, always anxious to do things. He was never depressed. He was definitely driven— he wanted to make himself very important."

RM's friends liked Betty. "She was a lady," said friend Dolores Fox. But Betty says she was left in the dark in regard to Meyer's obsessions. Maybe it was the times, maybe he was too timid—or maybe he just knew Betty wouldn't go for it. As associate Jim Ryan saw it, "I don't think her ideas were theatrically oriented. Betty thought Russ should go to work every day and carry a lunch box."

$ $ $

Betty would accompany Russ on visits to Lydia and Lucinda in San Leandro. "They never came to visit us, thank God." Betty didn't recall ever seeing a man present, so it is possible that Lydia's marriage to Howard Haywood had already ended. "They were rough people. They were not what you would call the elite." Betty described Russ's mother as "a rough housewife, a farm woman who lived and worked hard—she wasn't smooth at all. She would say that I was like a butterfly, that I was beautiful. She would make big compliments all the time, and you knew that she was trying to keep me as a friend of hers. I felt sorry for her. She tried too hard to be nice."

Storm clouds came quickly in the marriage. According to Meyer's autobiography, Betty unexpectedly became pregnant early in the union. Since she clearly wanted a child, RM hints that it might not have been an accident on her part. Meyer claims that he "browbeat" her into an abortion, arranging the operation through a Chinese American doctor whom Henrye Bowen, an early Meyer mentor, knew in Oakland. Betty, however, has never confirmed either the pregnancy or the abortion. In any case, any dream of a white picket fence was soon shattered. "Betty and RM not living happily ever after," wrote Meyer in *A Clean Breast*.

$ $ $

Around 1950 or so, war buddy Don Ornitz, now a photographer on magazine assignment for Globe Photos, came to visit the Meyers for a week with his wife and child. Although RM was still complaining about his friend's screaming child some five decades later, a momentous discussion occurred one day while he and Don were walking the streets of San Francisco. In the course of an argument over politics—Ornitz senior had been one of the Hollywood Ten, and Don actually had the audacity to invite Meyer to a Communist Party meeting—the conversation somehow turned to Meyer's future. Ornitz, recalling some natural-light portraits RM had done of his 166th comrades back at Wildbad Kreuth, suggested that Russ take advantage of the new girlie mag explosion by getting into glamour photography. Why, Ornitz himself was making good money from it. When Meyer complained he had no real experience, Don said, "What you lack in ability you'll make up for in enthusiasm."

Obviously Meyer needed little encouragement in this area— he'd already shot pictures of whatever strippers he could talk into peeling. Getting paid for such a task would be nirvana. Meyer hooked up with the Globe agency, and while the agency took 40 percent of the take on black-and-white shots and 50 percent for color, they had the skin magazine connections and could extract more generous fees than RM could ever wangle on his own. Meyer took to girlie photography hammer and tongs.

Perversely, Meyer found *cheesecake*—the most commonly used term for this photo work—offensive, preferring the bland assignation of *figure photography*. In later years he'd coin a colorful, much more crass, Meyerism for the endeavor: tittyboom. RM would shoot hundreds of layouts for magazines such as *Gent, Fling, Escapade, Frolic,* and scores of others. In our blasé age it is hard to imagine what an utterly clandestine affair photographing scantily clad women was then. Normal people just didn't do such a thing. Pulp writer John Bowers recalled "nearly fainting" upon seeing his first nude woman at a photo shoot. "Back then it was done sneakily, and as a result it was more exciting, because it was hidden and outrageous."

And it could also get you busted. Arv Miller, publisher and

editor of *Fling* magazine, had a retoucher on staff just to excise pubic hairs. "If there was one strand of hair you could have trouble," said Miller, and you had to be savvy about what could be gotten away with city to city or else you could lose your shirt. Due to a powerful Catholic faction, Chicago was a difficult territory, and Miller recalled a tense meeting with the God squad over an issue of *Fling* they found particularly offensive. "It was a face-to-face confrontation. They said, 'Girls with large breasts are pornographic.' That was an actual quote. The bigger the girls, the more obscene. I thought it was very funny, but I didn't laugh too much. They convinced my Chicago distributor not to put the issue out. Those were very rough days."

Selling the photos entailed more espionage. A magazine editor would be visited by a rep, "usually a Viennese guy," who would be carrying "a briefcase full of sets," as writer and former men's magazine editor Bruce Jay Friedman explained. "They were contact pictures of an individual girl, shot by one of his photographers." The editor would scan the contact sheets, circling with a grease pencil the shots that looked promising, then blowups would be made. The photographer didn't get to pick what was used; Meyer admitted he would "often completely disagree with the editor's choice." The sheer volume of RM's work meant not every Meyer pictorial is great—there's also the occasional lapse into "art" layouts (à la "naked girl with watermelon") or zany gag shots that are moldy at best—but when he connects, look out, because RM could make a dame look like she ruled the world.

Although it would take his second wife Eve to really light a match to his tittyboom career, Meyer met his first superstar in this department in the fall of 1950, and she would immediately (although unknowingly) cause the demise of his first marriage. Her name was Tempest Storm.

$ $ $

A self-described "freak with a forty-inch bosom," Blanche Banks stood at Third and Main and stared up at the Follies Theatre. It looked less than impressive in the cold light of day with its neon asleep. Blanche had already blown off her first appointment the day before. She had planned on being a Las Vegas chorus girl, not shaking her ass in some smoky flesh palace like the Follies. But this was Los Angeles, not Vegas, and the Follies was the only portal into a world Blanche desperately wanted to be a part of.

Life hadn't exactly been a bowl of cherries for Blanche, who was a mere twenty-two. Born March 1, 1928, in Eastman, Georgia, she'd been gang-raped by five men at the age of fourteen, endured attempted molestation at the hands of an alcoholic stepfather, escaped two failed marriages, and survived three abortions, the last of which nearly killed her. According to her autobiography, *The Lady Is a Vamp*, the only thing that saved Blanche were fantasies of movie stardom: "I did not have to accept a life of pain and degradation. I dreamed my way out of Eastman." Blanche was a brunette, embarrassed by her crooked teeth, but had been both blessed and cursed with the sort of figure that would put sweat on a man's brow: 39-24-39.

Cut to downtown Los Angeles, autumn 1950. There, in a shabby office behind the stage, a nervous Blanche came face-to-face with the matriarch of the Follies, a red-haired grandma named Lillian Hunt who also directed burlesque films shot right in her theater. Hunt barked at the young girl to take her clothes off, pronto. Lillian took a gander at Blanche's outrageous proportions, then bust a gut when Banks inquired as to whether her breasts were too big. Apparently this little sparrow with the big chest hadn't been in a burly-Q house before. "God didn't make boobs too big for my business," replied Hunt, who then instructed Blanche to shake a leg. "Let's see that pelvis move!" shouted Lillian, who noted the youngster's lack of grace and declared, "You just haven't got it." To which Blanche shot back, "I'm gonna make you eat those words one of these days."

Struck by Blanche's moxie, Hunt told her that if she laid off the men, booze, cigarettes, and sweets, she just might be a star someday and gave her the gig. Lillian also conjured up the monicker that made this dark-haired, porcelain-skinned beauty famous— Tempest Storm. Just how tempestuous Tempest could be soon became apparent when the newcomer got into a backstage dust-up with Follies headliner Lili St. Cyr.

Tempest had proved to be a quick study, and after only a handful of shows in the chorus line, Storm ascended to solo status, second-billed only to St. Cyr. The blond bombshell accused Storm of star sabotage, by way of dropping pins on the stage that pierced Lili's bare feet, and of copping St. Cyr's apparently trademarked running-of-the-fingers-through-the-hair. A showdown ensued, and Tempest, displaying the steely determination that has kept her afloat for over five decades of burlesque, pronounced St. Cyr a "so-called star." To keep the peace, Hunt quickly transferred Storm to Oakland's El Rey Burlesk Theater, where she was now a headliner making three and a half bills a week. Some punishment.

Tempest Storm soon became the star of her dreams, with Tinseltown wags declaring her infamous assets "the two biggest props in Hollywood." Sensational romances with Mickey Rooney, Nat "King" Cole, Hugh O'Brian, Trini Lopez, Sammy Davis Jr., Engelbert Humperdinck, and Elvis Presley would plaster her pretty mug all over the scandal sheets. But first came a whistle-stop at the El Rey, where she'd meet two men instrumental in kick-starting her career: Pete DeCenzie and Russ Meyer.

$ $ $

The El Rey Burlesk Theater was a fifteen-hundred-seat venue open from noon to midnight with a late show on Saturday, where mangled prints of B-movies unspooled between three live shows a day. Well known on the burlesque circuit, the El Rey featured the usual motley assortment of dancers, a chorus line, a small orchestra, and some flea-bitten comics.

A scrappy entrepreneur named Pete DeCenzie owned and ran the El Rey from its birth in 1950 until its demise eight years later. Oakland restrictions were such that "you couldn't take your clothes off as long as the lights were on," as burlesque queen Tura Satana recalled. Even stranger, "if you were nude, you could not move." DeCenzie's response was a contrivance called *Pictures in Poses*, during which the almost-bare froze in place to depict paintings by "the great masters." As long as they didn't move, it was art—and Pete didn't get busted.

Pete had been around the block a time or two and knew how to grease palms as well as wheels. With his graying buzz cut, bushy eyebrows, and flat, friendly face, DeCenzie looked, as one scribe for the skin mag *Adam* put it, like a "cross between a retired light-weight fighter who has let the pounds pile up and an amiable racetrack tout." Leisure time was devoted to his Australian show-girl wife, Yvonne, their two beloved dogs, and chasing skirt. "Pete was kind of a playboy; he loved the ladies," said Satana.

Born in Seattle, DeCenzie had broken into show business as a kid, working at another Oakland burlesque house as a "candy butcher"—grindhouse lingo for one who hawks sweets in the aisles during intermission. Pete worked carnivals, sold magazine subscriptions, toured with girlie shows, and even did a stint with notorious exploitation film potentate Kroger Babb, appearing as a phony doctor who'd pitch "educational" books to the rubes at-tending Babb's birth-of-a-baby shocker *Mom and Dad*.

Russ Meyer, who loved the arcane language of the carnival con, saw Pete as a master. "He had this great hype, and he was able to pique the curiosity of the unwashed. He was a real showman. It harkened back to when he was a carny man, a barker. 'Leap like a tuna, bark like a fox. Run up the stairs, rob your own trunk. Step right up here. Stop the sales. Everybody hold back. What we're go-ing to do is pick out six boxes, three of which will contain genuine Elgin watches. The others, of course, will have rewards not nearly so munificent.' " According to an amused Meyer, the booby prizes DeCenzie stuck in the loser containers were "torn pictures from film magazines of girls in shorts."

Pete DeCenzie would be a major catalyst in Russ Meyer's life. He believed in RM's talent and encouraged him, one added bonus being the nose street-savvy Pete possessed for sniffing out low-down movie titles and publicity campaigns. The two were off and on until 1963. "I liked him personally, he was honest," said Meyer. "Without DeCenzie and his farsightedness I would never have had the courage to go ahead."

Meyer first met DeCenzie, as he put it, "through the breast of Tempest Storm." In a fever after seeing Storm perform for the first time, RM phoned DeCenzie and launched into his free-prints-if-the-chick-will-pose rap. "I shot pictures of her and Pete thought that was just great. He was going to get publicity. I could've been some charlatan just trying to get into the girl's box." An amateur lensman himself, DeCenzie was knocked out by the quality of RM's work. A gargantuan Tempest in sweater and shorts soon graced a billboard that startled motorists on their way into town from the airport. "They'd have accidents," recalled a gleeful Tempest. "They had to take it down."

For the public at large, the first indication of Meyer's genius for capturing the female form is the dozen or so pictures he shot of Tempest strutting her stuff onstage at the El Rey that fall of 1950, some of which ran in the girlie mag *Follies* and which Meyer and DeCenzie sold via mail order. Fifty cents would get you a five-by-seven postpaid, and $2.50 bought the complete set of four-teen—"mailed in a plain envelope," promised the copy. Today they're not easy to find—there is no definitive book collection of Meyer's still work—but you can see them printed (albeit way too small) on a page of his autobiography. Eight-by-tens sometimes float through the ether of Internet auctions, and while not all of them are stunning, a handful are just fantastic.

There's just a girl, a stage, and some curtains in these black-and-white photos, but Meyer's dramatic, high-contrast lighting, razor-sharp focus, and bombastic sense of composition make for an event. This is the name of the game, ladies and gents. Tempest doing a backbend, barely touching the stage with her fingertips, her black mane cascading toward the floor as her pasties point heavenward. A low, wide-angle close-up of Tempest's astounding torso as she smiles innocently into the camera and pulls off her minuscule lace top. RM emphasizes her assets, but in a way that isn't freakish but mythic. She looks godlike, magnificent, an explosive figure of fun. One look at these photos and you completely understand Meyer's obsession with Tempest—lust looms large in every frame. Tittyboom, indeed. You can practically hear RM shouting, "Go, baby, go, go, *go!*"

$ $ $

Just for the hell of it, Russ decided to shoot a two-hundred-foot roll of 16 mm Kodachrome after hours at the Gene Walker facility. Meyer was playing with fire. Only Kodak itself could process the new film stock, and any non-clothed Tempest Storm shots coming through their lab in those very prehistoric days ensured that, as Meyer put it, "bells rang, lights flashed, a big sign probably went on and off on the wall winking, 'tits, tits, tits.' Everything would come to a halt." But RM schemed a way around it. The film was delivered very personally by a sexy young French girl named Susie, who gave the Kodak lab man a little something extra for sneaking the film through. According to RM, ol' Susie "took the seed" from the lab man right there "on Eastman Kodak's linoleum." "The power a woman packs between her legs," marveled Pete DeCenzie. Russ would repeat this line for years after.

But the crafty Meyer had made one dumb mistake. The can containing his footage bore the sticker of his employer, Gene Walker Films. When the inevitable gossip spread around the lab concerning RM's nudie movie, Kodak's Bob Antz put in a call to Gene Walker himself. "I got a roll of film, Gene. What kind of pictures are you doing these days?" Walker, a straitlaced type who served on the board of Stanford University, was not amused by Meyer's latest antics. "The chief called me in on the carpet and really read the riot act to me," said RM. "Bob Antz really enjoyed it all because he knew Walker was a little on the stiff side . . . he did that to needle Walker." The Kodak man then did an unexpected thing. "Antz normally would take film like that and put it in the bio-shredder," said Meyer. "For some reason he gave it to me." That little roll of celluloid would take RM a long, long way.

"When I showed this film to DeCenzie, he shit," said Meyer. "What really got him was the fact I shot it on good industrial film with inserts of close-ups of lips and nipples and so on.* He just said, 'Oh, my God.' " From all descriptions of the now-lost footage,

---

* Meyer told *Fling* magazine's Arv Miller that *French Peep Show* never got beyond pasties. Being this was 1952, it's hard to believe Meyer could get away with showing women completely topless, but who knows—the film hasn't been seen in nearly fifty years.

RM had made a standard short industrial film—only the product on display was a nearly naked female. DeCenzie then asked Meyer to shoot a filmed version of an El Rey show. So, directly after the day's shoot for Standard Oil's *Safe Every Second!*, RM smuggled the boss's Cine Special II 16 mm camera into the El Rey to crank out *The French Peep Show*. Approximately one hour long, the film is credited in a 1952 promotional pressbook as being directed and photographed by Russ Meyer—his first such credit.

The picture was a family affair, produced by Pete DeCenzie and written by the El Rey house press agent Ed DeVere, with sound and editing by Meyer's co-worker at Gene Walker, Chuck Schelling. It featured eight dancers, among them Lilly La Mont and Tempest Storm, plus a bunch of comics doing blackout bits. Even Pete's wife, Yvonne, sang a number. The elaborate two-color thirty-two-page publication made to promote the picture, filled with Meyer-shot El Rey girls alongside actual production photos of RM, DeCenzie, and Schelling, was undoubtedly sold in the aisles at intermission to rake in some additional dough.

DeCenzie distributed the movie himself, and Meyer no doubt learned a trick or two about film exploitation from this one-man band. Pete would travel from city to city, renting empty theaters, putting up banners, and drumming up publicity himself. DeCenzie brought a stripper along who'd get as naked as city ordinances allowed. Pete invariably gave his traveling companion the stage name Nana. When asked why, he said, "Who knows? She's my Nana, that's all. She puts on the poses for my spiel." After a few months spent squeezing every dime out of the locals, he'd move to a new town and start all over again. According to a 1958 *Adam* article, DeCenzie was still milking the picture six years after its release.

That same *Adam* story declared that *French Peep Show* had been "a small-but-rich uranium mine for the trio that shot it." Meyer maintained that both he and co-worker Schelling got a flat fee and that even Pete saw no real money from the enterprise due to the creative bookkeeping of some of DeCenzie's shadier burlesque cohorts. A mail order business DeCenzie and RM set up to sell pic-

tures of Tempest Storm from ads in the back pages of girlie magazines met a similar fate. "Pete entrusted it to one of his lieutenants
to keep track of the orders and send out pictures," said Meyer. "I
owned ten percent of it . . . so I brought myself to say, 'Hey, where's
my cut?' The lieutenant came up with the limp excuse that just the
night before, someone had broken in and taken all the receipts. I
knew the guy was lying, but Pete said, 'Gee, that's terrible, Ed.'
These were his friends." DeCenzie's lackadaisical business approach would later cause a great deal of acrimony among the
partners, particularly with Meyer's second wife Eve.

Unfortunately, *French Peep Show* is gone with the wind, a lost
film. No copies have surfaced since its original run. Even pack-
rat Meyer failed to hang on to a copy. RM later claimed that
Yvonne DeCenzie was yet another wife "hostile" to him, and that
after Pete's death she destroyed any remaining prints. It would
be a fascinating document to see, as it is the first celluloid expression of Meyer's mania. Burlesque films from that era—check
out Irving Klaw's *Varietease* (1954) and *Teaserama* (1955)—are
static one-camera/one-angle affairs, watchable only because of
their historical value, and for the chance to see legends like
Tempest, Betty Page, and Lili St. Cyr do their thing. But if the still
photos of Tempest are any indication, RM had given *French Peep
Show* his all.

$ $ $

RM was completely smitten with his new mammary muse. "Meyer
used to borrow my Cadillac to take Tempest out," said Jim Ryan.
"I know Betty never thought much of that idea." But Meyer was
too far gone to care. As he admitted, "I took pictures of Tempest
and became enflamed with the woman's tits, absolutely enflamed.
It was the thing that nudged me away from my first wife." Indeed.
Decades later Russ would confess to a passing business acquain-
tance that he outright walked out on Betty. He was a shit, a cad, a
heel, and what's more, he knew it. Said Meyer years later, "I remember thinking, 'Leave my wife and go off with this girl? Seems

like a good idea.' " Maybe RM wasn't so different from dear ol' Dad after all.

"He was a good man," said Betty. "I never ever could complain of anything Russ did. He was a very good husband and he behaved properly, until all of a sudden it became the parting of the ways. All I knew is Russ wanted to do his thing and I let him—in fact, I never tried to stop him. He decided he was gonna go. All of a sudden Russ wasn't interested anymore, and I told him to take all his belongings and to disappear. I was going over to my folks. That was the end of it. I didn't hang around, that's for sure."

Betty never remarried, and she spoke to RM only once more some years later, under rather unusual circumstances. "The FBI or the police did call me about his character. They said something about him making pornographic movies, and I said, 'I don't think Russ would do that.' Russ called and thanked me—he was very pleased to hear that I said that."

Betty professed to know nothing about RM's forays into the world of girlie photography while they were together. This was to be the first and last time Meyer kept his personal life and his work separate, and it was a miserable failure. Curiously, the only wife to get along with Russ's mother didn't last. No doubt Lydia saw some of herself in the "cows" that followed, and no doubt the same attribute attracted RM to these women like metal to a magnet.

$ $ $

RM was simply determined to do whatever the hell RM wanted to do, and right now he wanted to be cavorting between the sheets with the mighty Miss Tempest Storm. The very evening his marriage collapsed he spent the rest of the night with Tempest at the California Hotel, a flophouse across the street from the El Rey. She was conked out in bed, unaware of his marital woes (when interviewed for this book Storm wasn't even aware Russ had been married before his second wife Eve). The next day RM drove her down to L.A. for a return engagement at the Follies, taking his Olds convertible since the jealous frau of one of Storm's other paramours had dumped sugar in the gas tank of her spanking-new red Caddy. During the trip, an exhausted RM began to nod off, nearly plowing into the rear of a semi. When they arrived at the Follies, Meyer found his new assignation as stripper's escort immediately humiliating. He wasn't cut out to be a suitcase pimp, the kind of poor slob who trailed behind a dancer, rushing to gather up bits of discarded costume from the stage floor. "Peeler's retriever" was RM's derisive term for such a sap.

Worse yet, later that night in the sack, RM's pencil contained no lead. Blanche's beauty simply overwhelmed him. No doubt this was the closest he'd come thus far to his old dream girl, Margie Sullivan. Unbelievably, the great Meyer felt inadequate.* RM spent the rest of the night wandering the empty streets of seedy downtown Los Angeles, mulling over the mess that his life had become.

In the sobering light of day, Meyer drove Storm to the theater, passed the stripper her makeup kit, and bid her adieu. Gazing into the rearview mirror of his Olds, he watched this magnificent hunk of female sashay her shapely ass into the Follies and out of his life. Tempest was already riding high, but Russell Albion Meyer was going to be a star, too. He didn't yet know how, but somehow it would involve his two great loves: movies and tits. Really big tits. And it was gonna make him a shitload of money.

Once he had that moolah the women would come to *him*. Mother had always told her Russell he was special, and he wasn't about to prove her wrong. He'd show them all, even those Hollywood infidels who'd slammed door after door in his face after he'd returned from the war. RM stepped on the gas of his ragtop and headed north to Frisco.

---

* Tempest chuckled when I related Meyer's version of events. "A lot of men are like that. I had one guy who was crazy about me in Tahoe. I mean, he was a fabulous-looking guy, a big businessman. He made an appointment with a psychiatrist, and he said, 'Would you go with me?' and we get there and he said, 'Doctor, I'm in love with her, but I feel she's just too much woman to handle. I don't think I can follow all those powerful men she's had in her life!' I guess I intimidate men." Tempest and Russ would remain fond friends, though, and even decades later she was known to refer to him as "my photographer."

$ $ $

With his first marriage demolished, Meyer moved in with his old 166th buddy Bill Teas, the two of them living in an apartment above a gay nightclub called the Black Cat. When that got to be too much, RM relocated to a two-room flat at Lorraine Court, where his new roommate was Franklin Bolger, a highly amusing cabbie, cocksman, drunk, and sometime actor who'd later appear in a few Meyer films.

RM bounced around with a series of dames, all of whom he'd initially asked to photograph. There was Ysobel Marli, a hot-blooded waitress who nearly got RM killed when her ex kicked in the door of their fuck pad. When the cops arrived and asked for his name, Meyer, not wanting to besmirch his own sterling rep, responded, "Bill Teas." Meyer landed Marli in the sack but never got her to disrobe for the camera.

"Miss St. Louis" was an alias for a married blond dancer Meyer had first seen during the war and happily rediscovered at the Burbank Follies a few years later. The inevitable photo shoot took place somewhere in the valley in the middle of the night, RM heaving his equipment right past her indifferent mother, whose eyes remained glued to the living room TV late show. Next time he met Miss St. Louis it was for hot sex in her Chevy.

Meyer had first encountered stripper Lilly La Mont, the "Alaskan Heat Wave," at Portland Oregon's Star Burlesque while on business there for Gene K. Walker. Brunette, half Native American, "she had very soft white skin, like a marshmallow," as dancer Dixie Evans recalled. La Mont told Meyer a tale that he was eternally fond of repeating.

It seems that La Mont performed an occasional private show for a wealthy Portlander of German descent. He'd pick her up in a Mercedes-Benz and whisk her off to his fancy home in the suburbs. There he'd climb into a coffin, hidden under a sheet. With the flip of a switch inside the casket, "Night Train" began to blast away, Lilli dancing naked save for a pair of seven-inch heels. He'd peek at her through two eyeholes in the sheet until his trumpet sounded. According to RM, La Mont's summation was "I felt a little strange, but he gave me $200 and treated me like a lady."

Meyer later brought this depraved tableau to life in the opening
of 1979's *Beneath the Valley of the Ultra-Vixens.**

$ $ $

For Meyer, excitement now came in the form of motels, cameras,
and exposed film. RM liked nothing better than to gaze upon some
top-heavy wench caught in the slatted light of venetian blinds.
"Smile for the birdie" was his constant mantra. Too much was not
enough, nor would it ever be. This was a man with a big appetite,
and everywhere he looked was something fleshy to bite.

In *A Clean Breast,* Meyer documents each and every one of his
conquests in mind-numbing detail. Can it all be true? Hard to say.
RM's tales got bigger with every telling, and in maintaining the
legend he had an image to hawk. Many of his tittyboom layouts
featured the photographer in action—framing a shot, touching
up a model's makeup, carrying a tripod. Meyer was mythologizing
himself from the very beginning. There is a stunning self-portrait
from the early fifties taken with the aid of a timer. A somewhat de-
pleted bottle of Old Bushmill's Irish whiskey in one hand, a lit cancer stick in the other, and a Rolleiflex around his neck, Meyer
gazes heavenward while resting his head upon the truly nude bosom of Lilly La Mont, who looks upon her benefactor lovingly. The
sheer ego on display is impressive. Like any true artist, Meyer's
real subject was Meyer. Years later he'd boast that there were only
two directors whose names would sell a picture to the American
public when placed upon a marquee. One was Hitchcock. The
other? Russ Meyer, of course.

---

* Like so many women whom Meyer immortalized, La Mont would disappear into
the night. Dixie Evans bumped into her in Providence, Rhode Island. "She was
staying at this cheap broken-down hotel," said Evans. "She turned me on to gin,
we were drinking a lot of it." Dixie was to accompany the then-governor of New
York and his pals to a wild shindig upstate, and he wanted her to whip up a date
for a congressman friend. After seeing Lilly La Mont on a burlesque poster, the
fellas demanded Dixie bring her along. Evans tried to talk them out of it due to
La Mont's appetite for destruction, but they wouldn't have it. "We got about ten
miles and she said, 'I gotta have a drink!' We had to stop all the way there. These
guys were a little annoyed. And we got there and boy, was Lilly happy. Man, the
booze was flowing—and Thomas Dewey was there!" No one's seen La Mont since.

4

Love and Kisses, Eve Meyer

I just don't find it very fascinating to look at something that isn't a fantasy.
—RUSS MEYER

"Don't just stand there with your bare face hanging out," said Eve Turner on her first encounter with her husband-to-be. There was a lotta moxie packed into that throaty rasp. Russ drank in the dame as she invited him in. She was a real wowser—wasp waist, blond hair, blue eyes, "a face to sink a thousand Dungeness crab boats," and, most integral for boob scientist Meyer, a devastating pair of breasts that RM was wont to describe as "conically maddening." Dressed in a smart gray flannel suit, her beautiful, nylon-swathed gams sweeping down to stiletto heels with ankle straps, Eve had a soft, join-me-in-the-hayloft beauty. "I knew I'd marry her the minute we met," said RM, who'd refer to her as his Marilyn and name his filmmaking company Eve Productions.

Meyer had snagged her number by default one boozy night after seeing Dave Brubeck at a Frisco jazz club. Bill Coshow, the lawyer who handled his divorce from Betty, spoke of a sexy secretary he'd had in his employ, then scribbled her number on a business card he gave to Meyer pal Ray Grant. Ray, being a happily married man, palmed it off on Russ, who found the card a few weeks later as he was cleaning out his wallet and decided to give it a shot. Outraged her number had been bandied about amongst strangers, Eve let Meyer have it. "She was really pissed at me," recalled an excited RM, and thus hooked, conned her into a date.

It was there on the second floor of the Violet Apartments at 725 Leavenworth that Eve poured Russ a Scotch and soda, informing him right off the bat she absolutely detested moustaches. His offending facial hair would soon be duly sacrificed. For this was the beginning of a volcanic love affair, the greatest this self-described cad would ever know. For here stood the one woman who could handle Russ Meyer.

"Eve was a great intimidator," said Meyer proudly. Years later, when she worked behind the scenes hawking his skin flicks and collecting the take, he'd witness Eve angrily fling a $86,000 check in the face of a hapless Boston distributor who'd fallen behind. Declaring him a crook, she stormed out, leaving Russ to pocket the check with a smile.

One of very few women capable of swimming in the sea of finless predators known as the exploitation film business, Eve could spew forth the most vicious, vitrolic letter to a deadbeat distributor only to sign off "With love and kisses, Eve Meyer." More often than not they anted up. Few could resist this charming and sometimes diabolical southern belle. She possessed a high degree of financial acumen, had a throaty, unforgettable laugh, and was known to greet reporters wearing a Stetson hat and boots that pushed her already prodigious stature over six feet. Eve Meyer was a woman ahead of her time. As friend Floyce Sumners put it, "Eve was the first person that I ever saw wear pants and high heels."

And the first model to linger for any length of time in front of Meyer's still camera. Eve would quickly become, as RM succinctly put it, "a national institution," gracing the cover of countless men's magazines as well as the centerfold for June 1955's *Playboy*. Along with Betty Page, Diane Webber, June Wilkinson, Irish McCalla, and a handful of others, Eve Meyer was one of those archetypal amazons capable of giving many a fifties male fever dreams. Truly, she is as much a symbol of that decade as a pink Cadillac or a Douglas Sirk melodrama. Her image somehow conjures up those desperate drive-in fumblings with Bertha Lou's brassiere as well as the smell of the best ballpark hot dog you ever gobbled down. As American, the saying goes, as apple pie, Eve's living-doll figure and palpable joie de vivre made her the absolute perfect foil for Meyer's full-on style. She oozed wanton carnality, with what RM lovingly describes as "purported insolence" lurking never far from that tempestuous surface. You definitely got the idea that if a poor, unwashed sap such as yourself was lucky enough to be in the actual physical presence of such a beauty, a slap to the kisser was at some point not only possible but probable.

$ $ $

She was born Eve Turner in Atlanta on December 13, 1928. Working for Western Union, Eve was transferred to San Francisco, where she became a legal secretary for Pepsi company bigwigs. Eve liked to play poker, packed a fishing rod, and was a formidable cook who loved her turnip greens. Like Meyer, she'd been hitched once previously. RM fell for her "like a tall tree" but was somewhat flustered to find himself on the receiving end of a healthy dose of sexual aggression, with Eve "gang-tackling my jockeys from the outset." When he begged off during a particularly hot and heavy late-night session at her apartment, timidly suggesting they wait for their wedding night to close the deal, she sent him packing. Arriving home to Lorraine Court, a deflated Russ discovered the half-carat engagement rock he'd given her earlier that night in his pocket. Wily Eve had slipped the ring off her finger and back into his pants as a protest against his sexual restraint. When Russ rang, hoping to cool her down, she hung up. Things remained just as fiery for the duration of their relationship. He called her Peach; she called him Punkin. "They were absolutely astonishing together," said friend Irving Blum. "Where he was strong, she wasn't, and where she was strong, he wasn't. Eve was just right for him."

As RM's beloved Li'l Abner wed Daisy Mae in the funny pages of 1952, so too did Russell Albion Meyer wed Eve Turner at 2 P.M.

on August 2 of that same year at the Swedenborgian church on San Francisco's Lyon Street. In attendance was a horde of Meyer's combat buddies, their wives, and his mother. In his autobiography there is a picture of a radiant and delicate Eve checking her outfit in the mirror as Lydia lurks in the background, a grumpy bulldog in a drab dress. To say the least, Eve and Lydia would not become bosom buddies. Eve came to detest Meyer's meddling mother and she let everyone know it. No doubt Lydia considered Eve just another "cow" not good enough for her Russell.

Dolores Fox remembered the wedding as a stunning affair. "They had written their own vows. Eve was in a beautiful brown sheer shirtmaker's shirtlace dress."* Their betrothal led indirectly to Eve Meyer turning cheesecake. Eve had dabbled in a bit of modeling before but scoffed when RM asked her to disrobe for his Leica camera. He pestered her for months. "At first, Eve was cool towards my suggestion that she be my model," said RM. "In fact, you might say she was downright nasty." But Eve's picture on their wedding invite had caught the eye of Meyer's Globe Pictures rep, who, knowing Russ needed funds for the ceremony, suggested he shoot a few four-by-fives of his bride-to-be to see if they could peddle some glamour shots.† Eve relented, and on the very day of their nuptials Russ and Eve learned they'd sold their first cover portrait. It was far from the last.

$ $ $

Eve Meyer in her birthday suit meant money in the bank. From 1952 to 1958, Eve's body was on display in just about every men's pulp on the newsstand—*Night & Day, Fling, Modern Man, Photo, Frolic, Ogle*—and RM peddled 8 mm films and stills of her mail order as well. "From Eve I can obtain results that I cannot as a rule

---

* Meyer liked to tell an awful anecdote concerning their honeymoon night at the Highlands Inn on the Monterey Peninsula. Eve was on her period, and by the time they had finished screwing from one end of the suite to the other it looked like "a goddamn butcher shop."

† Eve tells a different tale in a 1958 *Modern Man* article, maintaining that Meyer was after her to model from the very first phone call.

get from any other model," wrote RM in his 1958 quickie paperback girlie photo opus, *The Glamour Camera of Russ Meyer.* "Call it closeness." Husband and wife, photographer and model. Meyer astutely realized that his desire for Eve charged their photographic collaborations in a particular and powerful way, something that went beyond shoot number 457 with model 168. RM found the arrangement with Eve thrilling, and not just because of the dough. "When you were through shooting you laid down the camera and jumped on her bones," said Meyer. "It was so good for our marriage."

But Russ could be an absolute bastard. All that mattered was the picture. He was not above referring to his models as props and remained indifferent to their discomforts, even when said model was his wife. Eve recalled cracking during one particularly grueling session. Meyer had her nude, kneeling in various contorted poses under Death Valley's white-hot sun. "The salt dug into my knees and the sun was cooking my bare back like a Fish[erman's] Wharf lobster," she said. Intent on finding just the right angle, Meyer ignored her complaints. "Finally I just couldn't stand it any longer. I just got up and stalked away, bloody knees and all." Meyer thrived on getting a rise out of his feisty wife, boasting that he had "obtained some of the most exciting pictures" right when she was ready to clock him.

Meyer was utterly obsessed with photographing Eve. "I'd ride her ass to get her to pose," he boasted. She'd eventually burn out on what she dubbed their "photosexual" relationship. "I got so I just hated that darkroom," she said in 1971. "For six years we never had a vacation from it, never went anywhere without Russ's camera." Indeed. Shortly after their wedding, he'd even be compelled to photograph the empty postcoital bed in Eve's apartment, publishing it almost fifty years later in his autobiography.

$ $ $

"I am a romantic," said Hugh Hefner. "My life has been a quest for a world where the words to the songs are true. A quest for that impossible ultimate romantic experience."

In November 1953, Hefner published the first issue of *Playboy,* and lurking within its pages was a nude shot of cover girl Marilyn Monroe, posing rather exuberantly against a red velvet backdrop, one of three such photos she'd done as a struggling actress hard up for cash in 1949. Hefner had bought the picture for 500 bucks, leaving only $100 in the budget to actually put together a magazine. The issue sold fifty thousand copies, thus enabling Hugh Hefner to quickly become "the first man to become rich by openly mass marketing masturbatory love through the illusion of an available alluring woman," wrote Gay Talese. "Prior to *Playboy,* few men in America had ever seen a color photograph of a nude woman."

E. M. "Mick" Nathanson, later the editor of several girlie books Russ Meyer shot layouts for, recalled the very moment he first laid eyes on a copy of *Playboy.* "I sort of looked over my shoulder to see if anybody was watching this pervert reaching for this magazine. I picked it up and quickly flipped through a couple of pages. I thought, 'My God!' " Nathanson put the magazine back and ran home to tell his wife what he'd just seen — "Nudity! *Full nudity!*"

These days it is a bit hard to grok the effect *Playboy* had on an unsuspecting nation. It was a strange time. "The Fifties were not *Happy Days* and *Grease,*" said playwright Robert Patrick, who maintained the decade was "more like the *Invasion of the Body Snatchers.* Americans were automated. All thought was suppressed. No one was honest with anyone. It is possible that during the entire 1950s not one true word was spoken in the United States."

Into this button-down arena marched *Playboy.* Pipe-smoking, never-break-a-sweat Hef offered men an irresistible package deal, a world of scarily flawless women, nifty appliances, and a fully equipped rumpus room. It all seemed to whisper, "Follow my direction, my boy, and ye too shall have pussy, plus a Cadillac with fins." "Hef's genius was to associate sex with upward mobility," said the Kinsey Institute's Paul Gebhard.

For its eighteenth issue in June 1955, *Playboy*'s centerfold would be none other than Eve Meyer, shot by husband Russ. Although he'd at least double the number in interviews, RM shot only three gatefolds for *Playboy* — Marguerite Empey (aka Diane

Webber), Yvette Vickers, and Eve—plus a handful of other non-foldable layouts. The most significant pinup would be his wife. Prior to the Eve centerfold, Hefner had just bought already existing shots from cheesecake photographers, invariably studio-shot "art" poses like the infamous Marilyn nude.

Hefner had other ideas. "I'm the guy who wanted to put it into a different sort of setting, make it less a sort of impersonal pinup, actually tell a little story." He had art director Arthur Paul sketch out a blueprint for Meyer, who turned it into a photograph: a nearly nude Eve lying alone by a roaring fireplace, not one but two wine glasses nestled in the shag carpet before her. Most potent of all, Eve stared back at the viewer as if to say, "Hey, buster, I've reserved this very spot for *you.*" With this centerfold, Hefner had catapulted the voyeur directly into the story, intensifying the deadly illusion of possibility. It was just one of those dangerous ideas whose time had come, like heroin or Twinkies.

Another man on a quest to turn the impossible into flesh, Meyer would follow Hefner's lead. They would not become friendly until some years later, after RM became a filmmaker. Although very different creatures, they would share a certain intensity and single-mindedness, as well as the curious fact that both lost their virginity relatively late in life at age twenty-two. And they seemed as impenetrable as their creations. If you spilled your deepest secrets, would either of them notice? These guys were owned by their dreams.

$ $ $

Booty from men's magazines enabled the Meyers to move into an ocean-view apartment on 47th Avenue. RM continued working for Gene K. Walker, but more and more the emphasis was on his own photography. One day Walker called him into his office and informed him that some of his clients weren't too thrilled to learn that Meyer had a second life cranking out skin shots for the likes of *Peep Show* magazine. Gene offered Russ a financial incentive to jettison the girlie mag work for good. Meyer was at a crossroads— back down, or finally go solo. He talked it over with Eve, but there was never a question what Meyer would do. Freelance work promised no steady paycheck, but Eve backed her man 100 percent. No longer able to slip into Walker's after hours to mooch off the photographic resources, RM assembled a darkroom in his apartment and taught Eve the ropes. Soon she was not only posing in the buff for his pictures but getting dressed to develop them herself.

"I am clearly in the business of producing glamour pictures for magazines for the express purpose of making money," wrote Meyer in 1959. "I won't go as far as to say this is the only reason; but I will say it is the primary one." But Meyer noticed a funny thing when it came to selling his product. Pictures of a modestly endowed model like actress Joan Collins sold only once, while more superstructured models sold over and over. RM's tastes seemed to jibe with many of the Joe Six-Packs of the world, so he zeroed right in on the area that interested him most. "I stress the bosom department in all of my photographs because I believe that this more than anything else says to me 'This is woman.'" The obsession was only beginning.

$ $ $

The zillion or so images Meyer snapped of Eve provided a very useful purpose: RM learned how to photograph a woman from every conceivable angle and in every setting. This allowed him to master the craft of photography. If the 1950 El Rey shots of Tempest Storm are the Meyer version of the Sun Studios sound—crude, gloriously rough around the edges, and straining to contain a thunderous energy—by the mid-fifties RM was early Elvis at RCA: a bit slicker, perhaps, but in full command of his talents.

Simply put, during his marriage to Eve, Meyer learned how to nail the big personalities of the women he was photographing on a tiny piece of film. At the same time he also figured out how to refine a sexy idea down to its barest essence. The best example of this is what I call the "female explosion" pictures, the penultimate of these being RM's cover shot of Virginia "Ding Dong" Bell for the August 1959 *Sir Knight* (volume 1, number 8, to be precise). The

picture is deceptively simple: Bell, in an outrageously skimpy burlesque costume, looking at the camera, hands behind her head,
sucking in her gut and sticking out her most ample stuff, standing in front of some paint-splashed "beatnik" mural. Other
photogs shot Bell, and, well, there's times when she looks like—
forgive me, Virginia, wherever you are—maybe she traveled a little
too long with the carnival (producer Dave Friedman, who made a
nudie movie with her, maintained she exuded zero sexiness in person). In Meyer's photo, Virginia's a fleshy firecracker, way too hot
to handle. Everything about this shot is perfecto: the pose, the
garish color, how Bell's crazy tangle of red hair sits on her head,
and, most of all, the way her big red lips are open much too wide
to suggest anything less than a misdemeanor. I mean, she's *too*
damned hot. It's so over the top it's funny. You know when you
drink a Coke too fast and it zaps your brain? That's the feeling this
writer gets, only head a little south. I look at this picture and see
those mythic Party Lights Claudine Clark sang of so desperately. I
hear far-off voodoo drums beating in the night. And I want to ride
Miss Bell like a pony, don't you?

Not too far in the future Meyer would apply these skills to motion pictures, and the effect would be deadly.

$ $ $

With photos of Eve selling like hotcakes, Russ Meyer's career with
Globe Photos exploded. West Coast Globe rep Charlie Bloch took
a liking to Russ and threw many an assignment his way. Along with
Andre de Dienes, Peter Gowland, Bunny Yeager, and others, Meyer
was one of the top glamour photographers of the fifties. He also
started shooting movie stars, although in a rare admission of failure he admitted that he did "a very inept job" with his first assignment, Ava Gardner.* He quickly found his feet, though, and went
on to photograph some of the most beautiful women of the decade,
among them Elizabeth Taylor, Tina *(Gilligan's Island)* Louise, Joan

---

* Eve Meyer accompanied him for this assignment, and Russ would tell more
than one person that Gardner had eyes for his wife. One dares not even imagine
that red-hot entanglement.

Collins, Lili St. Cyr, Ruta Lee, Mamie Van Doren, Barbara *(I Dream of Jeannie)* Eden, Fay Spain, Sabrina, Greta Thyssen, Gina Lollobrigida, Cleo Moore, Jill St. John, Joi Lansing, Jayne Mansfield, Yvette Vickers (as she sprawled bottomless on a couch near a turntable and records while shooting her scintillating *Playboy* centerfold, RM instructed her to sneer like Elvis), and Anita Ekberg, who Meyer declared was hands down the most beautiful female he ever photographed. This was the apex of his tittyboom period. Three women in particular from this era really lit up Meyer's viewfinder: Eve Meyer, Diane Webber, and June Wilkinson.

Meyer struck glamour gold for the second time with Diane Webber, a fine-featured, long-haired brunette whose earthy figure fit Meyer's rugged landscapes like the last piece in a jigsaw puzzle. She's the first of his nature nymphs, a reoccurring figure in his films best essayed by the actress Haji. A serious nudist, Webber possessed the slightly wacky appeal of an artsy, somewhat ethereal beatnik chick who'd dropped out of some East Coast Ivy League school to play bongoes and find the inner she. There's an offbeat glint in her eye, as if she might suddenly start talking about shamans or break into an inopportune interpretive dance at your parents' fiftieth-anniversary dinner.

RM shot Webber's second *Playboy* layout for the February 1956 issue, part of a slew of Meyer photos that show her at her most astoundingly voluptuous. The secret? According to Meyer, she was a few months pregnant, rendering her breasts even more enormous than usual. (Meyer would develop quite a knack for the knocked-up model, starring at least three slightly swollen females in his films.) He later shot a short feature of Webber entitled *This Is My Body* to accompany his 1959 opus *The Immoral Mr. Teas,* but later pulled it from circulation, bemoaning the crude fact that her body just wasn't the same after childbirth. She disappeared completely from the limelight once her modeling days were through, becoming a Van Nuys dance instructor, surfacing briefly as a somewhat unwilling interviewee for Gay Talese in his 1980 study of sexual mores, *Thy Neighbor's Wife.* As far as modeling went, Webber "did it for the money," said Meyer. "She looked upon the whole thing as being ridiculous." On to the next dame.

"This is the third girl I've found who is going to make me a fortune," said Russ Meyer of British model June Wilkinson in 1958. "The first was Eve, the second Diane Webber. Man, this is IT!" A tall, cocky blonde with a wicked smile, obscenely long legs, and a figure that would turn Barbie green with envy, Wilkinson had a good-sport aura that suggested she not only wouldn't mind a dirty joke but might know a few filthier ones herself.

Wilkinson first appeared onstage at age twelve as a ballerina but soon abandoned ballet, as she'd "begun to develop too much. Big bosoms and Swan Lake don't go together." By age sixteen June had a forty-one-inch bust and was already a striptease sensation in London. While touring America as "Miss Plastic Houseware," June happened to flip through a copy of *Playboy* in Chicago and came to the conclusion her body looked better than any of the women displayed. She promptly rang the magazine, and Hugh Hefner himself answered the phone. They shot a layout in the wee hours of that same night, due to which Hefner dubbed her "The Bosom." She was just seventeen years old.

Just prior to her Chicago trip Wilkinson had signed a movie deal with Seven Arts, and the studio hit the roof when they found out about the *Playboy* layout. Their solution was to capitalize on it, hiring the Rogers & Cowans publicity firm to make Wilkinson "the most photographed nude in America." The person they called upon to assist them in this quest was Russ Meyer, who was given a six-month exclusive. Due to the Seven Arts contract, Wilkinson made nothing, but according to one account Meyer reaped fifty grand from the endless photo sales. The pictures RM shot of Wilkinson are particularly electrifying. There's something unbridled about June, like a Roman candle in hot pants, and Russ was just the man to light the fuse.

One thing Meyer excelled at was the photo essay, a ludicrous little story that provided an excuse (however scant) for some female to drop her drawers. Typical is "Beauty and the Bust," a 1958 layout for *Adam* starring June. Meyer accompanies Wilkinson on a trip to "a smart modern building located in Van Nuys," Paulette's Custom Made Brassieres. Paulette Firestone is a cheerful Australian whose genius lies in making industrial-strength uplift sexy via such contraptions as "the Accentuator." "You've got to remember they're nothing but two big balls of fat," instructs Paulette. "No bone structure, no muscles—that's why they need support." Looking at this layout in these seen-it-all times is tantamount to decoding hieroglyphs—absurd, innocent, ignorant fun. At one point in the story Wilkinson is noted as having nicknamed her most famous assets "my chubbies."

$ $ $

Russ Meyer approached glamour photography with his usual fiendish intensity. Charlie Sumners recalled standing in a field with RM for three hours getting eaten alive by gnats waiting for the right cloud formation. He had a bugaboo for razor-sharp focus and would later fire a few camera operators and argue with an award-winning cinematographer over the same. That was Meyer—no detail spared, nothing left to chance. Meyer ripped out the passenger seat of his little German DKW so he could pack it full of equipment, then use it as a work space in the field. He'd load film into three M-3 Leicas, each ready with 125 mm, 50 mm, and 35 mm lenses. A Rollei camera was dragged along for color work (for still work, Meyer preferred black and white).

The artifical feel of studios and strobe lights left Meyer cold. Meyer preferred the flattering, warm look of open shade and natural light. Coarse textures were often his backdrop: big rocks, sand and surf, the weathered wood of old barns. Locale was all-important. An untamed landscape revved his engine. He went for simple but dramatic effects, such as a spirited close-up of a girl chewing on the ends of her hair. Meyer shot wide apertures— usually f 5.6—which made for shallow depth of field, resulting in soft backgrounds and a dramatic composition centered on the model. It was all about the girl.

If complete nudes were to be done, Meyer demanded that the model not wear undergarments for three hours before the shoot—they left wrinkles in the flesh. Russ liked makeup and lots of it. He combed through the model's wardrobe beforehand, leaning toward form-fitting capri pants, short shorts, and the boost of a merry widow corset. He liked nothing better than a too-snug sweater, a few buttons undone to highlight the treasures within.

"We never had a concept, we just had locations," said June Wilkinson. "It wasn't like doing a big *Playboy* shoot today. There was never a makeup artist, never a hairdresser, never a clothes consultant—it was 'OK, there's the camera, here's me, let's see what we can get.'" Wilkinson found RM to be the opposite of master Hollywood portrait photographer George Hurrell, who'd spend hours laboring over one shot. Meyer was in a frenzy to capture the moment, throwing himself into each shoot with the gusto of an action painter. "With Russ it was clickclickclick," said Wilkinson.

The shoot would start out early in the day with Meyer splurging for breakfast, invariably at "some kind of hole in the wall," as June recalled. "Russ was not comfortable in fancy restaurants." The pair would then zoom off to some remote locale where the entire universe boiled down to just a passionate, somewhat crazed shutterbug, one beautiful naked female, and the wild blue sky. Give RM a saucy dame, a transparent negligee, and a backlit clearing in the woods and anything was possible. There are Meyer shots of Anita Ekberg with only a towel as a prop that are hot enough to pop a thermometer.

"My glamour is of a very provocative nature," wrote Meyer. "There are those who say I have a reputation for exaggerated posing. . . . I heartily concur." Meyer liked his women to be comin' at ya, thrusting, stretching, kicking, bending their bodies into curve-crazy displays that make a mouth water. It's a pity Meyer never shot any kind of 3D, as his compositions beg for it. And all those low angles—his women look fifty feet tall, flesh skyscrapers. It's fitting that June Wilkinson would remark that Meyer came across like a little boy, because frequently the females in his photos and films are shot from precisely that kid's-eye view.

Meyer preferred intensive three-hour sessions with no break for lunch. Candy bars and a thermos of ice water were the only available fuel. "I have learned from unfortunate experience that taking a lunch break leads to difficulties," wrote RM. No sleepy or sluggish models for him. Nor was he keen on blasé, seen-it-all

types. As the shutter whirred, he'd force them to count their toes
or do something equally pointless just to break them out of their
mental rut. He'd cajole a model into endless chatter to free her
mind. If she was an actress, he'd have her recite lines from her last
part. The goal was to "direct her into expressing herself in a manner of 'unawareness' " to reach "plateaus" where the poses came
fast and easy.

Meyer was a powerhouse. What all of RM's women remember—and what they all responded to—was his galvanic energy.
He'd hurl one compliment after another at his models, and there
was no doubt he was genuinely excited to watch 'em strut their
stuff. "Russ was like a big kid. He would be *so* enthusiastic—'Oh,
June, that is great! Stick your breasts out, oh, oh, oh—huge! *Oh,
you look great*! That is *fabulous*!' And he'd make you feel like you *were*
fabulous."

But for all his lust, RM didn't lech. Wilkinson echoes the
words of many a Meyer model when she says, "Russ never made
any moves towards me, there was never any time that I felt uncomfortable. If he touched my naked body to move me, it was
never sexual." At this point, dare it be said, there was still something innocent about Russ Meyer. And one woman was never far
from his mind. "Russ used to talk about Eve all the time, all the
time," said Wilkinson. "How wonderful she was, and that he never
met anybody like her in his life. He was so in love at that time it
was unbelievable. He could not wait to get home to Eve every
night."

$ $ $

Despite his smashing success as a photographer, Russ Meyer had
another dream gnawing at his soul—that of the mighty silver
screen. Sometime in the early to mid-fifties he joined Local 659,
the San Francisco branch of the Hollywood cameramen's union,
shooting some military training films. More important, Meyer
then participated in his first exploitation movie, a tawdry, decid-
edly nonunion abortion exposé entitled *The Desperate Women*.
"The abortion racket," said Meyer, was "a very safe way to deal with

sex—showing it as a real crime." This sixty-nine-minute adults-only feature, circa 1954–55 (dates vary), dealt with "innocent women who put their lives and reputation into the shameful hands of men whose alliances are with the underworld," that is, the fiendish backstreet abortionist. (Meyer would revive this clichéd character—complete with Coke-bottle glasses—for a short scene in 1970's *Beyond the Valley of the Dolls*.)

RM shot the film completely on location, allowing its makers to peddle it as "a jolting documentary." A disapproving police chief chased the production out of San Francisco, into Berkeley and Oakland, but Meyer, always happy to outfox a cop, flashed his old war cinematographer's card to gain access to some army land at the base of the Golden Gate Bridge. Unfortunately the film is lost. All that remains is a handful of stills and a lurid campaign pressbook.

"Shall I Take the 'Easy' Way Out?" blared shrill ads featuring an angst-ridden Eve Meyer, for whom Russ had finagled a small part. It was the classic exploitation attack—prey on the ignorance and fears of the general public while simultaneously titillating them with promises of seeing the unshowable, in this case "facts of life heretofore only whispered [about] behind closed doors." The distributor helpfully provided copies of a cheap pamphlet whipped up for the film, "Sex—Happiness or Tragedy?" (written by an alleged doctor from the American Institute of Family Relations), to bilk the rubes in the audience out of a buck under the guise of "education." No doubt Meyer had learned a thing or two about the carny approach of the grindhouse world from Pete DeCenzie.

It was time for Russ Meyer to invade Tinseltown. After a brief stop in Canoga Park, he and Eve moved into a smart Hollywood home on Evanview Drive just down the street from Sammy Davis Jr. Meyer had done industrial films, cheesecake, and an exploitation picture. Now he'd combine all these disparate elements in one very idiosyncratic film. After a late-night poker game between Meyer and his cardsharp cronies, a plot would be hatched to pool some pocket change and make a rinky-dink flick starring a bevy of naked broads and one somewhat odiferous combat buddy. Who could've predicted the outcome? As no less than Ed Wood Jr. himself wrote, "*The Immoral Mr. Teas* changed the look of the nudie movies once and forever." Cinema would never be the same, and neither, certainly, would Russ Meyer.

5

The Immoral Mr. Meyer

Each film must begin with me. I am the idea. I've got to have the hard-on.

— RUSS MEYER

Pete DeCenzie was down on his luck. He'd been chiseled out of the El Rey Theater by political skullduggery. "It took a freeway to put me out of business," he said. "They built it right through the theater." Stopping in San Diego with his shopworn traveling girlie show, *Pictures in Poses,* he gave Russ and Eve a ring at their Hollywood home. Russ and Eve hopped in the car and headed south. Pete was still squeezing the last bit of juice out of *French Peepshow,* schlepping a tattered print from town to town. It was a far cry from the halcyon days of the El Rey and Tempest Storm.

Over dinner that night in a tony joint called Anthony's, DeCenzie, still gaga over Meyer's way with a movie camera, broached the subject of another collaboration. He wanted Russ to make a nudist picture. One of the stranger exploitation genres to hit it big in the fifties, nudist films were just that: cheap documentaries of average citizens awkwardly hiding exposed genitalia behind volleyballs. Meyer felt they generally escaped being busted on the grounds that bodies this fucking ugly couldn't possibly appeal to anybody's prurient interest. Posters for nudist films pitched beautiful and unlimited skin, but that was part of the grindhouse tease: promise them everything, show 'em nothing. Sagging asses were not for Russ Meyer. It was a matter of aesthetics. RM was about beauty; that is, a male fantasy of female perfection. As he so poetically put it, "The man on the street gets sick of seeing oatmeal on his wife's housecoat and curlers in her hair." Thus, no nudist colony exposé for Meyer. There had to be another way.

Meyer dropped Pete back at a flophouse too depressing for a nightcap. Bidding his friend DeCenzie adieu, he and Eve drove off into the night. But the seed had been planted—somehow Meyer was going to make his own movie. Once it was one for the history books, RM would fully credit his partner, even though he'd fall out with Pete like just about everybody else in his life. Meyer had to admit, "Pete DeCenzie supplied the fire, the urge, the desire."

$ $ $

DeCenzie went back on the road with his threadbare girlie show while a vague idea for a motion picture fermented in Meyer's fertile mind. Life on Evanview Drive was good. Meyer was shooting scads of tittyboom photos for Globe and, despite going out of their way to discourage him upon his arrival in town, the Hollywood cameramen's union now needed him. The advent of live TV shows meant more work than available bodies, and because of this Meyer was drafted into a very lucrative gig shooting stills for shows such as *Perry Mason*, *The Twilight Zone*, *Maverick*, *Gunsmoke*, *Rawhide*, and *The Fugitive*.

Out on location to cover the filming of James Dean's last picture, *Giant*, Meyer endeared himself to the sullen superstar by lending him a tripod for his after-hours amateur work. When it came time for Dean to do a scene pacing around his oil well, he took one look at the gaggle of still men clicking away and lost it, screaming, "No pictures! No pictures!" until he spotted Meyer: "Except for *him.*" Ever the bull in the china shop, RM would actually disrupt a *Giant* dialogue scene with his noisy Hasselblad, earning him a polite admonishment from director George Stevens. Once he'd seen the resulting magazine cover shot, Stevens sent Meyer a note saying that the annoyance had been worth it. Yes, life in Hollywood was damn good for Russell Albion Meyer. He'd even bought Eve a spanking new T-bird. And yet, *movies . . .*

Russ Meyer cut quite a figure in the mid-fifties. A tall, imposing beefsteak of a man with a buzz cut and black, bushy brows knit together over an apelike face, to say nothing of the knockout blonde on his arm who was not only his wife but an income-generating nude model, this commie-hating former combat photographer could've easily passed for one of the testosterone cartoons that burst off the cover of *For Men Only* or one of the other pulpy rags in which his pictures sometimes apppeared. Somehow the guy charmed you.

Those who knew Meyer at the time attest to his infectious enthusiasm, not to mention his unbridled appreciation for naked ladies. "Russ was a larger-than-life character, as odd as can be, very quick and quirky," said his friend Irving Blum. "I really adored him. His movies were funny—not always in the way he intended—and he was like that in real life. Droll at times and at others gravely serious—to the point of hardly being able to deal with him. The guy had a very short fuse.

"Russ took his game seriously, and if you took it as seriously as he, you were on his side. If somehow you stepped outside of that circle, he got pissed off. It could be anybody—a wife, a girlfriend, a business associate. Russ was a tiger. He wanted more than he had—and was determined to get it."

$ $ $

Pete DeCenzie showed up again a week or so later at Meyer's Evanview Drive doorstep, just in time for the weekly Wednesday night poker game. It was a tight bunch: a few of the usual combat buddies—Ken Parker, Paul Fox, and Bill Teas—plus new friend E. M. "Mick" Nathanson, editor of the skin mag *Adam*. And the lovely Eve, of course. "Her laugh was extraordinary," said Nathanson. "I'd be at some party with a roomful of people and hear this deep booming laughter. I'd say, 'Eve is here.'"

William Ellis Teas is a curious character in Meyer history. A member of the 166, Bill Teas took some of the most riveting combat photos of World War II. But Bill liked his vodka and orange juice more than any tour of duty. Visitors to his home saw stacks of pictures tossed aside, many with first-place ribbons attached. A shy, stout fellow with a quizzical Sylvester P. Smythe face adorned by a salt-and-pepper goatee, Teas didn't drive, dance, or swim. He had poor luck with women, with a tendency to fall for prostitutes. Bill "was always in love," said Meyer. "He was the ultimate gamesman." In Meyer's autobiography there's a Polaroid (no doubt snapped by RM) of a very elderly Teas resting his head between the naked silicone knockers of Meyer's latest flame. He looks rather happy there.

After the war Teas had worked for Meyer's boss Gene K. Walker, doing what RM called "bong films," slide shows that advance a frame every time a bong sounded. He'd lived with RM and his first wife in their San Francisco apartment, much to the annoyance of Betty. "Teas is the kind of guy that comes to have dinner and he stays a year," said Meyer. Bill had earned a reputation for being addicted to booze and poker, not to mention poor hygiene. "I couldn't stand it—he wasn't exactly a clean guy," said Betty. "We'd have to say things to get him to take a bath. Poor Bill Teas. He was a fine guy, but he was a dirty man." This flaw would not stand in the way of the very dubious sort of stardom that was about to descend on William Ellis Teas.

This night, with Teas the only remaining straggler from the Evanview Drive poker crew, DeCenzie and Meyer spent the wee hours kicking around movie ideas. Russ wanted to do something along the lines of a girlie-mag layout he'd just shot featuring some lech ogling a naked girl—the look-but-don't-touch game. Voyeurism was the technical name for it. In addition to Meyer's personal fascination with the subject, there was a built-in element of self-protection. Meyer was game to push the nudity content but knew that any touchy-feely stuff would land him in the joint. If DeCenzie was brokenhearted over his nudist documentary idea heading south, there is no record of it. Whatever Russ wanted to do was OK with Pete, who'd match him dollar for dollar. The two created a motion picture company named for their initials— PAD-RAM Enterprises—and the making of Russ Meyer's first real feature film was set in motion.

Now they'd have to round up some women, of course, but they'd also need a memorable doofus to play the Peeping Tom. Meyer's steely gaze landed on just the human question mark he needed, Bill Teas. "Teas had a satanic beard, liked orgies, hated water in any form and punched his hammy fist through windows when drunk," Meyer recalled. "I thought he would be perfect for the role."

DeCenzie made only one demand: first they had to have a title. Meyer was annoyed—they didn't even have a goddamn movie yet. But the old exploitation carny would turn out to be on the money. And right there on the spot, looking over at their improbable leading man, DeCenzie came up with *The Immoral Mr. Teas*. It was just odd enough to stick with you.

And so there on Evanview Drive, a stone's throw from the gleaming, moneyed studios run by the Hollywood big boys, came a loose plan to make a girlie picture: Meyer would direct and DeCenzie would produce, with Bill Teas their unlikely star. The only one left with nothing to do was Eve. But Russ Meyer was too lost scheming and dreaming to notice.

$ $ $

Take a peek at *The Immoral Mr. Teas* today and you'll wonder what all the fuss was about. It's just a quaint period curiosity featuring a bumbling dolt doing stale comedy of the sort associated with the baggy-pants burlesque comic. Although many of Meyer's irks and quirks are already on parade, the best that can be said for the film is that its colorful photography intoxicates in a warm, noonday-sun kind of way. But one has to keep in mind again that the late fifties were a time, as critic Kenneth Turan has written, "when nothing more than a glimpse of female flesh was enough to send strong men reeling and begging for more."

1959: Eisenhower was president, Charlton Heston in *Ben-Hur* was the top movie draw, and Bobby Darin's "Mack the Knife" wafted out of transistors everywhere. This was the year of the Cadillac Eldorado Biarritz, a gas-guzzling luxury car with a monster V-8 engine that cost as much as a house and sported foot-high tail fins. Suburban sprawl was spreading everywhere. Americans had money to burn.

Overt sexual content was creeping more and more into the culture. Somewhat tamed by 1959 (although Link Wray's "Rumble" managed to be banned by many radio stations, despite its being a mere instrumental), the salacious content of R&B and rock and roll had outraged powers that be everywhere. The beatniks had raised their own particular brand of ruckus with 1957's *On the Road* and *Naked Lunch*, published (albeit in Paris) in 1959. Still two years away from his first obscenity bust, Lenny Bruce made his television debut on Steve Allen's talk show, the host introducing him as "the most shocking comedian of our time."

The Hollywood motion picture business was busy coping with all sorts of new changes. The studio system was coming to an end, television was a dreaded competitor, and exhibitors had been trying every gimmick to keep audiences coming to theaters, including 3D and various widescreen attempts. The big studios were also turning to adult fare that couldn't be shown on the family TV — films like *The Moon Is Blue* (1953), *Baby Doll* (1956), *The Apartment* (1960), *Psycho* (1960), *Elmer Gantry* (1960), and *Walk on the Wild Side* (1962) meant sticking a toe into areas once reserved for that reviled strip of celluloid known as the exploitation film.

A 1961 newspaper article discussing efforts in the California Senate to reform the movie industry (which also references an upset parent who'd seen teenagers attending a drive-in showing of *The Immoral Mr. Teas*) paraphrases a Democratic senator angry over the previous year's Oscars, which had been given to two actresses playing prostitutes (Elizabeth Taylor for *Butterfield 8* and Shirley Jones for *Elmer Gantry*), Burt Lancaster's "preacher-seducer" *(Elmer Gantry)*, and to Best Picture of the year, *The Apartment*, a movie "based on a man permitting business associates to use his apartment for clandestine affairs."

Operating in the shadows of the Hollywood studio industry, the exploitation picture business had already been around for forty years by the time Meyer made *Teas*. Originally a scrappy bunch known as the Forty Thieves — "itinerant carnival people," as producer David Friedman describes them — these celluloid

confidence men made their living off the taboo. The lowdown titles of their films told the story—*Damaged Goods, She Shoulda Said
No, Please Don't Touch Me, Is Your Daughter Safe?, The Road to Ruin,
Race Suicide, Around the World with Nothing On, Fear of Childbirth,
Test Tube Babies, Narcotic Dens of the Orient.* Abortion, unwed mothers, sexually transmitted diseases, burlesque strippers, drug addiction, nudists, bloodthirsty rituals of faraway tribes . . . whatever
Hollywood couldn't show you, the exploitationers sold you—
although what wound up on the screen rarely delivered all the
lurid poster had promised outside. These were "films that showed
absolutely nothing, but had a heavy advertising pitch," as Meyer
noted.

Cranked out over a long weekend while no one was looking
and sometimes even sold from the trunk of a car, these two-bit
pictures starring yesterday's almost-stars were down-and-dirty affairs. They played inner-city grindhouses, drive-ins, and theaters
that happened to have a hole to fill or were available for rent. Distributors would shuttle their product state to state, cutting the
tattered print according to whatever local censorship laws would
allow, and in the case of sex hygiene pictures, a bogus doctor was
enlisted for an intermission spiel that ended in hawking "educational" booklets to the rubes. These independent rogues were
marginalized and detested by the mainstream film world, and yet
Hollywood would directly benefit from the censorship battles they
fought—and often wound up imitating their product once any
smoke had cleared.

Sex, or more accurately some promise of sex, was a major
ingredient of the exploitation picture. Until Meyer showed up,
those looking for illicit thrills got their fix either via stag films—
short, illegally made hard-core sex reels that were privately shown
(and which had been around since the beginning of the movie industry)—or from such exploitation fare as the aforementioned
nudist documentaries, sex hygiene pictures, or saucy melodramas
that had a moral tacked on the end condemning any hanky-panky
that had come before it (a device to blunt public outcry and censorship harassment). Sheathed in a velvet glove for the more so-

phisticated set was the foreign "art" film, like Roger Vadim's 1957 Brigitte Bardot wowser, *And God Created Woman*. Before she was Hedy Lamarr, Hedy Kiesler first appeared on these shores going for a nude swim in 1933's *Ecstasy*, and after numerous free-publicity court battles, the picture was a smash exploitation hit. Meyer ridiculed these films as well, complaining, "There's a lot of promise but never ... fulfillment. They would always cut to the curtain blowing."

With the utter craziness of the sixties right around the corner, times were ripe for change. And while Meyer might've regarded the nudist film with derision, producer Walter Bibo's costly court-room battle to free his 1954 color nudist epic *The Garden of Eden* from legal harassment eventually led to a federal judge declaring that "nudity per se is not obscene," a statement that certainly changed the rules of the game for the moviemakers like Meyer, and similar court cases were helping put state-run censor boards out of business everywhere.

Russ Meyer had arrived on Hollywood's doorstep at just the right moment to raise a ruckus. Meyer would bring increasingly higher budgets, a new level of technical sophistication, and a high-profile presence to the exploitation business. He'd be the link joining the exploitation world to the Hollywood studios. But first he'd birth a new sort of picture, called for obvious reasons the nudie-cutie, and this begat an entire genre known as the sex-ploitation film, unleashing new sexual freedom on the screen, not to mention the complete fury of those fire-and-brimstone types desperate to control what the general populace can see. Russ Meyer would drive them all crazy, and he'd relish every minute of the battle.

$ $ $

"It mustn't come across as some kind of great planning," in-structed Meyer years later while discussing *The Immoral Mr. Teas* with biographer David K. Frasier. "I did it as I went along." He'd stress again and again that the movie was just a dumb idea whose time had come. "*Teas* was a fluke, an absolute fluke. I had no real idea when I started. All I had was Teas, three girls, and my dentist and my attorney for assistants."

Irving Blum—a habitué of the Evanview poker soirées later to become a renowned art dealer—recalled the hazy origins of Meyer's movie. "A bunch of us evolved the idea of *Teas*. Virtually all of it was hatched at these poker games. I helped a little bit in writing it. It all evolved from a James Thurber story, *The Secret Life of Walter Mitty*." Mick Nathanson recalled Meyer's enthusiasm for French filmmaker Jacques Tati, to whose bumbling, bicycle-riding M. Hulot Teas certainly bears a passing resemblance. Nathanson remembers Meyer screening a bunch of unfinished footage for his friends and asking for their story input. Some woman whose name no one can remember offered up the psychiatrist ending that was used.

"Written on the back of a laundry ticket," the actual story of *Teas* didn't amount to much. Our straw-hatted hero Bill Teas delivers false teeth via bicycle. Mr. Teas is a figure of ridicule—even children bean the sad sack. The world at large fails to note his existence. He wanders around like the invisible man, staring at women who don't even notice he's alive. A shot of painkiller in the dentist's chair leads to naked reverie: Teas now sees women without clothes, even after the shot wears off. He spends the rest of the film helplessly ogling every woman in his path. Not one of them does he approach. "There was no contact, no attempt at lovemaking, no sex," said Meyer. And shockingly unlike the grindhouse wonders that preceded it, there was no punishment or apology for his behavior. The end of the film has Teas returning to his female psychiatrist's office for help. Instead she too appears before his eyes naked as a jaybird. "Some men just enjoy being sick," says our chipper narrator.

Nobody took Meyer's folly too seriously, except of course RM himself. "Frankly, I didn't have the most extraordinary conviction regarding the thing; it was absolutely a lark," said Irving Blum. "It was really Russ who had the drive and the will to see it through." Nathanson remembered Meyer—who smoked at the time—being so involved in a shot he didn't notice a lit cigarette butt burning away under his feet. This was what RM was born to do, and second-degree burns weren't going to intrude.

Meyer was also determined to shoot *Teas* on color Kodak film stock, and given the conservative nature of the company and the times, it might not have happened had it not been for a friend Russ had at Kodak, Ray Grant. "He put his job on the line," said Meyer. "He told his supervisors that we were making an experimental comedy filled with nudity and that he would personally be on the set at all times to make sure nothing objectionable was being done." In addition, Meyer had hooked up with a man named Adrian Mosser, who had just developed a revolutionary liquid gate process that minimized emulsion scratches in 16 mm to 35 mm blow-ups. Not only was Meyer making "an experimental sex comedy," he was now a technological guinea pig of great interest to the industry. "Even Walt Disney was curiously interested in what would happen," bragged RM.

So far, so good. But where was the female flesh? Rounding up women for *The Immoral Mr. Teas* wasn't as easy as RM had hoped. Models for still pictures were one thing, but if "you put 'em in a movie, it smacked of heinous stag films. It was almost slammer time," Meyer said. Earl Leaf, a well-known Hollywood glamour/celebrity photographer who lived in a thatched-hut Hollywood Hills hideaway and who appears as himself in an unbilled cameo (a number of the men in *Teas* didn't care to have their faces shown, adding to the odd, disembodied feel of the film), supplied one of his own models, Ann Peters, a Las Vegas showgirl and Meyer's favorite in the movie.

Pete DeCenzie brought in a pair from the burlesque circuit, Mikki France and Alaskan beauty Marilyn Wesley. Doris Sanders had modeled for *Adam*, Michelle Roberts arrived courtesy of a young guy Meyer described as "the heir to a vast fortune," one Paul Morton Smith, who Meyer claimed was "interested in breaking into photographing girls naked. And he wanted to get laid." Dawn Denielle was found walking down Sunset Boulevard. Meyer was ballsy and relentless: if he spotted a woman who measured up to his demanding requirements, he would "come on like a steam engine, telling them that they would all be stars. Lying through my teeth." Each of the women got a hundred dollars a day. "If any of those girls had lines to speak, [they] would've been dead," said Teas at the time, who felt compelled to remind the world at large that these beauties were "not actresses."

There would be one more nude, albeit uncredited and headless. June Wilkinson's naked torso materializes in a door panel as Teas juggles melons. In deference to her Seven Arts film contract, "Russ said to me, 'June, I beg you—I'm doing my first movie. I just want your breasts. I swear to you I won't show your face.' " Wilkinson was so grateful to Meyer for boosting her career that she even did the shot gratis. Many recognized that extraordinary cleavage anyway. "Breasts are like fingerprints," said Wilkinson. "No two are alike."

Padding the rest of the cast were friends Mick Nathanson, Pete DeCenzie (seen in the dentist's chair and managing a burlesque theater whose in-joke banner trumpeted past glory *French Peep Show*), combat buddy Ken Parker's daughter Paula as the Hula-Hooping brat who nicks Teas in the head with a rock, and Meyer himself, who appears as part of a burlesque show audience hollering for the main attraction. In lieu of a salary, Bill Teas was cut in for 2 percent of the gross (a deal Pete and Eve objected to that would cause a little anger down the line). "I got a lot more out of him because he had a piece of the action and I didn't have to pay him," said RM.

Discreet locations were another concern. Meyer's dentist Don Couch offered the use of his Van Nuys office (he also plays himself in the film, which he crewed on as well), an army buddy snagged a secretarial office in Brentwood, and Teas himself scored an ice cream parlor in Westwood. The rest of the interiors were done at the Meyer home, much to Eve's annoyance. RM also required outdoor locations, which obviously had to be free from prying eyes. An attorney friend offered his beachfront land in Malibu, and a lake was rented in the Malibu Mountains for a hundred dollars a day. Everything had to be done on the QT, as Meyer had to keep the cops at bay. Ken Parker, who worked as a police photographer, "had heard a rumble that they were going to bust us," said Meyer. Luckily they didn't quite know where the shoot was taking place (RM kept locations a secret until cast and crew had driven there), allowing Parker to act as a decoy, leading the police in the wrong direction as Meyer charged off in an Econoline van full of equipment and women.

$ $ $

The main shoot for *The Immoral Mr. Teas* was done over a long weekend sometime in 1958 and lasted approximately four days. "I always started with the girl with the biggest tits, and that was Ann Peters," said Meyer. "She had the best body, the most conical breasts." Teas recalled RM directing the silent "like one of the old timers" with a megaphone. "Sometimes we wouldn't even rehearse a scene. Russ would start his camera and yell at me, and something would come of it."

"I just had that built-in ability like any so-called photojournalist to make something out of nothing," said Meyer, who needed only the secluded lake, three naked girls, and a schlub in a straw hat to shift his imagination into high gear. Innocent shenanigans of the women paddling by in a canoe while Teas ogles not one but *a trio* of live naked women would constitute the film's big finale. Mick Nathanson remembers having to hide out of camera range behind the boat, physically propelling it as none of the nude girls inside could actually row. Nathanson also had to coax a dubious Teas to take a pratfall into the drink, and when viewing the movie later, members of the 166th were more excited by this accomplishment than by any epidermis on display.

The wild card was the immoral one himself. "Teas, to a large part, was a drunk when we were making the movie," grumbled Meyer, who maintained that the actor "was never terribly enthusiastic about anything. Unless it was crawling between the sheets with some chick." Just such a scenario nearly undid the production on the third night of shooting. Keen to control the minions, RM had cast and crew stay at his house in sleeping bags and on cots, with two of the women cordoned off in a bedroom. Late one night after shooting had wrapped and Meyer was asleep, Ken Parker and Teas demolished a fifth of vodka as Bill whined that since he was the star of the show, he was entitled to some girlie action.

As Parker drifted off to dreamland, Teas tried to slip into Marilyn Wesley's bed. When she pushed him away, a frustrated Teas decided to quit the production and, after calling a cab, charged into the bathroom, determined to shave off his now much-filmed goatee. At which point Parker—awakened by all the commotion—grabbed Bill's mitt mid-razor, "wrestled him back into the sleeping bag, paid off the cab driver, and saved my career," attested Meyer, who only learned of the incident later (Teas forever denied it occurred). After a mere half hour's sleep, Bill was back before the camera, doing, RM stated, "his best work on a blistering hot day at the beach, nursing a vodka hangover."

$ $ $

With the help of Gene Walker crony John Link and editor Igo Kantor, Meyer began to edit his "glorified home movie," and tinkering with those many bits and pieces of celluloid is an area where Meyer excelled. Don Couch, who worked on the picture, says the picture really had no script and that the actual story took shape only when RM started cutting.

"What made these films—what made any of my films—is all the post production," said Meyer. "Looking at what I had and saying, 'That ain't enough, we need more,' and then you go back and shoot a sign or a tin can or a lamppost." The original shoot might've been only four days, but once the picture began to take shape in the cutting room, Russ went to work methodically devising reshoots designed to polish any rough edges. In what would quickly become a Meyer tradition, *Teas* opens with a humorous industrial-film-style prologue. "Modern living is driving an ambitious civilization ever forward," intones the narrator as grand images of Meyer's America go marching by, such as a close-up of Mick Nathanson's fingers operating the push-button transmission of his shiny Nash station wagon.

Meyer had a real knack for photographing the shiny, new, and outrageous. Be it car, radio, or woman, Meyer made it all look like a million bucks. Eschewing flashy effects like zooms or tracking shots, he opted for endless angled setups, intricately intercut into dizzying musical montages that are just intoxicating, and *Teas* is no exception. Meyer's films are sturdy, functional, and efficient, just like an old Rambler, and the only thing he ever did to soup 'em up was to make them run faster and faster by way of the cutting room.

$ $ $

A film, especially a silent one, needs music, and Meyer found a kid hungry enough to come up with it. Edward J. Lakso—later to bless us with TV themes for the likes of *Charlie's Angels*—was an aspiring musician and writer fresh out of UCLA and desperate to get into the business. He first met the Meyers on the set of *Operation Dames*, a threadbare 1959 war drama directed by a war buddy of RM's that Lakso had scripted for a few grand and which Eve had starred in.

Lakso's initial encounter with Russ was a memorable one. RM had to do a location shoot with his wife and asked Edward to lend a hand. Off into nature they went, Lakso unaware of precisely what a shoot with Russ entailed. "Meyer goes, 'All right, Eve, do your thing'—and she strips to the buff! I wasn't expecting it and started dropping things." A nonplussed Meyer asked Lakso if there was something wrong. "It never occurred to Russ that you gotta prepare the average man for something like that."

Meyer offered Lakso two hundred bucks to score *Teas*. Anxious to stick a foot in the door, Lakso took the gig, inquiring as to how many musicians he could hire. "You can hire all you want—you're still only getting two hundred," was RM's response. Lakso joined two friends in some cheap Hollywood studio, and this meager trio, with Lakso manning that annoyingly unforgettable accordion, created the music for *Teas* off the top of their heads as a print of the film flickered before them. Whenever Teas appeared on screen, Lasko broke into a jaunty little march-of-the-tiny-man theme he'd come up with, instructing flute player William St. Pierre to improvise a solo "every time a girl with a breast shows up." When the first naked woman wafted by, St. Pierre—"a very straight guy"—"almost swallowed his flute."*

Although also credited with the narration of the film, Ed Lakso has no memory of writing the monologue. Nor did Meyer ever take full ownership, though it's certainly an embryonic version of his special brand of absurd wordplay (which would grow hilariously extreme in such later pictures as *Good Morning . . . and Goodbye* and *Cherry, Harry and Racquel*). When the professional hired to recite the narration pulled out due to pneumonia, RM offered the job to his friend Irving Blum, whose pompous, awash-in-reverb intonation added another strange layer of humor to *Teas*. Due to Blum's eventual standing in the hoity-toity world of fine art, his contribution remained largely a secret throughout the decades, although Meyer slipped him a print of the film, from which Blum got a lot of mileage at private parties.

Meyer and DeCenzie had laid out very few clams for the first shoot—$1,500 by one report. By the time additional inserts, editing, and distribution costs (including the 35 mm blow-up) were added in, the price tag came to everything they had: twenty-four grand. Although *Playboy* initially passed on a layout, finally running one in November 1961, *Adam* wrote a very welcome and "in those days unheard of" thousand-dollar check for a Ken Parker–shot photo spread of the production. This exorbitant fee would amount to peanuts when *Teas* was finally unleashed. Appreciative of Blum's help, Meyer offered him a percentage of the film's profits or a $1,500 buyout. "I took the buyout and ran," said Blum, who "could hardly believe it" when the picture proved to be a monster hit. "Russ was elated at the success, and, oddly, not too surprised. He kind of expected it. I never did."

But Blum certainly remembered how jazzed RM was when the film was completed. "I think this is *art*," he proudly told Blum, who chuckled at the memory. In the end Meyer would have the last laugh.

---

* Years later, Meyer called Ed out of the blue for another score. "By the way," said RM, "you are getting a raise—$300." Lakso, painfully aware *Teas* had gone on to make a fortune, wasn't amused. "I said, 'Stick it up your ass,' and walked out. Meyer was tight as a bastard."

$ $ $

When the movie was finally in the can, "we couldn't find anybody with the courage to screen it," said Meyer. "No one had ever seen as bare a film as *Teas.*" The picture had its world premiere in San Diego at 9 p.m. on Wednesday, May 27, 1959, at The Balboa Theater, where it was improbably billed with a Gary Cooper western, *The Hanging Man.* Classic exploitation teaser ads had ballyhooed its arrival: "For the first time—a combo of comedy and girls in a picture! Look! For Mr. Teas and his trusty bicycle on city streets tomorrow after noon! If your last name begins with 'T' stop Mr. Teas and get a free ticket! Extra! Bikini-clad Hollywood models hourly on mezzanine posing for amateur photogs!"

But *Teas* was a goner just as soon as it started to flicker. Twenty minutes into the picture the San Diego flatfoots rushed in, shutting the film down. The exact details of the bust were kept hush-hush. All mention of the film disappeared from the next day's newspaper, and the Balboa now had *Rio Bravo* filling the *Teas* slot. Word on the street was that DeCenzie hadn't paid local authorities "the patch," carny lingo for a bribe. It would take Meyer and DeCenzie a year just to get the print back.

In January 1960, *Teas* reopened at the Monica Theater in Los Angeles, breaking the house record on its opening night. *Variety* enthusiastically dubbed it "a perverted *Mr. Hulot's Holiday,*" praising its "amazingly good" photography. Due to the San Diego bust, though, nobody wanted to chance the picture in the rest of the country. *Teas* was too hot to handle. As RM put it, "A statement had been made: this is a film you shouldn't book because the police are going to get involved." It appeared that Meyer had been too adventurous for his own good.

But Pete DeCenzie would save their asses. Up in Seattle and still peddling his *Pictures in Poses,* Pete ran into a "fellow paisan" who just happened to be on the Seattle censor board. DeCenzie explained the little problem he was having with his new picture, and his friend arranged for *Teas* to be screened by the board. "They convened in a hotel room, which is unheard of," said Meyer. No way was DeCenzie going to forget the patch this time: he sprang for some Italian takeout, a few bottles of *vino*, and everybody sat back and enjoyed the show. Unbelievably, they passed the nudity-packed picture with one cut, an innocuous shot of Ken Parker's fully clothed wife Eleanor nibbling on his ear.* A censor board seal of approval went a long way in erasing the taint of the San Diego bust. *The Immoral Mr. Teas* opened in midsummer 1960 at Seattle's Guild 45th Theater and stayed for nine months. "Passing a censor board like that is like a license to steal," said Meyer. "A week after it opened Pete DeCenzie and I bought Cadillacs."

Teas broke records everywhere — Philadelphia, San Francisco, Washington, D.C. It played for three years straight in Los Angeles alone. The film would gross an unheard-of million dollars, making over eighty times what the sixty-three-minute picture cost. In October 1961, highbrow critic Leslie Fiedler wrote a long, enthusiastic review entitled "A Night with Mr. Teas," declaring the picture "a kind of imperturbable comedy, with overtones of real pathos." Of Meyer, Fiedler said, "I hope he makes a million." Much to Meyer's amusement, the critic also maintained that the filmmaker was indulging in pointed social commentary by placing Bill Teas in front of a bus-stop bench featuring a mortuary ad. Fiedler "read in all kinds of stuff," said Meyer. "I'm glad he did, but I had no message except big bosoms and greed . . . my cant is towards entertainment, not in creating some opus that has subliminal reasons for its existence."

When it came to analysis of his pictures, Meyer had a schizophrenic response, much like he did about everything. He'd laugh off any complex interpretations, yet a bad review would wig him out enough to fire off a handwritten attack to the critic responsi-

---

* At times Meyer said the the chewing of the ear was censored in Los Angeles and that Seattle passed the film without a cut. I could find nothing concrete on the subject. The history of the film's release is problematic to say the least, as Meyer suggests that the San Diego engagement was the very first public showing of *Teas*, with Seattle second. But newspaper articles attest to *Teas* opening in Los Angeles in January 1960, followed by Seattle in midsummer of that year. Outside of San Diego, the picture was subject to very little in the way of obscenity charges. Meyer ultimately prevailed in a legal action taken against the picture in Philadelphia. *Teas* had to lose sixteen minutes before passing the tough New York censor board, yet played uncut in nearby Atlantic City.

ble. RM claimed he was in it for the money, yet nothing pleased him more than serious interest in his films. In later years he'd bristle when lumped in with the hard-core industry. "I'm a class pornographer," said Meyer in 1979. "There's a difference. I spend fourteen months making a film. Not thirty minutes in a motel room."

$ $ $

Pete DeCenzie handled the distribution of *Teas* aided by an unexpected partner—Eve Meyer. Moving away from modeling, Eve had dabbled in an acting career but, according to RM, grew disgusted by casting-couch politics. But Eve proved to be a financial whiz, her astute investments making Meyer a fortune. Unfortunately, Eve and Pete butted heads over *Teas.* DeCenzie would entrust the picture to the same burlesque-world lowlifes who had robbed the partners on *French Peep Show.* "They'd fight strenuously over people Eve didn't trust, and with good reason," said Meyer, who felt the real damage to his friendship with DeCenzie was due to the simple fact that Pete "didn't like the idea of a woman having anything to do with business." Meyer would soon go it alone with his wife.

As *Teas* raked in the loot, its namesake grew tired of waiting for his 2 percent of the take to materialize. Meyer felt that "Teas would listen to the bartenders and they'd say, 'You have a piece of that show? You didn't get any money yet? The picture's making millions. You'd better check into it. These guys are cheating you, Bill.' It got to him. He was steaming, seething."*

Things came to a head one day when Teas charged up to Meyer's house in a rage. RM was developing prints in the basement when Teas "accused me of cheating him—'I want the money.' I said, 'Get the fuck out of here.' I literally chased him out

---

* Meyer claimed that Bill's paranoia was unwarranted, and if he'd hung in there he probably would've made ten grand or so. As it was, the exit of Bill Teas from the partnership meant a bigger tax cut for those left. "*Teas* made a lot of money, but the taxes that we had to pay were obscene," said Meyer, who maintained that his and DeCenzie's cut of the million-dollar gross amounted to "maybe $30,000 or $40,000 apiece."

of the darkroom. I was so angry that I was just ready to beat the shit out of him. He insulted my character. He just offended me."

Meyer went to Eve—who didn't care for Teas and hadn't been happy with Russ cutting him in—and instructed that she and Pete get rid of him. "So they bought him off for $750," said Meyer. Bill further angered RM by starring in a rarely seen early sixties non-Meyer nudie-cutie "sequel," *Steam Heat*.

The relationship between Russ Meyer and Bill Teas was a curious one. Never one to forgive a grudge, Meyer remained angry over the incident in perpetuity, wasting no opportunity to tell the world how "heavy into the sauce" Teas was. He blew a gasket when reporter Burr Snider did a look back on Teas and his involvement in RM's film in a 1981 *San Francisco Examiner* article. So enraged was Meyer that he dashed off a remarkable thirty-one-page handwritten memo in which he angrily corrects every factual error (ignoring his own misspellings), then goes on to accuse Teas of being soused throughout his stay in the service and drunk throughout the making of the film, being a weakling, and, perhaps worst of all, being too cheap to buy RM's first wife Betty a meal. Meyer ends the diatribe by suggesting that Teas and Snider go on a date to see that season's reporter-makes-fatal-mistake drama *Absence of Malice*.

Meyer seemed obsessed with what Teas thought of him. When biographer David K. Frasier was researching a never-finished article on Teas in the nineties, RM suggested that Dave tape-record an interview with Bill—then play it for Meyer so he could eavesdrop on what Teas *really* thought. Frasier declined to participate in that Nixonian melodrama.

$ $ $

"By the early 1960s sexual desire, especially male sexual desire, was economically legitimate," writes historian Eric Schaefer, and *Teas* definitely furthered that legitimacy, spawning well over a hundred imitators. Even *Time* took note of the film, maintaining that *The Immoral Mr. Teas* had "opened up the floodgates of permissiveness as we know it in these United States." Meyer would be uncharacteristically modest when held responsible for the decline of Western civilization. "The real driving force behind the increasing permissiveness of our society is Hugh Hefner," he said. "I simply put his illustrations to movement."

But Meyer had indeed done a very provocative thing. He'd made a technically polished, nudity-packed film completely unapologetic in its leering, and one that dared to poke fun at sex. "I don't know why people take love-making so seriously," he said. "It's pretty funny when you look at it."

And while *Teas* may seem "so innocent it is almost wistful," there lurks something diabolical under all that skin. Who exactly was Meyer's joke on? As usual with RM, the intention is not altogether clear.

Noted by Roger Ebert as "one of the canniest psychologists" of those who made sex films, Meyer "understood, instinctively or not, why men go to skin flicks." If you believe that many of these men might just attend such movies out of an inability to connect sexually with women in other, more direct ways, you have to conclude Meyer is exploiting a certain masochism in his male audience. Let's face it, looking ain't always living. For Mr. Teas mirrors all those poor saps—David K. Frasier writes, "who can never hope to meet, let alone attain, the fantasy women who excite their senses. The women in the film are all pinups come to life. They lack the emotional substance to make them real and are thereby immune to any form of relationship other than visual."

$ $ $

Meyer was an odd choice to be the one pushing any sexual boundaries. Here was a man with one foot in the commie-hating Norman Rockwell fifties and the other in some garish live-action Looney Tunes universe where Li'l Abner and Daisy Mae got naked and got down. This outrageousness would help carry him into the psychedelic sixties, although smoking his one and only joint merely put him to sleep. Strictly Black & White scotch for this gent, and straight up if you please. RM was squarer than your grandpa, but for some unknown reason he possessed a knack for latching on to the latest fad faster than Andy Warhol could silkscreen a soup can.

Meyer made clear he put sex on the screen the way he preferred it in bed, so it's a subject worth investigating. According to the women I talked to, RM's view of sex was Neanderthal at best. He didn't even care to get the vocabulary right. With a straight face he'd tell one writer how he might shoot a scene where a cop stops a woman and "she performs cunnilingus [sic] on him while he's writing out her ticket."

Romance and foreplay, that was for sissies. Nope, no kittens and flowers for Russell Albion. He liked his sex just the way he liked his food: meat and potatoes, skip the fancy sauces. RM just wanted to fuck, to get in there and "wail away at it." His terms for the act were more apropros of a boxing match: low body blows, stunts and grunts, hunkering down, doing the horizontal mambo.

No blow jobs, vibrators, whips, or chains for Meyer in his films or in his life. None of that kinky stuff.* He attended one wife-swapping party in his life, and only to watch. Perversion, RM declared, was simply "un-American." If a woman didn't get off just being in the presence of the man the *Wall Street Journal* dubbed "King Leer," well, that was her problem. A female servicing herself annoyed him—there was no RUSS in that equation. "What does a woman know about sexuality, anyway?" pondered Meyer as late as 1990. "They are the receivers, they're the catchers. You've got to be able to pitch."

America bought what Russ Meyer was pitching and it would make him a millionaire. If you put it under the simplest microscope, RM's universe was weirder than hell, but coming out of the sexual dark ages of the fifties it provided both release and relief. For a while his work hummed with a youthful exuberance that hid the dark shadows, a thar's-gold-in-them-thar-hills frothing at the mouth, more irresistable than the fanciest pack of lies from your favorite used-car salesman. RM had his big fat finger on the pulse of something. What was it? Who knows. Meyer saw the absurdity in sex at a time when it angered, bewildered, and frightened most everybody else. Despite the wacky visuals, it would soon become

---

* The big exception to the rule here, I guess, is Meyer's depraved 1976 picture, *Up!* But even then it's all played for laughs.

apparent that underneath it all RM was selling a rather whole-some and old-fashioned message, one that would quell Joe Six-Pack's anxieties: "normal" sex between man and wife maintains our moral universe. Meyer dragged the hairy sex monster into the noon sun and turned it into a seemingly innocent cartoon. Where Americans had shuddered, they now laughed. Of course, every-thing was funny to Meyer—underneath it all he believed in noth-ing. And in the end he'd become much like his own colossal, colorless everyman, a mean Mr. Teas. But that was a lifetime away. For now he was set to ride the sixties chaos rocket like Slim Pick-ens straddling *Strangelove*'s H-bomb, a-hootin' and a-hollerin' all the way down.

$ $ $

"He's still the first Sergeant in the Signal Corps," said Eve of her then–ex husband in a 1969 interview. "He never got over it." RM was just one of those guys who went barreling through life on a mission and let the chips fall where they may. He was Meyer, and Meyer did whatever he wanted.

He'd paid scant attention to Eve while making *The Immoral Mr. Teas*. She seemed annoyed with the whole enterprise, feeling that their happy home had suffered from the invasion. One day she came in to find Russ shooting the ridiculous dream sequence in which Teas hallucinates having a huge, bloody molar removed as dental assistant Marilyn Wesley cheerfully stands by, holding a gi-ant hypo and naked save for a nurse's cap. Eve took one look at this grotesque tableau and broke down, running from the house. Meyer chased after her, only to find his wife curled up in her T-bird, sobbing. It finally penetrated his thick skull: Eve felt left out. They might've fought like cats and dogs during her glamour photo shoots, but they'd done it as a team.

RM knew a way to rectify the situation in a hurry. His next movie would be called *Eve and the Handyman*, and you didn't need to tap the tarot deck to guess the female lead. Meyer would succeed in holding his fabulous marriage together, if only temporarily.

6

The Handyman

I made movie after movie . . . nothing else really mattered.

—RUSS MEYER

Modern Photo looks anything but modern. The place is a dusty, chaotic mess. Old family portraits hang on the walls; junk is scattered everywhere. Window displays have been bleached nearly colorless by the Los Angeles sun. You figure maybe you're in the wrong joint, but then start noticing Meyer regulars in some fading photos on the wall. A head shot of *Cherry, Harry and Raquel*'s Charles Napier lurks not far from a photo of *Beneath the Valley of the Ultra-Vixens'* Kitten Natividad appearing in a neighborhood parade. Traces of Meyer linger everywhere in this Figueroa Street shop. Bits of his movies were shot in this building, and I'd later learn that one of RM's last forays in public was warbling a karaoke "My Way" one boozy night in the bar next door.

Back in the depths of the repository, someone scuttling about in the shadows has heard me enter. Within seconds I am face-to-face with The Handyman himself, Anthony James Ryan. He is instantly recognizable from his many Meyer cameos, most frequently as the omnipresent, glassy-eyed strip joint patron. Al "Li'l Abner" Capp could've invented Ryan—thin, slightly hunched, a wide slash of a mouth, exclamation-point eyes behind black frames. He's The Man with One Expression, the walking, talking definition of "poker face." At times Ryan looks older than an un-wrapped mummy—he refused to state his age when asked—but there's a youthful fire present, accompanied by a sly sense of hu-mor. The guy's just a gas to be around, and, outside of combat buddy Charlie Sumners, no man has gotten closer to RM.

A sharp cookie, Jim Ryan speaks numerous languages and knows a bit about everything. "Ryan has all kinds of adventures in his background, some he won't talk about," said Meyer film editor Richard Brummer. "Secret government work here and there." De-spite his seemingly placid nature, one wouldn't want to cross him, even if he is way past qualification for an AARP card. Fellow Meyer actor Jean Duran recounted how Ryan was once forced to pull a blade on some street trash wreaking havoc throughout the neigh-borhood. "Jimmy took the knife and—*clickclickclick!*—cut all the buttons on his shirt," said Duran. "Don't go fucking with my old man, he'll take you out!"

Jim Ryan first met Russ Meyer at an August 1943 training ses-sion for combat photographers over at RKO. Another member of the 166th, Ryan didn't get to know RM well until after the war, when Meyer was just getting started in Hollywood and Ryan was running a commercial photography studio in Highland Park. In 1960, Meyer offered him a month's work at four hundred bucks a week to costar in his *Eve and the Handyman* film. Outfitted in striped overalls and cap, Ryan played a sort of new-model Mr. Teas. Meyer would be so fond of the character that he'd periodically coax Ryan into donning the old overalls for brief Handyman cameos, even in that grim final outpost of 2000, *Pandora Peaks*.

The Handyman was an apt part for Anthony James Ryan to play in a Meyer film, because that's the role he's essayed in RM's life. "Russ used to go to Ryan for everything," said former secre-tary Paula Parker. For decades Meyer relied on Jim to take care of business, whether co-producing, shooting second-unit footage, photographing stills, or cleaning up the many personal messes Russ left behind. "Ryan is a perfect Meyer crony—he's an old army buddy, he's soft-spoken, he's incredibly dependable, and he's always there for the emergency," said Meyer scriptwriter John McCormick. "Ryan is completely steadfast."

Not that one could expect Russ to show his gratitude. "I'm sure Ryan did more for Ryan than Meyer did for Ryan," said RM associate George Costello. Meyer became a millionaire, while Jim Ryan barely scrapes by. So why did Ryan stick with RM until the bitter end? "Meyer's problems were interesting," said Ryan. "His whole life was controversy. Meyer loved all that hullabaloo— women fighting, people screaming, cops and red lights flashing, neighbors complaining. He provoked people into something occurring."

"I think Jim lived quite vicariously off Meyer's hijinks," said John McCormick. Film distributor Jean-Pierre Jackson recalled Meyer forever chuckling over Ryan's checkered career with the opposite sex. His relationship with his late wife Jacqueline (whom he met on the set of *Eve and the Handyman*—she appears as a nude model in an art class) was rather tempestuous, as Jacqueline was a bit of a character herself, given to wearing SS uniforms as part of her obsession with the Third Reich. "Her whole room was covered in swastikas," said Jim. "It looked like a German Bund meeting."

Outside of Jacqueline (who, somewhat fittingly, wasn't exactly "built" in the way RM required), Ryan knew better than to get involved with any of the Meyer women. But he liked being around them, liked getting an occasional whiff of their perfume as they cried on his shoulder after big bad Russ had bawled them out. "For some reason they'd come talk to me rather than Meyer. I listened to them—and he didn't!"

The men in RM's movies are mere wisps of beings that are about as vague as Meyer's father: if the women are cartoons, the men are stick figures. In life, Meyer surrounded himself with some of the brightest, most talented guys around, but they weren't the most aggressive bunch. RM's was a world ruled by a king with no challengers. There was room for only one big shot: Russ Meyer. "I think Russ tended to romanticize the depth of his friendships with his male associates," said Meyer biographer David K. Frasier. "It would not surprise me if many of the people with whom he was close now express misgivings about the relationship." The fact that RM surrounded himself with such nonthreatening males suggests he wasn't as secure in his own skin as he appeared to be. It also meant that for guys like Ryan there would be no way to stand outside Meyer's shadow. "What a drag to work for a man who's a one-man show," said former RM crew member Stan Berkowitz. "You're nobody."

$ $ $

Before we jump back into Russ Meyer's post-*Teas* oeuvre and the making of it, let's take a look at RM's competition, the rogues who operated outside mainstream Hollywood in the underground world of the now-booming sexploitation business—and at just how separate Russ Meyer kept himself from them.

"I have no gods," said Russell Albion Meyer. "I'm impressed with a few films—*Sahara* with Humphrey Bogart. *Casablanca. Charley Varrick. Red Badge of Courage. A Bridge Too Far. The Bank Dick. Foreign Correspondent.*"

Meyer liked to present himself as a filmmaking primate who'd invented himself. He simply had no influences, and if pressed, made up fictitious ones with grand names, such as Chester Floodbank.* The truth was Meyer knew his motion pictures. He liked Sam Peckinpah, Don Siegel, Martin Ritt, David Lean, and a lot of film noir. He loved W. C. Fields, Mae West, and the Marx Brothers. He'd tell distributor and friend Jean-Pierre Jackson that the inspiration for the way some of his male characters are put upon came out of the 1947 Henry Hathaway espionage picture *13 Rue Madeleine.* David Prowse, who appeared in Meyer's 1974 picture *Blacksnake,* had worked with Stanley Kubrick on *A Clockwork Orange,* and Meyer grilled him on the director. "He loved me talking about Stanley Kubrick, because that was one of his big idols," said Prowse, who said RM wanted to know "everything I could possibly tell him about Kubrick."

"If you turned on the television he would always know what movie was on," said Roger Ebert. "I think that he must've gone to the movies a lot as a kid. You felt the knowledge was there, but you

---

* Actually, Floodbank existed; he was an old baggy-pantsed comic at the El Rey Burlesk.

didn't often talk about it because you usually talked about the project at hand."

Russ Meyer's work can be divided up (minus three one-off anomalies: *Fanny Hill, Mondo Topless,* and *Blacksnake*) into six periods, beginning with *The Immoral Mr. Teas* and its five "imitations," 1959–63; his four black-and-white "roughies," 1964–66 (culminating in *Faster, Pussycat! Kill! Kill!,* which introduced screenwriter John Moran); three color "soap operas," 1967–68 (two of them written by Moran); a pair of harder sex films, 1968–69; the two-picture 20th Century Fox studio output that signaled the arrival of Roger Ebert, 1970–1971; and the three self-conscious sex comedies of 1974–1979, all with varying degrees of Ebert input. Lastly comes 2000's *Pandora Peaks,* a fumbling, sad tombstone to his career that didn't even see a theatrical release.

$ $ $

"After *Teas* a lot of embarrassing bummers were made by people just jumping on the bandwagon," said Meyer. "I imitated myself six times." (Actually only five, Russ.) *The Immoral Mr. Teas* immediately jump-started an entirely new wave of sex pictures that came to be known as "sexploitation." Sexploitation ushered in a genre of (mostly) ultra-low-budget, American-made pictures that actually told a story (however marginal), had ample opportunity for sex within, and, unlike the exploitation films that preceded them, had no condemning moral tacked on at the end. Mr. Teas may have been immoral, but he was unapologetic about it—a new attitude indeed. And it sold tickets. Alabama-born producer/director/distributor David F. Friedman estimates that during the sixties heyday of sexploitation there were approximately 750 theaters in America hungry for the stuff. "Talk about business—back then, you got a new picture, and all the exhibitors were saying, 'When can I have it?' Selling? There was no selling."

Russ Meyer regarded nearly all of his competition with disdain. They churned out technically inferior product, crap with sprocket holes. And while Meyer would bring some imagination to the table with *Teas,* what followed in its wake certainly didn't up any artistic ante. Talent generally wasn't required to make a sex-ploitation film, only a loaded camera and a naked broad or two. These were pictures "as rigid in their construction as a medieval morality play," Friedman maintained. You stuck in something for everybody: a straight sex scene, a spanking scene, a lesbian scene, a rape scene, all simulated by a motley bunch of seminaked thespians who rarely if ever looked like they were even having fun, let alone actual sex. There were no sexploitation stars per se, just the latest available piece of flesh. "Our theory—Russ Meyer's, [sex-ploitation director] Bob Cresse's, and mine—was that every week the suckers want to see a new face, and a new set of tits," said Friedman.

The self-proclaimed Mighty Monarch of the Exploitation World, David F. Friedman did it all: exploitation, sexploitation, gore, hard-core. A jowly, moustached man whom distributors often mistook for RM, Friedman is charismatic, funny, and a great raconteur, but watch out, as he's got the cool, calculated stare befitting a carny (retired from the movie business, Dave now runs his very own midway attractions). In the flick of a cigar Friedman can ascertain your price tag, and before the stogie's ground out he's figured how to get you for a buck fifty less.

A notorious ham (he even appears in the sex scenes of some of his own pictures), Friedman, another Signal Corps graduate, worked for Paramount as well as exploitation pioneer Kroger Babb before teaming up with Herschell Gordon Lewis for a string of notorious films, most notably the landmark 1963 gore outrage *Blood Feast*, a picture that substituted the spectacle of bloody (if ridiculous) disemboweling for any sex.

In 1964, he moved to Los Angeles, founding with Dan Sonney (whose family had already been in the exploitation movie business for three decades under the banner Sonney Amusements) what became Entertainment Ventures, Incorporated, a mini-empire located at 1654 Cordoba Street, in the heart of what had once been Hollywood's film row. There, among the dusty, partially melted statues once featured in the Sonney family's traveling waxworks show (not to mention an infamous real-life mummy of Oklahoma petty criminal Elmer McCurdy), was a one-stop movie factory. Friedman even had his own printing company on the premises, which churned out florid one-sheets and pressbooks illustrated by the largely unknown great Rudy Escalera, who'd later turn to painting collectible plates for the *Reader's Digest* crowd. (Friedman had to keep a close watch on this one, as Rudy tended to paint women on the lardy side if left to his own imagination.) When not terrorizing their shrill-voiced Orthodox Jewish secretary Bea, Friedman and Sonney hosted a round-the-clock gin rummy game that drew in every sleaze merchant passing through downtown L.A. Even the ever-down-on-his-luck director of *Plan 9 from Outer Space*, Ed Wood Jr., stumbled into the Entertainment Ventures offices every once in a blue moon, sniffing around for a booze-money handout.

Friedman didn't have much contact with RM in the early years, outside of clashing with his uppity wife Eve at distributors' meetings. In 1973, Meyer—concerned about a Nixon-regime Supreme Court obscenity ruling throwing the decision of what's obscene back to individual states—was an unlikely attendee at Friedman's support group, the Adult Filmmakers of America Association, and the pair became friends. In the years to come, Friedman would testify on Meyer's behalf during his divorce battle with third wife Edy Williams, help RM get his film distribution in Australia, and introduce him to the home video market.

Meyer's pictures got wider exposure than most sexploitation, but he also spent much more making them. While Meyer loved moviemaking, David F. Friedman loved the con. Despite such title grabbers as *Trader Hornee*, *Thar She Blows*, and *Bell, Bare and Beautiful*, his pictures are insufferably dull, laboriously constructed grade-Z re-creations of grade B Hollywood product that exude a cynicism not dissimilar to that of some huckster selling twenty-five-cent peeks at a real, live two-headed baby in a jar. Friedman's trailers, however, are another story. Unable to advertise on television or in many newspapers, sexploitation pictures relied on the buzz generated by coming attractions, and Dave's were particularly irreverent and fast-paced. As Friedman admitted, "Our whole business was the old carny tease: 'Boy, we didn't see it this week, but look at the previews—look at what we're gonna see *next* week.' " The name of the game was get the "D.G.'s" (degenerates) into the theater, and making the actual film came in a distant second place. "I had the one-sheet and pressbook ready before the picture was even started."

Meyer admired Friedman's moxie and con-man charm. The latter may have churned out total crap, but he took it real seriously. RM described a visit to a Friedman production, a picture with "some stiff directing it. Dave would drop in when they'd have a love scene and say, 'Stand aside.' " Friedman "always came in with a coat over his shoulders, no arms in the sleeve. And he'd have some flunky take the coat off, and he'd say, 'All right, now *I'm* in charge.' And then he'd direct things so seriously it would wanna make you laugh. The motivation — 'Your old man is crazy, your child is a homosexual, this is affecting you, milady, despite the fact that you have breasts almost big enough to be in a Meyer movie.' Then he'd say, 'Alright cut! Gimme the coat.' Put it on, walk out. 'LUNCH!' That was Dave Friedman. And bless him for it."

"We were all independent characters," said Friedman. "We're talking about very unique people, people who did things that the average person would shun." Just like the mainstream film business, the main hubs of activity were New York and Los Angeles, and the usual clichés applied. "Hollywood producers made pictures to look like Hollywood product," said Friedman. "The New York producers made pictures to look like European product — a grittier, more art-house look." Friedman's being kind here, as a good percentage of the New York sexploitation pictures featured a sordid, ring-around-the-collar bunch you'd have gladly paid to keep their clothes on, while Los Angeles product boasted, naturally, the "best-looking dames in the world."

But while Hollywood had the slicker product, New York was home to the money mecca of the exploitation biz, 42nd Street and its formidable string of grindhouses, most of them clustered on one gaudy block and for the most part owned by the utterly ruthless Brandt Organization. Their goal was to exploit the exploiters, and the main terror in the family was the bald-headed, pinky-ringed Bingo Brandt; he constantly changed deals, lining his own pockets while shortchanging the filmmaker. Distributors lived in fear of the man because Bingo could make or break you on the Deuce. But not Eve Meyer. Marvin Friedlander, Meyer's New York distrib, would watch in amazement as Eve stood up to Bingo over a sour deal. There wasn't a man in the business who didn't shudder when it came to dealing with Bingo. Eve didn't flinch.

Strangely enough, the biggest sleaze pit in the world had to kowtow to one of the toughest censor boards in the country: the New York Board of Regents. Meyer tried and failed to get *The Immoral Mr. Teas* passed before turning to distributor William Mishkin, who finally got the picture passed by cutting it to forty-seven minutes—and taking 50 percent of the action. As usual, it took a bad deal to get onto the Deuce.

The New York City sleaze boys were a rough, tough, secretive bunch, characters to do Damon Runyon proud. Another RM, Radley Metzger, was king of the New York sexploitation world, and one of the exceptions to the rule there as Meyer was on the West Coast scene. Generally regarded as the two greatest talents in the field, Meyer and Metzger both made stylish, technically dazzling sex films that benefited from budgets that would cause other exploitationers to faint. Both men were also loners who had intense relationships with their mothers and female distributors, Ava Leighton in Metzger's case. But that's where the similarities ended. The West Coast RM serviced Joe Six-Pack, while his East Coast counterpart courted the intelligensia. "The most erotic films ever made," Meyer once said of Metzger's work.*

A silver-haired Leonard Bernstein look-alike, Metzger possessed a voluminous knowledge of motion picture history and had a predilection for wearing the occasional scarf. Radley made "serious" erotic films for the art-house crowd, delving deep into territory Meyer considered off-limits if not downright perverted. Bisexuality was the thrust of Metzger's 1972 *Score*, S/M the subject of his nefarious 1975 masterpiece *The Image* aka *The Punish-*

---

* David Friedman's late wife Carol knew and liked both RMs. According to her husband, she felt neither sexploitation director "had much use for" the female race.

ment of Anne. Under the alias Henry Paris, he directed what Meyer would never even consider: out-and-out hard-core.

Los Angeles had its own bunch of sexploitation auteurs and distributors, men like David Friedman, Lee Frost, Don Davis, Pete Perry, Harry Novak, and A. C. Stephen, aka Steve Apostolof, an Eastern European who talked of making "smoot pictures." By far the wildest character of the L.A. group was the notorious Bob Cresse, who partnered with a soft-spoken director named Lee Frost to form Olympic Pictures, an outfit responsible for such assaults on taste as *Mondo Freudo* and *One Million Years A.C./D.C.* A bug-eyed, sawed-off runt who looked like a cross between Erich von Stroheim and one of those carnival-prize chalk dogs from days gone by, Cresse was considered a "great little showman" by David F. Friedman, who'd met the young Cresse at—where else?—the carnival. "Bob was a bigmouth, with the balls of a burglar." A degenerate gambler, Cresse carried a gun, was fond of dressing as a Nazi, and routinely filmed women undressing behind a secret one-way mirror.

According to Friedman, Cresse was "not homosexual, heterosexual, not bisexual. He was totally asexual, and the greatest voyeur in the world. I think that more than anything else drove him into this racket. He was absolutely insane." Meyer was fond of recounting an apocryphal Cresse tale concerning the time Bob stuck his pistol in the mouth of a deadbeat exhibitor, who wisely paid up on the spot.

In later years Cresse, perusing the product in some adult bookstore, noticed two hooligans roughing up a woman outside in the street. Cresse gallantly charged out, pistol in hand, shouting that he was calling the cops. "We *are* the cops," announced one of the two undercover officers in the process of arresting a prostitute. Then they not only shot Cresse in the stomach, but put a bullet in his dog, too. "He was never the same, never worked again," said Friedman.

The L.A. mob was a crazy, fun-loving bunch. Although cutthroat competitors, they somehow managed to booze, gamble, and carouse as pals. Russ Meyer was the one exception. "He was never out on the town like I was," said Friedman. "We were at all the 'in' places, but Russ was never a part of it." Aligning himself neither with the exploitationers and certainly not with the mainstream, RM was, as he was fond of saying, truly a genre unto himself.

$ $ $

Outside of *Teas*, Meyer's first period—consisting of the five nudie-cuties Meyer made from 1960 to 1963—is the least interesting to discuss. Part of the problem is that three of these pictures—*Erotica, Europe in the Raw,* and *Heavenly Bodies*—have not been seen since their original distribution as Meyer withdrew them from circulation, adamant that they aren't his best work. All five films are *Teas*-like to varying degrees: 16 mm/35 mm blow-ups shot silent except for narration, with an average length just over sixty minutes, and featuring a simple, cutesy story that allowed for some no-contact female nudity.

The first *Teas* follow-up made in 1960, *Eve and the Handyman,* is the only Meyer picture to star wife Eve. Decades (and many films later) RM bitched that filmmaking was just hard work, but he'd admit to David K. Frasier that this was the one picture he'd actually had fun making. Meyer shot his second feature in and around San Francisco. Costarring with Eve was his 166th buddy Jim Ryan.

"Eve typed the script," said Ryan, which amounted to "just loose-leaf paper—it wasn't even a script, just a list of ideas. That's all we had to work with. I improvised some of the stuff." While the picture shared the same whimsical humor of *The Immoral Mr. Teas,* "it didn't have all the nudity in it," said Meyer. "Some." None of which featured Eve, as it turned out. Rightly concerned that RM was reluctant to show the goods when it came to his own wife, partner Pete DeCenzie bailed out right before production started. The Meyers continued alone.

"For a month I worked harder than I ever have in my life," said Eve, who rose before dawn to make breakfast for cast and crew, then packed lunches for everyone before driving fifty miles so she could essay her starring role. Then she'd schlep back home and feed everybody dinner.

There isn't much to the picture. Eve skulks around in a trench coat, beret, and red scarf spying on everyman plumber the Handyman. The Handyman bumbles around from job to job in his 1936 Nash pickup, blissfully ignorant of the beautiful blonde following him. An occasional naked lady appears. The big finale consists of Eve cornering the Handyman, seemingly flashing him by opening her coat. But no, we see that she's just wearing a display sign that reads, "Buy Strump brushes." But brushes alone don't get our plumber off. Eve then runs her brush through the Handyman's hair, which apparently does the trick, intercut as it is with trains coupling, a kettle boiling, and a rocket blasting off.

Visually, Meyer makes the most of this cornpone. *Eve and the Handyman* is a quaint little concoction, with one hoary sight gag after another—Eve serving up a two-scoop sundae adorned with maraschino cherries, Meyer cutting to her knockers, nudge, nudge, wink, wink. At one point the Handyman rolls a paintbrush across an empty canvas, and as the word "Mother" magically appears in big red letters on the blank white space, the sound effect of a bomb detonating is heard on the soundtrack. Nobody captures the flashy ephemera of modern life with RM's flair—in this case jukeboxes, pinball machines, and close-ups of Eve's beautiful kisser. Meyer makes capitalism look sexy, shiny, and new in that narcotic *Playboy* way.

Eve and the Handyman premiered May 5, 1961, at the Paris Theater in Los Angeles. The first ten thousand customers were promised free bathroom plungers, and members of the plumbers' union got in free. "Eve All Smirk, No Smoke," declared the *Los Angeles Examiner,* but the film was a certified smash and the dough continued to roll in. No one-hit wonder was Meyer.

Meyer missed his partner, though, and managed to bring Pete DeCenzie back into the fold for the next two pictures, beginning with 1961's *Erotica.* Ground out for a mere four grand, *Erotica* was a compilation of six vignettes, including "city girl who likes to swim in country stream" and "the legend and lore of bathing suits." Judging from the stills, it appears that there were two main attractions to the movie. The first, Miss Glendale, was an impossibly built credit manager for that city's Chevrolet dealership, and

RM had hounded Miss G relentlessly to work with him until she capitulated (afraid of being recognized, she let con man Meyer convince her that a mere pair of sunglasses would shield her identity from the world). Attraction number two was the truly astounding Sherri Knight and her fifty-five-inch bust. Two years before *Erotica*, RM had shot stills of Knight for the skin rags, and Meyer was wise enough to capture the dame on motion picture film at the same time. In RM's words, "Meeting Sherry [*sic*] for the first time might be compared to witnessing the launching of the U.S.S. *Ticonderoga*." A mink stole her only piece of wardrobe, Knight rolled around in the Malibu sand as Meyer snapped over a hundred stills with his Rollei, after which a hundred feet of Kodachrome 16 mm film chattered away in his Arriflex, and all this before any of the local boys in blue appeared on the scene. Shooting wrapped for the day and RM never saw Knight again. DeCenzie was knocked out by the footage and begged Meyer to stick it in *Erotica*.

Next came 1962's *Wild Gals of the Naked West*, a strange little crudity that's basically a plotless excuse for Meyer and his army buddies to play cowboys and Indians alongside a few scantily clad women, most notably men's magazine model Julie Williams and another RM personal favorite, Donna X, aka Trena Lamar. This is Meyer's first real collaboration with the fabulous Jack Moran (who'd provided some narration for *Erotica*), perhaps his greatest scriptwriter. Moran penned *Wild Gals* and plays the old coot cowboy narrator. Meyer loved to people his films with crazy characters, and this film marks the first appearance of one of the oddest creatures RM ever exalted to celluloid stardom, the toothless, "banjo-bodied" Princess Livingston. One can only guess in what dark corner of the world RM found this broad. A horny old grandma and nuttier than a loon, Princess had a cackle like a stuttering foghorn and a gleeful, glassy stare. She also told the filthiest jokes imaginable. "She was funny as hell," said actor John Furlong, who'd work with her in 1965's *Mudhoney*. "I don't know if she had any acting experience. I think she was running a motel in Hollywood." Furlong recalled a memorable moment during a break on the set of *Mudhoney*. "She was sitting on the porch and her skirt was kind of up. Sitting there with no underpants on!" Russ took one look at her undercarriage and muttered, "It's hairier than a blacksmith's apron!"

Meyer's fourth time at bat, *Wild Gals,* has its charms. The colorful cartoon sets and montages of rubber monster masks, gun barrels, and waggling breasts convey a jittery weirdness, a pre-Devo evocation of modern man absurdity. Meyer has a way of building tension with shot repetitions, hypnotizing the viewer in a very peculiar manner. Like the proverbial kid in the candy store, he's lost in the rhythm, overwhelmed with excitement to be showing us such crazy stuff—"Look at *this* and look at *this* and look at *this!* Now let's look at it all *again,* shall we?" RM's lust for life infects every frame. As does a borderline insanity, if you ask me. By the end of his career, repetition would take over everything, like a flip book on endless repeat.

If you're at all familiar with Meyer mythology, Jack Moran's closing monologue in *Wild Gals* becomes rather touching, RM's version of "Buckets of Rain" at the end of Dylan's *Blood on the Tracks.* Addressing the camera in his ridiculous fake moustache and Deputy Dawg hat, Moran's Old-Timer bemoans the fact that the "worst sin town in the West" has gone straight. "This town plumb died from good." Then comes a bit of philosophical musing, straight from the heart of Russ: "I ain't one to be sayin' evil's good, but a person needs a twinge of meanness in 'em—y'know. Somethin' for the good to work against. It keeps your blood movin'." There's a dreamlike montage of the film's characters fading into each other, a bit of D-cup Proust. "Seems like all I can see is yesterday." He's not even there yet and already Meyer is yearning for the past. But as the Old-Timer pontificates how "ol' Adam, he was a pretty straight-laced fella until Eve come along," an inevitable bit of evil—half-naked Trena Lamar—sashays in to end his big thoughts. Old-Timer ogles her as he picks up a bottle of booze and says, "What a combination: an eighty-year-old man, ninety-proof straight whiskey, and 100 percent pure woman!" Off into the desert the pair wander, the end.

Wild Gals would be the last joint effort with Pete DeCenzie, who complained that RM was holding back on the money shots by keeping the females in pasties. Both Pete and his wife, Yvonne, left in midproduction to return home to their dogs, and Meyer didn't appreciate being left holding the mop. When Eve fired one of DeCenzie's buddies over a distribution squabble, Pete tore into her, reducing Eve to tears. RM took his wife's side in the argument, and Meyer and DeCenzie would not meet again until decades later at an anti-censorship affair at San Francisco's Fairmont Hotel. RM suggested they meet for dinner to reminisce, but when Meyer arrived at Pete's Gaiety Theater, DeCenzie was a no-show. Meyer never saw him again, but paid for a DeCenzie tribute in *Variety* when he learned of his demise. "After Pete died, Russ almost got maudlin over him," said Dave Friedman.

$ $ $

In 1962, the newsreel-inspired Italian import *Mondo Cane* became a smash international hit (its theme song "More" was nominated for an Oscar), and it birthed a new exploitation film subgenre that some consider the precursor of reality TV. In the guise of educational travelogues, the mondo picture promised to sicken and disgust with the worst the world had to offer, while (initially in the series, anyway) balancing it out with more whimsical sights. Sometimes real, sometimes faked for the camera, it was yet another cinematic equivalent of the carnival freak show: do you *dare* look behind the curtain? See hell on earth, from a safe distance and for the cost of a movie ticket.

Meyer was outraged by what he felt was anti-American sentiment in *Mondo Cane*'s round-the-world freakfest—odd in itself since the few USA-inspired vignettes are no more cynical than those from the rest of the globe. He struck back by making his own sex shockumentary of European depravity using both actual travel footage and faked sex scenes, 1963's *Europe in the Raw*. Boarding the S.S. *France* with Eve, Meyer deliberately limited himself to short reels of film and cheap equipment in order to pass as a tourist and not the smut peddler he was. In Brussels he shot some fantastic footage of a dancer named Veronique Gabriel (he later recycled it in *Mondo Topless*) but ran out of luck in the red-light districts of Berlin and Amsterdam, where he realized that flashing a camera around might get him killed. In Amsterdam, RM tried to make up the difference by faking a Dutch nudist camp complete with windmills, adding the hot stuff back home.

Meyer then came up with a wild idea that would salvage the tenuous project. Noticing that Europeans were fond of carrying valises, he had a suitcase modified for a secret camera while in Copenhagen. "With a very obvious window built into the bag and the loud whir of the camera motor it would hardly take an Ian Fleming or an Allen Dulles to spot the thin subterfuge," wrote *Modern Man* magazine. Back into the fleshy fray went RM and his 16 mm eye-spy. Hamburg hookers chased Russ and Eve out of a bordello when one of the women smelled a rat. In Paris he shot footage of prostitutes trolling the notorious Les Halles district, tracking one hooker right up the stairs of some cheap flophouse and into her room. Foolishly believing that honesty was the best policy, Meyer revealed his camera and asked, "Photo?" The girl responded by running to an open window and shouting for a gendarme. RM hightailed it out of there, concocting a suitable staged ending for the cinema verité French footage back in the States, using a double for himself and a stacked Las Vegas showgirl named Veronica Erickson.

"Tits and War" was Meyer's summation of the picture after he'd intercut the European beauties with some of his old combat footage. The most intriguing of the three pictures withheld by Meyer, *Europe in the Raw!* did only OK box office, according to RM.

The year 1963 sent Meyer to the hospital twice, first for a hemorrhoid operation, then for an appendectomy. In order to have a money-generating project to work on while convalescing, RM spent five grand to hastily shoot his last pretty-naked-girls-plus-narration nudie-cutie—a purported exposé of the glamour photography biz called *Heavenly Bodies*—over a long weekend in Los Angeles. Eve, claiming an aversion to hospitals, didn't visit the ailing Russ during this time. "Eve was really pretty tough," recalled Jim Ryan, who said that her brand of TLC amounted to "Give him a drink and have him shut up." "Russ seeking downright pity did a real number on Mrs. Meyer," wrote RM.

Apparently Eve's indifference did a number on Russ as well. After eleven proud years of monogamous bliss, Meyer committed "joyful adultery" at the Hollywood Players Motel on Vine Street. His partner was the mysterious Janet Buxton. At least that's the alias she gets in Meyer's autobiography. Most likely, this is the same woman he nicknamed Miss Mattress, a married-with-children, baby-oil-loving wildcat who'd appeared in some of his films (she also shared Eve's December 13 birthday). "It is not a love affair," he told *Adam* magazine in the eighties. "It is strictly carnal." As he'd meet with her periodically over the years until he could no longer function, this was probably the most consistent relationship of Meyer's life. "We never spent more than three hours together at any one time," he'd boast to one reporter. "We go to a motel."

The Hollywood Vine Motel, the Disneyland Howard Johnson's Motel, the Le Baron Hotel in Anaheim, the Hyatt off Interstate 5 . . . Wham, bam, thank you ma'am. Meyer would even occasionally pimp Buxton to his friends, including a group of 166th buddies who chickened out at the last moment. There are reams of pages in RM's book documenting what seems to be his every sexual encounter with Miss Mattress in onomatopoeic detail, with every grunt, groan, and gush immortalized to a punishing degree. There are also scores of photographs of Buxton in the raw, although in each and every shot Meyer helps keep the Mrs.'s identity a secret by thoughtfully placing a paper bag over her head.

There was one more perverse wrinkle to his relationships with both his wife and Miss Mattress. "Eve truly wanted children," said friend Floyce Sumners. "She was desperate for children and she was just really unhappy that she didn't have any." Meyer was adamant that a family would only interfere with his many plans. Friend Dolores Fox felt that Russ resented anything that took Eve's attention away from him, even if it was merely a piano lesson. In spite of this, 166th buddy Charlie Sumners maintained that deep down Russ wanted children. "He always resented the fact that I had kids and he didn't. But he never really liked kids." Meyer seemed uncomfortable and impatient around children, unsure of how to act around them.

But while Eve wouldn't get the one thing she wanted most, his motel fuck-buddy would. According to Meyer, Miss Mattress bore him an illegitimate son. "The boy doesn't know and the father doesn't know," he said in 1979, adding that his son was now fifteen, meaning that he'd been born around 1964, while RM was still married to Eve. To most people, Russ would proudly express his indifference over the affair, but Rob Schaffner, a friend of Meyer's in later years, said that RM described more than once traveling to where mother and son lived in order to hide in a car and spy on his offspring. "He would sit there five, six hours just to get a look at him."

Charlie Sumners thought the whole thing was a fabrication on Meyer's part, just another tall tale. Meyer himself would deny the child's existence in Rolf Thissen's 1987 biography, yet he'd share the scandal with reporter after reporter. During a visit to Chicago in 1995, he'd jest to a roomful of fans that he'd named his son Mr. Mattress. At least one close friend doesn't doubt there's an heir. "I've seen a photograph of the kid," said biographer David K. Frasier. "It's obvious—this kid couldn't be anybody but Russ's son."

$ $ $

By 1963, the nudie-cutie fad was finito, and *Heavenly Bodies* stiffed at the box office. "The public just grew tired of seeing the same old thing," said RM. Had *The Immoral Mr. Teas* been his only credit, Meyer might've remained a curious footnote in sex film history. As it turned out, he'd just been revving his engines. "I realized nudies had had it. Women had been presented in every conceivable way. Now there was required—in addition to the exposure of flesh—some sort of story." Noting that foreign "art" films seemed to be making a comeback, RM started to concoct a new recipe for the sex film. And then a neon idea blinked on in his mind.

"I said, now I must do something like the foreign films, only it will be Erskine Caldwell and it will be a morality play and we'll borrow heavily from the Bible and I'll find a girl with giant breasts."

Exactly.

Top Lust, Top Hate, Top Heavy

No woman ever did anything after they worked for Meyer, by and large.
None of them. They've been to the top, where else is there to go?
They're through.

—RUSS MEYER

He cast a corpse. The broad doesn't have it. Tits aren't big enough.
She just doesn't do it, and if Meyer ain't feeling it in the grinch,
it's a no-go. Not one frame shot, and already RM is in a tailspin.
Deep inside he knows the picture's fucked. His co-screenwriter
and star James Griffith pushed him to cast Maria Andre, a redhead
he'd used in *Heavenly Bodies*, and he'd done so—reluctantly. RM
just couldn't come *up* with anybody else. "The worst part of making films is trying to find the women," he'd say later. "There was
only one Lorna, there was only one Uschi, there was only one
Kitten."

And then, at 4 a.m. in the carport of the Meyers' Evanview
home, just as Eve is sending RM on his way to *Lorna*'s location, a
funny thing happens. Eve hates that her husband's getting into actual smut films, perhaps sensing she'll lose Russ in the process, but
she stops pouting long enough to fork over a nearly forgotten test

Polaroid she'd socked away of a trashy, melon-breasted blonde, one who'd look good in the back of a pickup in a torn dress. A quick glance at this chick and RM's head nearly explodes. His fiery eyes lock on the small, shiny picture and don't let go. Lady Luck, as usual, was on RM's side.

He had to act fast—hell, they were supposed to start shooting in a few hours. Scrambling for the phone, Meyer gets James Griffith on the horn, tells him the good news, then instructs him to fire Maria Andre. "Pay off the other frail," he barks.

The errand boy is reluctant: "That's terrible! You agreed to cast her."

Meyer detonates. *"Fuck!* I have to *live* with this movie! It's *my* ass. You think I care 'bout principles? I care about the film. Lay a thousand dollars on her, say goodbye, then tell her Russell says he's sorry."

Shortly thereafter Meyer had his new starlet before the camera, shooting a scene in which, after another dud session in bed with her husband, a nude Lorna rises to stare longingly out the window. "I told her, 'I want you to be disturbed. He'd been lightning quick. You had no satisfaction. . . . I want to read it on your face.' What I wanted to say was, 'Read it on your big tits.'" There was a lot riding on this picture—37G, to be precise—and Meyer had yet to see his new leading lady lose her laundry.

RM and childhood chum Wilfred "Bud" Kues set up the equipment for the shot, then Meyer banished Bud from the room. "I shot without crew because I didn't want the leading lady rattled." Meyer also exited, instructing Lorna to disrobe, get under the covers, and call him back in when she was ready to go.

It was the moment of truth. The movie would add up to zero if she couldn't deliver the goods, and no doubt RM's heart was pounding out of his chest as he peered through the camera and whispered, "Roll 'em." But Lorna Maitland did not disappoint. She lay in bed sulking, then angrily threw back the covers and walked naked to the window, "with her big tits away from me," said an already relieved Meyer. "From the side I could see the confirmation of those dreadnaughts. Even when she bent forward to put on some sandals the configuration of those pregnant tits did not change one iota." Meyer, no doubt breaking a sweat as he squinted through the viewfinder, noticed her swollen nipple was brushing against a kneecap. It was just the sort of fetishistic detail Meyer reveled in. Dollar signs danced in his head as he muttered just two words to himself: "Box office."

$ $ $

A stiff swirl of cotton-candy blond hair, lips like a pair of overstuffed couches mating, a lethal-weapon body—there was something plain wicked about Lorna Maitland. Her terminally unimpressed scowl seemed to suggest your balls were not long for this world. A man-eater, to quote those fops of pop Hall and Oates. A Venus flytrap in a wighat, Jayne Mansfield's evil twin.

Born in Glendale, California, raised in Norman, Oklahoma, Barbara Joy had been one of 132 women to answer a *Daily Variety* cattle call for a new Meyer skin queen. Initially failing to make any sort of impression—"I was dressed with a rather secretarial look," the eighteen-year-old admitted—her determined manager, one Clancy Grass III, snapped a couple of Polaroids of the top-heavy Vegas dancer and pressed them into Eve Meyer's hands. It was RM who christened her Lorna Maitland—Lorna for a secretary who'd bewitched him back in his prewar pencil-pushing days, Maitland to provide classy contrast to the character's shit-kicker roots.

From here on out, nearly all of Meyer's leads would be played by strippers, go-go dancers, and other misfit entities not necessarily in possession of a Screen Actors Guild card. Dramatic ability was a welcome bonus but definitely not first in the job-description department, and over the years this led to some rather idiosyncratic performances. "A good actress! I'd rather have a big-chested stiff who can hardly pronounce her name."

Now, with the demise of the nudie-cutie, RM's films were moving from narration-only to spoken dialogue, and he was forced to deal with actual thespians, regarding them much as he did communists, feminists, and homosexuals. RM began heeding Otto Preminger's personal advice that actors should be treated like cattle.* "From then on I was a very difficult guy." He became particularly hard on his femme stars, giving direction only through an intermediary, offering no kind words of encouragement and no pats on the back for a satisfactory performance. And so the die was cast, with Meyer routinely playing sadist to his leading ladies, leaving his minions to wipe away the tears.

Meyer women would last for one film, two tops. Meyer likened the process to an affair. After poring over every inch of their bodies with his camera eye, he'd grow bored—and so would they. They just didn't glisten with the same excitement or take orders with the same gusto the second time around. "Once you've unwrapped them, the thrill is gone."

RM had observed ecdysiasts in action since the days of Tempest Storm and the El Rey, and his experiences had provided him with a rather special view of the female race. "Ninety percent of the strippers I've known have supported an old man who carries their makeup kits around," mocked Meyer. "These women need a servant; someone they can pussywhip."

Yes, these women invariably came with an accessory the director could've done without. The Ace, as Meyer dubbed him, was RM's bête noire. An Ace was an insecure and frequently unintelligent boyfriend or husband who, acting out of jealousy, would undermine and/or circumvent Meyer's power over an actress, usually during bedroom pillow talk once the day's shoot had wrapped. "In the morning when you start up again you can sense someone's been feeding that chick's computer," he groused. Thus RM went to great lengths to quarantine his cast in remote locations that were off-limits to outsiders, where he could lord over all as undisputed king. Outwitting the paramour of his latest glamazon was a never-ending game. "Russ's whole life was to not give the upper hand to the Ace," said Meyer, who referred to himself in the third person as often as Garbo. At any rate, Lorna Maitland would arrive at *Lorna*'s location alone, and by Meyer's preferred choice of star transport, Greyhound bus.

---

* For the record, the actors/cattle comparison is usually associated with Alfred Hitchcock.

Maitland is an interesting case in that Meyer always seemed a little disturbed discussing her. "She did a number on my head ... she wasn't going to be pushed around." Writer Gene Ross reported in the middle of an interview with RM that Lorna was the one Meyer star who "absolutely hated his guts." On page 84 of David K. Frasier's *Russ Meyer: The Life and Films,* there is a revealing production photograph of a nearly naked Lorna throwing a perturbed, angry look toward RM, who appears unsure of himself, maybe even cowering a bit. When Frasier's book was published, Meyer's gaze landed on this particular picture and he responded with utter fury, even though he'd personally OK'd each of Frasier's photo choices. This ugly little glimpse of reality was an absolute violation of the kind of fantasy RM peddled, and when Frasier returned the glossy, Meyer said he'd immediately destroyed it.

$ $ $

"We find the location and then we write the story" was Meyer's ass-backward way of doing things, and in this case bumping into old pal Bud Kues led him to explore a couple of depressed Sacramento Delta towns, Walnut Grove and Locke. The oddest places inspired Meyer—the more desolate and forlorn, the better. A sort of rural Chinatown founded in 1915, Locke had a tiny, claustrophic main street (which to this day is lined with dilapidated lean-tos that evoke Depression days) perfect for a *Lorna* sort of town, a place, as writer Nathaniel Thompson put it, "where everyone quotes the Bible and nobody follows its Commandments."

Lorna was shot in a couple of weeks in September 1963 with the usual five-man crew. It was a big gamble for Meyer. Not only was this a story with live dialogue requiring at least some pretense of acting, it was RM's first try at shooting in 35 mm, and the $37,000 budget was considerably more than any previous effort. This was the start of what Roger Ebert calls Meyer's "Gothic period," four mean-spirited pictures that would culminate in the monumental *Faster, Pussycat! Kill! Kill!*

"Without artistic surrender, without compromise, without question or apology, an important motion picture was produced:

LORNA—a woman too much for one man," went the hype. The picture opens with a frantic tracking shot down a lonely highway, a jazz combo wailing away as the broken white lines fly past. We halt for a preacher standing in the middle of the road who offers an ominous, abandon-all-hope-ye-who-enter-here monologue. The tracking shot picks up speed again, snaking through a dusty, dilapidated town and eventually landing on two reprobates exiting Al's Bar: sadistic Luther and his short, balding sidekick Jonah. On the prowl for women, they happen onto drunken Ruthie and follow her home. Luther barges into her abode and forces himself on Ruthie; she fights back; he beats her as Jonah, watching the action through a window, salivates. Afterward, Jonah voices tender concern that his friend might be hurt, but Luther waves him off, already lost in evil thoughts: "You know the one I really want!"

Lorna, the match that lights everyone's fire, is the sexually frustrated wife of noble but ineffectual James. While James is at work, Lorna is ambushed by The Fugitive, a sex-starved escaped convict. What starts out as rape ends in mutual satisfaction, and together they return to her home for further study. Hubby is ordered to fix his own dinner while Lorna fawns submissively over her attacker. Naive James defends his wife's virtue to his sadistic co-worker Luther, who delights in lusting after Lorna and undermining the husband's manhood at every turn. Meanwhile, The Fugitive socks it to wifey right in her wedding bed. Then James and his co-workers arrive for a final showdown during which Luther throws a knife that kills The Fugitive. Lorna falls onto him, impaling herself on a hook in her lover's hand, then James crawls atop his dying wife's body, mewling his love for her and asking forgiveness.* Our pompous Reverend, returning to wrap things up as Lorna turns into a pillar of salt, does a bit of preaching: "As ye sow, so shall ye reap."

Meyer opens his autobiography's chapter on *Lorna* with a

---

* You might ask exactly what James has to be sorry for, since he's used and abused during the entire movie. His sin is sexual inadequacy. Meyer's mind works like this: if James had only been able to satisfy his wife, none of this would've happened, so it's all his fault. This philosophy would be taken to its absurd zenith in Meyer's 1968 film, *Good Morning and Goodbye!*

definition of adultery. It is key to note that the first picture he made after breaking his marriage vows in a cheap Hollywood motel centered on exactly the same subject, only on film the philanderer is a woman who's punished by death. At times Meyer voiced the belief that his stories were "morality plays. I feel strongly about people getting their just deserts, if you do something bad you gotta pay for it." More convincing was his admission that bringing back the old-fashioned exploitation square-up ending—i.e., sinners must be punished—made for a bit of Bible Belt insurance. Sayeth RM in 1987, "The moralizing has nothing to do with my feelings . . . it's the whore that I am."

RM maintained to David K. Frasier that this black-and-white melodrama had been inspired by Italian neorealist film fare like *Bitter Rice*, only to backpedal a few minutes later: "Did I shoot in black and white for the purpose of grittiness and to emulate Italian masters? Horseshit! I didn't have the money to do it in color." Typical Meyer, this. He'd make a connection, then berate the interviewer if too much was made of it. RM also referenced ancient exploitation films like 1928's *Road to Ruin* when discussing *Lorna*, adding, "It's the same thing DeMille's been doing. Cut the guy's head off and throw him to the lions. The only thing new I brought was big tits."

Start off with Erskine Caldwell and the Bible, add some old-fashioned exploitation ballyhoo, mix in a bit of Lollobrigida-in-a-torn-dress "bending over, tits swaying"—not to mention the inevitable Meyer weirdness—and out comes a squalid, nasty picture, the first of two RM made with Maitland. It is a diabolical little nothing of a film, suffering from bland dialogue, leaden pacing, and, most surprisingly for Meyer (outside of the idiot preacher), little humor. An air of malevolence hangs over *Lorna*. It has a grimy, crime-scene-photo feel, RM's camera trailing Maitland like a shark after chum, and this makes for a shadowy, erotic reverie.

Best of all is a wild, zillion-Dutch-angles montage featuring a vivacious Maitland (dressed to kill in mere beads, a skimpy white fur, g-string, and big black vinyl belt) go-going away as neon signs for such swinging Hollywood hot spots as Why Not? Cocktails and Chicken in the Rough are superimposed one after another—along with a barely perceptible shot of flames leaping out of a burning building! Meyer shot Maitland's footage in his Evanview home, and Eve being away, the following day RM enjoyed a sweaty interlude à la *Lorna*, Janet Buxton splaying her meaty loins right in the bed Meyer shared with his wife.

$ $ $

Meyer's knack for discovering strange-looking, somewhat unsettling character types was in full force during his black-and-white pictures, and the latest find was Hal Hopper, *Lorna*'s Luther and *Mudhoney*'s equally depraved Sidney Brenshaw. Hopper had a lipless, reptilian mug with skin like a thrift-store wallet, lit up by mean, incandescent eyes. Previously Hopper had backed Sinatra in the vocal group the Pied Pipers and had written the theme song for the *Rin Tin Tin* TV show as well as the pop hit "There's No You," used in *Lolita* (Hal also provided *Lorna*'s lounge-lizard theme song). Strangely enough, he was also the guardian of Jay (*Dennis the Menace*) North, all of which somehow led him directly to Meyer. RM cohorts bequeathed him the title Hal Hamper after a startled motel maid found him lying drunk in a laundry basket sniffing panties.

From this film onward Meyer's men were basically set in stone, split between the two extremes on display in *Lorna*: James, the pretty-boy husband who's "everything that's nice, but strictly a bum bang," and The Fugitive, "a real shit, but everything in the sack hubby wasn't." The pussy-whipped and pussy-less schnooks in the audience were free to identify with impotent Mr. Yes, Honey, while the Neanderthal in the next row might fancy himself the psychopathic stud. It's not hard to guess where Meyer's sympathies lay, as you can't miss his utter contempt for the husband—listen to the limp, sickening way hubby coos to Lorna, "I love you." You almost expect Lydia to materialize and and berate one of these poor schmucks in the manner she decimated RM's stepdad Haywood. Meyer's take on the American husband would grow more brutal over time. They were lunch-pail-carrying saps, dopes chained to a piece of trim they rarely if ever got, and RM derived great satisfaction from ridiculing them, on film as in real life, where he might gleefully crack some no-tell motel's bed boards banging another man's wife. "I feel that it's important to really give that husband a bad, bad time," said King Leer.

$ $ $

"*Lorna* was the first dramatic naked-lady movie," wrote author and sexploitation director William Rotsler. "The films with nudity before then were more vaudeville than drama . . . with *Lorna* Meyer established the formula that made him rich and famous, the formula of people filmed at top hate, top lust, top heavy." The sex in *Lorna* (outside of the pathetic husband-and-wife encounter, which Meyer cuts away from) is all vicious, violent stuff—a new kind of combat footage. The goofy innocence of the nudie-cutie got blasted away by this latest breed of sex picture, the "roughie."

Meyer is sometimes credited by Roger Ebert and others with starting the "roughie" trend, but the 1963 David F. Friedman–produced, Herschell Gordon Lewis–directed "exposé" of smut photographers *Scum of the Earth* came first. Shot in black-and-white "so that it would 'look dirty,' like an old, scratched 16 mm stag film," *Scum of the Earth* is old-school exploitation and possesses none of *Lorna*'s nudity or stylistic pizazz, but both pictures share the same bad attitude, exemplified by a scene in *Scum* where the bald, cigar-chomping, pinky-ringed porno potentate rips into an "innocent" girl lured into his ring who wants out. The camera zeroes in for a close-up of his angry, sweaty mouth as he gives her the what for: "You act like Little Miss Muffet and down inside you're *dirty* . . . you're damaged merchandise, and this is *a fire sale.*"

That speech is the roughie in a nutshell (Friedman even claimed he coined the term). Once Friedman and Meyer had released the bats, scores of uglier sexploitation pictures were made, some more "roughie" than others. The titles speak volumes: *Bad Girls Go to Hell, Mantis in Lace, Abnormal Female, Rent-a-Girl, Caged Women, Chained Girls.* Between the Kennedy assassination, Vietnam, and them goddamn long-haired Beatles, the sixties brought attacks from every angle, and the grindhouse/drive-in crowd chose to take out many of their frustrations on the X factor that bewildered them most: women.

At the same time, these films were one of the only places one could see any sort of outside-the-norm sexuality portrayed, however crudely. One could make the point that exploitation pictures were by default somewhat less hypocritical than much of Hollywood's holier-than-thou product. Invariably these movies were cranked out by one person very quickly and for ridiculously low sums of money. Therefore you get to see what a time period really looked like and how men and women really treated each other. Nobody had the money or the time or maybe even the talent to hide anything. Meyer is perhaps unique in the exploitation business in that he crafts a very distinct fantasy world and yet you still get all of the above.

$ $ $

"My eyes bugged out of my head—we almost flew out of our seats," exclaimed author Rudolph Grey, vividly recalling seeing *Lorna*'s trailer with a fellow teenager at the Brooklyn Terminal Theater. "This girl coming out of the water with giant tits! It was the type of thing we always hoped to see, but never did. That trailer was meant to have impact, and believe me, it did."

"When you first looked at *Lorna*, you said, 'Shit, we're goin' to *jail*,'" said Fred Beiersdorf, head of Dallas's Dal-Art Films and one of Meyer's favorite distributors. Too much nudity, too much sex, too much violence, *Lorna* was a stick of dynamite that Meyer threw at the world with relish. "They were all afraid of it, and that's the wonderful thing," said RM. "When someone is afraid to show it, or concerned with prosecution, then you know you've got something."

Meyer was determined to bust *Lorna* out of the sex theater ghetto. As Beiersdorf saw it, "Russ didn't care about the money. He just wanted his pix to play in upscale situations. You had to fight for it, you had to fight for change. Russ was way ahead of his time." The result, said Meyer, was that *"Lorna* played the very best RKO houses in New York right down to skid row." One distributor in

Boston convinced the owner of the about-to-be-demolished Capri Theater to let *Lorna* play one week. It stayed for six months. A theater in Amherst, Massachusetts, was so mobbed that mirrors lining the lobby were cracked. *Lorna* was a money machine. "You'd open in a drive-in in some little Texas town and sell that sumbitch, every swingin' dick in the world would show up," said Beiersdorf. "And it does a zillion dollars!"

Drive-ins were extremely lucrative for guys like Meyer. Dave Friedman estimates that in just North and South Carolina alone, "there were four hundred drive-ins, half of them played skin—and here you were on the buckle of the Bible Belt." Of course, open-air venues enabled almost anybody to get a peek, which meant trouble from what Meyer dubbed "the tennis shoe brigade": preachers, little old ladies, and other prim-and-proper types determined to stamp out smut.

The simplest way of countering these moral crusaders was, once again, the patch. "I came from the old school," Friedman explained. "If there was some heat, you went down to see the chief or the sheriff and you said, 'Chief, what can I do . . . ?' 'Well, y'know, we need a new bathroom in the station. . . .' It cost less to patch than the First Amendment route." Increasingly, however, Russ Meyer found himself defending his pictures in court. RM maintained that charges were usually instigated by some ambitious district attorney seeking political advancement—cleaning up local dirt was easy publicity.

Between 1964 and 1968, *Lorna* was prosecuted for obscenity in at least three states—Maryland, Pennsylvania, and Florida. Meyer simply refused to back down.* Dave Friedman says it was independents like himself and Meyer who fought for their livelihood while the Hollywood majors watched and waited. "The majors should've kissed the independents' asses. Because the independents are the ones that fought the battles—the majors never took *any* stand against censorship." Preachers, payoffs, prosecution—

---

* *Mudhoney,* Meyer's next picture, was seized in Long, Texas. RM was informed he could have the print back if he admitted the picture was obscene. Allegedly, it remains there to this day.

"it was a game, like everything else," Friedman continued. "You won some and you lost some. A few of us played it well, like RM. Russ was one of the great fighters. He was never afraid."

Afraid? Hell, Meyer courted trouble. You couldn't buy the kind of press the tennis shoe brigade provided. Controversy equalled box office. As RM saw it, "If it were all so okay, who would care? Therein lies the secret of any so-called pornographer's success: it's the do-gooders that rise up and create all kinds of interest and publicity in this field."

$ $ $

Russell Albion Meyer, maker of roughies, had gotten much rougher to deal with in the bedroom. "Russ puts women down," Eve later said in a 1971 interview. "I don't think he likes women at all."

Things were not altogether cozy between Mr. and Mrs. Meyer in 1964. Eve clearly disapproved of the path his career was taking. The breezy voyeurism of *Teas* and its offspring was one thing; an out-and-out humpty-dance like *Lorna* was another. Eve "didn't like the idea of me making movies dealing with fucking. She didn't want me to get involved with other women." If she only knew. Eve also made the mistake of suggesting that Russ make a real (i.e., Hollywood) picture and leave the sex crap behind. The idea of "going straight" infuriated Meyer no matter who dealt it to him. He liked what he was doing and he was gonna do a lot more of it, come hell or high water.

At the end of the second week of the *Lorna* shoot, Eve checked into Adventist Hospital in Glendale for treatment of a serious infection, the details of which remain vague. Eve tried to keep it a secret to spare Meyer any further distraction, but a friend spilled the beans and, after the day's shoot at an old salt mine, Russ tore down in his car to join his sick wife. According to RM's autobiography, the first words from her lips were, "I can never have a baby, now. I hope you're satisfied."

Always a two-fisted drinker, Eve was hitting the bottle harder. According to friend Dolores Fox: "She was drinking a lot, and I think that's one of the things that Russ got angry at her for." Meyer liked a cocktail or two, but he was no boozer. "They would fight. When Eve would drink, she would get very nasty."

Jim Ryan recalled Eve ranting and raving over her husband's Diner's Club business expenses. Ryan shook his head and laughed about how prickly Eve could be where Russ was concerned. "She used to call me up and say, '*Ryan*, you *bastard*, what have you done with that fucker? You *bastard*, you *prick*!' " Jim was quite fond of Eve, but one day her foul mouth drove even the normally unflappable Ryan to crack. "I came back at her—'What are you doing, you *fuckin' cunt*, calling me a *bastard*?' She never did that again." In the heat of a business dispute, illustrator George King Carll—who created many of Meyer's memorable ad campaigns—wound up on the receiving end of one of Eve's infamous shotgun missives, this particular one blasting both George and Russ, "implying that we had a homosexual relationship. Can you believe that?"

"Eve was a free spirit," Dolores Fox went on to say. "She had a mind of her own. She said whatever she wanted to and did whatever she wanted to do." There is considerable evidence that one thing Eve wanted was other women, and a dismayed RM once suggested as much to Fox. In his autobiography, Meyer alludes to Eve "passing more time with her chickfriends . . . occasionally into the evening" around the time of *Lorna*, allegedly for something beyond needlepoint. Eve made a move on at least one of her female friends, and later came rumors of an affair with Christiane Schmidtmer, the wild German actress who'd previously gotten friendly with Russ. While visions of Eve as a switch-hitter might've made her only more appealing to most smut peddlers, who knows where it sat with "good, clean, wholesome sex" Meyer.

The great Russ/Eve love affair was sinking into the sunset, and Meyer's next picture would help drown it for good. Before returns on *Lorna* started rolling in, the couple was so broke that Meyer was forced to resume TV still work. An opportunity arose to work as a director for hire in West Germany, and RM asked his wife how she'd feel if he worked out of the country for a few months. Eve made it quite clear she didn't give a damn what her husband did.

Trouble ahead.

$ $ $

During his long flight overseas, Russ Meyer reflected on his disintegrating marriage. "The hell with it—I'm going to have a good time," he told himself. RM was about to experience both good and bad times in Berlin, the latter courtesy of Albert Zugsmith.

A dozen years older than Meyer, Al Zugsmith was a powerful and somewhat feared Tinseltown entity. During a five-year tenure at Universal, he produced *Written on the Wind*, *The Incredible Shrinking Man*, and *Touch of Evil*, then went on to direct some very odd exploitation films. Unlike Meyer, Zugsmith had a notorious reputation for molesting starlets. "One of the most lecherous men in Hollywood" was RM's summation of ol' Zuggy.

Based on the infamous John Cleland novel, *Fanny Hill* is a period piece set in London in 1748 and concerns a young girl who stumbles into a house of ill repute. Zugsmith had originally wanted Douglas Sirk to direct. When that fell through he turned to Meyer, to whom he'd been introduced at a *Lorna* screening by his son-in-law George Costello, soon to occupy a central role in RM's behind-the-scenes band of outsiders himself. Things went swimmingly at first. "Russ and I seriously considered making pictures together . . . he would direct one and I would direct one," said Zugsmith. Meyer was to receive a salary (deferred until the picture turned a profit) of $25,000. He agreed to the deal only if he'd also get a $200 weekly stipend, three-quarters of which he'd send home to Eve. *Fanny Hill* was a German-American co-production utilizing the Berlin facilities of Artur Brauner, a Polish Jew who'd survived World War II and rebuilt Germany's film business from scratch.

Nineteen-year-old Ulli Lommel—later to become an integral member of R. W. Fassbinder's entourage (Lommel maintains Fassbinder was a Russ Meyer fan, interestingly enough)—was cast as Fanny Hill's boyfriend Charles. He recalled that offscreen shenanigans were far more lurid than any brothel action in the movie, with the picture's producer as head pimp. "Zugsmith was what people considered the ugly American—cigar in his mouth, a really heavy American accent—and he showed up in Berlin with a

harem of women, all these young girls. Everybody in Hollywood
B-pictures between eighteen and thirty-five that had been discovered, and not yet discovered."

Fanny Hill's lead role was initially given to Jill Fromer, a sixteen-
year-old "discovery" George Costello found working in a San Fernando Valley ice cream shop, but on-location weirdness between
Zugsmith and Fromer's father led to her premature return to
the States. Zugsmith hired and fired two other actresses before
Artur Brauner cast Italian Leticia Roman for the part. "Zugsmith
changed his mind about casting every five minutes," said Lommel.
"Even during the shoot he wanted to change things around."

Zugsmith and Meyer clashed from the get-go. Zugsmith had
promised Meyer sole directorship of their first picture together,
but, according to RM, he was handed a contract immediately before filming commenced, stating that they were to co-direct. "Russ
knew it was all fucked up, but he stuck it out like a soldier," said
Lommel. "He was treated like a piece of shit by Zugsmith in front
of everybody." The German crew sided with Meyer, as did a sympathetic klieg light, which fell from the rafters one day as Zugsmith strode onto the set, narrowly missing his cranium.

Zugsmith pressured Meyer to broaden *Fanny Hill*'s comedy,
amp up the yucks. During the shooting of the scene where Lommel dresses in drag to sneak the lead character out of the brothel,
Zugsmith barged in, upset that the actor wasn't sporting any
cleavage. "He's a man," sputtered Meyer. "He doesn't *have* tits!"
Zugsmith proceeded to mince around with a pair of grapefruits
stuck under his sweater to illustrate his point. "Russ just lost it
completely, had almost a heart attack," said Lommel. "He said,
'*Fuck* the grapefruits!' "

Once the cameras started rolling, Leticia Roman revealed that
she had just gotten married—and pregnant. Zugsmith complained that she was too old for the part, Meyer complained that
she didn't take direction, and, according to Ulli Lommel, Roman
just complained. "Such a pain in the ass to work with! She didn't
want to be sexy, she didn't want to be anything. That was a disaster
in itself. They wanted to do alternate footage with her, and she
didn't want to show her tits."

In order to get his part, Lommel had been coaxed into signing an oppressive ten-year deal with Artur Brauner, only to wriggle out of it when his mother showed up on the set to announce that Ulli was underage. "Brauner went through the roof. He showed up in the middle of the shoot on his knees, begging me to let my mother sign this deal." To Lommel, the cast seemed lost and indifferent. Hollywood veteran Miriam Hopkins wandered around in "a world of her own" as Alex D'Arcy spun tales of his days as Clark Gable's understudy. *Fanny Hill* was a disaster. As Lommel concluded, "The experience was totally insane, totally unpleasant, total chaos."

Perhaps the ultimate insult for Meyer was Zugsmith's banning RM from the editing room. "I would have gone crazy if I hadn't known two remarkable women," said Meyer, referring to a couple of his personal favorites from *Fanny Hill*'s brothel. First RM cavorted with Christiane Schmidtmer, a sexy blonde who later became something of an Aryan icon playing Nazis on American TV. His second dalliance on the *Fanny Hill* set was with a German sprite named Renate Hutte, aka Rena Horten, and this one would last several years. Whereas RM's women tended to come from the darker, almost Wagnerian side of the street, there was something pastoral, even downright sunny about Rena, and those close to Meyer felt that she not only cared deeply for RM, but seemed capable of cheering up the workaholic curmudgeon. "Who really liked Meyer best? Rena," said Jim Ryan. "I always got the feeling he was happiest with Rena for a short period there."

Meyer, of course, still had a wife back home. When Eve informed him via transatlantic call that *Lorna* had gone through the roof in his absence, Russ decided to celebrate with a brand-new Porsche 365-SC, ordering his wife to wire him the four grand purchase price at once. Eve smelled a rat from this extravagant turn in her normally spendthrift husband but felt much better after going out and buying herself a mink coat of comparable value. Meyer got his wheels, and once the troubled *Fanny Hill* wrapped, he threw Rena in the passenger seat for a European mini-holiday, dusting off the old Leica at each and every pit stop to snap nudes of his new conquest.

Fanny Hill: A Memoir of a Woman of Pleasure was released in April 1965 and turned a modest profit despite some devastating reviews. About as far from a "roughie" as you could get, the picture still managed to offend. "A disgrace to the film industry . . . a setback for the business," declared *Variety*. "They said it couldn't be filmed, and it hasn't been," wrote critic Raymond Durgnat. Released to the home video market in the eighties, the picture is a bore, and perhaps the squarest credit on Meyer's resumé. RM's magic touch is apparent only in the casting of the bosomy brothel workers, particularly the boisterous Veronica Erickson (an oomph-girl blonde who'd done some uncredited body-doubling for *Europe in the Raw*) as a whip-wielding dominatrix. Eight years would pass before Meyer's next attempt at a period piece, and that would be a disaster as well.

$ $ $

Returning home to America, Russ Meyer now had to face the music, and after a solid night of squabbling with Eve, RM relocated to a motel. The Meyers were headed for divorce court. So what did Russ do? Talked Eve into putting up half the bankroll for *Mudhoney*, conveniently failing to inform her that his new girlfriend Rena was to have a starring role. The fact that Horten spoke no English didn't deter Russ. He just cast her as a deaf-mute.

Meyer was leaning in the direction of the nasty characters Hal Hopper played in his roughies, and for this RM was unapologetic. "We broke up because I'm a no-good son of a bitch," said Russ of his marriage. Time and again, he admitted that when it came to women, he was a philanderer, a pussy hound, and a heel. It defused any criticism by way of the trusty I'm-a-pig-I-know-it-and-so-what defense. "He makes his own immorality a virtue," said biographer and friend David K. Frasier. "I treat women very, very well," added Dave Friedman. "Russ didn't. I liked their company; I don't think Russ did that much. We all used women, of course. But you can use them and *like* them." "I don't like a woman that's too smart," offered Meyer in 1990, along with his magic recipe for a happy relationship: "Let's do what I want to do all the time."

"Russ was very strange with women," said Fred Beiersdorf. "They weren't a big factor. He could just take 'em or leave 'em the rest of his life. When I got divorced, I tried to talk to Russ. He said, 'Well, you didn't need her anyway.' Okay, Russ, but eighteen years of my life? He didn't give a shit. Tough-guy Russ didn't give a shit about anybody or anything—except makin' a movie. Eve was the best thing that ever happened to RM. He never realized what she brought to the table until after she was gone."

The Russ/Eve divorce wouldn't be finalized until 1968. It was amicable—according to Roger Ebert, they used the same attorney. Eve remained in business with Meyer as distributor of his films. On March 27, 1977, Eve was killed while on vacation in the Canary Islands. Two 747s collided on a foggy runway at the Tenerife airport, including the one Eve was on, wiping out 583 people in the biggest disaster of aviation history. The Meyers' friend Mick Nathanson found out at the newsstand. "I saw the headline in the newspaper, and there was the list of casualties right on the front page—there was the name 'Meyer, Eve, Hollywood.' That's all there was. I thought, 'Wow, that sums it up.'"

Eve was buried down in Sunnyside, Georgia. "They have a huge slab covering her, and they had put on it 'Eve Meyer, Killed in a Plane Crash in the Canary Islands,'" recalled Charlie Sumners, who visited the grave with RM. "Russ didn't like that and I didn't either." Sumners, who worked in a foundry, made a bronze plaque that read "Three Times a Lady." The next time Meyer came through he and Charlie epoxied it to her marker, completely covering the offending passage. "It's been there for a good many years," boasted Sumners.

There was only one Eve Meyer. RM bumped up against a lot of fabulous dames in his life, but none would ever be the ally she was. Somewhere deep inside, King Leer felt the loss. "Russ called me when Eve died. He was on the phone for ages, crying," said Charlie's wife, Floyce. "Russ cared for people. He really cared for people."

But nothing was that simple with Russell Albion Meyer. Near the end of his autobiography, Meyer stuck in a two-page tribute to Eve, filled with pinup shots he'd taken. Even here he'd hedge his bets. "And did I ever love her? Hell, yes! Maybe. I think so."

$ $ $

A return to *Lorna*'s steamy Sacramento Delta (this time Meyer had the audacity to pass it off as Depression-era Missouri), RM's next picture, *Mudhoney*, dropped a few new characters into the soup. Patient, hardworking, and liked by everyone, George Costello came aboard as RM's assistant director, dialogue coach, and all-around cleanup man. No challenge was too great for Costello, not even when it came to some buck-naked underwater body-doubling for an actor afraid of losing his toupee. George had brought Meyer the *Mudhoney* script, along with most of the cast, including a few that were to become RM stock players: man of a thousand voices John Furlong, who supplied frantic and highly amusing narration for many a Meyer epic; bug-eyed Mickey Foxx, a somewhat shady character prone to selling porno from the trunk of his car; and last but not least, the mighty Stuart Lancaster.*

A bald, middle-aged everyman with an insurance salesman's self-satisfied smile, his sonorous, self-important voice spewing forth Meyerspeak is somehow comforting no matter how many times I hear it. He functions as the cosmic guide for RM's sex-industrial universe, often delivering obtuse monologues that have one chuckling long after the movie ends. During interviews Meyer loved to paint Lancaster as the ultimate old pervert, going on at great lengths about the sick white coating of his tongue or how he'd fluster actresses by getting a hard-on in the middle of a scene. "I want willing hands hovering around," was Meyer's most frequent direction to Lancaster.

Lancaster was "a fun guy to be around, certainly not the typical actor," said Dave Friedman, who also used him in a few films. "He was a regular guy." A member of the Ringling circus family, Lancaster had blown his inheritance founding an acting theater in Sarasota, Florida, before seeking fame out west. Married six times, Lancaster was a severe manic-depressive who, according to

---

* According to John Furlong, one of Mickey Foxx's favorite RM tales came courtesy of some female who'd bedded Meyer. "Oh, Russ, I love you, I love you!" she exclaimed during the mutual exchange of wondrous body fluids. RM responded, "Look, just empty the balls and never mind all the dialogue!"

his last wife, Ivy Bethune, "studied every religion and had a million books on self-help. He was opposite of Russ. They were so different they didn't compete with each other. He made Russ laugh a lot." In concert with Furlong and Costello, very funny guys as well, Lancaster contributed a lot of mirth to RM's production day, much to the annoyance of the director himself, who was known to stomp around bellowing, *"I want no levity on this set!"*

$ $ $

Highly regarded by Meyerites, *Mudhoney* develops *Lorna*'s fever dream into a deranged Wal-Mart family portrait. "My homage to *Grapes of Wrath*," as RM put it. Although the convoluted script contains enough characters and plot twists to fuel an opera, it's basically the story of Sidney Brenshaw (again Hal Hopper), a mean old bastard who runs his tiny town through fear, intimidation, and rape. He sides with manipulative preacher Brother Hansen (Franklin Bolger), hoping to increase his stranglehold, but in the end Sidney can't control his all-consuming rage, and an angry mob (played by Meyer and his crew) hangs him in the town square.

Visually the picture is quite spiffy, with Meyer working to refine his tightly wound cross-cut collage style (there are enough cutaways of feet in this picture to satisfy any fetishist), but the script is unexceptional, and the jazzy dialogue so central to RM's wild style hasn't quite crystallized.

It's *Mudhoney*'s detailed ambiance that impresses most. The party scenes ooze a weird, wild energy teaming with real backwoods mental illness. What a memorably creepy bunch—as one scribe put it, "unforgettable grotesques ripped from the pages of some abysmal southern novel"—and all of them dancing spastically to some sweaty sax number on the stand-up Victrola. Appearing for her second and last Meyer film, barefoot Lorna Maitland shakes her stuff in a skintight dress as pantherlike Hal Hopper looks on, drinking from a flask and ready to pounce. Bearded Sam Hannah, shoeless in bib overalls, jumps around with a jug of moonshine in his hand while that ebullient harpie Princess Livingston, in sack dress and worn sneakers, eggs everybody on. Rena Horten, "the perfect female—can't hear, can't talk," watches happily in silence. There's something truly mad about these scenes, heightened by eruptions of evil, crazed laughter throughout the movie. In fact, *Mudhoney*'s total effect could be summed up in a single closeup of Livingston's cackling, toothless face. What's interesting is that you never get the idea that Meyer sides with the good in these pictures. Virtue, that's for chumps. The meek shall not inherit RM's scorched earth, and once again the yardstick is virility. "She's my woman, boy, my woman, and you know *why*?" Hopper snarls at the picture's wimpy good guy, Calif McKinney (John Furlong). "Because she needs a man, a real man, not some gutless boy!"

"My films can be taken on two levels: as parodies or as being completely straight. I guess they're both." Those who knew and worked with RM disagree over exactly when he realized how funny he was being, but *Mudhoney* seems to have been a turning point. Lancaster described a screening where one patron was "laughing so hard I thought he was gonna have a heart attack." This apocryphal event registered big on the Meyer Richter scale, as did reports of college students and other members of the "intelligentsia" yukking it up over the RM worldview. Once Meyer realized that there was an audience out there beyond the raincoat brigade, he went for it in a very peculiar way, making live-action cartoons that were to be "played seriously and straightforwardly, with no obvious tongue-in-cheek, but with situations and circumstances overblown and overdone. Do more, make it bigger than life, bigger, bigger, best."

Mudhoney was first released in 1965 as *Rope of Flesh*, with an awful ad featuring a silhouette of Sidney Brenshaw being hanged. Lynching did not prove to be a box office draw, so Meyer withdrew the picture, tightened the editing, and came up with a snappy new title by way of an odd word he'd plucked from, of all sources, Oscar Wilde—*Mudhoney*. Unfortunately, it was still a financial flop and thus no favorite of its maker. "I made a gamble with *Mudhoney* and failed. . . . The only reason I made *Mudhoney* was I was in love with a girl named Rena. . . . I should have not made the film." Meyer also held Maitland's postpregnancy cleavage responsible. "Her tits had kinda gone south."

According to Maitland's husband, Ben Rocco, Lorna should've gone on to much bigger things. "Angie Dickinson got the contract she was offered—two movies a year for seven years." When the call came in, Lorna was "sitting on the couch, half gone. In 1965, LSD was the happening thing, and she was one of the people who had trauma from it. In the seventeen years I spent with her, she spent a fourth of that time in mental institutions." Oddly enough, before Lorna would surrender to a vagabond life of cheap apartments and motels, she'd use go-go money to bankroll Lorna Records, whose sole release was one of the very first singles by Neil Young's intrepid band Crazy Horse, then known as the Psyrcle.

Meyer never saw Maitland again and didn't exactly break into "Auld Lang Syne" when her name came up. "It's not like we could meet in the Hotel Pierre twenty years later and have a tearful reunion. God, her tits must be down to her knees now."

$ $ $

Despite the telephonic screaming matches with ex-wife Eve and the occasional motel tryst with Miss Mattress, RM somehow kept it together with Rena Horten for a year or so, even living with her briefly in the Hollywood Hills. But the union was not meant to last. According to Meyer, Rena put him on the spot during the making of *Mudhoney* by trying to back out of the nude scene, after happily baring it all in front of a crewful of Krauts during *Fanny Hill*. "It represented a down deep solid lack of trust," said Meyer, who apparently never forgot the incident.

"They used to get in horrible arguments," said Jim Ryan, noting that Rena could be just as stubborn as Russ. "She'd say, 'I want to go downtown at 5 o'clock and he'd say, 'No, I can't go until 7.' Some trivial thing, and it would turn into a major argument." RM's buddies were fond of Horten. "Rena was pretty handy, she couldn't have been a nicer chick," said Fred Beiersdorf. "But Russ ran her off. Anybody who really tried to get close to him, he didn't want anything to do with."

Horten and Meyer remained good friends, although they were still bickering decades later. Meyer friend and scriptwriter John

McCormick witnessed RM once again exhibiting his frightful and defiant lack of knowledge on female sexuality at an eighties dinner reunion between Russ and Rena during which RM crowed about some sex partner "lubing up her pussy." As McCormick recalled, "Rena called him on it and said, "Russ, if it's *really* happening, she doesn't need to "lube up"! You just don't know *anything* about a woman!"

$ $ $

You can't get more exotic than Haji. She's a creature from a far-off land but who knows where to set her compass. "I came visiting here with my family from another galaxy, and we landed in Quebec," she'll calmly inform you, adding, "You earthlings are very strange people." With her English-mangling accent, moon-sized eyes, and jet black hair, not to mention makeup lovingly applied with a trowel, Haji had supporting roles in five RM pictures and is hugely memorable in every one of 'em.

Nearly every word from her extraterrestrial lips is quotable. "These people that talk about exploiting—you know who makes comments like that? Lesbians. I love being a woman. I love all those sexy negligees and the nylons and the high heels." Nature is Haji's bag, and she's been known to start the day at six a.m., body-surfing in her birthday suit. "I think a lot about all the little creatures in the ocean."*

Haji suggested many a leading lady to RM—Tura Satana, Erica Gavin, and Shari Eubank, to name a few—as well as working makeup and crew. Never an item, Meyer and Haji were close friends, one reason being that Haji was one of the guys. When Meyer had a reunion of combat buddies, it was Haji who brought the fellas beer. Although most definitely all woman, nothing about Haji is soft. Woe to the Mr. Hollywood who tries to talk his way into her pants in exchange for a part. "One guy asked me if I wanted to give him a little head. I said, 'What I'd like to do is bust your head!' "

---

* As of 2004, Haji is engaged to impressionist/comic/actor and (as far as I know) earthling Frank "The Riddler" Gorshin.

Born on January 24 of an unknown year in Quebec as Baby Girl Downes, she is mum on how she acquired the Haji moniker ("a long story" is all she'd reveal). She started dancing at age fourteen; a daughter Cerlette arrived soon after. A superb dancer, Haji was famous for undulating to "The Girl from Ipanema." She was shaking her stuff at some club in the Valley when Meyer first saw her in action and made his pitch: he was making a new picture called *Motorpsycho,* would she like to give it a shot? Initially she auditioned for a small part in the opening scene that later went to Arshalouis Aivazian, but on her way out to the car, RM called her back in. Haji was shocked to learn that Meyer now wanted her for the lead.

Meyer took his cast and crew deep into the barren scrub near Blythe, California. "Meyer loved the desert," said actor Charles Napier. "Asked him why one time and he said, 'Because you can die there.' " Conditions during the *Motorpsycho* shoot would've made an Eagle Scout blanch. Snakes and scorpions lurked underfoot; Meyer had the only trailer, which he shared with Rena Horten. Everyone else camped out, sleeping in "fart sacks"—Meyerspeak for sleeping bags. Cast and crew shared a tiny outhouse and showered beneath a water barrel perched atop wooden planks. "It was so cold that you would have to stop and pray before you went in," said Haji.

Meyer and Haji became fast friends following her forcible extrication from a fart-sack tryst with a co-star. Unhappily interrupted, Haji "clawed the shit out of me," said RM, who then installed her and the rest of the women cast members within the safety of his trailer. "I slept by the door with an axe handle," said Meyer, who from now on would go to absurd lengths to segregate men from women on his shoots. There would be no fooling around on his set, no hanky-panky. Meyer wanted all "vital juices" retained for the camera.

Echoes of RM's glory days as a soldier began to seep into the daily grind. He wouldn't simply tell an assistant to move the camera; he'd tell him to "hurl" the camera down a ravine, or "smash" the Arriflex into a corner. George Costello described the production style as "take the next hill." The battleground mentality invaded every aspect of the task at hand. "Two actors ended up in the hospital, one with a hole in his stomach two inches wide," reported one of the *Motorpsycho* leads, Steve Oliver. In the editing room, Meyer worked the crew until they were ready to drop. One evening Andre Brummer (who was scoring the picture under an alias) tried to head home for some shuteye after cutting music until well after midnight; instead, RM imprisoned him in one of his guest bedrooms, ordering George Costello to stand guard while Andre snoozed. Unfortunately, Costello was just as exhausted, fell asleep on his watch, and had to be dispatched to Brummer's home the next day by an apoplectic Meyer to haul Andre back in. During the mix Brummer's wife gave birth. "Andre couldn't appear because he was at the hospital," said his brother Richard, who filled in. "Russ was fit to be tied. That's not something that should intervene with the finishing of a Russ Meyer movie."

Although his brother withstood the making of only one picture, Richard Brummer would remain with Meyer off and on for the rest of RM's career. Brummer had military cachet—he'd also taken basic training at Camp Crowder—but the rest of his background was quite different from that of the usual Meyer associate, coming out of the New York City experimental film world of Maya Deren and Jonas Mekas, where he cut an influential 1954 short, *Jazz Dance.* A gentle, soft-spoken soul, Brummer recorded location sound and cut film for Uncle Russ, bringing a host of new ideas with him, not to mention a few of RM's best titles—*Motorpsycho* and *Faster, Pussycat! Kill! Kill!* Despite this, Meyer "wasn't particularly nice to Brummer," as actor John Furlong saw it. "He'd yell at him a lot."

"Meyer respected Brummer, because he was such a technician and such a stickler for detail," said actor Charles Napier, who described Brummer as "kind of like Harpo Marx out in the middle of the desert. We'd start to shoot and Brummer would go, '*Hold it!*' and it would just *infuriate* Meyer—'*What* is it *now???*' 'I hear a cup moving. A Styrofoam cup.' 'There can't be a fucking *Styrofoam cup,* we're in the middle of *Death Valley*!' And sure as shit Brummer would come up with a cup. That would piss Meyer off even more."

RM later boasted to one of his Hollywood film festival audiences, "There'd never be an extraneous noise with Brummer around!"

$ $ $

Weary of minor legal hassles over censorship that *Lorna* and *Mud-honey* had provoked, Meyer downplayed the nudity in *Motorpsycho* and emphasized a much more drive-in-friendly component: violence. No real story, just three young biker toughs terrorizing Anytown USA in a somewhat more salacious update of *The Wild One*. RM tapped into Middle America's growing youth-culture invasion anxieties with these sunglassed, amoral savages, their hepcat lingo and faithful transistor radio blaring one guitar-heavy doom tune.

Motorpsycho opens with a short boy-girl scene, its tension created by cross-cutting a handful of shots against a soundtrack that is silent but for three lines of dialogue, the squeak of a beach chair, and the *splunk* of a fishing line into the water. Meyer sucks you right into his skewed look at a pipe-smoking fisherman who blissfully ignores his buxom young wife to concentrate on rod and reel. Intent on having her needs addressed, she jumps into the water in front of him. "Now you've screwed up the fishing!" squawks hubby. "You've got the best there is on your line right now!" she shrieks, smiling demonically now that she's got his full attention. Wifey will be the first victim of the motorpsychos, but the rest of the women they attack will all suffer the same lack of primal attention from their mates. Once again it is Meyer's particular brand of sexual dysfunction that leads to doom and destruction.

Motorpsycho benefits from ever-greater camera work, and RM's pacing is beginning to speed up, but this is another dud script with unremarkable dialogue (courtesy of *Adam* magazine contributor Bill Sprague, who also co-wrote *Mudhoney*). There's just not enough flesh on display, and RM without dames means tedium. Haji is by far the best thing in the picture. An Anna Magnani in pasties, she's riveting, giving her all to such ridiculous moments as the one where Alex Rocco is bitten on the leg by a rattler. *"Suck it! Suck* on the poison, suck it out, suck it some *more,"* implores Rocco as he grinds Haji's face into his bloody wound.

RM's cameo as a paunchy, dumb cop sums up *Motorpsycho*. After gleefully peeking under the sheet at the battered body of one of the bike gang's victims being loaded into an ambulance, he mutters to the woman's husband, "Nothing happened to her a woman ain't built for." "Talk about politically incorrect!" enthused John Waters.

"A film that lacks any kind of good taste," was *Hollywood Reporter*'s verdict. "Meyer seems at times to be saying that the assault perpetrated on these women is no more than they deserve. But it is hard to tell just what his point is." Released in 1965, *Motorpsycho* packed the drive-ins, doing "a hell of a lot of business in the passion pits." While it might not be one of the greater Meyer efforts, its success would inspire RM to rebuild *Motorpsycho* as a muscle car with cleavage. "I told my wife, 'I've got a great idea, we'll do it with three bad *girls*. She said, 'Are you sure it's gonna work?' I said, Absolutely.'"

No shit. Although Eve would loathe the script and the picture, not to mention the mediocre box office returns, Russ Meyer was about to bang out a bona fide masterpiece: *Faster, Pussycat! Kill! Kill!*

Klieg Eyes on a Dry Lake Bed

I personally prefer the aggressive female . . . the superwoman.

—RUSS MEYER

Tura's a lady. Many who encounter her expect a fire-breathing dragon capable of executing a karate chop to the aorta. But she's just an old-fashioned gal. "I love being female and being catered to," said Miss Satana. "I enjoy men opening doors for me." Tura has the sort of pulse-racing effect on the id that few other women do, outside of, say, Ava Gardner, Tina Turner, and Tammy Wynette—sexy, proud, and heartbreaking all at the same time. "With all the beautiful women that exist in the world, she's one of the more fascinating," said director Ted V. Mikels, who not only put her in his no-budget epics *Astro-Zombies* and *Ten Violent Women* but romanced her as well. "Tura totally understands men," he said knowingly.

Spend any time around Tura Satana and you can't help but fall under her spell. One whiff of that perfume—Luna Mystique, if you must know—and you're a goner, my friend. She's got a smoky, mischievous chuckle that says life's a game and the deck's been marked, so we might as well laugh. Satana still gets a kick out of life and enjoys kicking it back. There's something noble about

Tura. She slugged her way through years of gin mills and flesh pits with nary a dent to her dignity.

Tura's led one hell of a life. Carrying her trademark props—hara-kiri knife, a Buddha, dazzling beaded costumes that weighed up to forty pounds apiece—she wowed the nation as a burlesque-headlining stripper. Her long, jet black hair, piercing stare, and lethally stacked figure added up to a cruel sort of beauty, one that commanded your absolute attention as she prowled the stage doing acrobatics, juggling fire torches, and twirling tassels. Nobody twirled a tassel better than Tura Satana. Lying on her back, she could make 'em go in opposite directions like "little propellers." Among her paramours she can count Hugh O'Brian, Rod Taylor, Billy Wilder, Elvis, a six-foot redhead named Tiger Lil, and at least one midget. Politically, I don't think she'd mind if you called her a hawk—Satana's pro-Bush, wants prayer in public schools, and loved *The Passion of the Christ*.

It is Tura's portrait of Varla in *Faster, Pussycat! Kill! Kill!* that stopped the clock forever. With her trademark Germaine Monteil eyeliner and Max Factor pancake, a Frederick's of Hollywood bra with specially made cups that ensured even cleavage with no unexpected pop-outs, and leather gloves—one of which inevitably holds a slim Nat Sherman cigarette—Varla's a gender-bending femme fatale who still packs a wallop nearly forty years later. Tura didn't have to do any research for the part. The tragic events of her childhood gave her a grim insight into the role that couldn't be begged, borrowed, or stolen. "Varla is the most honest, maybe the one honest portrayal in the Meyer canon," writes critic Richard Corliss. "Certainly the scariest."

$ $ $

Born Suvaki (*"Suvaki* means 'white chameleon' or 'white flower,' but in Cheyenne Indian it's *Tura"*) Yamaguchi in Hokkaido, Japan, on July 10, 1938, "my dad was a silent movie actor and my mom was a circus performer, a contortionist. He went to a circus, saw her there, and fell in love." Of Japanese, Filipino, Scotch-Irish, and American Indian blood, Tura spent part of WWII in one of California's infamous Japanese internment camps before relocating to Chicago. "This is where Varla was created in me," Tura writes in her as-yet-unpublished autobiography, *The Kick-Ass Life of Tura Satana*. "She was born in Chicago, on the Westside."

Tura was an excellent student and athlete, as well as leader of a scrappy little girl gang. In the early postwar years, she was constantly harassed for her oriental heritage and "fought my way going to school and coming back. I was constantly taunted about being a Tojo, a monkey-person." Further tormented by an extreme case of early developement—she was a 34C at age nine—Tura took to hiding her body in baggy clothes. The worst was yet to come.

On the walk home from an errand to a neighborhood bakery for her mother, the nine-year-old was cornered, thrown in a Chevy sedan and raped by five men, then tossed into an alley and left to bleed to death. Her assailants were never prosecuted, and Satana learned much later that it was rumored the judge had been paid off. "One thousand dollars for a little girl's virginity," she said. "I'm just lucky it didn't turn me into a man-hater. The only persons that were allowed to touch me were my father and brother. It was slow work until they could finally put their arms around me and give me a hug without me tensing."

Tura's father Juntaro taught her to defend herself. Satana went on to become a martial arts expert, achieving a green belt in aikido and a black belt in karate. "If I could help every woman this has happened to, I would," she writes in her autobiography. "It is in your spirit to conquer this degradation." Over the next fifteen years, Tura maintained she tracked down and exacted physical revenge on each of her attackers. "I made a vow to myself that I would someday, somehow get even with all of them. They never knew who I was until I told them."

After the attack, Tura was sent to reform school. "Everyone blames you for being raped, not the rapist," she writes. At thirteen she entered into a brief arranged marriage, then headed out to Los Angeles, where, with a fake ID, she worked as a B-girl and blues singer. She also did nude modeling for silent film star and 3D photographer Harold Lloyd, whom she credits with giving her the confidence to pursue a career. "I saw myself as a very ugly child. Mr. Lloyd said, 'You have such a symmetrical face, the camera loves your face. You should be seen, you should get into the entertainment industry.'"

Tura wound up in gritty Calumet City, Illinois, for the first time appearing nude onstage in an act called Galatea, the Statue That Came to Life. She was fifteen years old. Satana saw burlesque as a challenge she could easily master. "You have a thousand eyes looking at you. And you're trying to please all those eyes."

Tragedy continued to find Tura's home address. Her second marriage, to a jockey, ended when he was fatally trampled during a race. She went on a two-year bender, crediting friends in the burlesque world for saving her life. "Stripping wasn't the last step on the way down for me, it was the first step on the way up," she wrote in a 1957 article for *Cabaret* magazine entitled 'How a G-String Saved Me from Gin." Tura's downed nothing stronger than Diet Coke ever since.

Satana was a sensation onstage, and those lucky enough to have witnessed her dueling tassles haven't forgotten it decades later. "She had a number where she did acrobatics in high heels," said her hairdresser Peter Young. "It was something else. Even the waitresses would stop serving to look. She was so glamorous, a star." Director Ted V. Mikels first saw Tura dance in 1957 at the Silver Slipper in Las Vegas. He was instantly smitten. "Tura was just stunningly gorgeous. She had long hair goin' down to her buns, and she had it in a knot. She not only twirled fire tassels on her boobies, she flung her hair around like a watusi—a wild, crazy dance. She was just a real exciting person."

"Men were always after her—big, big names," said Peter Young. "She had boyfriends. A lotta them. Tall, good-looking men." Needless to say, she attracted a lot of uninvited suitors as well. In Danville, Illinois, one patron attended each and every one of Satana's performances. The last night, he asked if he could buy Tura a drink, confessed he was in love with her, then asked for her hand in marriage. Tura politely declined his request and left for the dressing room to pack her things.

"Next thing I know the sheriff is banging on my dressing room door," she remembered. "He takes me outside and there's this guy sitting behind the wheel of his car with a shotgun in his mouth—and his brains in the backseat." The same man who had proposed minutes earlier had restated his love in a suicide note. The story turns even more unbelievable with the arrival of Elvis Presley, whom Tura had been dating. "Elvis comes up in his Cadillac and away we drive," she said.

Tura was extremely devoted and kind to her friends and family, but she was also something of a loner. "She didn't have a lot of female friends," said Peter Young. "The other dancers would be extremely jealous of her. I never saw anything like it." And woe to the knucklehead who tried to put the make on Tura Satana. "She would let you know right off the bat, 'Don't even come near me, 'cause you're not gonna fuck me,'" said Young. "Tura was like a guitar: she wouldn't make noise unless you touched her. If you did, you were asking for it." Tura pulverized a six-foot Bourbon Street dancer named Honey and broke the jaw of another boyfriend who unwisely assaulted her. "When I was younger, I had a very short fuse," she said. "I'd lose my temper like *that*. I'd explode. And people would clear out of the way."

"A lot of girls were afraid of her," insisted Haji. "Nobody would dare use her makeup or hairbrush." But Haji wasn't afraid. The pair had danced on and off together since 1962, often at a swanky strip joint supper club on La Cienega Boulevard in Los Angeles called the Losers. The strange name came from its gimmick: a big lit-up billboard in front of the club that announced the latest unpopular figure in current events, from Richard Nixon to Fidel Castro. "Everybody always came by to see who the loser of the week was," said Haji. Owner Pete Rooney ran a tight ship, giving his dancers a sense of security by way of the baseball bat he kept behind the bar. Many a Meyer star was a Losers alumna, among them Tura, Haji, Erica Gavin, Kitten Natividad, Bebe Louie, and Shawn "Baby Doll" Devereaux, to name but a few. The club even had its own costume designer. "It was like a Las Vegas review show," Haji boasted. "Pete had a good eye for the ladies. Whatever a man's type was, he could find it at the Losers. We had Asians, black girls, blondes, brunettes, and redheads . . . it was like the United Nations."

The Losers was a world unto itself. There was a long mirror that ran the length of the dressing room, and there was definitely a pecking order as to the seating arrangement. "We'd be putting on our makeup and you'd talk to each other in the mirror—we all had our seats," said Erica Gavin. "Tura was at the very end—she had senority—then Haji." Gavin recalled being the new kid on the block, desperate to befriend the two dancers, who she thought were beyond cool. "Haji and Tura I loved," said Erica. "I wanted to fit in. They ignored me like I was nothing. Tura was the last one to talk to me. The first time she acknowledged me I immediately had this sense of 'Oh my God—*finally.*' " In all the time Gavin worked at the Losers, she never once saw Tura smile.

$ $ $

"I had men kicking the shit out of the women, so I thought, 'Why don't we do one where the women kick the shit out of the men?' " That, in a nutshell, was the concept for *Faster, Pussycat! Kill! Kill!*

Meyer had two ace screenwriters during his filmmaking career. Roger Ebert was one, and John E. "Jack" Moran was definitely the other. Ebert concocted witty, knowing, high-concept screenplays featuring some of Meyer's most outrageous characters and events, beginning with 1970's *Beyond the Valley of the Dolls.* Jack Moran ground out three rude, bitter scripts for Meyer that are far more human in a sweaty kind of way: *Faster, Pussycat! Kill! Kill!, Common Law Cabin* (in which he also starred), and *Good Morning . . . and Goodbye.* Moran had an ear for the way men and women verbally demolish one another, crafting a brand of bad vibes dialogue so sharp it could sever an artery. "That's the way Jack talked," said George Costello. "One-liners."

Jack Moran possessed one of those grizzled, haunted mugs routinely found at the track or an all-night check-cashing joint. Handsome, but with a flaw in the canvas, and sad, squinting eyes doggedly trying to see beyond a thousand regrets. An alcoholic, he lived and worked as a booze-store clerk in Hemet, a dusty outpost in the desert southeast of Riverside known as a cheap retirement sanctuary for those down on their luck. He was also a maniacal smoker. "One lung and he refused to stop," said RM.

Moran was a child actor who'd been in *Gone With the Wind* and played a space cadet in *Buck Rogers,* only to have a relative squander his show-biz fortune. He encountered one of Meyer's combat buddies during an unfortunate overnight stay in jail over writing bad checks, which led to his meeting Meyer. Aside from the threadbare *Wild Gals of the Naked West, Pussycat* was his first real piece of screenwriting.

Jack told Meyer his three requirements upfront: Writers Guild minimum paid in cash, a cheap motel, and a bottle of hooch.* With that, Moran slipped into some flophouse on Santa Monica and came out four days later. When he emerged, he had in his hands a finished copy of *The Leather Girls,* creating a diabolical world he obviously knew from the gutter up.

The plot concerns a day in the life of the Pussycats, three hard-driving, amoral strippers of amorphous sexuality. Varla is the leader, a psychopathic bully who controls through intimidation and sex. According to her pal Billie, Varla's "like the gas chamber . . . a real fun gal." Rosie is her hot-headed, masochistic lover, and Billie the party girl along for the ride. At a salt flats race course they encounter a squeaky-clean young couple, Tommy ("a safety-first Clyde," says a mocking Varla) and his half-pint girlfriend Linda. "Would you like to look under my hood?" Billie coos

---

* Moran's benders no doubt interfered with RM's deadlines. "He started getting on the sauce pretty good," said Meyer, who'd drag him over to his place, throw him in a room with a typewriter, and bolt the door. "I said 'I'm locking you inside. I'll be here in case there's a fire. When you're finished for the night, you get your jug.' He worked like a steam engine." According to John Furlong, Jack didn't always respond cheerfully to his internment in the Meyer labor camp. "Moran was always sayin', 'I'm gonna punch him right in the fuckin' face. In the shithouse, because he won't be able to get up.' " Jack got sober in the last years of his life and counseled others suffering addiction problems. To my knowledge Moran was never interviewed about his work with Meyer, which is too bad.

to Tommy. The Pussycats toy with Linda, pushing her around. "Honey, we don't like nuthin' soft," says Rosie. "Everything we like is *hard*!" Varla rips a stopwatch from around the terrified teenager's neck, shouting, "You overdress!" She runs Tommy off the track to keep him from winning the fast-car battles of the sexes that ensues ("I don't beat clocks, just people!"), then casually kills him with her bare hands. The trio jump into their bombs and flee, taking Linda as their hostage.

At a gas station the Pussycats spy The Vegetable, a muscle-bound hunk, carrying his crippled father, The Dirty Old Man. They discover that the Old Man's loaded. Billie wants to seduce The Vegetable ("Two of everything and some left over," she coos), but Varla's more interested in the Old Man's cash. They follow the pair to a remote and downtrodden ranch, where they wrangle an invitation to lunch. "That young'un . . . tender as a cottontail," says the lip-smacking Old Man upon eyeing the captive Linda. He's a pervert who depends on his half-wit son to drag girls back to the ranch so they can both have their way. Both are sexually dysfunctional, suffering fits when the local freight trains make their daily run. Kirk, the "normal" son, feigns ignorance of his family's secrets, and when a hysterical Linda escapes the ranch, the hapless Kirk brings her right back.

Everybody begins to unravel. During lunch, Billie gets soused, and Varla slaps her. Billie needles Rosie over her sexuality, and Rosie is devastated when she runs out of the house to find Varla in the arms of Kirk. "You're beautiful and I'm weak," says Kirk. "I want you." But Varla is too corrupt for the do-gooder Kirk. "What's he trying to prove?" she asks the Old Man. "Maybe that not everybody in the world is as twisted-up as we are," he responds. Varla plants a knife in Billie. Varla runs down the Old Man, and as he falls out of his wheelchair, his fortune falls out of his mobile honey pot. The Vegetable stabs Rosie. Varla crushes The Vegetable with her Porsche. The film ends near the railroad tracks when Varla is bested by little Linda, who smashes into her with a Jeep. She dies in the middle of a failed karate chop, Kirk and Linda walking off to an uncertain sunset. "I killed her like she was an animal, like she was nothing," sobs the corrupted innocent.

$ $ $

Armed with a crazy screenplay—a script Meyer says Eve wasn't fond of and had to be talked into co-financing—RM assembled one of his most exquisite casts. Playing Kirk was *Voyage to the Bottom of the Sea*'s Paul Trinka, a health food nut whose bad breath would have Satana complaining for the next thirty-five years. "I tried offering him breath mints, gum, everything," she said. Dennis Busch would play the muscle-bound, brain-dead "piece of mutton" The Vegetable (Busch also has the honor of being the only Meyer man whom John Waters "personally found sexy"). Ray Barlow played Tommy, Linda's straight-arrow boyfriend (apparently enunciation was none too easy for Barlow, as Lori Williams notes that "Ray had those big ol' caps on his teeth . . . he couldn't navigate those puppies for the life of him"), and bug-eyed Mickey Foxx popped in for a cameo as a gas station attendant.

Last but not least was Meyer stalwart Stuart Lancaster in a bravura performance as The Dirty Old Man, an unshaven, wheelchair-bound, female-hating lech who'd been crippled while trying to pull a woman from the path of an oncoming train. One memorable Lancaster moment occurs when The Dirty Old Man swigs some hooch to lessen the torture of the daily train whistle and, teeth grinding, lashes out at the distant locomotive: "Sound your warning . . . send your message . . . huff and puff and belch your smoke . . . and kill and maim and run off *unpunished!*"

Susan Bernard, later to appear as *Playboy*'s first Jewish Playmate in December 1966, played Linda, and was only sixteen at the time. "I was very ambitious—I read *Variety* daily and there was an ad and it said, 'All-American girl who looks good in a bikini.' I showed up." Susan's father, Bruno—aka Bernard of Hollywood—had worked with Meyer in Berlin shooting a layout on the production of *Fanny Hill*. Much to everyone's displeasure, Ruth "Brandy" Bernard accompanied her underage daughter to the set. "There was a choice between Susan and another girl, and Meyer really regretted it," said George Costello. "Because the mother was constantly nagging the whole way through. We would kind of laugh at her."

But the real casting came with the three devastating and fabulously odd Pussycats themselves. Lori Williams, an eighteen-year-old from Pittsburgh who'd already appeared in beach-party and Elvis movies, played Billie, the malevolently hedonistic non-brunette who'd rather frug than fight. "There was a 'big blonde' interview. Russ wasn't gonna hire me because he didn't think my boobs were big enough. He said, 'Well, maybe we'll pad you up,' and that's how I got it." Williams would contribute her costume: a skimpy bare-midriff sweater, go-go boots, and two pairs of white jeans that she wore on alternate days before cutting one pair down to make an outrageous pair of hot pants featured prominently in the movie. Meyer's only instruction to Williams was to swing her hips as hard as possible every time she walked.*

Haji was perfectly cast as the fireball Rosie, Varla's tortured lover. Meyer didn't let on about the lesbian relationship between the two until well into the shoot. In the scene where Rosie catches Varla making out with a man, Haji "didn't understand why I should be crying." For her, Varla was just a "big sister." Tura Satana was equally kept in the dark. "That was something Russ sprung on me," she said. "Back then that was a big no-no," but Tura understood the turf. "Believe me, in reform school, it was definitely there. I'm not gonna be anybody's bitch!" Satana recognized Varla's real mission: "Her gig was control."

Satana's agent Murray Weintraub sent her out for the part. Tura had already had cameos in major Hollywood pictures, most notably Billy Wilder's Irma La Douce, and was reluctant to audition knowing Meyer's rep. "There's no nudity in this thing at all," the agent assured her. Meyer would con both Tura and Lori Williams into ditching their duds for outdoor shower scene, but he'd show nothing (although one could argue by watching Tura's astounding just-above-the-nipples close-up that it was as close to the edge

* Williams confessed that like most everybody else, she was "a little afraid" of Tura. "One time she had words with Russ, who's pretty imposing himself, and I thought, 'Whoa! Back off from this one.' I kind of treaded softly around her." Williams found Haji to be "completely in her own world." Here's one for trivia buffs: Williams said that Carol Wayne—the busty "dumb blonde" who frequently appeared on Johnny Carson's late-night talk show—also auditioned for the role of Billie.

of nothing as it gets). Tura thumbed through the script and told Meyer, "I think she has to have a little more balls." She did a reading, and RM announced, "You are definitely Varla." (According to Satana, Meyer had been considering Haji for the role.) Tura Satana was a name Russ Meyer could love, and in the years following, he'd greet her by uttering it in a menacing growl, dragging out the syllables.

Shouting nearly every line of dialogue, whether she's scheming, seducing, or killing, Tura is simply magnificent as Varla. She's a murderous, evil villain, all right, but you want to get into her pants. "By the end of the film she seems almost supernatural," wrote critic Jim Morton.

Meyer and Satana: it was a clash of the titans. "We were always at sword's points," said Meyer, who had to admit Tura was "extremely capable. She knew how to handle herself. Don't fuck with her! And if you have to fuck her, do it well! She might turn on you!" In fact, the right for intercourse was Satana and Meyer's first battle. Once shooting was about to begin out in the desert, Meyer informed her of his production code: no connubial bliss.

"I can't do that," said Satana matter-of-factly.

"What do you *mean,* you can't do that?" barked Meyer.

"You better find somebody else, because I need it every day, and if I don't get it I get very cranky. If you want me to give you a good performance, I need to be relaxed. And *that* relaxes me."

"I knew she had me by the balls, because I couldn't very well discharge her," RM moaned later. He relented to Miss Satana, and it wouldn't be the last time.

But, Meyer had to ask, just who was going to fill her need way out here in the desert?

"Not *you,*" she shot back. "You're the director, and you're the producer. I'll find somebody, even if I have to pull on a gas jockey somewhere." She settled for the assistant cameraman. "Gil Haimson was my stud," she recalled, laughing. Meyer made her swear not to reveal to anyone else what she was getting away with.

Haimson blushed when asked to confirm. "I didn't conquer Tura. I was set up!" he blurted out. "Tura came on to me. I said, 'Russ'll have a fit!'"

After a day's filming the crew would assemble for dinner, and Meyer would shoot Haimson the greasy eyeball, unnerving him. Gil had no idea that RM was in on the deal until decades later. "I went over to see Russ and said, 'I've got to apologize for something,'" When Haimson confessed, Meyer started howling with laughter. "You son of a bitch! You were set up, Gil!" Satana was one of the mighty few who ignored Meyer's no-sex decree, and she always felt RM was a little miffed she didn't choose him for a roll in the hay.

$ $ $

The *Pussycat* shoot started out, appropriately enough, at the Pussycat Club, a Sepulveda Boulevard strip joint in Van Nuys. "I didn't think we were ever going to start the film until I finally got a call to come to that nightclub the following week," said Tura. The strip joint scene was the perfect setup for the assault to follow: unobtainable women lost in a taunting, frenzied dance as a bunch of sex-crazed slobs (played by the crew, of course) egg them on. Later that night, the group tore off for the south-central California desert, Meyer leading the way in his Porsche with Satana in the passenger seat (the car nearly got demolished during filming). *Pussycat* would be shot around Lake Isabella, Randsburg, and Johannesburg, the latter two a couple of mining ghost towns on the edge of the Mojave. The scenes at the Dirty Old Man's house were shot right outside the town of Mojave itself, at Ollie Peche's Musical Wells Ranch, a ramshackle old house with a spring supplying waters Ollie claimed were a gift from the sea. Five-foot Ollie raised German shepherds and "liked all the girls in the low-cut tops," said Tura. "He was totally all-male, and wanted to prove it to us."

After a few hours' rest, cast and crew saw the sun rise over Lake Cunniback, a cracked, desolate dry lake bed. Filmed in "glorious black and blue" (for economic—not artistic—reasons, Meyer made clear), *Pussycat* would take full advantage of this moonlike surface, which was, as critic Julian Stringer wrote, "a geometrically stark landscape that might suffice for a live-action remake of a Roadrunner cartoon." A master at using natural light with reflectors, Meyer relished shooting early in the morning or late in the day, when the low angle of the sun made it look like everybody's eyes were "just boring out of their sockets." Meyer had a mania about the on-camera blink. "He'd put a million reflectors in the hot sunlight," said Stuart Lancaster. "He'd say, 'Just hold your eyes open, you need klieg eyes.' He didn't want you blinking."

Tura Satana remembered that on their first day of shooting it was 110 in the shade. "We were out in a dry salt lake bed, so everything reflected off the salt back up at you and there was no shade anywhere. I'd get under one of the reflectors just to get out of the sun. After three hours of shooting I had a sunburn. I put oil on my body so the skin wouldn't look like it was peeling."

The first scene shot was part of the film's opening—the Pussycats screaming down the road in their sports cars. It quickly became apparent that Lori Williams had not only never driven a stick, she'd barely driven, period. "Of course Russ had asked on the interview, 'Do you know how to drive stick shift?' and I always said yes to everything on interviews. He was very upset, but there we were. I was stripping the gears and all that, but I learned. On the set. In that first shot."

Then it was time for the first big showdown: three bloodthirsty Pussycats versus Tommy and Linda, a pair of goody-goods described by Meyer as "so unctuously proud you want to throw up." The fight scenes had been choreographed the night before by Tura and Richard Brummer, who was also adept at martial arts and doubled for Ray Barlow (Tommy) in a few shots (he can be seen being mangled by Tura in some of the *Pussycat* stills). Satana was not impressed by Barlow. "Oh God, was he a chickenshit. I had to literally carry him thru all those fight scenes—'No, I'll get *hurt*.' Lucky I didn't break his goddamn neck!" Some of the falls were shot in reverse motion, so as not to ruffle Ray's feathers. A moment of humor came when they realized they had no fake blood for the big fight, and Costello stepped in to save the day. "I had chocolate syrup in a plastic robot, some cartoon character called Clanky. Tura thought it was great. I just filled her mouth with syrup." As soon as Meyer yelled, "Cut!" he bellowed, "Costello! I bow to your Clanky." The moment when Varla breaks Tommy's back was particularly memorable, due to an evocative sound effect added by Richard Brummer—the cracking of a walnut. "In Sweden, they censored the soundtrack, cut it out," said Brummer. "Too violent."

Susan and Brandy Bernard caused quite a stir on the *Pussycat* set. A former actress herself, Brandy didn't win any popularity contests with her offscreen portrayal of a meddling stage mother. "They were almost inseparable," hissed Tura. "I was surprised her mother wasn't in the scenes with her! So demanding—'My daughter is not getting enough dialogue. My daughter is not getting enough film time. My daughter is not doing enough in the scenes.'"

A precocious, chirpy sixteen-year-old raised by Hollywood royalty, Susan Bernard was the duckling among dinosaurs. "When I got there I went, 'Uh-oh.' The women were very different than me. They were bigger. I was five two and a half, protected by my mom, this charmed princess. They put on all this black eyeliner. And were older, led different lives. I used to imagine all these things about them—who they were, what they did—because I never met anybody like them. They were caricatures, cartoon figures come to life." Bernard didn't exactly become an honorary Pussycat. "Susan was a whiner," Haji complained. "She was a kid, and her mother was there to protect her. She was a little whiner, listen to her voice! Tura was always off to the side going, 'I'm gonna *kill* her.' I'd say, 'Whoa, girl, settle down!'"

From the first day of shooting, Brandy was agitated. "It was very primitive," said Costello of the lakebed set. "No trailer, working out of these cars . . . the mother thought it was gonna be like MGM out there. She expected the daughter to get some sort of star treatment." As crew man Gil Haimson recalled, "I think she wanted to take Susan off the picture because she got manhandled in a few scenes." According to Gil, Meyer was unmoved by Brandy's protests. "You signed the contract, that's it," declared RM.

Satana said she finally lost it when she heard Brandy refer to the Pussycats as "a bunch of whores."

"She goes or I'll go," Tura told Meyer.

"Oh, you wouldn't go," he replied.

"You wanna bet? Watch my fucking dust," she snarled.

According to Tura, Brandy Bernard's presence was pretty much nonexistent for the rest of the shoot.*

Bernard junior was a challenge in her own right. "Susan wouldn't cry, she would laugh," said Brummer, who recalled the teen breaking up during the scene where her boyfriend, Tommy, is killed. "Finally we heard this voice behind us." The voice belonged to Susan's mother, Brandy Bernard, who was lying prostrate across the white-hot hood of Meyer's Porsche. It would prove to be her one useful moment. "She was face up to the sun, with her arms stretched out like Jesus Christ. That hood would burn your skin. No joke. And she says, 'I'm in *pain,* I'm just burning up, *burning up!* You've got to cry—I won't get off here until you do!' And the kid starts to cry. Russ says, '*Action!*' and we start rolling the scene."

Bernard spends most of the movie bound and gagged, crying hysterically, or running frantically through the desert. Her emotions did not have to be manufactured. In talking about her *Pussycat* experience, Bernard compared it to tales of Hollywood directors ganging up cast and crew on an actor to extract the right performance. Susan thought that a similar number was being done on her head during *Pussycat.* "None of them really befriended me. I thought, 'Gee, this really is an experience.'"

She wasn't off the mark. Meyer had expressed his displeasure over what he felt were Bernard's tepid acting responses and, always ready to agitate his cast, he instructed Satana to provoke her.

"You want a reaction, I'll get one," Tura snarled. From that moment on, both Susan and her mother were prey. Satana went out of her way to wind them up, instructing Haji and Lori to do the same. "Russ was all for me scaring the crap out of her," she said.

---

* Susan disputes this, insisting that since she was a minor her mother had to be present. Other crew members memories are vague, but they recall Brandy fading away after the salt flats racing scene. "Russ really liked her," maintained Susan, who said that during a Pussycat reunion at the Egyptian Theater in the nineties, Russ went on about how great and supportive Brandy was. "I remember him acknowledging that in front of all these people," said Susan. "Russ was very much a gentleman." According to Susan, her mother was cognizant of *Faster, Pussycat*'s power right from the get-go. "I remember my mom saying this is going to be an important film one day."

Tura doesn't deny any of her unsavory ways. Susan Bernard would be standing there all gussied up in her perfect little red and white bikini and matching hair ribbon, cowering over the thought of what Tura might do next. Satana would just grab her by the arm and bark in her face. "And if it wasn't right, I'd grab her again! Or I'd give her a little push. *That* would get the adrenaline going." The end result was a great performance. Susan Bernard looks consumed by fear every second of *Pussycat*. "It worked," said Costello. "She was like a frightened little bird out there in the desert."

"I really felt Tura disliked me and really was after me," admitted Bernard. "It was frightening. She seemed very masculine to me, very masculine. I thought she was actually capable of hurting someone physically. I felt that there was something in there that said, 'This is real.'"

$ $ $

Outside of the snafus that came early on in the production, the *Pussycat* shoot went smooth and fast. Meyer even let the cast improvise dialogue at times. He might've been a control freak, but he was wily enough to abscond with any good ideas that came his way. Tura came up with some snappy repartee for the scene at the gas station where Mickey Foxx yammers on about seeing America first as he ogles her chest. "You won't find it down there, Columbus," she tells him. Lori Williams actually got a bit schnockered to do her drunk bit at the Dirty Old Man's dinner table. "I don't think I drank but a couple times in my life," she said. "I came right from high school."

Killing downtime at the Adobe Motel in Johannesburg, Tura would amuse both herself and Haji by letting a hairy spider crawl up her body and into her hair. "A very contented tarantula," said Satana. "Mickey Foxx was deathly afraid of it. I said, 'Mickey, he's not gonna hurt ya, c'mere.' He said, 'No, no, no!'"

The biggest dust-up on the *Faster* set came between RM and Satana, and it was during the memorable man-versus-machine scene where Tura crushes the Vegetable against a wall with the

Porsche. Satana felt that the tires should be shown spinning in a close-up, and she took Meyer aside and told him so. Russ didn't want to take the time. Tura pressed harder; still Meyer said no. "You stubborn son of a bitch!" she yelled, smashing her fist into a wall. "Bam! I broke my hand." After a short to trip to the hospital, she went right back to work. No one knew about the accident but Meyer. As for the tire, "we did it his way. And then Russ looked at it and he says, 'That sucked.' I said, 'No shit.' " So they dug a hole and they redid it." Satana got her way, broken appendage notwith-standing. "Meyer's like talking to a wall when he's got his idea," said George Costello. "Nobody's gonna thwart him. Tura has that same kind of defiance. In a way it kind of worked for them."

Richard Brummer recalled that "each girl wanted to outdo the other in their death scene. And those death scenes were done in order, so Tura had to have the best death scene." She felt a mouth-ful of blood would be a crowning touch, so once again Costello turned to Clanky the Robot. Running Tura down in a Jeep proved memorable for Susan Bernard. Susan was another actress unfami-lar with a stick shift, so a crew member hunched down below to change gears for her. "It was really scary. I thought I'd smash into Tura, just kill her—but by that time I think probably I wanted to!"

Once the film was over, Bernard went back to teenage life. She felt, of course, like she'd been through Meyer's war. "I didn't really talk about it, because I think it's something you can't explain—it was so surrealistic, it's almost like this . . . dream. Then you wake up and it's over.

"Russ was way ahead of his time. He didn't victimize women, he empowered them. They took the action, they took the aggres-sion—even Linda, my character. She may have been a victim, but in the end she was a hero. She gets in a car, she drives a stick shift, and kills Tura."

$ $ $

The *Pussycat* crew consisted of the usual suspects: Fred Owens, George Costello, Walter Schenk, Chuck Schelling, and Richard

Brummer. (Gil Haimson and Meyer army buddy Bill Tomko* helped on photography.) Chuck Schelling had been working for years as Meyer's collaborator in the cutting room, and the approach had been workmanlike. With *Pussycat*, Schelling departed, allowing Richard Brummer to step in, immediately bringing Meyer up to date on the latest editing techniques. While working as soundman on the shoot, Brummer recorded wild lines that could be used to replace flubs, which proved extremely useful for Meyer in particular as the actors he used were often far from experienced. Brummer also recorded wild effects, such as the sounds made by each of the Pussycat's cars. He also managed to speed up the cut itself. "I said to Russ I thought the film could be better paced if we could overlap the dialogue. And he said, 'How would we do that?'" Brummer went through the picture and marked bits of shots that could be lost if dialogue overlapped onto the next one.

This was a new concept for Meyer, who'd previously cut picture and sound simultaneously on a one-track Moviola. Enlightened by Brummer, he soon purchased a two-track Moviola to accommodate sound editing, and from now it would be a contest to see just how fast the picture could run. Meyer's machine-gun montage style was now free to fully develop and, some fifteen years before MTV, was way ahead of its time. One has only to look at pre-*Pussycat* Meyer films to see the impact Richard Brummer had on RM's style. It was also Brummer who, somewhat inspired by the current release *What's New, Pussycat?* concocted the film's bombastic title. Meyer immediately jettisoned *The Leather Girls*, although it would play Britain under that title as well as *The Mankillers*.

Everybody connected to *Pussycat* had something unique to offer. A mélange of theremin horror, sax-blasting noir, and saccharine melodrama, the *Pussycat* score was by Russian immigrant Bert Shefter and Polish export Paul Sawtell. Sawtell scored over five hundred movies, with classic noirs *Raw Deal* and *Born to Kill* among them. The robust theme song, played by a manufactured "group" called the Bostweeds, is sung with "What's New, Pussycat?" bom-

---

*When Tomko realized how rough a picture *Pussycat* was, he pled with Meyer to take his name off the film. It remains on the credits.

bast by Rick Jarrard, who also penned the in-your-face lyrics. Jarrard would later produce Jose Feliciano as well as Jefferson Airplane's *Surrealistic Pillow,* and in recent years he's worked in the Christian music field (Russ Meyer, "White Rabbit," and God— quite a résumé).

$ $ $

Nineteen sixty-six: the tumultuous year of *Who's Afraid of Virginia Woolf, Blonde on Blonde,* the 13th Floor Elevators—and *Faster, Pussycat! Kill! Kill!* With *Pussycat,* Russ Meyer had created something truly unique. He'd been feverishly cranking out one picture after another, and maybe that allowed him to fire on all cylinders this time. "One of the most unrelenting from the most unrelenting of filmmakers," wrote reporter Louis Black. "A dusty, violent film . . . this is a mean Meyer." Yes, but also a beautiful one. The sumptuous high-contrast black-and-white cinematography is sharp as a razor, colder than ice. Meyer's trademark low-angle shots make the Pussycats look like fifty-foot amazons—as Julian Stringer put it, "human Chevys." "You don't know whether these women want to have sex with you or kill you—and you don't care!" wrote trash film critic Joe Bob Briggs.

"Meyer's characters, men or women, have no personalities— what they have are attributes," writes critic Myron Meisel. In this picture it seems like an asset. The inhabitants of this film lumber around like archetypes in a subconscious nightmare, incapable of introspection or restraint. Meyer biographer David K. Frasier nails it when he writes, "One never gets the impression that a larger world exists beyond this emotionally supercharged microcosm. The operatic, primal passions of Meyer's characters, like the physical endowments of the women, are too big—so big they overshadow the lesser emotions of reality."

Pussycat's sublime, serious-as-death tone would soon be abandoned for a more arch approach. "It's the script, I think—Jack Moran," said one of the film's most ardent admirers, John Waters. "I think he understood Meyer more. I'm not so sure if Russ had a little bit of revisionist thinking later, because he certainly wasn't making these movies for an art audience or for hip people. I don't know how much irony he really had. He was not kidding. Russ was hardly looking to appeal to *me*. Or highbrow critics."

Pussycat capped Meyer's great black-and-white melodrama period. It is one of RM's masterpieces—the other being 1970's *Beyond the Valley of the Dolls*. But while the arctic nothingness of *Dolls* may be its main virtue, *Pussycat* wears a black heart on its sleeve. The freaks come out at night, and this is the one time our man from the 166th truly embraces and stands up for them. Meyer may have been a twisted, bizarre fellow, but he let his women go-go-*go* freely, and with abandon—in fact, no man present in his films can ever stop the dance. To the world he may have looked like (and even presented himself as) a leering Frankenstein, but deep inside that misfit heart Meyer recognized that even a monster picks a flower or two before, say, tossing a child into a lake. Aside from its ending, which, like many a RM picture, slightly deflates into a by-the-numbers action picture, *Faster, Pussycat! Kill! Kill!* hits like a punch in the face, yet feels like a kiss. Its "message" can be summed up in two lines of its dialogue. "What do you want?" Kirk asks Varla. "Everything—or as much as I can get," she responds. It's eat or be eaten, and Varla is nobody's hamburger.

"For the first time on screen we will see a woman kill a man with her bare hands," Russ Meyer boasted, but when *Faster, Pussycat! Kill! Kill!* was unleashed on the public in early 1966, it was a complete loser commercially. "It just died, laid an egg," said RM. "No one cared." *Pussycat* was just too extreme. Exhibitors were uncomfortable with the lesbian overtones, and black-and-white pictures, even low-budget ones, were on their way out. "People complained when I didn't show Tura Satana's big tits naked," noted RM. After heading in his most interesting direction as a filmmaker, he would immediately abandon it. *Pussycat* had failed the Meyer test: no asses in the seats. End of story.

$ $ $

But *Faster, Pussycat! Kill! Kill!* managed to find friends in funny places. Riding through the dirty streets of Baltimore in his vehicle of choice—a somewhat used Buick sedan of an indiscriminate (but plain) color, a teenage John Waters had been transfixed by lurid ads from the local black station blasting out of his car radio. He motored on over to Carlin's Drive-in to check this *Pussycat* thing out. "I was completely blown away. A redneck lesbian killer drama, and because it was black-and-white, somehow arty. They were homicidal oversexed lesbians, which was right up my alley. Talk about strong women, my God. They were feminists, but in a Las Vegas kind of way. I went to see it the next night and the next night. I *kept* taking people to see it. I took Divine, who loved it because of the exaggerated women. It was just so amazing."

For a brief moment Waters was film critic for the *Baltimore Free Press*, and in his initial May 3, 1968, column suggested *Pussycat* be shown as part of a five day "Shock-a-Thon" film festival he wanted to put on in celebration of the recent collapse of the Maryland Censor Board. *Pussycat*, Waters wrote, contained "enough first rate shock scenes to open the most jaded film-goer's eyes." John also wrote a gushing fan letter to Meyer, which would eventually lead to a rather unique friendship. In his 1981 book *Shock Value*, Waters dubbed Russ Meyer "the Eisenstein of sex films," and famously declared *Faster, Pussycat! Kill! Kill!* to be "beyond a doubt, the best movie ever made. It is possibly better than any film that will be made in the future."*

Pussycat refused to die. "My films are like a reptile you beat with a club," RM boasted. "You think you've killed it, but then it turns around and gets you on the ankle." This was never truer than with *Pussycat*. It just seemed to keep building momentum over the years. In 1983 came the majestic recording of the *Pussycat* theme song by the Cramps, bringing a legion of new fans Meyer's

---

* Waters was happy to elaborate when it came to Russ Meyer's impact on his film-making style. "Looking back on it, that kind of monotone that Tura talks in really was an influence. My characters speak in the same great loud, shouting tone. Certainly *Female Trouble* has some Russ Meyer in it—how Divine looked as Dawn Davenport, that kind of evil Las Vegas homicidal showgirl with those arched eyebrows. And yet, my star was a man with big tits.

"I'm surprised somebody hasn't remade *Faster, Pussycat! Kill! Kill!* It'll be terrible, but I bet someone very definitely will remake that movie in the next ten years."

way; RM himself admitted in the nineties that *Pussycat*'s newfound success was "largely because a punk-rock group called the Cramps make references to it."

The film became a major seller for Meyer with the advent of the home video market in the eighties. "Lesbians and fags are crazy about it," was Meyer's crass boast. In 1995, *Faster, Pussycat! Kill! Kill!* had a major theatrical rerelease and played to packed houses nationwide. It would also reunite the three Pussycats, who had more or less lounged in obscurity in the years since. Their appearance at screenings and conventions now brings out rabid fans who are often covered in tattoos of their favorite Pussycat. Although Satana, Haji, and Williams don't see a dime from any of the film revenue—though for a while Tura received overseas royalties on video sales—the trio seem a little nonplussed by the picture's second life. "Russ was a little ahead of his time," said Haji. "You just didn't see women taking over and beating up men in those days."

In September 2002 the Pussycats went on a triumphant two-month tour of Belgium, Denmark, Finland, Holland, and Switzerland. "I felt like a rock star," said Lori Williams. "They had people standing in the auditorium, lined up outside around the building. They'd play the movie and we'd do scenes from it. There were people with candles, somebody had a tattoo of me on their arm." The other Pussycats found that time had brought on a mellower, gentler Tura Satana. Lori went as far as to call her "spiritual." "She's very generous," said Haji. "No matter what you need she'll open her magic little bag and she'll have it for you. She's like Mary Poppins!"

The fact that Tura Satana's talents haven't been utilized in more films is criminal, and even Meyer realized an opportunity had been missed. "I really made a mistake," he said. "I should've used her in another film." RM readily admitted that Tura was the heart of the movie—and that maybe the friction between them had pumped blood into it. "He said, 'I couldn't have done it with anybody else,'" Tura recalled. "The way he said it made me feel very, very special." "She and I made the movie," said Meyer.

"We had this confrontation that was constantly, 'Who was the strongest?' Not physically strongest, *mentally* strongest. I could never put one over on her, and nor could she really with me."

In hindsight, Satana recognized that a lot of the fuel for Varla came from the terrible childhood assault all those years before and "the anger that never left me. I was never able to really put a closure to it. I eventually got even with those guys—it took years—but the anger stayed. Because I could never erase the fact of what they did." It's not necessarily easy to move Tura Satana, but she's genuinely touched by the response she continues to receive from this one scrappy little film.

"Y'know something? It makes me very humble. I get e-mail from women all over the world—Italy, Spain, Japan, Brazil, China. I'd hate to tell you how many women say, 'Thank you for showing us we can be feminine and still be independent. We don't have to rely on men.' I'm happy I've had an influence on females this way." Tura let out an evil little chuckle. "Can you imagine being a Susan Bernard all your life? If I get a flat, I change my own tire.

"You don't have to be a namby-pamby. You can still be feminine and have balls."

Shit Floats

I'm proud of my life / But don't ask me why.

— "PRIMITIVE," THE GROUPIES

"You couldn't kill that broad with an axe," says psychopathic cop Barney Rucker in *Common Law Cabin*. The broad in question? The lovely Babette Bardot, of course.

Tanned, blond, and gigantic, with a harsh, cubist kisser that sends some wags in search of an Adam's apple, Babette Bardot is one of Russ Meyer's scariest superstars. It's definitely attack-of-the-fifty-foot-woman time with ol' Babette. "I'm the fourth cousin of Brigitte Bardot," yaps our BB, who also modeled for Picasso at age fourteen before becoming a two-grand-a-week stripper. Everything about Babette is too much—that slightly deranged, hysterical femininity, an incomprehensible Swedish-French accent, a body so overripe that flies might be interested, and let's not forget the tongue-waggling/thumb-sucking monster red lips that look like they could swallow a Hummer. With flesh quivering in all directions, there is something abstract about Babette, something a little Paul Klee . . . RM claimed to have enjoyed a dalliance with BB. A daunting task, if you ask me, like attempting to mount a float from the Macy's parade. But then Russell A. Meyer is not just any man.

And only Meyer could dream up Babette's raunchy unveiling,

the simply maniacal *Mondo Topless*. This is the film that convinced me Russ Meyer was mad. Shot in five days in 1966 for the princely sum of twelve grand, *Mondo Topless* is a plotless stripper "documentary" made to cash in on the then-raging topless dancing craze and is Meyer at both his most threadbare and pure.* Hard to endure straight through its sixty-one-minute totality, *Mondo Topless* is best savored in short, concentrated blasts that allow you to linger on the chrome-plated, neon-lit nuttiness of it all—a line of cinematic coke, but much better for you (right). "My films have a lot of vignettes," said Meyer in 1990. "You can just look at one vignette every now and then. Or another. And that may be the reason why people buy them—you don't have to look at the whole damned movie again." Absolutely.

$ $ $

Mondo Topless began with Meyer filming Babette Bardot running amok back at Ollie Pesche's ranch, one of the main locations for *Pussycat*. Meyer unearthed Babette at the Pink Pussycat on Santa Monica Boulevard, and she rounded up the other "buxotics" he'd shoot undulating in the desert—Sin Linee, Darla Paris, Diane Young, and the exquisite Pat Barringer. He brought back an old favorite from his early sixties film work, Trena Lamar (now dubbed Donna X), grabbing some truly frenzied stuff of her bouncing around in a cramped motel room, her only props being some beads, a reel-to-reel tape recorder, and a dress with no ass.

Meyer augmented this new material with footage purloined from his past films, mainly staged footage of strippers—Denise Duvall, Gigi La Touche, Veronique Gabriel—doing their nightclub routines from *Europe in the Raw*. One of the more fetishistic soufflés Meyer has ever concocted, the scene featuring Veronique Gabriel is especially mesmerizing. With the precision of a surgeon,

---

* The utter failure of *Faster, Pussycat! Kill! Kill!* had drained Eve Productions dry. "By the time we got around to *Mondo Topless*, we were in dreadful shape," said Meyer. "We barely had enough money to produce a film that cost $12,000." As Eve had been against *Faster, Pussycat* from the get-go, one can only imagine the screaming matches that took place in its aftermath.

Meyer's quick cutting between close-ups chops Gabriel into op-art chunks, mutating her performance into a meditation on shiny black patent leather belts, fishnets, high heels, diamond earrings, snapping fingers, and blood red lips. The sequence wouldn't look out of place in Michael Powell's *Peeping Tom*.

Last to arrive to the *Mondo Topless* scene was Darlene Gray, aka Candy Morrison, aka Vivienne Cornoyer of—I shit you not—Maidenhead, England. A pigtailed pipsqueak with breasts the size of Yul Brynner's shiny head, Gray was discovered by RM's favorite Melrose Avenue flesh wrangler, Andy Anderson. Anderson took one look at her impossible physique and got Russ on the horn, telling him to haul ass and bring plenty of film. Meyer gave her the once-over and, characteristically nervous his latest filly might vanish, treated Cornoyer to dinner, then imprisoned her in a hotel overnight. When Darlene inquired as to what she should wear for the next day's shoot, Meyer responded, "Max Factor's 'Light Egyptian.' " And nothing else. That morning at 3 a.m. Meyer whisked little Darlene off to the Chocolate Mountains, where he shot footage of her frugging through the wilderness, in her tiny hand a compact and streamlined symbol of all things US of A for Meyer, the transistor radio. Darlene stops vibrating only long enough to relax in a luxurious mud puddle. "I got her at her absolute prime," said RM. "I only photographed her one day and then she disappeared. Never saw her again." Meyer bosom buddy Roger Ebert panted that Darlene was "undoubtedly the most voluptuous actress Meyer has *ever* used in a film."

Ostensibly an exposé of the ecdysiast lifestyle, the *Mondo Topless* soundtrack originally featured Meyer doing the Q&A with the dancers on display. When Richard Brummer cut the track, he suggested dropping RM's questions, resulting in absurd monologues that lull the viewer's brain into sexy negative space as Meyer's bombastic images assault the eyes. "Color makes me feel sex." "All you're doing is a dance, it has no meaning whatsoever." "Even if it does excite them, this is good." "There seems to be something subtly sadistic going on here," deduced Ebert. Bingo, Roger.

$ $ $

Mondo Topless leaps out of the gate at a dizzying gallop. We see a street sign that reads "Twin Peaks." A telegraph stutters on the soundtrack. "San Francisco is calling!" Cut to Babette Bardot buck naked and squished behind the wheel of a snazzy auto, careening around the crazy-quilt Frisco streets like a pinball. A bent travelogue of the city unfolds, complete with untoward remarks about the Coit Tower and obtuse ruminations on cablecars. Cheapo rock music by the-never-heard-from-again supergroup the Aladdins blares endlessly on the soundtrack, all thin, brittle guitars and leering sax. There's no plot, no logic, and no men, outside of a narrator (barking in an insistent, grave tone previously reserved for cattle auctions or reporting the *Hindenburg* crash) who implores, "You've only dreamed there were women like these, but they're REAL, unbelievably REAL in *Mondo Topless*"—only minutes into the picture and it's referencing itself already!?!*

But relief is in sight because, as Ernie K. Doe once sang, "Here come the girls, girls, *girls.*" It's as if RM perused his one-armed viewers and thought, "OK, you want tits? You're gonna drown in 'em! *Suffocation by way of the bosom!*" Blammo! Denise Duvall and "her tempting, teasing dance of the muff!" Gigi La Touche, the Girl with the Throbbing Guitar! Bleached blond Pat Barringer, looking like a Sunset Boulevard Cleopatra as she swings precariously from a telephone tower (wonder how RM sweet-talked her into that one). It is a world reduced to hamburgers, hot pants, and hood ornaments. The movie never stops moving. Ass shaking! Cut! Chrome fender! Cut! Breasts quivering! Cut! Car radio! Cut! Tape recorder! Cut! Cut! CUT!

There is a shot here of Babette Bardot that once seen will remain tattooed on your eyeballs forever. Certainly Babette's big blond head, tanned carcass, and non-outfit of white bra, black panties, and tiny high heels would in and of itself be enough to

---

* The narration was done by the great John Furlong, who said that Meyer just threw a legal pad at him covered with long, scribbled monologues, then pushed him in a closet, covering him with a blanket to deaden the sound. Aided by a flashlight so he could see the words, Furlong bellowed into a mike and hoped it would all soon be over.

raise the dead, but Meyer has positioned her out in the desert right alongside a railroad line. As she's frantically frugging away, a huge locomotive barrels down the tracks toward the camera. Bardot, in broken English, informs us, "I try to project a childlike-to-woman quality." Whatever you say, Babette. Big trains, big women, big dreams . . . bad intentions drenched in testosterone. Meyer visually invades these women with the same sort of I'm-gonna-eat-you-alive gusto he displayed tearing into a blood-red steak. This is manly-man filmmaking at its most erect, spurting forth with a macho attitude not dissimilar to, say, a cock-swaggering Howlin' Wolf bellowing "You'll Be Mine" to some over-come front-row female at Theresa's Lounge on the Southside of Chicago late one sweltering summer night in 1961.

After a while, though, RM's enforced euphoria becomes unbearable—you just want to scream, "Uncle!" It's like cheese doodles. You have one, it's pretty good. But then the bag's gone, you feel sick, that crappy orange dust is stuck to your fingers, and you're wondering why. *Mondo Topless* is a tune with one note, a *Metal Machine Music* with hooters. It's ever so giddy and upbeat on the surface, and so completely depraved underneath. When aliens excavate the ruins of planet Earth in 2525, would you rather they found a copy of some anemic, technically inept, politically-correct-to-the-point-of-screaming-boredom John Sayles film? They'd learn a lot more about us humans watching a top-heavy Lorna Maitland pulling a burro up a hill!

$ $ $

RM dismissed *Mondo Topless* as "a quickie," but—unlike *Faster, Pussycat*—it was drive-in gold, and in later years became a hot seller on the home video/DVD market. There's certainly nothing else quite like it. "Russ was a great filmmaker," said John Waters. "He really knew how to edit films and he really knew how to shoot them. Like nobody else. You could immediately tell it was a Russ Meyer movie. He had his own style—he made industrials about tits.

"Russ was a fetishist. He did the whole macho thing, certainly, but he was so obsessed by tits. It was a wonderful perversion to me, like somebody who likes big dicks. It was a big, big part of his personality. He could barely *talk* about anything but tits. But not many people turn that into a film genre!"

Waters related a tale about Meyer visiting his Baltimore apartment and perusing John's vast collection of books. "I see him lunge at a volume and pull it out," said Waters. "It was *The Mellons*. It was about the family. But he thought it was about tits! I'm not makin' that up. I saw him *lunge*. Russ said, 'Oh,' and put it back. It really made me laugh."

$ $ $

Where does one begin to sing the praises of Alaina Capri? Is it the staccato, far-from-cuddly personality, or maybe the imposing jet black coiffure, with nary a hair out of place? The blasé but armed-with-razors tone that could render any male within 150 yards impotent? Perhaps it's the iceberg gaze that seemed to imply, "You're the run in my stocking, you little ant"? The full lips that whisper, "No dice, Casanova"? At the end of the day it may be the breath-taking narcissism on display that impresses the most. You just get the feeling that nobody in the world matters to this chick but her gold-plated-bitch self. Elizabeth Taylor in a Pez wrapper, a sweet, sweet nutcracker indifferent to cries of lust or pain. Something about Capri's beautifully arrogant mouth says, "I can't count to ten and it doesn't matter." Regrettably, Capri only made a pair of pictures for RM, but after all these years the mere utterance of her name still lights a fire in the loins of those in the know. Absinthe in a bad bikini, that Capri, and good to the last drop.

One of eight kids, Aelina Tuccinardi grew up in Inglewood, California. "I won Miss Muscle Beach," she recalled. "Russ Meyer saw my picture in the paper." He then shot some photographs of the sixteen-year-old on the beach in Malibu. Their paths would cross again. Aelina studied acting at UCLA—"I was a natural." She then got under the wing of music impresario Oliver Berliner, who renamed her Alaina Capri and stuck her in a femme pop trio called the Loved Ones. "We looked like three sisters. None of us really sang before they put us together. We got jobs on our looks."

Right before the Loved Ones were leaving for a gig in Japan, Berliner saw an ad "looking for buxom girls to put in a movie. He sent my picture to RM." Meyer wanted her for his next picture. Her only professional acting experience thus far had been a small walk-on next to Jerry Lewis in *The Delicate Delinquent.* In contrast to her conniving, Meyer-induced screen persona, Capri was really just a nice lady who'd eventually wind up teaching grade school. Being dropped into the Meyer world was like a trip to another, more squalid dimension. When asked about her co-star Babette, Alaina laughed. "She was kind of wild. She said she kept milk in her boobs so they'd always be big." Exactly what that means I don't know, but it's certainly not hard imagining big ol' Babette muttering it.

There are those who say that RM really had the hots for Capri. He did seem to take particular care in composing her shots, which often look dreamlike. "Russ kind of protected me," said Capri. "He didn't put me in the same category as the other women. I was Miss Innocent."

$ $ $

In his seminal 1973 *Film Comment* article on Meyer, Roger Ebert more or less dismisses the two films RM made with Capri, *Common Law Cabin* and *Good Morning and Goodbye,* as lesser works, "essentially soap operas whipped up to display voluptuous actresses." Let me get this straight—you're saying that's a minus for Meyer, Roger? These two unrelenting hatefests are silver bullets of badness oh-so-tightly packed with RM's soiled, despairing view of humanity, the sort of sad bile usually found in the dime-store novels of Jim Thompson. Both made in 1967, these are among Meyer's most entertaining pictures, and benefit greatly from more acidic wordplay from the mighty John Moran.

First up was *Common Law Cabin,* a film permeated with a very specific sort of flop-sweat desperation, the kind, let's say, that drips off a one-hit wonder awaiting the reception of an ill-fated second album.

The plot, such as it is: alcohol-damaged skipper Cracker (John

Moran) cons Martin (John Furlong) and Sheila Ross (Alaina Capri) into taking a trip to Hoople's Haven, vacation spot from hell. Martin is a pathetic shell of a man with a fatal heart defect, resigned to being a kick-ball for his venomous, deeply unsatisfied wife, Sheila. Along for the ride is Barney Rickert (Ken Swofford), a psychopathic cop on the lam with a million in hot rocks. Getting a whiff of the testosterone her husband sorely lacks, Sheila eyes him like a hungry cat. "Must you pant?" asks hubby wearily. "It's an animal trait." "It's the bitch in me, dear—or don't you remember?" sneers Sheila, still taking Rickert in. "It has been such a long time."

Hoople's Haven turns out to be a miserable dump, its downtrodden boozehound host Dewey Hoople tortured by incestuous thoughts about his daughter Coral (yet another slightly pregnant Meyer beauty, a German export by the name of Adele Rein). Dewey's bitter girlfriend Babette attempts to entertain the unfortunate visitors with a screaming, torch-wielding dance, the finale of which has her jumping off an imposing precipice into the river below.*

Things quickly unravel at Hoople's Haven as the participants reveal themselves as human scabs unable to refrain from picking each other to death. "I only say what you think so you'll hear how lousy it sounds," Babette tells Dewey. Rickert schemes to take over the place, striking evil alliances with just about everybody but Dewey. He also seduces Sheila, rapes Babette, and paws Coral. "Wake up, old fool," Sheila tells Dewey. "I'm not your daughter. I'm not even your friend." Martin slaps his wife; she spits in his face. Sheila and Babette sneer at each other. "I really feel for that broad," says Babette of her rival. "That's the problem—everybody feels." Their hatred for each other culminates in the river, where, balanced precariously on the shoulders of the menfolk, they get into a vicious catfight, somehow inducing a fatal heart attack in Martin. When Sheila is asked if she knew about her husband's

---

* It's crew member Jack Lucas in drag doing the actual jump. Meyer wanted Lucas to shave off his very unwomanly goatee for the shot, but he refused, so it was photographed in a long shot. As Lucas recalled, "I put the godamn fright wig on and this Babette bra and away we went."

heart condition, Babette hisses, "She knew his bank balance—why worry about his heart?" Coral romps with late arrival Lawrence Talbot III (Andrew Hagara), a young heir on the run for reasons never explained. Rickert knocks Babette out with a punch in the face, then shoots both Cracker and Sheila. After a big tussle in Cracker's boat leaves Rickert adrift in the river, the unmanned vessel plows into Rickert's skull, killing him. Dewey walks off into the sunset with Babette, pleased that his daughter's boyfriend is worth $40 million. That's all, folks.

From its pompous opening narration—"Where does a river begin?"—*Common Law Cabin* is one long wallow in a blasé sort of disgust for the human race, in this case exemplified by a bunch of losers in brightly colored bathing suits trapped on a weedy moonscape, awaiting a ship they know will never come in. Everybody's corrupt and life's a con game. Somehow Meyer gets a lot of belly laughs out of this brutal conceit.

This was one of RM's kookier casts. A lipless, red-faced dark cloud of the Burt Lancaster variety, Ken Swofford is a worthy addition to Meyer's malevolent manimals. John Furlong is perfecto as the sad clown of a husband, Franklin Bolger is a suitably pathetic pie-eyed popeye, and newcomer Andrew Hagara contributes one of the worst performances ever in what I believe is his only appearance on the silver screen. And the women? Yet another collection of gaudy billboards advertising Meyer's crackpot notions of femininity—what's not to like? Just watching Babette Bardot attempt to chop wood with a machete is worth the price of a DVD.

$ $ $

There are about ten thousand good *Common Law Cabin* stories, so let's go through all of them, okay?

The picture was set to be shot in Hawaii, but problems with film unions put the kibosh on the deal, as Meyer just couldn't justify the expense. "Russ was furious," said Richard Brummer. "We didn't do a rewrite—he literally tore all those pages out of the script that referred to Hawaii." Meyer relocated the production to a remote nowheresville on the Colorado River near Yuma, Arizona. The principal location was a small shack on an ugly, sunbeaten hunk of land accessible only by boat. Of all the crazy places that RM chose for celluloid immortality, this was perhaps the most despairing. In place of the lush tropical island that had slipped away was a landscape as bleak as a ghost town with no ghosts, and shot in color to maximize the dread. Hollywood it wasn't.

Jack Lucas accompanied Meyer to scout for locations, and remembered the moment RM found what he was looking for. "We had to hack our way through the reeds to get onshore. Here's this beat-up ol' torn-down, fallen-apart place—a sheepherder's cabin." Lucas dressed up this shabby lean-to as Hoople's Haven, a vacation "resort" more suitable for a POW camp. Grass skirts, Hawaiian shirts, and leis—all holdovers from the pre-torn script—only underscore the cruel irony.

Cast and crew were imprisoned downriver in a bunch of tattered bungalows run by an old river rat who bettered herself by selling the entourage marked-up six-packs of beer. RM's headquarters consisted of a rustbucket trailer augmented by a tent annex with a frequently willing Babette Bardot ensconsed inside. The camp was phoneless, forcing Meyer to communicate with his minions via walkie-talkie. Power was supplied by generators, and an unemployed steamboat hash slinger doled out the production cuisine—chicken-fried steak, day in, day out.

Every morning at four the group rose, scarfed down a greasy breakfast, then hiked to a tiny dock where they boarded a pair of motorboats that putt-putted through the predawn chill to Hoople's Haven. Sandbars would rise in the river during the night as flow was cut from the dam upstream, and Meyer would jump into the water to physically dislodge the vessels. "I can still see Russ in that river pullin' that boat," said a disbelieving Ken Swofford. "Like Humphrey Bogart in *African Queen.*"

So there they all were. A Swedish-French stripper, a pregnant fraulein, a schoolteacher, a bewildered pretty boy, and a few actual but somewhat desperate thespians. A band of outsiders in the middle of nowhere, all at the mercy of Russell Albion Meyer, the sun frying their minds as they shot a feature film in a decrepit hut that shivering pygmies would hesitate to enter. Something was bound to go wrong. Indeed, just about everything did.

Andrew Hagara—the picture's male "love interest"—was a mere babe in the woods, and the delicate, refined actor didn't exactly fit in with the he-man Meyer posse. "First of all, he showed up with a full-length mirror and under his arm," said John Furlong. *"And* a little stuffed green frog." Hargara took one look around at the cramped, dirty quarters where the actors were staying and meekly inquired as to where he was to sleep. A hulking, barely clothed Ken Swofford threw back the threadbare sheets on his cot and bellowed, *"Get in, kid!"* A terrified Hagara fled for the leading ladies' bungalow.

Meyer rode the poor guy the rest of the shoot. One afternoon as he stumbled over his lines for the nth attempt, RM just lay facedown in the Arizona dirt and moaned—within earshot of Hagara—"Shit, *I* was the one who hired him." At the end of the day Meyer would reward each actor with a little nip of booze from his private stash. "Whoever Russ was mad at that day didn't get a shot," said Swofford. "Andrew would be standing there with his cup hanging out. I don't remember him ever getting a drink.

"When Hagara started the picture, he looked like Tab Hunter," Swofford continued. "After two weeks of Russ he looked like Franchot Tone. He had aged thirty years."

Meyer's boozy old pal Franklin Bolger spent most of the time in an alcoholic stupor. Frank nearly totaled a boat, not to mention crew and camera, during a shot in which RM wanted the Cracker character to beach the vessel right next to the camera for dramatic effect. "Bolger drives the boat up on the shore," reported Richard Brummer. "He was very timid, coming up very slow. Russ said, 'C'mon, now! This has got to be an exciting scene—I want you to bash that boat right up on the beach! Just *bash* it right in there!' Here comes Bolger with that boat full speed and hits the mudflats. The boat keeps coming. The cameraman dives, pulls the camera away, and the boat comes almost all the way up to Russ. The shot was ruined, of course. And Russ said—very calmly—'OK, Frank. This time give me a *medium* bash.' "

Franklin was always good for a chuckle or two. Apparently Bolger had an unnatural fear of pumas. "If a forest ranger would come up, he'd go, 'Have you heard any new reports of . . . *pumas*?' The guy would look at him kind of funny and go, 'No.' He was always worried about pumas." Enlisted as a crew man when not acting, Bolger would squat behind a cactus to defecate into a sack in between takes. "We'd hear this cry of 'Food for the pumas!' and he would fling this paper bag of his crap across the desert," said Richard Brummer.

In order to record the dialogue for the boat scenes, soundman Brummer had to hide in the bow with all the equipment. "The boat starts to leak. And the water starts to rise. And I have open 110-volt wires that I'm sitting in the water with. I'm watching the water rise as I'm continuing to record, because Russ had not said cut yet. We got the shot—just before I might've been electrocuted!"

The fact that French-Swedish Babette was playing mama to Deutschland's Adele Rein and that neither navigated the English language too gracefully only added spice to the casserole. "Adele had a Kraut accent and Babette had a French accent," said Ken Swofford, who recalled the scene where Dewey Hoople bemoans the fact that he's made his family suffer in poverty and Babette is supposed to console him by saying, "Oh, Dewey, you make me rich." "And Babette goes, 'Aaah, Dewey, you make me *retch*.' Furlong and I are standing there just looking at each other. Russ goes, '*Cut!* Beautiful!' Furlong goes, 'Russ, she said, "You make me retch." ' He goes, '*What?!?*' and turns on the tape recorder, and there it was—'Dewey, you make me retch.' Russ goes, 'Ah, fuck it, it's a comedy.' " On to the next fabulous scene.

Meyer had his own rather unusual technique to inspire great performances from his leading ladies—one to rival Strasberg, Adler, Stanislavski, and all the rest of the greats, but with none of the fuss. He'd just have George Costello go up to an actress right before a scene and shake her as hard as he could. *Shake* her! "Meyer would say, 'Go shake the girls now, George. Go shake Alaina, get her ready, shake her up.' He'd have me shake them before the take to get them in some sort of physical mood or emotional state, get them more involved. This was ongoing. He had me shake them all. I'd grab 'em by the shoulders and give 'em a big shake. This was Meyer's version of the Method. It sounds ludicrous now, but this really happened." (Which female was Costello too apprehensive to shake? Tura Satana, of course.)

Although she'll remain nameless, one actress induced much unintentional mirth when she announced to her fellow thespians, "Russ says if we do real good we might make the Canus Film Festival." John Furlong chuckled when I asked him about Meyer's disdainful attitude toward the theatrical arts. "I don't think he knew a goddamn thing about acting. I remember Alaina Capri wasn't moving her face enough, so he said, 'Give me some Ben Turpin!' She didn't know who the hell Ben Turpin was! A lotta times he'd mention these older actors and nobody knew who the hell they were." Ken Swofford concurs. "Russ'd be doing a scene and he'd go, 'Babette! On this one give me an Edgar Kennedy! And she'd go, 'An *Eeeee*dgor *Keeeee*nedy???' She had no idea what Russ was talking about." Swofford maintains that Babette also had a wandering eye, which only added to the particular challenge of acting alongside her.

At one point in the film Swofford was supposed to hit Babette with his satchel of stolen goods. "Babette turns around and hits me in the face with a boob. It just flew out and hit me in the face. Russ goes, '*Cut!*' I go, '*Leave it in!* For God's sake, that's a movie first.' "

$ $ $

Meyer didn't exactly handle the endless mishaps of making *Common Law Cabin* calmly. "Russ would have seventeen tantrums a day," said Ken Swofford. "One of the things he did was try to discombobulate everyone." If it was a fight scene, he'd whisper offending things that one actor supposedly said about the other, "so the guy would be mad and maybe actually punch someone." If it was a love scene, he'd tell an actor that the leading lady said he wasn't delivering the goods. "If Russ had upset enough people, he had achieved his objective," Swofford continued. "I think he thrived on that. You know that term 'drama queen'? Russ was a drama king. He liked turmoil and he liked to see people go against each other."

Swofford enjoyed Meyer as a character but saw him as a bully. "I think he had a lot of contempt for women and he enjoyed making them uncomfortable, making them cry.* I saw it." Get the king to chuckle, though, and he backed off. "You figured out very early on if you could make Russ laugh, you were free from abuse. . . . He could actually smell fear on someone and boy, that was the end of it. There was a lot of latent sadism there."

More often than not, it was George Costello who drew the short straw. Not only did he tend to all the minutiae on set—each night after the shoot he had to round up that day's footage and, pilled up to keep his eyes open, speed through the dry river beds, making the hour-and-a-half drive to Yuma to ship the footage to the lab.

"Russ would humiliate George in front of people," Swofford admitted. At one point Swofford and John Furlong showed up on set out of costume. Meyer barked at them to put on their suits. Furlong told Meyer they didn't have to bring their outfits, as Costello had informed them they were working as grips that day. Meyer went berserk, rounding up cast and crew. It was lecture time.

As Swofford recalled, "Russ goes, 'Now listen to me: George has the mind of a two-year-old!'" Meyer started jumping up and down, spittle flying from his lips as he shouted, "George has the mind of a two-year-old! Don't listen to George!" Growing more agitated, he demanded that those present join in. "We're all yelling, 'George has the mind of a two-year-old! And he's stamping his feet in rhythm—'*George has the mind of a two-year-old!*'" Meyer repeated it to the point of insanity. It was these moments when many felt

---

* Swofford's wife visited the set, and of course Meyer immediately put her to work moving gear with the crew. As Ken recalled, "We go out in the boat and Russ turns to me and he goes, 'Jesus Christ, you made a good choice. My wife can't lift *anything!*' That was how he rated her. A good lifter."

RM had truly gone off his rocker. A momentary snafu would trip some diabolical inner switch, and in a matter of mere seconds Meyer would accelerate from zero to a murderous sixty. "I don't know how George didn't have a complete physical collapse," said Swofford.

The scripted Babette-Alaina catfight in the ice-cold river provided another opportunity for Meyer to torment George. "Russ thought our legs were too thin," said Swofford. "So he has Costello take his pants off and run through the water while he shoots close-ups of George's legs. We're just standing there, George is running through the water, punch drunk and no sleep for a week, running through this freezing water while Russ is shooting his legs."

At the end of another grueling day, Meyer was frantic to finish a scene before the light faded, and instructed Swofford and Furlong to haul equipment pronto. "Russ points a mile down this muddy beach and says, 'Take these reflectors down there,'" recalled Swofford. "So Furlong and I change into our coveralls and we're sloggin' down the beach with all these reflectors." John got his foot stuck in the mud as wind blew the reflectors out of his hands. An exhausted and fed-up Furlong bolted upright and muttered, "Goddamn it, Swofford, as soon as I get back to Hollywood, I'm gonna suck a dick! How long could it take? A few minutes and you're a star!"

At one point in the movie Swofford fires off a round from his gun. Furious that the shots weren't visible on camera—the blanks didn't physically eject like actual bullets—Meyer loaded the weapon with actual lead and started screaming at Ken to fire directly over the camera. "I was so pissed off," said Swofford. "I came running through the sand dunes and I fired these real bullets right over Russ's head while he was standin' by the side of the camera. He goes, 'Good. They all ejected.' And I thought to myself, 'Well, by God, that's pretty good—the bullets whizzed by and he didn't even *blink.*"

One final anecdote sums up the miserable fantasia that was *Common Law Cabin.* Heading down river on the cramped motorboat with the rest of the troupe, Swofford accidentally knocked

Meyer's annotated script into the water. *"That's the master script!"* yelped an apoplectic RM. "Don't worry, Russ," said Swofford. "Shit floats!" Everybody on the boat broke up—except of course Meyer, although Ken maintained that he saw the humor in it "eventually."

$ $ $

Common Law Cabin was originally called *How Much Loving Does a Normal Couple Need?* Theater managers complained that they couldn't fit the damn thing on their marquee (the *Los Angeles Times* refused to run even the title, declaring it "lewd"). George Costello thought of the new, improved title *Common Law Cabin,* but the picture failed to set the world on fire under either obscure banner, although somehow this comparatively tame effort found itself banned in Fort Worth.

Meyer chalked up the picture's failure to too much hanky-panky on the set, namely, his many mutual exchanges of wondrous bodily fluids with Babette Bardot. Those low body blows had softened his resolve, and even worse, RM had not interfered when others had managed to sow a few wild oats during the production. But no more. Meyer would remain ever vigilant. If he was dumb enough to actually be screwing the leading lady, damn it, they'd just sleep in separate motel rooms until the picture wrapped. Stan Berkowitz, who later wrote about Meyer and crewed on one of his pictures, said that RM truly believed if he slept with his actresses "the movie would be no good. There would be no hunger for her while he was shooting. Russ had to *want* the actress while he was making the film."

$ $ $

Ken Swofford would go on to bigger and better things, including the television series *The Virginian* and a starring role in *Bless the Beasts and Children,* a picture directed by Meyer's old 166th nemesis, Stanley Kramer. Swofford caught up with Russ in the seventies at a memorable party at RM's swanky manse on Mulholland Drive. Ken walked into the shindig to find that Meyer had installed a bunch of projectors showing his own movies on the walls. "Only Russ would do that. You can't imagine going to Hitchcock's house and there's twenty projectors playing all of *his* movies!"

The year 1967 also saw the release of the outrageous Alaina Capri vehicle *Good Morning . . . and Goodbye,* a picture with an even badder attitude than the one that preceded it. A favorite among hard-core Meyer aficionados, this one really rolls out the blood-red carpet on the subject of man/woman collision. And, boy, does the bile fly. "My people don't make love, they compete," said Meyer, and here was the ultimate proof.

The story of "eleven losers in a game that all of us play . . . high rollers that always crap out," the focus here is on the lovely Boland family. "A lush cushion of evil perched on the throne of immoral- ity," the insatiable Angel (Alaina Capri) is "a cesspool of marital pollution . . . a shameless, brazen, bulldozing female prepared to humiliate, provoke and tantalize." Her hapless, impotent husband, Burt (Stuart Lancaster), a wealthy farmer who possesses every- thing—"everything except manhood," as he's "always staggering before the summit of sexual communion." Add daughter Lana (Karen Ciral), "the latest version of the farmer's daughter," a seventeen-year-old both envious and sickened by her stepmother's predatory sexuality. "The valley punchboard, that's my mom," she mutters to horny boyfriend Ray (Don Johnson—and no, not *that* Don Johnson).

There are few Meyer moments as mortifying as our introduc- tion to Angel and Burt—we see the unhappy couple in bed, Angel disgusted with her husband's sexual shortcomings, weak-chinned and weary Burt frozen against the pillow, the covers pulled up tight to his face, his pained gaze staring into the nothingness of the night while our chilly narrator drones on. "The dead-quiet, complete void of uselessness . . . the giving up, the evaporation of passion . . . the finality of something lost and now leaden . . . the ending of something that never was."

Angel spends most of her time brutalizing Burt. "You store your nuts away like a squirrel. Got the message, husband?" She relishes broadcasting the sordid details of her flagrant affair with cigar-smoking hard-hat Stone (Patrick Wright), a loutish, arrogant, amoral fuck machine who hops from bed to bed when not breaking rocks in the hot sun. Angel and Stone spend as much time trading insults as they do in the sack. "Big tipper, big lover, big man, *big deal*," she taunts. A dejected Burt jeeps out to the country to drown his sorrow in nature, only to stumble upon the Catalyst (Haji). "A child of Gypsies deserted . . . a honeycomb with no takers," the Catalyst is a mysterious half-naked sprite—mute outside of an occasional meow—who kick-starts Burt's limp libido by way of a blood-drinking ritual that culminates in the return of his virility and a spirited romp in the hay.

A triumphant Burt rides home, instructing his wife, "Turn in your travel card, I'll be booking all your action from now on." Their drunken daughter, smoking a cigarette, swilling a beer, and fresh from being deflowered by Stone, crashes the party before they can consummate their connubial bliss. An enraged Burt charges to the gravel pit and, aided by Stone's white-trash co-worker Herb (who also hates Stone for buggering his wife, Lottie, during a company lunch break), conquers his nemesis with his bare fists.

Burt returns to the love nest to finally sock it to Angel, as the narrator boils happiness in life down to one thing only: sex. "That three-letter word makes a mockery of the four-letter ones that try to cheapen it."

$ $ $

Blasting off with yet another preposterous opening line—"How would you define nymphomania?"—to its final shot of an exuberant Haji bounding naked through the desert in slow motion, *Good Morning . . . and Goodbye!* is, as biographer David K. Frasier has written, the most potent distillation ever of Meyer's cracked personal philosophies. Everything wrong in this world can be traced back to Burt Boland's impotence. "Order is restored only *after* Burt's mystical sexual regeneration," wrote Frasier. "In Meyer's cinema, 'good' healthy sex is the operative imperative that ensures contentment and maintains cosmic order."

It should also be noted that cars are very important to the

Meyer universe. These garish heavy metal chariots are symbolic of the loveless gargoyles they transport: hungry creatures whose antennae are always at attention to find a new victim or fend off a possible attack, men and women who have reached that point beyond sad and remain desperate to hold on to whatever meager crumbs of power they have hoarded for the rest of their wintry lives. In other words, Meyer people. The women even refer to each other in vehicular terms. "Stay off the shoulders, this isn't a freeway," Angel hisses to a clumsy waitress making google eyes at Stone. "I'm sorry," she blandly replies. "I didn't see your tail lights."*

Trolling around in a gold convertible Caddy, the ever-superior Capri is a riot as Angel, a character who is, as Frasier notes, "driven to be a whore not because of any choice she's made, but by the sexual inadequacy of her husband." Stuart Lancaster is stunning as well, putting a poetic face on Burt, the most pathetic of Meyer's cuckolded half-a-man husbands. Built like a tree trunk and subtle as a sledgehammer, Patrick Wright is the embodiment of Meyer's square-jawed macho man archetype, the aptly named Stone ("where other men are mere flesh and blood, he is fashioned of steel"). In a role she was born to play, Haji is the Catalyst, slinking around the woods doing primitive dances with obscure, odd hand movements that bring to mind a belly dancer with a strangely graceful form of Tourette's. Perhaps channeling Bette Davis circa *The Petrified Forest,* Megan Timony delivers a memorably overblown performance as hillbilly wife Lottie. And the extreme-looking Karen Ciral, sporting a mug not unlike a sunburned candy apple, appears suitably disturbed as Lana.

$ $ $

---

* A little observation on Meyer's women courtesy of John Waters: "They act like female female impersonators. I have never met a woman that just walks around acting like *that*. My favorite scene in *Good Morning . . . and Goodbye* is where Alaina Capri's so horny she just drives to a construction site all dressed up in a Cadillac and leans on the horn till somebody comes over . . . that's so great. If it was played by men, that could be a gay porno movie scene. A man going to a construction site and having sex with construction workers *is* in plenty of gay porn. But this is *a woman* doing it."

Apparently the dismay contorting Ciral's face was real, as an event on the first day of the *Good Morning . . . and Goodbye* shoot suggests. "Meyer had contacted General Motors and got a brand spanking new 1967 red convertible to use in the movie," said George Costello. There was one problem no one was aware of: Karen Ciral didn't know how to drive. "This girl was a little afraid of Meyer. Nobody gave her a trial run, Meyer just said, 'Get in and take off! Hurry!' By now the poor girl looked frightened, she was fumbling a bit. Meyer got that look on his face, started yelling at her, stomping his feet. We'd gone through three takes. He likes one take."

Costello tried to calm Ciral down, to no avail. "In the background Meyer's got his eye on the camera lens, and as soon as we stopped trying to soothe her, he would start screaming. This was the fourth take, he's really pissed off now, and she's just totally rattled. Meyer yells, '*Goddammnit, take off!*' So she just guns the fuckin' car, spins in this gravelly road, and winds up smashing into this bridge abutment."

Haji watched in disbelief. "She gets out crying—and Russ is going, 'Shoot that, shoot that!' She crashed the car and Russ is telling the cameraman to get her crying so he could use it in the film!" Meyer and Costello ran down to the local Chevrolet dealership and, laying on a thick and greasy 'We're from Hollywood' rap, waltzed out with yet another freebie ragtop. As far as Karen Ciral goes, "Meyer waited for her to recover from her trauma," said Costello. "I think he felt a tinge of guilt. Meyer was more destructive than the car crash."

Wearing not much more than some weeds in her hair and flower petals on her breasts, Haji was definitely in her element as The Catalyst. She never complained about Meyer's crackpot ideas, even though she tore up her feet running naked through a grove of stinging nettles. "I'd do anything for a great shot, like put fish in my mouth. I did things Russ couldn't believe. I'm a nature girl. I picked my wardrobe every day. I'd run into the woods and make my costumes out of leaves and rose petals. I was a real loner, I was happy being in the woods."

Haji did have a rare disagreement with RM during the

shoot—she felt he was chintzy when it came to The Catalyst's menagerie. Being the symbol of nature, Haji desired an entourage of real animals around her—a mountain lion, rattlesnakes, tarantulas crawling up her arm. Meyer balked, but Haji was undaunted: "I was determined to have a wild creature in the film." She borrowed a friend's pet reptile for the shoot, hiding it in a chocolate chip cookie box on the flight to the location. When George Costello picked Haji up, he asked her what was in the box. Due to Haji's incomprehensible accent, "snake" came out sounding like "snack." Thinking he was going to score a cookie, George stuck his hand in the container—and freaked. "The box and the snake went flying," said Haji. "George threw the snake—and it flew, it just didn't drop. The snake landed on the benches and was slithering on the seats. Everybody cleared out of the airport." Once the movie wrapped, Meyer took Haji to dinner to tell her she had been right in requesting her personal zoo.

Stuart Lancaster endured many a Meyer-made agony making this picture. Take the scene where he steps into Haji's rope snare and hangs upside down from a tree. "When I was screaming in agony, I wasn't acting. The rope was cutting into my ankles." Meyer did nearly twenty takes of the scene, much to Lancaster's chagrin. "I'd eaten a big lunch and I kept throwing up carrots." During the climactic battle with Stone, an exhausted Lancaster—perched in the boiling sun on the scorching-hot lip of a bulldozer—couldn't stop squinting, and Meyer went ballistic. Lancaster's attempt to maintain a shred of modesty in his love scenes with Capri only led to further humiliation. Stuart tried to maintain some decency by wearing brief coverage. "*Lose* the jockstrap," barked RM. "*Hurl* it in the corner!" Trapped in a production-crowded room with the windows locked shut and the hot lights cooking his hairy back as he waited for Meyer to set up the scene, Stuart actually fell asleep atop Alaina. "Lancaster *lost interest*," complained RM. "The scene is out of the picture." Meyer didn't speak to him for three days.

There is one more rather humorous detail concerning *Good Morning . . . and Goodbye*. The bulk of the film was shot in the same house cast and crew stayed in, saving RM a good deal of money.

Apparently Meyer scored the location by servicing the young Russian widow who owned the place. "This woman he had the relationship with, my God, she looked more like a man," said George Costello. "Husky. We referred to her as the Tractor Driver."

Jack Lucas was with Meyer the day he clinched the deal. "I remember when Russ came back, he said, 'Yeah, we got this all squared away. Of course, I had to bed her down. Boy, that broad's got a clitoris the size of a walnut.' Russ always was brilliant with words."

$ $ $

Good Morning . . . and Goodbye went great guns at the box office (maybe it was the gotcha title, maybe it was Capri's chassis—in the roll of the loaded dice that was the exploitation biz one never knows), but back at Rancho Meyer, the bodies began to pile up. The demands of success just seemed to bring out the von Stroheim in RM. First the axe fell on cameraman Wady Medowar—who'd also crewed the previous picture—due to a fogged camera shot. Then came the sudden departure of longtime Meyer crony Fred Owens.

"We're by the pool one day and we're having one of those times when our Alaina is simply not getting the dialogue right," recalled soundman Richard Brummer. "And we get to take eleven—very rare in itself. And Russ turns around to Fred Owens, who was operating camera, and asks, 'What's the footage?' Jack Lucas, the camera loader, says, 'Eight hundred and forty feet.' And Russ slowly turns around and says, 'On a *four-hundred-foot magazine?*' Everybody just stopped talking. Because when Russ gets that look of fire in his eyes . . ." Meyer had gone on shooting takes after Lucas had allowed the film to run out. From the smoke pouring out of RM's ears it was plain to see that someone would have to pay for this most egregious error, and fast. But strangely enough, it wasn't the head of Jack Lucas that would roll this particular day.

"You know what Russ did?" said Brummer. "He didn't fire Jack, because Jack was the loader—his job was simply to watch the footage counter. He fired his good friend and army buddy Fred

Owens, because Owens, being the camera op, was in charge of the camera. It was his responsibility. Fred was devastated, almost in tears." Lucas was relegated to whipping boy for the rest of the shoot, after which he quit, even though he'd worked with Meyer on and off since the early sixties. "By that time I'd just about had a bellyful," said Lucas. "He rode me pretty heavy."

Alaina Capri said sayonara after her second picture because she felt Meyer had betrayed her by showing too much of her flesh. "Russ told me it was going to be *alluding* to nudity—it even says in the script 'alluding to nudity'—and I saw the thing, and you could see me. I was really upset. I never really talked to anybody on the set again."*

Next up was Stuart Lancaster, who later related his expulsion to writer Kris Kilpin. One night Lancaster took Meyer to a movie, pointing out some actress he thought was deserving of a part. "Her tits aren't big enough," Russ commented in a voice loud enough to be heard by the entire audience. Lancaster tried to stress her theatrical abilities, and Meyer stormed out of the theater to sulk in his Porsche. When Stuart tracked him down in the parking lot, Russ bellowed, "Be at my house at 9 a.m. and bring your attorney. I'm breaking your contract!" They made peace, only to have Meyer snap again when Lancaster gently hinted to Russ that maybe he should put his talents to use on some more worthwhile material. "He turned livid and ripped the phone out of the wall," Stuart told writer John Donnelly. "He didn't speak to me for a couple of years." Meyer wouldn't put Lancaster in another role until four years later with *The Seven Minutes*.

---

* A schoolteacher after leaving show business, Capri hid her infamy as a Russ Meyer superstar. Despite receiving a ton of fan mail, RM honored her wishes and never gave out any information on where to find her. "I was embarrassed by those pictures because I thought, 'Oh my God, if my family or anybody sees me in these pictures, they're gonna think I'm a bad person,' " she said. Throughout the years Capri lived in absolute fear she'd be outed one way or another to her friends and family. When tracked down by the author for an interview, she finally gathered the strength to tell her now-grown children. "They said, 'Mom, we *saw* them. You hid them in your closet.' I said, 'You mean you *know* about this?' 'Yeah, we've known ever since we were twelve years old.' " Capri was both floored and relieved.

Worst of all was the loss of screenwriter John Moran, who had just burned out completely on RM's rough and rowdy ways. "Meyer's main thing was keeping Moran on schedule," said George Costello. "He'd be constantly on Moran's ass: 'Keep writing, keep writing!' Moran was trying to write as best he could, but it's hard to do with somebody shouting at you." Meyer would not find another truly exceptional screenwriter until the arrival of Roger Ebert in 1969.

Meyer did gain one new dance partner in the midst of all the defections. *Good Morning . . . and Goodbye!* benefits from a very humorous score, with a very heavy-handed Verdi's *Anvil Chorus*—complete with the macho clank of a hammer—trumpeting Stone's every intrusion upon the screen. For the next few Meyer pictures, Igo Kantor would assemble wry, witty bits of film library music that cut back and forth between a variety of cheesy, ultra-Hollywood "now" sounds, emphasizing Meyer's montage technique while adding another level of sophisticated humor to RM's always bold palette.

$ $ $

Duly noting a trend toward hardtop indoor theaters—much safer bets, RM felt, than drive-ins, where at any given moment members of the tennis shoe brigade might "accidently" peer over the fence, causing some bingo-haired, Bible-thumping old biddy to see her first act of sexual congress in thirty-seven years and experience a heart attack, but not before writing her congressman—Meyer now made a conscious decision to concentrate once more on rougher, sex-and-violence fare. The picture that resulted from this decision was 1968's *Finders Keepers, Lovers Weepers*.

Unfortunately, *Finders Keepers, Lovers Weepers* is Meyer on autopilot. The story concerns a cheating couple (Anne Chapman and Paul Lockwood) who get caught up in a bar heist. Aside from good performances by new Meyer mini-regulars Lavelle Roby and Gordon McLeod, this is one lackluster cast, headlined by Chapman, an odd Canadian dancer who resembles nothing so much as a wax museum replica of Olivia de Havilland, albeit slightly melted. And the tepid dialogue makes clear that not just any dummy Meyer locked in a closet with a typewriter could concoct his weird brand of talkfest. This is just a TV movie with tits. It has that tired ambience of one of those smoky strip joints that Meyer was so fond of, but only at about five minutes past last call.

When *Finders Keepers* comes up, the philandering sex scene intercut with demolition derby crashes is touted as an example of moralizing Meyer—cheating couples, colliding cars, the wages of sin is death—but RM cares like the PTL Club cares. It just feels like a crass joke whose only purpose is to enliven an otherwise dull movie. The film's most memorable scene involves Jan Sinclair shaving Paul Lockwood's chest as she rambles on about her Mennonite childhood and incestuous relationship with her brother (the sex later in the scene is intercut with childhood flashbacks of the siblings—in full Amish costume—flying a kite). "Who told Meyer that watching a plump girl shaving a guy's chest is exciting?" complained one reviewer.

"Meyer *loved* that scene," said George Costello, present in some anonymous, fetid room above a Santa Monica bowling alley where the foul deed was committed for the benefit of celluloid. "You had to be there. Meyer was smacking his lips filming that one. He was *really* into it. It went way beyond just normal filming, it became personal. The crew just gave each other looks. We were used to it."*

Costello himself pops up in the strangest places in this film, if you know where to look. As usual, once he got into the cutting room, Meyer polished the film with some pickup shots, in this case adding some close-up gropes to a scene with Chapman. "Meyer was doing a closeup on her breasts," said Costello. "He had me stick in my hand and feel her up. That's when I discovered her breasts weren't real."

George was again utilized—below the neck only—to stuff more flesh into a sex scene with Chapman in the pool. "Meyer had

---

* Discerning viewers will note that Paul Lockwood's chest looks hairless to begin with and certainly doesn't match the hairy-chested close-ups RM cuts in. "You know whose chest got shaved?" said Costello, laughing. "Jim Ryan's. Meyer volunteered him. The other actor had no hair on his body!"

me go nude in the pool because the actor didn't want to lose his toupee," reported an amused Costello. For such a technical perfectionist, RM sure didn't mind some very sloppy, mismatched underwater inserts. (Check out the scene with Babette and Ken Swofford tangling in the river during *Common Law Cabin*. During postproduction he added footage of Costello and some woman in a blonde Babette wig bumping pelvises to beef up the nudity. They were obviously not shot in a river, but paddling around back home in Meyer's pool!)

But more important, what's a Meyer film without a meltdown? "The maddest I ever saw Meyer get was the time Nick Wolcuff took his bacon," said Costello. Wolcuff had played a sheriff in *Mudhoney* and returned as the cathouse bouncer in *Finders Keepers*. "Nick was a lovable, heavyset Russian guy—a gentle, nice man who wouldn't hurt a fly. Meyer's cooking breakfast, and he set on a plate some just-cooked bacon. Nick and I were standing in the kitchen prepping to do a scene." RM turned his back, and it was at this moment Nick Wolcuff made a fatal error. He innocently filched a piece of the fried pig fat and happily began to munch. Meyer went absolutely mad. "Without any warning, Meyer jumps up and screams, *'Goddamn it, keep your pisspaws off my bacon! I hate you bastards always eating my breakfast!'* Meyer took the whole damn plate and and smashed it against the wall, bacon and eggs flying everywhere. Poor Nick. He just melted."

$ $ $

For some unknown reason *Finders Keepers, Lovers Weepers* was a big hit, even hitting the legit houses in May 1969. The Meyer imprint delivered a certain sort of jolt, and right now America was buying. Russ Meyer was a brand name, and he simply refused to go away. He kept cranking out pictures, and they kept making money. Lots of it. Meyer was on a roll. Big shots like Vincent Canby of the *New York Times* were reviewing his product. RM was making more and more cross-country pilgrimages to tub-thump his latest release. Although he still couldn't curb his impulse to answer a bad review with a curt missive from his own angry hand, Meyer had learned a thing or two about handling the press since the days of *The Immoral Mr. Teas,* when reporter Mike Wallace had taken a bite out of our high-class pornographer during a mysterious and rarely spoken about "hatchet job" in the fifties. "I used to defend my films. Now who cares?" said RM. "They can call me whatever they want. I admit to everything."

Cognizant that many of his critics were merely poor working stiffs surviving deadline to deadline, he'd take reporters and reviewers out on the town for steak dinners while regaling them with tales of the flesh. Here was a smut peddler who was refreshingly blunt and not one to hide behind lofty ideals. Consequently, Meyer got oodles of ink. He could trot out set-piece anecdotes— Hemingway assisting in the loss of his virginity, dear mother Lydia pawning her wedding ring for little RM's first camera—and the press ate it up. "When people meet me they expect to find some slimy guy wallowing in his own pool of saliva," Meyer told Ellen Goosenberg. "I'm just some guy from Oakland living out my fantasies on film, foisting my personal tastes on the world. I give the people what they want."

$ $ $

By the time of *Finders Keepers,* RM had made fourteen pictures, and outside a few financial flopperoos (primarily *Mudhoney* plus *Faster, Pussycat! Kill! Kill!* and *Common Law Cabin*), most had made bank and a few had made a fortune. Meyer was forty-five years old. He answered to no one. It wasn't the Battle of the Bulge, but hell, it wasn't bad. He'd made a pile of loot and conned a lot of beautiful woman out of their big brassieres. The fact that he'd exchanged wondrous bodily fluids with more than a few of them was just icing on the cake.

Meyer had grabbed the world by the balls with *The Immoral Mr. Teas.* He'd reinvented himself and the sexploitation game with *Lorna,* then reached a creative plateau with *Faster, Pussycat! Kill! Kill!* It was time for Sgt. Meyer to lob another hand grenade.

The Look of Love

The Great American Dream is to run into a woman that has no principles whatsoever—and a greedy pussy.

—RUSS MEYER on *Vixen*

Her tangle of long brown hair barely held at bay by a loud seventies brown scarf, Erica Gavin is Vixen, and she's seducing a new victim. This time it's Janet, the tipsy, unsatisfied wife of a friend. Vixen is one scary but entirely irresistible creature, the siren on the rocks, and she's cheerfully bedded everyone in sight, including a Mountie and her own brother. "Basically this is a woman that is a racist, a sex fiend, an incest partner, a lesbian," said Gavin. "[And] an all-American girl that saves a plane from being hijacked by the communists." In other words, your typical Meyer heroine.

The first female whom Meyer would allow to drip sweat on-screen, Erica Gavin remains the most natural of his superwomen, and what she may lack in heavy appendages she certainly makes up for in heat. *Vixen*-era Gavin is fleshy in the most delectable way, lust personified, sporting a pair of thick, antennaelike eyebrows more appropriate for one of those disquieting translucent masks hanging by an elastic band on the joke shop wall. Her inviting lips alternate between bratty smirk and sullen pout, those bottomless brown eyes radiating "Danger Ahead." Hardheaded, none too consistent, and utterly magnetic, Gavin's most important asset is passion: whatever the complications, when Erica decides to give all, look out. Gavin, like Meyer, doesn't kid around.

Gavin's partner for *Vixen*'s thespian lesbian tango is one Vincene Wallace, who plays Janet, a clueless redhead with all the depth of a puddle of rain. RM has swathed her in vivid red lingerie and parked her atop an equally blood-colored bedspread. There could never be enough red in a Meyer picture — it was his favorite color — and with her pale skin, insouciant lips, and moronic, sexy little topknot, Vincene's the dumb cherry atop a maroon cake.

The ever-sensitive Meyer has taken to calling Wallace "baby" when directing her on the *Vixen* set. "My name's *Vincene*," mutters the redhead. RM has already torn Wallace a new one for wanting to whip up steak curry for the cast in her downtime. Meyer sentenced her to slate takes instead. "You're being paid to make a *movie*," barks the maestro. Decades later Meyer would claim that Wallace was the first actress to defeat his no-casting-couch policy, staining the *Vixen* laser disc commentary with a rare tale of post-shoot hanky-panky.

Wallace looks a bit dazed, but who wouldn't be when faced by Meyer as well as with the human tornado that is Erica Gavin? This girl-on-girl scene is *Vixen*'s deal-closer, and it is far from running smoothly. RM has provoked Gavin to the point of hysteria. For weeks she's been trapped with an all-male crew in a cramped red farmhouse on six acres straddling the California/Oregon border. A million miles from nowhere, the joint is owned by Meyer childhood crony Wilfred "Bud" Kues, a man who is said to get a big kick out of eyeballing the smutty proceedings. As usual, RM is utilizing natural light, but silver reflectors brighten the small room to a painful degree. It's a scorcher of a day, over a hundred on the thermometer, and even the walls seem to be perspiring. A reporter and photographer from the very manly *True* magazine huddle in the corner. The atmosphere is tense. Will Gavin deliver the goods, or flake once more?

Thus far Meyer's terse instructions have been high-concept: "Turn on the sex. Be voluptuous, evil, sinful. Look satanic. Conceive of yourself as a female animal." Gavin is nervous about the lesbian scene and, clueless as to the inner workings of actual Sapphic love, Meyer regales Gavin with a tale told to him by some AC/DC jailbird. Both her and her cellblock paramour achieved climax by "banging pussies," legs locked like "two scissors."

But thoughts of human shears only serve to send Erica into an inner freakout, and she grows more passive with each take. "You're ruining the *most important scene* in the movie!" screams Meyer. She runs for the shelter of her room, where, between crying jags, Gavin is comforted by George Costello, ever the good cop to RM's bad.

The sympathetic Costello goes so far as to slip Erica a can of Treesweet grapefruit juice purloined from Meyer's private booty, unleashing a juggernaut that eventually dooms Costello to a thirty-year exile. George commits the unpardonable sin of fraternizing with the enemy, and with one of Meyer's prized fillies yet. As Gavin saw it, "Once you become a Russ Meyer girl, in his mind you almost become like the Virgin Mary—no one can fool around with you." But Meyer would have no one but himself to blame for the Gavin-Costello affair. "He pushed her right into George's arms," said Haji.

Sick of waiting for his erratic starlet to get it together, Meyer's fuse is burning shorter by the second. But some dumb little bit of wisdom Costello imparts to Erica clicks. It's a simple idea: just treat little Miss Vincene like she's the woman and you're a man. We have lift-off. Vixen pounces on the woozy redhead like a vulture, barely pausing to spit out the bones, the room silent save for the two dames kissing and pawing each other. Big belly to the floor, Meyer's in a trance, his Arriflex camera gently swaying to the crotch opera unfolding before him. It's what Meyer referred to as "umbilical cord" moviemaking—just the actors, the camera, and Russell Albion, humming together like a thousand beehives. Yeah, he's definitely feeling it in the old grinch, and after the scene oozes to a halt he yells, *"Cut!* I've gotta change my shorts." RM has broken the bank on this one.

$ $ $

One of Meyer's most amusing creations, Vixen is a calculating bitch, but she pulls the strings with such gusto you want to surrender. And in a direct reversal of fates befalling Meyer's past heroines, she is not punished for her sinful ways, but celebrated—Vixen is sixties sunshine to Varla's black night. "She's a healer," proclaimed RM. "She makes everybody well again through sex." Meyer, once again cannily adapting to changing times, created a heroine who not only played upon men's fears but offered female viewers a vengeful chuckle or two, and RM maintained that women in particular readily responded to Vixen's calling-all-the-shots attitude, turning the movie into a racy but acceptable couples date. "This was the basis for *Vixen's* huge success. Once you have that happen, your gross doubles, even triples. It's not just the raincoat brigade."

Ground out in six weeks, the picture cost a paltry $72,000 and earned $7 million in its first year alone, $1 million of that from a record-breaking forty-three-week run at Chicago's Loop Theater, a 606-seat grindhouse with a $2 admission. A fifty-four-week stand at the Starlite Drive-in in the tiny town of Elgin, Illinois, made the *Guiness Book of World Records*. "The film that put Meyer on easy street," is how RM described *Vixen*. "It was a barn-burner."

By Meyer math, *Vixen* eventually returned a whopping $15 million plus. That's a lot of clams, and the attention of a sleeping giant known as 20th Century Fox was definitely aroused. No matter how much he wanted to strangle her, Meyer would always credit Erica Gavin for achieving his improbable entrée into the Big Time. While at Fox a few years later making *Beyond the Valley of the Dolls*, a puzzled tech noticed Erica wandering the set and asked RM who was the spaced-out ingenue in the doorway. "She," replied the man who never forgot a favor, "is the reason I'm here."

Russ Meyer and Erica Gavin: a clash of wills the likes of which had not been seen since Meyer and Tura Satana locked horns. Unconquerable women brought out the best in Meyer, and *Vixen* in particular was a bloodless boxing match between director and star. By her kooky nature alone, Gavin pressed every button RM had; he in turn went out of his way to torment, belittle, and be-

devil his latest nude ingenue. So much so, in fact, that some witnesses went as far as to declare it love.

$ $ $

Vixen was birthed in a West Hollywood Laundromat located at
Santa Monica and Robertson. Inside, Meyer and Jim Ryan were
shooting the shit while tending to RM's soiled boxers. Meyer had
been addled—maybe even panicked—by the big guns muscling
in on his territory.

An ill wind was blowing out of the world's ass, and its name was
hard-core pornography. A fascinating 1969 profile on Meyer in
True magazine* found him wringing his hands over whether the
explicit Swedish "art" film *I Am Curious (Yellow)* would make it
through customs. All of a sudden people were having sex, Doing
It, right on screen. "The whole business will be ruined," RM
moaned. Pass it did, and it would rip the panties right off Meyer's
world. Meyer had promised everything and shown nothing—that
was an essential part of his con. Now they were passing the stuff
out on street corners like a Port Authority hooker. By 1970's *Mona*,
hard-core features would be shot in America.

Let's make one thing perfectly clear: RM was not against the
showing of hard-core—he was no hypocrite—but that didn't
mean he had to like it. He detested it for aesthetic reasons. For
Chrissakes, it was all pimply asses and motel lighting, nothing
more than "roping sperm" meeting "an open-faced oyster." No sir-
ree Bob, not RM's style at all. Meyer is *not interested* in What Lurks
Below the Waist. No mystery there. Besides, said RM, if he did
make hard-core, "I don't think my mother would like it."

---

* Author Burton H. Wolfe (who also penned the introduction to Anton LaVey's
notorious *Satanic Bible*) was called in to make the rather bland men's magazine
more "now," the initial attempt being the Russ Meyer profile. The first in-depth
portrait of Meyer, it provoked the usual angry response from the man himself,
who wrote in to suggest that Wolfe just might be a dirty commie. "I have a hunch
the guy who wrote is a little on the pinko side," he told Roger Ebert at the time.
The article also resulted in a deluge of negative letters from readers, and, according to Wolfe, the magazine folded shortly thereafter.

It had been Meyer who'd invented the game, Meyer who'd upped the ante, and now any talentless hack capable of zooming in on some garishly lit gash splayed open in a no-tell motel could trump his hand. From now on, Meyer would be continually lumped in with such charlatans, and it stung. Did these imbeciles care about machine-gun editing, razor-sharp focus, the beauty of the female form? You wouldn't find a Meyer girl spreading her legs in some no-budget porno.* (Although John Lamb's successful court battles over his 1965 nudist documentary smasheroo *The Raw Ones* made full frontal nudity legally A-OK for the exploitation crowd, and furtive glimpses of pubic hair would soon start showing up in Meyer films.)

Threat number two was Tinseltown itself. "It is hard today to stay one step ahead of the majors," he complained. "Why should the man on the street shell out to see a Russ Meyer movie when he can see nudity in *Blow Up*, lesbianism and masturbation in *The Fox*, and blood 'n' guts in *Bonnie and Clyde*?" The upscale Canadian R-rated Keir Dullea–Sandy Dennis lesbodrama *The Fox* in particular wound Meyer's clock.

All this meant that the competition was closing in. But Russell Albion Meyer was at his best with his back against the wall. It was strike-first-lest-ye-be-struck time. "Jim, we got to make the sexiest film ever made," he announced to Ryan, his ever-present consigliere, and as the big coin-driven dryers hummed, *Vixen's* story was plotted. A script was quickly fleshed out from the Meyer-Ryan treatment by another one of RM's improbable scribes, this time actor Robert Rudelson, one of the *Finders Keepers, Lovers Weepers* thugs. This would be no hard-core film, but it would have wall-to-wall sex, including lesbianism, incest, and interracial couplings. Not to mention the fish fondling.

$ $ $

---

* Meyer actually convinced himself there were no big-busted women in porn. He got into a heated argument over the matter during a 1990 interview with *Fling* magazine's Arv Miller. "They're all built like a hoe handle," snarled Meyer. "I just don't even want to think about it."

Meyer ran off to scout locations, leaving the impossible task of finding the lead in the hands of George Costello. "I wanted a girl to come on like the Superchief," said Meyer, and George would deliver the goods. On May 16, 1968, *Daily Variety* ran Costello's tiny casting call ad for "Vixen, the Female Fox." Erica Gavin, yet another dancer at the Losers, saw the ad while sitting in a dentist's office and decided to audition for the role of a "technically inter-esting young Caucasian woman." Why not, she thought — "the seed of Russ Meyer's name had already been planted" by Haji and Tura. Erica showed up for the cattle call, where a sheepish Costello — who'd already seen over three hundred women — snapped a topless Polaroid, and soon she was summoned back to meet the boss.

"George and Russ were both there," she remembers. "I think George knew he had a good one — he was sorta proud to present me to Russ. Russ wanted to see my tits. I felt that he was harmless. When he asked me to take my shirt off, it was like a doctor . . . very clinical. There was nothing sleazy about it." Dismissing her sup-posedly lacking rack (Erica: "Here I'm thinking, '*These* are small??' "), Russ explained his big idea, which had been imparted to him by Costello: women would relate to Gavin because of her "normal" (by Meyer standards) body. RM had a hunch George was right. As simply as that, Erica was hired. She was now a leading lady, albeit a $350-a-week one.

Gavin was a true Hollywood starchild, the kind RM would soon poke fun at in *Beyond the Valley of the Dolls*. Born Donna Graff on July 22, 1947 (the name change occurred at age nineteen when she needed a fake ID to dance topless at the Losers), Erica's parents were both actors — before being blacklisted, Fred Graff starred op-posite William Holden in the 1950 noir *Union Station*. Following a traumatic split between her parents, teenage Erica was hell on wheels, smoking pot and dropping LSD "almost every day." She fled home at seventeen, running off with an artist she met at Hollywood High. When drug dealing landed him in the joint, Gavin began dancing for the Models A-Go-Go agency to pay the rent.

Erica wound up in an Oxnard bar and, starting at ten in the morning, shook her ass fifty minutes on, ten minutes off, for seven hours a day. This wasn't a world she knew. "I was in so much pain—you had to wear three-inch heels. I walked into my apartment, took off my shoes, and the tears started to flow."

Like many a Meyer dame, Erica looks back with mixed feelings about what she was doing and why. "Sex has always been a really weird thing for me because I was molested for a long period of time when I was a kid," remembered Gavin, who says a neighbor abused her for nearly a year when she was ten. Relationships with the opposite sex were problematic at best, and taking off her clothes for money didn't simplify matters.

"I always felt that men were looking at my body, and I didn't like that. But what a weird thing for me to go into—topless dancing. You don't want people to like you for your body, yet you're out there saying, 'This is what I am, I'm *all* about my body.'" More to the point, she told writer Steve Sullivan, "Down deep inside, there's a part of Erica who always felt that the only reason any man was with her was to fuck her."

At age nineteen, Gavin showed up at the Losers for a Sunday amateur night, and owner Pete Rooney hired her on the spot. It wasn't easy to break the ice with Losers luminaries like Tura Satana and Haji. "When you first join a crew like that, honey, they're ready to massacre you," Erica recalled. "I was kinda quiet. I was so involved with myself. They realized I wasn't some kind of bimbo dumbass. I wasn't there to steal their man or to be better than them. I was just trying to make a fucking living." During her Losers stint Gavin did a bullfighter routine complete with cape and south-of-the-border eye makeup that would inspire the fabled *Vixen* brows. At times she was so zonked on drugs other dancers had to cover her ass. "I was stoned all my life," said Gavin. "I mean *really* wasted."

Now Erica was Vixen, and come the end of June 1968, she boarded a Greyhound bus bound for Miranda, California, where she was transported down a dirt road in the redwoods to the small farmhouse that would be her home for the next four weeks or so. Outside of some extra work and a one-afternoon no-budget bumblefuck called *Erika's Hot Summer* that saw light of day only in the wake of *Vixen*'s success, she had no real experience in front of the camera: "I had never made a movie before. I had no clue." And no preparation whatsoever for the man, the myth, and the madness that was Russell Albion Meyer.

$ $ $

The Bud Kues ranch was a typically grim Meyer outpost. RM, Gavin, and other cast members stayed in the farmhouse; the crew was relegated to tents on the lawn. Meals were cooked by the lethal Chef Meyer; according to sound man Richard Brummer, breakfast amounted to "one inch of bacon fat." RM seemed particularly amused that the crew had not only to bathe with a cold-water hose, but defecate in full view of everyone by way of a makeshift open bathroom. "The girls could use the toilet in the house," said Brummer. "The crew was supposed to use this throne that was on display." Meyer would rise at 5:30, squeeze some fishing in, fry up some chow for the gang, then bore down on moviemaking until well into the evening.

Vixen's plot is strictly no-frills. Tom is a workaholic "bush jockey"—pilot for hire—married to the beautiful Vixen. Tom flies Dave and Janet King, a handsome young couple, to his Canadian lodge where, unbeknownst to her husband, Vixen seduces them both. Vixen also beds her biker brother, Judd, and harasses his friend Niles Brook, a black draft dodger. When not scheming, seducing, or manipulating, Vixen coos utter devotion to her husband, who remains blissfully unaware of his wife's endless philandering. Along comes O'Bannion, an evil redheaded Scottish commie intellectual complete with walking stick. He plans to hijack Tom's plane to Cuba and coaxes Niles into coming along for the ride. During the flight, O'Bannion reveals himself to be a racist, and the men get into fisticuffs. Vixen pilots the plane while Tom knocks out O'Bannion with a monkey wrench. Niles picks up O'Bannion's gun, wanting to turn the plane back to Canada, but Vixen talks him out of it and, after landing safely, the draft dodger runs off. A new couple appears, wanting Tom to fly them somewhere. Vixen studies the attractive pair while smiling in sharklike anticipation, and—shades of some fifties sci-fi shocker like *The Blob*—the movie freeze-frames on her face and on pops "THE END?"

Meyer shot a lot of the aerial footage for *Vixen* at a rather dramatic little location atop a mountain in the redwoods. "No buildings, just a landing strip," said soundman Brummer. "At either end of the landing strips, you flew off the top of the mountain." Brummer remembers seeing his Nagra tape deck "literally float in the air" while the pilot flew sideways and nearly upside down for the shots required for the film's tumultuous, in-air climax, and at one point the pilot coolly told the soundman, "Y'know, I'm not supposed to do stunts in a Cessna. We may lose the wings any minute." Dialogue sequences with the actors were shot on the ground with the crew hiding below and occasionally rocking the plane to simulate flying.

Vixen benefited from a great lineup. Garth Pillsbury plays one of Meyer's most blissfully ignorant husbands, the pipe-puffing mannequin Tom; Harrison Page is the uppity but nice-guy African American draft dodger Niles (Michael Landon would later hire him for TV work based on seeing *Vixen*); red-bearded Michael Donovan O'Donnell essays the evil commie O'Bannion with just the right twinkle in his eye; and Vincene Wallace convinces as the sexily dumb Janet King. (Squished in for a brief cockney-accent cameo is Meyer stalwart John Furlong.) But the movie belongs to Erica Gavin, even though she felt like the odd one out during filming. When not embroiled in mind games with the filmmaker, she'd retreat to her quarters, consoling herself by spinning a vinyl copy of her theme song from the Losers, Sergio Mendes' hit "The Look of Love."

$ $ $

At least at first, Gavin saw Russ as a father figure, and when Big Daddy was pleased—as when Erica came up with the famous *Vixen* eye makeup—everything was groovy. "As soon as he said, 'I love those eyebrows,' that was it. Anything to make him happy. Because he was just looking for anything to be unhappy. He was just such a grump sometimes."

The early part of the shoot was fun. Richard Brummer got to the production late, as he had just wrapped up work on *Incubus*, a curious, all-Esperanto horror picture starring William Shatner. Outfitted in his "traveling clothes"—a suit—Brummer arrived to find George Costello in a complete frenzy. No time to unpack or change, said George. They had to run to the town square and swipe some colored lights luckily left on a big tree since the holidays. "Next thing I know, I was climbing up a pine tree taking down Christmas lights and resetting them for the fish scene," said Brummer.

Ah, yes—the infamous fish scene. During a barbecue, a yellow-dressed Vixen comes on to Dave in a novel fashion: by grabbing an about-to-be-fried trout, sticking it down her cleavage to shake her seafood-stuffed jugs, then slipping it into her mouth to suggestively suck on its head. Shot late one night with the crew bone-weary from a grueling day's work, Gavin remembers the scene as a rare instance when she actually pleased RM. Although understandably apprehensive about sticking the slimy, odorous corpse (freshly caught by Meyer) between her lips, Erica got into the swing of it, and RM was ecstatic.

"I don't know how he got me to be so free," said Gavin. "The one thing about Russ is when you're doing something right, he gets excited. He elicits it just by letting you know you're doing good. It's like patting a dog—'Good girl!'" Costello recalled how Meyer just kept squeezing Gavin for more, more, more. "That was another Meyer fascination scene, blowing this fish. He'd shout out all this dialogue—'Make love to that fish! *Suck* on that fish, *suck* on that head.' He was getting off on that one. He'd give this little chuckle to himself. Like he's got one here. Something special."

Battle lines were drawn between Meyer and Gavin the day they shot Vixen abusing Niles, all the while coming on to her brother Judd by flashing her yellow bikini and snarling, "We'll let the shine watch so he'll have something to tell his grandchillun." "It was so fucking hot," Erica remembered. "It wasn't one of Russ's good days, everything was pissing him off. I was squinting because of the reflectors, and I was sweating. He didn't like that—'C'mon, it's not that hot—stop sweating!' I was, like, 'How do I stop sweating??' He said, 'Just *think* of it being *cold*,' and then put more reflectors on me."

Gavin had problems hurling racial epithets at Harrison Page. In the course of Meyer's alleged indictment of racism Vixen calls the actor "spook," "spade," "sambo," "chocolate drop," "Buckwheat," and "black prince of the Congo." Meyer wanted her to be "meaner and meaner, inflammatory and racist," said Erica. "My parents taught me you never say the N-word, ever. I had never even *heard* those words before Russ, much less said them—I wanted to ask Russ, 'What the fuck is a pickaninny?' "*

Page had a mad crush on Gavin but also saw Meyer's side in his battles with the female lead. "Truthfully? I thought Erica was extremely gifted but spoiled and difficult—this kind of dilettante," he said. "She just behaved so irrationally, stormed off I don't know how many times. And George would woo her back. Erica was a star with no experience whatsoever—and behaved like a star, believe me. She stomped around a lot. You always heard her coming." Those with any acting experience found the casting of Erica Gavin a bit puzzling. "She was terribly amateurish in her line delivery," recalled Garth Pillsbury. "Meyer was always going, 'Erica, just say the lines.' This was her first film, and she had the lead."

Costello sensed that Meyer was doing a number on Gavin, and felt sympathy for her. "She was the wounded flower. During the shooting she was ready to quit several times and I had to talk her out of it. Because Meyer was browbeating her . . . it was just the wrong approach. It scared Erica, demoralized her. She just became totally afraid of him. She wouldn't argue when he started yelling, she'd just go into this shell. That's when he'd send me in to negotiate—'George, go see what you can do with *that girl*.' "

---

* In 1997, Meyer would express his admiration for Harrison Page, stating that in the middle of the scene where he tries to attack Gavin he paused to ask RM if he really wanted to go through with it, as it might alienate the "white folks." Meyer also said he was hurt that the "well read" Page (who made "a good income") rebuffed his attempts to maintain a friendship, as Meyer "needed a good dose of the Negro to be able to understand their problems." When I related this info to Page, he seemed nonplussed.

Costello followed orders, not knowing he was writing his own death sentence.

Oddest of all was the fact that when Harrison Page went out walking at night after the day's shoot, he'd catch Meyer peeking into Erica's room, obviously in an excited state. "He would look at me and I would pretend like I didn't see him," said a somewhat bewildered Page, who actually thought that Russ and Erica were a couple playing some kinky game and kept the incident to himself. "As far as I'm concerned they could've had that worked out together. . . . I felt the reason he was so hard on her is because they had a relationship."

All these years later Gavin was stunned to hear that others felt Meyer was obsessed by her. "See, I never got that Russ was interested in me in any kind of way. Because Russ gave me no inclination. He made me cry a lot. He knew that I wanted to be perfect. And I wanted him to love me. I guess there were a lotta things that nobody knew about him, like his looking through my window! For some reason it doesn't even offend me. God, Russ is such a clumsy teddy bear—one, I guess, who likes to look in windows and masturbate.

"What I really loved about Russ is underneath that harsh exterior I knew there was mush. Mush. I feel that inside him was just this tender loving person that thought he had it covered it up by being so fucking butch. Trying too hard. I always remember Russ scratchin' his ass and pickin' his nose. He would like to act gross as possible—I think Russ wouldn't mind taking a shit in front of you. I mean, he never let anyone slide. The dirtier it was, the harder it was, the hotter it was—if he could've made the work any worse, he would've. Russ *loved* the fact that I had to run through the brush barefoot and it hurt like hell on my feet. He kept making me do it over and over and over. The more sensitive you were, the more Russ would go for the jugular."

$ $ $

What a crazed triangle: Gavin thinking Meyer hates her, Meyer thinking Costello's in love with Gavin, everybody else thinking

Meyer's in love with Erica, and George Costello oblivious to it all. It's a wonder somebody didn't die. They almost did.

One day during downtime a few of the cast members decided to mosey over to a stream not far from the house. When Meyer realized they were MIA, he became unglued, running out to a second-story balcony with a gun that he fired repeatedly in the air as he screamed, 'You bastards, *Come back*!' Costello and the crew were frozen with fear in the nearby kitchen. "That was the worst. We thought he'd start turning the gun on *us*. Maybe he was going nuts."

Pillsbury was among the infidels who had wandered away. "Suddenly I hear these gunshots go off, and we're in the middle of nowhere. I thought, 'Jesus, what the hell is that?' I come back to the cabin and there's Russ sitting there with a gun. Somebody told me that Russ took his fist and smashed it into the cabinet and got the gun out." Garth felt the real source of Meyer's anger was the bond developing between Gavin and Costello. "I really thought it was possible he was going to kill George," he said.

Pillsbury's wife Jacqueline recalled the intensity of the situation. "Russ said, 'Nobody leaves tonight. You're all gonna stay here. In the compound.' That was the word, *compound.*" Garth had somehow talked Meyer into letting him and his wife stay at a nearby motel, and they got the hell out of Dodge before RM could restrain them. As they sped away, Jacqueline ducked down below the car window just in case Russ decided to open fire. They figured the one point in their favor was the fact that he had a movie to make and, as she reasoned, "It wouldn't do him any good to kill the actors."

As if the production itself wasn't fraught with melodrama, once Meyer got to the cutting room a major technical snafu was discovered. "The camera had been running slow, less than twenty-four frames per second, so if you played the sound as it was supposed to sync up with picture, it would sound like Mickey Mouse — in sync, but high-pitched," said Richard Brummer, who had to sync the picture syllable by syllable, a painstaking task. The unexpected benefit was that the faulty camera speed actually "made the action faster, which *improved* the movie," said Brummer, chuckling. "Russ always wanted it to move faster anyway. Now he had a film that was innately faster."

Unfortunately a sped-up picture left the film running short, and Brummer, cutting picture for Meyer for the first time, asked the boss if he should stretch scenes to pad it out. "Cut it as tight as you can, tighter than a drum, and I'll fix it," ordered Meyer, who flew off to the Northwest and shot some airport footage that brought the running time up to seventy-two minutes, a barely acceptable length for a feature. Next Meyer and Brummer labored over a rather novel teaser trailer, which "had no scenes at all, just the title changing colors," said Richard. "We said in the narration that the picture was too hot to show you any part of it." (Roger Ebert later reported that people were actually showing up at Chicago's Loop Theater just to peek at the *Vixen* trailer.)

$ $ $

That August, Meyer ran out of scratch and, confident he had a winner, went begging to Eve to bail him out for an additional half of his take (according to Meyer, his ex had pulled funds out of the production at the last minute, angry RM had cut the crew in for distribution returns). They ceased bickering long enough to agree on terms for which proved to be a wise investment. *Vixen* would be the last offering under the banner of Eve Productions.

It would also be the last Russ Meyer picture for George Costello. While in the editing room Meyer somehow learned of the treasonous little can of Treesweet grapefruit juice that Costello had slipped Erica, and he just couldn't let go of it. Brummer was adding a lot of wild lines to correct deficiencies in Gavin's performance, and because of the camera problems he also had to spend time resyncing lines. An impatient Meyer had to find a culprit. "He blamed the performance problems on George!" said Brummer. "Not on anything he did or Erica did. George was persona non grata. In Russ's mind it grew. This was now disloyalty."

Costello's marriage was kaput largely because he'd devoted every minute of his time to Meyer, and now his relationship with RM was heading south because of his involvement with Erica

Gavin. He moved in with her, the brief affair tightening the vise a notch further. Jim Ryan had a good relationship with Gavin—she had Polish roots, and Ryan, speaking the language, called her by a Polish nickname, Slavka—but he made sure not to get too close, as he knew it had meant curtains for Costello. "George had moved in with her in the Valley somewhere," he said. "I never said anything. I thought Meyer wouldn't want to know."

The fact that RM was up to his old habit of working everybody around the clock didn't help matters. The editing crew ate only when and where Meyer wanted to eat. They broke only when Meyer said it was time to quit. "I think he had the need to control everybody associated with him," said Costello. "And his feeling was he was paying us well, so we should be totally dedicated as he was. He verbalized that several times—that we should feel just as he does about these films. For the most part everybody was gung-ho—but when he became too possessive, to where you couldn't leave or go down the street, then it became too much, against human nature. You couldn't be out of Meyer's *sight*. I was at that point where I'd had enough."

Late one evening at the Meyer compound Costello let RM know that he was leaving for the night. "I told him I had to go and visit my child—I lied. Evidently he checked up on me." When George showed up for work the next day, Meyer confronted him, and all of the anger building up came out like a cannon shot. Seething with rage, Meyer snarled, 'You *lied* to me! You *lied* to me!" To which George calmly replied, "Well, Russ, if that's the way you feel about it, okay. I'll see ya later." Costello walked out the door. "That was the end of it," he said. "Excommunicated."

Jim Ryan might've have been RM's eternal right-hand man, but as far as the actual productions went, since the making of *Mudhoney* George had been indispensible. "Russ doesn't give credit where credit's due," said Haji. "If he said, 'Jump,' Costello would say, 'How high?' But it wasn't because he was a pushover, it was that he felt so part of Russ's world. He must've wore five hats and he never had an ego trip about him. George never came on to anybody on the set—he had a lotta class and style. I have so much love and respect for him. George was the glue that kept everything together."

Haji was one of the few brave souls who attempted to mend the fence between the two men, but the mere mention of the Costello name sent Meyer into a complete fury, roaring at Haji, "George *betrayed* me!" Haji shot back, "If it wasn't for George, Erica would've left the movie," which only made Meyer hotter. Haji felt Russ was being petty and not copping to the real reason behind the break. "Russ had a real crush on Erica Gavin," she said. "I know it for a fact. Russ just fell in love with Erica."

Gavin had truly become a femme fatale. "It was really bad," she said. "Russ was just never ever going to talk to George again, and I felt horribly responsible. Now I think Russ was just absolutely floored that someone other than him was having an affair with me."

A few years later when Meyer made it to 20th Century Fox, Costello couldn't resist calling for a job. "I thought maybe he would let me back into the fold," he said. Meyer took the call, said, "You've got a lot of nerve, Costello," and hung up. How dare that scoundrel call *now*?

George received a missive in his mailbox shortly thereafter, consisting of a curt "Costello, you've got a lot of gall." Below that loomed that big Meyer signature, and inside the letter was a yellow feather—an arcane reference to *The Three Feathers*, a 1939 British film concerning a British officer who is given yellow feathers for fleeing service the night before battle.

Back at the Meyer manse, the inevitable plaque for *Vixen* was placed upon the wall of fame. Glued to the cheap wood was a single can of Treesweet grapefruit juice. Meyer would tell interviewers it represented the liquid needs required by a member of the *Vixen* cast that "nearly broke me," but those close to the fray knew better. This cheapo, shiny can was now the symbol of George Costello's betrayal. Meyer would not speak to Costello for another thirty years.

$ $ $

"A sexual steeplechase," *Vixen* is one of Meyer's plainest scripts, and stylewise the picture is equally low-key, giving off a TV-movie blandness that only serves to heighten Gavin's rabid performance. This is a square's fantasy all the way, and Meyer delivers exactly what the old codgers were a-hopin' and a-wishin' for while eye-balling those freewheeling hippie chicks skipping around town with no damn brassieres on. Although somewhat dated, the Gavin-Wallace lesbian escapade still packs a laughable sort of punch—Erica's so keyed up one feels she just might explode on-screen. For once Meyer lets a sex scene build tension and play out instead of cutting away to some hyperactive montage. There are the usual amusing Meyer touches, such as the melody from *The Volga Boatman* bleating ominously on the soundtrack when the commie shows up. But the main attraction here is Erica. You just can't take your eyes off of her.

Vixen inaugurated an image that would recur ad infinitum in RM's films: a floor's-eye view of sexual congress atop bare bed-springs (George Costello suggested the angle). The shot of a female ass grinding into the metallic coils was to be a much-noted Meyer trademark, not to mention the cause of many a bellyache from actresses who resented the reddened "spring-rings" left upon their stinging derrieres. Another relatively new visual obsession was the sight of some naked, barefoot broad running with abandon through the fields and streams of Mother Nature.

Vixen was the first American-made release rated X via the new MPAA ratings system. Meyer voluntarily slapped an X on the picture, and MPAA potentate Jack Valenti personally sought out RM during a post-Oscar bash to commend him for this noble deed. Meyer would soon grow to loathe both Valenti and the ratings board, declaring the all-too-broad rating a commercial "skull and crossbones," but right now he loved being the first offender, and that ominous big black *X* on the one-sheet was guaranteed to stop Joe Six-Pack in his tracks. A loud, lurid campaign underscored the forbidden fruits to be seen on screen. "Is she woman or animal? TOO MUCH for one man."

The picture opened nationally on October 15, 1968. By the

end of January it had cracked *Variety*'s top ten grossers. In February, Meyer rounded up Erica Gavin and Harrison Page and flew to Chicago to attend some promotional ballyhoo for *Vixen*'s Windy City premiere at Oscar Brotman's Loop Theater, a grindhouse that critic (and Meyer adversary) Gene Siskel declared "the movie cesspool of Chicago." *Vixen* was one hot potato: a nervous Brotman pushed back the opening a week to allow city prosecutors a look-see. Meyer had bought Erica a dress for her one *Vixen* promotion, and suddenly Gavin had to face a gaggle of angry feminist protestors, then get eaten alive on a local TV talk show by Betty Friedan. The picture broke all records at the Loop, and in the pages of the *Chicago Sun-Times* Roger Ebert would declare *Vixen* "the best film to date in that uniquely American genre, the skin flick."

Even the poison-pen reviewers had to chuckle over this "ludicrously topical" picture, and notices were far from bad. *Playboy* deigned to call *Vixen* "the most wholesome dirty movie of the year." Kenneth Turan jumped off a cliff in praising Erica Gavin for the *Washington Post:* "The look of calculated lust with which she views every living thing is worth the price of admission, as striking in its own right as any of the more famous close-ups of Garbo or Dietrich."

Most important, *Vixen* made fuck-you money, the kind of loot (Meyer claimed it eventually tallied $26 million) to which even the bigwigs couldn't say no. MGM distributed the picture overseas, and in Los Angeles, Meyer managed to place *Vixen* with the Loews Theaters. Meyer gloated that this was the first time he had gotten one of his adult pictures "into first-class theaters in LA, before it was just the art house thing. The majors have pushed me into a position of respectability."

$ $ $

Money, money, money. The coffers were so full even Eve was off his back. But all was not well in the temple of Meyer. One inevitable response to *Vixen*'s rampaging success was anger. Conservative,

frequently pro-religious censorship advocates were beyond outraged over the picture's unabashed carnality, and this ragtag but
vocal group went on the attack.

January 22, 1969: The projectionist and manager of the Weis
Drive-in, Macon, Georgia, are arrested by Bibb County sheriff's
officers and their print of *Vixen* confiscated. Bail is set at two
grand apiece. A year of litigation ensues.

May 1, 1969: Accompanied by state police, a county prosecutor—besieged by anti-*Vixen* petitions from local clergymen—
barges into the projection booth of the 31 Drive-in in Niles,
Michigan, a scant four minutes from the film's end. Once *Vixen*
concludes, the officers allow the twenty patrons in attendance to
flee, but duly note the presence of a minor in the audience. They
arrest manager James Bowers and projectionist Electus M. Slater
for exhibiting an obscene film and contributing to the delin-
quency of a minor. *Vixen* is seized and Bowers and Slater are
thrown in the hoosegow. The hysteria in Niles is such that when
Vixen flickered on the drive-in screen Slater's son Pete felt that it
was as if "one big tit" had thrown its pear-shaped shadow over the
town. "People was raisin' hell," he said. A month later in Oshkosh,
Wisconsin, the local DA threatens the manager of the Grand Theatre with arrest if he doesn't excise the film's sexual content. He
complies, but Meyer himself pulls the film, proclaiming the ad hoc
censorship a contract violation.

October 3, 1969: The vice squad charges into the Five Points
Theatre in Jacksonville, Florida, where *Vixen* has been packing
them in for five weeks straight. The picture is stopped and the
print seized. "How come it took you so long to come and get it?"
asks Mormon projectionist Carlos Starling as he hands the reels
over to John Law. Theater owner Sheldon Mandell is charged with
one of mankind's great crimes: projecting "an obscene, lewd, las-
civious, filthy and indecent picture depicting graphic visual and
audio representation of a physically attractive female engaging in
sexual intercourse with a Mountie." "Why don't you leave town,
you dirty old man?" is but one message subsequently left on Mandell's answering machine. The bust only increases business.

March 16, 1970: A nine-man, three-woman jury convicts Illiana

Drive-in Theater owner Jack A. Butler on obscenity charges for exhibiting *Vixen*. He faces a thousand-dollar fine and a year at the
Illinois State Penal Farm.

May 26, 1970: Monroe, North Carolina, Center Theater manager James Gregory is fined $250 for showing *Vixen*. Reverend
Glenn Gaffney signs the warrant and is the prosecution's expert
witness. And who but the rev would know better?

On and on it went, from Texas to St. Louis to Pennsylvania.
Meyer was now a smut-film King Kong, swatting one dive-bombing
prosecutor after another. He would later claim he endured twenty-
three prosecutions in one year, defending *Vixen* to the tune of
$250 G's. "Censorship is the wrong word," he'd crow. "It's perse-
cution!"

For Russ Meyer, the showdown of showdowns over *Vixen* came
in Cincinnati, Ohio, a town with "a history of making war against
the bare breast" and whose infamous censorship campaigns
have been fodder for books, documentaries, and the odd made-
for-TV movie. There was just no way the good German Catholics
on the Ohio River were going to open their arms to *Vixen*'s
smutty charms. "Hamilton County," RM muttered, "is a bastion
unto its own. There is no hardcore. There is no softcore, even.
It's bust time."

On September 22, 1969, the Guild Arts Theater at 782 East
McMillan Street in Cincinnati was reopening with *Vixen* following
a $25,000 renovation when the long arm of the law stopped
everything. "The night of the first raid, there was a news photographer hanging around across the street," said owner Pete Gall.
"For the hell of it, I turned off the lights so they couldn't get any
pictures." The reporter walked across to the Guild and let the cat
out of the bag—the theater was about to be paid a visit by Officer O'Leary. The bust "was no last-minute deal," said Gall. "It was
planned."

Meyer's lawyer had another print shuttled in the very next day,
and Gall ran it on the assurance that he wouldn't have to pick up
the legal tab. *Vixen* was seized again. This was just the beginning of
a well-orchestrated attack. A politically connected lawyer claiming to be a "concerned" private citizen was at the center of it all,

and he would prove to be a formidable adversary, one who would throw a very expensive wrench in Meyer's smut machine. His was a name that could always elicit a curse from RM's lips. "I was arrested so many times," said Meyer. "Charles Keating did everything he could do to put me in the iron hotel."

$ $ $

Born in Cincinnati on December 4, 1923, the rangy, six-foot-four, thin-lipped and bespectacled Charles Keating Jr. looks like a Madison Avenue Ichabod Crane as painted by Grant Wood. A product of poverty, he became a self-made dynamo in the legal world after a stint as a navy fighter pilot. Keating was not unlike Meyer: a risk taker, devout workaholic, and control freak who thrived on chaos, and whose whims could suddenly move valued employees to the persona non grata column in a process his staff likened to Amish shunning. Intimidating and inscrutable, Charlie was a skilled manipulator who loved big bands, had a profound distaste for commies and homosexuals, and "never saw a lawsuit he didn't like."

"Anyone who ever tells you he understands Charlie Keating is either lying to you or making a big mistake," said a key aide. "He is the most complex, enigmatic human being you will ever come across." Keating and Meyer would share one other extremely significant peccadillo, but RM wouldn't learn of it for another twenty-five years.

Unfortunately for Meyer, whom Keating referred to as "that criminal," Charlie's pet hate was pornography, and in 1970 alone he traveled two hundred thousand miles to convert others to his anti-porno gospel. He was Richard Nixon's only appointee to the Presidential Commission on Obscenity and Pornography, and when the committee's report found attacking smut in the courts somewhat pointless, an angry Keating blocked its release until his and other commission members' dissenting opinions were tacked on in a huge appendix.

Charlie had first been enlisted in the fight by a local Catholic Church leader in 1956, and took to it with the Bible-thumping

Russ Meyer (*top right*) with childhood playmates, the Filipovitches—Lou, Pete, and Martha. "Russ was one of the nicest guys I ever knew," said Pete Filipovitch. "I don't think there was a mean bone in his body." (*Courtesy Martha Robbins*)

Sergeant Russ Meyer, photographed by fellow combat photographer and best friend Charles Sumners. "I really didn't want the war to end," said RM. "It was the best time I ever had." (*Charles Sumners*)

Russ Meyer reluctantly resting a leg mangled in a Jeep accident, Metz, France, 1944. "Russ would get so involved in makin' the picture that he would forget about the danger," said Charlie Sumners. (*Charles Sumners*)

Tempest Storm, *Frolic* magazine, October 1952. Meyer
had a brief affair with the stripper, but decided
against the occupation of "peeler's retriever."

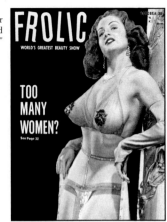

Russ Meyer and first wife Betty Valdovinos on a
trip to Hollywood, January 1951. "Betty
thought Russ should go to work every day and
carry a lunchbox," said Jim Ryan. *(Paul Fox,
courtesy Dolores Fox)*

Russ Meyer and camera circa 1950. "Russ,
with his big, huge hands, would tenderly
handle that camera like it was a lover," said
longtime love and Meyer superstar Kitten
Natividad. *(Paul Fox, courtesy Dolores Fox)*

Russ and Eve Meyer, newlyweds, 1952. "Where he was strong, she wasn't, and where she was strong, he wasn't," said Irving Blum. "They were absolutely astonishing together." (*Paul Fox, courtesy Dolores Fox*)

Eve Meyer as photographed by Russ Meyer, *Frolic* magazine, 1954. "Eve was a great intimidator," said RM.

Grimy early fifties ad for buy-'em-direct-from-Russ mail-order photographs of wife Eve. "I got so I just hated that darkroom," she said later.

FROLIC
THE MAGAZINE OF ENTERTAINMENT
Are Bosomy Beauties A Fad?
EVELYN WEST VS. KINSEY

EVE
4 - "New" "Spectacular" "Blow-ups" EMPHASIZING HER NOW 41" VOLUPTUOUS BEAUTY
$ 1°° Post Paid
EVE
P.O.Box 3634
San Francisco 19, Calif.

Virginia "Ding-Dong" Bell, photographed by Meyer for *Sir Knight*, August 1959. One of the best of Meyer's "female explosion" pictures. "My glamour is of a very provocative nature," wrote Meyer. And how.

Meyer was cinematographer for this late-fifties exploitation shocker starring Eve. "The abortion racket," said Meyer, was "a very safe way to deal with sex—showing it as a real crime."

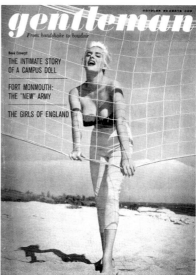

Various RM-shot June Wilkinson magazine covers, late fifties to early sixties. "Breasts are like fingerprints," said Wilkinson. "No two are alike."

Fling magazine cover of Virginia Gordon by Meyer, 1959.

Ad for Meyer's first smash, 1959's *The Immoral Mr. Teas.* "We couldn't find anybody with the courage to screen it," said Meyer. "No one had ever seen as bare a film as *Teas.*"

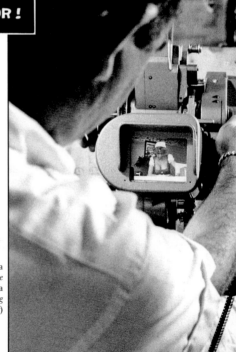

The view over Meyer's shoulder as he sat at a Moviola assembling his 1960 picture *Eve and the Handyman.* "Cut, cut, cut, cut, cut—get a rhythm," RM told David K. Frasier. "A *punishing* rhythm." (*Ken Parker, courtesy Paula Parker*)

The luscious Veronique Gabrielle doing her thing in *Europe in the Raw*. Meyer would use the mesmerizing footage in 1966's *Mondo Topless* as well.

RM shooting the 1961 nudie-cutie western *Wild Gals of the Naked West*. "I made movie after movie," said Meyer. "Nothing else really mattered." (*Paul Fox, courtesy Dolores Fox*)

Ad for Meyer's 1963 sex shockumentary, *Europe in the Raw*. "Tits and war," proclaimed RM.

The mind-boggling Tura Satana, Miss Japan Beautiful, circa the late fifties. "Men were always after her big, big names," said Peter Young. "She had boyfriends. A lotta them." (*Courtesy Tura Satana*)

Lorna Maitland, photographed by Meyer for *Fling* magazine, 1965. "A good actress!" scoffed Meyer. "I'd rather have a big-chested stiff who can hardly pronounce her name."

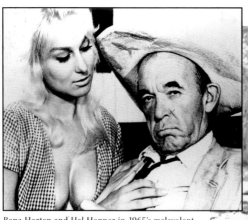

Rena Horten and Hal Hopper in 1965's malevolent Meyer melodrama, *Mudhoney.* "Rena was pretty handy. She couldn't have been a nicer chick," said Fred Beiersdorf. "But Russ ran her off."

"Sound your warning . . . send your message . . . huff and puff and belch your smoke . . . and kill and maim and run off *unpunished!*" The Vegetable's sudden moment of impotence upon hearing the train in *Faster, Pussycat! Kill! Kill!*

The outrageous triumvirate from 1966's *Faster, Pussycat! Kill! Kill!*—Tura Satana, Lori Williams, and Haji. "I personally prefer the aggressive female," said Meyer. "The superwoman."

Alex Rocco and Haji during a high-angst moment in *Motorpsycho*, 1965. "I came visiting with my family from another galaxy," mused Haji. "I think a lot about all the little creatures in the ocean."

"You've only dreamed there were women like these, but they're *real*, unbelievably *real!*" Pat Barringer in Meyer's 1966 mammary-overloaded masterpiece, *Mondo Topless*. Note the ubiquitous Meyer prop, a transistor radio.

The hapless cast and crew steel themselves for another trip to the remote location for 1967's *Common-Law Cabin*. The boat would sometimes run adrift, forcing Meyer to jump in the water and tug it along, "like Humphrey Bogart in *The African Queen.*" (*Courtesy Alaina Capri*)

The bleak view over Meyer's shoulder as he directs Alaina Capri and Babette Bardot in *Common-Law Cabin*. "Meyer loved the desert," said actor Charles Napier. "Asked him why one time and he said, 'Because you can die there.'" (*Courtesy Alaina Capri*)

Nothing but the best for Meyer stars: *Common-Law Cabin* star Alaina Capri doing her own on-location makeup. (*Courtesy Alaina Capri*)

The great Anthony James Ryan, Meyer confidant and clean-up man, not to mention star of the silver screen, behind the counter at Modern Photo, 2003. "I think Jim lived quite vicariously off Meyer's hijinks," said John McCormick. (*Jimmy Vapor*)

The chest-shaving scene with Jan Sinclair and Paul Lockwood from 1968's *Finders Keepers, Lovers Weepers.* "Meyer was smacking his lips filming that one," said George Costello. "He was *really* into it."

IS SHE WOMAN...
OR ANIMAL?

Only today's society could make such an animal a woman ... Or such a woman an animal.

RUSS MEYER'S

VIXEN.

X RATING

INTRODUCING ERICA GAVIN AS VIXEN. RESTRICTED TO ADULT AUDIENCES. IN EASTMANCOLOR. PRODUCED AND DIRECTED BY RUSS MEYER. AN EVE PRODUCTION.

The feral Erica Gavin in an ad for Meyer's X-rated 1968 smash, *Vixen*. "Basically this is a woman that is a racist, a sex fiend, an incest partner, a lesbian," said Gavin. "[And] an all-American girl that saves a plane from being hijacked by the Communists."

Russ Meyer shooting *Vixen*, photographed by Erica Gavin. "I wanted him to love me," said Gavin. (*Courtesy Erica Gavin*)

Erica Gavin and Meyer lieutenant George Costello confide and conspire during the shooting of *Vixen*. Meyer terrorized the actress, pushing her, said Haji, "right into George's arms." (*Courtesy Erica Gavin*)

Teutonic bombshell Uschi Digard and RM share a moment in Meyer's pool for *Cherry, Harry, and Racquel.* "The dedication of a Watusi gun-bearer," said Meyer of the actress. "She'd run over bare coals and cut glass."

Ad for Meyer's human comic strip, 1970's *Beyond the Valley of the Dolls.* RM considered the picture his masterpiece.

Roger Ebert and Russ Meyer, circa 1970. According to Erica Gavin, Ebert was "awestruck" by Meyer's world. "Russ took him under his wing. . . . It was like, 'All right, kiddo, I'm gonna show you what tits 'n' ass is all about.'" (*Courtesy Roger Ebert*)

Beyond the Valley of the Dolls: John La Zar (*left*) as the sexual question mark Z-Man, posing between takes with RM screenwriter Manny Diez. Meyer surveyed John's new rack and muttered, "Y'know what you need, kid, after this? A good Western." (*Courtesy Manny Diez*)

The ferocious Edy Williams, star of *Beyond the Valley of the Dolls* and Meyer wife number three. "I don't think I've known any woman who made me happier or more unhappy," said RM. "She's the ultimate bitch and the ultimate sex symbol."

The Seven Minutes, Meyer's 1971 flop for Fox. "A losing battle of mind over mattress," said *Playboy.*

Ad for 1979's *Beneath the Valley of the Ultravixens,* starring the fabulous Kitten Natividad. Said the actress of her director, "When he wanted me to cry he'd say, 'Pretend they're beating your dog.' When he wanted me to look sexy, he'd say, 'C'mon, baby, jerk off the whole world.'"

Beyond the Valley of the Dolls all-femme supergroup the Carrie Nations (Cynthia Myers, Marcia McBroom, and Dolly Reed). "Showgirls on LSD" is how John Waters described them.

The marriage of Russ and Edy, 1970 (*left to right:* David Gurian, Edy, Russ, Erica Gavin). Said Edy, "I thought, 'Hey, this will be swell—like Humphrey Bogart and Lauren Bacall, y'know?'" (*Peter Borsari*)

Ad for Meyer's 1976 atrocity *Up!* starring the delectable Raven De La Croix. She recalled being "thrown and whipped and raped and punched throughout the whole thing."

Jim Ryan and a stogie-smoking Meyer prepare to shoot the *Supervixens* scene in which Shari Eubank smashes an axe into her boyfriend's car. (*Paul Fox, courtesy of Dolores Fox*)

Meyer's sex life was the stuff of legend, worthy of tabloid headlines.

Russ and his beloved wolf-dog Harry, circa 1980. Screenwriter John McCormick was shaken after Harry sank his teeth into his arm. "I never told Russ about it," said McCormick. "I knew he'd take the dog's side." (*Paul Fox, courtesy Dolores Fox*)

Porn star Viper about to unleash her new implants on a roomful of Vegas fans as disgusted Russ Meyer buries himself in his autobiography manuscript, 1990. "Meyer couldn't keep up with the adult industry, and it passed him by," said Porno vet Bill Margold. (*Bill Margold*)

RM and combat buddy Charlie Sumners document another 166th reunion with Meyer's old wartime Eyemo camera. As reporter Kay Hively recalled, "RM was directing a movie the whole time we were here.'" (*Charles Sumners*)

The utilitarian bed of Russ Meyer, 1990. Note the box of tissues on left. Said Jane Hower of Meyer's lovemaking, "Very straightforward— hug, kiss, touch and put it in." (*David K. Frasier*)

Meyer's last paramour, stripper Melissa Mounds. Recalled Jim Ryan, "I'd say, 'Meyer, you bought her an engagement ring for three thousand dollars and she loses it?' He said, 'It's worth it.'" (*Dolores Fox*)

Russ Meyer, 1998. "Russ is losin' it," Charlie Sumners told his wife. (*J. Scott Wynn*)

brimstone of a backwoods preacher, the kind Meyer had lampooned in *Lorna.* "I'm only one guy," intoned a solemn Keating. "It is not possible for me to do this alone. If the majority wants it, we'll have public decency." Charlie's first big victory: the conviction of an elderly woman for selling sex aids out of her schoolyard-vicinity candy store. Lady Justice fined the old biddy a hundred bucks.

On November 1, 1958, Keating founded Citizens for Decent Literature, a somewhat loony but powerful watchdog group (sporting four senators and seventy House members on its honorary committee) that would have Meyer reaching for the antacids more than a few times. *Hustler* publisher Larry Flynt, who would take his battle with Keating to the Supreme Court and win, writes in his autobiography that the CDL "provided a vehicle for its staff members to pursue their own obsession with smut in a socially sanctioned way and condemn it at the same time. Freud would have a field day: several guys sitting around watching porno flicks, saying, " 'God, that was disgusting—would you rewind the film and play it again?' " Keating was completely and wholly obsessed with wiping out smut, so much so that it made even potential allies uncomfortable. Appearing before a House subcommittee, Charlie had to be restrained from reading aloud from an ode to sadism entitled *Love's Lash.* He seemed to delight in shocking reporters by whipping out filth, and further unnerved one scribe when he uttered "a scatological term which somehow reaches the apex of revulsion."

In 1965, Keating entered the motion picture biz, producing a threadbare Citizens for Decent Literature "exposé" just this side of exploitationville called *Perversion for Profit.* This laughable little gem exhibits almost as much flesh as a Meyer opus, specifically notes the smut world's "preoccupation with the female breast to a point where it has become a fetish," and puts forth the ludicrous claim that "75 to 90 percent of pornography ends up in the hands of small children."

On September 19, 1969, *Vixen* unspooled in Cincinnati. One week later, Keating went on the attack, writing a letter to Safety Commisioner Henry Sandman complaining that the picture was obscene, and by way of an Ohio nuisance law demanding an injunction to prevent the picture from being shown. "It is my preference that action be taken by police," wrote Keating, who filed suit in Common Pleas Court the day of the first print seizure. Sandman and members of the vice squad had already slipped into the Guild, seen *Vixen*, and decided to prosecute, and after a final Monday night showing it was seized at 11:30 p.m. "Keating orchestrated the whole thing," said Pete Gall. "He was pushing to get rid of these theaters."

Meyer's lawyer for obscenity charges was Elmer Gertz, a colorful Chicago attorney who'd defend Jack Ruby, Nathan Leopold, and Henry Miller during his six-decade career. In the rest of the country, Gertz was able to get nearly all of the charges against *Vixen* dismissed via a First Amendment defense. In the press, Meyer utilized *Vixen*'s crazy "political" banter as relevant commentary. "I'm violently anti-communist, which gives my films social significance," he'd boast to one reporter, while commenting to another, "Strangely enough most of the litigation has been associated with or near the Mason-Dixon line, which convinces me the frank racial exposition of the film is the primary reason the picture is being harassed."

The tune being whistled by Meyer fell on deaf ears within the Ohio legal system, however. The cards were stacked against *Vixen* in Hamilton County, and Pete Gall recalled an incensed Keating denouncing Meyer's name in particular when snooping around his theater one night. "The difficulty was that Keating's family ran Cincinnati—the newspaper, the courts, the state attorney's office," said Elmer Gertz. *Vixen* was facing a judge with a long history of anti-pornography actions, Simon L. Leis Sr. ("Simon Leis," moaned Meyer at the mention of his name decades later. "It sounds like the name of someone who stabbed Christ. The name *bespeaks* evil!")

The assistant city solicitor attacking the picture in court was a devout Catholic ex-Marine known for mounting aggressive frontal assaults—and who, amazingly enough, also went by the name of Simon Leis. "We were up against a judge whose son was the prosecutor!" complained Meyer. Charles Keating and Simon Leis Jr.

were sort of the Lennon and McCartney of anti-porn, later making life miserable for Larry Flynt. Clearly Keating and his Citizens for Decent Literature group aided other *Vixen* attacks outside of Ohio. The September-October 1969 issue of the CDL's *National Decency Reporter* newsletter announced that their in-house legal counsel would be "happy to assist with prosection in any area of the country."

Meyer and company fought back. "Mr. Keating intimidates people," Gertz charged in court, accusing Keating and his cronies of engaging in a "conspiracy" to deprive Meyer and the general public of their civil rights, arguing that *Vixen* was already being shown in forty states, not to mention nineteen theaters in ten Ohio cities. During the trial, Gertz trotted out nine witnesses for the defense, among them psychologists, professors, and one local citizen and Knights of Columbus member who testified that *Vixen* had "Billy Budd–Christlike" themes that gave it relevance. A California physician was the prosecution's only witness. He maintainted that the "unrealistic hoax" of Vixen's "male lust" was "one of the major causes of marital discord."

On November 17, Leis granted Keating a permanent injunction against *Vixen* in five Ohio counties on the grounds it was obscene. In a twenty-two-page opinion in which he quoted the prosecution's sole witness extensively, Leis branded Meyer a "cancer on society," one of those "unscrupulous men who have taken advantage of lack of censorship and capitalized on it" and who, if not stopped, "will infest society with a disease which will kill it." The only thing Leis did not grant was Keating's request that all box office receipts be turned over to the state. Charlie was now the victorious white knight of anti-smut, boasting that Judge Leis had "set a precedent whereby a private citizen could himself take measures to stop the pornographers from polluting the hearts, minds and souls of Americans."

In Columbus, Ohio, on July 21, 1971, the Ohio Supreme Court upheld the ban, ruling in a 5–2 decision that "purported acts of sexual intercourse solely for the profit of the producer and exhibitors cannot constitute the communication of an idea or thought protected by the First and 14th Ammendments." Gertz would claim he heard the judges laughing aloud while screening *Vixen* behind closed doors. Of course, *Vixen* could be shown if Meyer cut the sex out—which would leave little more than some footage of a plane flying and a cockamamie argument or two. Although the U.S. Supreme Court refused to hear the case, Meyer, a man not used to losing, had lost big time.* *Vixen* has not played in Cincinnati since those two days in 1969, and legally, it still can't— when a screening was attempted on a local university campus in 1984, authorities threatened seizure and arrest.

Ironically, the court battle didn't vanquish the Guild Theater, as national publicity from the case only jacked up post-*Vixen* business. "My God, did we pack that house," said Pete Gall. "It was a blessing in disguise." But paranoia remained high. Before entering the theater, Gall had patrons sign a statement admitting they were knowingly seeing pictures containing nudity (even the vice cops had to add their John Hancock, much to their dismay). In addition, Gall had to put up with the Cincinnati papers changing David F. Friedman's *Trader Hornee* to *Trader Horn* and refusing to run the title *Love Is a Four-Letter Word*. While legally unsuccessful beyond the *Vixen* brouhaha, the attacks by Keating and Leis had a chilling effect on adult entertainment in southern Ohio. The harassment just wasn't worth it.

In the late seventies, Keating and Leis zeroed in on their new target, Larry Flynt. The battle got extremely personal. In their 1993 Keating biography *Trust Me*, Michael Binstein and Charles Bowden report that Keating held Flynt accountable for the rape of a daughter, and when the porno potentate was shot in an anonymous attack that left him paralyzed from the waist down, there were those (including, unbelievably, Keating's own son) who suggested Keating might've been involved. To this day, Flynt's at-

---

* RM would forever sing Elmer Gertz's praises after he waived a large chunk of his fee upon losing the case. Perhaps the funniest moment of the legal battle came during a screening of the film for the U.S. Supreme Court, which refused to hear the case. Upon witnessing the ridiculous capitalism/communism argument that occurs in the hijacked plane at the end of *Vixen*, Justice Thurgood Marshall drolly muttered, "Ah, the redeeming social value."

tempt to sell *Hustler*'s wares in Hamilton County is being thwarted in the courts by Leis.*

According to David F. Friedman, the majors didn't lift a finger to help in the censorship battles, although they'd certainly benefit from the freedoms that ensued. It was the exploitation mavericks like Meyer who smashed the locks for everybody. "He fought the big, big fight to ensue the First Amendment rights of every American citizen," said Friedman. But for Russ, it was just another game. He'd win the next round, and the fifteen after that. Let somebody try to stop *Meyer*. RM was at his best when the chips were down. "In the final analysis, you have to be a man," he told authors Kenneth Turan and Stephen F. Zito. "You ain't worth a shit if you don't finally stand up to something."

$ $ $

There is a sublime epilogue to the Keating-Meyer saga. Charles Keating would go on to become a very rich, powerful, and arrogant figure in the banking industry, but it all went to hell in the end. In 1993, Keating was convicted of fraud in the Lincoln Savings and Loan scandal and sentenced to 151 months in jail (the conviction was later overturned, although in 1999, Keating, now seventy-five, pled guilty to four counts of fraud to avoid a retrial). Countless retirees—some of them perhaps members of CDL's "tennis shoe brigade"—had lost their life's savings due to the swindle.

---

* Sheriff of Cincinnati since 1987, Simon Leis has remained unrelenting in his prosecution of obscenity cases. In 1990, 121 sheriff's deputies in SWAT uniforms halted a museum exhibition of Robert Mapplethorpe's photographs. Leis lost the case. In 1995, his Computer Crimes Task Force raided the home of a local cyber bulletin board operator, seizing twenty-three computers and the e-mail of six thousand people. The result was a class action suit filed against Leis that may cost the city a fortune. Still, Leis does have his fans, even in the smut industry. "I think he's probably done more for the adult industry than any single person in America because of the national attention he gave Larry Flynt," said Larry's brother Jimmy. "Simon has been more responsible for the success of Larry Flynt and *Hustler* than any other person." Speaking through a representative, Leis maintained that he had "no clear recollection" of the *Vixen* case.

A gleeful Meyer laid out a hundred bucks for Charlie's mug shot, which he then printed in his autobiography. But the best was yet to come. When Meyer perused an article on Keating's downfall in the *Los Angeles Times*, certain passages screamed out. Keating liked to "peer down the blouses of secretaries he has hired," wrote Binstein and Bowden, who stated that a dozen women on Charlie's staff had had augmentation done. First came an "unexpected" bonus, quickly followed by "huge new breasts." Opposite a page showing a passbook from a canceled Meyer bank account at Keating's notorious Lincoln Savings and Loan, RM reprinted the most salacious excerpts from the article in *A Clean Breast*, and directly below the text lurked a picture of Meyer, his grinning mug between the mammoth knockers of some frail. "*Et Tu*, Charlie?" asked Russ.

$ $ $

There was no such punch line for Vixen herself, Erica Gavin, and no rest for the wicked. After another bumpy ride with Meyer in 1970's *Beyond the Valley of the Dolls*, Gavin drifted through miserable low-budget affairs like the never-released, shot-in-Tunisia Larry Buchanan epic *The Rebel Jesus* (in casting that would have Charlie Keating frothing at the mouth, she played Mary Magdalene, although illness forced her to bow out). Jonathan Demme's 1974 women-in-prison *Caged Heat* was her last film of any note.

On the commentary track for the *Vixen* laser disc, Meyer callously suggests that succumbing to the Hollywood casting couch would've been best for Erica. Truth be known, Gavin had plenty to endure due to the *Vixen* legacy. She recalled a trip to the Beverly Hills Hotel to see a "producer" for what she thought was a part. She was greeted by a gross middle-aged troglodyte swathed only in a robe.

"I didn't know what to do, so I basically let him fuck me," said Erica. "I was afraid my agent would fire me. On his dresser he had all these bottles of perfume. They were all the same and they weren't even in wrapping paper, they were wrapped with a bow. Afterwards, he gives me a bottle of the perfume and two dollars for my parking. Do you know what a piece of shit I felt like? I felt like I didn't even deserve to be living. This guy was never making a movie. When I tried to do other things after *Vixen*, nobody was like Russ. They were *all* out to fuck you—period. Whereas Russ was into putting you into a movie. And not fucking you."

But Gavin was a cat with nine lives. She floated around the fringes of the rock scene, running with such luminaries as Love's Arthur Lee, the Patti Smith Group's Lenny Kaye, and Aerosmith. She did too much of everything, including heroin and speed. Erica quit acting, and for nearly twenty years she worked at the posh Melrose Avenue clothes store Fred Segal's, then became a buyer for Barney's, whereupon she and John Waters became friends.

"I knew her from wealthy show business dinner parties," said Waters, who was stunned by the svelte, "chic" post-*Vixen* Gavin. "She looked like a model." According to John, few knew of her previous notoriety. "I don't think when they were buying designer outfits from Erica in Barney's they were thinking, 'Is she *woman* or is she *animal*?'" said an amused Waters.

The Meyer-Gavin relationship remained ever contentious through the years. RM stayed angry at her for losing weight after *Vixen*, not to mention the treachery involving George Costello. In 1976 Erica gave a rare, candid interview and took a few swipes at Meyer, marking her as one of few in the inner circle brave enough to offer any kind of criticism of the Great One.

RM was infuriated, responding decades later with a chapter in his autobiography entitled "The Other Side of the Coin," in which he prints a cheerful handwritten note from Erica sent just after *Vixen*, a polite (if chilly) response from Meyer, and then the interview where she trashes him. Accompanying the text is a *Vixen* shot of Gavin holding up a small compact mirror, mesmerized by her own image. It's a wonder she didn't get a yellow feather in the mail.

At Gavin's lowest ebb in the eighties, she got a Christmas card from Meyer out of the blue. He knew of her troubles and wanted to wish her the best. Inside the card was three hundred bucks. A small gesture from the man who'd made a mint off her naked body, but it got to her. Erica called him, and they had a few laughs. How did Russ know she'd end up a gay designer, exactly the character she played in *Beyond the Valley of the Dolls*? In that comically gruff voice of his Meyer uttered a crass remark about how she liked "all that pussy." Somehow it warmed the cockles of Erica's knocked-around heart, and she actually braved the many phobias she had at the time to attend a Meyer birthday party, even if she soon fled. They now enjoyed an affectionate truce.

The eighties were Gavin's nadir. She quit working and spent long periods alone, afraid to leave her abode. Anorexia nearly stopped Erica's clock forever, and she traced the obsession with weight back to the first time she saw *Vixen* on the big screen. "I was shocked. Shocked. Everything was so big, just huge, including me. I could see my pores, a little zit that was on my chest . . . And knowing everyone else sees it, too! It was traumatic."

After *Vixen*, said Erica, "people started to look at me. Scary. That's why I became anorexic. It's all how men see women—it was me wanting to become invisible by shrinking myself so that no one would look at me anymore. I almost killed myself by starving. I was one hundred and forty when I made *Vixen*. I went down to seventy-six pounds. My lowest weight. I was hospitalized three times.

"I'd just turn sideways and you wouldn't see me. I didn't *want* anybody to see me. I just wanted to be a nonsexual entity, androgynous. No tits, no ass, nothing feminine, nothing soft. And it kinda worked. No one came around me, y'know?

"I can see why Marilyn Monroe, anybody who has any fragile part of them, there's no fuckin' way they're gonna make it through. I've seen people end up tossed on the lawn after they OD'd. They'd been in L.A. for nine months and that's what became of them. They come here with all these dreams—'I'm gonna be a star,' all that. Y'know what? It's so, so not that way. It'll eat you up. It'll fuckin' eat you up."

$ $ $

Tracking down Gavin these days is a daunting task. She's the rock star of the Meyer women, the Elvis figure whispered about but rarely seen. Yes, she'll meet me. No, she won't. Yes, no, maybe so. More phone calls, then the waiting. Filmmaker and friend "Colonel" Rob Schaffner gives fifty-fifty odds on her waltzing through the door. Hours go by. Another phone call. She's on her way. The odds go up to eighty-twenty. More waiting. "Erica only comes out at night," says Schaffner. "She really *is* Vixen, dude."

Finally, after one aborted meeting and even more phone calls, Erica consents to meet at an all-night L.A. coffee shop aptly named Swingers. It is three a.m. when she arrives. Wiry, angular, painfully alive, Gavin resembles an improbable collaboration between Gustav Klimt and Walter Keane. Life has thrown a few well-placed punches, to say the least. The voluptuous Vixen body is long gone, chipped to the nub as purposefully as one would strip a car, and she's down to the sinewy fighting weight of say, Iggy Pop.

Infamous for clocking an ex-manager in broad daylight whilst attending a fan convention a few years back, Gavin's no slouch in the tough-cookie department, yet one feels that the slightest of slights could send her scurrying back into that starless Hollywood fog to hide for another year or ten. All the hoop-jumping is worth getting to Erica, though. Plug into her socket and the juice is enough to fry you for good. Gavin's a born provocateur. After a few minutes you either want to kiss her or kill her—there's no middle ground. Even during a simple trip to the mini-mart, Erica drives like she's auditioning for the remake of *Bullitt*.

Meyer's cinematic image of Erica Gavin and her subsequent time on earth have dovetailed in eerie ways. She feels that RM had an almost supernatural—albeit unconscious—power when it came to the roles he cast people in. "Russ sees your subconscious, and then he has you become it. He has this vision of you that's very real and very natural, before you even see it. That's his gift."

Erica shakes her head, smiling, and addresses the one who isn't there. "Russ, you motherfucker! How did you know I was going into clothing? How did you know I would become a sex fiend and actually start masturbating while driving down the street, looking at guys *and* girls? How did you know I was going to end up liking women? How did you know all the things I was gonna be? Who predestined what?"

Gavin laughs. "It's the Twilight Zone. Russ saw beyond without even knowing. It's weirder than you even know."

The Watusi Gun-Bearer

All that counts is to get the film done, no matter what you have to do. Lie, cheat, steal, bunco, con—get it out.

—RUSS MEYER

Uschi. Two syllables that evoke sweet dreams. There, beneath a ravenous grin that somehow managed to be more pornographic than old 42nd Street in all its glory, lurked a fleshy, sun-baked carcass with more curves than the Coast Highway—the sort of filthy figure that could even make a macramé dress look inviting. To a pimply adolescent, encountering an image of Uschi Digard for the first time was akin to the thrill of seeing Godzilla: taller than the tallest skyscraper and breathing fire. "Who cares about acting ability and character development when you were presented with nipples that would show up in satellite photos?" wrote Uschi fan Mike Accomando in his treatise "I Love Uschi: Thanks for the Mammaries." "You could tell it was more than a paycheck with her.... She shows an exuberance for sex that bordered on berserk."

Uschi Digard, aka Digart (and a zillion other aliases—for Meyer's *Cherry, Harry and Raquel* she's Astrid Lillimor) was a seventies soft-core queen. Her credits are infinite, as she appeared in a ton of magazine layouts and cheap sexploitation movies ("Who else can say they appeared in films about the sex lives of Robin

Hood, Casanova, Pinocchio and Bigfoot?" writes Accomando). But it is her work with Meyer that exalts her to some sort of immoral immortality, particularly her performance as the maniacal milkmaid in 1975's *Supervixens*.

Other than a handful of endearingly bland, contemporaneous interviews—"I'm living for right now. . . . We live behind clothes, and why?"—little is known about the real Uschi. She was born August 15, 1948 (some say a few years earlier; unfortunately, some also say Uschi isn't her real name), in Bismarck, North Dakota (!) and raised in Scandinavia. Speaking some nine languages, Digard worked as a translator before falling into nude modeling. According to Uschi, Meyer saw her first magazine layout sometime late in the sixties and went gaga. "We've been together ever since that day," she said in 1976.

When it came to taking Meyer production punishment, Uschi was not unlike Haji: one of the guys. "The dedication of a Watusi gun-bearer," said Meyer, who gave Uschi associate producer credit on two of his pictures. "She'd do anything. She'd run over bare coals and cut glass. I mean literally! She was that kind of chick." Like most Meyer women, Digard never ventured into hard-core. "I made my reputation by the tease," she said. "Everything was simulated."

Meyer, however, has suggested otherwise in both his autobiography and interviews, maintaining that there were times Uschi wanted real stimulation in order to make the fake look real. RM told writer Dan Scapperotti that the two "had a great love affair" off and on for years. "One of the most aggressive sex partners anyone could hope to find," added Meyer, who confessed to having spent a weekend in Vegas with both Uschi and Babette Bardot, a mind-melting concept akin to having a couple of the heads of Mount Rushmore parked in your living room (but sexier, of course).

Digard's initial foray into the world of Russ Meyer was 1969's *Cherry, Harry and Raquel,* but the movie would have to fall apart first, creating a black hole only a supernova like Uschi could fill.

$ $ $

Meyer's sixteenth production cost $90,000, some of the cash coming from co-producers Jim Ryan and Thomas J. McGowan. McGowan, who had first encountered Meyer at Camp Crowder, was an old crony of Ryan's—he'd made a 1956 short in the Amazon starring Jim—who'd gone on to work at major studios, directing the 1966 all-feral kiddie extravaganza *Born Free*. McGowan sank $38,000 into *Cherry, Harry and Raquel* and wrote the screenplay under the pseudonym Tom Wolfe. By the end of the affair, RM would complain that McGowan had done nothing but sit under an umbrella and watch Meyer sweat, while McGowan bitched that he never saw a penny from the hit film after getting his initial investment back. The ten-week shoot took place in the rugged desert canyons of Panamint Valley—"a terrible fucking place," according to McGowan, and undoubtedly a location Russ Meyer could love.

The concept for *Cherry, Harry and Raquel* came during a visit to Charlie Sumners during which RM and Sumners saw the latest Clint Eastwood picture, *Coogan's Bluff*. Meyer grabbed a pad and started scribbling, the result being a nearly incomprehensible action picture involving drugs, lesbianism, and a mysterious Native American assassin named Apache. The movie starred Meyer stalwart Franklin J. Bolger, along with a few new faces, including (most ruefully for RM, as we shall see) an English woman named Linda Ashton, a Miami Beach showgirl with an ICM agent boyfriend. The male lead was another Meyer discovery, sort of a knockabout yang to Uschi's sparkler-bright yin.

There is something frightening about the head of Charles Napier. I say that with full admiration. As RM was fond of saying, he's got six more teeth than Burt Lancaster and is perhaps the only man who can simultaneously smile out of one side of his mouth while sneering out the other. Napier is the archetypal Meyer manly man—testosterone made flesh, square-jaw determination in the shadow of a Stetson hat, and headed straight for your daughter. No doubt you've seen Napier's mug on either TV or the big screen, playing the paranoid CIA operative, the psychotic redneck sheriff, or the sadistic coach, but it was RM who made him a star.

Perhaps to show his appreciation, Napier became the first

actor to grace a Meyer picture with full frontal male nudity. *Cherry, Harry and Raquel* contains one shot where, accompanied by an equally unclothed Larissa Ely, Napier runs toward the camera wearing nothing more than boots and Stetson. "Next thing I know it gets picked up by United Artists, and there I am galloping across the screen naked as hell," said Napier. "AP gets a hold of it, calls my mother. I weathered the storm."

The Meyer-Napier relationship was a combustible combination. Take the ill-fated *Blitzen, Vixen and Harry,* a picture Meyer was planning to do in the early eighties. According to Roger Ebert, "Napier was reluctant to commit, because he had been doing a lot of work with Jonathan Demme and others. I think that Napier always had his eye on a mainstream career and was conflicted about working for Russ. Russ felt this was disloyal."

Napier has his own version of the story. "We were gonna split this thing fifty-fifty, and that was Meyer's idea, because he got on a guilt trip—let's face it, I made the guy a lot of money, right? We'd worked on it a year, and we were out in the desert scouting locations, and finally he just said, 'I can't do it, I can't do it.' I stopped the car. I said, 'How come?' 'I just can't stand to think of *an actor* having that kind of money.'" Despite the squabbles, these are two men cut from a similar cloth, and Napier would give RM his beloved wolf-dog Harry, one of the more significant partners in Meyer's life.

Napier ran into Russ Meyer by accident, as chaperone for a friend on her way to an audition. "I had a lady friend who worked as a stripper. She goes, 'You go down there with me, I don't trust this guy.' West Hollywood off Sunset, as I recall. New Cadillac convertible outside, good neighborhood. Russ was a pretty formidable-looking guy in those days, y'know. Big bearish guy, very brusque and abrupt, had that World War II pencil moustache. You could tell he was eccentric just by looking at him, which sort of interested me."

RM immediately zeroed in on Napier. "Who are you and what do you want?" Napier explained that he was there to play bodyguard for his friend.

"Are you an actor?"

"Well, yeah, I'm trying to be," replied Napier, whose career up till then consisted of one episode of *Star Trek*, a couple episodes of *Mission Impossible,* and two nudie westerns.

"You been in the army?"

"Yeah, I've been in the army, why?"

"I've got a part here that you might be interested in," said Meyer, totally ignoring the girl.

"How 'bout her?" asked the actor.

"Tits aren't big enough."

"Right in front of her!" marveled Napier. The dancer stormed out, and RM had himself a new leading man. "It sounded like fun, man—get a buncha chicks with big tits and run around the desert," Napier recalled.

On location in Panamint Valley, Charles Napier quickly learned that making a Russ Meyer movie wasn't exactly "fun." "I didn't see a lot of people around—it began to take on a thing more like a commando raid than a movie, y'know? Secrecy. Whispers. Secret telephone calls. We shot from daylight to dark, and all my scenes were in the middle of nowhere. Maybe Jim Ryan or Richard Brummer would be there and that would be it. He could've hired a full film crew, but he wanted to control it himself. You'd be locked in the room of some neighborhood house for an interior with the people who owned the place in the living room, wondering what the hell is going on in there—or you'd be planted under a yucca tree in the middle of Death Valley, with Ryan standing there with binoculars and a thirty-ought-six. Pretty bizarre film training."

When cast and crew gathered for meals, no one spoke. "Tension started building from day one, because Meyer made it build," said Napier. "He had control over everybody from the beginning. And you couldn't leave because there was no place to go. There's no way back, there's no way out.

"He got you out there alone and started pitting one against the other. Calling the chicks, telling them we were faggots—and telling us the women were dykes. By the time you got ready to film, we were all ready to kill each other. When we were havin' a kiss and a hug and a hump, you did it with gritted teeth."

$ $ $

Drug boss gangster Franklin (Franklin Bolger) wants another smuggler killed, a mysterious Native American known as the Apache (John Milo), so he enlists the services of crooked sheriff Harry (Charles Napier) and second in command Enrique (Bert Santos) to bump him off. Harry emerges from a bloody showdown in the desert to write a book about the tale. That's ostensibly the plot of *Cherry, Harry and Racquel*, but don't pay too much attention to it, because RM didn't.

As with any Meyer production, injuries were inevitable on the front lines. In one scene a white '55 Plymouth was supposed to careen down a hill and explode, but the car refused to die. "I was the powderman on that show," said Richard Brummer. "We threw that car off the cliff three times. The first two times it still ran." Finally Brummer took a five-gallon can of gasoline, doused the car, then wrapped some paper around a rock, lit the paper, threw the rock and ran like hell. "Before I could get far enough away, it blew up and blew me five or six feet." Brummer wound up with a concussion.*

Near the end of the film, in a scene where Napier is shot by Apache, they ran out of blanks. Meyer started frothing at the mouth, and Brummer again came to the rescue. "After the yelling and screaming about how negligent everybody is, I said, 'Russ, I think I can do something. I can make a fake blank, but the Indian has to miss.' " Brummer emptied out some shells, then replaced the gunpowder with wadded-up toilet paper held together with chewing gum. Once again he cautioned Meyer that the shot would have to miss, because it would still pack a punch. "Get to the first take, the Indian aims, he shoots, and Napier does a complete flip in the air! Down on the ground and

---

* "Meyer loved crashin' all those cars, blowin' 'em apart," said Charles Napier. "He hated anything mechanical, except for the camera. Once I was with him in Hollywood in a brand-new Porsche, and he couldn't figure out how to shift gears. He literally ripped the gear shift out of the thing, broke it." Napier said Meyer went berserk. "We got out and he kicked this car—and kept kicking." A crowd gathered to watch RM bash the car with his shoe.

he doesn't get up! Russ says, 'Cut! Terrific, terrific!' And Napier says, 'I'm *shot*!' "

"Man, that was brutal," Napier recalled. "This thing hit me in the shoulder and flattened me. A knot jumped up on my shoulder the size of a baseball. It hurt like hell after I got up. I knew I'd been shot, I started bitchin' and screamin' and yellin'. Meyer didn't say anything. Nobody said anything. After I finally stopped cussin' everybody out, I said, 'Let's go.' I wasn't about to wimp out on him, and we went on and finished the scene. Nothing was ever said about it. It's pretty bloody in the movie. If shit like that happened today, it would wind up on the front of the *L.A. Times* and people would get fired."

Toward the end of production came the scene that nearly derailed the movie completely: Charles Napier finds Linda Ashton buried naked in a dune and gradually uncovers her sandy body. Meyer was already at odds with Ashton over her pets, a pair of Pomeranian pooches she'd lock in the room of the dive motel where the cast and crew were trapped. The dogs crapped everywhere, and the motel owner—according to RM, "like Chill Wills, only fatter"—was going nuts.

Things went from bad to worse doing the scene in the dunes. "While it was being shot, Russ was putting different lenses on, including long lenses," said Brummer. "Of course, she's nude in that scene. Between takes the girl looked very strange at Russ. And after we got back, she was getting testier and testier. She starts in on Russ—'You were using a telephoto lens in that scene. You were photographing my private parts in close-up!' He couldn't convince her what he was doing was taking close-ups of an elbow or a hand, which is exactly what he was doing. It certainly wasn't her box—Russ isn't interested in that."*

---

* In the confusion, they hadn't gotten the proper reverse angle shots of Napier looking down at Ashton. Back home in West Hollywood, Meyer took Napier up on the roof of his house, shooting close-ups of Charles so all that was visible was the actor and sky. Down below in the house Brummer ran the scene back and forth on the Moviola and shouted out descriptions so Meyer could match the footage shot in the desert. The scene plays seamlessly in the movie.

Ashton walked off the production, leaving Meyer in deep shit. Not only did he have an incomplete movie, but once Brummer had finished cutting it as tight as possible (per RM's wishes, missing scenes or no) the picture ran short. The footage Meyer added simultaneously increased the running time and decreased any possibility for a comprehensible story. He hauled his camera to the San Diego–Mexico border, shot one of his best industrial film montages of signs, boats, fences, and nude women, then slapped on a drug-smuggling narration that afforded Meyer the opportunity to go on a rather whimsical anti-marijuana rant. After that, he came up with an even nuttier idea: dragging his new cast addition, Uschi, into the desert to "symbolically act out the missing footage" as the nonsensical character Soul, which supposedly "added an air of mysticism" to the film.

More like an utter absurdity. *Cherry, Harry and Raquel* is the point in Meyer's work where melodrama meets abstraction head-on—it's as if a *Man's Adventure* hack had been slipped a tab of Ecstasy halfway through writing some macho action tale. Thus there are gleefully nonsensical blasts of Uschi Digard throughout the picture: Uschi nude save for a huge Indian headdress and leather boots, galloping through the desert, jumping up and down on an outdoors couch, striking poses atop various cars; Uschi nude in a pool with a French horn atop her head, beating water with a tennis racquet; Uschi as a nude switchboard operator who speaks no English stationed in the middle of railroad tracks. Personally, my favorite tableau is an exquisite shot of a buck-naked Meyer in the pool (looking businessman-serious, despite his lack of laundry), using an old black phone to ring his film distributor Jack Gilbreath while Digard rests her imposing jugs next to a poolside champagne glass. The image is so preposterous and beautiful.

The first opening of the film—there are three—is a complete assault. An obtuse text crawls up the screen as Meyer bombards us with lightning-fast cuts of Uschi bouncing off the walls of his house, rubbing breasts with some chick, and chomping on phallic vegetables, all intercut with the Hollywood sign, Coit Tower, the Capitol Records building, planes taking off, and God only knows what else. Here is Meyer revisiting the maniacal abstraction of

Mondo Topless and putting it to a (tenuous) narrative—something he'd take to the max on his next picture, *Beyond the Valley of the Dolls*. This is a good thing, since the rest of *Cherry, Harry, and Raquel*—aside from some ingenious visual touches like a striking car-chase-as-bullfight—suffers from anemic dialogue and a pedestrian plot. Only when the TV movie disintegrates and Uschi explodes upon the screen does the film come to life. Digard's crazed exuberance matches Meyer's rampaging camera to a tee.

$ $ $

Robert Pergament, the son of one of Meyer's distributors, was anxious to get into the film business. RM put him to work cleaning prints, running errands, and learning the ways of the cutting room. Pergament dropped an armload of film cans when he first glimpsed the daily routine at RM's Vista Grande home. Meyer was cutting film poolside as Uschi floated nearby, both stark naked. Said a nonplussed Pergament, "I don't know how he could see the Moviola out there in the glare of the sun."

It was in the cutting room that Pergament learned one of the great secrets of RM's editorial style: the removal of blinking eyes. "His movies got kind of cutty because he didn't want anybody blinking their eyes—so all of a sudden, bam! And I thought, 'Gee, well, okay, this is something I'm learning—when I start cutting, don't let anybody blink.' I'd go watch a movie in a theater and say, 'God, he missed an eye blink. Look at all those eye blinks.' It's a good thing I *wasn't* cutting!"

$ $ $

Cherry, Harry and Raquel was another smash for Meyer, and right on the heels of the red-hot *Vixen*. Said distributor Fred Beiersdorf, "When you had a new Russ Meyer picture comin', the screening room would be packed. Every exhibitor in the world would wanna see what's cookin'. You were a major player, a big, big gross."

Meyer was on a roll. Even the hoity-toity critics were taking note. "*Zabriskie Point* in gym socks," wrote Roger Greenspun in an enthusiastic *New York Times* review. "*Cherry, Harry and Raquel* is a rotten film, yet the celluloid stinks with harsh vitality," sniffed Aljean Harmetz in the same paper.

A most significant article on RM appeared in the *Wall Street Journal* on April 24, 1968, a little before *Cherry, Harry and Raquel*'s release. Beneath the title "King Leer: 'Nudie' Filmmaker, Russ Meyer, Scrambles to Outshock Big Studios," Steven M. Lovelady reported a detailed overview of Meyer's career and the impact of his films on Hollywood. We are also told that RM's first movie had a forty-to-one return on his initial investment, a record that "has been matched only by *Gone With the Wind.*"

Hollywood took note, and 20th Century Fox executives Richard Zanuck and David Brown (a team later responsible for such blockbusters as *Jaws* and *Driving Miss Daisy*) read the *Wall Street Journal* story with particular interest. The mainstream picture business was in a near-fatal slump—America just wasn't buying what Hollywood was selling (by 1970, unemployment in the industry reached an all-time high of 42 percent). Fox in particular was coming off a string of big-budget flopperoos and desperately needed a hit. Zanuck and Brown decided they'd talk to this guy Meyer.*

RM drove down to the Fox lot in a beat-up Jeep Charles Napier had piloted in *Cherry, Harry and Raquel*, its police flasher hidden beneath a snood. Meyer wondered what all the hubbub was about, figuring it would amount to zilch. Yep, just some Tinseltown bullshit, like the time American International Pictures tried to rope

---

* In countless interviews as well as in his own book, Meyer told a much different tale of how he landed at Fox. He claimed Richard's father—legendary mogul Darryl F. Zanuck—was the person initially responsible for bringing him in. Allegedly Zanuck senior wanted to see *Vixen* and was told by RM's distributor that no prints were available for a private screening. So Zanuck and playwright Abe Burrows ventured to 42nd Street to see the film. "If this putz can do that for $70,000, imagine what he could do with a million dollars!" was the infamous quote Meyer attributed to Zanuck senior. Both David Brown and Richard Zanuck told me there was no truth to the story and that at that time Zanuck senior was no longer actively involved in moviemaking at the studio. Roger Ebert had no memory of his involvement, either. Nor did his New York distributor Marvin Friedlander, the one Zanuck supposedly contacted for a print. Another Meyer mystery.

him into doing that *Beach Blanket Bingo* crap. In fact, if Meyer is to be believed, he fell asleep while waiting in Zanuck's office, daydreaming about the previous day's liaison with Miss Mattress.

Zanuck told Meyer the score. *Valley of the Dolls* had been a big moneymaker for Fox. They wanted to make a sequel, but the scripts churned out by Jacqueline Susann, the author of the *Dolls* book, were losers. A small fortune had dribbled down the drain, and Fox still had nothing more than a title: *Beyond the Valley of the Dolls*. Now they no longer wanted Susann, but they sure wanted to exploit that juicy title. Zanuck gave Meyer five grand and told him to come up with a treatment.

After the meeting, Meyer drove his Jeep "like a yahooing cowboy" around Fox's New York City set for *Hello, Dolly!* What was happening was truly unbelievable. Russ Meyer, the self-described high-class pornographer, was being given free rein to create a movie at a major Hollywood studio. In no time at all he'd have a million-dollar budget, plus a hundred-man crew to do his every bidding. "I'd been trying to get into Hollywood through the back door all my life, and suddenly the red carpet was being laid out for me." The mountain had come to Meyer.

"As I drove out of the studio after Richard Zanuck said go ahead, I was overcome by this insane laughter. I felt I had pulled off the biggest caper in the world." The caper had just begun.

12

Strapping On Fox

They're all whores, those Hollywood people. They wouldn't do anything good for anybody.

—RUSS MEYER

Richard Zanuck and David Brown were not the only ones who'd taken notice of Russ Meyer's appearance in the pages of the *Wall Street Journal.* On May 8, 1968, two weeks after the article appeared, came a short letter to the editor commending the paper for acknowledging RM, whom the author compared favorably to Howard Hawks and Henry Hathaway. "Is it not time for a major studio to sign Mr. Meyer? His films are more alive and interesting than most current action pictures costing twenty times as much. And his heroines, heaven knows, are technically interesting as well." It was signed Roger Ebert.

Long before becoming America's thumb of cinematic judgment, prior to winning the first Pulitzer awarded for movie criticism in 1975, Roger Ebert was Russ Meyer's unlikeliest partner in crime. He wrote the screenplay for what Meyer considered his masterpiece, *Beyond the Valley of the Dolls,* and, under various aliases, contributed to three more Meyer pictures, and at least an equal amount of unrealized scripts. It was Ebert who came up with the final title of RM's autobiography, *A Clean Breast.* Other than

John Moran, Roger Ebert was Meyer's greatest screenwriting collaborator. "He writes the words, I put in the music," said RM. "Just
like Rodgers & Hammerstein." Although he stopped reviewing
Meyer's pictures once he became involved in them, Ebert remained an outspoken supporter of RM's work in the press, au-
thoring the first major in-depth appreciation of Meyer's entire
oeuvre in a landmark 1973 article for *Film Comment*.

"An odd and talkative kid," Roger Ebert was born June 18,
1942, in Champaign-Urbana, Illinois. He was a movie buff early
on. "Television came late to Champaign-Urbana, and so, for my
age, I spent more time at the movies than most other American
kids." He started his newspaper career at the tender age of fifteen,
as a sportswriter for the *Champaign-Urbana News-Gazette*. "His father died while we were working there," said co-worker Betsy
Hedrick, who maintained that Ebert suddenly became "an instant
grown-up."

One day around 1959 or so, Ebert ventured across the street
from the *News-Gazette*'s offices to the oldest and smallest theater
in town, the Illini, and wandered into a showing of the *The Immoral
Mr. Teas*. "College students jammed the place," said Ebert. "There
were lines down the street. I think the movie ran for two years."
Sitting there in the dark theater, Ebert connected with *Teas*.
"Russ's film was unlike any similar adult film that had ever been
made—it wasn't smutty, it looked great, it was positive, and it was
cheerful, like all of Russ's other films. Russ had a very healthy, go-
ahead, unapologetic way of celebrating the female form." Ebert
followed RM's career with interest, unaware he'd become a major
player in it after that one little letter to the *Wall Street Journal*.

Eagle-eyed Meyer took notice of the dispatch and wrote Ebert
an appreciative note, suggesting they meet. "I found him to be, as
everyone did, one of the most fascinating men I ever met—he was
smart, funny, extroverted, robust, no bullshit," said Ebert, who made
the trek to California, where he watched RM and 166th buddy Fred
Owens shoot an underwater pool scene with Uschi Digard.

Ebert was also on hand when Meyer came to Chicago with Erica Gavin and Harrison Page for the opening of *Vixen*. His most

distinct memory of that visit was watching RM and army cohort Gene Abrams teeter on a ladder in downtown Chicago in zero-degree weather, struggling to affix giant plastic letters spelling out "VIXEN" to the Loop Theater's marquee (Ebert said the letters were so large, the city made the theater remove them, lest the wind blow them off to whack some poor passerby in the head). This was quintessential Meyer: anything for the movie. Ebert was impressed.

Meyer and Ebert shared a certain satirical sense of humor, not to mention a love of movies and food. But perhaps most important, Ebert had, to Meyer's delight, "that wonderful sickness about him. Bosomania." Yes, Roger Ebert was "freako over tits." RM went to great lengths to elaborate this point for the benefit of the press. "Ebert is more debauched than I," Meyer told Kristi Turnquist in 1979. "Ebert is truly a Jekyll and Hyde. We've got to make that clear. He is more into breasts than I could ever hope to be . . . he is absolutely possessed. He's always nudging me, saying, 'Look at that girl!' " The pair were known to heatedly debate the finer points of their fetish with the grave import of art historians arguing the authenticity of a newly unearthed Van Gogh: RM chided Ebert for liking dames with "pendulouso" hanging breasts instead of the up-thrusting, rounded bosom Meyer preferred. Ebert described RM's particular taste as "the guns of Navarone."

Meyer reveled in revealing Ebert's sexual proclivities to the press, cheerfully recounting one night early into the writing of *Dolls* when there was a small get-together at his home including Uschi, Ebert, and some wanna-be starlet who had stripped before Meyer earlier that day at Fox in hopes of getting a part. "Roger got head right on the edge of the pool," boasted RM. "Flapping like a seal. A great scene!" (After which Meyer declared there would be no more exchanges of wonderous body fluids until *Dolls* was completed.)

Ebert had some clarifications in regards to this tale. "I will leave it to Russ to tell his version of this story, since it is more action-packed than mine. The auditioning actress and the girl in the pool were two different women, nor did both events happen on the same day. Actually it's surprising Russ would tell this story the way he does, since he was adamant about *not* connecting the 'casting couch' with his sex life."

Meyer was particularly fond of relating his version of how Ebert had first encountered June Mack, an immense African-American dominatrix who'd go on to star in *Beneath the Valley of the Ultra-Vixens*. "They started to talk, and she described to him, y'know, her whole act. And Roger turned white . . . June finally said, 'Okay, what do *you* want?' And Roger told her, "Everything but the shit and the piss.' " (When asked to confirm this, Ebert had this to say: "I could tell you some stories about June Mack, but that one doesn't ring a bell. It sounds more like a scripted line. I think that if I was talking to June Mack in answer to that question, I would've said, 'Tits.' ")

Not unlike John Moran, when it came to remuneration for his work, Ebert "would have conditions," said Meyer. "For example, he wanted to have screenwriter's money, no salary, and he wanted to drink—he doesn't drink now—and he liked to have a lot of good booze and good food . . . at the end of the week he would have to have a girl with outrageous proportions." Countered Ebert, "I did not require a girl at the end of every week, nor, for that matter, did I get one."

Whatever the details, it was a hell of a team. A paunchy war vet and a somewhat nerdy, bespectacled film critic—neither of these guys were exactly matinee-idol material, and the image of the two of them drowning in a readily available sea of cleavage is a rich one. According to Erica Gavin, Ebert was "awestruck" by Meyer's world. "Russ took him under his wing. Roger was like the son that Russ never had, who'd just gone into puberty and Russ wanted to show him all the whorehouses. It was like, 'Alright, kiddo, I'm gonna show you what tits 'n' ass is all about.' " There are those who felt that RM used the promise of female flesh as a means to lull Ebert's busy mind into submission and thus the critic was somewhat blinded by the Meyer myth. "Then again, I'd believe everything I was told if some outsized mammarific apparition (controlled by King Leer) was pressing her casabas against my distended member," said one anonymous observer.

And so it was that when 20th Century Fox opened its pearly

gates, Russ Meyer got on the horn to Chicago. "I called Ebert. I said, 'You gotta get your keister out here. It's the big time.'" Added Roger, "It was a military campaign, and I was a recruit."

$ $ $

Ebert got a taste of what he was in for on that first night in Tinseltown, when Meyer took him to his favorite Hollywood Boulevard eatery, Musso and Franks. Roger had planned to lose some weight on his time off from the paper, and was about to order some fish when RM stopped him. "Russ forbid that. He said, 'When you're working for me you're gonna eat well, because you have to have your energy.' And he ordered me lamb chops and a baked potato."

Meyer put Ebert up at the Sunset Marquis, at the time the somewhat dusty lodgings for such notables as blacklisted screenwriter Abe Polonsky, comic Jackie Gale, and actor Van Heflin, as well as freak-show crooner Tiny Tim and his fiancée Miss Vicki. "It was very cheap in those days, nineteen dollars a night," said Ebert. "No room service, but you could cook in your room. Russ would pick me up every morning in his big Cadillac. We'd drive off to Fox."

Where Ebert would write. And write. "When Russ didn't hear the typewriter, he'd say, 'What's the matter?' To him typing and writing were the same thing. If you weren't typing, you weren't writing." Meyer and Ebert blasted through a 127-page treatment in ten days. Within three weeks they had their first draft, and in six weeks the script was done. (Given a typewriter and locked in a closet by Meyer, Manny Diez would contribute a few uncredited scenes after Ebert's departure.) Turns out someone actually worked fast enough for RM.

$ $ $

As Roger Ebert notes, Meyer's plots could be summed up in either a sentence or not at all, so for *Dolls*, let's go with the sentence Ebert gave *Time* magazine: "It's a camp sexploitation horror musi-

cal that ends in a quadruple ritual murder and a triple wedding."
Kelly McNamara, Casey Anderson, and Petronella Danforth (re-
spectively, Dolly Read, Cynthia Myers, and Marcia McBroom) are
the Carrie Nations. They come to Hollywood intent on the big
time, and there encounter sex film star Ashley St. Ives, lothario
Lance Rock, lesbian fashion designer Roxanne, omnisexual teen
music tycoon Ronnie "Z-Man" Barzell, and a cast of a thousand
crazies. Sex, drugs, and death result. Fullfilling Meyer's bent desire
for "the picture to end in a positive way," the survivors indeed
marry, including the group's manager, Harrison Allsworth, who
can miraculously walk again despite a live-on-TV suicide attempt
that left him wheelchair bound.

Originally, Fox had asked Meyer to drum up a sequel to *Valley
of the Dolls*; RM and Ebert screened the Mark Robson–directed
tear-jerker, ignored Susann's two attempts at a follow-up screenplay, then proceeded in their own frenzied direction. *Valley* star
Barbara Parkins was under contract to reprise her Anne Welles
role, but Meyer deemed her too expensive for his budget. (He'd
actually asked his former leading lady Alaina Capri—a dead-
ringer for Parkins—to take the role, but she'd just had a child.)
Any ideas of an outright sequel were scotched after Susann, incensed upon hearing Fox was going forth with smut king Russ
Meyer in her place, went to court to get an injunction, and when
that failed, Susann sued Fox outright.* Early drafts of the Ebert
screenplay feature returning characters from *Valley* as well as a sex-
novel authoress named Ashley Famous, surely a playful jab at Su-

---

* With Susann on the offensive, Fox was anxious to distance any claim that *Beyond* was the offspring of *Valley*. Ads for *Dolls* read, "It's not a sequel . . . you've
never seen anything like it before!" In his autobiography Meyer revealed that an
alternate ad campaign was prepared that had the movie titled *Russ Meyer's Dolls*.
    A disaster for Fox, Susann's suit wasn't settled until after her death in August
1975. "The trial began in Pasadena with twelve old ladies who drive very old
cars, and for whom Russ Meyer was anathema," said David Brown, who believed
that the simple act of showing *Beyond the Valley of the Dolls* to the jurors sank
their defense. "They exhibited the picture and that was enough. We lost everything." Susann's widower Irving Mansfield collected $1,425,000 in a settlement
from Fox.

sann herself. (The character became sex film star Ashley St. Ives in the end, the name change due to concerns over reprisal from the then-powerful Ted Ashley talent agency and the career switch undoubtedly made to avoid further trouble with Susann.)

In the hands of Meyer and Ebert, *Dolls* became its own animal, possessing a crazy anarchy not seen before in a studio film. With Fox's cash, RM was going for broke. "He made it clear that the key word in the title was 'beyond,' " wrote Ebert. "*Dolls* was supposed to be a satire of an exploitation movie in which the very genre itself would come under attack." But there was no master plan at work. "We never talked about our purpose," Ebert admitted. "We only talked about the plot." Thus the character Z-Man was suddenly revealed to be a woman in the film only when Ebert happened to invent a scene where "he" reveals his breasts.* "I said, '*Russ!* You're not gonna believe this! Z-Man's a woman! He's been a woman the whole time.' " RM's response? "You can never have too many women in a picture." Not that anything was changed in the previous 174 pages to foreshadow such an outrageous conceit; this was just another oddball explosion in a picture full of them. Wrote Ebert, "Meyer wanted everything in the movie except the kitchen sink." From Roger he got it.

Russ Meyer had arrived at Fox at just the right moment. The studio was near collapse following a string of big-budget flops like *Star!* and *Hello, Dolly!* Fox publicist Jet Fore, who'd become a life-long friend to both Meyer and Ebert, begged for their help. "He told us one night that our job was to save the studio, because everybody was going to *Easy Rider* and all they had were two war pictures and a Western. Of course, it was *M*A*S*H*, *Patton*, and *Butch Cassidy*, but they didn't know they were gonna be hits."

And with that Meyer and Ebert rode into Fox with their six-guns blazing. And while they didn't exactly wear white hats, in their own demented way they did help "save" the studio, with a

---

* "*If* he was a woman," notes Ebert. "I don't know what Z-Man was . . . maybe he was a transsexual. I never answered that question in my own mind." In the October 27, 1969, draft of the script, Z-Man/Superwoman is described as a transvestite.

picture that would outrage not only the studio that made it, but most of America.

$ $ $

Roger Ebert had arrived in Los Angeles the same week the gruesome Sharon Tate murders hit the papers. "This cast a pall over Hollywood—the notion that you live this lifestyle, but it could lead to your death. And that seemed to dovetail with the message of the original *Valley of the Dolls*. So I said, 'Russ, that was about three actresses that found fame and fortune, but some of them were destroyed by booze, drugs, and sex. Let's just make 'em an all-girl rock trio. Have them come to Hollywood, and have some of them be destroyed the same way.' He went for it." This cross-fertilization of Charles Manson and Jacqueline Susann birthed the Carrie Nations, a femme band that was a far cry from any group muddied by Woodstock. "A hippie in Hollywood was certainly very different than what a hippie anywhere else was," noted John Waters. "The Carrie Nations hardly looked like hippies. They looked like showgirls on LSD."

"Everything was unmentionable, but nothing was unimaginable," wrote Joan Didion of Los Angeles in 1968–69. "This mystical flirtation with the idea of 'sin'—this sense that it was possible to go 'too far' and that many people were doing it . . . black masses were imagined, and bad trips were blamed." Not only was coverage of the Manson murders everywhere you looked, the mayhem at Altamont was another indication all was not groovy with the Woodstock Nation. Even Hollywood was going a little berserk: among the top twenty grossing films of 1969 were such shockers as *I Am Curious (Yellow)*, *Three in the Attic*, *Midnight Cowboy*, and *Easy Rider*. An X-rated United Artists film had won the Oscar, for chrissakes—John Schlesinger's *Midnight Cowboy*—and Dennis Hopper's hippie freakout *Easy Rider* proved, at least for a moment, crazy longhairs could be boffo box office, and to the tune of $40 million. No wonder Meyer turned his X-ray vision on the youth culture, and what a strange set of peepers to be seeing it through.

"Russ was not affected by the love generation," said John

Waters. "The sixties *never* affected him. He certainly wasn't into drugs or gay people or hipness—he didn't pretend to be either. Russ was untouched by hipness, in a way." But Meyer was also a permanent kid. He never grew up! He understood excitement, excess, youthful energy, thumbing your nose at everything. At the same time there's that curmudgeonly Mother Meyer side of RM: everybody is shit, young or old. Put those two elements together, add Ebert's *Mad* magazine zaniness, and you begin to get where *Beyond* is coming from.

Not to mention that Russ Meyer and Roger Ebert were two very unlikely prospects to chronicle the Los Angeles music scene. Although RM frequently utilized rock's beat to propel his films, "he hated it," said editor Richard Brummer. Meyer's preferences leaned more toward big bands and Dixieland, with an occasional shot of Engelbert Humperdinck. "I like rock and roll," Ebert insisted to this author, but withering comments from his work might suggest otherwise. For example, in his review of *Dead Man*, Ebert writes, "A mood might have developed here, had it not been for the unfortunate score by Neil Young, which for the film's final thirty minutes sounds like nothing so much as a man repeatedly dropping his guitar." Of Bob Dylan he's written, "Since he cannot really sing, there is the assumption that he cannot be performing to entertain us, and that therefore there must be a deeper purpose." Ebert on *The Last Waltz:* "The overall tenor of the documentary suggests survivors at the ends of their ropes.... These are not musicians at the top of their art, but laborers on the last day of the job."

So how did these two outsiders research a satire on the current rock scene? They made it up. "We wanted the movie to seem like a fictionalized exposé of real people but we had no real information as inspiration for the characters," wrote Ebert. So, although the spark behind Z-Man had been fiendish pop producer Phil Spector, Ebert happily admitted that neither he nor Meyer had ever met or even knew much of anything about the man. Likewise for Randy Black, a vague approximation of Muhammad Ali.

Meyer went to new extremes with the look of the film, lighting each scene as if "there were eighty-nine searchlights," said *Dolls* composer Stu Philips. "Like a comic strip." From the gibberish people talk to the hollow "now" sound of the score to the movie's brash visuals, nothing registers as remotely real in this film, down to the big-mama voice raging out of pipsqueak Dolly Read. "That inauthenticity is perhaps the point of *Beyond the Valley of the Dolls,*" wrote critic Stuart Klawans. "Here is sixties youth culture as seen, and warped, by a World War II vet. . . . Mr. Meyer had by this time reduced other social milieus to burlesque. Now it was the hippies' turn."

$ $ $

Richard Zanuck (now president of Fox) and David Brown were in Cannes when they received the Meyer-Ebert treatment, and on September 8, 1969, they sent an enthusiastic three-foot cable giving the green light. Despite some reservations about all the debauchery and murderous mayhem present in the pages sent, everything would remain in the finished film save one scene, and curiously enough it involved a studio mogul character named Maurice Fruchtman attempting to get in the pants of Casey Anderson during a bogus script reading. It was cut (which had Cynthia Myers miffed, as this was her big scene—and the tenuous explanation why she becomes a man-hater who falls for lesbian fashion designer Roxanne).

Zanuck and Brown approved a million-dollar budget (nearly the same amount had already been blown on Susann's treatments). Meyer vowed to come in under and did, shooting almost the entire film on existing sets and paying none of the actors (outside of Fox contract player Edy Williams) more than $500 a week. For his trouble, RM received $80,000 and was given 10 percent of the profits, his own suite of offices, and access to Darryl F. Zanuck's private steam room. "Russ was on friendly turf—at least cash-friendly," said Brown. Meyer had a few demands of his own—mainly the freedom to bring in members of his own cast and crew. "It was my shot at making a film for a major studio. I thought I might not get to make another, so I was damn well going to make the film I wanted to make."

Incredibly, the studio let Meyer do exactly that, with little or no interference. "Russ did this as an independent movie under Fox's banner," said composer Stu Philips. "Russ made a certain kind of movie at a certain price, and we didn't want to mix in," explained David Brown. "We approved the script and the making of the movie, and he brought it in under budget, under schedule. That was good enough for us." According to Ebert, one man whom Meyer butted heads with was his esteemed director of photography, Fred Koenekamp, who the next year won an Oscar for his work on *Patton* (which, ironically enough, utilized some of RM's combat footage). Meyer had the cojones to question his DP's focus (a picture could never be sharp enough for RM). According to Ebert, Koenekamp felt that "no other director—let alone some sleazeball from poverty gulch—had ever been so demanding. Russ was a perfectionist."

The music for *Beyond the Valley of the Dolls* was also created on Meyer's terms. Over the objections of Fox music head Lionel Newman, RM insisted on bringing in Stu Philips, who'd produced and co-written the title song for *Cherry, Harry and Raquel;* Bill Loose, responsible for many Meyer soundtracks of the seventies; and old standby Igo Kantor (*Dolls* was his last for RM, as he'd enrage Meyer by not being available due to his own directorial work). Lynn Carey, a knockout blonde with a voice so huge that Philips had her stand across the studio from the mike, recorded the vocals Carrie Nation lead singer Kelly McNamara was to lip-sync. The daughter of actor Macdonald Carey, Lynn became infamous for her group Mama Lion's shocking cover photo of Carey breast-feeding a lion cub. "They put pablum on my nipple and he actually was sucking. He had no teeth, thank God. I had visions of being destroyed." Carey, who had appeared in *Lord, Love a Duck,* herself had a figure that could quell an angry mob, and Meyer in fact asked her to be in *Dolls,* but she declined, although somehow she'd muster the courage to pose for *Penthouse* in 1972. Carey co-wrote a couple of numbers for the picture, most notably "Find It," the high-octane opening song, which she wrote on the spot with Philips and which was somehow inspired by the opening scene in which Erica Gavin gets a mouthful of lead. "I pictured this woman getting married in a nuclear sunset after her head's been chopped off," said Carey. "It's a bizarre song." Much to Lynn's dismay, political infighting resulted in her vocals being replaced on the actual soundtrack album by unknown Ami Rushes.

Like *Ben-Hur, Dolls* seemed to have a cast of thousands, among them some of the most alluring young creatures Tinseltown had to offer. RM found three new stunners to play the Carrie Nations. Marcia McBroom, drums, was a black former New York fashion model. Out front were two ex–*Playboy* centerfolds, English import Dolly Read and Cynthia Meyers, a wide-eyed Ohio innocent still known to use the word "gosh"—and whose 39DD-24-36 body earned her a legion of particularly rabid fans.

In loyalty to his veteran thespians, Meyer shoehorned as many as he could fit into *Dolls:* Erica Gavin, Harrison Page, Lavelle Roby, Duncan McLeod, Charles Napier, Garth Pillsbury, Bert Santos, Joe Cellini, Veronica Erickson, and Haji, wandering through the picture wearing nothing but black body paint. The film is also blessed by Henry Rowland playing exiled Nazi Martin Bormann, the first of three such appearances in RM's films. Pam Grier, in her debut film role, is alleged to be present as well. Looking more toothless than ever, a bewigged Princess Livingston boogaloos through *Dolls* with a lizard-tongued Stan Ross, famous for his TV work on Milton Berle's *Texaco Theater.* The party scenes in *Dolls* dazzle, capturing, as Ebert has pointed out, the lunatic energy of a Jack Davis cartoon. "I grew up in Hollywood," said Erica Gavin. "Russ captured it. That party is so disgustingly, pukey Hollywood." Hugh Hefner himself visited the *Dolls* set, devoting a *Playboy* layout to the film and its women in its July 1970 issue.*

---

* Meyer would tell at least two interviewers that Elvis Presley also visited the set. "Bullshit!" said Dolly Read. "Never happened."

$ $ $

The big secret to Meyer's direction on *Dolls*? None of the actors were told the movie was supposed to be funny. "You create the greatest satire in the world if you direct everybody at right angles and don't say it's a comedy, just play everything straight. If you try to make it funny, it doesn't come off," RM told David K. Frasier decades later. "Two actors on *Dolls* understood—John La Zar and Michael Blodgett." The rest were left to stumble around in the dark. A baffled Charles Napier would confront Ebert with the observation, "You wrote this, Roger. It reads like a comedy to me. But, hell, Russ treats it like Eugene O'Neill."

Shooting began on December 2, 1969, and continued for approximately three months. In the eye of the *Dolls* hurricane sat big Papa Russ and his starlets, a gaggle of girls saddled with the uneasy task of making Daddy happy. No doubt the making of his first big-budget picture upped the stress a notch. "Meyer was a man on the edge, always ready to explode," said Stu Phillips, who witnessed Meyer constantly barking at the girls to lose weight. "He was very hard on them."

Dolly Read vividly recalled tooling along Pico Boulevard in her brown Dodge Dart on the way to 20th Century Fox to interview for her part in *Dolls*. Looming above the street was a gigantic billboard for Barbra Streisand in *Hello, Dolly!*, which our Dolly took as an omen: "I knew I was gonna get the part." Her excitement was soon tempered by repeated clashes with Meyer. "Russ scared me to death—I thought he looked like Charles Manson. He had these wild eyes, those eyebrows. You didn't want to get on the wrong side of him. And he knew it. Everyone was on eggs around him. He was like a serial killer director."

Early on, Meyer leveled Dolly at a rehearsal meeting with other members of the production when he asked to inspect her merchandise. "He wanted to see my boobs. And I was quite proud of my boobs. So I showed them, and Russ was just so horrible. He said, 'Well, they've *really* drooped.' I was devastated. He knew how to push buttons.

"He kept telling me I was gonna be fired during the rehearsals," Read went on to say. "Russ would tell me at least two, three times a day that I could be easily replaced, I had to put more into the singing. I was an absolute wreck." Much to Meyer's annoyance, Read was spending weekends in Palm Springs with her future husband, comedian Dick Martin. "Russ wanted her to stick around and do rehearsing," said Meyer's assistant, Manny Diez. "He would not speak to her." So he spoke to Diez, who then relayed his comments to Dolly.

When Dolly's parents arrived for a visit from the UK, Meyer then confounded Read with his gentler side by having a couch with a fold-out bed delivered to her apartment. Over the Christmas break, he took Dolly, her parents, and fellow Carrie Nation Marcia McBroom on an all-expenses-paid trip to San Francisco. And when an exhausted Read ended up in the hospital following production, RM was the first to visit her, a dozen red roses in his hand. "I think Russ loved women," said Dolly. "But he wanted to dominate them, be in control." She felt Meyer had "a great deal of anger inside of him that was probably a sad anger. Russ liked beauty, prettiness, but then he wanted to destroy it—and then have the ability to restore it."

Erica Gavin had a particularly hard time on the *Dolls* set. In the aggressively tasteless opening minutes of the picture she's shown lying asleep in bed. Oblivious to a gloved hand clutching a gun invading her space, she instinctively sucks on the barrel before getting her brains blown out.* Erica saw the slaughter as symbolic. "I was Russ's favorite child until *Beyond the Valley of the Dolls* and his new Hollywood clique. Then I was an adopted Cinderella, a leftover that didn't quite cut it. I wasn't his star anymore, I wasn't his important girl. And all these other girls were."

---

* The gloved hand belonged to actor John La Zar, who told me he killed time on the day-long shoot for the scene by playing with Erica Gavin's nether regions. "He did not!" an angry Gavin responded. "Unless I just don't remember—which is highly possible." Erica admits to being so zonked on drugs during those years that "anyone could say anything about me and it might be true."

Gavin had lost considerable weight after the shock of seeing herself in *Vixen,* and RM, further perturbed that Gavin had jettisoned her Spock-like *Vixen* eyebrows, took it as more betrayal. "Russ would say, 'Can you feed her? Can you get her to *eat?*' " recalled Cynthia Meyers, whose on-screen dalliance with Gavin raised blood pressures for many a viewer. "I said, 'Erica, do you like milkshakes?' "*

Intrigue bubbled after Gavin had managed to talk RM into hiring one of her fellow dancers from the Losers for the party scenes—a notorious Asian chick by the name of Bebe Louie. "Bebe Louie had long black hair. She was very exotic," said Haji. "She wore those sleeveless Japanese dresses, and would stand in one spot and shimmy and her dress would crawl all the way up to her butt. And she'd be swingin' her hair. Bebe brought the house down." Erica had a tortured affair with Louie that went on for ten years. "She was probably the first girl I was really in love with. She had the most gorgeous little cone tits. Everything about her was perfect. She'd walk around naked with no makeup, nothing. Just take her and put her into my veins, okay?"

Cynthia felt Bebe Louie did everything she could to undermine Gavin's performance. "Bebe threw a few daggers with her eyes and all of a sudden Erica's run off to her trailer. I was like, 'You kissed me yesterday, what's wrong today?' " Gavin laughed when I asked about the grip Louie had on her. "Bebe was a fucking cold bitch, man. I liked to live vicariously through her. She would just tell people to get fucked if they fucked with us. And Bebe was very possessive. She didn't like anybody else around me." Other romances revved up the *Dolls* set—John La Zar confessed that during the wrap party he was actually caught by his then-wife

---

* Apparently inspired by the TV actor Bill Bixby (star of *The Courtship of Eddie's Father*), Myers insisted she had an actual orgasm during the scene. Expressing her concern over playing such an intimate moment while having dinner with the actor, "Bill said, 'Blow their minds. Don't try to fake it, just do it.' " The orthopedic surgeon Myers was engaged to at the time wasn't so supportive, as she found out when she took him to see *Dolls.* "This poor guy from Minnesota, he almost had a heart attack—he kept getting lower in the seat . . . he had beads of sweat all over his forehead. The poor man couldn't take it, he thought I was a lesbian!" The couple broke up soon after.

while entertaining a *Dolls* actress in his trailer—and Michael Blodgett seems to have bagged any female who fell for his dubious charm.

"In 1969–70," said Blodgett, "this town was just sizzling . . . it was a drug culture. Sex was wide open. There weren't any diseases or problems." No doubt this contributed to many off-camera soap operas that mirrored the *Dolls* action on-screen. "There was arrogance, there was pettiness, there were sexual flings," said Charles Napier. "Meyer orchestrating it all, feeling good. I was relegated to a small part, but I also had a producer's role—which was to spy on everyone else and report to Meyer. Who was doing what to whom, who was havin' an affair. I was like his secret KGB."

"Russ would play one against the other," said Dolly Read. "I had the feeling he was playing Erica against me. And me against Erica." Read felt that RM was easier on the male actors, although he did make use of a clash between John La Zar and Michael Blodgett. "John was a classically trained actor and Michael liked to wing it," said Manny Diez. "Michael would never do the scene twice the same way. For him it was a party. La Zar took it very, very seriously." Things came to a head during rehearsals at RM's spiffy new Avenue of the Stars Century Towers apartment. "La Zar went after Blodgett, and Russ and I had to separate them," said Diez. So what did Meyer do? He made them stay in the same trailer during production. "Russ did that on purpose," said La Zar.

Blodgett is memorable as one of the oilier characters of the *Dolls* ensemble—Lance Rocke, a despicable Don Juan with limpid eyes, feathered bangs, and a self-satisfied smirk. Dolly Read took great pleasure in derailing Blodgett during one of Meyer's trademark through-the-bedsprings love scenes. Right before the take, Dolly, gazing intently upon some imaginary imperfection on his face, murmured, "Uh-oh," then, halfheartedly, "It's fine, it won't show." Blodgett panicked. "Cut! Cut! Makeup! *Makeup!*" "He was *too* pretty," Read chuckled. "Blodgett had an ego so enormous that I just loved to get him. He was so full of himself."

There are two supernovas in *Dolls*: John La Zar as Z-Man and Edy Williams as Ashley St. Ives. They play essentially the same part: irresistibly malevolent sexual predators, unsettling alien creatures that exist only to charm and overpower the humans they're about to swallow whole. As a land shark in a crocheted bikini, with a lion's mane of honey-brown hair and a glint in her eye perhaps shared only by the criminally insane, Edy talks in the unsettling throaty purr of a Marilyn on Quaaludes, uttering such memorable profanities as "You're groovy, boy. . . . I'd like to strap you on some-time." Personally, I find Ashley to be a hell of a lot scarier than Z-Man/Superwoman, which is saying something. Edy Williams is so intense you feel she might jump right off the screen and take a bite out of you. "Her idea of sexuality was the flaring of the nos-trils," said RM. Not the most popular figure in the Meyer circle, Edy, some cruel wags felt, was only playing herself. Director and star would soon be married.

With his menacing good looks and ridiculous pseudo-Elizabethan doggerel, La Zar's Z-Man is one of Meyer's most pe-culiar creations: an Adonis sporting a secret vagina. Z-Man's delivery is as odd as Ashley's. Listen to the way La Zar tortures meaning out of Superwoman and you won't be surprised that the inspiration for his performance was Olivier doing Richard III. Z-Man owns many of the most beloved lines of dialogue in the movie, such as "This is my happening and it freaks me out!" Not to mention "You will drink the black sperm of my vengeance!" (Meyer was so fond of the last line he repeated it to greatly dimin-ished effect in two later pictures.)

The film climaxes in a wild four-character masquerade orgy that ends in same-sex couplings. Lance Rocke, dressed only in leopard-skin briefs as Jungle Boy, partners off with Z-Man, who's now become his alter ego, Superwoman. Outfitted as Robin, the Boy Wonder (with Cynthia Myers wearing the actual togs Burt Ward wore for the *Batman* TV show), Casey Anderson slinks off with fashion designer Roxanne, herself costumed in a slightly vague Catwoman-with-cape get-up (too bad, as in an early draft she was dressed as Batman). The two women manage to get it on, but some-how it's a little more difficult for Superwoman and Jungle Boy, and after one embrace ("My first movie kiss was kissing another man," groused La Zar) things become even more convoluted as we dis-cover Z-Man/Superwoman is actually a woman. Then the mood turns murderous, as the end result of these sexual hijinks is death for all involved. As *Village Voice* critic Michael Musto noted, the movie's "gay content is deliriously unenlightened ... where the mere suggestion of queerness practically drives characters insane."

Transformation into womanhood wasn't easy for La Zar, who insisted on wearing sideburns as a reassurance of his masculinity. "The thing I didn't want to do is wear the prosthetic tits. I begged not to do it." The rubberized knockers were created by John Chambers, who'd won an Oscar in 1968 for his work on *Planet of the Apes*. "They had to bake the motherfuckers," said La Zar, who spent two weeks with cleavage. "They had to shave my chest every morning and glue 'em on me." At some point toward the end of La Zar's ordeal, Meyer surveyed John and his boobs and muttered, "Y'know what you need, kid, after this? A good Western."*

$ $ $

Despite her not-ample-enough-for-Russ bosom, soon-to-be-wife Edy Williams was the walking, talking embodiment of Meyer Female Philosophy 101, and she knew how to pitch it. "The way Indians could sniff out buffalo, Edy can sniff out flashbulbs," wrote reporter Burt Prelutsky. "At the mere mention of the word 'camera' her lips automatically moisten and her teeth part." Decked out in some skimpy concoction designed to make passersby walk into walls, she'd muse to one reporter, "There is a certain satisfaction in frustrating men. I'm getting back at them and it's a good feeling." In her prime, every day was a press conference for Edy. "You mustn't let a man feel too sure," she instructed. "Instead of giving him your whole box of candy, you've got to ration it out one piece at a time."

Five feet eight inches, most of it long hair and legs, she was born Edwina Beth Williams in Salt Lake City on July 9, 1942,

---

* La Zar said playing Z-Man wasn't exactly the best thing for his career. He'd go out for interviews, and people would express their surprise that he wasn't like his crazy character. "If I was really like that, I'd be in San Quentin," La Zar replied. *Dolls* certainly didn't shoot anybody to stardom. "Nobody came out of that movie," said Charles Napier.

and raised a Mormon. "I'm a baaaad Mormon. I drink and I
smoke. *Shoot!*" With the help of her mother—"She made some
of the dresses I wore—or didn't wear"—Williams racked up
wins in many a beauty contest: Miss Sherman Oaks, Miss Beverly Hills, Miss San Fernando Valley, Miss Los Angeles. In January 1967, she became a contract player at 20th Century Fox.
Before Meyer came along, her acting career consisted of bit
parts in *The Naked Kiss* (Williams does a cameo as a cigarette girl
in a whorehouse; listen for her few lines, as the mannered delivery is already cemented in place) and *I Sailed to Tahiti with an
All-Girl Crew.*

Ebert takes responsibility for introducing Meyer to Edy in the
Fox commissary. Both RM and Manny Diez maintained it was
Richard Zanuck who insisted that Williams be cast in *Dolls.* "Russ
did not want her," said Diez. But Meyer and Williams had a thing
or two in common. "He conned everybody," said Edy. "Russ is really a schemer. He was telling me, 'Oh, *you're* going to be the star.
You've got the greatest role in the whole film.' Well, he was telling
the same story to all the other girls, too."

On the set, Williams proved to be no pushover, and by her own
admission she behaved like "a spoiled bitch." A few years later Edy
complained to writer Tony Crawley, "I didn't look too good in *Dolls.*
I was on downers." Although Williams was most famous for wearing next to nothing in public, nudity on the silver screen was another matter. "I am really inhibited. When I first met Russ on *Dolls*
I had never even done a nude scene. I had to take off the bottom
part, my panties. . . . I was shaking. I even cried afterwards. I felt
like I'd been disgraced. Russ and I got really close after that."

The classic Edy/*Dolls* moment occurs when Ashley St. Ives
pulls up in her Rolls-Royce to seduce sad-sack pretty boy Harris
Allsworth in its sumptuous backseat, musing loudly during the act
over whether a Bentley or a Rolls was better for doing the dirty
deed. A clash between two forces of nature like Edy and Russ was
inevitable. Williams wasn't used to a director who not only wanted
her naked, but demanded she hold her own light reflectors. Edy
stormed off the set, but by the time she returned, something
about this crazy chick had already clicked with The Ultimate

Voyeur. "I really met my husband when I was seducing another guy in the back of a Rolls-Royce. It was bizarre."

$ $ $

Unsurprisingly, a major Hollywood studio proved to be far smuttier than any Russ Meyer set. One Fox executive bitched to Meyer that Erica Gavin wouldn't "swing," while Cynthia Myers complained that another tried repeatedly to "meet" with her. But outside of the evening spent poolside with Ebert, RM didn't indulge during the *Dolls* production. "People could not believe Russ could be around such beautiful women and not be bedding them all— and he wasn't bedding *any* of them," said Manny Diez.

He did pimp for his friends, however. Diez related what must be the most curious casting-couch tale of all time, one which involves RM, and yet doesn't. Jet Fore, Meyer's publicist buddy at Fox, had become enamored with a Vegas showgirl and unwisely told her he could get her in Meyer's movie. Because he was fond of Fore, RM begrudgingly agreed to see the girl. "She and Jet come in to the secretary's office, and she was spectacular. Six feet, an endless series of fabulous curves," said Diez. Meyer met with her, dispatched the pair, then beelined for Manny's office.

"Russ comes in and closes the door, which was very unusual. He said, 'Did you see her?' I said I had. Now, to be in this picture, this girl would've done him in a New York minute. So Russ says, 'OK, here's the deal: I've told her Manny Diez is the one who decides if she's gonna be in this picture. I told her to come back tonight at six.' We hadn't started *Dolls* yet, everybody went home at five. He said, 'You can fuck her on your sofa or you can fuck her on mine, but tomorrow you will give me a full report.' And I had a giant problem with this, because I really can't do that with a total stranger—I just can't!"

At six, the guard buzzed, telling Diez his visitor had arrived. "Everybody was gone, I was in the office by myself—and she walks into the office with an obviously gay guy. And I thought, 'Oh boy, I'm off the hook, because I'm not here alone with her.' " Even though Meyer had her in mind only for the nude walk-on part that

Haji ended up with, he instructed Diez, "Build this up, make her think she's got a line, give her something to read."

"So I felt even worse. I've got a page of the script. And I give it to her and I say, 'See this piece right here? You learn that.'" While she studied her line, Diez bullshitted with her pal about how they'd driven down from Vegas in a Volkswagen. A few minutes later, "she opens the door, sticks her head out, and says, 'I'm ready.' I go inside, close the door, sit on the sofa next to her, and say, 'Let me have the line.' So she says it. I give my line, she gives her line. I thought, 'That's enough of this nonsense,' so I stood up, walked to the door, and said, 'Fine. As far as *I'm* concerned, you've got the part.'

"I'll never forget the look on her face—the typical deer trapped in headlights. Because she thought, 'This guy's gonna want head, he's gonna want something.' She said, 'That's *it?*' I said, 'Yeah.' So she got up, gave me a big hug, and she and the guy leave. The next morning Russ said, 'How did it go?'

"I shoulda lied. Shoulda said she was great. But I told the truth. Russ was livid. How *dare* she? 'Cause he wanted me to get laid. He picked up the phone and called Jet and said, 'Jet, that cunt's not gonna be in the picture.' End of story."

$ $ $

With shooting completed, Meyer hunkered down in the editing room. RM claimed that once the movie was cut, he proceeded to "recut the entire picture, even though I had two picture editors. This took three months." Meyer outdid himself here, because the pace of *Dolls* is brutal; like its maker, it never stops. If you look at the script, you'll find that he's snipped away every extraneous bit of dialogue—and some that are not so extraneous. Anything to keep the picture moving, regardless of whether it made sense. "Cut, cut, cut, cut, cut—get a rhythm," Meyer told David K. Frasier. "A punishing rhythm. Pummeling the audience." The trailer is even more extreme: barely registering blips of outrageous images covered with overheated text, the earnest narrator shouting RM's bombastic hype.

Dolls is rich with all sorts of absurd personal touches: Meyer scoring a beheading with the mighty 20th Century Fox logo theme; Ebert's homage to *Citizen Kane* during the death of Harris Allsworth; Meyer naming one lead after an obscure character actor (Porter Hall) and another—the abortion doctor Downs—after a particularly despised 166th commanding officer. Perhaps the only legitimate complaint about *Dolls* is that, like so many other Meyer films, it feels a bit too long. Meyer sets the bar so high there's no way to maintain such a fevered pitch, and the picture sputters to a close. "I always have seven endings," said RM. "How do you come down? 'The End' never got anybody a laugh."

Meyer tangled with the MPAA over the movie's rating. According to RM, Zanuck had instructed him to make an "R minus" picture—as hard as possible without losing the R. But the MPAA slapped on an X. At the studio's insistence, RM returned to the ratings board three times to plead his case, to no avail.* Meyer would bitterly complain forever after that the picture got the dreaded rating because of who he was, not what it contained. "I think so, too, because I don't think there was anything in it that really deserved an X," said Richard Zanuck. Meyer was doubly indignant because he'd cut nudity to get an R and, with the release date looming, it was too late to put any of it back. "There was never any other version than the one you've seen—but there could've been," maintained Ebert. "Russ always regretted that, because he had great nude scenes."**

Fox was not happy to be saddled with another X. Unfortunately *Dolls* would be tainted by association with the lingering stink of Fox's *other* X-rated scandal, the disastrous Raquel Welch–Rex Reed sex change epic *Myra Breckenridge* (one Fox

---

* Meyer and the ratings board were not exactly the bitter enemies one might think. "We rather enjoyed him, actually," said board veteran Al Van Schmus. "Russ took his creations with a sense of humor. He'd say, 'I'm gonna send a picture over.' I'd start laughing, and I'd say, 'OK, Russ, you've got an X immediately.' "
** A number of bits were cut from the movie, including a fashion-shoot *Blow-up* parody and a background scene of Kelly McNamara at her mother's funeral, in which her coffinbound mother (played by an "aged" Dolly Read) relates the facts of her life in couplets with music. "Almost like rap," according to Read.

board member had simply quit in disgust due to the studio's involvement). Based upon the celebrated Gore Vidal novel, the movie version was an incomprehensible mess. Undiscerning (and invariably offended) viewers lumped the pictures together, and unfairly; *Myra*'s chaos was the result of ineptitude, while that of *Dolls* was lovingly designed. The result was Fox's distribution arm wanted to dump *Dolls* in wide release and be done with it. Meyer fought them and Zanuck backed him up. According to RM, when told there were no theaters available for a special release on such short notice, Zanuck barked, "Well, then *buy* one." *Dolls* premiered at the Pantages Theater on Hollywood Boulevard on June 17, 1970. It took in $7.5 million in its first six months, becoming one of *Variety*'s top grossers of the year. Financially, it was a hit. The reviews were another story.

$ $ $

Dolls is a diabolical achievement. There is something so peculiar and particular about its brand of nothingness. Unlike *Pussycat*, which possesses certain passions, however bizarre, this picture is defiantly empty, a glittering, glowing void in a gold frame. It's a genuinely nihilistic picture, utterly cynical about humanity. "I have no message," boasted RM, and here's the proof: a picture that seems to exist only to thrust a big middle finger to the world.

The critical reaction to *Dolls* was violent, as if Meyer had abducted the critics' children and shot the family dog. "Utter garbage," sniffed Stanley Kauffman of the *New Republic*, who felt the film's climax went "past trash into obscenity. . . . If this is what 20th Century Fox needs to save itself, why bother?" Critic John Simon found *Dolls* to be "true pornography. . . . The only people it can arouse are those whose idea of sex is totally divorced from reality." "As funny as a burning orphanage," said *Variety*. "A treat for the emotionally retarded, sexually inadequate, and dimwitted . . . a grievously sick mélange of hyper-mammalian girls . . . a totally degenerate enterprise," wrote a disturbed Charles Champlin in the *Los Angeles Times*. In a lengthy companion piece covering both *Dolls* and *Myra Breckenridge*, Champlin went on to bemoan the "breakdown" the films represented, there being "not a damn thing redemptive about either one of them." "He thought it was the end of the film business!" chuckled Meyer. "It was really great to have that sonofabitch go off. . . . I was in SATANIC glee!"

Screw awarded the film a mere 11 percent on its infamous phallic-shaped review chart—the Peter Meter—and demanded that the severed head of Meyer be hoisted high in Times Square. And at the opposite end of the spectrum, RM's old nemesis Charlie Keating agreed, holding a rally in Hollywood to protest the picture and demanding that both Meyer and Richard Zanuck be "arrested and jailed."

Even those who'd defended RM in the past were vexed. "Meyer's earnestly vulgar sensibility . . . has become patronizing," said Vincent Canby in the *New York Times*. "Maybe *Dolls* represents the end of what he can do," mused Leslie Fiedler, the highbrow critic who'd championed RM at the beginning of his career. For some the outrage still simmers over thirty years later: *Los Angeles Times* critic (and longtime Meyer admirer) Kevin Thomas declared to this author that *Dolls* is "a piece of shit. There's something unsavory about it, unattractively decadent, godawful and depraved."

At the time, fingers were pointed at Roger Ebert, who some felt had turned RM into a parody of himself. (Meyer fans seem to be divided over his scriptwriters: there are Roger Ebert and John Moran camps, Beatles-versus-Stones style.) "Ebert forced Meyer to acknowledge what he was all about," wrote Myron Meisel, declaring it "a disaster." Even John Simon found the union a mismatch: "It is as if Harold Robbins had collaborated on a novel with Gore Vidal."

Back in Chicago, Ebert was feeling the heat. Fellow local critics Mike Royko and Gene Siskel demolished the picture, leaving a glum Ebert to ponder, "Will this be a bad thing for my career?" "I was so close to it I didn't know what to think," said Ebert, who admitted he was "shocked" by some of the gory touches Meyer slipped into *Dolls*. Meyer soon arrived in town with Edy Williams in tow, and they dragged Ebert off to the Roosevelt Theater, where the trio watched the picture with a live audience. When the crowd went wild, Roger felt redeemed. "That movie really does play," he said. "It really plays."

Meyer maintained that he threatened to throw Siskel out a skyscraper window for giving his pal Roger such a hard time. Although Ebert would contribute to a number of other Meyer projects under various pseudonyms, he would not contribute to RM's second Fox picture, ending his "Hollywood" screenwriter career. Ebert's boss at the *Sun-Times* had given him an ultimatum: either keep the gig as a film critic or become a full-time screenwriter. "I went for the job security," said Ebert. "I've always wondered what would've happened if I'd gone to Hollywood—would I have become a screenwriter or a director? Maybe I would've destroyed my life. Who knows."

Despite indifference from Fox, who Meyer continually maintained was "ashamed" of the movie, *Beyond the Valley of the Dolls* has taken on a life of its own. Although fairly hard to see over the years due to poor prints and a spotty video release history, it has become a bona fide cult classic, with maniacal fans crowding revivals to mouth every word of dialogue. Mike Myers is said to have acknowledged the movie as a major influence on his Austin Powers franchise, and as recently as 2003 *Dolls* enjoyed another successful and well-reviewed theatrical run. As RM liked to say, you couldn't kill the picture with a stick.

For the filmmaker, there was no question where it ranked in his oeuvre. "The ultimate Russ Meyer film has already been made—*Beyond the Valley of the Dolls,*" said RM in 1977. "Something special happened with that film. . . . I'd never be able to approach again."

$ $ $

It's hard to say which people found more surreal: the triple marriage at the end of *Dolls* or the next legal union of Russell Albion Meyer. On June 27, 1970, Meyer wed Edy Williams. Friends and enemies alike were stunned. "He didn't like Edy—that's what was so weird," said Erica Gavin. "And all of a sudden he's getting *married*?" But Meyer made clear that he got off on the sordid nature of it all. "We were an extraordinary couple: a sex bomb with an old pornographer."

The ceremony took place at the posh Bel Air Hotel. In attendance were *Dolls* cast and crew, various war buddies, and, pipe firmly in hand, Hugh Hefner, accompanied by his current girlfriend, cornfed *Hee Haw* cutie Barbi Benton. Critic Kevin Thomas recalled Edy's dramatic entrance, swathed in "a Marie Antoinette dress with an overskirt pulled back and draped . . . only Edy didn't put the underskirt on."

"You talk about a cartoon!" exclaimed Manny Diez. "There must've been a couple of hundred guests there. About thirty yards away from me there's this man standing there looking at all this. And it was Buck Hall, first assistant director on *Dolls*. I walked up to Buck, put my arm around Buck's shoulder, and said, 'Buck, why are you standing here?' He was just . . . looking. And he shook his head and said, 'Why?' That's all he could say. 'Why?' Because everybody thought this was a giant mistake. Nobody could understand it. Nobody."

Edy claimed to be optimistic. "I thought, 'Hey, this will be swell—like Humphrey Bogart and Lauren Bacall, y'know?' " But the newlyweds quarreled even on their wedding night. "No pussy," wrote RM in his autobiography. This was a union born to implode, a tormented, angry dance. Edy was a high-maintenance filly and just as stubborn as Meyer, who always let it be known that whatever he wanted to do came first. "He ignores me," moaned Williams to writer John London. "That really exasperates me. The audacity to come in and see me lying in bed and go into the living room to read scripts. It blows my mind. And turns me on."

Such a glamorous couple deserved a ritzy Hollywood home, even though RM couldn't have given a shit. "Russ was a very modest guy, he didn't like ostentatious things," said Manny Diez. Meyer asked Diez if he knew a real estate agent for something in the $100,000 range. "Next thing I know they're living in a two-million-dollar house. It was a star house, fabulous, but not for Russ—he'd be living in a tent somewhere. That's what Edy wanted."

Rumored to be the former residence of film noir icon Lizabeth Scott, the house in Coldwater Canyon was both palatial and secluded. Meyer referred to it as Xanadu, his Castle-on-Mulholland. It had a swimming pool that extended into the living room, crystal chandeliers, Louis XIV furniture, a fireplace you could stand in, plus a two-way mirror in the bedroom. Not to mention a touch of trailer park as soon as the Meyers moved in. When Stu Philips visited he was stunned at what a pigsty the joint was. Beer cans and bottles filled the fireplace; newspapers and magazines were stacked everywhere. "The place looked like nobody had cleaned it. It was almost disgusting to walk in there." Meyer liked to recount a discussion he had with Edy's mother. "Your daughter doesn't do dishes," complained RM. "How can she do dishes when her eyes are on the stars?" responded Mom.

Meyer's friends were not impressed by the naked ambition of the new Mrs. Meyer. David Friedman recalled Russ and Edy making a visit to his Cordova Street office in downtown L.A. "Edy said to me, 'Is that your car?'" When Friedman nodded, she said, "'Hmm, that's interesting. That's bigger than Russ's car.' I knew right then and there, here's a low-class broad. Edy was a mistake."

Williams was known for her jealousy, and Meyer later confessed that he continued to see both Uschi Digard and the ubiquitous Miss Mattress, Janet Buxton (RM even admitted to having filmed one of their sweaty couplings at his editing suite on the Fox lot, but strictly for his own edification). Richard Brummer remembers Edy coming into the editing room and peering over his shoulder as he cut, studying the female face fluttering on the Moviola screen. "She grabs Russ when he gets back to the cutting room and says, 'That's why you went up to Bakersfield! You were screwing that girl!' Edy was convinced what she saw was evidence of foul play. And Russ was not gonna hear this from her. He walks out of the cutting room, she follows him, *screaming* as he walks up the street trying to get away from her."

Edy has her defenders. Jim Ryan found her to be a smart cookie and appreciated what she had to put up with living with the King. Each morning Meyer would hand her a decree of daily duties scrawled out on one of his ever-present yellow legal pads—Clean This, Fix That, Don't Do This, Call Me at 0700 Hours. "She came to me with the list and said, 'Do you see what he's doing? He's driving me crazy!!' I said, 'Edy, would you rather be back working for $750 a week for Fox?' " If Edy thought life was to be a series of Edy Williams films directed by Russ Meyer, she'd misunderstood. She was now a prisoner of war in Camp Meyerville. "He wanted to be the star, and anytime I did anything I got yelled at . . . He didn't want me to be in the limelight. He wanted me to stay at home. He didn't want any guests in the house for the first year."

Decades later, Meyer would claim that Edy had taken one look at Lydia, in failing health and wheelchair-bound, and said, "I don't want your mother around here. She's a cripple." In almost the same breath he maintained that Edy had suffered a miscarriage after slipping by their pool while engrossed in an article on herself in the *Los Angeles Times*. RM told David K. Frasier that when it came to this wife, his particular weakness was the fact that he "could not stand being embarrassed, and that's one way she knew how to get me. She'd throw a tantrum in the middle of the fucking *desert*. Bedouins would come in out of nowhere." But then there were those ten fabulous seconds when they got along, some of them even in the sack.

Mused Meyer, "I don't think I've known any woman who made me happier or more unhappy. She's the ultimate bitch and the ultimate sex symbol. Nothing in between."

$ $ $

Critics might've held their noses watching *Dolls*, but the picture raked in the dough. Meyer was riding a big wave. In February 1970, Yale held its very first film festival—a two-day Russ Meyer retrospective. Richard Schickel, covering the event for *Harper's*, favorably compared RM to Walt Disney. In May, Fox announced they'd given the filmmaker a three-picture deal, with a $150,000 salary for the first one alone. The studio sweetened the deal with a pair of new Corvette Stingrays for him and his missus. Meyer was clearly amused by such studio excess. "If your luggage is broken, they'll repair it—at enormous cost to the stockholders."

"We're exceptionally pleased with Mr. Meyer's work," proclaimed Richard Zanuck. "We sincerely feel that he can do more than merely undress people." In July 1971, the Museum of Modern Art paid homage to Meyer by screening six of his films in New York City. The audience went gaga over *Beyond the Valley of the Dolls.* "It was fantastic," said RM, who compared navigating the frenzied crowd that night to a "bullfight. They were just trying to rip Edy's clothes off." An ecstatic Meyer noted that once he and Edy slipped away from the fans, they managed to re-create the lusty Bentley/Rolls scene from *Dolls,* this time in the back of a Big Apple limo.

Meyer preferred the assignation of filmmaker rather than director. The latter, he felt, referred to "someone who takes himself seriously, who wears suede shoes and leather vests." Well, suddenly Russ Meyer had taken to wearing gaudy neckerchiefs. He, too, had become A Director. RM was living in a mansion with a sexy young starlet, had signed a three-picture deal with a major studio, and had plenty of cash in the bank. Not bad for a high-class pornographer.

Meyer had big plans, places to go, people to see. "The sex film?" mulled our King Leer. "I think it's on the way out. I want to get into horror films. Suspense, mystery." He was the man with the Midas touch, the one who could do no wrong.

And then everything went kaflooey.

$ $ $

Meyer's three pictures for Fox were to be a project called *The Final Steal,* a film based on Irving Wallace's best-seller *The Seven Minutes,* and, oddest of all, *Everything in the Garden,* a housewives-who-become-hookers Edward Albee play that Jerome Kilty, another renowned playwright, was to adapt for the screen. Meyer planned to do *The Final Steal* first, from a script by Manny Diez involving nerve gas, stolen diamonds, and a double-crossed Native American seeking vengeance. RM was considering casting Johnny Cash as the latter. Unfortunately, Zanuck and Brown had other ideas. They'd made a very expensive deal with author Irving Wallace for three of his best-sellers and, as previous director Richard Fleischer had left the project, someone was needed to helm the author's most recent hit. Meyer's camp maintained that Russ had no interest in the property. "They shoved *The Seven Minutes* down his throat," said Manny Diez.

But Meyer felt he could use this tale about the politics of censorship as a way to get back at the only person who'd ever beaten him—Charles Keating. RM even stuck a group in the movie called the Strength Through Decency League (after Keating's Citizens for Decent Literature). Fox executives arranged a meeting between Meyer and Irving Wallace, then "more or less talked Russ into it," as producer David Brown remembers. "He agreed, like a good soldier." Meyer told reporters that it was his "most fervent hope and desire to hold a spectacular world premiere . . . in Cincinnati, Mr. Keating's home town."

Where *Dolls* had been anarchy, *The Seven Minutes* would be studio-square. Brown laid down the law: the picture must get an R rating. Meyer even sent the MPAA a script before production began for insurance. This time when *Dolls* music contributor Lynn Carey submitted a soundtrack song, Fox's Lionel Newman—whose hands had been tied on Meyer's initial effort for the studio—rejected it because it contained the lyric "lay of the land." "Instead they used 'Midnight Tricks'—which is about a hooker!" noted Carey. As usual, Meyer packed the crew with combat buddies.

The plot revolves around a controversial book, also called *The Seven Minutes,* referring to the average time it takes a woman to achieve orgasm. In hopes of getting the volume declared obscene, conservative power mongers attempt to blame the tome for inciting a rapist, overlooking the fact that the accused didn't commit the crime. The climactic court battle in the film reveals that author J. J. Jadway is actually pornography-fighting retired movie star Constance Cumberland (Meyer's big twist: in Wallace's book it's a male Supreme Court justice). She provides the court with concrete proof that the accused couldn't have committed the crime—he's impotent. Yes, a limp pecker is the root of all unhappiness in the land of Meyer, and the movie ends in bed with the hero defense lawyer about to get it on with his new girlfriend. Once again, the world's problems are solved by some good, old-fashioned fucking.

Meyer assembled a cast of "real" film and TV actors—Yvonne DeCarlo, John Carradine, J. C. Flippen, Philip Carey, Wayne Maunder—to stand alongside Meyer regulars Charles Napier, Henry Rowland, Stuart Lancaster, Uschi Digard, and wife Edy (she balked at a nude scene during which she gets slapped on the ass, so RM fired her; according to him, Edy "begged" to be reinstated). On the set, Meyer was up to his usual dictatorial shenanigans with the pneumatic Mora Gray, who was forced to do so many takes of the opening running-down-the-street scene that her feet bled.* Whatever his initial misgivings, Meyer had high hopes for the picture. "The plot is advanced through dialogue," he boasted, declaring, *"The Seven Minutes* will be beyond all doubt the finest movie I've ever made."

With close-ups of gnashing alpha-male square jaws arguing the politics of smut in place of the usual parade of oversized bosoms, *Minutes* contains Meyer's usual ace camera work and machine-gun editing, but it adds up to zilch. RM was not a fan of character development; the people in his movies were never more than cardboard. And frankly, Meyer's dullsville without the dames. The fleeting moments the criminally underutilized Shawn "Baby Doll" Devereaux lights up the screen is the only time *Minutes* really ticks. And although the movie cost more than twice what Meyer had spent on *Dolls*, it feels about as sumptuous as an old episode of *Judd for the Defense*.

The Seven Minutes opened in the summer of 1971, and Meyer got his sneak premiere in Cincinnati, to no avail. "The first night in every theater was packed," he recalled. "And the next night: three people. Why? The audience knows." So did the critics, who were more than happy for another chance to carve up RM. "Talky censorship brings out the dullard in Meyer . . . a losing battle of mind

---

* Meyer originally wanted to cast Rena Horten in Gray's role for the sole indulgence of having his ex-girlfriend in a split-screen conversation with his current wife, but Edy talked him out of it (apparently ex-wife Eve, who'd suffered a similar indignity on *Mudhoney,* thought this a riotous idea). Meyer got a real kick out of sneaking Uschi into a stag movie sequence, as she was far from a favorite of his wife. According to Manny Diez, as an in-joke they outfitted the pornographer in the stag scene "the way Russ dresses—boots, black pants, and a maroon V-necked sweater. That was his uniform."

over mattress," said *Playboy*. "Tedious," said Kevin Thomas in the *Los Angeles Times*. "Tepid," said Jay Cocks in *Time*. "Success . . . has spoiled King Leer," concluded *New York* magazine. "A tombstone for the dead talents of Russ Meyer," sneered Al Goldstein in *Screw*. Author and director—who'd sung each other's praises in the press—suddenly ended their lovefest. Irving Wallace groused that Meyer had ignored his countless pages of script suggestions and that the filmmaker was a "bull in a china shop" when it came to complicated issues like obscenity and censorship. "I took on an impossible task—to try to make a good movie from an Irving Wallace book," countered Meyer, now disowning the picture.

Complicating matters was the fact that Fox's David Brown and Richard Zanuck had been ousted before production had even begun. According to Brown, the lingering stench of their two X-rated offspring *Dolls* and *Myra Breckenridge* contributed to their exit, even though *Dolls* had been a big moneymaker. "It undermined the authority of Mr. Zanuck and myself. The board of directors weren't happy with it, Darryl F. Zanuck wasn't happy. We were members of the board, so we got an earful. Directors are waspy characters. They don't like that kind of material. They like *The Sound of Music*."

Zanuck and Brown hightailed it to Warner Bros., taking Meyer with them. There Meyer commenced work on *Choice Cuts*, a rather unique Jerome Kilty cryogenics horror script about a twisted doctor who revives the severed head of a criminal whose body parts have been donated to Vietnam vets. Unbeknownst to the doctor, there's a tumor in the brain, and the head commands its wayward limbs to kill the bodies they've been stitched onto. A girl in love with the head rounds up the parts, hoping to reassemble her lover—after somehow managing to get intimate with the jarred cranium, that is. RM was given fifty grand to develop the property, only to be ordered to clear out of the studio in a matter of hours when Zanuck and Brown lost another power play. "They had a man out there painting my name off the car park," said RM. "That's the final blow in Hollywood. . . . The day before they had been saying how great my work was."

As Jim Ryan observed, RM remained stoic in the face of such

disaster. "Meyer said, 'We'll make something else—what do we need these guys for?' " But he would not work at a major studio again. According to Charles Napier, "I think he feared ridicule more than anything in the world. Meyer feared he would not be recognized as a filmmaker. He *wanted* to be accepted. I saw that when we went to Fox. He'd never admit it, he'd want to say he was always a lone wolf, but I've never seen him so pleased with himself as when he was on that lot."

In years to come, RM turned bitter on the subject of "Pope" Zanuck and "Cardinal" Brown. He'd compare Brown to the colonel in *The Red Badge of Courage* who'd ingratiate himself to the troops before the battle, then go off to a big breakfast as his men were decimated. And Meyer would seethe over his former producers disparaging the movie they'd encouraged him to make. Typical Hollywood hypocrites, thought Meyer. "Zanuck was always telling me how great it was to see my car in the lot on Sundays, but I don't think he'd ever seen one of my films." (In his autobiography, Meyer states that Zanuck arranged a screening of *Vixen* only to walk out after five minutes.)

Although Zanuck and Brown never called on Meyer to make another movie, they both purported to have warm feelings for the man. "I liked him," said Zanuck. "I thought he was very direct, very honest. . . . He was a filmmaker. I thought he had the potential of doing other than what he'd been making a life's work out of. Russ never really did that. Maybe he was just uncomfortable. I think the whole Hollywood scene may have been too much for him to swallow. Russ wasn't quite the master and commander all at once as he was in his own operation."*

Hollywood still thought it had the occasional use for Meyer, however. According to a girlfriend who was present for the call, in the eighties RM was contacted by a critically acclaimed mainstream director with a long, distinguished career. He was looking for underage girls, and thought Meyer was just the man to help him. RM hung up the phone in disgust.

---

* David Brown, who also maintained he "liked Russ very much," compared RM to another "rambunctious, maverick, skilled storyteller with an agenda all his own" whom he'd worked with—Michael Moore.

$ $ $

Next RM tried to mount a $750,000 independent horror picture to be filmed in Georgia, *The Eleven*. The Meyer–Jim Ryan–Manny Diez script concerned eleven people who are killed by their sins: a slumlord devoured by cockroaches, a gossip columnist whose ears explode from a thousand chattering voices, and so on. Ryan did extensive preproduction work on the picture, with shooting set to start in March 1972, but investors got cold feet at the last minute. "We got $5,000 prep money, but that was the end of it," said Ryan. "They changed their minds."

RM's next picture would at least get made, but that's where the good news ends. For some unknown reason Meyer had a bee in his bonnet to do a period piece about slavery. The uncredited inspiration for *Blacksnake* came from a script by Manny Diez, but he had a falling-out with Meyer when the director wanted to play fast and loose with what had been written as a historically accurate account. The result was a convoluted mess that seemed to exist only as an excuse for the cast to exchange racial epithets and the white female lead to whip nearly naked black men. Inexplicably, Meyer would compare the finished picture to both the 1935 Errol Flynn swashbuckler *Captain Blood* and the TV sitcom *All in the Family*.

The $400,000 independent feature (shot in Panavision, no less) began its six-week shooting schedule in April 1972 in Barbados (Ryan insisted Meyer let him grease the local political wheels alone, fearing RM would offend the locals). Then, just days before the cameras rolled, the female star—an Italian Anita Ekberg doppelgänger—was hospitalized following an overdose. The part went to second choice Anouska Hempel, a slim English blonde Meyer kindly described as having "two backs." There was surprisingly little nudity in the picture. When a disappointed David Prowse, playing a zombie, commented that not one of the female leads was endowed in the Meyer tradition, RM replied, "Sex is out, violence is in. This film will have every conceivable death you can think of—death by hanging, by double-barreled shotgun, by whipping, by machete, by crucifixion and by shark."

Meyer arranged for first-class accommodations for cast and

crew at the swanky Sam Lord's Castle, but to say he failed to hit it off with the English and Barbadian cast is an understatement. "Working with the characters he'd chosen turned out to be a very, very harrowing experience," said Prowse. "They all were looked after hand, foot, and finger. Nothing was too much trouble and they were leadin' Russ on a merry dance." The homosexuality of David Warbeck disturbed RM even before the actor led a successful strike for teatime breaks. The actors "would sit in the hot blistering sun of the tropics in the middle of a cane field and drink hot tea at four o'clock," said soundman Richard Brummer. "In porcelain ware, served by knowing servants." According to David Prowse, "Anouska Hempel didn't want to know anything whatsoever about sex on the screen."

Meyer had gone to great lengths to import a huge anaconda into Barbados, as snakes weren't indigenous to the island. One of the actors thought it would be amusing to set the animal loose in RM's room, but it promptly slithered out the window and was run over by Meyer and Ryan returning from dinner. They managed to recapture the snake, which, as Prowse recalls, was "OK, with only a few tire marks on him—but from then on he became vicious and hard to work with." Richard Brummer had to tape the reptile's mouth shut for a scene where Anouska discovers the snake in her bathtub and has it thrown out the window.

From runaway snakes to testosterone-fueled fights over stunning slave girl Vikki Richards, *Blacksnake* was a troubled shoot, with Meyer suffering alone, in silence. However, there was one night when the cast assembled for dinner when RM decided to share his displeasure. "He'd obviously had a very, very bad day," said Prowse. "There were about ten or twelve of us at this dinner and he stood up and berated the whole table. 'I'm fed up with your attitudes, the fact you're bitchin' all the time. I'm not getting what I want from you as actors.' And then he said, 'I only wish you all had the same attitude as Dave Prowse here.' I started cringing."

When Prowse returned to the States, Meyer drove him to the airport, where the actor handed RM a bottle of whiskey before boarding his plane. "I gave it to him as a going-away present. Russ said, 'Y'know, you're the first person that's ever given me a present at the end of a movie.' And he burst into tears."

David Prowse would go on to play Darth Vader in *Star Wars* (oddly enough, he learned that George Lucas had used James Earl Jones to overdub his lines via a cable from Meyer, who'd just seen the movie). With *Star Wars* a monster hit, RM grabbed *Blacksnake*, slapped on yet another title—*Slaves*—and released it in England, with "Starring David Prowse" in big letters on the poster.

The making of *Blacksnake* had dragged on for a little over a year. According to Jim Ryan, Meyer was so strapped for finishing funds that he forged his mother's signature to get the $100,000 needed for release prints out of her account. Ryan had scraped together nearly a third of the budget, putting himself months behind in house payments in the process. "I thought we had a winner." How wrong he was.

$ $ $

Blacksnake had the usual forty-six Russ Meyer endings, but for its theatrical run, the final exclamation point was a trailer for what was to be Meyer's next opus, featuring Edy Williams waterskiing nude. *Viva Foxy,* aka *Foxy,* from a Roger Ebert script, was planned as a $400,000 vehicle for Edy. It was another period piece, set in South America in the 1920s, in which Williams would play a bombshell named Foxy McHugh, a character she compared to *Vixen.* "She used men and abused them and had a ball. That's what *Foxy's* gonna be about. She's gonna do all the things that men have done. I'll be a female guerrilla. I'm gonna be the power behind two thrones."

It was not to be. "We went to Europe, the three of us, for the casting of *Blacksnake*—sort of a ménage à trois, but I didn't get any ménage," said Jim Ryan. "Meyer and Edy were fighting at the time about his controlling her, mainly." Edy had assumed she was starring in *Blacksnake* as Lady Susan. To pacify his spouse, RM shot a nude layout of her sprawled across the Barbados beach that ran as a *Playboy* spread. According to Edy, when they returned to Los

Angeles, she asked for the layout loot to purchase "a pretty coat" and Meyer told her he'd already spent it. "I was so hurt that I picked up the biggest rock I could find. I could hardly lift it, and I threw it through the windshield of his Porsche. He got so mad he smashed my Corvette." Meyer would re-create a downhome version of these events for his next picture, *Supervixens*.*

Viva Foxy was on again, off again throughout 1972–73. "Have you any idea how frustrating it is to want something more than anything in the world, and there beside you is the man who could give it to you—but won't?" lamented Mrs. Meyer in the press. RM publicly claimed to have abandoned the picture due to a recent Supreme Court ruling, but Ryan maintained the real reason was because the couple were constantly at each other's throats.

While RM was in Barbados struggling through *Blacksnake*, Edy was photographed in the tabloids cavorting with an African American actor named Ed Hall. And then one day Mrs. Meyer just decided to "pack everything I own and leave that mansion. I left my false eyelashes and my padded bra and financed my own trip to the Cannes Film Festival." Edy filed for divorce, accusing her husband of "disappearing acts" and announcing to the press, "I am a sex symbol and I don't want to be alone." Meyer moved out of the Mulholland Drive estate and into a Hollywood apartment. In *A Clean Breast*, he claims to have later returned home to find Edy in bed with a younger man. The marriage over, the divorce battle was about to begin.

Said Edy, "I trusted Russ. I thought he was more than just someone who wanted to take my clothes off. But I was wrong. He said, 'All I want you for is fucking and cooking.'"

Said Russ, "I just couldn't picture myself making twenty films starring Edy Williams."

$ $ $

---

* At times Meyer would arrive at his Mulholland home and find Edy had chained up the entrance to the home, at which point RM would pop the trunk of his black Porsche and retrieve what he called his "spare key"—a pair of bolt cutters.

Blacksnake opened in the spring of 1973 to universal indifference. "The blacks hated it, the whites hated it," Meyer admitted, conceding that the movie was "sort of like *Mandingo* without the sex." RM retitled the picture *Sweet Suzy, Duchess of Doom* and tacked on a prologue featuring a naked, busty black chick, but the damage had been done. Financially devastated, Jim Ryan came within two hours of losing his home in a sheriff's sale. "I put a lot of money in it. Lost it. It hurt me. It hurt Meyer, but he had the funding to withstand it. I didn't." Ryan never let on to RM and, despite their long association, refused to turn to him for help. "I knew him well enough not to do that."

Russ Meyer had to wonder just what the fuck had happened. Just a few short years before it was top o' the world, Ma. Since then there had been a string of flops, fizzled projects, and a marriage made in hell.

Things were rather painfully summed up at a showing of *Blacksnake* at the 1973 Dallas Film Festival. When the screening was over, Meyer stood for the requisite Q and A. "A guy got up and shouted, 'Where's the broad with the big tits?' And like a hundred students stood up and said, 'YEAH!' It was like a James Cagney prison epic with the tin cups." The incident unnerved RM. "One thing I knew right then and there—I was doing the wrong thing, and I damn well better get back to what I do best."

13

Run Like a Gazelle, Dear

I really dig violence. —RUSS MEYER

It was way past midnight in Franklin Towers. Russ Meyer puffed on a slender cigar and downed the last of his Bombay martini—just the way he liked it, so cold his teeth hurt. It was unlike him to be boozing so late. RM hated the lack of company, but he'd managed to rope no one into dinner. Just as well. Meyer had to face facts: his career and his personal life were both in the shithole. His last two pictures had been bombs, total flops, and his marriage to Edy was zipping toward divorce court faster than a speeding bullet. Fuck. All washed up in Tinseltown and the world laughing at Russell Albion Meyer. Action was required, drastic action. No time to waste.

Meyer knew he had to return to what he did best: big bosoms and square jaws. He'd turned his back on the formula that had made him one very rich male chauvinist pig. RM had to lose the fat head and get humble, ASAP. It was time to make another umbilical cord movie: a handful of actors, the camera, and himself. Go deep into the desert, push people to the end of their goddamn rope. Just like old times.

It was a daunting challenge. The skin game had changed radically in the few years he'd been away. Nineteen seventy-two had brought a vogue (albeit brief) for both lowdown and highbrow X-rated movie hits. *Deep Throat* was hard-core porno, an excuse to wallow in a particular Meyer bête noir: the blow job. *Last Tango in Paris* had Hollywood icon Marlon Brando buck-naked and doing explicit sex scenes. "What is there left?" moaned RM. "I mean, the idea a few years back of Brando, an Oscar winner, putting butter up some broad's ass and jumping her . . . it's hard to compete with that."

Meyer would later call September 19, 1973, "an important day in my life." Without telling a soul, he hopped aboard a plane bound for Hawaii, then checked into the Mauna Kea Hotel. Over the next seven days he'd crank out one complete script and loosely sketch ideas for two others. A return to the world of X-rated sex and violence, *Supervixens* would unleash Meyer's most memorable (and misanthropic) macho man: Harry Sledge, the greatest role of Charles Napier's weird career. And this time RM was gonna have not one but *seven* gravity-defying women, bringing them in one after the other, "every reel, like a new linebacker." He'd attach the *super-* prefix to their names—everything about this movie was going to be XXL—naming some of them after characters that had brought him fame and fortune in the past: SuperVixen, Super-Lorna, SuperHaji, SuperSoul.

RM was going for broke. Count Meyer out, did they? The infidels were sadly mistaken.

$ $ $

Fed up with acting, Charles Napier was working as a correspondent for *Overdrive,* a magazine for the independent trucker. RM sweet-talked him into leaving his job to take the lead in *Supervixens,* so the pair went location hunting, roaring off in Napier's International Scout. "We headed toward the Colorado River, toward Laughlin, Nevada—the middle of nowhere, all desert country—and we get about halfway there and he goes, 'Let's go north.' I go, 'There's no fucking road.' Meyer says, 'We don't need a road, this is four-wheel drive. We'll either make it or we'll die. You're either with me or you're not.'

"So we're driving this endless wasteland and now Meyer's really excited—'We may not make it, we could die here, we don't have any water.' We immediately get lost, of course. We had to sleep out the night under the stars. It was getting kinda hairy.

"The next day we keep heading north, and there's a strange-looking hill. And he screams, '*Stop here!*' And he jumps out, he bolts. He starts climbin' this mountain, straight up. It was a mound that looked like a woman's breast." Napier charged after him, reaching the top after twenty minutes, and found Meyer in a frenzy. "He stood there cursing at the gods, saying, 'Here I will make *history*!'

"I said, 'What's gonna take place here?' An excited RM replied, 'We're gonna chain a chick down to the top of this mountain, and we're gonna abuse womanhood like it's never been abused. And I'm gonna take out my hatred on every cunt that ever fucked me over in my life.'

"It became a hate trip against Edy, and Meyer made a movie out of it. And I was his alter ego."*

$ $ $

We see a tow truck tearing through the desert, pulling the hulk of a dead VW Bug. A scratchy record of Nazi marches is our sound-track. Behind the wheel of the pickup is infamous Nazi fugitive Martin Bormann (Henry Rowland), proud owner of Martin Bormann's Super Station, where Clint Ramsey works as a gas pump jockey. One of the blanker slates in Meyer's cavalcade of manhood, Clint is terrorized by jealous, insatiable SuperAngel, whose sole mission in life is provoking him into an angry screw.

The wild *Supervixens* opening sets the stage for the utter havoc to follow. Clint is pumping gas for SuperLorna (the demonically

---

* Napier is tremendous in *Supervixens*, and according to crew member Stan Berkowitz, the main reason was because Napier agreed to work with Meyer again only if he refrained from offering the actor any direction. "I witnessed this," said Berkowitz. "Chuck looked at the script and said, 'I'm gonna rewrite my part, I'm gonna direct myself—stay outta the way.' RM said, 'Okay, fine.' Napier was the one guy that intimidated Meyer."

sexy Christy Hartburg) when SuperAngel calls the station to check up on her old man. SuperLorna slips into the rest room, donning a devastating outfit—red halter top, boots, white hot pants, pig-tails. Slinking out of the ladies' room, SuperLorna starts go-going, pulling Clint's attention away from the phone. Angel detects a woman in the background, suspects the worst, and gives Clint the third degree, but he manages to calm her momentarily. "You make her look like a boy," Clint lies. Gleeful over the putdown to her competition, Angel purrs, "Come on home to our big bed. SuperAngel's got a *big need.*" Martin Bormann yells at his employee to get back to work and Clint hangs up on SuperAngel. Enraged, she calls back, only to have SuperLorna answer. "Get off the line, bitch," hisses SuperAngel. "Can't wait to strap on your groovy old man," says SuperLorna with an evil smile, dropping the phone into her cleavage, the canyon between her massive breasts causing Su-perAngel's telephonic curses to actually echo.

A nasty spat between Angel and Clint summons psychopathic cop Harry Sledge to the scene. Sledge later returns for an illicit li-aison with SuperAngel, but when he is unable to close the deal, SuperAngel's taunts drive him to brutally murder her. Bormann worries that Clint will be blamed for the crime and slips him money to hit the highway, where our innocent hero is beset by sex-crazed sirens who beckon from haylofts and even a dune buggy's bucket seat. Eventually Clint runs into SuperVixen, the reincar-nation of his dear departed, although he's too dumb to recognize it. Harry Sledge returns, the trio entering into a weird déjà vu that brings the movie full circle. The climax of the film has a lingerie-clad SuperVixen spread-eagled and bound to a mountaintop, Harry Sledge lighting a stick of dynamite parked between her legs. Clint comes to the rescue and love saves the day as Sledge acci-dentally blows himself up.

Supervixens hits 80 mph right out of the gate and never slows to a legal speed. This film returns Meyer to that same hyperkinetic universe of *Beyond the Valley of the Dolls,* although RM has ex-changed the glitz of Hollywood for middle America's dusty byways, where Meyer's blue-collar surrealism explodes. Faded gas stations, last-chance motels, and gleaming brass beds that overwhelm otherwise threadbare bedrooms supply the backdrops for a mythic, mini-mart soap opera of hate. Meyer maintained that his films were live-action cartoons, and *Supervixens* is self-consciously so—right before Harry Sledge meets his end from the stick of dynamite is his hand, a hapless What, Me Worry? close-up of his face is set against a car horn imitating Roadrunner's familiar *beep beep* to let us know he's a goner.

Supervixens is a technical tour de force for Meyer. The editing is magnificent—RM boasted that the film contained over three thousand setups and that no single shot was over three feet long. The beyond-busy soundtrack gooses the rhythm as well. Way before Scorsese concocted hyperactive, wall-to-wall soundtracks for the likes of *GoodFellas* and *Casino,* Russ Meyer was there, using layers of music, dialogue, and effects to achieve a headache-inducing white noise, not unlike three TV stations murdering a radio. And just when you're ready to scream, he brings the soundtrack down to a mere tap-tap of high heels on gritty asphalt and the squeak of a swinging screen door. The music here functions as a constant barrage of exclamation points, with silent-movie themes, sitcom pap, and Dixieland jazz running against snippets of ditties so familiar they barely register—"Here Comes the Bride," "Dixie," "Glory, Glory, Hallelujah," "When Johnny Comes Marching Home."

Wild imagery is what one remembers most from *Supervixens.* Deaf and dumb SuperEula (Deborah McGuire, who later married Richard Pryor), her ebony body struggling to break free of a white bikini festooned with red hearts, signing away frantically as she zooms off in a dune buggy railjob; Lute the farmer (Stuart Lancaster) maniacally screwing his very vocal Austrian milkmaid wife SuperSoul (Uschi Digard) as Clint works the soil and "Turkey in the Straw" blasts on the track. And on and on and on. It really *is* a comic book come to life, spilling over with loud, vivid colors, particularly Meyer's bold reds, which seem to pop up everywhere.

Supervixens has an amazing, hostile energy. Men and women spar in a manner that would make a boxer wince. Martin Bormann asks himself in German—subtitled for the audience's convenience—"Is the fucking you get worth the fucking you get?"

Although it's somewhat hard to hear the dialogue amid all the chaos, the bedroom banter between Clint and SuperAngel is far from lovey-dovey. "Gotta play the man-eater," Clint sneers. "Angel number one, screw everybody else . . . money, a shitpile of it, just lay it on Angel . . . buy, spend, give it away, rip off any jerk that says no to her." As the battle escalates he shrieks, "Say one more thing about my mother and I'll bust you in the jaw!" The parallels between Clint/SuperAngel and Russ/Edy were purely intentional. "I wrote the dialogue," said Jim Ryan. "I just copied what Edy would've said. *Supervixens* was almost all Edy Williams."

$ $ $

If there was ever a Meyer movie that truly approximated war, it is *Supervixens*. Shooting in and around Palo Verde Valley, California, and Quartzsite, Arizona, in March and April 1974, Meyer had cast and crew ensconced in shabby little cabins "that these migrant workers had abandoned in the Arizona desert," according to actor Charles Pitt. Roger Ebert, who roomed briefly with Meyer to contribute to the script, added that the closet was just "a broomstick hanging from the ceiling. The shower water ran down a sloping floor and right outside into the desert. There was no drain."

Ebert chuckled while recalling crew member Stan Berkowitz, "some kid who I think was a film student at UCLA." It was Berkowitz's job to dig holes for the pay phone Meyer carried around for scenes—and redig it when RM decided it wasn't the right height. Said Ebert, "The guy is complaining to me, 'I'm studying Bergman and Antonioni and here I am diggin' a hole!' Russ repeated that for years." Perhaps the spirit of *Supervixens* is best exemplified by the powderman in charge of the picture's many explosions, Harry Wohlman. "He had a Toonerville Trolley kind of truck, full of explosives," said editor/soundman Richard Brummer. "That guy would sit outside those explosives, smoking a cigarette. He had several fingers missing."

Meyer charged around the desert like a pirate, a cigar in his mouth and a .45 on his hip. "We worked our way up from Yuma through the Copa Game Range. No permits, nothing," said Charles

Napier. "I don't know why the rangers didn't catch us. Meyer's answer to that was, 'We'll give them a blow job. Forget about a permit. Anybody can be bought.'"

At the end of the physically grueling shoot Napier found himself attempting to recover at the Little Lake Motel in Long Pine, California, RM laid out next to him. "We're sittin' up there in the room, Meyer's in one bed, I'm in the other. We'd been filming for three weeks. I'm beat, he's beat. And I said, 'Have you had enough?' And Meyer goes, 'Yup. I've had enough now. I've beaten myself down to my knees. I can barely walk, but I did it.' I said, 'Ya gotta really kill yourself, don't you?' 'Yup. Physically, mentally and every other way, or else it won't succeed.' That was Meyer, man."

$ $ $

Russ Meyer's newest superstar was SuperAngel Shari Eubank, a very funny brunette who remains the most corn-fed and all-American of Meyer's many cuties. A former cheerleader, homecoming queen, and sorority girl from Farmer City, Illinois, Eubank was, according to Haji, "very forgiving, very naive, and a little too sensitive for this business." "We never discussed sex," Shari informed a reporter in reference to her family. "One night my father called us all out to a barn to see a calf being born."

Meyer had nothing but praise for Eubank and "the way she was dragged over that damn mountain in the movie—she never complained. And every rock just reached out and bit you." By the end of the film she'd be perched naked upon the mountain's very pinnacle, a crew member hiding behind her (and out of camera range) with his palm extended in a catcher's mitt, allowing Eubank to perch there safely without gouging her ass on volcanic rock.

Haji, playing *Supervixens'* nude bartendress SuperHaji (whom Napier found "a little distracting—she used to do makeup with only sneakers on"), found Eubank for Meyer. "Shari was working at the Classic Cat as a dancer. She was a damn good actress and didn't even know it. But Russ brings these things out in you." Although there was certainly no Meyer-Eubank romance, Haji felt that she was "another one Russ kinda had a thing for. I know he liked her."

Eubank actually had two roles in *Supervixens,* a somewhat confusing gambit Meyer would later repeat with Kitten Natividad in 1979's *Beneath the Valley of the Ultra-Vixens.* It came about by accident. According to Ebert, Meyer was short one Supervixen during the time when there were still a few dying embers left in RM's marriage. "The final character was supposed to be played by Edy, and she said she wouldn't do it because her career had reached the point where she didn't want to take off her clothes." Meyer, whose shot of his wife nude on her back in their pool for *Playboy* had gone on to become a popular poster, was dumbfounded, telling her, "We can't have six naked vixens and for the climax have you with your clothes *on.*" Ebert says he told Edy she was out of the movie, sinking any hope of staying out of divorce court.

Instead of a new actress, it was decided that Shari Eubank would be brought back at the end of the film after SuperAngel's death to play another character — SuperVixen — and RM brought Ebert in to figure out how. "He told me we had to explain how come she was still alive, so I told him that we would put a bathtub on a mountaintop — that's where she was last seen, dead in a bathtub — and have the sun rising behind it and play 'Thus Spake Zarathustra' as she stood up in a white gown, backlit by the sun. This would be her resurrection."

Next they had to get that bathtub up the mountain. According to Ebert, "Napier went into a truck stop and said, 'Any of you guys wanna be in a Russ Meyer movie?' Six truckers came out, and they all got paid with beer. Their job was to carry the bathtub up to the top of the mountain." Meyer shot the scene, but when Ebert saw the finished product, it wasn't in the movie.

"I said, 'What happened to that scene?' And Russ said, 'I tried it, but y'know, it was just too implausible.'" The idea of Meyer finding *anything* implausible is a rich one. "What was hilarious was at one point in his next film, in a montage involving sex, there was a cut to six guys carrying a bathtub up a mountaintop." Meyer saved the footage, and "used it as his 'symbolism.'"*

---

* Meyer's next film was *Up!* (1976). I couldn't find any bathtub shots, but with Meyer's quick cutting, that doesn't mean it isn't hiding in there.

$ $ $

Pretty boy Charlie Pitt, whom Edy Williams had met in an acting class, was to play Clint Ramsey. "Edy and I got on extremely well— I underline *extremely*—and she had me come up to her mansion on Mulholland Drive. I had just got into Hollywood, a kid from Fort Pierce, Florida. She just thought I was so hot."

Edy suggested Pitt for a role in *Supervixens*, escorting him down to Meyer's Ivar Street office, where RM growled, "You got good bones, kid, but can you act?" Meyer shot a screen test of Pitt scrubbing vehicles in a Pasadena car wash. "I like the way the kid moves," declared Meyer. Adds Pitt, "I knew how to juggle, so I was throwing the Windex around. He got a kick out of that. I sing pretty good, so I sang for him in Italian. Russ said, 'Well, it sounds a little fag.'" Pitt was miffed when Meyer later allowed Charles Napier to warble a little ditty in *Supervixens*.

Meyer and Pitt clashed from the get-go. RM bitched that the actor was too frisky with his leading ladies, to which Pitt happily pleads guilty. "What are they for? Quote me: 'What are they *for*?' It's like putting a chocolate cake in front of you—you're supposed to try and not eat that?" But Meyer also offered his own brand of encouragement to the rookie, informing him early in the shoot, "I need more from you. Ryan looked at the dailies. You're dull as shit, dull as shit."

"I still carry a scar from that movie," revealed Pitt. During the big finale on the mountain top, the dynamite's magnesium fuse fell on him "and left a hole in my chest the size of a quarter. I jumped up in the middle of the shot—I'm supposed to be unconscious. Meyer said, 'What the fuck are you doing?' I screamed, 'I'm on fuckin' fire, Russ!' 'That's no excuse to ruin a shot! C'mon, be a *man*, Pitt!' It was always 'Be a man,' never 'Let's see some serious acting, what's your motivation?'" In that same scene, Charles Napier throws a knife that lands in Pitt's leg. "Meyer was shooting a close-up of my face. I was supposed to react like I'm getting knifed. He kept saying, 'It's not enough. C'mon, Pitt, *c'mon!*' Finally Russ just clubbed me right in the calf of my leg with his fist. It got the reaction he wanted."

But Pitt's greatest humiliation would come during the rambunctious hayloft sex scene with Uschi Digard (who plays, of course, SuperUschi). Pitt remembered the scene as "a lot of dust, not very romantic at all . . . when I'm supposed to jump up and zip my pants up very fast, I caught my irving in the zipper. It hurt like hell, and I turned around to scream. Meyer said, 'Now, that's the kind of reaction we want. That's what I call *acting!*' "*

Crew member Stan Berkowitz felt RM had deliberately set out to instigate friction with Charles Pitt. "Meyer likes strife, and he creates it when there's no purpose for it," said Berkowitz. "He's superstitious. Russ actually told me that when a shoot went well, without problems, the movie was not a hit. But those movies that were ridden with strife, misery, and all sorts of disasters happening, those were the hits."

$ $ $

Supervixens is one entertaining, poisonous piece of work. Meyer lays his cards on the table early on with the drawn-out, frenzied killing of SuperAngel, but the twisted, vengeful face of Harry Sledge is really the main attraction here. Napier's macho cop wears mirrored shades, carries the requisite oversized nightstick, and, strangely enough, is given to wearing saddle shoes in his downtime. "Built like a brick shithouse. Biceps, triceps, lats, pectorals," boasts Harry, donning for the film's climax a rather fey combat ensemble of fatigues, beret, and wrist bazooka. Sledge is

---

* Pitt would further irritate Meyer by testifying for Edy in the divorce proceedings, and trashing the director in a 1975 newspaper article, stating, "I have no intention of working again for Russ Meyer." RM would excerpt the article in *A Clean Breast* alongside an autographed glossy of the actor whereupon he thanks Meyer for giving him his big break in show business.

These days you can find Charles Pitt on his website promoting his new career as "America's Tenor," singing a blend of pop and opera he's dubbed "popera." According to his hype, "Madonna calls him 'the sexiest tenor alive.' " Also on the site you'll find pictures of Pitt demonstrating his acting ability by interpreting such themes as 'Matador,' 'With a Horse,' and 'Romancing a Woman.' Curiously, *Supervixens* is not listed on his lengthy resumé, although duly noted are such milestones as *King Frat, Bog,* and *Skatetown, USA.*

impotent and orally fixated on his stogie, yet when SuperAngel heads south on his suddenly rigid body, he mutters, "Knock that queer stuff off . . . we're gonna do this my way or no way at all." SuperAngel gets a kick out of needling Harry, cooing, "I like a good cigar, but I take it out of my mouth on occasion." Her reincarnated alter ego will repeat the line near the end of the film.

When Harry meets SuperAngel—who functions, according to one critic, as "the embodiment of evil, malice and all castration anxieties"—for their illicit rendezvous and fails to perform, she takes Harry's flaccid "prune prick" member as a personal attack. "What the hell's wrong with you? Not ready, with my beautiful body? You got a lotta nerve . . . all those muscles, except the one that really counts." SuperAngel throws a drink in Harry's face and we're off to the races. For Meyer, beautiful women are cruel, narcissistic figures of torment that can't be vanquished. "Regardless of who holds the social, economic, or political power, women, because of their bodies, are sexual objects of desire," writes journalist Louis Black. "Even if men are physically stronger, they're nothing before women, who have that ultimate power."

Harry Sledge is driven berserk by this vaginal mojo. As SuperAngel, who has locked herself in the bathroom to escape his rampage, turns on a radio to nonchalantly go-go what will be the final few minutes of her life away, Harry hacks his way in with a butcher knife. "What's the matter, Superstud Harry? All your other muscles gone limp, too?" Harry plunges the knife into SuperAngel, then drags her into the bathtub, the water turning crimson as he strangles and repeatedly stomps on her. A blood-drenched Angel feebly tries to pull herself up over the edge of the tub. "Lousy lay, huh? . . . You're quite a turn-on yourself," sneers Harry as he drops the radio into the water, electrocuting her. Meyer tried to explain away the numbing brutality of the scene as a "satire" on violence. Napier—who helped create it—disagreed: "There was nuthin' satirical about it." Crew member Stan Berkowitz shuddered recalling how spent Shari Eubank looked at the end of the shoot. "The makeup was gone, she was in a tub of blood-red water . . . I almost threw up."

During an interview, Napier described the genesis of the scene. "We were in a restaurant one night discussing ways to dispatch the chick. Somebody overheard and called the cops—thought we were getting ready to murder somebody." The scene was shot not on location but in Jim Ryan's Los Angeles home—"I still use the bathtub," said Ryan with a chuckle—and he scripted the dialogue the night before right in the room they used. "I just visualized Edy," he said once again. It seems that Edy's ire fueled more than just Meyer alone.

The final bizarre touch in SuperAngel's murder scene is the briefly glimpsed two-foot cock Napier sports. The actor said that he came up with the idea, telling Russ it was the only way to show any "redemption" for Sledge. "So we had to stop shooting and sent somebody into town for a dildo. Which we named Wilbur. Kept it in a case. Then Meyer got carried away and wanted to put it on all the guys." In fact, once *Supervixens* was finished, RM tested the picture on a tour of six East Coast colleges, claiming that "the girls complained they weren't getting their fair share, so I re-edited it and put in a lot of shots of male nudity I'd left out." At least one woman wasn't so crazy about the inserts Meyer added. According to Haji, "When Shari Eubank saw all this stuff in the finished picture, she freaked out. She ran out of the theater crying." Meyer's love of phony phalluses would be carried to absurd lengths in his next picture, *Up!*

$ $ $

"Russ Meyer comes bolting out of the burning Sonora desert, with the vengeance of a mad Visigoth lusting to regain his throne!" screams the pressbook for *Supervixens*. Billboards featuring a heart-stopping image of the criminally abundant Christy Hartburg in her red halter top wreaked havoc in places like Raleigh, North Carolina, where, said RM, "the townspeople insisted they be taken down. That was on a Saturday. By Sunday the film had grossed double what it had before."

Meyer, back on top. After debuting at the Rotterdam Film Festival—where, according to RM, Europeans were distressed by the film's violence—*Supervixens* had its official U.S. premiere in Dallas on April 2, 1975. The film was a smash hit, eventually earning $17 million worldwide on an investment of $221,000.

Meyer certainly knew he had a hit after a college campus screening in Austin, Texas. "When it was over, a hysterical woman ran up and told me *I* ought to have a stick of dynamite up my ass. Any time I generate that much of a reaction I know I'm really doing something right." According to RM, the funniest response to the film came from Shari Eubank's father, who—sitting next to his daughter—attended a showing packed with her friends and family in Milwaukee, Wisconsin, not far from Shari's hometown. The unbelievable shot of Eubank completely nude atop the mountain pinnacle appeared on the screen. *"Mah God, Shari,"* the father gasped. "Dad, I told you not to come," shushed his daughter. The rest of the audience cracked up.

By the end of 1974, Charles Napier was destitute, living in a trailer he'd parked in a lot Meyer owned on Sunset Boulevard. A truckers' strike had ended his gig at *Overdrive*, and other than the work for RM, his acting career had amounted to nothing. "I figured this was about it: thirty-nine years old, pounding the pavement, just another failed actor," Napier told Roger Ebert. "Then Meyer released *Supervixens.*"

Over at Universal, Alfred Hitchcock himself requested a private screening. Next thing Napier knew, somebody was knocking on the window of his truck, telling him he had an appointment to keep. "Hitchcock evidently loved the brutality in this film. His favorite scene was me stomping the chick in the bathtub." The actor headed for the studio, fearing it was some sort of joke. He was ushered into Hitchcock's office and instructed not to talk. The director had him turn around once, and Napier suddenly found himself signed to Universal, a check for $5,000 in his pocket. "I went out and rented a little apartment and just sat there for two days, I was so happy to be indoors." A *Supervixens* check for eight grand arrived the next day—Meyer had cut the actor in on the profits. Napier never looked back, working continuously in film

and TV for such directors as Jonathan Demme, John Landis, and
Sylvester Stallone.*

$ $ $

The blind fury on display during the *Supervixens* bathtub murder
impressed and disturbed audiences and reviewers alike. "Truly one
of the most impassioned expressions of the battle of the sexes ever
filmed. Grisly . . . shocking . . . visceral," wrote Kevin Thomas in the
Los Angeles Times. In the *Hollywood Reporter,* Arthur Knight worried
that Meyer was encouraging audiences to "enjoy vicariously" *Supervixens'* ultraviolence. "Although not hardcore, its X is abundantly earned." Both critics also favorably compared the sequence
to the shower scene in *Psycho,* although Knight felt it lacked
"Hitchcock's sense of detachment," attributing to Meyer "a rage
in the man that makes him positively revel in violence."

Meyer continued to divide critics, with reviews for *Supervixens*
all over the map. "Meyer is the best comedy director working in
America today," gushed Dave Kehr in the *Chicago Reader,* ranking
the director with ace animators Chuck Jones and Tex Avery. Others felt RM had traded his talent for empty self-parody. The *Village
Voice's* Andrew Sarris saw Meyer as "auditioning for role of the
Frank Tashlin of the seventies . . . another talent lost to pop attitudizing." Perhaps the most interesting interpretation of the film
came from Ken Emerson in the *Boston Phoenix.* Emerson saw *Supervixens* as a repressed homosexual nightmare and felt Harry was
actually in love with Clint, whom the critic saw as the "archetypal
gay porn figure—the ingenue in blue jeans." His conclusion:
"*Supervixens* is for men who hate women and love each other."

---

* The year 2003 brought Napier's most unsettling credit. He appeared on the
syndicated *Dr. Phil* talk show with his wife, Dee, the topic being the pitfalls of
show business. Napier, now sixty-seven, admitted he was depressed over his current career and the dwindling roles he was being offered. "Dr. Phil, can you help
my husband get over his depression about his career and his fame?" asked Dee.
"I'm at the groveling stage of my career . . . you're my last shot," Napier told the
host. Harry Sledge fans everywhere wept.

$ $ $

Meyer had another war to face, the inevitable divorce from Edy, and this would be one gory battle to the death. Jim Ryan had to run interference for RM on the *Supervixens* set, taking Mrs. Meyer's frequent angry phone calls. "She was mad about everything," said Ryan, recalling a particularly rabid tirade during the film crew's time in Blythe. "She called me up and said, 'That son of a bitch!' Not even hello. She said, 'You tell that son of a bitch I just bought a thirty-eight-caliber and I'm gonna blow his fuckin' brains out if he comes through the door.' This is at four o'clock in the morning. I had to call Meyer and say, 'Look out—Edy's gonna shoot you.'" According to editor Les Barnum, RM was so paranoid that Williams would steal the *Supervixens* negative, he had a huge vault installed in his home. Meyer also attended dubbing sessions for the picture "disguised" in his 166th combat uniform, apparently, according to Barnum, "so Edy wouldn't recognize him."

The ever-quotable Williams held court for reporters at her now-husbandless Mulholland Drive estate. "Russ apparently expected me to just stay home and be a housewife," she told the *National Police Gazette*. "Me? In this day of the liberated woman, this is just not possible." Edy also claimed RM had "hit me and knocked me down."

In July 1975 Meyer had his wife evicted from their home. "Russ gave me the house as a wedding present," Edy sniffed to gossip columnist James Bacon. "Now he wants it back." She added that she'd be "waiting for the sheriff in my bikini."

"The divorce was very unfriendly," said Jim Ryan. "Edy had two or three high-powered attorneys there, Meyer had two. It was an expensive thing—I think he had a $100,000 bill." Edy was demanding not only the house but a share of the profits from *Supervixens*, saying she'd helped in its creation. It all came to a head in Los Angeles Superior Court before Judge Paul G. Breckenridge in October 1975.

Much to Edy's dismay, Jim Ryan testified about the phone call where she'd threatened to shoot Meyer. One press report said that RM had claimed his wife "had attacked him with a knife and kicked him in the groin," forcing him to obtain a court order preventing her "from using a gun or any dangerous weapon" against him. The day after Ryan's testimony, Edy, wearing a yellow T-shirt that read "FREE! Almost," held court for the press, not only to deny she'd threatened Meyer, but to deliver a plea to directors and producers everywhere. "I don't think my talent is just in being naked," she said, adding she'd like to "play a person with feelings and not be treated just like a piece of meat."

In November, Judge Breckenridge ruled very much in Russ Meyer's favor. Edy was entitled to nothing from *Supervixens*, 50 percent from the sale of their home, and $900 a month for only twenty-eight weeks. He noted that Williams had been an actress for fourteen years previous to her marriage, maintaining that "if she has the talents her lawyers believe, most assuredly she will find employment." A bitter Edy complained to the press that Meyer had "planned the divorce like he was Hitler."

Edy went on to date mobster Mickey Cohen—"my Sir Galahad," she told *People* magazine—and to a career that mainly consisted of appearances at various public events wearing as little as possible, or, in the case of the Cannes Film Festival, even less than that. An "intercontinental starlet," Roger Ebert dubbed her. Film roles were few and far between, something she blamed on Meyer and *Beyond the Valley of the Dolls*. "I got typecast as the porn star . . . it makes me really furious."

The eighties brought harder times. Williams surfaced in a few porno films, doing soft-core lesbian scenes. In 1995, Edy went hard-core (talked into it by none other than ubiquitous porn fixture Ron Jeremy, according to writer Luke Ford), doing girl-on-girl "with someone half her age" in the unforgettable *Snatch Masters 6*. As Ford cruelly notes, "The scene reveals more of Williams than most people want to see—including her many liver spots." Hollywood is a chilly place.

Russ Meyer lived to count his loot another day. He would never marry again. RM maintained that, yes, he'd wanted each of his three unions to last "the rest of my life, but it never worked out. They all wanted to change me. 'Why don't you go straight?' they'd say. Or they'd complain about my working Sunday. But I'm not about to change."

$ $ $

The next addition to Meyer's stable of tomatoes was the marvelous Raven De La Croix, a stunner with long black hair, big sad eyes, and an unmistakable New York accent. "I'm a strong woman, but I'm not an aggressive male stuck in a female body." She keeps tabs on the other Meyer dames, offering a helping hand whenever needed. "I'm the cosmic mother."

Raven manages to be old-world and outer-space at the same time. She can talk a mile a minute about working with Meyer, break into Mae West for a bit, then veer off into discussions of "goddess energy" that somehow don't have you running for a vomit bag. Raven's a searcher, a romantic, but despite the frequent excursions into the fantastic, there's no bullshit about her. She's lived nine lives, a few of them even on this planet.

Raven's been an ordained minister and spiritual counselor, worked in drug rehab with prison inmates, and rubbed elbows with a Hells Angel or two. "I love the roar of a Harley," she told *Iron Horse* magazine. "I dig the iron." One of her more famous escapades involved sneaking onto prison grounds to make love to her then husband, right under the nose of armed guards in a nearby gun tower. In the eighties De La Croix brought a touch of class to the strip circuit with her mix of elaborate costumes, fantasy, and old-school burlesque.

Born in Manhattan in August 24, 1947, Raven was one of eight kids. Her exotic looks come from the blend of her father's Comanche Indian heritage and French blood on her mother's side. Raven grew up poor with an alcoholic stepfather, losing herself in old musicals on TV. By the time she met RM, she'd worked in the music business and as an exotic dancer and was raising a nine-year-old son, Matoux.

De La Croix's entry into the movie biz was "the traditional Lana Turner story of being discovered in Schwab's." Raven was chowing down in Joe Allen's, a West Hollywood eatery, when Meyer's then casting agent Samantha Monsour spotted her. After one glance at Raven's 38DD-28-36 figure, RM didn't even ask her to take off her top and wouldn't see her naked until she was already parked in front of the camera. "He goes, 'I'm only paying a thousand dollars a week and we'll be shooting three to five weeks,' " Raven recalled. "I didn't know I was already hired. He didn't even ask."

$ $ $

Meyer's next picture — 1976's *Up!* — is, at least on the surface, his most extreme. Defenders maintain that in his later films, RM is mocking the constraints of plot, but I think it's just evidence of an increasing indifference (at least one Meyer insider, Stan Berkowitz, sees *Up!* as early evidence of what would become RM's long mental decline). Suffice it to say this picture has something to do with the murder by piranha of Adolf Hitler, rape, death by chainsaw, another stupid cop, and the illegitimate daughter of Hitler and Eva Braun. That and naked women chattering endlessly as they run through the woods. Plus loads of aberrant sex, which, from a director who saw any deviation from the missionary position as un-American, is curious indeed. Perhaps a capitulation to smuttier times, this is really the first RM movie to feature plenty of simulated sex, and to no great effect. There's oral, anal, S/M, homosexuality, much gratuitous violence, and a plethora of freakishly large rubber phalluses. It is also the only Meyer movie that feels a tad sleazy. Like *Supervixens*, one feels plenty of anger — "Russ has me being thrown and whipped and raped and punched throughout the whole thing," notes Raven — but this picture lacks the shot-out-of-a-cannon intensity that made RM's previous film so appealing. *Up!* is largely a pointless, indulgent spectacle akin to watching punk rock mess G. G. Allin lob his own waste at ducking but expectant fans. You peek in amused but detached disgust, hoping none of it gets on you.

The editing in *Up!* is surprisingly languid for Meyer (longtime editor Richard Brummer wasn't aboard). Without the typical punishing rhythm, the result lacks pizzazz. For me, the best part of the film is the one sequence that plays like Meyer truly gave a shit and that's the absolute insanity of the first five minutes. In a dark dungeon, a nude Adolf Hitler indulges in some S/M play with a woman in a zippered vinyl face mask while he is whipped, then buggered by a man in Pilgrim drag sporting a ridiculously large unit. An Asian woman named Limehouse stops by to sound a gong and sit on der Führer's face. A naked black woman looks on and, for no apparent reason, stirs a steaming cauldron. Old pervert Hitler, speaking in German without the benefit of subtitles, provides a nonstop monologue for nearly the entire sequence. It's hard to fathom what Meyer was intending here, except perhaps the complete alienation of his fans. According to his French distributor Jean-Pierre Jackson, Meyer relished the fact that his followers hated the beginning of *Up!*

The doting attention Meyer pays to Hitler's rape—it feels like it might lurch into gay porno at any moment—and the rather disquieting way RM has his often bizarre male leads strut their stuff raises an obvious question about his sexuality: Meyer, a closet case? This idea will no doubt be heresy to his fans and is definitely a minority viewpoint in the RM camp, but it has its supporters, most specifically Erica Gavin, who felt Meyer's whole macho routine was a little forced.

"Russ was extremely homophobic," said Gavin. "I think he had a lot of feelings that he didn't understand toward his army buddies and guys—it was almost like if it hadn't been such a no-no, Russ could've easily been in a relationship with a man. He created that closeness in the army—it was his way of doing it without it being sexual. The feeling I always had was if he would've allowed himself to *have* feelings, that his feelings would've been for men— and that's why tits 'n' ass were such a big thing to him, because that made him definitely straight."

Personally, I think it's an easy pop-psychology out to rely on closet homosexuality to sum up an increasingly complex character. Both Charles Sumners and Jim Ryan—his closest male friends—dismissed any notion of a gay RM. Though *Up!*, to the shock of many a Meyer fan, is full of actors sporting gigantic prosthetic peckers, and this raised a few eyebrows. "I had to rub my eyes, like in a cartoon," said a delighted John Waters. "I thought, '*What?!?*' Really kind of shocking for Russ. I was always amazed that he did that. Russ seemed like the type that big dicks would make a little . . . nervous. I thought that was great." Of course

Meyer maintained that those elephantine cocks were just a little something extra for the ladies. "I don't care for faggots," he bluntly informed critic David Ansen in 1975.

What shocked observers more was the increasing violence in Meyer's films. RM certainly wasn't alone in the raping and pillaging department: the seventies had led to ever-violent movies, including two 1971 pictures by filmmakers Meyer greatly admired, Stanley Kubrick's *A Clockwork Orange* and Sam Peckinpah's *Straw Dogs*. 1973's *The Exorcist* broke more taboos. The ultra-low-budget sicko "documentary" feel of 1972's *Last House on the Left* and *Texas Chainsaw Massacre* (1974) had upped the ante for the drive-in crowd. 1976—also the year of Meyer's *Up!*—saw the release of both *Carrie* and the ultimate "art" violence picture of the decade, Martin Scorsese's *Taxi Driver*. (It should also be noted the MPAA was notably more friendly to violence than sex—most of the pictures listed herein got R ratings.)

Your academic types might suggest all this carnage was a response to Watergate, Vietnam, and the death of the sixties, but in RM's case, I'd just say it was PES—post-Edy syndrome. An increasing bitterness toward women had metastasized within Meyer's films, as *Supervixens* attests (a picture, let's not forget, largely inspired by his tanglings with the ex-wife). However preposterous the execution, the way Meyer now combined sex and violence so explicitly and so casually left audiences and critics queasy. "As a dysfunctional, violent-oriented male, Russ is breaking new ground," said Raven De La Croix of *Up!* "It doesn't really have a happy message."

$ $ $

Poor Raven De La Croix—I always felt that she deserved a better Meyer picture than *Up!* One of Meyer's superior actresses, she has a real flair for comedy. Aside from the usual sprinkling of Meyer's combat cohorts, *Up!*'s cast consists of new and generally unimpressive faces. Raven is the standout, although Ed Schaaf—a former part-time golf caddy who had answered a *Daily Variety* ad—is an uncanny Hitler (RM's standby Nazi, Henry Rowland, somehow decided to pass on playing a nude, violated Führer, although he does dub the voice). Meyer returned to the Miranda, California, cabin where he had shot *Vixen* for most of *Up!* The day Raven arrived, Meyer was riding the actors in usual hard-nosed fashion, directing a scene where a nude girl in an Indian headdress is in bed, riding local cop Homer Johnson (the square-jawed Monte Bane). De La Croix quickly adapted to Meyer's boot camp ways and took to calling the director "Chief."

RM put Raven through the wringer. When Meyer had her swing nude through the air over the camera, Raven came flying down and knocked the cameraman over. She hung off a cliff with no safety net below. In another scene, as she's being violently dunked in a river, De La Croix, who'd almost drowned as a child, was stricken with panic. RM kept yelling, *"Put her under again!"* Raven noted the sadism in Meyer's approach. "If you pissed him off in any way, he would rewrite the script for the other character to degrade you."

And Meyer made Raven run. And run. And run. Through the woods, down winding roads, across raging rivers — delivering some mightily verbose dialogue (recorded live) all the while. "Run like a gazelle, dear," he'd instruct her. If Raven made even the slightest stumble, he'd scream, "Cut!" and have her start from the top. "She has great feet," informed Meyer. "You can run Raven through a bed of hot coals." No matter that her soles looked like hamburger at the end of the day. No human frailties were allowed for RM's amazons.

For some unknown reason Meyer also drafted Raven as his Inspector Clouseau. One morning before it was even light out, Uschi Digard, working as an associate producer/crew member on *Up!*, came in to tell Raven that Russ wanted to see her. When she reported to a dour Meyer, he immediately starting grilling her: "De La Croix, *who ate my salami*?" "I knew I had to take this seriously," Raven recalled. "Food was his thing."

"Who took my salami?" Meyer demanded.

"He didn't want it to be the crew, because then he was gonna have to lock up his food," Raven recalled.

"Can you tell me anything?" asked Sgt. Meyer.

"Give me some information," replied Cpl. De La Croix.

Meyer took her to where the salami had last been seen, hanging outside on the back porch. Raven told Meyer to give her a few minutes, and RM stormed off into the house.

De La Croix sat there, bleary-eyed in the predawn chill, asking herself, Who ate the salami? "All of a sudden I see this little face with little hands peep out. *Raccoons.*"

Uschi came out to summon her for a progress report on the investigation. She addressed a grave-looking RM. "It's the raccoons, Chief. I saw the raccoon that took your salami. And they were coming back for more, sir." Case closed.

"Okay, you got twenty minutes before the bell rings."

Raven went back to her room to grab a few minutes more shut-eye before Meyer had her back before the camera, once again running naked in the woods.

$ $ $

Up! was hardly the barn-burner that was *Supervixens*. Fred Beiersdorf, one of Meyer's distributors, said the picture merely did "OK." Meyer and De La Croix hit the road for a thirty-five-city promotional tour.* Although RM dismissed Raven's pursuit of the spiritual as a bunch of malarkey, he found himself unable to curb a certain fascination.

One night as they were heading out for their evening meal, RM stood before Raven, "sort of like Clark Gable. All dressed up, charming, his heart attached to his pants. He had that look on his face, and I knew that this was the offer, this was the moment, and I said, 'You look really great, Russ. Really handsome. I'm really glad we're friends. Let's go to dinner.'"

Raven saw Meyer as a kind of eccentric grandpa. But she had great affection for the old coot—and pity for King Leer: "He doesn't know how to make love to a woman, from any woman I've

---

* Meyer slipped a rave review of *Up!* attributed to one Martin Bormann into the film's newspaper ads. The *New York Times* pulled it after a day, although it continued to run in other dailies.

ever talked to that's ever been with him. He has no clue of what to do with these breasts he's so fascinated with. None at all."

$ $ $

When Meyer was in the editing room busy with *Up!*, he dreamt up a final touch that would render the film even more incomprehensible. Shari Eubank had suggested that RM might want to use a dancer she knew, and Shari turned out to be on the money. Meyer decided to create a new character for this female, The Greek Chorus, to narrate the movie nude on-screen and further confuse the already convoluted story. He asked Roger Ebert to whip up something in a hurry. "Russ said, 'You've got to write some dialogue for the Greek Chorus. It doesn't matter what she says, she just has to say something. And it should sound kinda poetic.'" So I just pulled down the first book of poetry I had, and paraphrased poetry by H. D. Hilda Doolittle always wrote under the name 'H.D.' She was an imagist poet, a contemporary of Pound. Nobody has ever noticed that. Maybe RM fans and H.D. scholars aren't the same people."

Armed with Ebert's lofty gobbledygook, Meyer took The New Girl out in the woods, stripped her down, and made her recite all this complex, arcane narration while she hung from trees and hid in bushes, although he'd later dub in another girl's voice to obliterate his new paramour's Spanish accent. He scared The New Girl and made her cry. But Meyer would fall hard for her, and as far as the women in his life went, he'd place her second only to Eve. They'd fuck, fight, and film off and on for the next four years.

Meyer was in a fever over the broad, and he was gonna use his movie camera to cut her up like a steak—RM's next film would be a loony jigsaw puzzle assembled out of endless disembodied close-ups showing her every naked inch. Her name was Kitten, and she was one hot tamale.

The Ultra-Vixen

I don't need any of that connubial bliss stuff. I imagine I'll probably end up a lonely old man.

—RUSS MEYER

Everybody loves Kitten. She's got a big heart, a big temper, and of course, mythic mammaries. Natividad's battled booze and drugs and, during a low point in the eighties, even slid into that crass wango tango known as hard-core. She's survived a double mastectomy (Russ contributed $11,000 to her operation costs—"one tit," joked an anonymous friend), and is determined to rebuild her fantastic physique. No doubt some people would find that desperate. I find it inspiring in a cuckoo sort of way. Like Meyer, Kitten wants to one-up reality at any cost. "I have a metal cast of my fanny," Natividad once informed reporter Jessica Berens. "I just sold one to a doctor in Madrid. I only have two left . . . I must reorder. Some guy in the Valley made it."

Kitten Natividad is one of Meyer's wackiest dames. The living embodiment of funky delirium à la James Brown's "Hot Pants," everything about Kitten was too much—outrageous body, "Is it a wig?" hair, industrial-strength makeup, and the most overheated line delivery this side of Edy Williams. In some ways, Kitten was also along the lines of Uschi—a dedicated soldier ready for anything—only Kitten kept going long after the cameras had run out

of film. Critic Ted Mahar recalled Natividad making an unforgettable Meyer-orchestrated entrance at a Portland, Oregon, reviewers' screening of *Up!* "Kitten comes out in a jumpsuit zipped up to
her neck—'Hello, I hope you like me!'—and she zips it all the way
down. She's got nothing under the jumpsuit. None of the people
present reported what she did. Everybody enjoyed the show and
kept it to themselves."

Later that same evening Meyer took Mahar and Natividad out
for a steak dinner, during which "he pulled open her shirt and said,
'Aren't those the most beautiful things you ever saw?' Kitten looked
down, smiled, and blushed mildly—not because her breasts were
exposed, but she was receiving a compliment. It was like Russ had
said Kitten had gotten straight A's on her report card." Much to
Meyer's great glee, wherever Kitten went, craziness—and much
publicity—ensued. When she returned to the City of Roses three
years after *Up!* to promote *Beneath the Valley of the Ultra-Vixens*, she
was thrown off the campus of Portland State University. "Offering
no resistance, the pneumatic Natividad went quietly with officers," according to the campus paper.

In *Shock Value*, John Waters wrote about a memorable evening
spent with RM and Natividad at Meyer's favorite Hollywood eatery,
Musso and Frank's. "Kitten gave out nude photos to the waiters,
and the maître d' treated Russ as if he were Cecil B. DeMille." Natividad's pants were too tight for her to step up into Meyer's GMC.
So RM wrapped his meaty paws around the back of her legs and
lifted her in, writes Waters, "as she squealed, 'Ohhhhhhh, Russ!'"

Movie critic Kevin Thomas recalled a trip to the cinema with
the crazy couple. "Being the English major that I was, I ventured
into conversation with Kitten," said Thomas, who started discussing Meyer's films, describing Russ as "essentially a puritan."
Kitten said, 'Boy, you aren't kidding—I can't get him to go down
on me!' Well, it was the one and only time I have ever seen Russ
blush. Beet red." According to a highly amused Waters, "She told
me that she taught Russ how to eat pussy. I thought, 'Well! I just
met you.'"

Natividad was a raunchier kind of Meyer girl, and some of his
other superstars needed time to adjust. Haji, in attendance when

RM later proposed to Kitten, was shocked when Natividad nonchalantly popped a boob out of her dress in a local eatery. "I looked at Russ like he was a gentleman. I was totally embarrassed. I was very private and shy. I said, 'I'm not going out with this girl anymore.' It took me a long time to make friends with Kitten—then I learned how kind and wonderful she is." Roger Ebert maintained that Natividad was, "loyal to Russ right to the end. They loved each other, and it was sexual at various times, but it was always a friendship."

Even Meyer's combat buddies warmed to her. "Kitten I liked," said Charlie Sumners. "She was so frank and aboveboard. No pretense." Charlie's wife Floyce recalled a reunion of the 166th that included a tour of Oral Roberts University in Tulsa. Kitten picked up many knickknacks in the gift shop, and among all the fine, upstanding military folks present, the stripper "was the only one who bought something religious out of our whole group," said Floyce. "We thought that was so funny."

$ $ $

Francesca "Kitten" Natividad was born on February 13, 1948, in Juarez, Mexico. The first of nine children, Kitten was born when her mother was just sixteen. By age fourteen, Natividad was housecleaning for actress Stella Stevens. Exposure to the world of movie stars hooked her on show business, and she became determined "to grow up and be gorgeous and loved and coveted by all!"

Kitten started dancing in 1969 and eventually held not one but two prestigious titles, Miss Nude Universe and Miss Nude Cosmopolitan. Hipped to Natividad by Shari Eubank, Meyer ventured into the Classic Cat to see what Kitten had to offer. Determined to make an immediate impression, she introduced herself by sneaking up behind RM and resting her big knockers on his back. Ironically, it was Natividad's second husband, wig importer George DeMoss, who encouraged her to pester Meyer for a part. "The first time I went to read for him, he asked me to dinner. I said, 'I'm married.' He said, 'Oh. Well, I was just asking for dinner.' When Russ wanted something, he went for it. He didn't care if you were married," Natividad laughed. "He didn't care if *he* was married."

Kitten was soon smitten. "I saw different little things that impressed me. How Russ, with his big, huge hands, would tenderly handle that camera like it was a lover. He was so good to it. He had these big fat fingers, yet he could gently open the lens and click it—it was just marvelous. Then when he wrote a check out, ooooh—what perfect, beautiful handwriting for such a massive hand." As for Russ's craggy visage, Natividad instructed the press that RM had "a sexy face, sort of perverted." To one reporter in 1979 she helpfully explained, "I have a father complex thing." And why was Russ gaga over Kitten? "Because I mother him," she revealed.

Eventually Meyer invited Kitten to lunch at a Hollywood watering hole called Michael's. "I was thirty years old and never drank," said Natividad, who nervously downed a martini after RM ordered one. "I drank one martini and it was okay. By the second, I started throwing up at the bar. Then I went to the bathroom, threw up, and passed out." RM got a hat check girl to revive her by sticking amyl nitrate under Kitten's nose, while Russ struggled with her bushy pubic hair as he zipped up her pants.*

Somehow Meyer managed to drag Kitten back to his lair. "I woke up naked. And Russ said he took my clothes off so I wouldn't throw up on them. But then I said, 'Why are *you* naked?'" Meyer actually admits in his autobiography that he had his first roll in the hay with Natividad while she was still unconscious.† And thus began their grand and tempestuous affair.

Russ went right to work on his new project, concentrating first on redoing Kitten's bargain-basement Tijuana boob job. According to both Roger Ebert and Haji, RM had previously been against augmentation, but Meyer set about rebuilding Kitten like he was souping up a T-Bird. RM took Natividad to a Dr. Tippit in Las Vegas, who properly augmented her breasts for $3,500. "You can

---

* RM would maintain the two things that caused him the most trouble with censors were the bathtub scene in *Supervixens* and Natividad's hairy pudenda.

† "Oh my God, that's not *nice!*" said Kitten, who burst out laughing when I repeated this tale. "Now you see why I thought Russ had some sort of mental illness?"

get them for $1,200, but they are not nearly so good—those kind droop," Kitten instructed the press. (RM also set her up with a $100-an-hour voice coach to demolish her thick Spanish accent.) From here on in Meyer starlets became so massive Meyer boasted they could only be measured in "hat sizes."

As for the sexual rewards that followed, "Kitten Natividad was the champion, without a doubt." In interview after interview, Meyer would describe Natividad as an insatiable sex maniac who would eat you alive if she wasn't satisfied nightly. Funnily enough, Kitten complained the same about Russ, who, she felt compelled to point out, "had a beautiful, huge cock with a big head. After a while, you don't like him banging you that hard all the time! It had to be twice a day, morning and night. Four o'clock in the morning—whether I got up or not. You can never have a head-ache with him, y'know?"

The fame bestowed upon her by Meyer alleviated any mi-granes, however. "I really enjoyed just looking at my name up there," said Natividad of seeing *Up!* on a theater screen. "So *huge.* The biggest I've ever seen it." Kitten would star in RM's next film, playing two confusing roles à la Shari Eubank in *Supervixens.*

$ $ $

Meyer filmed the $233,000 *Beneath the Valley of the Ultra-Vixens* in eight weeks during 1977, shooting most of it (outside of a few days spent along the Colorado River) in a new Hollywood Hills house on Arrowhead Drive he'd bought specifically for the production, as its A-frame construction allowed him to stick the camera any-where.* RM's home became a very personal smorgasbord of strange, colorful sets: one space filled with piñatas, sombreros, and Mexican flea-market junk; another completely neon-blue down to the bed frame and springs. The sadistic violence that had

---

* *Beneath* crew member Bruce Pasternack went from working with Russ Meyer to Orson Welles, and he found the two directors to be the same sort of miserable enfants terribles. "They were very, very similar in terms of their personality," said Pasternack. "They both wanted to control absolutely everything and everyone around them."

proved so unpopular in Meyer's last two pictures was now abandoned, although he'd have characters bleed in different colors
(black junkyard man Mr. Zebulon bleeds white; the gay dentist
bleeds pink; etc.) Apparently this was RM's retort to critics of his
past cinematic bloodshed, although cowriter Roger Ebert
thought it an obtuse gambit at best. "I don't think anybody can
understand it," said Ebert, who, despite being an outspoken critic
of exploitation gore in such pictures as *I Spit on Your Grave*, maintained he never took Meyer violence "very seriously. It was a cartoon, but sometimes I thought [Russ] lost control of the tone."

Believe it or not, *Beneath*'s ludicrous plot had been somewhat
inspired by Kitten having introduced Meyer to anal sex, a sport he
found absurdly repellent. With Roger Ebert manning the typewriter under the pseudonym R. Hyde, director and scribe spent a
week dreaming up the story of Lamar Shed (played by Ken Kerr),
who "can't look a good fuck in the eye"—that is, he can only function sexually with wife Lavonia (Kitten Natividad) á la rear entry.
In the course of salvaging his marriage, Lamar not only gets saved
by radio preacher Eufaula Roop (the big blonde Ann Marie, *Playboy*'s Little Annie Fanny made flesh), but endures coitus with the
immense Junkyard Sal (June Mack) as well as with Lavonia's alter-
ego, Spanish stripper Lola Langusta (Kitten again).

Perhaps only a county away from *Supervixens*, this world of
"beautiful people, driving terrible cars and living in squalor . . . all
oversexed" (and all sporting intricate names RM had nicked off a
Georgia map) benefited from one of Meyer's stronger casts. Much
beefier than in his *Good Morning . . . and Goodbye!* days, Pat Wright
plays macho sex machine Mr. Peterbuilt with one-stroke-away-from-
a-heart-attack intensity, giving new meaning to the term *grudge-fuck*.

Providing the obtuse *Our Town* on-screen narration is The
Man from Small Town, U.S.A., the cosmically bland Stuart Lancaster, in overalls and a plaid red hat, gazing into the camera with
the earnestness of a Home Shopping Network rep conning you
into calling in your credit card number to buy a Christmas elf fig-
urine. You simply haven't lived until you've seen Lancaster barge
into a tiny mountaintop shed to interrupt some young buck
humping Soul (Uschi Digard) with the immortal admonishment,

"Now son, if you plan to be around to see your fifteenth birthday, you'd better pull out that *thing* you call a *dick* and let your father show you how it's done."

A huge African American woman with a mug not unlike a sexy Jabba the Hut, June Mack was a dominatrix and madam who tooled around in a Rolls when not polishing off tubs of ice cream. As Roger Ebert put it, "She had so much silicone goin' on that you didn't know where it stopped and the body began." RM had seen an ad advertising her services in the *L.A. Free Press* and sent it to an interested Ebert. Before long her massive body was parked in front of Meyer's lens essaying the role of Junkyard Sal. According to Ebert, Meyer's favorite June Mack tale involved the scene where she entertains Mr. Peterbuilt in a pile of leaves in the back of a garbage truck. "Shout like you love it!" barked Meyer. Mack shot back, "What do *I* know about love?" The image of this ebony mountain of flesh in a hot pink nightie, clapping Lamar's feet together while they go at it—well, it's a vision you can't erase (upon gazing upon the big-breasted behemoth that was June Mack, Charles Napier muttered to the critic, "You got your night cut out for you, Ebert").*

Despite such impossible eyefuls as June Mack, *Beneath* clearly belongs to Kitten. Meyer—who at the time said of Natividad's body, "I know every nook and cranny, every depression and elevation"—photographs her flesh like a cartographer charting heretofore unmapped wilderness. Shots of Natividad's eyes, lips, breasts, and ass function as the dominoes in the *Beneath* game. RM is visibly obsessed with Kitten, lost in her painted smile, and it's a beautiful thing to experience. Here Meyer takes his industrial-sex-film approach straight to the moon, cramming in many crazy and masterfully cut montages, using what editor Richard Brummer called "musical repetitions" of radio towers, street signs, old trucks, and people fucking on steering wheels to create a magnificent blue-collar sex farm that is equal parts Roy Lichtenstein and

---

* Mack was murdered not long after making *Beneath*. According to Ebert, a drug dealer was going to shoot her boyfriend. "She stood in front of the guy to protect him and took the bullet."

Hee Haw. When *Beneath*'s motor is hummin', there's nothing quite like it. "Meyer had carried everything that we had developed to an extreme," said Brummer (amazingly, most of the film had been shot silent and then dubbed in postproduction, a painstaking editorial tour de force by Brummer).

There are sequences that absolutely dazzle, such as the opening where Ann Marie screws Martin Bormann in a coffin, bringing to life the tale that Lilly La Mont had related to Meyer years before. Shots of Ann Marie in a white mesh jumpsuit, chewing gum as she twiddles with Pong, her face lit only by harsh, video-game light, evoke a grotesque beauty. The scene where Lavonia, sexually frustrated one hot summer night, taunts her husband with the sound of a sex aid as he tries to study in the next room is a sublime assault only Meyer could engineer. "I wanted a symphony of vibrator, calculator, and crickets," said RM, who zeroes in the sort of details nobody else would ever bother with, such as a bed frame caster leaving dirty grooves in the carpet as it jerks to and fro from Kitten's gyrations.

But when *Beneath* is bad, it's dire, with infantile doo-doo humor and cringe-making homophobia again exposing RM as the primate he is. And while expertly cut, the film goes on forever. And ever. Released in 1979, *Beneath* is at once the best and the worst of Russ Meyer, but critics were consistently unkind. "Russ Meyer's films were funny ten years ago; today they're juvenile," said Gene Siskel. English critic Tony Rayns felt that the director had turned into a machine stuck on repeat. "It may be that Meyer, certainly one of the American cinema's true mavericks, in his total independence, will never recapture the freedom of invention that he discovered during his brief soujourn at 20th Century Fox but will condemn himself to endless varations on the formula he pioneered with *Vixen.*"

Dave Kehr, who'd championed Meyer as recently as *Supervixens,* saw *Beneath* as a "strangely unsatisfying" case of style obliterating content. In Kitten Natividad, "with her big round eyes and polished cheeks," he detected "an eerie resemblance to Howdy Doody," and it's clear that Kehr was disturbed by the director manning the puppet strings. "It's one thing to stylize a landscape, something else to stylize a person," he wrote. "There's a lot more to lose."

Meyer's more-more-more aesthetic was becoming a headache-inducing less. Many critics simply felt exhausted, beat up by the Meyer oeuvre. Myron Meisel noted that RM's "last few films frantically seek to top themselves," while Kehr opined that "after a certain point the audience can't take it anymore." Meyer had become the cinematic equivalent of a carny operating a ferris wheel, determined to run the ride faster and faster, unaware or perhaps unconcerned that some of his customers were being thrown screaming into the night air.

The emptiness at work can't be denied. Meyer, at the top of his game in terms of photography and editing, has nothing new to add other than his visual vivisection of Kitten. One can deflect criticism by declaring that It's Only a Cartoon, but if that were true I don't think a viewing of *Beneath* could leave you feeling so utterly spent in such an unsavory way. Due to RM's potent, almost childlike obsession with Kitten, I happen to love this movie, but it's awfully hard to defend in its entirety.

He-man Meyer once more flaunts his lack of introspection, his disinterest in women as anything more than animatronic pinups or receptacles for his sperm, and his contempt for just about everything under the sun with this film. "I'm not a sensitive person," he sneered. He had no patience in life, let alone for a script. Where could it all lead, other than down a cold, narrow, sporadically bedazzling dead end? Of course, the very idea of a kinder, gentler Meyer makes one puke. One great thing about him is that he just didn't give a fuck. "If I wasn't so into tits I probably could've been a great filmmaker," says Our Hero in summation.

Maybe critic David Ansen had RM's number after all. "This is precisely Meyer's limitation as a filmmaker — behind his bracing mockery is the compulsive guffaw of a high school student too scared to step out of the self-protected shade of parody. It's all finally just a goof."

$ $ $

In Kitten, Meyer had found a Marlene for his Von Sternberg. "He's a genius, a real genius," Natividad crowed. "When he wanted me to cry he'd say, 'Pretend they're beating your dog.' When he wanted me to look sexy, he'd say, 'C'mon, baby, jerk off the whole world.' I gave all the stagehands hard-ons, which Russ says is the biggest compliment in this business." RM's personal life bled further than ever into the cinematic, and the no-sex-while-filming rule was completely abandoned. When the crew would break for lunch, RM would disappear with Kitten, who'd then return with half her body makeup eaten off.

"It was very, very sexual," Natividad said of making *Beneath*, with RM continually egging her on. "I was screwing so hard I broke the bed a few times. The walls fell and everything." Kitten would look at Meyer "and I could see that his penis was . . . erect, and it was oozing. I didn't want to say anything, because then everybody would look. But the guy had a hard-on. And it was *oozing.*"*

When Kitten wasn't getting down in front of the camera, she was getting it on with Meyer, who expected her to deliver the same sort of pile-driving passion she'd put on-screen. "We were really going at it every night. And it was very, very hard, because they'd pick me up at 5:30 a.m., I'd work until about six or seven at night, then I had to wait for Russ to do his cocktail hour and calm down. We'd go have dinner, we'd come back, screw. It would be twelve midnight, he'd drop me off at home—to my husband." George DeMoss, the man who'd pushed Kitten into Meyer's arms, was by

---

* As usual, Meyer was intent on blocking the ooze of others. According to Natividad, he had it in for *Beneath*'s Ken Kerr. "We had a little liaison, and Russ was not happy about that. He never spoke to him again. Russ wanted to control everybody's sex life. He was eccentric—or crazy. What did he get out of it? I said, 'Russ, you won't let any of the guys get any pussy, but you're getting pussy every night.' He said, 'Well, I'm the *director,* I'm *Russ Meyer.*' It was so weird."

By the end of *Beneath,* RM would alienate not only Kerr but the picture's associate producer as well, his longtime ally Uschi Digard. According to editor Les Barnum, when Meyer chewed Uschi out for not following orders, a furious Digard revealed she'd not only done exactly as told, she'd tape-recorded his instructions, at which point she proceeded to play them for RM. Uschi exploded at a crew dinner. "Right there at the dinner table, right to Meyer's face, Uschi said, 'I will not work for this man again, he is crazy!' " Barnum recalled. "Russ didn't do anything. He kind of took it and continued to eat his dinner."

now seething with jealousy. He challenged RM to put up his dukes, then, after seeing Kitten tooling around in it, smashed up Meyer's Mercedes.

The drama was "wearing me out," Kitten confessed. "I was breaking out in hives." Finally I said, 'Look at me—I look worn out! I'd go, 'Russ, ya gotta let me go home and sleep.' He'd go, *'Makeup concealer!'* " One of the girls would slather on the pancake to hide the bags under Natividad's eyes, then it was on with the show. But Russ Meyer would take a bizarre and frustrating detour before putting *Beneath* to bed.

$ $ $

Russ Meyer and the Sex Pistols. It had more potential than Godzilla versus Megalon. Were there any two forces more arrogant, provocative, and obnoxious? In 1977, the Pistols were the essence of thumbing your nose, and Meyer had made a career out of it. The mastermind pimping this idea was of course Malcolm McLaren, the oft-reviled Svengali behind the band. The Sex Pistols were causing a big ruckus in England, and Warners was intent on breaking them in the States.

McLaren thought a feature film would be just the ticket for the Pistols, and he'd already considered Peter Cook, Stephen Frears, and Ken Loach for the director's chair. Now he set his sights on Meyer, admiringly declaring him to be "the epitome of American fascism." So McLaren flew to Los Angeles to meet King Leer. Wisely, Meyer brought along a young friend who could decode and deflect the hip Englishman: Rene Daalder, a young Dutch filmmaker and screenwriter active in the Los Angeles punk scene. Daalder and McLaren hit it off immediately.

"Malcolm McLaren was this very intellectual art school product—serious Marxist leanings, informed by the Situationists," said Daalder. And then there was Russ—unpretentious, commie-hating, frequently farting Russ. RM would begrudgingly admit that "McLaren was sincere. He really was a zealot, he had fire in his eyes," but the two clashed immediately, with Meyer soon fobbing McLaren off on Daalder, who put the agent provocateur up for a month in Los Angeles. "I don't know if either of them understood how far apart they were," said Daalder, adding that although RM's house was mere minutes away, the vibes between them were such that "it was almost impossible to have Malcolm go there on his own."

Daalder and McLaren banged out a treatment for the Pistols movie with the working title *Anarchy in the U.K.* Meyer perused the work, which, according to Daalder, centered on the grim, grimy "actual story of the Sex Pistols," and threw it right into the nearest trash can. Reality? That was for dummies! Meyer hated the treatment "because it was depressing," according to Daalder. "Depressing—that's the last thing that a Russ Meyer can ever be. But a Sex Pistols movie *has* to be depressing."

RM immediately set out to undermine McLaren's plans. There was no way Meyer could make some downer cinema verité band hagiography. So RM got Ebert on the horn—he'd whip up something fast *and* remember to put in the tits. McLaren had to get it through his Situationist skull that he'd hired Russell Albion Meyer and, as Daalder put it, "Z-Man and Martin Bormann were going to march right through *whatever* it was gonna be." In June 1977, Roger Ebert installed himself at the Sunset Marquis Hotel and, with a great deal of input from McLaren—who gave Meyer and Ebert a crash course in punk rock and Pistols, thrashed out a script with the unforgettable title *Who Killed Bambi?*

M.J.,* a rich, decadent rock star, gets his kicks being chauffered through the countryside, lazily searching for some deer to shoot. He has his driver dump his latest kill in front of some poor family's home, a little girl opens the door, sees the bloody carcass, and exclaims, "Mummy, they've killed Bambi!" M.J. then tries to corrupt the Sex Pistols, as does their head-game manager P. T. Proby, with such distractions as a mad rapist, a sexy Scotland Yard operative named O, and an arcade game that pokes fun at Scientology's fabled E-Meter along the way. The little girl returns at

---

* Intended as a swipe at Mick Jagger; in some versions of the script, it's B.J.

film's end, avenging Bambi by way of a .357 magnum blasting a fat hole in M.J.'s celebrity face. *Bambi* was to be, Ebert later wrote, "a statement of anarchic revolt against the rock millionaires, and the whole British establishment." Meyer, who was going to appear as an on-camera narrator, described the picture as "a combination of *A Hard Day's Night* and *Beyond the Valley of the Dolls.*"

With the script somewhat complete, the entourage set out for London. Meyer and McLaren weren't exactly becoming bosom buddies. On the flight over, "Russ insisted on sitting on the aisle because McLaren had his bondage pants on," said Ebert. "Russ said, 'If we get in a crash, you're gonna get those goddamn straps twisted around the chair and we'll all die.' " The chaos that seemed endemic to McLaren was beginning to chafe RM, and in the absence of a signed contract, he demanded to be put up in style and paid weekly in cash.

In England came the inevitable summit meeting of Meyer, Ebert, McLaren, and the Sex Pistols. It was a surreal collection of egos. As Ebert later wrote, both he and Meyer were "a little nonplussed, I think, to hear Johnny Rotten explain that he liked *Beyond the Valley of the Dolls* because it was so true to life."

Pistols band members Paul Cook and Steve Jones got on with Meyer. Jones had no clue who RM was before a copy of *Faster, Pussycat! Kill! Kill!* won him over ("I love the bird in it, she was fuckin' *awesome*," he said of Tura Satana). Jones was also impressed by Meyer's chutzpah. "He was a Hollywood guy, American, dressed kinda loud. I thought he was great."

Not surprisingly, Rotten plus Meyer made for a toxic cocktail. "If I had a tape recording of any one night in my life, it would be the night Johnny Rotten, Russ Meyer, and I went out to dinner," said Ebert. "We went to Beauchamp Place, behind Harrod's. And at one point Rotten was being obstreperous. And Russ said, 'Listen, you little shit—we won the Battle of Britain for you. And we can come over here and beat *you*, too.'

"What Russ didn't take into account was that America didn't fight in the Battle of Britain and that John Lydon was Irish, not British. But this didn't register with Johnny Rotten, either, because he was impressed. At this point—when he was supposed to be the bad boy of Britain—here was a guy who called him a little shit and said he would knock his block off. I think Rotten liked that."

Not according to JR, who later maintained that he completely lost interest in the project on the spot. "After I met Russ Meyer, this dirty old man, I felt really shabby about the whole thing," he wrote in his autobiography. "I didn't want to know from there on. . . . I hated Russ Meyer from the first second I saw him—an overbearing, senile old git."

Meyer, happily exhibiting his anti-Irish prejudice, complained that all Rotten did was pick at his scalp, his nose, and the green film on his teeth. Worst of all, little Johnny was vociferously anti-American. "He was proud of his bomb-throwing countrymen, the IRA," said a disgusted RM, who maintained that if the IRA requested Rotten "to throw a bomb, he'd probably run the other way."* Still, Meyer admitted, "Rotten definitely had charisma."

Sid Vicious had his own problems with Meyer. At McLaren's behest, Ebert had written a scene in which the doomed bass player has sex with his mother (Meyer had already cast Marianne Faithfull for the role) and then shares heroin with her. At this, Vicious drew the line: "Well, I don't mind balling her, but shooting up—forget it!" Meyer later made the preposterous claim that had the movie happened, Vicious would "still be alive." Roger Ebert reported that at the time of *Bambi*, McLaren had Sid on a weekly retainer that translated into about $14 in U.S. funds. "He had nothing to eat," said Ebert, who recalled that Meyer, driving Vicious (in some tellings it's Rotten) home one night, bought him a much-needed dinner: "two six-packs of beer and a big can of pork and beans."

Rene Daalder saw the Pistols and RM as a case of two angry worlds colliding. Meyer was Mr. Can-Do, always ready to go-go-go. "Every morning the phone would ring at 5:30 a.m., a military wake-up call. If Russ heard in your voice that you were still somewhat sleepy, he would find it disgusting." The Pistols, on the other

---

* Meyer once boasted in an interview he got threatening calls from the National Front due to working with the Pistols. No one present who I interviewed remembers this.

hand, "were not at all about energy. Sick every morning, incapable of moving a limb, totally lethargic British guys."

By this point in the game Rotten and Vicious totally despised McLaren, and *Who Killed Bambi?* became emblematic of his scheming megalomania. Now the Pistols had been relegated to performing monkeys in a Russ Meyer film. Rotten, particularly annoyed he'd been consigned to play a sex fiend, was determined to wear a garish hippie outfit for the role to thwart what he surely regarded as a Hollywood version of punk. According to director Julien Temple, who picked up the pieces after Meyer left (and decades later put together the one great Pistols visual document, *The Filth and the Fury*), it was during the *Bambi* debacle that McLaren really lost control of the band. "The group broke up largely because of that film," he said.

Still, the project staggered along. McLaren drove Meyer around London, amused by the director's determination to avoid showing a single red double-decker bus in the film, and his fascination with arcane British street signs, "names like Wopping, Battersea, Bayswater, names that conjured up sexual connotations." Ebert polished off another round on the script and flew home. Sets were built near Heathrow, and Meyer summoned Fred Owens and Jim Ryan to join him in London.

In mid-October 1977, Meyer shot the opening scene, where M.J. kills the deer that's dumped on the little girl's doorstep. With *Blacksnake*'s David Prowse as the chauffeur, all went well. "They'd already seen the dailies of the stuff they'd shot and had put a work print together of the first scene," said Jim Ryan. When Steve Jones saw the footage, "I didn't really know what to make of it, 'cause I didn't even bother reading the script." He admits he was still looking forward to "the birds with big tits."

Three days into the shoot it became apparent that they were already out of money. McLaren had never finalized a deal. "Reams of contracts were prepared, document upon document for producing and financing of the film," Sandy Lieberson, then of 20th Century Fox, told Craig Bromberg. "And Malcolm was continually changing his mind." With increasing chaos surrounding the project, Fox's stockholders were getting cold feet—particularly one of its more famous board members. "We just happened to meet the Fox guys who axed us in an elevator in Portugal," recalled Jim Ryan. "They said, 'Well, this is off the record—[stockholder] Princess Grace said, 'We don't want another X picture from Meyer.'" Yes, none other than Grace Kelly hammered the final nail in *Bambi*'s coffin.

Would *Who Killed Bambi?* have made a great film? Who knows. "What a tragedy! It could've been a screamer!" insisted RM, who found Ebert's script to be cinematic gold. Steve Jones thought Meyer was clueless when it came to the band's music, complaining that as far as RM was concerned, "we were the Monkees." "It was totally doomed," said Rene Daalder. "It could never have happened, really." Meyer's best pictures may approximate the energy of rock, but he had little interest in the actual stuff, and one of the world's most exciting bands might've been squandered in the process. "Almost without exception, motion pictures are a very unfortunate match with rock and roll," maintained Daalder. "Ultimately you're going to pervert or corrupt the spirit. It just can't be done."

$ $ $

Who Killed Bambi? collapsed in a tangle of lawsuits from both sides. Even director Julien Temple was dragged into the fray in 1980, during a promotional tour for *Rock 'n' Roll Swindle*, the film that finally resulted in the aftermath of the Meyer debacle. He told reporter Todd McCarthy that Meyer had "personally shot a deer with a pistol" while filming *Bambi*. RM, furious that someone would accuse him of such a stunt, took Temple to court for libel, extracting a printed public apology from him in the pages of *Screen International.* "He loved to sue people," said Kitten Natividad.

Meyer was devastated by the sudden demise of *Bambi*. He'd thought this would be his ticket back into the big leagues, and at age fifty-five, Meyer no doubt realized the opportunity wasn't going to present itself again. "That experience drove me to not make more films for quite a time. It's depressing to have a project collapse like that. I traveled to New Zealand and Switzerland just to get away from it."

Meyer went into a tailspin. "He would go into deep depressions and get diarrhea," said Kitten. "I knew when Russ had diarrhea he was depressed. He'd get up, his pants would be all soiled. I'd go, 'Russ, *God!* Go take a shower!' He wouldn't sleep all night. He'd be in a dark room, sitting and staring. 'Russ, are you coming to bed?' Nothing. 'Russ, are you coming to bed?' *'Leave me alone!'* " Natividad said these down periods could last weeks. "I think he was sort of manic when he was depressed. He'd be really, really low, and then when Russ was working, he was working, working, feverishly working. Y'know, we could *never* stay home and watch TV. Never. Because he had to work. And if he wasn't working, he was screwing—or asleep."

$ $ $

Eventually Meyer finished and released the film he'd shot before the *Bambi* fiasco, *Beneath the Valley of the Ultra-Vixens.* Not only were the critics harsh, but the outlets for a Russ Meyer picture were drying up.

Meyer encountered increasing resistance from theaters due to his constant X ratings. While RM had jumped on X in its infancy, he now considered it a liability. Meyer criticized the MPAA every chance he got. He particularly loathed the MPAA's all-powerful potentate Jack Valenti, whom he saw as a glad-handing shill for big-studio interests. "The rating board is our censor board, plain and simple," charged Meyer. "If you get an X rating, there are a lot of newspapers and television and radio stations that won't take advertising." In the late seventies theaters were proliferating inside shopping malls, and mall owners forbade X material—it clashed with a wholesome family atmosphere.

X was the one rating Valenti had failed to copyright, a prime reason being, notes author Jon Lewis, "to keep the studios out of the dirty picture business." The message seemed to be: Make a picture that goes too far for Hollywood and we'll trap you in the gutter. Thus Robert Aldrich's lesbian psychodrama *The Killing of Sister George,* the hard-core *Behind the Green Door,* and the soft-core *Supervixens* were all slapped with (and many filmmakers say marginalized by) the same rating, whether MPAA-designated or self-imposed. Could Joe Six-Pack discern the difference between triple-X porno and a Meyer X? They were a galaxy apart, yet all that registered with the public was the one scarlet letter. "It had a bad connotation because of the hard-core people," said Meyer. Yet when RM had some of his older pictures rerated R, business fell. The X was Meyer's albatross.*

As previously stated, big studios and major directors were routinely exploring subjects that were formerly taboo. One only had to catalogue some of the major's pictures in the decade preceeding *Beneath*. Male hustlers in *Midnight Cowboy*. Wife-swapping in *Bob and Carol and Ted and Alice*. The ultraviolence of *The Wild Bunch, Straw Dogs,* and *A Clockwork Orange. The Exorcist*'s obscenity-spewing devil-child masturbating with a cross. Box office superstar Marlon Brando's shenanigans in *Last Tango in Paris*. The sexual politics of *Shampoo*. Teen prostitution in *Pretty Baby*. An Oscar-winning director—Roman Polanski—appearing in drag in *The Tenant*. The pressbook for the 1974 Columbia Pictures–distributed soft-X import *Emmanuelle* spoke volumes: "X has never been known for its elegance. Or for its beautiful people. Or for its intelligent story line. X has been known for other things. At Columbia Pictures we're proud to bring you a movie that will change the meaning of X." This was bullshit, of course, as what was being peddled was no loftier than anything Russ Meyer had to offer, but since *a Hollywood studio* was doing the selling, hell, it must be art.

Guys like Meyer had busted down the doors, enabling the studios to waltz in after him, throwing big bucks around in the process. "The exhibiting game is now based on the advertising

---

* Surprisingly, Richard Heffner, the controversial chairman of the MPAA's ratings board from 1974 to 1994, and a man who publicly battled such directors as William Friedkin and Brian De Palma over ratings cuts, agreed with Meyer. "I wanted to change X at the beginning, I thought it was an abomination," said Heffner. "I do recognize that it was a mistake on the part of the founders, meaning Valenti. I thought it was so clear they ought to make the change away from X before it killed the system—and it did kill the system in terms of giving the Russ Meyers and others the chance to beat us over the head with it. When the NC-17 [rating] came it came really too late—twenty-five years too late."

dollar," he noted. "The majors pump all that money in. They get one hundred and forty theaters, and put up an advertising budget of half a million dollars." A small fry like RM could no longer compete.

Meyer saw the handwriting on the mall. "The days of *Vixen* are gone." *Beneath the Valley of the Ultra-Vixens* would be Russ Meyer's swan song, the last theatrical release of his career.

Which makes the ending of *Beneath* all the more poignant. Meyer stands on a desert mountainside, surrounded by his equipment. The crew has left and he's packing up his movie camera alone. He addresses the audience, his voice dubbed by John Furlong doing a passable Bogie impression. He yells for Kitten—who's gyrating wildly in the vicinity—telling her it's time to go home. It was a retirement from which Meyer would not return.

$ $ $

"We fight all the time," Kitten told a reporter in 1979. "We can't stand each other. But it seems to work." By this time, Meyer had queered the relationship by trying to control Natividad like he did everything else. For Kitten, the reality in the bedroom was a long way from what they'd created on the silver screen. "I'm glad to make a movie where I'm the superior one . . . but then when I try to live it out in real life, Russ wants to cut my head off."

Stuart Lancaster's wife Ivy Bethune saw Kitten trapped in "a masochistic relationship. She was very good to Russ, she would do anything to please him. He showed her off a lot, but you felt it was as if you took a dog on a leash—they'd better do certain things, or else. My own feeling about Russ was that though he was sexually attracted to women, he thought very little of them and never really related to them as people. Kitten always suffered because he treated her as he had the others."

According to some, the passion between Meyer and Natividad sometimes turned violent. "Kitten gave him a couple of vicious cuts," said Jim Ryan. "Busted his head right open. Chair, I think." Meyer distributor Fred Beiersdorf, who put Russ and Kitten up on a trip to Texas, spoke of "fistfights in the house."

Natividad emphatically denied all of this. "We never hit each other. *Never!* I don't even think I broke a dish—I *like* my things." However, she admits that Meyer "liked women to be violent, he got off on it. He wouldn't hurt me, but he would yell and scream about my family or my friends or how dare I do that stupid movie. He'd wind me up. After he got me all upset, Russ didn't want to stay there and argue. I knew that once he split, I wouldn't see him for six months. He'd hide out somewhere. Vegas."

When Meyer walked out after one particular screaming match, Kitten "ran out naked after him—stark naked, not a stitch of clothing. I said, 'No, you're not gonna go, you're not gonna go, you'll have to run over me!' Then he started the car. I just jumped on the hood, everybody in the neighborhood watching me. I hung on by the windshield wipers.

"Everything was just about RM. Period. You really couldn't talk about anything except RM. He had me all brainwashed—'I am the best! In *my* movies there are no stars, because *I am The Star! I am!'* That's why I think our relationship went south. One time Russ had to work late, so I had a girlfriend come over. We were listening to that song 'I Will Survive' and we were dancing. Russ opens the door and goes, '*I guess I'm not needed here.*' And he slams the door and leaves. He couldn't stand for me to have fun."

Nor did RM have any use for Kitten's close family ties. When her sister would join them for dinner, her Meyer-induced uneasiness would render her silent. "He'd go, 'That sister of yours. She doesn't say a *word*! And I fed her that steak!' "

Despite the many battles, marriage was discussed while the couple was in Europe for the *Bambi* ordeal. "He goes, 'Let's go to Amsterdam and get your diamond there.' That scared me. To tell you the truth, Russ just didn't seem normal. I thought, 'Something's not right here.' He said, 'Look, I want your tits bigger. Will you double your birth control?' Screw up my health? *No!"*

While in London with RM, Kitten started going to the gym, cutting back on the chocolates and booze. It enraged Meyer, who liked company while feasting on both. Natividad even returned to her husband, but RM lured her back with the promise of children.

Then Kitten fell for a younger guy, with Meyer still refusing to admit defeat. "We'd go to lunch and Russ was just hoping to get lucky. He'd carry a briefcase. I said, 'What's in the briefcase?' He'd open it and it was a bottle of champagne with two glasses. And he said, 'I got a room, too,' then point upstairs. I'd say, 'All right, let's go.' "

Although Kitten would come and go in RM's life until very late in the game, she had to make her escape. "By the time I was forty, I was worn out."

$ $ $

Mother Meyer remained cantankerous to the very end. Lydia spent her final days wheelchair-bound in a rest home, and RM would express his eternal gratitude to both Uschi and Kitten for visiting and caring for her. Meyer even paid for Uschi to take Lydia to visit relatives in Germany, but after one day abroad she wanted to return to the States. Jim Ryan then had his sister take Lydia to Hawaii. Once again, it was one day, then home.

"Lydia was not really with it most of the time," said Ryan, recalling vicious fights she had with staff at the Sepulveda Convalescent Hospital, where she spent her final years. According to Jim, discourse from Lydia often boiled down to 'fucking Jews,' 'goddamn niggers.' And right in front of the people — 'You dirty nigger, you ain't gonna touch me. Get outta here.' That's not the thing to say to those people, because they have ways of retaliating." Lydia would find her false teeth missing or her glasses stepped on, then put in an angry call to her son.

Charles Napier remembers tagging along with Jim Ryan and Meyer for one Lydia outing. "We would pick her up and we'd go through the Hollywood Hills looking at the Christmas lights. Meyer would talk to her. She was senile, incoherent. She thought he was a doctor. We'd go to a bar and he'd order her a cocktail. He's wiping her mouth, making sure she isn't spilling anything on herself, expounding on tits and ass, and I'm trying to keep a straight face." The rest of the visit consisted of "running her over curbs in this wheelchair — bangin' her around, bam crash, back to the rest home. It was that kind of bizarre funny-but-not-funny, y'know what I mean?" Roger Ebert recalled Meyer pushing Lydia across four lanes of traffic just to take her out for a meal. "We wound up in a topless restaurant that was attached to a motel across the street from the rest home."

Lydia succumbed to cancer on March 21, 1979, her son's fifty-eighth birthday, and just days short of turning eighty-two. Meyer was out on the road with Kitten promoting *Beneath* when the call came in. "We were in Houston. Russ went on doing interviews and the opening of the film. He got diarrhea because he stayed up thinking of his mother and he didn't sleep and he cried. He got kinda sick." Once back in Los Angeles, Meyer was consoled by Roger Ebert. "I went and talked to him, sat with him for a while in the evening. He was crushed." Meyer was deeply touched by Ebert's kindness, and when Roger's mother passed away RM flew to Illinois for her funeral.

Meyer packed Lydia's body into his GMC Suburban for the trip to her final resting spot in Stockton. Kitten stayed behind. "I said, 'Do you want me to go with you?' And he goes, 'No, I wanna be alone with her.' " From then on he'd spend every Christmas at her gravesite. He'd tell friends he was going to dedicate all the proceeds of his autobiography to cancer research.

Meyer, a mama's boy to the end. He had never really been able to commit to any other woman. His first marriage to Betty was over in a flash. Eve lasted longer then most, but eventually that, too, went to hell in a handbasket. And then came the parade of cows, as his mother was so fond of calling them. Meyer kept Lydia at a distance, but her shadow hovers over everything in his life, and I don't think it's a coincidence that RM's film career basically ends with her death.

"I think Russ was a very lonely person," said Meyer production associate and editor Les Barnum. "He really wanted to be close to other people, and I think he was envious of those who had solid family relationships. Russ really tried—he was very gracious and magnanimous at times—but his films always won out. There was just that look in Russ's eye that meant the fiends of hell were risin' up. There was always a demon lingering in the background. It's terrible, but there's that line in *Arsenic and Old Lace*—'Insanity runs in my family, it practically gallops.' "

Lydia, the only one who had truly believed in him, was gone. But there was that omnipresent living ghost, The Poor Dear. Lucinda still called Meyer's office incessantly, often in hysterics, insisting she'd been assaulted or raped, desperate for her brother to set her free.

15

Mondo Meyer

Lose your dreams and you will lose your mind.
—JAGGER-RICHARDS, "Ruby Tuesday"

Throughout the eighties and much of the nineties, reporters hungry to spill some ink on a slow news day made the trek out to Hollywood to RM's Arrowhead Drive home, aka the Russ Meyer Museum, paying their respects to King Leer. Dressed in Ralph Lauren chino shorts, a *Beyond the Valley of the Dolls* T-shirt, and some old-school bling consisting of a diamond-encrusted Rolex alongside a gold ring and bracelet both bearing his name, a crusty, well-oiled Meyer held court, often holding in his huge mitt a piece of celluloid from a film he'd never finish. He had become a caricature of himself, a walking, talking hooter-hungry legend of lech, and his palaver was always the same. "They must be cantilevered. They must be defying gravity. You've got to have *huge* breasts, casting *long* shadows. Just so the women don't buckle at the knees." The walls of his home echoed his words, as they were plastered with photos showing "dozens and dozens of women with large and sometime very, very large breasts," wrote journalist Louis Black. "It is overwhelming . . . too much flesh. It is nice to go outside and find the California sun."

Meyer would live in the Arrowhead Drive house until the end of his life. Even when RM was mentally intact, he didn't exactly keep it according to the lifestyles of the rich and famous. All of its five rooms functioned as offices to some extent, while plaques, pictures, and Meyer memorabilia crowded every inch of the walls and even the ceilings. Overnight visitors of lesser status stayed in the guest house by the pool, while for the A-list, Russ rolled out a cot and you "slept amongst boxes," according to friend Paul Fishbein. "There were no clean towels, no soap, no shampoo. Russ had no idea how uncomfortable it was staying there."

Meyer's 166th buddy Fred Owens came to visit RM in the late seventies shortly after he moved into the Arrowhead home. "Fred worried about Russ like a brood hen," said Roger Ebert. "He didn't feel that Russ understood the pleasures of life. He worked too hard. Fred said, 'Well, look at this place—there's nuthin' here but office furniture! Every chair in the house has wheels on it! There's no place to sit down in this house, unless you're *working*! My wife and I, we have a couple of easy chairs, one on either side of the fireplace. We sit down, stretch out our legs, read the paper, have a drink, do whatever you feel like doin'.' " Every time Ebert saw RM he "would quote that and just roar with laughter." For Meyer, "it was all work. There was no easy chair."

When Garth Pillsbury and his wife Jacqueline Mayo attended a party on Arrowhead in the late eighties, both were struck by the lack of atmosphere. "I don't know what Stalag 17 looked like, but a stalag is where I was," said Mayo. "Aluminum chairs, steel-topped sinks, paper plates, cheap stuff from Sears—it looked like a commandant's office. It just didn't look like a place in the Hollywood Hills. More like the outskirts of Kansas City, or near a penitentiary." When neighbors complained that sets Meyer had discarded in his yard were an eyesore, he retaliated by painting his house the garish orange and green that adorned his home video boxes.

$ $ $

The eighties, a crap decade. Ronald Reagan, Huey Lewis and the News, *Top Gun*—need I say more? If you were unfortunate enough to be around, it seemed like ten years that didn't happen at all. In the wake of 1977's *Star Wars*, Hollywood turned more and more to

high-priced, often indistinguishable blockbusters seemingly designed to sell sequels, action figures, and lunch boxes. Such
assembly-line corporate crap only reinforced the idea of Meyer as
a renegade cobbler whose down-home product had only been influenced by his crotch, and even though he didn't release a single
film during the decade, the eighties were very good to him indeed.
RM had stuck around long enough to become a bona fide icon.
"Like an old hot rod, he has aged gracefully from Public Enemy to
American Classic," declared the *Soho Weekly News*.

Projects came and went. *The Jaws of Lorna; The Jaws of Vixen;
Blitzen, Vixen and Harry; Mondo Topless, Too; Up the Valley of the Beyond;* an ill-conceived color remake of his 1966 masterpiece entitled *Kill, Kill, Pussycat! Faster!*—all were announced, all faded away.
"I don't care about making another movie," said Meyer in 1988. "I
got all the money I'll ever need. You gotta be hungry to make a
movie. I don't have the desire, the urge." What other filmmaker
would have the guts to admit the fire was gone? Meyer's three-
volume autobiography stopped abruptly once it got past 1979's
Beneath the Valley of the Ultra-Vixens. No more films, no more life.

There was plenty of life to be squeezed out of the past, though.
One day Meyer ran into Dave Friedman ("at, of all places, Frederick's of Hollywood," Friedman recalled), and Dave said he wanted
to show RM something. Friedman took him a few blocks away to
the videocassette operation he was a partner in. This was in the
earliest days of video, and Meyer, amazed, saw dollar signs. It was
just like what Friedman's old exploitation crony Dan Sonney used
to say: a movie's like a bag of flour. Every time you tap it a little
more money comes out.

Meyer had shrewdly held on to the rights of all of his films,
save for *French Peep Show, Fanny Hill,* and the two Fox-backed pictures. He owned twenty movies outright and began putting them
out on video himself, right from his home. The price tag was outrageously steep—$79.50 a tape, $50 wholesale—and RM didn't
waiver. He did no advertising, took no credit cards, and when you
called in your order, odds were good that Meyer himself would answer the phone. The market had opened a whole new audience for

his films. In 1984, he'd tell a reporter he was shipping ten thousand cassettes a year. Video, said a jolly RM, was "going to swell my ego even more."

RM bridled at the term *cult*, but he certainly qualified for one. His pictures were perfect for the home video market. Strange pictures featuring strange characters, not to mention sex, and nothing that graphic meant they were somewhat suitable for parties. The built-in mystique of having to be in the know enough to buy them direct only increased their hip appeal. Plus, as Meyer has pointed out, you can start watching in the middle, stay only ten minutes, and still have a good time.

Meyer started receiving all sorts of accolades. The British Film Institute put on a major retrospective in 1983; the Chicago Film Festival honored him in 1985; a flood of revival circuit bookings included a seventeen-and-a-half-hour marathon at the Boston Film Festival. RM did a walk-on as an adult video store clerk in the John Landis segment of the 1987 anthology film *Amazon Women on the Moon*. In 1990, Roger Ebert would review *Wild at Heart* and boldly declare, "Russ Meyer invented the cinema of David Lynch twenty-five years ago." Tim Burton attended one of RM's birthday parties and paid tribute by casting Meyer stock player Stuart Lancaster in bit parts for *Edward Scissorhands* and *Batman Returns*. A Meyer biopic was under discussion, and inexplicably RM wanted Robin Williams to play him on the silver screen.

One massive film project obsessed Meyer throughout the eighties—*The Breast of Russ Meyer.* Meyer had talked about doing an anthology film forever. One titled *Hotsa, Hotsa* was announced as early as 1972, but by the next decade the idea had morphed into something truly epic. RM began condensing his films down into trailer-length capsules, with documentary footage he'd shot of the people and places in his life in between. He went back to Cincinnati to relive his battles with Charles Keating and returned to Europe several times to retrace his every footstep during the war. "The film is unrelenting . . . the scenes are cut by three feet, four frames each, so you get a rhythm," RM told writer Paul Sherman. "It will either lull you to sleep or give you nightmares."

The more one heard about *Breast*, the more extravagant it became. By 1985 Meyer was telling *Variety* it had already cost nearly
$2 million and, depending on who he was talking to, he claimed it
was anywhere from twelve to seventeen hours in length. "You've
heard of *Berlin Alexanderplatz*? Well, this is *Meyerplatz.*" The first
seventy minutes would cover his childhood "in a very abstract
sense. A naked woman in a tree, watching. The gazebo. 'Rosebud.'
Ferries turned on their side in the mud. A railroad track. What
does it all mean? If you don't understand, tough shit." Six new
buxom Meyer discoveries would be featured in *Breast*, and, using a
self-timer, he'd even shot Kitten and himself doing the horizontal
mambo. "It's a tone poem," said RM of the massive project. "It will
be my song."

In the meantime, Meyer's mammary obsession had only in-
tensified with age, if that's possible. As Kitten Natividad observed,
"He was going a little bit crazy, because he started using girls that
were bigger and bigger and bigger and bigger ..." Advances in
augmentation made the ridiculous possible, and RM was now im-
mortalizing women who seemed more suited to the pages of medical textbooks. The bosom had become so all-encompassing in
Meyer's mind that the body was now a mere appendage, a tit
transport mechanism that otherwise served only to annoy and
distract. "Mount Baldy wasn't big enough for him," said friend Rob
Schaffner.

Meyer went through all sorts of overseas espionage to shoot
the truly freakish Tundi, a nineteen-year-old Hungarian who
spoke no English and resembled a giant triangle made flesh. Her
measurements, threatened RM, would render "all the others obsolete." Entering his sixties, Meyer was no longer averse to the
casting couch. The gentlemanly filmmaker was now an official
dirty old man, and sex became a requisite of the shoot. RM
boasted to a reporter of laying down the law to an English lass who
was his latest discovery: "We are going to be intimate. That's part
of the deal."

$ $ $

Rock and roll had begun namechecking Meyer. First and foremost came the Cramps, followed later in the decade by groups named after RM's films, such as Seattle grunge outfit Mudhoney. Germany gave birth to the Charles Napiers, and an alt-metal outfit called Manhole elected to face the future simply under the name of a favorite Meyer superstar: Tura Satana. And still the infection spread. The Bangles played gigs as the Carrie Nations, White Zombie paid tribute with its 1992 track "Thunder Kiss '65," and Janet Jackson's black-and-white video for "You Want This" plundered *Faster, Pussycat! Kill! Kill!* for inspiration.

In 1987 came the inevitable. Meyer, now sixty-five, was asked to direct his first music video. The L.A. hair metal band Faster, Pussycat needed MTV fodder for their debut single, "Don't Change That Song." Could anyone be more qualified to direct it than the man responsible for their name? Initially, RM balked at the request. By the time he relented, there was a list of demands to be met, primary among them: three girls with big breasts, no silicone, and no porno stars. Keisha, a hard-core "name," actually slipped into the cast and was immediately recognized by the crew, but Meyer remained oblivious. Even Kitten Natividad tried to get in on the fun, marching into the production office with her own weighing machine to prove her moneymakers' worth. "Eight and a half pounds," she announced, hefting a boob out, but the scales did not tip in Kitten's favor.

At this time music videos were exhausting a plethora of technological advances with a can-you-top-this fury. Meyer treated the music video world with disdain, "always pretending to have one foot out the door," as producer Dave Ewing observed. He immediately laid down ground rules: no dollies, no zooms, and no extra stuff, just a list of shots longer than the Bible. Assistant director Brent Bowman saw RM as "stuck in a certain way of filmmaking. He operated his motion picture camera like a still camera."

Meyer wanted to shoot the video outside Modesto in an area he dubbed "the tit hills," which, he claimed, looked just like a field of firm bosoms in the right light. Ewing actually traveled to the location with Meyer but found the landscape to be rather flat-chested. They wound up shooting on a soundstage, the video's "plot" consisting of a bunch of top-heavy girls worshiping a vintage jukebox as the band mimed in front of a screen showing clips of Tura Satana and her girl gang in action. Whoopee.

Five hairspray addicts sporting more makeup than Babette Bardot, the band Faster, Pussycat was a touch on the fey side for our former combat photographer. "He kept calling them 'the or-chestra,' " said Ewing. Meyer was particularly rough on lead singer Taime Downe, begging him not to wear a dress. "With all his makeup, it made him look like Renee Taylor doing a bad number in the Catskills," complained RM. "Russ didn't give the band their due as stars—Russ Meyer was the star," said Ewing. "They started out idolizing him; by the end they didn't want anything to do with each other."

On the set, Meyer was "demanding, demanding, demanding," said Brent Bowman. RM hated the cameraman and ran the girls ragged. "It had the feeling of a big game," said Ewing, who liked Meyer but found him exhausting: "You felt like the weight of the world was on you when you were around him."

The end result was, according to Ewing, "a terrible video." For Bowman, the most memorable moment came one night as the crew chowed down on pizza. An inquisitive Meyer asked the pro-ducer, "You're a pretty healthy guy, but you eat all this junk. What's your stool like?" "No one had ever asked me what my stool was like, except for my doctor," recalled a nonplussed Bowman.

In 1991 Meyer shot his second and last video, for "Soul-twister" by German rocker Jean Park. Once again, the now-tired reference point was *Faster, Pussycat! Kill! Kill!* Meyer shot Park lip-syncing in the Mojave as three wenches reenacted scenes from the old workhorse. Leading the pack was RM's current girlfriend Melissa Mounds, outfitted in cringe-inducing eighties workout spandex (and seen washing Meyer's car). Music video should've been a cinch for the fastest cutter in the West, but the opportu-nity had come too late to matter. Clips intercut from the original film only pointed out how truly spectacular Meyer's women had once been—and how little he seemed to care about what he was doing now.

By now, Meyer "was a caricature of himself," as "Soultwister" producer Gary Adelman saw it. "He kind of played the role of RM, and he had his routine down." One scene for "Soultwister" was shot in front of Meyer's house, the director lying on the ground shooting up as Richard Brummer stood across the street holding a reflector. "He yells to Dick, 'Move the goddamn reflector to the right spot,'" recalled Adelman. "Russ said to me, 'That's what film-making's all about—you can yell at people.'"

$ $ $

One way or another, Meyer yelled at a lot of people in the eighties. "Russ started changing," said Haji. "He starting believing his own press. It was like a drug to him."

Even though they no longer had business together, Meyer's longtime distributor Fred Beiersdorf tried to maintain their friendship. RM, unfortunately, began to have fits if Fred didn't return his phone calls immediately. "He lost his sense of humor," said Beiersdorf, who was dismayed by what he saw when he visited Meyer on Arrowhead Drive. "I said, 'Russ, you got all this money and you're sittin' here like a goddamn hermit! Why don't you enjoy it?' But his enjoyment was to make other people's lives misery." A popular routine involved threatening to take people out of his will. One day Fred would be out, the next day Jim Ryan. "Every day I'd hear somebody off, every day," said Kitten Natividad, who continued to float in and out of RM's life. "I'd say, 'Yes, Russ.'"

With 1974's *Pink Flamingos* (starring jumbo drag queen Divine, infamous for scarfing down a dog dropping during the movie), John Waters had become a notorious filmmaking force himself. He continued to befriend and champion Meyer. RM even attended a premiere after-party for one of John's early films, during which Waters happily noticed a very odd couple. "Russ and Divine were sitting there together," he recalled. "Divine was scared of him, I think. Russ was uncomfortable. You could just see him thinking, 'What the fuck am *I* doing here?' "*

Not unlike Meyer, the John Waters imprint soon crossed into the mainstream as a touchstone for all things depraved. By the eighties, Waters had an impressive three-film oeuvre of his own and a highly influential book to his name, *Shock Value*. According to Kitten Natividad, all that success caused Meyer to start taking a dislike to him. If someone became a bigger phenomenon than Meyer, RM "got jealous," said Natividad. "He'd ignore the person."

In 1985, Waters wrote an article for *Rolling Stone* entitled "John Waters' Tour of L.A.," and one of the primary stops was the museum Russ Meyer called home. By now, Waters had gotten friendly not only with Meyer but also with some of his stars. "Every one of the women I met were great. They were all nice, they were all funny, they were all smart. They were like old showgirls basically, and I mean that in a good way." Waters, of course, intended the article as a sort of tribute. Problem was, he included RM's address.

"I remember telling him, 'Russ, to be in there I have put your address in, because it's a tour. He said yes." When fans started showing up at Meyer's front door, he went berserk. Eventually word got back to Waters, who called RM to clear up the situation. "I said, 'But Russ, you said it was okay. I have it on tape.' " Meyer then blamed the wine they'd shared over dinner. John should have *known better*. He hadn't *really* said yes.

Waters was clearly pained to talk about the falling-out with Meyer. "He started saying really mean things about me in the press, which shocked and hurt me. I never answered Russ in the press. I *never* said nasty things about him—and I still am not saying nasty things about him. I don't know why, but from what I hear, he got nasty to a lot of people, so I guess I just joined the club." Meyer stopped speaking to the man who'd done so much

---

* Waters never felt Meyer cared much for his pictures. "I just don't think he quite got it. Russ understood the exploitation angle, he respected me as a carny—he thought Divine eatin' dogshit in *Pink Flamingos* was funny. I don't think Russ got that they were exploitation art films. I might be wrong, but he certainly never *gushed*."

to bring his films to a new audience, although when *Faster, Pussy-cat! Kill! Kill!* was rereleased theatrically in 1995, RM put the in-famous "best movie ever made" Waters quote front and center in the ad campaign. "*That* was really ballsy," said John. Reporters who visited Meyer's home would see a Polaroid of Waters—af-fixed to RM's toilet.

Meyer even started grousing about the recently married Roger Ebert during interviews. "His wife really doesn't feel all that keen about me," said RM. "She's afraid that he might get something in his shorts. . . . I like the idea of him . . . cheating on his wife."

$ $ $

In the mid-eighties, Rolf Thissen, German author of several film books, undertook a biography of Meyer. With RM's blessing, he came to Hollywood, interviewed the director, then pored over his archives. Everything went swimmingly until he showed the man-uscript to Meyer so corrections could be made. RM labeled the book "libelous," once again blaming the booze enjoyed during the many dinners author and subject had shared. RM took the matter to court. Surely Thiessen knew better than to actually *print* what Meyer had told him.

The Thissen book was published in 1987. In the course of in-terfering with it, Meyer had thought again about his own autobi-ography, something he'd started years earlier during a trip to Europe. RM was further encouraged by William Kahrl, a *Sacra-mento Bee* reporter who'd written a reverent 1982 Meyer piece that so moved RM he later included it in his book. Suddenly Meyer's mission in life was to tell his story. Yellow pads filled with RM's characteristic oversized scrawl began to pile up everywhere. He got a literary agent involved, who, after perusing a draft in 1986, wrote back with some very on-point suggestions. RM then for-warded her note along with the manuscript to some combat bud-dies and Roger Ebert, requesting a detailed critique from each and every one of them. There turned out to be some agreement on her criticism, particularly when it came to lugubrious plot synopses and excerpted reviews RM included within passages on each and every film.

So what did Meyer do? He instructed his friends that he was doing it his way, thank you very much. Then he wrote the agent and told her he'd be publishing it himself. In the same communique, RM quoted the interview with Eve where she'd suggested he had the talent to make "better" films, then pointed out that his wife had been wrong, too. The time had come to put these women in their place, once and for all!

Called *Russ Meyer: The Rural Fellini* before being christened *A Clean Breast* by Ebert, this "fuck-and-tell book" was regarded by Meyer as "the most important thing I've ever done. I purged myself." Everything else in RM's life fell by the wayside as he grew more and more obsessed with The Book. Meyer sent flyers out to all his video customers in the mid-eighties, encouraging prepublication orders at $70 a pop. By the time it was finally published in 2000—now three hefty volumes and costing $350—he'd lost a few friends, gained some angry fans who'd paid for the book over a decade earlier, and filed at least one lawsuit over a printing mishap. "He kept adding to it, like the Winchester House," said Meyer friend and other biographer David K. Frasier. "He'd still be adding to it, except that he got ill."

$ $ $

Meyer's constant companion throughout the eighties and early nineties was Harry, a 130-pound wolf-dog hybrid that had been given to him by Charles Napier. "He probably loved that dog more than anybody else," said David K. Frasier. Harry made a strong impression on RM's visitors. "I'm the biggest dog lover in the world," said Meyer friend Paul Fishbein. "Harry is the only dog I've ever been scared of." Harry had a low moan that made the hair on your neck stand up, and "crystal-gray-blue eyes that looked right through you," as screenwriter and RM crony John McCormick wrote. Guests recall Harry pacing outside the patio door, drooling foam while Meyer dumped that night's leftovers—steak, mashed potatoes, salad, maybe a dog bone or two—into a big bowl for his friend. Meyer let Harry have the run of the Arrowhead house when they were alone, and the place came to smell strongly of half-wolf piss.

Funnily enough, "Harry liked women," according to RM's longtime assistant Paula Parker. But just like his owner, men were another story. One night screenwriter John McCormick came to take Meyer out to dinner, and while RM was upstairs getting dressed, McCormick came face-to-face with Harry. The dog terrified him, so he was relieved when Harry began to rub up against him in a friendly manner. He started to pet the dog, scratch his stomach. At which point Harry chomped down on McCormick's Armani-clad arm, holding it in a vise grip and refusing to let go. When the dog finally got bored and set him free, a shaken McCormick ran off to the bathroom to tend to his bloody puncture wounds. "I never told Russ about it. I knew he'd take the dog's side."

$ $ $

Meyer traveled yearly to the Consumer Electronics Show in Vegas, a big shindig for the home video market where RM personally hawked his tapes from a little booth, a couple of his posters providing the only fanfare. Porno veteran Bill Margold frequently had the space next to Meyer, who'd "sit in his booth scowling, writing voluminous notes on his book." RM had no use for the porno sellers surrounding him, and the feeling was generally mutual. Said Margold, "Meyer couldn't keep up with the adult industry, and it passed him by." David F. Friedman recalls making the rounds of Vegas strip shows with RM, landing in "a real typical greaseball joint — great-looking broads, table dancing, lap dancing. Russ is watching this, and he said, 'These girls are degrading themselves. This isn't stripping.' Russ wanted to see an old-fashioned strip. A lap dance turned him off. We had one drink and blew the joint."

It was at the 1987 CES show that Meyer met his next tit-throb. A recent divorcee in her early forties parading around in an Elvira get-up, Jane Hower was clearly looking for a good time. When the big-balconied blond part-time strip-o-grammer sailed past

Meyer's booth, RM took one look at her cleavage and threw her a business card. When Hower returned home to Seattle, she promptly won a celebrity look-alike talent show by performing as Dolly Parton, miming a wicked "9 to 5." The prize was a trip to Hollywood. Accompanied by a Liza Minnelli doppelgänger she'd befriended, Hower decided to look Meyer up when she got to town.

They met at the hotel bar, Meyer inquiring as to Hower's age. Forty-three, she told him. "His face kind of sagged." RM then "leaned over the table to get a better look—he picked up the candle on the table and held it up on one side of my face, then on the other. He was impressed." Meyer then told her he was fifty-eight. He was actually sixty-five.

Heading out for dinner in Meyer's white TR3 roadster, the talk naturally turned to Hower's own headlights. RM asked if they were real. When Hower responded in the affirmative, he asked for a feel. "So he's driving with one hand and grabbing me with the other. He's got ahold of the left breast, trying to feel with his fingers for the nipple, and I said, 'Three inches more to the right.' He just about went off the road."

Hower was more than a little nervous. As far as she knew, Meyer was just some Hollywood porno guy—but they clicked immediately. "We ended up in the hotel room and I took my top down. Oh my! The first time he saw me naked I thought he was gonna collapse. Yeah, breasts are a big thing to him. No act." Soon Hower was experiencing sex at the hands of the master. "Very straightforward—hug, kiss, touch, and put it in. It lasted a fair amount of time, not three strokes and you're done. Nothing too bold. The minute we were through makin' love, it was up out of the bed, into the bathroom, hot soapy water—I never saw a guy move so fast. He was fastidiously clean."

Hower assumed it was just a one-night stand, but Meyer began calling her nightly. On December 16, 1987, eagerly anticipating their second rendezvous, he sent two bras—34E and F—along with specific instructions to wear whichever fit best under a tight sweater. During their time together RM snapped some pictures of Hower in the buff, carrying one in his briefcase next to the beloved shot of Mom. Jane made frequent trips to Los

Angeles on Meyer's dime, and he'd visit her in Seattle as well. He'd brag to pals that the trips north were a write-off since he had a working history with a local film lab, Alpha Cine.

When she'd visit Meyer at his home, he'd sit by the pool, immersed in revising The Book. One day Hower, swimming naked so RM could click the occasional picture, decided to stimulate herself with one of the water jets. "I liked it a whole lot—and it pissed him off a whole lot. Russ didn't like the fact that I could get pleasure off a stream of water."

Hower got the full measure of Meyer's eccentricity when she and RM spent time at Roger Ebert's Indiana vacation home with a few other couples. "We all couldn't sleep, because Russ and Jane made so much noise," said fellow guest Paul Fishbein, who insisted that Ebert was still talking about it when he bumped into him some ten years later. Oddly enough, it had all been an act. "When we got alone in the bedroom, Russ wanted to make noise—we weren't actually making love, but he wanted it to *sound* like we were. Oh God, he wanted to put on a show. I didn't know if I could stand the embarrassment of it. But I moaned and groaned." Jane then whispered to RM, "Are you happy now? Can we go to bed?"

Despite such charades, things seemed to be getting serious between the two. Meyer met Jane's parents and Hower met the combat buddies, a few of whom were amazed that RM was dating someone relatively close to his age. But after a year and a half, Meyer suddenly cooled. Phone calls became infrequent, visits were postponed. Hower's next trip to Los Angeles would prove to be her last. "When he picked me up at the airport, I just sensed that somethin' major had changed. We went back to his place, and of course made love as soon as we got there, and that was the dead giveaway. 'Cause as soon as he took his clothes off I could tell he'd been with another woman. Big time. He *smelled* of it. In fact, Russ commented on it. He says, 'Aaaaah, it even *smells* like sex!' I felt terribly insulted that he would come to me unwashed from another woman."

Once his seed had been spent, RM told Hower that he'd have to take her to a hotel, as he was "having some work done" at the Meyer manse. She knew it was a ruse. By this time Jane had fallen hard for Russ and was deeply hurt. Hower tried to keep the relationship going, but Meyer finally admitted in a letter that there was another woman, boasting that he'd met and impregnated this new conquest on June 26, 1989, and was looking forward to fatherhood.

The romance kaput, Meyer continued to write Hower now and again for nearly ten years, trying to talk the already beyond-abundant Hower into getting augmentation surgery.

$ $ $

Two women would come to dominate RM's life in the nineties. One was a rather harsh-looking stripper sporting a wicked, feathery mullet and lacking the crazy class of previous editions; the other was a ruthless secretary with a voice so shrill it could drive you to drink. In a twisted scenario that could have come straight from the poison pen of Meyer's old screenwriter John Moran, the stripper would be convicted of brutally assaulting RM, starting a bloody chain reaction that left the assistant in complete charge of his very being.

Both women were somewhat undersized and not particularly well liked by the RM crowd. They were certainly not your typical Meyer broads. You could almost call them the Anti-Vixens.

Janice and the Handyman

*I am chauvinistic. I don't care to have business with women in
the film game.*

— RUSS MEYER

It was a little before 2 a.m. on May 27, 1999, when Paul Fishburn
heard his doorbell ring. As the dog barked, Fishburn went down-
stairs to check the peephole of the front door to see just who was
out there at this ungodly hour. "It's Russ Meyer," said a voice in the
night. Fishburn opened the door to find his seventy-seven-year-old
neighbor standing there, his head covered in blood that had oozed
down onto his shirt. "I have been assaulted." Fishburn let his
wounded neighbor in, asking whodunit. "Well, I'm not sure," said a
dazed but guarded RM. Paul's wife Donna got a towel and tended to
the wounds. The old guy looked pretty beat up. There were cuts and
bumps all over his noggin, a big gash near his eye.

Paul asked if there was still somebody in his house. "There
could be," mused Meyer. Ten minutes later the police and para-
medics arrived on the scene. Officers Miller and Hightower tried
to pry out of Meyer just what had occurred, and once again he
vaguely suggested there might be someone lurking within his
home. When the officers entered RM's house, they came face-to-
face with one Melissa Mounds, a blond, unsmiling former stripper who stood five foot three, Meyer's current paramour. "She was

emitting an odor of an alcoholic beverage," Miller would testify in court. "Her eyes were bloodshot and watery. Speech was slightly slurred." As a final touch, he added that there was a "wobble to her walk." Mounds, who did not appear to be hurt, feigned ignorance regarding Meyer's injuries. She would change her tune a few hours later when the police returned to slap on handcuffs.

They took Mounds over to Fishburn's house, where Meyer sat in a breakfast nook with a coffee. "She was frightened," Donna Fishburn later testified. "And she said, 'I hope they do not arrest me.'" On the way to the hospital, RM told Officer Miller he was starting to remember: he had awakened on his couch to find Melissa looming over him, pummeling his face with her fists.* Mounds then explained that she had grown tired of being yelled at and had decided to fight back. The next day a restraining order was granted to keep Mounds away from Meyer and his home.

It was a pathetic turn of events for the once mighty and seemingly indestructible Russell Albion Meyer. I'd once discussed with Erica Gavin the defining characteristic of the men in RM's films. "Weak," she maintained. Now Meyer had been pinned to his own canvas. "God, what a person won't do to have sexual access to a women with mammoth majungas," said friend and biographer David K. Frasier.

$ $ $

Born Debra Masson on October 9, 1959, the owner of these particular majungas had posed for men's magazines as Angela Parker before reinventing herself (and her bustline) as Melissa Mounds, appearing as the first centerfold for *Hustler's Busty Beauties* in 1988. According to agent Eleanor Bucci, Mounds made $3,000–$3,500 a week in those days, not counting tips and money from fan Polaroids. "Melissa could be booked fifty-two weeks a year. Everybody liked her. There wasn't a club owner or a fan who didn't

---

* Later Meyer told friends that he'd been hit with a hammer and that he was saving the souvenir of his assault to mount on a plaque for the museum.

like Melissa. She was just a sweet person. Didn't have a scheming bone in her body, although I tried to put some in."

Mounds would testify in court that she first met Russ Meyer in Las Vegas around 1979 and initiated a relationship with him five years later, although nobody in Meyer's camp remembered seeing her around until the end of the eighties. In his autobiography, Meyer dates their first photo shoot together as April 4, 1988, at his vacation home in Palm Desert. RM became absolutely obsessed with Mounds, intent on making her his next star. "She was greedy for penis, very greedy," he told the press. Meyer insisted that the saline implants inside her huge, terrifying orbs were embedded deep behind the breast, attached to the rib cage. "You can dig your fingers in there up to four or five inches and not encounter a foreign substance," he enthused. Mounds was the woman RM had told Jane Hower he'd impregnated at age sixty-seven, on a mission "to get some sort of heir going. It would have pleased my mother, God bless her soul." Melissa lost the child, reportedly miscarrying after a fall during a trip with Meyer to the Moscow Film Festival in July 1989.

Melissa was an odd addition to the Meyer menagerie. "She was kinda simple," said RM friend Dolores Fox, who took Mounds shopping for a dress at the request of Meyer, who'd set her up with a bank account. "When we went to pay for it, she did not know how to write a check." Richard Brummer saw Melissa as "a homebody. Liked to cook, clean. She could've been a terrific mother. She wanted that kind of a life. That's not Russ's life." But many friends were dubious about her intentions. "There was a sort of classlessness about her," said David K. Frasier. "I don't think Melissa cared very much for Russ. It was the money." Meyer complained to friends that Mounds had a lot of needy family members.

The romance was on and off for a decade. In January 1991, Meyer shot footage for a Melissa Mounds feature film that was to be narrated by her. RM tinkered with it for years, abandoning it whenever he was pissed off at her, which was frequent, as Charles Napier attests. "He'd call and say, 'Sweet Melissa this, sweet Melissa that.' Then it turned to 'That bitch, she tried to kill me with a hammer. *Have her locked away forever.*' The usual Meyer love triangle."

Meyer bought her cars (including one van he christened the Moundsmobile), wedding dresses, and glittering baubles. "He gave her three engagement rings," said Jim Ryan. "They'd get in a fight and break up. She'd be gone out of his life, and suddenly they'd be back together again. I'd say, 'Meyer, you bought her an engagement ring for three thousand dollars and she loses it?' He said, 'It's worth it.' "

In Roger Ebert's opinion, "Melissa was bad news." But there was no convincing Meyer. David K. Frasier said their one and only argument took place when RM asked whether he should marry Melissa Mounds and have a child. When Frasier told him it wasn't a good idea, RM erupted. "I'll have anything I want to have, because Meyer's a selfish, self-centered son of a bitch." Frasier recalled Meyer hunched over the Moviola, transfixed by Melissa's image. "He said, 'Look at the evil. The *evil!*' Russ just thought that she had a real demonic presence, a real sexual rapaciousness. He loved it."

"Russ had this cassette," said screenwriter John McCormick. "The Righteous Brothers singing 'Unchained Melody.' He and Melissa, that was their song. He was fishing for the cassette in the back of the Suburban, and while he was fishing for the cassette, he cut himself on a piece of broken neon tubing. His fingertips were bleeding as he put it into the tape player. It was supersentimental for him—I was more concerned about the blood. He wasn't even fazed. 'That's our song.' "

$ $ $

By 1990, RM had abandoned his gargantuan, umpteen-hour anthology film *The Breast of Russ Meyer.* "It was totally unmanageable," he admitted at the time. "I would have never completed it."*

---

* Although some footage would end up in 2000's swan song *Pandora Peaks,* exactly one and a half minutes have surfaced of the original, unadulterated *Breast,* in the 1988 Jonathan Ross–hosted Meyer documentary for British TV. We see maps illustrating the 166th's route during World War II, then RM zooming along in a car, retracing the path. Meyer is shown filming with his old Eyemo camera, then the picture cuts to old black-and-white footage Meyer shot during the war. Intercut with this is Kitten Natividad riding in the backseat of his car nude— RM ignores her to concentrate on his camera. Atlanta stripper Tami Roche is shown sitting in a tree naked. Apparently she plays Meyer's guardian angel in the film. Too bad more of this project can't be seen—it's fabulous stuff.

Instead he threw himself deeper into the autobiography, now a maze with no exit. Although many around RM would be driven over the edge by the project, the burden fell mainly on three men: George King Carll—who'd worked with Meyer since the mid-sixties, creating advertising campaigns for the majority of his films—helped RM assemble the initial text and layout, then retouched the twenty-four hundred photos in the book; biographer David K. Frasier worked on the editing; Larry Christiani attended to the final layout and typesetting. "I thought this was going to be a little job. 'Maybe I'll make a few thousand bucks on it,'" said Christiani. "What I thought was gonna be a short thing turned into ten years.

"We would sit down, shoulder to shoulder, hours on end, going through every single line and every single word," Christiani continued. "Russ was directing us. I would have no doubt his fingerprints are on every single movie frame that he ever shot. That's the way he treated the book—every word." If Christiani slipped in a typeface that varied even minutely from what had come before, RM caught it. "He was a real eagle eye."

Once Meyer became aware of the process called kerning—adjusting the space between letters and words—there was no controlling him. "He would get a printed page, and let's say there'd be a word like *develop*. He'd say, 'The *e* is too close to the *d*, the line doesn't look right,'" said Frasier. By changing the spacing of words, it often threw the line off visually. Amazingly, the way the text looked to RM suddenly took precedence over what it meant. Meyer would whip out a thesaurus and replace words on the spot, rewriting the book as Christiani was trying to put the layout to bed. "He would change words," said an exasperated Christiani. *"He would change words.* We went through every single page doing this."

Near the end of the book, Meyer included an interview Frasier had done with him that had already seen print in a film journal. RM started monkeying with the text, replacing and changing words as he saw fit. The fact that he was rewriting an already published interview didn't concern him in the slightest. "The amount of hours we spent kerning and changing, I don't know," said Christiani. "It was hundreds of hours. It just got out of hand. It was just crazy."

Meyer demanded that the thousands of black-and-white photos he wanted to include be printed in duotone, a prehistoric process involving a one-color overlay that added a sense of depth to the images — and which computers couldn't assist with at the time. As the years went by, Christiani faced another problem as he tried to keep on top of the latest software innovations. "If I updated my files to newer versions, it would cause the text to reflow, and we'd done so much manual kerning that I *couldn't* have it reflow. I ended up keeping an old computer that was just ready to die, because I couldn't run the older software on the newer computers."

RM would disappear for months, maybe even a year, then suddenly materialize with a new version of the text in his hands. According to Frasier, Meyer kept "every incarnation" of the book around, so they all began to bleed together. "You never knew what version you were working on. It was impossible . . . If there's a telephone pole fifty feet away, rather than walking directly to the pole, Russ would dig a hole, go underneath the pole to the next town, then parachute in. Meyer loved hardship. And when there wasn't hardship, he'd create it."

There was more than enough hardship to go around on *A Clean Breast*. First to fall was RM's longtime associate George Carll. "He was with Meyer constantly — literally like a scribe," said Frasier. "Ninety percent of what I was doin' was photo retouching," said Carll. Meyer was a maniac about the pictures, particularly when the subject was breasts. Each pair had to look firm and round and be pointing heavenward. "It was a bitch. He was pretty critical about it."

Carll, having marital problems at the time, was not only working with Meyer, but also living with him at the Arrowhead Drive house. When RM and Melissa Mounds ran off to Russia for a retrospective of his work, Carll was left with nothing to do. He wanted to take a couple of weeks off and reconcile with his wife. Of course, Meyer accused him of holding up his book. "We had a violent argument in the garage," said Carll. "He stood right in my face. I swore he was gonna hit me." Carll was then excommunicated, joining the ever-lengthening list of Meyer Betrayers.* "The irony of this was that the book didn't come out for over eight years past that time," said David K. Frasier.

RM poured an endless amount of time and his own funds into the autobiography project. Meyer got into a dispute with his Hong Kong printer over damaged paper, taking them to court. Printing costs alone ran into the hundreds of thousands. "I think he knew all along he would probably never make money," said Christiani. "We ran the book out three or four times for printing, and then he would change things. It kept looking like we were at the end—I kept hearing over and over, 'This is the end, this is the end,' and he'd come back with a huge rewrite."

Christiani felt that one force driving all the chaos was Meyer's mortality. "As I worked on it over the years, I wondered if he didn't want it to end. The book's done, his life's over. He never said that to me directly, but I just got that feeling. He did not want it to end."

$ $ $

Pandora Peaks arrived during one of the frequent disappearances of Melissa Mounds. Peaks came to RM through the efforts of Morgan "Tex" Hagen, editor of *Hustler's Busty Beauties* magazine and a huge Meyer fan. Another scientific marvel of boob engineering, Pandora at least had some of the spunk of Meyer's classic old-school dames. She had started stripping in September 1990 and by April of the following year Meyer was shooting a layout of her for German *Playboy*.

A smart cookie with ambition, Peaks knew how to keep RM happy without getting too deep in the Meyer mire. The two

---

* Meyer was friendly with a reporter named William Kahrl. According to Dave Frasier, once George Carll was banished, William became "The Good Kahrl," George "The Bad Carll."

weren't involved, although Pandora was savvy enough to let the world think so. "I didn't have a problem being on Russ's arm and letting him have his glory. I wasn't gonna be a romantic figure in his life—*he* might've presented me that way. Russ was very kind to me. I was his girl of the nineties. It would've been Melissa, but she just wasn't there. She could've been very jealous of me." Meyer filmed Peaks for a feature that wouldn't see light of day until 2000. "For years he'd say to me, 'Six months, it's gonna come out in six months,'" said Peaks, who was kept on a $9,000 weekly retainer during filming.

Meyer's next project was another *Busty Beauties* sensation, Letha Weapons. Assuring Letha that "there wouldn't be any sex, or whatever," Meyer talked her into coming out to his home in Palm Desert for some pictures. "I was sleeping in his bed and everything, but he never tried to make a move on me. The whole time we hung out, he's goin' on and on about my hair. I didn't want to disappoint him by taking my wig off—a blond bob with bangs. So I left it on for, like, two days." RM accidentally barged into the bathroom to find Weapons wigless. There were no further compliments concerning her coiffure.

A few days later Letha left for a dancing gig in Corpus Christi. To her shock, Meyer showed up at the club. "He had come there with an engagement ring to propose to me. I never had even had sex with the dude. He was like, 'I have an engagement ring for you, I wanna marry you, blah blah blah. I was like, 'Huh?'" To sweeten the deal, RM told her he wanted to shoot her for German *Playboy*, promising her $7,000 for one week's work. When Letha, who already had a commitment to appear in Howard Stern's *Butt Bongo Fiesta* video, told Meyer she'd do it if he'd limit the shoot to a few days, RM got angry.

"He was raising his voice, pissed off. Up until that time he'd been totally nice to me, a gentleman, and then the second he hears I'm not gonna do exactly what the hell he wants me to, he just turned to like an obnoxious jerk-off. Howard Stern was only paying me fifty dollars, but it was the principle of the matter. I knew this photo shoot didn't take more than a day, so I was being very generous giving him three or four. He's trying to take all my time and be possessive—'Well, you have to choose! You either do this photo shoot with me or do Howard Stern! You're not gonna do both.' I said, 'Y'know what? You can kiss my ass. Just forget it.' "

Meyer still wanted to spend the night in her hotel room, but Letha refused. When she got back to the hotel there was a missive from Meyer awaiting her. "And in the card it says I owe him three hundred for his round-trip ticket and fifty dollars for his hotel stay! I was like, 'Oh, I do not even *think* so.' I got on the phone and talked to his secretary, just let her have it. I said, 'Look, you tell this motherfucker that he invited *himself* here—he's trying to propose to me, I don't even know this fool, and he shows up sayin' I owe him his *airline ticket*?' I was irate. I never talked to him again after that."

$ $ $

Right to the bitter end, Russ kept a close watch on all his 166th buddies, organizing their reunions. When Bill Teas died, Meyer took his ashes to the next 166th get-together in Joplin, Missouri. As Charlie Sumners recalled, "We were all sittin' around, and Russ said, 'I have Teas' ashes.' Teas loved to drink and he loved vodka, so I said, 'Well, I have a suggestion—why don't we just get a fifth of vodka, stir Teas's ashes up in it, and all have a cocktail.' That didn't go over too well. Russ still has Teas's ashes." Meyer took the deaths of his comrades hard, calling up friends to weep openly over the latest loss. And by this time they were dying with some regularity. Roger Ebert noted that when actor Henry Rowland—RM's beloved "Martin Bormann"—passed, Meyer took out a full-page tribute in *Variety.*

For Meyer, the hardest death of all was that of wolf-dog Harry in 1993. Although Harry's hips had given out and he was falling apart in general, "Russ wouldn't put him down," said secretary Paula Parker. "The dog was shitting all over the room." For Harry's frequent trips to the vet, Meyer summoned an ambulance. And when Harry finally gave up the ghost, RM called the man who had brought the dog into his life. "When Harry died, man, I answered the phone and he was sobbing unbearably," said Charles Napier.

"Russ goes, 'He's gone,' and I knew who 'he' was. I talked to Meyer like the dog was a member of the family—'You want me to come down, you want to have a service?' He had to treat Harry like he was a human. You could never refer to Harry in front of Meyer as an animal." Harry was buried beneath Meyer's deck, then RM had the requisite plaque made in his honor.

One night, returning to his Palm Desert home from dinner with Charlie Sumners, RM suddenly slammed on the brakes in front of a small church. Meyer went in, leaving Sumners in the car. "It shocked me!" said Charlie, a Baptist who'd never discussed religion with his best friend. "Russ got back in the car and said, 'You didn't expect me to do that, did you? I was praying for Lucinda.' " Others remember RM visiting the church to communicate with his mother. "I turn to God," Meyer confessed in 1995. "I find myself going to a little wayside chapel. I'll say a prayer for people who need help."

And yet no one knew how Meyer felt about his own mortality. Said Kitten Natividad, "He never discussed death—even though it was all around him."

$ $ $

In 1995, Mike Thomas at Strand Releasing suggested to RM that *Faster, Pussycat! Kill! Kill!* be rereleased theatrically. Thomas was a great friend and fan of Meyer's; he booked his films on the revival circuit and even helped Meyer shoot a scene or two for *Breast.* According to Thomas, RM had taken "a fatherly attitude" toward him.

Meyer was excited by the prospect of resuscitating *Pussycat,* consulting with Thomas on every detail. Everything went swimmingly until they got to the one-sheet. RM wanted the original poster re-created, down to the paper stock. Of surpassing importance to Meyer was that the red—the only bit of color in the otherwise black-and-white poster—be matched exactly. The printer went to great trouble, painstakingly mixing the color to get it just right.

Although RM wanted to inspect the posters as they came off the press, the printer provided short notice, so Thomas took his vintage original down there and compared the two himself. To Thomas's eyes the new one-sheet seemed perfect, but Meyer took one look and hit the roof. Unfortunately, Thomas's original poster had faded, and thus they'd matched a slightly different red. "Hardly anybody could've ever told the difference—but Russ noticed. Strike number one." Meyer wanted them to run the poster again, threatening to sue. "Already the paper it was printed on was expensive," said Thomas. "We didn't have the resources to go out and print more posters for a crazy man over a shade of red."

The movie became a smash hit on the revival circuit, playing to packed houses. Thomas said it grossed a half million dollars— not bad for a nearly thirty-year-old picture that had flopped the first time around. *Pussycat* then went into the secondary stage of release, playing smaller cities for two or three days at a time. "Meyer started bein' offended when we wouldn't do well in some town where we probably *never* had a chance of doing well. He started taking those failures seriously, became kind of like the wounded bear, and lashed out."

Meyer suddenly demanded a $350 daily guarantee—"an arbitrary figure which would go up depending on his mood," said Thomas. The shit really hit the fan in Miami. RM didn't like the advance publicity done there, and he tried to pull the print at the very last minute, after it had already been advertised. Meyer relented, but that was the last straw. Thomas was exhausted by dealing with his hero, even though he'd originally planned on re-releasing the rest of RM's catalogue theatrically.

"I knew how Russ could be, and I just wanted to get out before we turned into archenemies. Before he sued us, or who knows what. I just didn't wanna find out."

And yet RM could be incredibly kind when you least expected it. He bailed out numerous combat buddies and ex-girlfriends financially. Screenwriter John McCormick was also among the fortunate after a deal to do a Meyer picture at Carolco collapsed. "I couldn't get arrested in terms of writing gigs, couldn't get anything going, and one day Meyer just pulled up in front of my house in the Suburban, came in, and said, 'I need you to write a screenplay for me,' and wrote me out a five-thousand-dollar check. It was like manna from heaven, and it saved my ass. Russ discerned my trouble—I certainly didn't tell him."

$ $ $

Throughout this time, the Meyer/Mounds doom train continued its intermittent ride to hell. In Febuary 1994, Mounds filed a lawsuit against Meyer over a bite to the face she'd received a year earlier from Harry. Melissa settled out of court, some say to the tune of a hundred grand. Mounds gave up stripping that same year, leaving her with no income, and when she discovered she had throat cancer, RM picked up the tab for treatment. "She was a real mess," said Haji. "I liked her, but she had no goals in life. She'd get up in the morning and she had nothing to live for or do."

Except report to Sgt. Meyer, that is. "He was a very controlling, moronic idiot," said Melissa's agent Eleanor Bucci, who was literally spat on by RM at a video convention in Las Vegas after Meyer decided she was partly to blame for his troubled relationship with Mounds. "She couldn't call me on the phone—he would go through the phone records. He was a possessive person, really quite nasty. He promised all kinds of things, then he showed his colors. She was almost a prisoner. He didn't want her to go anyplace. It was like putting a teacup over a butterfly. He just smothered her. She was very unhappy; she'd call me up and cry."

Copious amounts of alcohol didn't help matters on either side. "Russ was not a drunk," said Roger Ebert. "He drank in a social way. Russ worked too hard to have time to get drunk." Without any real projects to drive him—and with Melissa by his side—that changed. "Melissa was just an alcoholic and they both got drunk together," said Charlie Sumners, recalling a comical visit the two lovebirds made to his home in Alabama. Although Sumners lived in a dry county, Mounds borrowed a car and somehow managed to find beer, which she hid outside. "She didn't want Russ to know she was drinkin', and Russ didn't want her to know he was drinkin'. I would fix his drink in a can of 7-Up and she'd slip outside to drink hers—and take her a swallow of cough medicine so we couldn't smell it on her." Meyer later paid for Mounds to attend rehab at the Betty Ford Center, but she checked out early. "She won't listen to them," said RM.

$ $ $

Friends started to suspect that something was wrong with Meyer. The word *Alzheimer's* was whispered. The fear that RM had expressed to Manny Diez some twenty-five years previous was now becoming a reality: he was losing his mind. That magnificent brain, so all-powerful and detail-cognizant, was beginning to get hung up on repetition, not unlike a Meyer editing sequence. Charlie Sumners first noticed it in the mid-nineties on a trip overseas. "He would irritate the tar out of me, because every time we stopped he would go through every damn thing in his bags. He had money from all different sources—he had French francs, German marks, Portugese money. He had about five billfolds, and every time we'd stop he'd count his money. When I came home, I told my wife, 'Russ is losin' it.' "

For years, Meyer tinkered endlessly with the Pandora Peaks movie and then, whenever he was on good terms with Melissa Mounds, abandon it to work on her film. It seemed like he'd never finish either one (the Mounds film remains unfinished). "Russ finally entered into a phase of his life where he just was always perfecting things and never finishing them," said Roger Ebert. "I think it was part of his disintegration."

Richard Brummer lived in Meyer's Palm Desert house, editing the Pandora Peaks film in RM's garage cutting room. "We were working on it in fits and starts. He was already not in good shape, already forgetting." When RM asked for a section of the work print, Brummer would make Meyer "write a note that he had received it, because later in the day he would say, 'Where is it?' I'd say, 'I gave it to you.' He said, 'No, you didn't.' And I would have to say, 'Well, here's a note that says you did.' "

Getting ever stranger, Meyer had a urinal installed in the middle of the editing room. "Up until that time, he would open the back garage door and piss on the piece of lawn between us and the next house," said Brummer. "The neighbors began to complain, because not only did the grass die, but it also began to be odorous. So he put in the urinal, which he wanted me to use as well."* Alas, Brummer preferred the privacy of the bathroom inside the house, which irritated Meyer, along with Richard's habit of getting up early in the morning hours and using a hairdryer and electric toothbrush. "He didn't like the noise of it. I had to close all the doors. He says, *'You think I still don't hear it?!?'* It upset him beyond reason."

After one of their many breaks, Meyer summoned Brummer back to Palm Desert to resume work on *Pandora Peaks*, this time with a catch: RM was working with a scriptwriter, and he didn't want Richard disturbing him with that thunderous hairdryer/ electric tootbrush racket. Meyer wanted Brummer to come to work just the way he woke up—no blowing of hair, no brushing of teeth. "I'd rather stay in a motel," was Brummer's response. Meyer was furious. He made Brummer stay in Hollywood to cut the film, communicating with the editor only via written notes. They eventually made up, but not before RM trashed Brummer in an interview with a German magazine, accusing Richard—who'd now worked with him off and on for over thirty years—of being disloyal.

In 1996, Pandora Peaks appeared in the Demi Moore feature *Striptease*, and RM got it in his head that he was going to shoot stills for the Moore movie. "That just didn't happen," said Peaks. "I felt really bad. He got cantankerous; he wanted it to be on his rules. Russ was just too difficult to deal with." The following year, Peaks appeared in *Playboy's Voluptuous Vixens II*, a home video hosted by Russ. At one point a haggard, wild-eyed Meyer ruminates on the merits of the term *glamour.* "I don't care for it myself. I'd much rather say, 'This girl's built like a brick shithouse.' " Meyer's brief clips seem heavily edited, with the vixens surround-

---

* According to David K. Frasier, Meyer was known to piss in his own swimming pool at the Palm Desert house. When RM asked him if he'd like to take a dip, Frasier wisely refrained.

ing him looking genuinely uncomfortable. It saddened Pandora to see RM obviously deteriorating.

Kitten Natividad, working for RM at the time, realized things were out of whack "the day Russ stacked up the desks. One day we came in and he had desks on top of desks, all very neat and organized. And he said, 'See, now we have lots of room. Your desk is up there.' And I said, 'Yeah, but how am I gonna sit up there?' He goes, 'I didn't think about that.' He started getting kinda weird."

Natividad joined Meyer and Ebert for a night out at the Academy Awards. At dinner, Russ kept asking if he had ordered. Then Meyer announced he had to call Melissa. "He didn't know how to dial the phone . . . that night was a bad night," said Kitten. "The next day he was okay. He'd say, 'From now on I'm gonna remember things, I'm really gonna remember things.' "

Up! star Raven De La Croix came by with her boyfriend Michael Ziton to visit Meyer. They realized RM was heading south when he asked for Michael's help setting up magazine racks—on the exterior of his house. "These interviewers came and he started talking about children and sex," said Raven. "I almost fell on the ground." RM continued to give interviews right up into 1999, and they got progressively weirder and filthier.

Charles Napier came by to see Meyer. "It's eleven o'clock at night, we're drinking, all of a sudden he looks up and he goes, 'Who in the hell are you?' When Meyer was getting really bad, he called and said, 'Y'know, I can act—I want you to direct me.' I said, 'I know you can, Russ. Pick a script. I'll direct you.' Of course, he'd forget about it the next day. He'd call up in the middle of the night, just out of his head. It's a terrible disease. He was bizarre when he was *himself*—when it was Alzheimer's, you never really knew. I said to Ryan, 'Did you guys take his guns away?' "

Napier took Meyer to the set of a movie he was appearing in. "During the day he sat around watching. I could see he was getting upset. 'These fuckin' people don't know what they're doing.' And he started trying to take over. I hadda hustle him off—he was getting ready to fuck it *all* up. Once I got him out, he goes, 'I want to go home.' It became a thing where it was a very unpleasant situation to be anywhere with him."

Even taking RM to his favorite restaurants became impossible. He'd yell at the help, then pull his member out and whiz on the floor. His behavior bordered on the poetically surreal at times. Rob Schaffner recalled Meyer scurrying out to his GMC Suburban and, a can of spray paint in his hand, writing "RYAN SITS HERE" on the passenger-side door. Combat buddies from the 166th were also becoming alarmed by Meyer's condition. "At our last reunion up in Joplin, he was in bad shape," said Charlie Sumners. "He had on a pair of shorts, old scuffy shoes, and his old World War II hike jacket. Shocked everybody."

George Costello—whom RM had excommunicated back in the *Vixen* days—bravely came to visit and make his peace with Meyer. Once RM figured out who his old friend was, he enlisted Costello's help for a shoot he was doing out at the Salton Sea. "When we got back, Jim Ryan told me he didn't put film in the camera. None of the pictures that we spent all day taking came out." In September 1999, Meyer attended a fourteen-day retrospective of his work at the Egyptian Theater in Hollywood. Sporting blood on his neck from an unattended shaving cut, a gaunt, gray, nearly spectral RM made one of his last public appearances.

$ $ $

The Betty Boop voice. That's the first thing people mention when Janice Cowart's name comes up. High, grating, impossible to ignore. "She has a squeaky voice that Russ hated," said Kitten. "He used to tell her, '*Ugggh*, your *voice!*' He thought that she was a good worker. He never hit on her, because she wasn't the way he liked women. And I guess it bothered her. He thought she had a fat ass and no tits." Natividad giggled. Cowart's reputation definitely precedes her. Richard Brummer smiled somewhat wryly when I mentioned her name. "Janice can be very sweet. Don't cross her."

An army brat born January 9, 1949, Janice had been recommended by Meyer's accountant, Phil Cooperman, and the two met years before Cowart came to work for RM in 1988. "One of the reasons she got into this better and deeper and thicker than anybody is the new computer age," said longtime RM secretary Paula Parker. "She has a brother who is a computer programmer." Whereas everything had previously been done by hand, the Internet age left Meyer out in the cold—and completely dependent on his new hire. Web sites? E-mail? Janice could take care of all that. Everybody liked Cowart in the beginning, even Kitten Natividad. "When she first started, she was nice to everyone—'Oh, is this Kitten? Hold on, I'll get him for you. It's *Kitten*, Russ!' Then later on it was, 'Well, I don't know—he's really busy right now.' You could see her changing. She took over."

While Cowart would be all sweetness and light with Meyer himself, having to work with her was a trial, according to Paula Parker. "She logged everything. She spent more time logging and keeping info than she did working on the company. It was just totally bizarre to me. Everything I did wrong was noted down." For years Parker had gotten along fine with Meyer. After Janice arrived, she could do nothing right. If Paula forgot to put a stamp on a letter or happened to leave the air conditioner on when she left, Cowart went straight to Russ. "She'd have to tattle on everything I did." And what drove Cowart? "She used to always say," according to Parker, " 'I want to own my own business, I need my own business.' "

Kitten, who briefly rekindled her relationship with RM during one of Melissa's absences, came to work for Russ, driving him places, running errands. It was a bad time in her life—she was broke, facing breast cancer, and had a serious drinking problem (she's sober now). Giving her a gig was Meyer's way of throwing her a few bucks. Cowart maintained that she liked Natividad at first, but things turned sour. Janice felt that her drinking was endangering Russ, and she alleged that "[Natividad] was caught taking swigs from RM's liquor bottles on the job and became very difficult to deal with ... whenever possible, she was making Russ take her out to expensive restaurants and bringing along her friends, often four or more at a time, and I would see the credit card receipts on Monday. In addition, she took Russ to liquor stores and charged a lot of booze to his credit card, which she would then take home ... Later she tried to sue Russ without success, and basically we had a very unpleasant relationship at the end. I was very disappointed because she was the one person I felt would be with Russ to the end, to visit him and cheer him up, but it didn't turn out that way."[*]

Other observers felt that Cowart saw Natividad's relationship with RM as a threat. "She was mean to Kitten," said Haji. "And she knew she had cancer, she was sick, and this chick had no compassion at all. Russ was always there for Kitten—sometimes he complained about it a little bit, but he was always there. And Janice took that away from her." Added Paula Parker, "She needed insurance, and Janice made sure that she didn't get it. This is how cruel the woman is."

Cowart's job was to run a business, and she was concentrating on the bottom line. "Kitten wanted Russ to pay for her health insurance, and when she came up with a policy with a very high premium I asked her to do some research on alternative plans so that we could make a decision on what was the best one," said Janice. "Kitten became irate at this request, and did not want to do any further research. She complained to Russ, who agreed with me, and time passed and nothing got done so the matter was dropped.

"You might note that over the years Kitten had been very successful and made a lot of money but had no savings and had not been responsible enough to get health insurance for herself, so now she looked to Russ to help her."

$ $ $

Love him or hate him, Meyer was an honest guy. "I often would say that Russ lives his life in one compartment," said Roger Ebert. "Many people have different compartments—a family compartment, a work compartment, a sex compartment." Ebert was impressed with Meyer's insistence on mixing everybody together, offering apologies to no one. "Russ wouldn't take the sarge out one night and Kitten out the next night. All the girls got to meet

---

[*] Said Kitten, "I was drinking a lot . . . I was not all there mentally, either. It's not all Janice. I was fucked up . . . but she's a screwball, anyway."

all the army buddies. Russ taught me not to try to hide so much. To just affirm whatever it is you are or whatever it is you want." Paula Parker agreed, noting that things became markedly different with Janice Cowart on the scene. Doors were suddenly shut, conversations whispered. "Russ was out front, told you what he thought in front of your face—but he put somebody in position who is the total opposite. Secretive, hiding behind this and that."

Friends began to feel cut off. "I saw her start to manipulate and push everybody out," said Parker. "She was in his ear all the time." Meyer's French distributor and friend Jean-Pierre Jackson concurred. "I had excellent relations with Russ for more than fifteen years. From the point Janice went in, things began to crumble. The letters from Russ were less and the notes from Janice more . . . It was so progressive I didn't realize what was happening." Jackson wound up in French court defending his right to distribute RM's films, maintaining that Cowart lost the battle not once, but twice. "She's not professional, she understands very little. I don't think she's very bright. Russ means business, Janice means ego."

Lee Blackman, a lawyer who'd engineered some lucrative deals for Meyer, was also out. Jim Ryan thought Blackman did a good job and was sad to see him go, but the bottom line, said Ryan, was that "he and Janice had a problem." Longtime friends were incredulous that a mere assistant seemed to be pulling the strings in the Meyer empire. "Nobody can get access to him," RM's old exploitation crony Dave Friedman complained in 2003. "I can't figure out at what point she got control. I don't know where she came from."

Cowart's relationship with Meyer himself was a curious one. "Russ referred to her as 'the battle-axe,'" said Rob Schaffner, who remembered sitting in the lower level of Meyer's house working on photographs for RM's book as Janice loomed in the shadows. "She'd be sitting up there where the computer is, fucking eavesdropping on anything we were talking about. I had many lectures of, 'Well, Rob, you really shouldn't talk about titties.' I go, 'We're down there looking at naked chicks' tits! What do you *mean* we shouldn't be talking about fuckin' breasts!?' And he's goin', 'That fuckin' battle-axe.'" According to Shaffner, Meyer had a rather unique secret location for clandestine talks in the bottom of the house. "Mr. Teas was cremated and on his couch. Russ had him in an ammo box, and we'd always have to, quote-unquote, 'go near Teas.' To actually talk about anything, to be just enough to be out of earshot. And that drove her crazy. She'd come down the stairs and start spying."

Friends felt that Meyer grew intimidated by Cowart over time. Dave Friedman had dinner one night with RM at Musso & Franks. "He insisted I come up to the house next day, and I get there and he's showin' me the house, of course I've seen it a thousand times—I said, 'Who's the other broad?' Russ got all uptight. He said, 'Shhhhh.' He was totally coherent then, but suddenly there was a fear." Kitten Natividad recalled discussing her booze problem with Meyer. "He knew I was drinking a lot. I go, 'I need it.' He goes, 'Don't let Janice see you drink.' I went, '*Whoa!* Even *he's* afraid of her now!' " Some felt that Cowart was literally transforming. "Haji told me, 'Janice thinks she's Russ Meyer,' " said Kitten. " 'She talks like him sometimes, acts like him . . . uses some of his words.' "

In the opinion of some, Cowart's power increased as Meyer became more and more enfeebled. Erica Gavin recalled an agitated Meyer complaining about Cowart's domination at a dinner with RM and Jim Ryan at the French restaurant Pinot, one of Meyer's favorite haunts. "He would go to Jim, 'Y'know, if you don't do something, she's gonna take over my entire business. She's trying to *take* my business.' It was like a broken record—he kept going back to that the whole night. It just haunts me, that last dinner." Paula Parker and her boyfriend recalled being at a party with a confused RM, who asked them, "Do I own my own company?"

Meyer and Kitten came over to Raven's for dinner one night. The pair arrived to find no hard liquor, so they trotted off to Ralph's supermarket, returning with armloads of alcohol. Raven's live-in boyfriend, Michael, was amazed. "They had vodka, they had whiskey, they had beer, wine, liqueur, Courvoisier, tequila . . ." As the booze flowed, tempers flared. Kitten started ribbing RM, telling him he should be more generous with his fortune. Meyer wasn't amused. "He'd listen and his eyes would slit," said Raven.

"Russ turned into Gollum." They stumbled out after a big fight. "Janice calls me a couple days later screaming at me—'Why is there a ninety-seven-dollar alcohol bill?' " said Raven. "Janice calling about his money? About how *Russ* spends *his* money?"

$ $ $

After decades of being institutionalized, RM's half-sister Lucinda finally gave up the ghost on February 27, 1999. There would be no more panicked calls to Meyer's office, no more whisperings of dark plots. But Lucinda's funeral was bedlam. When Raven De La Croix and Michael Ziton arrived at the funeral home, Janice and RM employee Julio Dottavio were there alone. Then Kitten, Haji, and Tura meandered in. And they all waited for Russ and Melissa Mounds, who was back in the picture once more. "About a half an hour later we hear all these voices in the background," said Michael Ziton. "You hear Russ Meyer, *'Where is this place, fer God's sake? Where the hell are we goin' here?'* He walks in with his girlfriend, boobs up to here—it was like a *show,* man. We all sit down, he goes up to the front, he goes, 'Aaaah, that's *my sister* there. What a gal, what a girl.' "

Meyer and Mounds were visibly drunk. According to Ziton, RM rose to say a few words, pacing back and forth in front of the coffin: "Dad was a police officer, a real bastard. My sister and I were really close, and our favorite thing to do was pick cantaloupes. And eat cantalopes together." Things got weirder. "His girlfriend goes, 'How about some pictures, honey?' " recalled Ziton. "He goes, *'Fabulous idea.' "* Somebody located Meyer's camera. "He's standing in front of the coffin, he's trying to hug the dead body—'Okay, you taking a picture?'—he's *posing* her," said Raven. "I wanted to cry."

Then Melissa stood up and announced, "We're gonna miss dinner! And we have to get this body outta here, 'cause this place closes at nine-thirty!" Tura instructed her to say a prayer. "Our Father . . . ," Melissa began. "Our Father . . ." Silence. Clearly plastered, Mounds had forgotten the rest. "Don't you know the goddamn Lord's Prayer?!" shouted RM.

The entourage proceeded to a nearby eatery called the Blue

Dolphin. Taking RM Films employee Jesse Bryner with her, Mounds got up to leave. To retrieve Lucinda's corpse. She and Meyer were going to haul the body up to the Stockton cemetery where Lydia was interred. More turmoil ensued when Melissa returned. "We almost dropped her," she reported. There was a big hullabaloo over ice, which RM wanted in order to prevent Lucinda decaying. In the midst of this, Cowart signed Meyer's name on the bill. According to several witnesses, Meyer was livid, insisting he was fully capable of writing his own signature, and telling her to never do it again.

Cowart recalled it a bit differently. "For some time it had been RM's habit to give me the credit card receipt and ask me to calculate the tip and write it in, then he would sign and give me the receipt for safekeeping . . . I remember Russ being somewhat upset at the size of the bill . . . There were some people at the table that night that had ordered quite a bit to drink and the bill was quite large, so Russ was upset about that, not that I had signed the receipt."

Out in the parking lot, Mounds almost shut the car door on Meyer, causing another explosion. Screeching out of the lot, they drove off, Lucinda's body bouncing around in the back of the GMC, possibly on ice. Jesse Bryner* had the unfortunate job of manning the wheel, later testifying in court that Mounds berated her elderly beau the whole way home.

"She said she hated him. She said, 'Where are you? You don't even know where you are.' She was yelling that she was going to go home when we got back to Russ's house, that she was leaving, which would've left Russ with the body. And he didn't have a driver's license, so he would've been stranded with the body."

$ $ $

---

* Curiously, Meyer regarded Bryner with suspicion even though Jesse was on the payroll. "He never trusted him because he felt that he was Janice's 'boy,'" said David K. Frasier.

Meyer and Mounds continued to stumble through the Hollywood nights. At some point the pair got thrown out of a party at the Playboy mansion due to some drunken antics that left Mounds with a sprained ankle. "If you're going to do something, do it big," boasted RM. "They sent us home in a limo."

Back in the first week of June 1998, the police had been summoned to RM's Palm Desert home. Meyer was temporarily MIA. They found Melissa Mounds out by the pool, "a loaded gun by a cool drink" at her side, according to court testimony. Mounds informed the police that Meyer had threatened her with the firearm. Melissa told the court that RM's guns were everywhere. "One time I went to get my shoe from under the bed, I pulled a gun out. It went off this close to my head." Meyer's attorney pointed out that she'd scrawled a little note next to the bullet hole in the wall that suggested otherwise: "Melissa shot this hole through the wall in a fit of rage."

At this same time Meyer wound up in the hospital with a badly injured hand. He told doctors he'd fallen, but Janice Cowart later testified there had been an argument over a vehicle. "She [Mounds] was upset that he was not going to buy her the car. He told me several times that she hit his arm with a rock."

The relationship with Melissa was falling apart, and for the last time. She didn't like staying at the Hollywood house. "Living in the office atmosphere all the time, nothing is private. We weren't getting along." Mounds had been making sporadic trips to visit family in Ohio and decided to move there. On May 24, 1999, she told Meyer she needed a truck, $1,000 spending money, and $49,500 to buy a mobile home. "And when Janice came we discussed it with her," Mounds claimed. "There were no problems." An appointment was made for 11 a.m. on Thursday the twenty-seventh at the office of Meyer's lawyer.

Something went awry, though. Meyer, Cowart, and Mounds got into a squabble. "There was ongoing arguing pretty much the whole day," said RM employee Jesse Bryner. According to Cowart's testimony, Meyer parked himself on the couch in the upstairs office of his home. "He seemed somewhat intimidated and fearful."

Mounds—who, Cowart maintained, "smelled like alcohol"— would periodically barge in. "She was very agitated, pacing the floor, saying that she had to get out of there, that she wanted to leave, that he was going to have to give her money. She was saying her life was going nowhere."

Cowart described Mounds bullying Meyer. "She started to berate him . . . about his medical condition, about his memory, telling him that he was crazy and didn't know what he was doing, that he was pathetic.* I thought she was going to hit me." According to Cowart, Mounds spent the next day recovering in bed, but things flared up again the night of the twenty-sixth, the day before the appointment with RM's lawyer.

Cowart said she received a number of calls from Mounds. "She was just sort of saying, 'Russ is going to have to give me $49,500, and he is going to have to give it to me this morning, and that's the way it is.' " Melissa maintained she only called Janice once. "Russ was missing and I was worried . . . he took off down the street."

When Meyer returned, he and Mounds argued over his drinking. "I asked him to please lay off the gin. He got a beer and poured gin into the beer . . . he likes to spike it up." As Mounds explained, "He doesn't like . . . to have anybody tell him that he can't drink his alcohol . . . or that he's lost his memory. He gets very, very angry. And he got angry at me and yelled, 'Nobody is going to tell me that I'm crazy and that I can't drink or do whatever I want.' "

Mounds maintained that it was a little before 1 a.m. when things spun totally out of control. "He pushed me against the wall . . . then he put his hand around my neck. He was just raging—'Nobody is going to tell me I can't drink!' After he grabbed my throat, I punched him. . . . I was defending myself. I only hit him once." Those who know Meyer scoff at the idea of him lunging at a woman. Then again, he'd never before been a heavy drinker, and his mind was on the fritz.

Mounds was arrested, at which time the police discovered she

---

* Mounds denied this in court. "I did not belittle him. . . . Russ and I had our arguments . . . a rocky relationship, but I wouldn't do that to him."

had an outstanding DUI from December 1997. She would be charged with three counts: inflicting corporal injury on a spouse, violence used against a spouse (curious, as Meyer and Mounds were not married), and willfully causing injury to an elder. She was held on $10,000 bail.

The incident hit papers across the country. When Rob Schaffner went to see how Meyer was holding up, RM seemed unfazed. "Like usual, Russ opened the door in his bunhuggers, scratchin' his ass. He had a huge shiner and a gash on his head— he was totally amused by the thing—'Wow, can you imagine? I really haven't done a flick in, like, twenty years and look, I'm still in the fuckin' paper.'" The one thing that annoyed Meyer was the "elder abuse" idea.

The trial took place that July and painted a bleak picture of Meyer's present state. Meyer was barely coherent on the stand but still somehow managed to be his amusing self. When asked if Mounds was after his money, he responded, "Well, it's a natural feeling on the part of people that don't have as much money. They'd like to get some." His account of the assault was rather elegant. "I can recall I was laying on a couch. And I was attacked on that given evening or afternoon, whatever the case may be. And I felt severely injured. . . . I was being struck by a very strong person, and I think probably by a strong woman." The court testimony is frequently compelling. Cowart expounded on RM's condition: "He gets confused. He doesn't know what day it is. He doesn't like to address it." Mounds got in a dig or two at Cowart: "She has manipulating [sic] him before. She is coaching him." Meyer defended Cowart: "She has been a very close confidante and honest lady."

In early August 1999, Melissa Mounds was convicted of all three counts against her and sentenced to sixty days in jail, forty-five days on a work crew, 104 Alcoholics Anonymous meetings, one year of domestic abuse counseling, and three years' probation. There are those who feel that Mounds got a bit of a raw deal, pointing out that in his condition, Meyer couldn't discern reality anymore. "That disease started settin' in so bad, he started getting really weird," said Paula Parker. "He used to say things like, 'Paula, last night people were chasing me, beating at my door.' He was makin' up things that couldn't possibly have happened. I think that maybe Melissa got railroaded a bit."

Melissa Mounds did not walk away empty-handed, though. According to Jim Ryan, Meyer's lawyers were concerned about any future legal action involving her and whatever photographic or film work she did for RM. To send her on a permanent vacation, she was given Meyer's Palm Desert home plus a sizable amount of cash. (Curiously, RM's will still lists the residence among his holdings.)

$ $ $

In August 1999, David K. Frasier was summoned to Meyer's home in hopes of salvaging the autobiography RM was no longer capable of finishing. He was shocked to find Meyer limping, being carted around by a driver. The morning after RM had welcomed Frasier, he greeted him with, *"Dave! When did you get here?"* Frasier was troubled by what he saw. "Russ's dementia was pronounced."

The situation only became more grim as Frasier looked over the latest incarnation of the autobiography. Meyer had ripped pictures out of porno magazines and slapped them into the layout. Photographs of the recently departed Melissa Mounds were shoved in everywhere.* Dave took Janice aside and told her he was wasting their time being there. The book was already done. Russ was just monkeying around.

"Well, are you gonna tell him?" asked Cowart.

Steeling himself, Frasier sat down and told Meyer there would be no more additions or changes to the book. They'd worked on it for a decade and it was over and done.

"Well, I guess we don't have a book then, right?" asked RM.

---

* On page 1186 of *A Clean Breast*, alongside a Melissa Mounds interview completely concocted by Meyer, there is a shot of a German porno video box with a female on the cover that looks very much like Mounds. "During the time of the book Russ had found out she had done hard-core," said Frasier. "He wanted to write something really, really vitriolic, just slamming her." Dave talked him out of it.

Frasier assured Meyer they had a great book, they only had to go back to the previous finished version. Ever so delicately Frasier explained the situation to Meyer, assuring him they had a fantastic tome. To his relief, RM seemed to accept the news.

"I'm thinking, 'Great, it's settled,' but then an hour later Russ said, 'Oh yeah, I found somethin' else I want to put in the book.'"

It was beginning to dawn on Frasier just how far gone Russ was. "We tried to put together a millennium calendar, and he had thousands of slides. They had tried for months and months to make selections. We couldn't even get through that. He'd get distracted. We couldn't even get thirteen shots."

There was a sad goodbye between the two men at the airport. "I realized that was the last time I was gonna see him," said Frasier. "See, the one tragedy vis-à-vis Russ and myself is that we never got to celebrate the book coming out. Because that was our war."

$ $ $

Friends worried that no one was looking after Meyer. During his last visit, David K. Frasier noticed that RM was wandering around in shit-stained shorts and voiced his concerns to Cowart. "Most people don't want to walk around in fecally encrusted clothing . . . that bothered me. I didn't come right out and tell her—I did say, 'Well, I hope that if Russ is going to be kept here there's going to be more of an attempt to manage his hygiene." Frasier said Cowart later apologized in regard to Meyer's appearance.

The fact that RM was limping during that last visit also concerned Frasier. Talk of a stroke was making the rounds. But nobody really knew the facts, because Cowart—allegedly to protect Russ—not only insisted on keeping his condition a secret, but legally threatened anybody who talked about it in the press. "One thing that sort of hurts me a little bit is they never told me any of this—the fact that Russ had a stroke, or that he was developing dementia," said Frasier. "I'm not the sort of person that would've talked to *Entertainment Tonight*. If they needed somebody to go out there tomorrow, I'd go."

Cowart admitted in an email response that she kept many of

Meyer's intimates in the dark. "Everyone is entitled to his privacy. There was nothing to be gained by publicizing his decline, nor would Russ have wanted it. Let me ask, did you hear all the details of Ronald Reagen's [sic] 'long goodbye'? There is a reason for that."

There were other complaints. Paula Parker related the time Cowart got upset because Meyer had suffered an accident, taking a dump on the floor and blaming it on an invisible friend. "Well, she threw a fit—'Russ! Come up here!' And she got *mean* with him. That upset me. She started reprimanding him like you couldn't believe—'I can't do this, this is disgusting.' She talked to him like a mother to a two-year-old. I was very embarrassed for him. And I cleaned it up. She didn't want to touch it. She said it was a health issue, she didn't want to get sick." Kitten Natividad said that Janice called her up in a panic to help with another accident, even though Kitten had already been fired from her job. She arrived to find Meyer covered in his own waste. According to Natividad, Cowart "just let him wallow in this shit for five hours because she didn't want to go in the room and clean him up. She would let him die in shit, because she doesn't wipe her own ass, y'know?"

Haji backed Natividad up. "I saw Kitten wipe the crap off the floor from one end of the house to the other. And Janice would be in the other room yelling."

Cowart doesn't deny these incidents occurred. "Early on, there was a time when Russ was suffering from diarrhea on several occasions and there was no way to convince him to get cleaned up. I did hire carpet cleaning services several times." Janice credits Natividad with coming to the rescue. "She bathed him and cleaned him and it was not a pleasant situation, but she did it in a very caring way. She loved Russ and was very, very nice to help. I was never involved with Russ in an intimate manner and it would have been very uncomfortable for him and inappropriate for me to be bathing him or even seeing him undressed."

At least three of the Meyer women (who requested not to be named for fear of repercussions) told me that in 2001 they called the authorities over their concerns about what was going on inside the Arrowhead Drive home.

"Someone called the Adult Protective Services on several oc-

casions to report some sort of mistreatment of Russ by me," said
Cowart. "We never knew who called. However, since this wasn't
true, the social workers that came out thought that Russ was very
well cared for and the calls were not merited." According to Cowart, on the third alleged complaint the then "head honcho" of
Adult Services came out for an inspection and told Janice that she
was "very impressed with RM's living conditions and his appearance. I mentioned, 'Well, I guess we'll be seeing you again,' and
she asked me what I meant. I told her this was the third visit, and
she got very upset and said, 'We don't allow people to use our office to harass someone,' and that was that.

"None of the actresses like Kitten, Raven, Haji, Erica, Tura, or
any of the 'girls' were aware . . . that [Meyer's home] had been
cleaned up, straightened up, and simplified to help with RM's care
and well-being. RM's doctor wanted a calm serene atmosphere so
Russ would be able to cope with what was to come."

$ $ $

The Melissa Mounds assault case had set loose a juggernaut in
Russ Meyer's life. Because of the elder-abuse charges that resulted
from the Mounds beating, Meyer's case was turned over to the
California Department of Welfare. Complicating matters was the
fact that RM had no immediate family. Jim Ryan said that if
Meyer's lawyers hadn't acted fast, the company's assets could've
been seized and RM might've wound up in a home. But Meyer
had put a living trust in place. Around the time of the assault it
involved just a handful of people—Jim Ryan, accountant Phil
Cooperman, lawyer Glenn Alperstein, and, last but certainly not
least, Janice Cowart, who would testify that she was added to the
trust "probably as a direct result" of the Mounds case.

The matter wound up in court, and while the Welfare Department backed off—"they had already started the procedure to
seize," said Ryan—the one thing the court insisted on was that
Meyer have around-the-clock care. RM was legally declared to be
suffering from dementia and incapable of managing his own affairs. He was said to be suffering with Alzheimer's or multi-infarct

dementia—clots blocking small blood vessels in the brain, leading to destruction of brain tissue. Doctors wouldn't know the exact cause of RM's dementia until an autopsy was performed. "We haven't got a firm diagnosis," said Ryan in 2003. "I told Meyer 'A pubic hair is growin' in your brain.' "

What all this meant was that somebody had to officially watch over Meyer and manage his health. "We had a meeting at the lawyer's of the people named as conservators in the living trust," said Ryan. "They said, 'Somebody's got to take over the physical problems with him being declared incompetent.' " Ryan already had his hands full trying to maintain his photo business while tending to his own ailing wife. "I didn't open my big mouth—it ain't my bag, as they used to say."

Apparently it was Janice Cowart's bag, because she volunteered. On June 19, 2000, she was granted conservatorship of Russ Meyer's physical being, which, according to the court documents, gave her absolute control over six very interesting points:

1. Power and right to fix the residence or dwelling of the Conservatee.

2. Power and right to access confidential records and papers belonging to the Conservatee.

3. Power and right to consent or to withhold consent to marriage.

4. Power and right to give but not withhold medical consent.

5. Power and right to limit the Conservatee's right to control his own social environment and contacts and/or sexual contacts and relationships.

6. Power and right to contract on behalf of the Conservatee.

According to Meyer's friends, the effects of the conservatorship were immediately felt. "When Janice came to power—when Russ signed the papers—I'm telling you a demon came out, and she became very mean," said Haji. RM's cronies no longer felt welcome. George Carll took Meyer out for dinner with Jim Ryan: "We drove all over East L.A., places he remembered. He enjoyed the ride. We ended up in Chinatown, had some food. We were gone for two, three hours. I didn't realize anything was the matter. Well, Janice was all over my ass for takin' him out—she says, 'You've got him all riled up.' After that it was strictly cold city."

David K. Frasier felt that he was expendable once Cowart had gotten his help in extracting the final version of *A Clean Breast* out of Meyer. He got very little information out of the company afterward and felt, like so many others, that his calls inquiring as to RM's health and well-being were blown off. "I guess I called at inopportune times, because I was always told, 'Well, we're busy here now.' After a while it's like hitting your thumb with a hammer. I can see where people would feel they have been cut off and they've been distanced. Ideally, I don't think it would've taken much effort to say, 'Well, Russ is doing well today, we're taking him out.' That's all I wanted."

Even Charlie Sumners—Meyer's best friend since World War II—got the cold shoulder. Intially he liked Cowart and sympathized with her attempts to protect RM. "I think Janice is afraid that all of this will just snowball, so she's kinda built a wall around him and kept everybody away—including me. I try not to think about it. Last time I talked to Russ, Janice would tell him what to say.... I've tried to call out there, but I can't get through."

"Many of RM's friends could not understand the concept that, as he became more ill, Russ could not talk on the phone anymore," said Cowart. "Instead they liked to believe that I was preventing him from contacting them. Russ could not dial the phone anymore. You don't know how many times I dialed Charlie Sumners and brought Russ to the phone to attempt a conversation. I did this with many other friends as well ... I know at one point Floyce Sumners viciously attacked me on the phone, accusing me of 'preventing' Russ from talking to her or Charlie, which really surprised me, since he had seemed so nice before. I repeatedly asked her and Charlie to come out to visit Russ one last time and even offered to pay their plane tickets, as Russ often did, but they never came. Russ loved Charlie like a brother so it was very sad that they didn't visit one last time."

Floyce Sumners, widow of Meyer's closest buddy (Charlie passed away in 2004), and who herself was by all accounts a dedicated friend to Russ Meyer for over forty years—in his will, Meyer left his mother's belongings to Floyce—was emotionally devastated upon hearing Cowart's statements. "That's a lie. She never invited us out and offered to pay our way* . . . I can't believe she'd talk about Charlie like that . . . this breaks my heart." Floyce pointed out if it hadn't been for her late husband, Janice wouldn't have even met Russ, as Charlie had saved his life during World War II. As far as a trip out to California for "one last time," Charlie Sumners was simply too ill to fly the last year of his life. "But [Janice] didn't know that, because she would not answer our calls . . . Janice shut everybody away. She did. Everybody."

$ $ $

Fearing that her access to Meyer would soon be cut off, Haji talked fellow Pussycat Lori Williams into a clandestine visit one weekend when Janice wouldn't be there. "It was just really sad," said Williams. "He was sitting in a chair, like a hard card-table chair. The pictures were taken off the walls, all the posters, everything— but there were all the remnants of what had been there, all the glue marks and the holes and the tape. It looked like somebody had moved and he was sitting in the middle of it. It was pretty bad. And he had this nasty lady that was cooking some kind of slop for him. I definitely did not get the idea that there was lots of TLC going on. I don't think that anybody was abusing him, but it was grim." But at least Meyer seemed to remember them, posing for pictures to document the occasion. According to Haji and Lori, Cowart went ballistic when she got wind of the visit. "As soon as she heard that, the rules all changed—'Nobody's allowed to ever come here.' And that was the end of it."

---

* Floyce did confirm that Cowart did offer to pay her travel expenses for RM's memorial service, as noted later in this chapter.

To one degree or another, Cowart had made enemies with all the Meyer women I spoke to. RM's friend Rob Schaffner listened as she badmouthed one after the other.* "She'd go, 'Y'know, these whores keep callin' me. . . .' I go, 'Y'know what? They're not whores, Janice—they worked with Russ.'" Said Kitten Natividad, "It's very, very strange. She thinks it's terrible that we girls make money with our clothes off—but it's not terrible for her to get a paycheck every week from it."

Meyer had often supplied his former stars with videos, posters, and stills at cost so they could pull in a meager income from fan conventions, but Cowart has all but cut that off. "She became so penny-pinching and cheap!" said Haji in 2003. "Didn't care about the girls anymore, didn't help us out or anything." Lori Williams concurred. "Janice makes you pay for every little thing, which is really sick. Then she threatens us when we do the shows. Russ would be *outraged* if he knew, especially if he knew she threatened to sue Tura. It's unbelievable . . . she has no limits to how far she goes with this nonsense."

Counsel on behalf of RM Films sent threatening letters to Kitten Natividad, Tura Satana, and Rob Schaffner, instructing them not to talk about RM's health even though his illness was a matter of public record. Sometimes the aggression has been downright comical, as in a March 3, 2003, e-mail Julio Dottavio—acting as a representative of RM Films—sent to the Webmaster of the Velvet Hammer burlesque troupe site, which had posted an old interview with Meyer. Dottavio accused them of selling stills (which they clearly weren't) and making up the interview (which had been previously published in 1995), then threatened legal action within forty-eight hours. Nothing came of it.

Meyer may have been an egomaniac and a brute, but he always publicly acknowledged his debt to and affection for the women in his films, and the fact that his estate disrespects and even harasses the women that made him famous strikes many as a

---

* A wildly entertaining character in his own right, "Colonel" Rob Schaffner has got to be the only hard-core pornographer Meyer ever befriended. Schaffner's filthy and low-down 2000 home video release *Camp Erotica* is dedicated to "Russ Meyer and the men of the 166 Photo Corps."

disgrace. It has caused a great deal of hurt and anguish among RM's former stars. "I am part of Russ's life and his legacy and all that, and I shouldn't be thrown to the trash like this," said Kitten Natividad.

"The women who starred in RM's films were not allowed to see Russ for many reasons," said Cowart. "Most of them did not respect his privacy and spoke about his illness to the press just so they could get attention. Many of them tried to take advantage of him financially and brought around uninvited guests who often tried to get RM to enter into some sort of business project that was not in his best interest ... The women you mention wanted to visit for themselves, not for Russ. It was not a positive thing. The court appointed me to protect Russ and his privacy, which is what I did.

"Russ was a very private person who was embarrassed when he could not function socially as he had in the past. A number of invited people continued to visit but it was very painful for them and also for Russ. He would often become furious after they left or insult them when they were here. The doctors advised us there was no point to having these people visit as Russ would forget by the next hour."

"Janice says she does it all for Russ's sake," said Floyce Sumners in 2004. "I said, 'Janice, how can you say that, when you cut off everyone who's cared for him?' She even went so far as to tell me that people didn't really care for him, they were just moochers, just used him."

"The whole thing is ironic, because one of the things that Russ wanted through his company is that all his personal friends be a part of his business, and she wasn't even a personal friend," said Paula Parker. "The worst thing is to take your support team away when you're leaving, you're at the end days," said Raven.

"Now if Kitten was in charge? He would've died so happy, this guy," said Haji in 2003. "Janice hasn't got that kind of sensitivity or imagination that she would allow—in his own home—the Pussycat girls and Kitten to come up and have a party. So what if Russ doesn't remember us? We remember *him*. I'm telling you, he might not have remembered it all, but he would've had a ball."

But that sort of merry shindig would never happen, and RM's

friends were all left in limbo as to the progression of his affliction. Said Haji, "I told Jim Ryan the other day, 'So, Jim, I can't see him anymore? You know what you're telling me, Jim? You're telling me the next time I'm gonna see Russ Meyer is in a coffin.' " Most poignantly, Erica Gavin asked, "When Russ passes away, are we even gonna know?"

$ $ $

At some point Meyer's beloved museum at Arrowhead Drive was dismantled. "They said Russ got violent and started writing obscene things on the pictures and he would start destroying them," maintained Kitten Natividad. "It would upset him and make him horny or whatever." Ryan was told that a nurse who specialized in Alzheimer's suggested they be removed, as they stirred partial memories that confused and agitated Meyer. All the pictures and plaques were taken down, aside from a few on the ceiling that couldn't be reached. "They haven't thrown it away," said Ryan. "It's preserved. All the pictures are piled in a heap." Friends were disturbed that RM had been stripped of his all-important past. "I think that would be the ultimate blow for him," said Jean-Pierre Jackson. "He was living on souvenirs."

Meyer spent his end days facing bare walls that echoed with the soothing sounds of Guy Lombardo and Bing Crosby. "Passive music that keeps him calm," Ryan explained. "He's under medication." Measures were taken to ensure that RM complied with his prescription schedule. "They've got television cameras on him all the time. He'd fake taking the pills and then throw 'em away— he'd say, 'I don't like 'em, they make me feel funny.' "

Ultimately, Ryan defended Cowart, maintaining there was nothing nefarious going on with Meyer's care. "What's nefarious? There's three different nurses and housekeepers and they have to cook his dinner, get him to the toilet, give him a shower and shave him, cut his hair. Somebody supervises that, and they've done a good job. He looks great all the time. You'd never know there's anything the matter with him. He's lost weight, he's in the sun and got a suntan." Ryan maintained that the estate went to great

lengths to obtain the newest imported drugs in hopes of rehabil-
itating RM's mind, but to no avail.

There is no question that Janice Cowart had one tough gig.
She'd been hired as an office worker and now she was caretaker of
a sick old man. Meyer was often belligerent and uncontrollable
even when his brain was functioning properly. "He's strong, too,"
said Jim Ryan, recalling the way Meyer grabbed Cowart during
one outburst. "She was really scared—but she was able to say,
'Russ! Your mother wouldn't like that!' " Ryan backed up Janice's
claims that she was only protecting Meyer and his business. "She's
rather blunt as far as doing things to keep his privacy. She doesn't
want him to be disturbed, because when he gets disturbed, it dis-
turbs everybody there. He's upset all that day, then he gets fighting with the medical assistants, the nurses, the housekeepers. It
takes him a day to settle down after these encounters."

There are those in Meyer's circle who wondered why Ryan allowed events to unfold the way they did, some even suspecting
darker motives—a ridiculous claim if you know the man. Erica
Gavin felt he was simply oblivious, that Ryan "would never expect
evil out of people. He's like the movie he's in—the Handyman."
The last time he saw Gavin, Meyer, who always got a chuckle when
it came to Ryan and the opposite sex, expressed the opinion that
Jim was somewhat bewitched by Janice Cowart.

$ $ $

Despite Janice Cowart's desire to be head honcho of her own business, Paula Parker saw "weakness in her. She always had to have
somebody around helping her make a decision."

Enter one Julio Dottavio. Originally hired by Meyer to do
some remodeling in his home, in recent years Dottavio's stature
has grown by leaps and bounds at RM Films, with this vaguely
handsome sometime graphic artist of South American/Italian descent acting as Janice's right-hand man. When Jim Ryan arranged
a meeting with director John Landis, hoping at the time to make a
movie out of Meyer's autobiography, Julio was there at Janice's

side. Dottavio now enjoys the title of Director of Operations for RM Films.

Born in 1956, Dottavio has worked as a Class B general contractor, real estate developer, designer for numerous architectural firms, and a schoolteacher. He also pointed out that he possesses "a Bachelor's of Arts Degree in Architecture at City University of New York and completed one semester of classes towards a Master's of Fine Arts in Interior Architecture."

On the subject of Julio Dottavio, Janice Cowart waxed poetic. "A sea of predators surrounded Russ as he became more ill and vultures that were hoping to make money or get attention through RM's work and legacy abounded. It was as if God sent Julio, a decent and kind person, secure in himself, to help me stave off the evil people who were trying to use Russ. Julio has been a good friend who gave me confidence and helped me make decisions that were best for Russ and the company. I was overwhelmed with the situation and will always be thankful to Julio for his compassionate caring and willingness to help. I hadn't met too many people like that around Russ."

Julio Dottavio arrived on the RM Films scene circa 1994. At the time Meyer was concerned that aftershocks from a recent earthquake might knock down his chimney and damage his vast memorabilia, so he asked Dottavio, then doing remodeling work in the neighborhood, to take a look. Julio did the inspection free of charge, and according to Dottavio, a wondrous friendship then began. "[Russ] liked to talk to me because I was familiar with art and recognized his wonderful style. We became good friends, he reminded me of my distant father who was the same age and had a similar personality. He grew fond of me and repeatedly invited me to dinner. I had to turn down many of the dinners because I did not want him to pay and it was getting a little excessive for me."

Once Dottavio's work in the area was done, he told RM he wasn't going to be coming by as much. Meyer, said Julio, "got very sad. He was a very lonely man searching for just a sincere friendship . . . Realizing how lonely he was, I tried to be a companion to him . . . We would talk for hours sometimes, and he was very protective of his money, especially when it dealt with the women who had been in his films. 'These women,' he said, 'are only after a free meal.' He didn't trust them. He would often say, 'I trust you because you are hard working just like me—like the Germans say, 'Work and sausage.' " Julio stressed that Meyer never forgot the one time Dottavio drove RM to see Lucinda on a Christmas Eve after she'd gone into respiratory arrest. As Cowart elaborated, "The hospital was urgently asking Russ to come and it was Julio Dottavio who was willing to drive Russ all the way to Norwalk at 4 p.m. on Christmas Eve in horrendous traffic."

Dottavio maintains that RM eventually "gained complete trust" in him "and would repeatedly say that he only trusted me. Even when he was ill he would say this over and over. He would also say, 'I want you to take care of the business, I trust you.' " The way Julio tells it he was Meyer's only real friend. "I was there to listen when everyone else ignored him. Most of the people who visited him just wanted a free meal. I sincerely felt sorry for Russ, who was surrounded by many vultures after his money." This is the one tune that gets played over and over: Janice and Julio versus the vultures.

When I asked Floyce Sumners what Dottavio was like, she said, "Really, really good-looking," with her husband Charlie adding, "Really, really married." Dottavio "thought he could break into film," Floyce maintained. "Russ told us that Julio wanted Russ to build a new house so he could do the work—Russ said, 'I don't need another house.' " (According to Dottavio, Meyer had "numerous projects in mind" for Julio to do "but couldn't decide on one.")

David K. Frasier recalled getting a call from Russ toward the end of their work on *A Clean Breast* where he expressed misgivings about Dottavio. "He mentioned something about some handyman Janice knew that he didn't really like or trust all that much. I mentioned that to Janice—'Oh, that's not right, nothing's happening there.' She was sort of defensive about it. She was just *real concerned* that Russ had been speaking about the possible relationship" between herself and Dottavio. "Shortly after that they made it so Russ couldn't call out much." (Cowart took issue with this, stating that

Meyer's private number has remained the same until the current day, although "Russ did have an additional phone line that was changed when certain people were trying to take advantage of him.")

Among other duties, Dottavio is now the curator of the Meyer estate. Those close to RM are stunned that the job of Meyer archivist is now held by an outsider with perhaps no specific credentials for the gig. "Russ would roll over in his grave," said Erica Gavin. "I *know* that Russ hated Julio," she added. *"Hated* him. He didn't want him anywhere near the house."

Cowart insists that Meyer was one of Julio's biggest fans, with the only problem being that RM was simply jealous of Dottavio's way with the ladies. "When Julio was working for Russ in 1998 and 1999, Russ had a lot of women around, and since Julio is a nice-looking and very gracious guy, the women tended to pay attention to Julio. Russ did not like this because he always wanted to be the center of attention. I think the conflict was that Russ did not want competition from a younger man, so sometimes he would act like he didn't want Julio around, but when no women were present Russ liked Julio a lot."*

$ $ $

"These films are my legacy, they are my children," Meyer once said, but his movies seem to be living as raggedy orphans these days. Whatever the opinion of Janice Cowart and Julio Dottavio as RM's caretakers, it is hard for Meyer fans not to get angry over the current presentation (or lack thereof) of his films. Theatrical showings of Meyer films are priced so high that revival houses don't

---

* Apparently Cowart believes that all roads lead to Julio Dottavio, as she felt that her problems with Kitten Natividad were somewhat due to Kitten being spurned by Julio. "In my opinion part of her animosity towards me began because she liked Julio, who had been kind to her because he felt sorry for her because of her cancer surgery, and when he didn't ask her out, she thought it was because he liked me, which really wasn't true at all." Funnily enough, Kitten felt that Janice never forgave Natividad due to outspoken comments she made regarding Janice's relationship with Dottavio.

want to bother with them (*Faster, Pussycat! Kill! Kill!* costs $500.00 for a single screening).

Then there are the DVDs. "Quality only Russ Meyer could approve," it says on the back of the DVDs, which are sold by the company for a whopping $39.95, but the quality of the product underwhelms. Meyer did charge top dollar for his home videos in the eighties, but he utilized top-of-the-line transfers at the time. The current releases rely on the same twenty-year-old masters, ignoring the technological advances of recent years. There are no extras, save for some shoddily presented trailers (the one for *Pussycat* skips during play, and fans have reported glitches in the *Up!* DVD) and a short, poorly written biography by Dottavio. The DVDs even look cheap. As Meyer friend and fan Rob Schaffner put it, the artwork resembles "something you'd buy at Pic 'n Save." Julio Dottavio is credited with package design, his name appearing nearly as often as Meyer's, right on the covers. "Russ would've gone berserk if he'd seen this," said Frasier. There are numerous complaints about RM's DVD product from his fans on various cult-movie websites. "The state of DVD has gotten to the point now where they ought to remaster everything and restore it and do it right," said Roger Ebert.

Cowart maintained that to describe their DVDs as shoddy was "a ridiculous assertion. We have had a great deal of praise and very few complaints. Our sales figures have been outstanding with no returns. The new packaging and box covers have increased sales and all our dealers love them." Once again she blew a trumpet for Dottavio, the mastermind behind the RM Films of today. "The Co-Trustees were pleased to be able to hire Julio as Director of Operations, and we were lucky that he agreed to work with RM Films, becasue it is Julio, who over the past five years has kept the company profitable. He has successfully negotiated creative lucrative licensing deals with Canada, Japan, and England as well as many other projects . . . He is a savvy, experienced businessman who Russ trusted and liked very much."

For all of Cowart's alleged computer know-how, the prehistoric RM Films website looks tacky and fails to provide for credit card

ordering. According to Jim Ryan, Meyer's film negatives are deteriorating and Jim wants to release *Europe in the Raw* and other
long-unseen works but can't find support within the company.
"Nobody wants to put up the money to do it."

What many find most galling is the fact that Janice Cowart has
never shown the slightest interest in Russ Meyer's work. RM complained to friends that she never sat through one of his films. "She
has contempt for Russ's movies," said Jean-Pierre Jackson. Clearly,
Meyer's intentions are being ignored. As recently as August 26,
1997, Meyer listed David K. Frasier as the first to be consulted in
regard to decisions concerning his work in case of his demise.
Frasier hasn't been asked for input on anything since the publication of *A Clean Breast*.

$ $ $

In 2000, *Pandora Peaks* was released as a home video. The crude
Julio Dottavio cover features an image of Peaks that looks like it
was cut out with a child's scissors, and what is contained on the
tape inside is just as unrefined. All the ingredients are there—big
boobs, hopped-up narration, a zillion cutaways—but the film is
flaccid and borderline unwatchable. It is the work of an old pervert
who can no longer pretend otherwise. Against narration by Meyer
himself, we see Peaks dancing among the oil rigs with Handyman
Jim Ryan hobbling along behind. Intercut with this is footage from
the aborted *Breast*, much of it featuring Hungarian mammary monster Tundi, her voice-over narration dubbed by Uschi Digard.
While it's amusing for those in the know to see Meyer and Charlie
Sumners revisiting various 166th European haunts, mugging for
the camera when not fishing, the sight of a grizzled Meyer in baseball cap and muscle tee, ogling Pandora as she wobbles her whop-
pers, repeatedly mouthing "A-OK" to the camera in a style that
would make Benny Hill blanch—well, it makes one pine for the
days when Meyer made such ridiculousness add up to something.
"For somebody who wants to see the tits, even they don't come
right away," admitted editor Richard Brummer. "There's an element

of anger that takes away from the satire." And thus RM's film career went out with a whimper, not a bang.

That same year, *A Clean Breast* was finally unleashed on the public. Housed within nauseating baby blue boards festooned with Meyer's gold-lettered signature, it was a three-volume set, 1,213 pages in all, with over twenty-four hundred pictures—and only available by mail order from RM Films for the jaw-dropping price of $350 plus shipping. This was Meyer's chance to set the record straight, and when it comes to the nuts and bolts of specific events, that's exactly what he does. Interspersed with details of each film's production are endless excerpts of reviews, with the final volume containing detailed synopses illustrated with clever film-strip still sequences. The book has no ending: after *Beneath the Valley of the Ultra-Vixens*, Meyer's life simply ceases, fading away to mediocre nude layouts of his last busty beauties, Pandora Peaks, Letha Weapons, and Melissa Mounds.

"That book will be worth a fortune someday," said John Waters. "I think it's an amazing document." The narrative is full of bizarre Meyerisms and the pictures are often stunning and hilarious, but the gory details of one sexual encounter after another—down to the timing of every grunt and groan—quickly become tiresome. His one-dimensional world is much more dynamic on film; the flatness of the page brings out the flatness of the person. *A Clean Breast* is one long Meyer monologue, never more than skin deep. Mere paragraphs are devoted to his childhood and mother Lydia, and RM is incapable of bringing his larger-than-life women—Eve, Edy, Rena, Uschi—to life. This is Meyer's closing statement, the summation of everything he thought and stood for and accomplished over the many years of an action-packed existence. There is not one genuine insight to be found.

$ $ $

Russ Meyer was fond of recounting some quote by Charles Keating that basically held RM responsible for the decline of Western civilization. Meyer wanted Keating's words carved into his tombstone, with "I was glad to do it" chiseled directly beneath. Certainly it's no idle boast for RM. Sex has gone so mainstream it's not even smutty anymore. Welcome to a world where, as Howard Hampton writes, "everybody gets off and nobody's satisfied." A TV star's homemade porno tape evokes a yawn. Pop stars author arty erotica books, and rappers have taken to porn like hamburger to a bun. And hardcore itself has become, as Hampton states, "a treadmill devoted to increasingly calisthenic exercises in futility." Big boobs remain big business—teenagers get implants on Mom's credit card, and Hooters restaurant is a billboard-friendly national chain. "Sex today has nothing to do with revolution anymore," said writer Erica Jong. "It's about capitalism and protecting little profit centers."

The old warriors refuse to die. Deep inside that hermetically sealed Tinseltown fantasy factory known to aficionados simply as "the mansion," a curiously square jaw that has been sans trademark pipe for over seven years now and his brittle bones comforted by the finest silken pajamas, Hugh Hefner holds court with his seven cookie-cutter blond girlfriends, plus a newly remade/remodeled Pamela Anderson. Perhaps the gang is discussing the finer points of saline implants, or the joys of Viagra. A few miles away Edy Williams stares at the bare walls of her abode and wonders just what happened to all those flashy dreams. Two and a half hours outside of Los Angeles, smack dab in the middle of a broiling, unkind desert of the sort that only Russ Meyer could love, a seventy-six-year-old Tempest Storm shakes her somehow still-intact stuff, the closing act of a shambolic, affectionately retro annual burlesque shindig known as Miss Exotic World.

Used, abused, and still a bit nutty after all these years, Meyer's women fight to scratch out some sort of a living, waiting for the break that never came post-RM.* They were too far ahead of their time, too big for this planet, and financially they have benefited the least from the work they helped to create. But somewhere out

---

* In 2001 came the home video release of William Winckler's *The Double-D Avenger,* a non-Meyer low-budget comedy reuniting Kitten Natividad, Haji, and Raven De La Croix. It's nice to see the women get work, but this mediocre, unfunny work only serves to remind how singular Meyer's talent was.

there a fourteen-year-old scowling bad seed of a girl is seeing *Faster, Pussycat! Kill, Kill!* for the first time and thinking to herself that the world can't be all bad if Tura Satana's in it.

As a filmmaker, Meyer stands alone. His untamed visions have inspired countless filmmakers, rockers, and artistes of all stripes— as recently as November 2003, Quentin Tarantino—whose *Kill Bill* films certainly qualify as Meyeresque to some degree—talked reverentially of *Faster, Pussycat* in the *New York Times* and told another interviewer he'd "give up five years of my life" to have worked with a circa-*Pussycat* Satana.

Movies, TV, rock videos, reality TV hellcats like Anna Nicole Smith . . . if you squint, it's not hard to discern the ghost of Russ Meyer flitting about. Much of the stuff is sexless and grim, though—*Girls Gone Wild*, anyone?—and completely devoid of the vulgar exuberance of Russ Meyer at his best. Big-budget remakes of his films seem inevitable—Courtney Love starring in a *Beyond the Valley of the Dolls* is excruciatingly easy to imagine. But RM's world can't be replicated in these jaded, numb times. It's funny—who would've thought one would long for the days of Meyer's wholesome depravity? Who could've predicted that RM would come to represent class, however crass? One way or another, Meyer's films will prevail, despite their many imperfections. They are just too rambunctious, too original, and too evocative of an America now gone. As long as men and women continue to connive ways into each other's pants or wallets, Meyer's big bosoms and square jaws will captivate.

For a while there RM succeeded in getting the world to chuckle over sex, a subject that still short-circuits this country. A single tit can stop a nation—witness the night in 2004 when Janet Jackson's wardrobe "malfunction" disturbed the sanctity that is American football. If only Meyer had been able to provide some play-by-play commentary for that debacle. It was such a plastic and strange event, as was the hysteria that ensued. These days it sometimes feels like we are all trapped in a Russ Meyer film, and not one of the good ones.

$ $ $

And what was to become of Russ Meyer, the man? "Russ was so vi-brant, so, so alive," said Tura Satana. "To see him now, it's just—you wanna cry, you really do. He's like a Popsicle." Tura last saw Meyer in 2000, as did Kitten. "So RM's only pleasure would prob-ably be eating, huh?" she mused in 2002. "I'm supposing a drink is out of the question. God, he loved his cocktail hour."

Outside of his handlers, few saw Meyer in his end days, except for the occasional brief visit from Jim Ryan and, whenever he was in town, Roger Ebert. "Russ dug his own grave, in a sense," said Raven De La Croix. "He brought it all on himself. Russ became the character in his films, abused by women, taken advantage of. He made his fear come true."

"It's almost biblical, isn't it?" said David K. Frasier. "No love in RM's life, so he dies alone sitting on a Costco folding chair." Nine-teen ninety-nine was the last year Frasier saw Meyer in the flesh, and the great man had already turned into a drooling shadow of his former self. One bright California day during his stay, Frasier took RM out for a little jaunt in the immediate neighborhood. On the scrubby hillside behind them the infamous Hollywood sign shone big and white in the sunlight. "I don't think I've ever felt closer to Russ than during those walks," said Frasier. Meyer, almost like a child, would gather up leaves from the street—"only the very reddish orange ones," said Frasier—and stick the stems into the buttonholes of his shirt. "June Wilkinson is coming over for a photo shoot and I'm going to place these leaves all over her body," announced a beaming RM. "Nice memory," Frasier told me.

Of course, there was no photo shoot. And no pending visit from June Wilkinson. But that was reality, after all, and Russell Al-bion Meyer never gave a damn about that.

Postscript

In early September 2004, an ailing Meyer, suffering from pneu-monia, was taken to the Glendale Adventist Medical Center. It wasn't his first bout. After a couple of weeks he was sent home on September 18, and that day, in bed and surrounded by his care-takers, Meyer suddenly began gasping for breath. An ambulance was called, but he was pronounced DOA at the hospital. He was eighty-two years old. The news wasn't made public to friends until three days later, outraging many of those close to him.

Janice Cowart had micromanaged Meyer's life until the last minute and beyond. Rob Schaffner, a friend of RM's for twenty years, had discovered what hospital Meyer was in during his last bout of pneumonia, and only wanted to slip in for brief moment and say a final goodbye to his friend. Cowart found out he'd called the hospital, and she went ballistic, telling Schaffner's wife Chris she'd have guards escort Rob off the property if he dared to show up there.

Meyer's service took place at the Old North Church in Forest Lawn Memorial Park, in the Hollywood Hills. Both the viewing the day before and the service were private, with a strict guest list compiled by Cowart. This seemed highly inappropriate for a man who not only loved the company of his friends and fans but also loved mixing them all together. (Schaffner, who was not on the list, still managed to sneak in and give his old friend a final salute. To the mirth of many, another crony of his absconded with Janice's guest list. It should be noted that the estate did offer to pay travel expenses so at least two of RM's old friends could attend the service, Tempest Storm and Floyce Sumners.)

I counted fifty-five heads at RM's service, a paltry send-off for a king like Meyer, but that's what you get when you lock out the world. Still, many of the fabulous women he made famous managed to show, all of them dressed to the nines: June Wilkinson, Tura Satana, Haji, Kitten Natividad, Alaina Capri, Erica Gavin, Raven De La Croix, and a few others. Dressed in the requisite black, Janice Cowart sat in a front pew "like the grieving widow," as Rob Schaffner cruelly observed. By her side was the ubiquitous Julio Dottavio.

For anyone the least bit familiar with Meyer's life the service was an outrage. The man who'd made such fun of organized religion in his movies was given a cookie-cutter ceremony, with canned songs interrupting a bland sermon. The Presbyterian minister mispronounced RM's name as "Mayer" and, as if apologizing for Meyer's existence, babbled such dubious statements as "Russ was not a voyeur." One only hoped RM, lying there in his coffin back behind the minister, would suddenly rise from his casket and end all this punishing monotony by way of a loud fart.

The only moment of actual emotion came courtesy of Roger Ebert, who stood up and, graciously thanking Janice and Julio for taking care of RM, shared a heartfelt and funny remembrance of his deceased compadre. Glancing at the back of the church, spying a crony of Raven De La Croix's up in the rafters surreptitiously videotaping the event for a documentary Raven's putting together on Meyer, I had to laugh. Cowart would find out about the clandestine recording, and the next day De La Croix played me a recording of an angry phone call full of veiled legal threats she'd received from her. Janice also complained that Haji tried to photograph RM in his coffin. "How tacky is that?" said Cowart.

At the end of the service, everybody shuffled out of the church, pausing in front of RM's open casket to pay their respects. He was dressed in a cheap suit and sported nary a speck of his trademark gaudy gold jewelry, nor — sins of sins — the slightest physical evidence of his combat career. So much larger than life while alive, Meyer now looked very small, tragically mundane. Life had been never-ending hand-to-hand combat for Meyer. Had he won the battle? Had he lost? That I can't tell you, but as I stood there silently staring at the man, a line Gene Mustain and Jerry Capeci had written of John Gotti came to mind: "For a while, he was what he wanted to be, which is only what we all want."

Yes, one mustn't feel too sorry for Russell Albion Meyer, despite his long, sad journey to the end of the Hollywood night. Russ wouldn't want it that way. RM wasn't interested in anybody's help. He was too good for that. After all, he was Meyer, and Meyer needed no one. Mother Lydia had made certain of that. No, there had been no repenting or regretting. Meyer had given the world the finger and lived to tell the tale. As Roger Ebert maintained, when it came to his life, "Russ never apologized."

$ $ $

A few days later, Meyer was to be interred up north in the Stockton Rural Cemetery, buried between mother Lydia and half-sister Lucinda. Janice Cowart reportedly has a fear of flying, so that Sunday she, Dottavio, and Ryan were taking the body by train ("not unlike the burial of President Lincoln," quipped one RM associate). There was a meager turnout at the gravesite: Cowart, Dottavio, Ryan, a few close friends. According to one witness, Cowart choked up recalling how Meyer had complimented her at the end of each and every day she worked for him. Julio Dottavio also reminisced, although, according to one spy, "he didn't have the kind of memories that would bring a tear to your eye." As of February, 2005, it looks like Meyer's tombstone will indeed carry the Keating quote previously mentioned as well as RM's wicked retort.

$ $ $

And what about the fabled Meyer will? It had been the subject of endless discussion among both his friends and enemies. RM—as a tribute to his mother, who died from the disease—left the bulk of his fortune to both the Kenneth J. Norris, Jr. Comprehensive Cancer Center and the Memorial Sloan-Kettering Cancer Center. A few of his stars, girlfriends, and associates are to receive the sum of approximately $5,000 each (a 1999 amendment to the will states that Melissa Mounds was specifically disinherited), and some closer associates (including a few army buddies) are to get $15,000 apiece. Meyer left instructions that his house and its endless memorabilia remain intact, a monument to himself.* RM also left a final stinger attached to his last wishes: should anyone contest the will, that person is to be immediately disinherited. Apparently most of the many recent codices Meyer had added to the will in fits of anger or joy have been discounted due to his dementia, although there are those who are already questioning whether the 1998 document that's been chosen by his estate could be declared invalid for the very same reason.

---

* The will specifically states that Meyer's archive be available to historians of merit. Apparently this author doesn't qualify, because permission was denied by the estate.

The will states that Meyer's trust be run by three consecutively appointed candidates from the following list of six people: Janice Cowart, Phil Cooperman, Jim Ryan, David K. Frasier, the late Charles Sumners, and a friend (unknown to this author) by the name of James Gaspar. According to one source, for quite a while the Meyer trust was (and may still be currently) run by only two trustees, Cowart and Ryan, with Cooperman having dropped out some time ago. If this is true, it would appear RM's instructions are being ignored. It seems that Julio Dottavio has a great deal of input concerning anything to do with Meyer's archives, despite no apparent mention of his name in the will in regards to the matter.*

Additionally, the will calls for the creation of a three-person committee overseeing any and all decisions relating to Meyer's work in all its mediums. The committee members are to be picked consecutively from the following list of Meyer's associates: Janice Cowart, Jim Ryan, Charles Sumners, a filmmaker friend named Mike Carroll, David K. Frasier, Warren G. Harding, Fred Owens, Bill Newhouse, and George Carll (Sumners, Owens, and Newhouse are all deceased). To my knowledge, no such committee has been set in motion thus far, and at least some of those listed had no idea that they have been so chosen by Meyer.

No doubt the will of Russ Meyer is destined to cause as much controversy as everything else in his life. "I just hope this is what Russ wished for," said his old secretary Paula Parker. "That's the only thing I'd like to know. Would Russ be glad? Maybe he would find all this very exciting. He used to kid about how he had his will all tangled, just so everybody would be all screwed up—so he was controlling people, even from the grave."

At the end of the Los Angeles service, I had watched as Janice Cowart, Julio Dottavio, and RM's caretakers climbed aboard a large stretch limo that whisked them away, ostensibly to Meyer's home, which was only a ten-minute drive. By contrast, a frail-looking Jim Ryan got into a beat-up '87 Oldsmobile, which failed

---

* About seven and a half pages have been redacted from Meyer's will so each beneficiary knows only what they are getting, so until an unedited copy comes into circulation, one can't make any absolute statements concerning the will.

to start on the first two tries, although it eventually puttered off. Who should be blamed for this injustice? I wondered. "The Handyman," Ryan had pretty much given sixty years of life to Meyer, and as far as many were concerned, RM should've left him a huge chunk of dough. But then I recalled something Meyer had said to a friend about his good buddy Jim Ryan: "The day after I die, Ryan'll go out and buy a Cadillac." Although Anthony James Ryan remains on the board of Meyer's trust, it looks like he won't be tooling around in a shiny new Caddy after all.

$ $ $

The morning of Meyer's Los Angeles service, Dave Frasier, staying at an old haunt of RM's in Burbank, the Safari Inn, walked a few blocks to the nearby Talleyrand restaurant, an old-school coffee shop. Meyer loved its horseshoe booths and on numerous occasions had taken Frasier there to chow down. Dave wanted to pay tribute to his old friend with a final breakfast in RM's honor. When Frasier arrived, the place was packed. A waitress hustled him off to a booth, which, eerily enough, was the very same one Frasier had sat in with Meyer the last time they were there.

Looking down at the tabletop, Dave noticed a pile of ones, obviously a tip the waitress hadn't pocketed yet. As he studied the top dollar bill, the hair on Frasier's neck stood up: somebody had inked a large, loud set of initials near the center of the dollar that simply read "R.M.," and within those bold letters the same hand had scribbled a big smiley face. Perhaps, just perhaps, Russ Meyer was off somewhere in the afterlife, looking down (or up, as the case may be) to have one last laugh after all.

Epilogue: Smell of Female

The point is of no return—and you've reached it!

—VARLA, *Faster, Pussycat! Kill! Kill!*

The Friend drove the long, winding road up to the Meyer manse. He tried to see RM every time he was in town. He wasn't aware that he was one of the few allowed in. Meyer and The Friend went way, way back. Let's just say they'd fought a war together.

He pulled up to the house, which had long since been painted normal colors—as opposed to the neighbor-provoking orange and green. Parked under an awning was a familiar GMC Suburban, the one Meyer called the Kampfwagen, the one with "Patton's Photographers—166 Signal Corps" on the tailgate. The Kampfwagen had a flat and looked like it hadn't been driven in a long, long time.

They'd had a lot of fun in this place. Movies. Food. Women. Laughs. In addition to everything else, RM was the only guy he'd known who'd built an entire museum to himself and his love of the female breast. But now all the walls were bare. Muzak played, and a closed-circuit TV system made sure that Meyer took his pills. Apparently he didn't always want to take his medicine.

A nurse ushered Meyer into the room. He looked great—better than ever, in fact. Strong as an ox, and tan as hell, too. Somebody had even cut his hair. Yes, RM looked fit as a fiddle. The only problem was, he didn't recognize his visitor. Or himself.

The Friend sat for a few minutes to reassure himself he'd made the effort. Truth was, he didn't know if he'd be making the journey again. He held his emotions in check, knowing it would do no good to express them.

The nurse came in to give Russ his bottle of water. He had to have his bottle. Three times a day. Meyer slurped it down like a child, then the nurse retrieved the empty container and left.

As The Friend got up to go, he noticed RM gazing in the direction of the nurse's exit. Russ paused a moment, then, looking The Friend directly in the eye, slowly patted his chest, quietly mouthing two unmistakable words.

"No tits."

Source Notes

All author interviews are listed at the head of individual chapter source notes. Most of them took place between 2002 and 2004.

Interviews with Meyer from David K. Frasier's archive are referred to in source notes as *DFA*. These interviews were done 8/16–17/90, 8/19/90. A small portion of this material was published in *Cinefocus* 1.2, Fall 1990, and reprinted, albeit somewhat changed, in Meyer's autobiography. At times my transcriptions of these interviews vary slightly from Mr. Frasier's.

A listing of individual articles utilized for my research on this book would run hundreds of pages, so I have only noted what is quoted in the text. At the risk of throwing Frasier's name into the text once again, this book benefited greatly from his bibliography work in *Russ Meyer: The Life and Films*. Suffice to say I have been through the entire Frasier archive of 1,148 pieces of text, plus hundreds more articles and books published since then. Full info on any book listed in the chapter source notes can be found in the bibliography. Meyer's *A Clean Breast* autobiography is referred to as *ACB/RM* in the chapter source notes.

I regret to say the following people either declined or ignored my interview requests: Bill Moore, Malcolm McLaren, Taime Downe, Artur Brauner, Ron Vogel, John Landis, Rick Garrard, Stephen Hunter, Melissa Mounds, Shari Eubank, and Bunny Yeager. Due to constraints on the interview process, I declined to speak with both Edy Williams and RM's former counsel, A. Lee Blackman. Attempts to reach Charles Keating Jr., Donna Scott, Rena Horten, and Uschi Digard proved unsuccessful. Uschi, Rena, Donna: if you're out there and reading this, drop me a line via jimmymcdonough.net. I'd love to hear your side of the story. Readers who've enjoyed this work might want to check out my biography of Andy Milligan, *The Ghastly One*. It mirrors this book in many strange ways.

Books and Articles by Russ Meyer

Dixie Sparkle. All–Eve Meyer digest. Mid- to late fifties. Uncredited.

The Glamour Camera of Russ Meyer. Whitestone Publications, 1958.

"The Low-Budget Producer." *The Movie Business: American Film Industry Practice*. Edited by A. William Bluem and Jason E. Squire. Hastings House, 1979.

"My Friend Cleavage." *Oui*, vol. 5, no. 8, August, 1976.

A Clean Breast, Adolph Albion Schwartz (Russ Meyer), three volumes. Hauck Publishing, 2000.

Meyer contributed countless layouts to such men's magazines as *Night and Day, Playboy, Gent, Adam, Escapade*, and many others. He also wrote occasional articles to accompany his layouts. Three are listed below; I'm sure there are many more.

"The Full Figure," *Candid Photography*, Fawcett Book 318, 1956. Fawcett Publications.

"Commercial Glamour," *Photographing Glamour*, Fawcett Book 412, 1959. Fawcett Publications.

"The Glamour Technique of Russ Meyer," *Famous Photographers Photograph Beautiful Women*, #46, 1963. Whitestone Publications.

Books About Meyer

Frasier, David K. *Russ Meyer: The Life and Films*. McFarland and Company, 1990.

Green, Doyle. *Hips, Lips, Tits, Power: The Films of Russ Meyer*. Creation Books (UK), 2004.

Jackson, Jean-Pierre. *Russ Meyer, ou, Trente ans de Cinéma Erotique à Hollywood*. (France) PAC, 1982.

Thissen, Rolf. *Russ Meyer, der König des Sexfilms*. W. Heyne (Germany), 1987.

Woods, Paul A. *The Very Breast of Russ Meyer*. Plexus (UK), 2004.

Selected Reference

Binstein, Michael, and Charles Bowden. *Trust Me: Charles Keating and the Missing Billions*. Random House, 1993.

Butterfield, Ralph, editor. *Patton's G.I. Photographers*. Iowa State University Press, 1992.

Cohan, Stephen, and Ina Rae Hark, editors. *The Road Movie Book*. Routledge, 1997 (UK).

Friedman, David. F., with Don De Nevi. *A Youth in Babylon: Confessions of a Trash-Film King*. Prometheus Books, 1990.

Gertz, Elmer. *To Life: The Story of a Chicago Lawyer*. Southern Illinois University Press, 1990.

Fenton, Harvey, editor. *Flesh and Blood Compendium*. Fab Press, 2003 (UK).

Flynt, Larry, with Kenneth Ross. *An Unseemly Man*. Bloomsbury, 1996.

Harris, Marlys J. *The Zanucks of Hollywood: The Dark Legacy of an American Dynasty*. Crown, 1989.

Lewis, Jon, *Hollywood v. Hardcore: How the Struggle over Censorship Saved the Modern Film Industry*. New York University Press, 2000.

McCarthy, Todd, and Charles Flynn, editors. *Kings of the B's: Working Within the Hollywood System*. Dutton, 1975.

McDonough, Jimmy. *The Ghastly One: The Sex-Gore Netherworld of Filmmaker Andy Milligan*. Chicago Review Press, 2001.

Philips, Stu. "Stu Who?" Forty Years of Navigating the Minefields of the Music Business. Cisum Press, 2003.

Pomerance Murray, editor. Bad: Infamy, Darkness, Evil and Slime on Screen. State University of New York Press, 2004.

Ross, Jonathan. The Incredibly Strange Film Book. Simon & Schuster, 1993 (UK).

Schaefer, Eric. Bold! Daring! Shocking! True! A History of Exploitation Films, 1919–1959. Duke University Press, 1999.

Schneider, Charles Editor. Cad: A Handbook for Heels. Feral House, 1992.

Spitz, Marc, and Brendan Mullen. We Got the Neutron Bomb: The Untold Story of L.A. Punk. Three Rivers Press, 2001.

Storm, Tempest, with Bill Boyd. The Lady Is a Vamp. Peachtree Publishers, 1987.

Sullivan, Steve. Bombshells: Glamour Girls of a Lifetime. St. Martin's Press, 1998.

———. Glamour Girls: The Illustrated Encyclopedia. St. Martin's Press, 1999.

———. Va Va Voom! Bombshells, Pinups, Sexpots and Glamour Girls. Rhino Books/General Publishing Group, Inc., 1995.

Sumners, Charles Eugene. Darkness Visible: Memoir of a World War II Combat Photographer. McFarland Press, 2002.

Thompson, Stephen, and The Onion. The Tenacity of The Cockroach: Conversations with Entertainment's Most Enduring Outsiders. Three Rivers Press, 2002.

Tomko, William J. Turan. Photo by Signal Corps. Manuscript privately printed by Tomko.

Turan, Kenneth, and Stephen F. Zito. Sinema: American Pornographic Films and the People Who Make Them, Praeger Publishers, 1974.

Vale, V., and Andrea Juno, eds. RE/SEARCH #10: Incredibly Strange Films. RE/SEARCH Publications, 1986.

Wallace, Irving. The Seven Minutes. Simon & Schuster, 1969.

Waters, John. Shock Value: A Tasteful Book About Bad Taste, Dell 1981.

———. Crackpot: The Obsessions of John Waters. Scribners, 2003.

Introduction: Bigger than Life

JM interviews: Hugh Hefner, Erica Gavin, David K. Frasier, Roger Ebert, Richard Brummer, Lux Interior, John McCormick, Stan Berkowitz, Arv Miller, David F. Friedman, Lou Filipovitch, Raven de la Croix, Charles Napier, Tura Satana.

John Furlong, the man responsible for the opening narration of Faster, Pussycat, informed me that he was utilizing his best Richard Burton impression. News to me.

"Hi Mom, sorry . . . you tomorrow" . . . "I'd never . . . John Ford films," My Christmas with Russ: Road-Tripping, Grave-Visiting and Plotting "Up the Valley of the Beyond," John McCormick, L.A. Weekly, 12/9–15, 1994. Highly recommended by the author.

"High-class pornographer," RM to Dan Huff, " 'High-Class Pornographer' Enjoys Flak, All the Way to the Bank," Tucson Citizen, 11/13/79.

"A directness . . . in Hollywood films," "Russ Meyer: King of the Nudies Takes a Bow, Roger Ebert," Chicago Sun-Times, 1/9/83.

"I love vulgarity," Helmut Newton, Autobiography, Helmut Newton, Nan A. Talese/Doubleday, 2003.

"I don't pretend . . . express trains!" RM to Stan Berkowitz, "18—Count 'Em—18 Couplings and an X-Rating: Russ Meyer in Hollywood," UCLA Daily Bruin, no. 79, 1/7/70.

"Meyer is both for . . . a kind of style," Alan Brien, "The Vampire in the Dark," *London Sunday Times*, 11/25/79.

"In Meyer's film world . . . possess the 'square jaws,'" *Lips, Hips, Tits, Power.*

"The first time . . . the psychedelic state," Jeff McDonald to Jaime Pina, "Jeff Macdonald of Redd Kross," *Hollywood Book and Poster News*, 12/86.

"I'm laughing at the world," RM to Charles Petzold, "He Puts a Grin in Skin Movies." *Philadelphia Daily News*, 4/28/69.

"I believe . . . the heaving bosoms." Roger Ebert, "Russ Meyer Busts Sleazy Stereotype," *Chicago Sun-Times*, 11/15/85.

"I won't become . . . has huge breasts," RM to Steven Smith, "Soft-Porn King Makes No Apologies," *Eugene Register-Guard*, 9/27/79.

"Like an explorer . . . for bigger bosoms," Catherine Chapin, "Meyer's Core Is Soft, but He Thinks Big," *Charlotte Observer*, 8/5/79.

"The pneumatic . . . man," RM to Taffy Jacaway, "X-Rated Producer Lets Hair Down, Down, Down, Down," *Tacoma News-Journal*, 7/4/75.

"As distinctive . . . to her husband," Kristen Hatch, "The Sweeter the Kitten, the Sharper the Claws," *Bad: Infamy, Darkness, Evil and Slime on Screen.*

"I get an idea . . . a movie," RM to Dan Yakir and Bruce Davis, "An Interview: Beyond the Big Breast—Can Russ Meyer Keep It 'Up'!" *The Thousand Eyes* magazine, vol. 2, no. 4, 12/76.

"I'm in it . . . no bones about it," RM to Jackie Brooks, "Assessment of X-Rated Movies," *The State*, 8/5/79.

"I'd probably make 20 RM films," RM to Phyliss Braden-Lowe, "Beneath the Valley of the Ultra-Meyer," Pop Arts Entertainment Supplement to the Portland State University *Vanguard*, circa 1987.

"I would hit upon . . . a budget," RM, "The Low-Budget Producer," see Books and Articles by Russ Meyer.

"*Carried* it," Roger Ebert, "Russ Meyer: King of the Nudies." *Film Comment*, Jan/Feb 1973.

"Every film is exploitation . . . same game," RM to Menetaos Toutsidis, "Film Is 'Full of Sex Fun,'" *The News*, Adelaide, Australia, 5/4/81.

"Meyer films don't . . . their audiences," David Ansen, "Russ Meyer: Auteur of Sleaze," *The Real Paper*, 7/30/75.

"I don't let . . . action," RM to Robert Baum, "When Russ Meyer Brought His Raven to Lunch," *Patriot Ledger*, 10/30/76.

"It's my genre . . . really matter," RM to Ellen Goosenberg, "Supervixen Russ Meyer," *The Drummer*, 7/29/75.

"I deal with . . . beyond women," RM to Tom Teicholz, "Movies: Tit for Tat: Russ Meyer," *Interview*, 1/86.

"Four F's," RM cited by Gordon Burn, "Rising Below Vulgarity," *Sight and Sound*, vol. 6, issue 12, 12/1996. Original source of quote unknown.

"Russ not only . . . in women," Haji to Ronald L. Smith, "Haji: from Pussycat to Double-D Avenger!" *Phantom of the Movies' Videoscope*, no. 45, Winter 2003.

"His women had an exuberance . . . films anymore," Camille Paglia, quoted on lukeford.com. Origin of quote unknown.

Paglia and Tura Satana: Ann Magnuson, "Russ Meyer: Thing King of B Movies on DD Cups and XXX Ratings," *Details*, 3/93. Magnuson reports that "Tura Satana is Camille Paglia's wet dream!" She goes on to say that Paglia saw Meyer's films at a grungy New Haven porn theater while she was in grad school.

"Deals a body-blow to the idea that women are victims" . . . "an unexpected celebration of bad-girl empowerment," B. Ruby Rich, "What's New, Pussycat?" *Village Voice*, 1/11–17/95.

"Hopefully it's my dick," RM to Paul Fishbein, "Interview: Russ Meyer," *Adult Video
News*, vol. 1, no. 4, 6/83.

"I love to put sex . . . erotic and funny," RM to Tony Rayns, "Dolls, Vixens, and Supervixens in the Films of Russ Meyer," *Late Night Video*, vol. 2, no. 2, 1983.

"Who knows more . . . Russ Meyer?" RM to Howard Gensler, *Premiere*, vol. 2, no.
9, 5/89.

"I portray sex . . . in bed," RM to Craig Trigger, "Russ Meyer Keeps Few Secrets:
I'm in the Business for Greed, Lust." *Miami Hurricane*, 11/19/76.

"Former prizefighter now operating a successful chain of South American brothels," John Simon, "Meyer's Blue Heaven." *The New Leader*, 7/20/70.

"Genuine, impure, adulterated, no-bullshit working class American," Richard
Corliss, "Film: Cherry, Harry & Raquel!" *Village Voice*, 6/11/70.

"Like Marlon Brando . . . in the culture," D. K. Holm, "Nocturnal Emissions" column, *Movie Poop Shoot* website, 9/27/04.

"I figure if it's good . . . the world," RM to Jackie Brooks, "Assessment of X-Rated
Movies," *The State*, 8/5/79.

Crying over *Casablanca*: RM to Karin Winegar, "Porn King: Russ Meyer Still Up-
front with Films and 'Fillies,' " *Minneapolis Star*, 7/2/79.

"Meyer's life . . . as Churchill's," Roger Ebert, "The Immoral Mr. Meyer," *Playboy*,
vol. 42, no. 6, 6/95.

"Who'd know more . . . is mine," RM to Alison Mayes, *Calgary Herald*, 9/6/95.

"Everyone . . . story," RM to David Frasier, *DFA*.

RM boots in Ireland story: Harvey Fenton, "Thanks for the Mammaries: Russ
Meyer," *Flesh & Blood Compendium*, Fab Press, 2003 (UK).

"Never let the chink in your armor be exposed," RM to David Frasier, *DFA*.

"It's not supposed . . . the last," Lux Interior to Randy Harward, "Got Cramps?"
Salt Lake City Weekly online, 10/21/04.

"Is there . . . paintings," Roger Ebert to Nancy Spiller, *The West*, 12/27/87.

"In the end . . . lust and guilt," Gordon Burn, "Rising Below Vulgarity," *Sight and
Sound*, vol. 6, issue 12, 12/96.

"It could be . . . America," David Thomson, "Big Bosoms, Square Jaws—The Tale
of a Red-Blooded American," *The Independent*, UK, 9/26/04.

OK, so I fibbed a bit: The fantastic Jimmy Wages can't be located on a "scratchy
old 45," as his few recordings for Sun were never released. But most of them
can be found on a 1995 CD, *Let's Bop: Sun Rockabilly Volume 1*, AVI Records.

Lux Interior would like it known that he considers Russ Meyer to be "the American Tinto Brass."

1. Mother Meyer and the Poor Dear

JM interviews: Manny Diez, Tura Satana, Paula Parker, Fred Beiersdorf, Jane
Hower, Warren Harding, Dolores Fox, Richard Brummer, Betty Meyer, Jim
Ryan, Charles Sumners, Charles Napier, Jean-Pierre Jackson, Kitten Nativi-
dad, Lou Filipovitch, Darlene Filipovitch, Pete Filipovitch, Martha Robins,
David K. Frasier, Raven de la Croix, Tom McGowan, George Costello, Erica
Gavin, George Carll, Harry Downard, Joe Longo, Dixie Evans.

"The question always. . . . Yes!" RM to John Waters, *Shock Value*, see Bibliography.

Example of RM denying mother's dimensions: *Russ Meyer, der König des Sexfilms*.

RM's whispering paranoia: JM interview with Bruce Pasternack.

"Mother influence . . . did was right," RM to Kristine McKenna, "The Big Boob Theory," *Los Angeles*, 6/2000.

"She was a very God-fearing . . . success in me," RM to Farnum Gray, "Skin-Flick King Recalls Career Low," *Atlanta Journal*, 1/12/73.

"Anything I achieved was because of her," RM to Maggie White, "The King of the Nudies," *Downtowner*, no. 31, 4/30/79.

RM middle name: State of California birth certificate (and amended version) for Russ Meyer.

"I hope they both die!" *E! True Hollywood Story* documentary, *ACB/RM*.

"He was a bastard . . . a damn," RM, *E! True Hollywood Story* documentary (see Filmography).

"When I was young . . . Job's turkey," RM to Archer Winsten, "Russ & Friends Come to Town," *New York Post*, 5/12/79.

Meyer on Vixen and brother Judd scene: "The most animalistic sequence that I've put in a picture," RM to Paul Fishbein, "Interview: Russ Meyer," *Adult Video News*, vol. 1, no. 4, 6/83.

"I love farting . . . fart any day," RM to Alan Platt, "Uncle Dirty," *Soho Weekly News*, 5/24/79.

Brownout over Denver: JM interview with David K. Frasier.

"Sexually I was a late bloomer," RM to Steve Hogner, "Russ Meyer: The Amiable Bear of Erotic Cinema," *Austin Statesman-American*, 5/5/75.

"I make Al Capp cartoons come to life," RM to Murry Frymer, " 'Ultra Vixens' is an Assault to the Senses." *San Jose Mercury-News*, 9/23/79.

"If she moved . . . was enormous," RM to Cory Turczyn, "T&A Q&A," *Pop Cult* website interview, 2002. Interview done 1995.

"I used to . . . her shrine," RM to William L. Kahrl, "Peep Show Becomes Fine Art: The Transmogrification of Russ Meyer," *World's Fair*, vol. 2, no. 4, Fall 1982.

"From then on . . . looking for," RM to Hope Urban, "Russ Meyer," *Velvet Hammer Burlesque* souvenir program, 2/14/95.

"Most people . . . with someone," Kevin McGovern to Taylor Clark, "Panty Man," *Willamette Week*, vol. 30, no. 51, 10/20/04.

Background on the UniveX camera: *The UniveX Story*, Cynthia A. Repinski, Centennial Photo Service, 1991.

RM trip to Catalina: Aljean Harmetz, "Oh, Those Beautiful Dolls!" *New York Times*, 12/21/69.

"It's kind of a curious . . . the mattresses," RM to Michael Holden, "Russ Meyer," *Loaded*, no. 4, 1994 (UK).

"My heart jumped . . . beat accounting," RM to R. Allen Leider, "Russ Meyer Thinks Big," *Porno Movie Girls*, no. 1, 1976.

RM training with Ruttenberg: *ACB/RM*.

2. Sgt. Meyer

JM interviews: Charles Sumners, Tom McGowan, Warren Harding, Harry Downard, Floyce Sumners, Richard Brummers, Bill Tomko, Kay Hively, Jim Ryan, Jean-Pierre Jackson, Alaina Capri.

General background on RM/the 166: *ACB/RM*; *Darkness Visible/Patton's G.I. Photographers/Photo by Signal Corps*; and the *Shooting War/At Risk* documentaries (see Filmography).

"I really didn't want the war to end . . . to approach," RM to Ted Mahar, "Russ Meyer: Part Patriarch, Part Pariah," *The Oregonian*, 11/3/88.

"The excitement . . . of fear, really," RM in *Shooting War* documentary.

"I'm probably the greatest voyeur of them all," RM to Jon Casimir, "King Leer: A Life," *Sydney Morning Herald*, 9/3/90.

"Nothing can match . . . that yet," Meyer to Aljean Harmetz, "Oh, Those Beautiful Dolls!" *New York Times*, 12/21/69.

RM not shooting the faces of the dead: *Shooting War.*

"He would always . . . cut that scene,' " RM to D. K. Holm, Steve Fugett, Pat Holmes, *Cinemonkey*, vol. 5, no. 2, Spring 1979.

"Destiny wonderfully upon us," RM, *ACB/RM.*

Stars and Stripes RM article info, *ACB/RM.*

"It really shook us . . . were scared," RM, *At Risk* documentary.

"In the war . . . wondrous game," RM to R. Allen Leider, "RM Thinks Big," *Porno Movie Girls* no. 1, 1976.

"It was like something . . . sitting in the back," RM to Philip Thomas, "Russ Meyer," *Empire* no. 70, 4/95.

"The quail . . . used to say," RM, "My Friend Cleavage," *Oui*, vol. 5, no. 8, August 1976.

"A newfound tingling . . . burst asunder," *ACB/RM.*

"Rather play cards," RM to Dale Ashmun, "Mondo Russo: Russ Meyer Interview," *Film Threat*, no. 15, 1988.

"Comprised . . . mission instead," E. M. Nathanson, new afterword to *The Dirty Dozen*, Regenesis Press, 2002.

"Knees had turned to jelly," "damn careful," RM at UCLA *Dolls* panel, quoted from "Russ Meyer, Roger Ebert and 'Beyond the Valley of the Dolls,' " *Movie Talk from the Front Lines*, Jerry Roberts and Steven Gaydos, editors. Meyer also relates the story in the *At Risk* documentary, putting Charlie Sumners in the middle of the action.

"Last good war," RM to Karin Winegar, "Porn King: Russ Meyer Still Up-Front with Films and 'Fillies,' " *Minneapolis Star*, 7/2/79.

"I love finding . . . a broad," RM to Tonmy Mastroianni, "Beneath the Valley of the Skin Flicker," *Cleveland Press*, 8/23/79.

"By and large . . . embrace them," RM to David Frasier, *DFA.*

"I am a rabid anti-Communist," RM to Roger Ebert, "Why Meyer Is King of the Skin Flicks," Chicago Sun-Times, 2/16/69.

"Vicious capitalist," RM to Ellen Goosenberg, "Supervixen Russ Meyer," *The Drummer*, 7/29/75.

"Meyer uses his productions . . . the war," Roger Ebert, "The Immoral Mr. Meyer," *Playboy*, vol. 42, no. 6, 6/95.

"Working with Russ . . . a whorehouse," Charles Napier to Nathaniel Thompson, *Mondo Digital* website.

"I have never . . . never can," RM to Aljean Harmetz, "Oh, Those Beautiful Dolls!" *New York Times*, 12/21/69.

3. Tittyboom or Bust

JM interviews: Evelyn West, Tura Satana, Tempest Storm, Dixie Evans, Jim Ryan, Arv Miller, Betty Meyer.

"Tits are a means to an end," RM to Doug Royalty, "Oral Treats Lighten Meyer's Load," *The Daily Illini*, 6/19/79 1016.

"couldn't begin . . . certainly suffice," *ACB/RM.*

"Sturdy jockstrap," *ACB/RM.*

"I went at it . . . nothing would stop me," RM to Dale Ashmun, "Mondo Russo: Russ Meyer Interview," *Film Threat*, no. 15, 1988.

"Industrial films . . . do everything," RM to J. Cook, "Look at All the Naked Ladies," *Forbes*, vol. 122, no. 92, 9/18/78 p.39.

"Browbeat"/"Betty and RM not living happily ever after," *ACB/RM.*

"What you lack in ability you'll make for in enthusiasm," RM, countless interviews, such as "Hellcats for a Modern World," Beth Accomando, *Hypno*, vol. 4, issue 5, 1995.

RM on "cheesecake": *Glamour Camera.*

"Nearly fainting"/"Back then it was done sneakily, and as a result it was more exciting, because it was hidden and outrageous," John Bowers quoted in *It's a Man's World: Men's Adventure Magazines, the Postwar Pulps*, Adam Parfrey, Feral House, 2003.

"Usually a Viennese guy" . . . "a briefcase full of sets" . . . "They were contact pictures of an individual girl, shot by one of his photographers," Bruce Jay Friedman, *It's a Man's World.*

"Often completely disagree with the editor's choice," RM, *Photographing Glamour.*

"Freak with a forty-inch bosom" . . . "I did not have to accept . . . of Eastman" . . . "God didn't make boobs too big for my business," Tempest Storm with Bill Boyd, *The Lady Is a Vamp.*

"Cross between a retired lightweight . . . racetrack tout," "Who knows . . . my spiel," "a small-but-rich uranium mine for the trio that shot it," Roger Turrell, "Portrait of a Burlesque Producer," *Adam*, vol. 3, no. 1, 1958.

"He had this great hype . . . girls in shorts," RM to David K. Frasier, *DFA.*

"I liked him personally, he was honest," ibid.

"Without DeCenzie . . . go ahead," ibid.

"Through the breast of Tempest Storm," ibid.

"I shot pictures . . . the girl's box," ibid.

"Took the seed"/"on Eastman Kodak's linoleum," RM to Dan Scapperotti, "50s Legend Russ Meyer," *Femme Fatales*, vol. 6, no. 10/11, 4/98.

"The power a woman packs between her legs," Pete DeCenzie as quoted by RM, Bill Mooney, "Russ Meyer: Up the Valley of the Beyond," *BB Gun*, 1998.

"The chief called me . . . riot act to me," RM to David K. Frasier, *DFA.*

"Bob Antz . . . needle Walker," ibid.

"Antz normally . . . gave it to me," ibid.

"When I showed this film to DeCenzie, he shit," ibid.

"What really got him . . . 'Oh my God,' " ibid.

RM on *French Peep Show* pasties: Arv Miller, "Between the Valley of My Ultravixens," Part One, *Fling*, vol. 31, no. 6, issue 159, 3/90.

Additional background on DeCenzie, French Peep Show: "Some of My Breast Kept Secrets: An Interview with Russ Meyer," Paul Sherman, *Filmfax*, no. 28, 8–9/91.

"Pete entrusted it . . . his friends," RM to David K. Frasier, *DFA.*

Yvonne DeCenzie "hostile," RM to Ashmun, "Mondo Russo."

"I took pictures . . . my first wife," RM to David K. Frasier, *DFA.*

"I remember thinking . . . good idea," RM to M. J. Simpson, "American Peep Show," *Total Film*, 2/97 (UK).

"Peeler's retriever," *ACB/RM.*

"I felt a little strange . . . like a lady," Lilly La Mont quoted by RM, Jonathan Ross RM documentary, see Filmography.

4. Love and Kisses, Eve Meyer

JM interviews: Floyce Sumners, Dolores Fox, Hugh Hefner, E. E. "Mick" Nathanson, June Wilkinson.

"I just don't . . . a fantasy," RM to Gil King, "A Chat with Russ Meyer," Swank.

"Don't just stand . . . hanging out," Eve Turner quoted by RM, ACB/RM, vol 1.

"A face to sink a thousand Dungeness crab boats," "conically maddening," ACB/RM, vol 3.

"She was really pissed at me," RM to Sergei Hasenecz and Charles Schneider, "A Clean Breast: Titillating Talk with Russ Meyer," Cad: A Handbook for Heels.

"Eve was a great intimidator," Faster, Pussycat! Kill! Kill! laser disc audio commentary.

"A national institution," RM to Hasenecz and Schneider, Cad: A Handbook for Heels.

"Like a tall tree," "gang-tackling my jockeys from the outset," ACB/RM, vols. 1 and 3.

At first, Eve . . . was downright nasty," RM in Fling, 1961, exact date/issue unknown, quoted by Sullivan, Glamour Girls.

"From Eve . . . it closeness," RM, The Glamour Camera of Russ Meyer.

Meyer honeymoon story: JM interview with Dave Ewing.

"When you were through shooting . . . her bones," RM to Steve Sullivan, Eve Meyer chapter, Va Va Voom!

"It was so good for our marriage," RM to Hasenecz and Schneider, Cad: A Handbook for Heels.

"Obtained some of the most exciting pictures," RM, Glamour Camera.

"The salt dug . . . bloody knees and all," Eve Meyer to Larry Teenan, "How Eve Meyer Was Changed into Cheesecake," Modern Man, vol. 8, no. 3, 9/58.

"I'd ride her ass to get her to pose," RM to Joel Judd, "Big Tits and Square Jaws," Gent, 5/86.

"Photosexual," "I got so I just hated . . . without Russ's camera," Eve Meyer to Jane Wilson, "What's a Nice Girl Like You Doing in a Business Like This, Eve? (Well, Maybe Crying All the Way to the Bank)," Los Angeles Times West magazine, 5/9/71.

"the first man . . . a nude woman," Gay Talese, Thy Neighbor's Wife, Dell, 1981.

"The fifties were not Happy Days . . . in the United States," Robert Patrick to Michael Dale, "Robert Patrick's 'Hollywood at Sunset' Premieres with TOSOS II Theatre Company," Internet article, 3/4/04.

"Hef's genius was to associate sex with upward mobility," Paul Gebhard to Gretchen Edgren, The Playboy Book: Forty Years, General Publishing Group, 1994.

"I am clearly . . . the primary one," "I stress the bosom . . . 'this is woman,' " RM, Photographing Glamour.

Eve and Ava: JM interviews with David Frasier, Jim Ryan.

"Sneer like Elvis," RM as quoted by Yvette Vickers, John O'Dowd, "Yvette Vickers: On Music, Movies . . . and Men," Psychotronic Video, no. 39.

"Did it for the money . . . being ridiculous," RM to Steve Sullivan, Diane Webber chapter, Va Va Voom!

"This is the third girl . . . this is *it!*" RM, "Beauty and the Bust," *Adam,* vol. 3, no. 1, 1958.

Additional background on Wilkinson: "June Wilkinson: The Goddess' Magic Endures," *Best of Glamour Girls Then and Now,* vol. 2, Winter 1997.

"Begun to develop . . . don't go together," June Wilkinson to Ian Johnston, "June Wilkinson," *Psychotronic,* no. 20, Spring 1995.

"The most photographed nude in America," Steve Sullivan, *Va Va Voom!*

"A smart modern building located in Van Nuys," "You've got to remember . . . two big balls of fat," "No bone structure . . . need support," "Beauty and the Bust," *Adam,* vol. 3, no. 1, 1958.

"My glamour . . . heartily concur," RM, *Glamour Camera.*

"The abortion racket . . . a real crime," RM to Dale Ashmun, *Film Threat,* no. 15, 1988.

"A jolting documentary," *The Desperate Women* pressbook, author's collection.

"*The Immoral Mr. Teas* changed . . . forever," Ed Wood, Jr, *A Study in the Motivation of Censorship, Sex & the Movies,* Edusex Press, 1973.

I believe the very first Eve magazine cover—she's credited as Eve Turner—is *Night and Day,* 11/52 (half a cover, actually, as *Night and Day* always split their covers between two models).

5. The Immoral Mr. Meyer

JM interviews: Irving Blum, E. E. "Mick" Nathanson, Don Couch, June Wilkinson, Ed Lasko, Dave Frasier, Jim Ryan.

Meyer has stated on a few occasions that the shoot he did for *Giant* snagged him the cover of *Life* magazine; the only *Giant* cover for *Life* I found does not feature a Meyer photograph.

RM repeatedly claimed that the inspiration for *Teas* was a "voyeur" girlie picture layout for *Playboy;* I could not find it. Possibly it was done for another men's magazine.

"Each film must begin . . . the hard-on," RM to Gregory Poe, "Russ Meyer," *Exposure,* no. 3–4, 1989.

"It took a freeway . . . the theater," Pete DeCenzie to Roger Turrell, "Portrait of a Burlesque Producer," *Adam,* vol. 3, no. 1, 1958.

"The man on the street . . . curlers in her hair," RM to Candice Russell, "This Man Has Wild Fantasies," *Miami Herald,* 11/30/75.

"Pete DeCenzie supplied the fire, the urge, the desire," RM to unknown, *Wildest Films,* vol. 1, no. 5, 1966.

"Was always in love . . . ultimate gamesman," RM to David Frasier, *DFA.*

"Bong films," RM to Phyliss Braden Lowe, "Beneath the Valley of the Ultra-Meyer," *Poparts*/Supplement to PSU *Vanguard.*

"Teas is the kind of guy . . . a year," RM to David Frasier, *DFA.*

"Teas had a satanic beard . . . the role," RM to Burton H. Wolfe, "King of the Nudie Movies," *True,* 3/69.

"When nothing more . . . begging for more," Kenneth Turan, " 'Immoral Mr. Teas' in Retrospect," *Washington Post,* 3/23/73.

"Preacher-seducer," "based on a man permitting business associates to use his apartment for clandestine affairs," from 1961 UPI article by Jerry Reynolds, publication and exact date unknown.

"Itinerant carnival people," David F. Friedman to David Chute, "Wages of Sin," first half of two-part article, *Film Comment*, vol. 22, no. 4, 7–8/86.

"films that showed . . . advertising pitch," RM to David Frasier, *DFA*.

"There's a lot of promise but never . . . fulfillment. They would always cut to the curtain blowing," RM quoted by Luke Ford, Internet biography, lukeford.com. (It should be noted that Meyer himself cuts away from a sex scene to a curtain in *Lorna*.)

"It mustn't come across . . . I went along," RM to David Frasier, *DFA*.

"Teas was a fluke . . . for assistants," RM to Robert Cross, "The 'Skin Flicks' of Producer Russ Meyer," *Chicago Tribune*, 2/16/69.

"Written on the back of a laundry ticket," RM to David Frasier, *DFA*.

"There was no contact . . . no sex," RM to R. Allen Leider, "Russ Meyer Thinks Big," *Porno Movie Girls*, no. 1, 1976.

"He put his job . . . being done," RM to David Frasier, *DFA*.

"An experimental sex comedy," "Even Walt Disney . . . what would happen," RM to Arv Miller, "Between the Valleys of My Ultra-Vixens," Part One, *Fling*, no. 159, 7/90.

"You put 'em in a movie . . . slammer time," RM to David Frasier, *DFA*.

"The heir to a vast fortune," ibid.

"Interested in breaking into . . . get laid," ibid.

"Come on like a steam engine . . . my teeth," RM to Nathan Rabin, 1995 interview, *The Tenacity of the Cockroach*, 2002.

"If any of those girls . . . not actresses," Bill Teas to Burr Snider, "The Blue Movie That Started It All," *San Francisco Examiner*, 11/18/81.

"I got a lot more . . . pay him," "had heard . . . bust us," "I always started . . . Ann Peters," "She had the best . . . conical breasts." "I just had that built-in . . . out of nothing," "Teas, to a large part . . . making the movie," RM to David Frasier, *DFA*.

"Like one of the old-timers . . . come of it," Bill Teas to Burr Snider, Burr Snider, "The Blue Movie That Started It All."

"Was never terribly enthusiastic . . . some chick," RM to Braden-Lowe, "Beneath the Valley of the Ultra-Meyer."

"Wrestled him back . . . saved my career," RM to Burton Wolfe, "King of the Nudie Movies."

"His best work . . . vodka hangover," RM to David Frasier, *DFA*.

"Glorified home movie," RM to Alex Bennett, "Screw Interview with Russ Meyer: The Barnum of Boobs," *Screw*, no. 411, 1/17/77.

"What made these films . . . a lamppost," RM to David Frasier, *DFA*.

"In those days unheard of," ibid.

"We couldn't find anybody with the courage to screen it," RM to Rick H. Berger, "Laugh at the Establishment: Meyer's Sexploitation Films Soft-core," *Daily Trojan*, 1/8/76.

"No one had ever seen as bare a film as *Teas,*" RM to Braden-Lowe.

"A perverted *Mr. Hulot's Holiday,*" "amazingly good," "The Immoral Mr. Teas," *Variety*, vol. 217, no. 9, 1/27/60.

"A statement had been made . . . get involved," RM to David Frasier, *DFA*.

"Fellow paisan," RM to Turan and Zito, *Sinema*.

"They convened . . . unheard of," RM to David Frasier, *DFA*.

"Passing a censor . . . steal," ibid.

"A week . . . bought Cadillacs," RM to Barney Hoskyns, "Thanks for the Mammaries," *New Musical Express*, 1/22/83.

"A kind of imperturbable . . . makes a million," Leslie Fiedler, "A Night with Mr. Teas," *Show*, vol. 1, no. 1, 10/61.

Teas New York cuts, JM interview with distributor William Mishkin, see McDonough, *The Ghastly One*.

"I'm a class pornographer . . . a motel room," RM to Murry Frymer, " 'Ultra Vixens' Is an Assault to the Senses," *San Jose Mercury-News*, 9/23/79.

"They'd fight strenuously . . . with business," RM to David Frasier, *DFA*.

"Teas would listen . . . steaming, seething," ibid.

"Accused me of cheating . . . offended me," RM to David Frasier, *DFA*.

"*Teas* made a lot of money . . . $40,000 apiece," RM to Paul Sherman, *Filmfax*, no. 28, 8–9/91.

"So they bought him off for $750," ibid.

"Heavy into the sauce," ibid.

Meyer's unpublished thirty-one-page handwritten response to Burr Snider is dated 11/29/81. A fascinating, heartfelt document.

"By the early 1960s sexual desire, especially male sexual desire, was economically legitimate," Eric Schaefer, *Bold! Daring! Shocking! True!*

"Opened up the floodgates of permissiveness as we know it in these United States"—an interesting quote. Despite much digging by both myself and Dave Frasier, the location of this quote was not tracked down in any *Time* article on Russ Meyer or any search of the magazine in general, despite its having been referenced in countless articles, such as "Russ Meyer at the Floodgates," Ross Woodbury, Gross Valley, Nevada *Mountain Messenger*, 10/3/79.

"The real driving force . . . to movement," RM to Tricia White, "Russ Meyer Is Porno's DeMille," *Las Vegas Sun*, 3/23/77.

"I don't know why . . . look at it," RM to Richard Seeley, "Russ Meyer Enjoys His Work." *Detroit Register*, 11/28/79 921.

"So innocent it is almost wistful," Turan, " 'Immoral Mr. Teas' in Retrospect."

"One of the canniest . . . skin flicks," "Russ Meyer: King of the Nudies," *Film Comment*, vol. 9, no. 1, 1–2/73

"Who can never hope . . . other than visual," Frasier, *Russ Meyer: The Life and Films*.

"She performs cunnilingus [*sic*] on him while he's writing out her ticket," RM to David Rosenbaum, "The Man Behind the Casabas," *Boston Phoenix*, vol. 4, no. 31, 8/5/75.

"Wail away at it," RM to Sergei Hasenecz and Charles Schneider, "A Clean Breast: Titillating Talk with Russ Meyer."

"Un-American," RM to Don Safran, "Britain's Townsend Due," *Dallas Times Herald*, 4/20/69.

"What does a woman . . . to pitch," RM to David Frasier, *DFA*.

"He's still the first Sergeant . . . got over it," Eve Meyer to Burton Wolfe, "King of the Nudie Movies."

6. The Handyman

JM interviews: Richard Brummer, Jim Ryan, Jean Duran, Paula Parker, John McCormick, Jean-Pierre Jackson, David Frasier, Stan Berkowitz, Dave Prowse, Roger Ebert, David Friedman, Marvin Friedlander, John Furlong, Dolores Fox, Charles Sumners, Rob Shaffner.

"I made movie . . . really mattered," RM, *ACB/RM*, vol. 2.

"I have no gods . . . *Foreign Correspondent,*" RM to Diana Loevy, "Son of Beyond the Valley of the Dolls," *Home Video,* vol. 2, no. 6, 5/81.

"After *Teas* . . . six times," RM to David Frasier, *DFA.*

"As rigid . . . morality play," David Friedman to David Chute, "Wages of Sin," second half of two-part article, *Film Comment,* vol. 22, no. 5, 9/86.

"Our theory . . . new set of tits," ibid.

"Our whole business was . . . see *next* week,' " David Friedman on the DVD commentary track to his picture *The Defilers.* Something Weird has released a number of Friedman-made or -distributed titles on DVD, most containing very entertaining and informative commentaries by the mighty monarch. They are essential for any student of exploitation history.

"I had the one sheet . . . even started," Friedman, *Defilers* commentary.

"Some stiff directing . . . bless him for it," ibid.

"The most erotic films ever made," RM to Scott Eyeman, "The Survival of Russ Meyer," *Exit,* 7/30/75.

"For a month I worked harder than I ever have in my life," Eve Meyer to Jane Wilson, "What's a Nice Girl Like You Doing in a Business Like This, Eve? (Well, Maybe Crying All the Way to the Bank)," *Los Angeles Times West* magazine, 5/9/71.

"Eve All Smirk, No Smoke," *Los Angeles Examiner,* 5/8/61.

"City girl who likes to swim in country stream," "the legend and lore of bathing suits," uncredited review, "Erotica," *Filmfacts,* no. 5, 1962.

"Meeting Sherry . . . U.S.S. *Ticonderoga,*" RM, *ACB/RM,* vol. 1.

"Banjo-bodied," ibid.

Description of *Europe in the Raw* shoot, "Thanks for the Mammaries: Russ Meyer," *Flesh & Blood Compendium,* Fab Press, 2003 (UK).

"With a very obvious . . . thin subterfuge," unknown author, "Europe in the Raw," *Modern Man* magazine, Winter 1963.

"Tits and War," ibid.

"Russ seeking downright pity did a real number on Mrs. Meyer," *RM/ACB,* vol. 1.

"Joyful adultery," ibid.

"It is not a love affair . . . strictly carnal," Veronica Vera, "Veronica Vera's New York," *Adam,* vol. 31, no. 12, circa 1980s.

"We never spent . . . to a motel," RM to Tommy Mastroianni, "Beneath the Valley of the Skin Flicker," *Cleveland Press,* 8/23/79.

"The boy doesn't . . . doesn't know," RM to Norman Dresser, "Things Mostly Big and Busty in Russ Meyer's Standards," *The Blade,* Toledo, Ohio, 7/19/79.

"Jest to a roomful of fans that he'd named his son Mr. Mattress," reported by Michael Flores, "Breast of Russ Meyer—the Interview," *It's Only a Movie* newsletter, no. 5, 1995.

"The public just grew tired of seeing the same old thing," RM to David Frasier, *DFA.*

"I realized nudies . . . sort of story," RM to Tony Crawley, "History of the Blue Movie [Part 5]," *Marilyn Chambers' Best of Club,* no. 15, 1981.

"I said, now I must . . . with giant breasts," RM to Turan and Zito, *Sinema.*

7. Top Lust, Top Hate, Top Heavy

JM interviews: David Frasier, Douglas Kues, David Friedman, Rudolph Grey, Fred Beiersdorf, Dolores Fox, Jim Ryan, George Carll, George Costello, Ulli Lommel, E. E. 'Mick' Nathanson, Charlie Sumners, Ben Rocco, John McCormick, Haji, Charles Napier, Andre Brummer, John Waters.

"No woman . . . they're through," RM to David Frasier, *DFA*.

Opening description based on David Frasier's interviews with Meyer, *DFA* and *ACB/RM*, "Interview," *Cinefocus* 1.2, Fall 1990; various other interviews.

"The worst part . . . only one Kitten," RM to Dale Ashmun, "Mondo Russo: Russ Meyer Interview," *Film Threat*, no. 15, 1988.

"I told her, 'I want you . . . your big tits,' " RM to David Frasier, *DFA*.

"I shot without . . . facing a crowd," ibid.

"With her big tits away from me," ibid.

"From the side . . . one iota," ibid.

"Box office," ibid.

Maitland background: "Lorna," two-part article, *Fling*, vol. 10, no. 1/2, 3–5/67, uncredited, probably by Arv Miller. Features many great photos by Meyer.

"I was dressed with a rather secretarial look," Lorna Maitland, *Mondo Topless*.

"A good actress . . . her name," RM to Jan Golab, "Return from Beyond the Valley of the Dolls," *Los Angeles*, vol. 31, no. 12, 12/86.

"From then on . . . difficult guy," RM to Jim Morton, *Research: Incredibly Strange Films*.

"Once you've unwrapped them, the thrill is gone," RM to Ron Base, "Meyer Mammary Films Smothered the World," *Toronto Sun*, 1/14/76.

"Ninety percent . . . they can pussywhip," RM to Rose Raidt, "I Couldn't Survive on the Raincoat Brigade," *Up the Creek*, vol. 1, no. 32, 8/17/79.

"In the morning . . . chick's computer," RM to Morton, *Research: Incredibly Strange Films*.

"Russ's whole life was to not give the upper hand to The Ace," RM on either one of the laser disc commentaries or *ACB*. Misplaced at press time, apologies.

"She did a number on my head," RM to Gene Ross, "Russ Meyer: The Brains Behind the Breast, Boormann and Beyond," *Adult Video News*, vol. 2, no. 4, 6/87.

"Absolutely hated his guts," ibid.

"We find the locations and then we write the story," "Close-up, Russ Meyer," author unknown, *This Week*, 11/26/87.

"Where everyone quotes . . . its Commandments," Nathaniel Thompson, *Mondo Digital* website.

"Gothic period," Roger Ebert, "Russ Meyer: King of the Nudies," *Film Comment*, Jan.–Feb. 1973.

"Without artistic surrender . . . for one man," *Lorna* theatrical trailer.

"My stories are morality . . . you gotta pay for it," RM to Turan and Zito, *Sinema*.

"The moralizing . . . whore that I am," RM to Gene Ross, "Russ Meyer: The Brains Behind . . ."

"Did I shoot . . . in color," RM to David Frasier, *DFA*.

"It's the same thing . . . big tits," ibid.

"Bending over, tits swaying," ibid.

"Everything that's nice, but strictly a bum bang," RM, *ACB/RM*.

"A real shit, but everything in the sack hubby wasn't," ibid.

"I feel that it's important . . . a bad, bad time," RM, *Beneath the Valley of the Ultra-Vixens* laser disc commentary.

"*Lorna* was the first dramatic naked-lady movie," William Rotsler, publication/date unknown, quoted by Luke Ford, "Russ Meyer," lukeford.com.

"The films with nudity . . . top heavy," William Rotsler, *Contemporary Erotic Cinema*, Penthouse/Ballantine, 1973.

"so that it would 'look dirty,' like an old, scratched 16 mm stag film," David Friedman.

"They were all afraid ... got something," RM to David Frasier, *DFA*.

"Lorna played ... skid row," RM to Frank Thistle, "King Leer," *Adam Film World*, vol. 7, no. 6, 9/79.

"A theater in Amherst, Massachusetts," as reported by Turan and Zito, *Sinema*.

"The tennis shoe brigade," RM to Sunny Shubert, "Sex in My Films Just for Laughs," *Bloomington Herald Telephone & Bedford Daily Times-Mail*, 6/29/75.

"If it were all so okay ... in this field," RM to David Frasier, *DFA*.

Mudhoney seizure in Long, Texas: *ACB/RM*.

"Russ puts women ... women at all," Eve Meyer to Jane Wilson, "What's a Nice Girl Like You Doing in a Business Like This, Eve? (Well, Maybe Crying All the Way to the Bank)," *Los Angeles Times West*, 5/9/71.

"Didn't like the idea ... other women," RM to David Frasier, *DFA*.

Eve illness, "I can never have a baby, now. I hope you're satisfied," *ACB/RM*.

Christane Schmidtmer/Eve affair: JM interview with Jim Ryan, other sources.

"Good, clean, wholesome sex," RM to Roger Ebert, "Why Meyer Is King of the Skin Flicks," *Chicago Sun-Times*, 2/16/69.

RM flight to Germany: *ACB/RM*.

"One of the most lecherous men in Hollywood," RM to Harvey Fenton, "Thanks for the Mammaries: Russ Meyer," *Flesh & Blood Compendium*.

"Russ and I ... direct one," Al Zugsmith to Todd McCarthy and Charles Flynn, *Kings of the B's*.

Artur Brauner background: *Fritz Lang: The Nature of the Beast*, Patrick McGilligan, St. Martin's Press.

"He's a man ... doesn't have tits!" RM as quoted by Uli Lommel, JM interview.

"I would have gone crazy ... remarkable women," RM to Paul Sherman, "Some of My Breast Kept Secrets: An Interview with Russ Meyer," *Filmfax*, no. 28, 8–9/91.

RM buying Porsche: *ACB/RM*.

"A disgrace to the film industry ... a setback for the business," Dale, "Fanny Hill: Memoirs of a Woman of Pleasure," *Variety*, 3/17/65.

"They said it couldn't be filmed, and it hasn't been," Raymond Durgnat, "Fanny Hill," *Films & Filming*, vol. 12, no. 8, 5/66.

"We broke up ... son of a bitch," RM to Kristine McKenna, "The Big Boob Theory," *Los Angeles*, 6/2000.

"I don't like a woman that's too smart," "Let's do what I want to do all the time," RM to Arv Miller, "Between the Valleys of My Ultravixens," Part Three, *Fling*, vol. 31, no. 6, issue 161, 9/90.

Eve Meyer plane crash: *World Disasters: Tragedies in the Modern Age*, Keith Eastlake, Henry Russell, Mike Sharpe, Fitzroy Dearborn, 2001.

"And did I ever ... I think so," RM, *ACB/RM*, vol 3.

"I want willing hands hovering around," Stuart Lancaster to Kris Gilpin, Interview: Stuart Lancaster," *Draculina*, no. 11, 1990.

"My homage to Grapes of Wrath," RM to Allen Greenfield, "Direct It: Russ Meyer Tells You How," *Video Review*, vol. 2, no. 6, 12/81 1128.

"Unforgettable grotesques ripped from the pages of some abysmal southern novel," from a fanzine I have only one page of. I'd love to identify the author.

"My films can be taken ... they're both," RM to Maureen Koch, "Inter/View with Russ Meyer and Edy Wlliams," *Andy Warhol's Interview*, no. 19 2/72.

"Laughing so hard ... a heart attack." Stuart Lancaster to John Donnelly, "Stuart Lancaster," *Psychotronic Video*, no. 17, Winter 1994.

"Intelligentsia" "played seriously . . . bigger, best," RM to William L. Kahrl, "Peep Show Becomes Fine Art: The Transmogrification of Russ Meyer," *World's Fair,* vol. II, no. 4, Fall 1982.

"I made a gamble . . . made the film," David Frasier, *DFA.*

"Her tits had kinda gone south," RM to Hasenecz and Schneider, *Cad.*

"It's not like . . . her knees now," RM to David Glassman, "Director Meyer Gives Thanks for the Mammaries," *UCLA Daily Bruin,* 1/24/80.

"It represented a down deep solid lack of trust," RM to Morton, *Research: Incredibly Strange Films.*

"I came visiting . . . in Quebec," Haji to Matt Maranian, "The Best of the Breast! Russ Meyer's Vixens Speak," *Boing Boing,* no. 14, 1995.

"You earthlings are very strange people," Haji to Ronald L. Smith, "From Pussycat to Double-D Avenger," *Phantom of Movies Videoscope,* no. 45, Winter 2003.

"These people . . . the high heels," Haji to Beth Accomando, "Faster, Russ! Go! Go!" 1996 article of unknown origin, reprinted online.

"I think a lot . . . the ocean," Haji to Maranian, "The Best of the Breast! Russ Meyer's Vixens Speak."

"One guy asked me . . . bust your head!" Haji to Jewel Shepard, *Invasion of the B-Girls,* Jewel Shepard, Eclipse Books, 1992.

"Fart sacks," RM to Dale Ashmun, "Mondo Russo: Russ Meyer Interview," *Film Threat,* no. 15, 1988.

"It was so cold . . . before you went in," Haji to Nathaniel Thompson, *Mondo Digital* website.

"Clawed the shit out of me," RM to Ashmun, "Mondo Russo."

"I slept by the door with an axe handle," ibid.

"Vital juices," ibid.

"Two actors ended up in the hospital, one with a hole in his stomach two inches wide," Steve Oliver to David Lees and Stan Berkowitz, "Russ Meyer, One-Man Movie Machine Is at It Again," *Los Angeles Times Calendar,* 1/7/79.

"There'd never be . . . Brummer around!" RM speaking at the Los Feliz Theatre, 12/11/87, as reported by Kris Gilpin, *Draculina Fear Book,* no. 2, 11/93.

"A film that lacks . . . his point is," James Powers, " 'Motorpsycho!' Is Exploitable," *Hollywood Reporter,* vol. 186, no. 45, 8/13/65.

"I told my wife . . . Absolutely,' " RM to Chris Willman, "Return of the Ultrapussycats," *Los Angeles Times,* 12/11/94.

8. Klieg Eyes on a Dry Lake Bed

JM Interviews: Tura Satana, Ted V, Mikels, Peter Young, Haji, Erica Gavin, George Costello, Richard Brummer, Lori Williams, Susan Bernard, Gil Haimson, John Waters.

Harold Lloyd's 3D pictures of Tura Satana: *Harold Lloyd's Hollywood Nudes in 3D!* Suzanne Lloyd, Black Dog & Leventhal Publishers, 2004. Note: Despite Lloyd's expertise as a stereo photographer, the stereo effects in this book are poorly executed, so don't expect much in the way of 3D.

"I personally prefer . . . the superwoman," RM to Jerry Stein, "Films Starring Flesh," *Cincinnati Post & Times Star,* 3/24/73.

"Varla is the most honest . . . the scariest," Richard Corliss, "Thanks for the Mammaries," *Time* online, 8/2/02.

"This is where Varla . . . on the Westside," Tura Satana, *The Kick-Ass Life of Tura Satana,* unpublished manuscript, reprinted by permission.

"If I could help . . . I would," ibid.

"It is in . . . this degradation," ibid.

"I made a vow . . . not the rapist," ibid.

"I saw myself . . . entertainment industry," ibid.

"Stripping wasn't . . . the way up," Tura Satana, "How a G-String Saved Me from Gin," *Cabaret*, 1/57.

"A lot of girls . . . or hairbrush," Haji to Matt Maranian, "The Best of the Breast! Russ Meyer's Vixens Speak," *Boing Boing*, no. 14, 1995.

"I had men kicking . . . out of the men?' " RM to Nathan Rabin, 1995 interview, *The Tenacity of the Cockroach*.

"One lung and he refused to stop," RM to Sergei Hasenecz and Charles Schneider, *Cad*.

"He started getting on the sauce . . . steam engine," ibid.

"By the end . . . supernatural," Jim Morton, *Research: Incredibly Strange Films*.

"A geometrically stark . . . Roadrunner cartoon," Julian Stringer, "Exposing Intimacy in Russ Meyer's Motorpsycho! And Faster, Pussycat! Kill! Kill!" *The Road Movie Book*.

"Just boring out of their sockets," RM, *Faster, Pussycat! Kill! Kill!* laser disc commentary.

"He'd put a million . . . you blinking," Stuart Lancaster to Kris Gilpin, Interview: Stuart Lancaster, *Draculina*, no. 11, 1990.

"So unctuously proud you want to throw up," RM, *Faster, Pussycat! Kill! Kill!* laser disc commentary.

"One of the most unrelenting . . . a mean Meyer," Lewis Black, "Faster, Pussycat! Kill! Kill! Staying Abreast with Russ Meyer," *Austin Chronicle*, 6/9/95.

"Human Chevys," Julian Stringer, "Exposing Intimacy in Russ Meyer's 'Motorpsycho!' And 'Faster, Pussycat! Kill! Kill!' " *The Road Movie Book*.

"You don't know whether . . . don't care!" Joe Bob Briggs, "Russ Meyer," syndicated column, exact publication unknown, 7/4/02.

"Meyer's character's . . . are attributes," Myron Meisel, "Over, Around, Through and Beyond the Valley of the Super-Meyers," *Reader: Los Angeles Weekly*, vol. 1, no. 14, 1979.

"One never gets . . . emotions of reality," David K. Frasier, *Russ Meyer: the Life and Films*.

"For the first time . . . her bare hands," RM quoted by Arthur Knight and Hollis Alpert, "History of Sex in Cinema," *Playboy*, vol. 14, no. 1, 6/67.

"It just died . . . one cared," RM, *Faster, Pussycat! Kill! Kill!* laser disc commentary.

"People complained when I didn't show Tura Satana's big tits naked," RM to David Frasier, *DFA*.

"My films are like a reptile . . . on the ankle," RM to Kenneth Turan, "Russ Meyer, Almost an American Institution," *Washington Post*, 11/9/76.

"Largely because a punk-rock . . . references to it," RM to Jan Golab, "Return from Beyond the Valley of the Dolls," *Los Angeles*, vol. 31, no. 12, 12/86.

"Lesbians and fags are crazy about it," RM to Barney Hoskins, "Thanks for the Memories," *New Musical Express*, 1/22/83 62.

"Russ was a little . . . in those days," Haji to Matt Maranian, "The Best of the Breast! Russ Meyer's Vixens Speak," *Boing Boing*, no. 14, 1995.

"I really made . . . in another film," RM, *Faster, Pussycat! Kill! Kill!* laser disc commentary

"She and I made . . . really with me," ibid.

"You don't have to be a namby pamby you can still have balls and be feminine,"
Tura Satana to Susan Barrows, "Tura," *Tease*, no. 5, 1995. Satana said the almost exact same words to me as well.

9. Shit Floats

JM Interviews: John Waters, Alaina Capri, John Furlong, George Costello, Jack Lucas, Ken Swofford, Haji, Richard Brummer, Igo Kantor, Lavelle Roby, Gordon
McLeod, Jim Ryan.

Background on Babette Bardot: "The New Bardot," Dale Roberts, *Dapper*, vol. 5,
no. 4, 4/69.

For more (albeit in a non-Meyer context) of the fantastic Pat Barrington/Bar-
ringer, see Something Weird's DVD of two William Rotsler films, *Agony of
Love/The Girl with the Hungry Eyes.*

Candy Morrison (aka Angela Carter, aka Vivianne Cornoyer or Moyer) layouts
(all? by RM), *Fling*, 1/67, 3/67, 1/70.

"My films have a lot . . . damned movie again," RM to Jim Goad, "Just a Couple of
Boobs Talking," *Los Angeles Reader*, 1/12/90.

"By the time we got . . . cost $12,000," RM to David Frasier, *DFA*.

"Max Factor's 'Light Egyptian,' " RM to Steve Hogner, "Russ Meyer: The Amiable
Bear of Erotic Cinema," *Austin Statesman-American*, 5/5/75.

"Undoubtedly the most voluptuous . . . in a film," Roger Ebert, "Russ Meyer: King
of the Nudies," *Film Comment*, Jan.–Feb. 1973.

"There seems to be something subtly sadistic going on here," ibid.

"A quickie," RM to Vince Staten, "Russ Meyer Reflects on his Pneumatic Career,"
Louisville Courier Journal, 5/6/89.

L.A. Times refusing *How Much Loving* ads: Burton H. Wolfe, "King of the Nudie
Movies," *True*, 3/69.

"My people don't make love, they compete," said RM to David Hale, " 'A Dirty Old
Man': Russ Meyer Goes Beyond Valley of Skin-Flicks," *Fresno Bee*, 3/18/77.

"Order is restored . . . maintains cosmic order," David K. Frasier, *Russ Meyer: The
Life and Films.*

"Driven to be a whore . . . her husband," ibid.

"*Lose* the jockstrap . . . *Hurl* it in the corner!" plus details of the Stuart Lancaster
exit: Kris Gilpin, "Interview; Stuart Lancaster," *Draculina*, no. 11, 1990.

"He turned livid . . . pretty heavy," Stuart Lancaster to John Donnelly, "Stuart
Lancaster."

"Hatchet job," RM to John Hartl, " 'King Leer' Back with a Downer Called 'Up!' "
Seattle Times, 1/23/77.

"I used to defend . . . to anything," RM to Ron White, "Exploit? Of Course Art Ex-
ploits," *San Antonio Sunday Express-News*, 10/17/76.

"When people meet me . . . what they want," RM to Ellen Goosenberg, "Supervixen Russ Meyer," *The Drummer*, 7/29/75.

It should be noted that "Primitive" by the Groupies (quoted at the head of the
chapter) is credited to the Groupies and Nick Venet.

10. The Look of Love

JM interviews: Erica Gavin, George Costello, Harrison Page, Haji, Jim Ryan,
Richard Brummer, Garth Pillsbury, Jacqueline Pillsbury, Pete Slater, Pete Gall,
David F. Friedman, John Waters, "Colonel" Rob Shaffner.

Opening scene based on Burton H. Wolfe's excellent article "King of the Nudie Movies," *True*, 3/69; "From 'Vixen' to Vindication: Erica Gavin Interviewed," Danny Peary, *Velvet Light Trap*, Fall 1976; and author interviews.

Background on Erica Gavin: "Erica Gavin: To Hell and Back," Steve Sullivan, *Glamour Girls Then and Now*, Spring–Summer 2002. An incredible article documenting in detail Gavin's tortured life.

"The Great American Dream . . . greedy pussy," RM, *Vixen* laser disc commentary.

"Basically this is a woman . . . the Communists," Erica Gavin, *E! True Hollywood Story* documentary (see Filmography).

"Banging pussies" . . . "two scissors," Gavin to Sullivan, "Erica Gavin: To Hell and Back."

"Once you become . . . fool around with you," ibid.

"She's a healer . . . through sex," RM, Jonathan Ross documentary (see Filmography).

"This was the basis . . . the raincoat brigade," RM to Arv Miller, "Russ Meyer: Between the Valleys of My Ultravixens," Part Three, *Fling*, no. 161, 7/90.

"The film that put Meyer on easy street," RM to Dan Scapperotti, "50s Legend Russ Meyer," *Femme Fatales*, vol. 6, no. 10/11, 4/98.

"It was a barn-burner," RM to Arv Miller, "Russ Meyer: Between the Valleys of My Ultravixens," vol. 31, no. 5, *Fling*, 1990.

"She . . . the reason I'm here," numerous interviews, such as this one with Stan Berkowitz, "18 — Count 'Em — 18 Couplings and an X-Rating: Russ Meyer in Hollywood," *UCLA Daily Bruin*, 1/7/70.

"The whole business will be ruined," RM to Burton H. Wolfe, "King of the Nudie Movies," *True*, 3/69.

"Open-faced oyster . . . roping spermatozoa," RM to Craig Reid, "Russ Meyer," *Adam*, vol. 25, no. 5, 5/81.

"It is hard today . . . *Bonnie and Clyde*?" Steven M. Lovelady, "King Leer: 'Nudie' Filmmaker, Russ Meyer, Scrambles to Outshock Big Studios," *Wall Street Journal*, 4/24/68.

"Jim, we got to make the sexiest film ever made," RM to Arv Miller, "Russ Meyer: Between the Valleys of My Ultravixens," Part Three, *Fling*, no. 159, 3/90.

"They're all built . . . think about it," RM to Arv Miller, "Russ Meyer: Between the Valleys of My Ultravixens," no. 160, 7/90.

"I wanted a girl to come on like the Superchief," RM to Dan Scapperotti, "50s Legend Russ Meyer."

"Almost every day," Erica Gavin to Steve Sullivan, "Erica Gavin: To Hell and Back."

"Down deep inside . . . to fuck her," ibid.

"White folks" . . . "well read" . . . "a good income" . . . "needed a good dose of the Negro to be able to understand their problems," RM, *Vixen* laser disc commentary.

Vixen trailer attendance: Roger Ebert, "Why Meyer Is King of the Skin Flicks," *Chicago Sun-Times*, 2/16/69.

"Nearly broke me," RM to Turan and Zito, *Sinema*.

"A sexual steeplechase," RM to Maureen Koch, "Inter/View with Russ."

Meyer and Edy Williams, *Andy Warhol's Interview*, no. 19, 2/72.

"Skull and crossbones," RM to Lee Beaupre, "Can't Risk Investors Coin Anymore Russ Meyer Cancels $400,000 'Foxy'; Raps 'Schlock' Films as Spoilsports," *Variety*, 271, vol. 8, no. 5, 7/4/73.

Oscar Brotman and Vixen: Dorothy Storck, "Director Russ Meyer: He Sees Everything with the Naked Eye," *Chicago Today American*, 2/15/69.

"The movie cesspool of Chicago," Gene Siskel, "Next: 'Karate Rape in Harlem,'" *Chicago Tribune*, 12/2/73.

"The best film . . . skin flick," Roger Ebert, "Vixen," *Chicago Sun-Times*, 2/24/69.

"Ludicrously topical," William Wolf, "Russ Meyer's 'Vixen,'" *Cue*, vol. 38, no. 20, 5/17/69.

"The most wholesome dirty movie of the year," Unknown, "Vixen" *Playboy*, vol. 16, no. 8, 8/69.

"The look of calculated . . . Garbo or Dietrich," Kenneth Turan, "'Vixen': Top of the 'Skin Flick' Heap," *Washington Post*, 8/13/69.

"This is the first time . . . position of respectability," RM to unknown, "Russ Meyer Extends Mileage His Esoterica Erotica Pics," *Hollywood Reporter*, 4/29/69.

"How come it took you so long to get it?" Carlos Starling quoted in "Halts 'RM's Vixen' After Receiving Summons," author unknown, *Boxoffice*, vol. 95, no. 26, 10/13/69.

"An obscene, lewd . . . with a Mountie," *National Decency Reporter*, vol. 6, no. 9–10, 8–9/69.

"Why don't you leave town you dirty old man?" "Lawyers Attack Obscenity Law," Otis Perkins, *Florida Times-Union*, 10/8/69.

Illiana Drive-In details: "Jury Rules 'Vixen' Obscene," Bill Acton, *Danville Commercial News*, 4/16/70.

Center Theater details: "Movie Obscenity Conviction Appealed," author unknown, *National Decency Reporter*, vol. 7, no. 5–6, 5–6/70.

Prosecuted 23 times: RM to Middleman, "Russ Meyer and His Boobs," *Video Trade Weekly*, no. 58, 1/13/83.

"Censorship is the wrong . . . persecution!" RM to Ron Chepesiuk, "Hollywood or Bust," *Gallery*, 3/91.

"A history of making war against the bare breast," Binstein and Bowden, *Trust Me: Charles Keating and the Missing Billions*.

"Hamilton County . . . bust time," RM to Craig Reid, "Interview/Russ Meyer," *Adam*, vol. 25, no. 5, 5/81.

"I was arrested so many times . . . the iron hotel," RM, *Vixen* laser disc commentary. For the record, none of Meyer's associates could recall RM ever being arrested.

"Amish shunning," Binstein and Bowden, *Trust Me: Charles Keating and the Missing Billions*.

"Never saw a lawsuit he didn't like," ibid.

"Anyone who ever tells you . . . ever come across," ibid.

"That criminal," Charles Keating to author unknown, "Appeals to Public—Keating Assails Courts' Stand on Smut," *Cincinnati Enquirer*, 3/10/71.

"I'm only one guy . . . have public decency," Charles Keating to Gloria Anderson, "Who Charles Keating Thinks He Is," *Cincinnati Enquirer Magazine*, date unknown.

"Provided a vehicle . . . play it again?'" Larry Flynt, *An Unseemly Man*.

"A scatological . . . of revulsion," Richard L. Gordon, "The Other Keating: Crusader in the Fight Against Pornography," *Cincinnati*, 6/70.

"It is my preference . . . by police," "Russ Meyer's 'Vixen' seized in Cincinnati," *Boxoffice*, vol. 95, no. 25, 10/6/69.

The Guild Arts Theater details: "'Vixen' Seized, Hearing Is Continued," author unknown, *Cincinnati Post*, 9/23/69.

"I'm violently . . . social significance," RM to Virgina Kay, "Virginia Kay Byline," *Chicago Daily News,* 2/13/69.

"Strangely enough most of the litigation . . . being harassed," RM to Bill Ornstein, "Russ Meyer Finds Sex Censorship Mostly Racial," *Hollywood Reporter,* vol. 210, no. 6, 3/3/70.

"The difficulty was . . . state attorney's office," Elmer Gertz, *E! True Hollywood Story* documentary (see Filmography).

"Simon Leis . . . *bespeaks* evil!" RM to Gary Morris, "An Interview with Russ Meyer," *Bright Lights,* 4/96.

"We were up against a judge whose son was the prosecutor!" RM, *Vixen* laser disc commentary.

"Will be happy . . . of the country," *National Decency Reporter,* Vol. 6, no. 9–10, 9–10/69.

"Mr. Keating intimidates people," Elmer Gertz as reported by Libby Lackman, "Judge to Decide Whether to Stop Movie 'Vixen,' " *The Cincinnati Enquirer,* 9/27/69.

"Billy Budd–Christlike" . . . "Unrealistic hoax" . . . "male lust" . . . "one of the major causes of marital discord," author unknown, "You Be the Judge," *National Decency Reporter,* 11–12/69.

"Cancer on society" . . . "unscrupulous men who have taken advantage of lack of censorship and capitalized on it" . . . "will infest society with a disease which will kill it," " 'Vixen' Obscene, Judge Leis Rules," author unknown, *Cincinnati Enquirer,* 11/18/69.

"Set a precedent . . . of Americans," author unknown, "Presidential Commission—For or Against Obscenity?" *National Decency Reporter,* 11–12/69.

"Purported acts . . . 14th Amendments," quoted in "High Court Upholds 'Vixen' Censorship," author unknown, *Cincinnati Post & Times Star,* 7/21/71.

1984 attempted *Vixen* screening: "Second Copy of 'Vixen' Confiscated," author unknown, *Cincinnati Post & Times Star,* 9/24/69.

Rape allegations, Flynt/Keating: Binstein and Bowden, *Trust Me.*

"Ah, the redeeming social value," Thurgood Marshall quoted by Jon Lewis, *Hollywood v. Hard Core.*

"He fought the big . . . American citizen," David Friedman, *E! True Hollywood Story* documentary (see Filmography).

"In the final analysis . . . up to something," Turan and Zito, *Sinema.*

Current Simon Leis hijinks, see also: "Hustler Owner May Face Charges," Denise Wilson, *Cincinnati Post,* 6/18/03.

"I think he's probably done more . . . any other person," Jimmy Flynt to France Griggs Sloat, "An Army of One," *Xavier* magazine, Fall 2004.

"No clear recollection," e-mail correspondence with author.

"Peer down the blouses of secretaries he has hired" . . . "unexpected" . . . "huge new breasts," Binstein and Bowden, *Trust Me.*

11. The Watusi Gun-Bearer

JM interviews: Tom McGowan, Jim Ryan, Charles Napier, Richard Brummer, Burt Santos, Robert Pergament.

"All that counts . . . get it out," RM to David Lees and Stan Berkowitz, "Russ Meyer, One-Man Movie Machine Is at It Again," *Los Angeles Times Calendar,* 1/7/79.

"Who cares about acting . . . on berserk," "I Love Uschi: Thanks for the Mammaries," Mike Accomando, *Something Weird Blue Book,* no. 1, 1997.

"Who else can say . . . Bigfoot?" ibid.

"I'm living . . . and why?" Uschi Digard to Kern Williams, *Journal News*, Hamilton, Ohio, 4/26/75.

"We've been together ever since that day," Uschi Digard to Otto Dekom, *Morning News*, Wilmington, Delaware, 12/21/76.

"The dedication of a Watusi gun-bearer," RM to Arv Miller, "Russ Meyer: Between the Valleys of My Ultravixens," Part Two, no. 160, 7/90.

"She'd run over bare coals . . . that kind of chick," RM to Sergei Hasenecz and Charles Schneider, *Cad*.

"I made my reputation . . . was simulated," Uschi Digard to unknown, *Celebrity Sleuth*, issue and date unknown.

"Had a great love affair," RM to Dan Scapperotti, "50s Legend Russ Meyer," *Femme Fatales*, vol. 6, no. 10/11, 4/98.

"One of the most aggressive sex partners anyone could hope to find," ibid, also on RM's *Supervixens* laser disc commentary.

"Like Chill Wills, only fatter," RM to Ross and Stan Berkowitz, "Russ Meyer, One-Man Movie Machine Is at It Again."

"Symbolically act out . . . air of mysticism," RM to Mark Baddeley, "Thanks for the Mammary," *Video*, 3/83 (UK).

"*Zabriskie Point* in gym socks," Roger Greenspun, "Russ Meyer's Film 'Cherry, Harry and Raquel' Opens," *New York Times*, 4/23/70.

"*Cherry, Harry and Raquel* is a rotten film . . . harsh vitality," Aljean Harmetz, "Oh, Those Beautiful Dolls!" *New York Times*, 12/21/69.

"Has been matched only by *Gone With the Wind*," Steven M. Lovelady, "King Leer: 'Nudie' Film-maker, Russ Meyer, Scrambles to Outshock Big Studios," *Wall Street Journal*, 4/24/68.

"Like a yahooing cowboy," RM to Nicholas Von Hoffman, "Dirty Movies Are His Bag," *Washington Post*, 11/5/69.

I'd been trying to get into Hollywood . . . the red carpet was being laid out for me," RM to John Anders, "A Frank Visit with Russ Meyer," *Dallas Morning News*, 4/13/75.

"As I drove . . . in the world," RM to Kevin Thomas, "King of the Nudies Takes on Biggest Film Caper Yet," *Los Angeles Times Calendar*, 11/30/69.

12. Strapping On Fox

JM interviews: Richard Zanuck, David Brown, Roger Ebert, Stu Philips, Cynthia Myers, Erica Gavin, Dolly Read, John La Zar, Gordon MacLeod, Harrison Page, Lavell Roby, John Waters, Lynn Carey, Igo Kantor, Hugh Hefner, Charles Napier, Manny Diez, Kevin Thomas, Richard Brummer, David Prowse, Al Van Schmus.

When contacted for an interview, guitar great Ed King—member of the *Beyond the Valley of the Dolls* band Strawberry Alarm Clock and later of Lynyrd Skynyrd—informed me that the only memory he had of making the movie was falling asleep on the toilet at home and missing his 6 a.m. wakeup call.

"They're all whores . . . good for anybody," RM to MJ Simpson, "American Peep Show," *Total Film*, 2/97.

"Is it not time . . . technically interesting as well," Roger Ebert, ". . . And a Critic," *Wall Street Journal*, vol. 171, no. 91 5/8/68.

"He writes . . . Rodgers & Hammerstein," RM to Ted Mahar, "Meyer 'King Leer' of Soft-Core Cinema," *Sunday Oregonian*, 4/29/79.

"An odd and talkative kid," Roger Ebert, "Thought Experiments: How Propeller-Heads, BNFs, Sercon Geeks, Newbies, Recovering GAFIAtors, and Kids in the Basements Invented the World Wide Web, All Except for the Delivery System," *Asimov's Science Fiction* online article, issue 0501, 1/2005.

"His father died . . . there," Betsy Kedrick as quoted by Paul Wood, "Profile on Bravo Features Ebert," *News-Gazette* online article, 1/18/2003.

"That wonderful . . . Bosomania," RM to Harvey Fenton, "Thanks for the Mammaries: Russ Meyer," *Flesh & Blood Compendium*.

"Freako over tits," RM to J. Scott Wynn, *Shock Cinema*, no. 13, 1998.

"Ebert is more debauched . . . Look at that girl!' " RM to Kristi Turnquist, "Russ Meyer: Porno Potentate and Proud of It," *Willamette Valley Observer*, 9/28/79.

"Pendulous," RM to Edward Guthmann, "Russ Meyer: Running the Gauntlet of Vice," unknown Portland, Oregon, paper.

"Roger got head . . . Great scene!" RM to Carel Rowe, "Russ Meyer," *The Perfect Vision*, exact date/issue unknown, circa 1990, UK publication.

Meyer, no more exchanges of wondrous body fluids: *ACB/RM*, countless interviews.

"They started to talk . . . the piss,' " RM to David Chute, "Beyond the Valley of Russ Meyer," *Boston Phoenix*, 5/22/79.

"Would have conditions . . . outrageous proportions," RM to Hope Urban, "Russ Meyer," *Velvet Hammer Burlesque* souvenir program, 2/14/95.

"Then again, I'd believe . . . my distended member," confidential source.

"I called Ebert . . . the big time,' " RM, *E! True Hollywood Story* documentary (see Filmography).

"It's a camp sexploitation . . . triple wedding," Roger Ebert quoted by unknown author, *Time*, "Populist at the Movies," vol. 95, no. 13, 3/3/70.

"He made it clear . . . come under attack," Roger Ebert, "Russ Meyer Busts Sleazy Stereotype," *Chicago Sun-Times*, 11/15/85.

"Meyer wanted everything in the movie except the kitchen sink," Roger Ebert, "Russ Meyer: Ten Years After 'Beyond,' " *Film Comment*, no. 16, 7–8/80.

"Everything was unmentionable . . . bad trips were blamed," Joan Didion, *The White Album*, Simon & Schuster, 1979.

"A mood might have developed . . . dropping his guitar," Roger Ebert, "Dead Man," *Chicago Sun-Times*, 6/96.

"Since he cannot really sing . . . must be a deeper purpose," Roger Ebert, "Masked and Anonymous," *Chicago Sun-Times*, 8/15/03.

"The overall tenor . . . day of the job," Roger Ebert, "The Last Waltz," *Chicago Sun-Times*, 4/19/02.

"We wanted the movie . . . inspiration for the characters," Roger Ebert, "Russ Meyer: Ten Years After 'Beyond,' " *Film Comment*, no. 16, 7–8/80.

"That inauthenticity . . . was the hippies' turn," Stuart Klawans, "It's One Long Dirty Joke but Hey, Man, It's a Classic," *New York Times*, 11/17/02.

"It was my shot . . . wanted to make," RM to Jon Casimir, "King Leer: A Life," *Sydney Morning Herald*, 9/3/90.

"You create the greatest satire . . . Michael Blodgett," RM to David Frasier, *DFA*.

"You wrote this . . . Eugene O'Neill," Roger Ebert, " 'Dolls' triggers flood of great memories," *Chicago Sun-Times*, 2/7/03.

"In 1969–70 . . . diseases or problems," Michael Blodgett at UCLA *Dolls* panel, quoted from "Russ Meyer, Roger Ebert and 'Beyond the Valley of the Dolls,' " *Movie Talk from the Front Lines*, Jerry Roberts and Steven Gaydos, editors.

"Her idea of sexuality is . . . nostrils," RM to Jonathan Ross, "Russ Meyer at the NFT," *The Very Breast of Russ Meyer.*

"Gay content is . . . characters insane," Michael Musto, "Good Pill Hunting," *Village Voice,* 11/20–26/02.

"The way Indians . . . her teeth part," Burt Prelutsky, "What's a Sex Symbol to Do?" *Los Angeles Times Calendar,* 4/28/74.

"There is a certain satisfaction . . . it's a good feeling," Edy Williams to Ted Mahar, "Sex-Bomb Reaps Revenge on Men," *The Oregonian,* 8/26/70.

"You mustn't let a man . . . one piece at a time," Edy Williams to Brad Castleman, "Edy Williams Sheds Mate Who Made Her Star of Nude Movies," *National Insider,* 8/19/73.

"I'm a baaaad Mormon . . . shoot!" Edy Williams to Susan Pile, John Moran, Patrick Tiloen Close, "Getting Intimate with Edy Williams," *Interview,* no. 34, 7/73.

She made . . . didn't wear," Edy Williams to Dorothy Manners, "Edy Williams Giving Up Sex Symbol Status," *Los Angeles Herald-Examiner,* 3/14/71.

"He conned everybody . . . other girls, too," Edy Williams to Susan Pile, John Moran, Patrick Tiloen Close, "Getting Intimate with Edy Williams."

"I spent about three months being a spoiled bitch," Edy Williams to John London, "Edy Williams is Five Feet Eight Inches Tall, with Tawny, Dark Auburn Hair, Sensuous Lips and Titillating Hips, Who Says So? Edy Williams," *London Evening News,* 2/12/72.

"I didn't look too . . . on downers," Edy Williams to Tony Crawley, "Swank Interview: Russ Meyer & Edy Williams," *Swank,* vol. 19, no. 12, 2/73.

"I am really inhibited . . . close after that," Edy Williams to Susan Pile, John Moran, Patrick Tiloen Close, "Getting Intimate with Edy Williams."

"I really met my . . . was bizarre," Edy Williams to John London, "Edy Williams is Five Feet Eight Inches Tall . . ."

"Swing," RM to Lowry and Black, "Russ Meyer Interviewed."

"recut the entire . . . three months," RM, "The Low-Budget Producer," *The Movie Business: American Film Industry Practice.*

"Cut, cut, cut . . . the audience," RM to David Frasier, *DFA.*

"I always have seven . . . a laugh," RM to Bob Andelman, "The Happy Pornographer: Revealing Conversation with Russ Meyer," *Gainesville* magazine, 11/1/79.

"R minus," Zanuck as quoted by RM, Richard Cuskelly, "Russ Meyer Abdicating Title of 'King of the Nudie Movies,' " *Los Angeles Herald-Examiner,* 4/12/70.

Zanuck: "Buy one!" *ACB/RM.*

"I have no message," RM to Stephen Hunter, "King of the D-Cups Is Back with Another Vixen," *Baltimore Sun,* 5/21/82.

"Utter garbage . . . why bother?" Stanley Kauffman, "Myra Breckenridge and Other Disasters," *The New Republic,* vol. 163, no. 3, 7/18/70.

"True pornography . . . divorced from reality," John Simon, "Meyer's Blue Heaven," *The New Leader,* vol. 53, no. 15, 7/20/70.

"As funny as a burning orphanage," Murf, "Beyond the Valley of the Dolls," *Variety,* vol. 259, no. 6, 6/24/70.

"A treat for the emotionally . . . totally degenerate enterprise," Charles Champlin, *Los Angeles Times,* date unknown, quoted by RM in *ACB/RM,* vol. 2.

"Breakdown . . . either one of them," Charles Champlin, "Breakthrough or Breakdown in Film Standards?" *Los Angeles Times Calendar,* 7/5/70.

"He thought it was the end . . . SATANIC glee!" RM to Scott Morrow, "Adventures in the Skin Trade," *Los Angeles Weekly*, vol. 10, no. 3, 12/11–17/87.

Screw's 11 percent: Dan Mouer, "Muck & Meyer: Beyond the Valley of the Dolls," *Screw*, no. 71, 7/13/70.

"Arrested and jailed," Charles Keating quoted by unknown author, "650 Protest Smut in Pix at L.A. Rally," *Daily Variety*, vol. 135, no. 35, 1/26/71.

"Meyer's earnestly vulgar sensibility . . . has become patronizing," Vincent Canby, "Screen: 'Beyond the Valley of the Dolls': Russ Meyer Presents a View of Show Biz: Film Seems to Parody His Earlier Efforts," *New York Times*, 6/27/70.

"Maybe *Dolls* represents . . . he can do," Leslie Fiedler, "Beyond 'Beyond the Valley of the Dolls,' " *American Journal*, vol. 1, no. 5, 1973.

"Ebert forced Meyer . . . a disaster," Myron Meisel, "Over, Around, Through and Beyond the Valley of the Super-Meyers," *Reader: Los Angeles Weekly*, vol. 1, no. 24, 4/13/79.

"It is as if Harold Robbins . . . with Gore Vidal," John Simon, "Meyer's Blue Heaven," *The New Leader*, vol. 53, no. 15, 7/20/70.

"The ultimate Russ Meyer . . . approach again," RM to John Stanley, " 'Blazing Bosoms' and the King of Sexploitation," *San Francisco Chronicle*, 3/17/77.

"We were an extraordinary . . . an old pornographer," RM to M. Caen, "Russ Meyer: sein these," *Video News*, no. 17, 2/83 (France, article translation by A. J. Ryan).

"I thought, 'Hey, this will . . . Lauren Bacall, y'know?' " Edy Williams, *E! True Hollywood Story* documentary (see Filmography).

"No pussy," RM, *ACB/RM*, vol. 2.

"He ignores me . . . turns me on," "I spent about three months being a spoiled bitch," Edy Williams to London, "Edy Williams Is Five Feet Eight Inches Tall . . ."

"He wanted to be the star . . . for the first year," Edy Williams to John Stark and Michael Alexander, "Famous for Her Nude Romps in the World's Pools, Edy Williams Tries to Make One More Splash," *People*, vol. 26, no. 26, 6/29/87.

"I don't want your mother . . . a cripple," Edy Williams as quoted by Russ Meyer, *Faster, Pussycat! Kill! Kill!* laser disc commentary.

"Could not stand . . . out of nowhere," RM to David Frasier, *DFA*.

"I don't think I've known . . . in between," RM to Beth Winakor, "People . . . and Things," *Chicago Sun-Times*, 11/17/76.

"If your luggage . . . to the stockholders," RM to Tony Crawley, "History of the Blue Movie: Part Six: Show 'Em," *Club International*, vol. 5, no. 6, 6/81.

"We're exceptionally pleased . . . merely undress people," Richard Zanuck to A. H. Weiler, "Meyer to Make 3 More Films for Fox," *New York Times*, 2/17/70.

"It was fantastic . . . rip Edy's clothes off," RM to Turan and Zito, *Sinema*.

"Someone who takes himself . . . vests," RM to Joyce Haber," exact source unknown at press time.

"The sex film . . . suspense, mystery," RM to Terry Kay, "Russ Meyer Unnoticed in Company of His Wife," *Atlanta Journal*, 7/12/71.

"Most fervent hope . . . home town," RM to unknown, "Meyer Readies a Treat for Smut Crusader," *Daily Variety*, 1/27/71.

Williams "begged" to be reinstated—RM to Dan Scapperotti, "50s Legend Russ Meyer," *Femme Fatales*, vol. 6, 10/11, 4/98.

"The plot is advanced through dialogue," RM to Stan Hieronymus, "King of the Nudies Russ Meyer Says They've Shown All There Is to Show," *Champaign-Urbana News Gazette*, 3/28/71.

"The Seven Minutes will be beyond all doubt the finest movie I've ever made," author unknown, "Beyond the Valley of the Nudies," Panorama section, *Chicago Daily News*, 4/3–4/71.

"The first night in every theater . . . audience knows," RM to Ed Lowry and Louis Black, "Russ Meyer Interviewed," *Film Comment*, vol. 16, no. 4, 7–8/80.

"Talky censorship brings out the dullard in Meyer . . . a losing battle of mind over mattress," unknown author, "The Seven Minutes," *Playboy*, vol. 18, no. 10, 10/71.

"Tedious," Kevin Thomas, " 'Seven' Attacks Censorship," *Los Angeles Times*, 9/8/71.

"Tepid," Jay Cocks quoted in *Filmfacts*, "Seven Minutes," vol. 14, 296–298, 1971.

"Success . . . has spoiled King Leer," *New York* magazine quoted, ibid.

"A tombstone for the dead talents of Russ Meyer," Al Goldstein, "An Oscar for Meyer's Weenie," *Screw*, no. 124, 7/19/71.

"Bull in a china shop," Irving Wallace to John Leverence and Sam Grogg Jr., "Irving Wallace—The Interview: The Author of the Word," *Journal of Popular Culture*, vol. 7, no. 1, Summer 1973.

"I took on an impossible task . . . an Irving Wallace book," RM to unknown, "Russ Meyer Tells Press That He's Returning to 'What He Can Do Best,' " *Boxoffice*, 12/16/74.

"They had a man out . . . my work was," RM to Cameron Mackay, "The Pneumatic World of Russ Meyer," *Penthouse* (UK), 2/81

"Zanuck was always telling . . . one of my films," RM to David Lees and Stan Berkowitz, "Russ Meyer, One-Man Movie Machine, Is at It Again," *Los Angeles Times Calendar*, 1/7/79.

"Two backs," RM, *Screw* cable TV interview, date unknown.

"Sex is out . . . by shark," RM quoted by Dave Prowse, JM interview.

"She used men . . . behind two thrones," Edy Williams to Pile, Moran, Close, "Getting Intimate with Edy Williams."

"A pretty coat . . . smashed my Corvette," Edy Williams to Ruth Batchelor, "Edy Williams: 'I Think They Censor the Films Too Much,' " *L.A. Free Press*, no. 568, 6/6–12/75.

"Have you any idea . . . but won't?" Edy Williams to Donald Zec, "All About Edy: (Front Girl for the New Fifties)," *Daily Mirror*, 2/14/72.

"Pack everything . . . Cannes Film Festival." Edy Williams to Batchelor, "Edy Williams: 'I Think They Censor the Films Too Much.' "

"Disappearing acts" . . . "I am a sex symbol and I don't want to be alone," Edy Williams quoted by Lawrence Van Gelder, "Notes on People: This Book May Be Dangerous," *New York Times*, 6/28/73 210.

Edy in bed with a younger man: *ACB/RM*, vol. 2.

"I trusted Russ . . . fucking and cooking,' " Edy Williams to Batchelor, "Edy Williams: 'I Think They Censor the Films Too Much.' "

"I just couldn't picture . . . Edy Williams," RM to Lowry and Black, "Russ Meyer Interviewed."

"The blacks hated it, the whites hated it," RM to Louise Lague, "Russ Meyer: Back in the Soft Core Business," *Washington Star*, 6/29/75.

"Sort of like *Mandingo* without the sex," RM to David Rosenbaum, "The Man Behind the Casabas," *Boston Phoenix*, vol. 4, no. 31, 8/5/75.

"A guy got up . . . the tin cups," RM to Dan Yakir and Bruce Davis, "An Interview: Beyond the Big Breast—Can Russ Meyer Keep it 'Up!' " *The Thousand Eyes* magazine, vol. 2, no. 4, 12/76.

"One thing I knew . . . do best," RM to Christine Nieland, "Russ is Back in the Valley of the Vixens," *Chicago Daily News*, 10/19–20/74.

Some *BVD* trivia: distributor Jean-Pierre Jackson told me the only fight he ever got into with Meyer was over the titling of the 1980s French reissue of the film. Jackson insisted on *Hollywood Vixens*. Meyer had wanted *Hollywood Vixens Au Lait* (translation: *Hollywood Vixens with Milk!*).

13. Run Like a Gazelle, Dear

JM interviews: Charles Napier, Jim Ryan, Charles Pitt, Roger Ebert, Stanley Berkowitz, Haji, Richard Brummer, Erica Gavin, Jean-Pierre Jackson, John Waters, Fred Beiersdorf.

Background on Raven de la Croix: Steve Sullivan, "Raven de la Croix: From Russ Meyer to the Realm of the Spirits," *Glamour Girls Then and Now*, no. 14, 2–3/99.

The prehistoric superimposed lightning effect that pops on during the *Supervixens* Shari Eubank electrocution scene came from the laboratory set-up used in James Whale's 1930's Frankenstein pictures, courtesy of Whale's effects man himself, Kenneth Strickfadden. "We went over to his house and he had the stuff in his backyard in a garage," said Jim Ryan. "We brought the camera over there and filmed the sparks off it."

"I really dig . . . violence," RM to Terry Box, "Porn's Disney," *Corpus Christi Caller*, 11/20/76.

"What is there . . . compete with that," RM to Tony Rayns, "Dolls, Vixens, and Supervixens in the Films of Russ Meyer," *Late Night Video*, vol. 2, no. 2, 1983.

"An important day in my life," RM to Pat H. Broeske, "After Two Flops, the 'Nudie King' Is Back in the Ring," *Southeast Daily News*, 9/20/74.

"Every reel, like a new linebacker," RM to Gary Morris, "Russ Meyer's Supervixens," *Bright Lights*, vol. 1, no. 2, Spring 1975.

"We never discussed . . . a calf being born," Shari Eubank to Jason Thomas, "The Development of Supervixen," *Chicago Sun Times*, 5/1/75.

"She was dragged . . . bit you," RM to Craig Reid, "Russ Meyer," *Adam*, May 1981.

"A little distracting—she used to do makeup with only sneakers on," Charles Napier at UCLA *Dolls* panel, quoted from "Russ Meyer, Roger Ebert and 'Beyond the Valley of the Dolls,'" *Movie Talk from the Front Lines*, Jerry Roberts and Steven Gaydos, editors.

"I like the way the kid moves," RM quoted by way of Charles Pitt to A. Leigh Charlton, "Super Camp Meets Super Raunch in 'Super Vixens,'" *UCLA Daily Bruin*, 5/23/75.

"I have no . . . Russ Meyer," Charles Pitt to Charlton, "Super Camp Meets Super Raunch in 'Super Vixens.'"

"Regardless of who . . . that ultimate power," "The Abreasted Development of Russ Meyer," Louis Black, *Austin Chronicle*, vol. 8, no. 10, 11/6–12/98.

"The girls complained . . . I'd left out," RM to Jean Dietrich, "Russ Meyer Approaches Moviemaking as Mostly a Question of 'X-cellence,'" *Louisville Courier-Journal*, 6/11/75.

"When Shari Eubank . . . theater crying," Haji to Ronald L. Smith, "From Pussycat to Double-D Avenger," *Phantom of the Movies*, no. 45, Winter 2003.

"The townspeople . . . it had before," RM to Ellen Goosenberg, "Supervixen Russ Meyer," *The Drummer*, 7/29/75.

"When it was over . . . something right," ibid. (italic emphasis my own).

Eubank's father seeing *Supervixens:* RM to Craig Reid, "Interview/ Russ Meyer," *Adam,* vol. 25, no. 5, 5/81.

"I figured this was . . . released *Supervixens,*" Charles Napier to Roger Ebert, "This Is the Man 'Rambo' Fans Hate," *Chicago Sun Times,* 6/30/85.

"I went out . . . be indoors," ibid.

"Truly one of the most . . . visceral," Kevin Thomas, "Violence Bared in 'Supervixens,' " *Los Angeles Times,* 5/14/75.

"Enjoy vicariously . . . abundantly earned," Arthur Knight, "Russ Meyer's 'Supervixens,' " *Hollywood Reporter,* vol. 236, no. 27, 5/21/75.

"Hitchcock's sense . . . in violence," ibid.

"Meyer is the best . . . America today," Dave Kehr, *Chicago Reader,* vol. 4, no. 5, 10/25/74.

"Auditioning for role . . . pop attitudizing," Andrew Sarris, "Reflections on the New Porn," *Village Voice,* vol. 20, no. 35, 9/1/75.

"Archetypal gay . . . blue jeans," Ken Emerson, "Russ Meyer's 'Supervixens,' " *The Boston Phoenix,* vol. 4, no. 31, 8/5/75.

"*Supervixens* is for . . . love each other," ibid.

"Russ apparently . . . just not possible," Edy Williams to John Austin, "Uncensored Interview: Marriage Isn't for Sex Symbols Says Edy Williams Who Would Rather Play the Field," *National Police Gazette,* vol. 179, no. 2, 2/74.

"Hit me and knocked me down," ibid.

"Russ gave me . . . it back" . . . "waiting for the sheriff in my bikini," Edy Williams to James Bacon, "Bikinied Edy Waits for the Sheriff," *Los Angeles Herald-Examiner,* 7/1/75 193.

"from using a gun or any dangerous weapon" reported along with details of case in "Sexpot, Skinflick Director Break Up," author unknown, *Dayton Daily News,* 11/6/75.

"I don't think my talent . . . a piece of meat," Edy Williams at press conference, reported by Myrna Oliver, "Now She Wants to Shed Mate [Seeks New Role]," *Los Angeles Times,* 10/17/75.

"If she has the talents . . . find employment," Judge Breckenridge quoted in "Actress Denied Share of X-Rated Movie's Profits," *Los Angeles Times,* 11/6/75.

"Planned the divorce like he was Hitler," "Edy Williams' Dirty Divorce," author unknown, *Modern People,* 1/4/76.

"My Sir Galahad," Edy Williams to John Stark and Michael Alexander, "Famous for Her Nude Romps in the World's Pools, Edy Williams Tries to Make One More Splash," *People,* vol. 26, no. 26, 6/29/87.

"Intercontinental starlet," Roger Ebert quoted in ibid.

"I got typecast . . . really furious," ibid.

"The scene reveals . . . liver spots," Luke Ford, lukeford.com.

"The rest of my life . . . about to change," RM to Norman Dresser, "Things Mostly Big and Busty in Russ Meyer's Standards," *The Blade,* 7/19/79.

"I love the roar . . . dig the iron," Raven de la Croix to Lobo, Raven de la Croix profile, title unknown, *Iron Horse,* date unknown.

"I don't care for faggots," RM to David Ansen, "Russ Meyer: Auteur of Sleaze," 7/30/75.

Martin Bormann quote: "Meyer Fakes Quote," *Variety,* no. 285, 1/12/77.

Another curious fact about *Supervixens:* Meyer claimed in a number of interviews that Roger Ebert had "a piece of the film" ("Proud of His Escapism," Jack Garner, *Democrat and Chronicle*, 7/17/79). In an e-mail to the author, Ebert stated he received no profits from *Supervixens*.

14. The Ultra-Vixen

JM interviews: Kitten Natividad, Kevin Thomas, John Waters, Les Barnum, Ted Mahar, Haji, Charles Sumners, Floyce Sumners, Bruce Pasternack, Roger Ebert, Richard Heffner, Ivy Bethune, Fred Beiersdorf, Richard Brummer, Lavelle Robey, John Furlong, Renee Daalder, Steve Jones, Jim Ryan, Dave Prowse, Charles Napier.

Background on Kitten Natividad: Steve Sullivan, "Kitten Natividad: Russ Meyer's Most Bodacious Babe," *Glamour Girls Then and Now*, no. 11, 4–5/86, 8/17/90.

"I don't need . . . lonely old man," RM to Mike Henderson, "A Conversation with the King of Hard Core," *Seattle Post-Intelligencer*, 6/21/77.

"I have a metal cast . . . made it," Kitten Natividad to Jessica Berens, "Return of the Ultravixens," *The Observer*, 7/22/01.

"Offering no resistance, the pneumatic Natividad went quietly with officers," Sue Iggulden, "Porno Star 'Kitten' X-pelled from Campus," *Portland State University Vanguard*, vol. 54, no. 56, 4/27/79.

"Kitten gave out nude photos . . . as if he were Cecil B. DeMille," John Waters, *Shock Value*.

"As she squealed, 'Ohhhhhhh, Russ!' " ibid.

Background on Kitten Natividad: "Kitten Natividad: Russ Meyer's Most Bodacious Babe," *Glamour Girls Then and Now*, no. 11, 4–5/86.

Kitten meets RM: *ACB/RM*.

"He has a sexy face, sort of perverted," Kitten Natividad to Leigh Weimers, "Meyer's Living His Fantasy as King of Porn Producers," *San Jose Mercury-News*, 3/10/77.

"I have a father complex thing," Kitten Natividad to Bob Hicks, "For King of the Soft Cores, It's Lust and Profit," *Oregon Journal*, 4/26/79.

"Because I mother him," Kitten Natividad to Maggie White, "The King of the Nudies," *Downtowner*, no. 31, 4/30/79.

"You can get them for $1,200 . . . droop," Kitten Natividad to Bob Porter, "Russ Meyer: He's the Father of Mainstream Movie Nudity," *Dallas Times Herald*, 3/19/79.

RM on censor problems involving Natividad's pubic hair: Dan Scapperotti, "50s Legend Russ Meyer," *Femme Fatales*, vol. 6, no. 10/11, 4/98.

"Kitten Natividad was the champion, without a doubt," RM to Michael Holden, "Russ Meyer," *Loaded*, no. 4, 1994 (UK).

"World of beautiful people, driving terrible cars and living in squalor . . . all over-sexed," RM to Kent Beyda, "Russ Meyer," Search and Destroy, no. 10, 1978.

"You got your night . . . Ebert," Charles Napier as quoted by RM, Jonathan Ross interview, "Russ Meyer at the NFT," *The Very Breast of Russ Meyer.*

"I wanted a symphony . . . crickets," RM to William Kogut, "Hitting Them over the Head with a Sledgehammer: Russ Meyer Exposes Himself," *Oregon Daily Emerald*, 10/4/79.

"Russ Meyer's films were funny . . . juvenile," Gene Siskel, "Meyer's 'Ultra Vixens' Goes Beyond the Valley of the Shadow of Boredom," *Chicago Tribune*, 9/6/79.

"It may be that Meyer . . . with Vixen," Tony Rayns, "Beneath the Valley of the Ul-travixens," *Monthly Film Bulletin*, vol. 47, no. 552, 1/80.

"Strangely unsatisfying," Dave Kehr, "Only the Style Survives," *Reader: Chicago's Free Weekly*, vol. 8, no. 48, 8/31/79.

"with her big . . . Howdy Doody," ibid.

"It's one thing to stylize . . . more to lose," ibid.

"Last few films frantically seek to top themselves," Myron Meisel, "Over, Around, Through and Beyond the Valley of the Super-Meyers," *Reader: Los Angeles Weekly*, vol. 1, no. 24, 4/13/79.

"After a certain point . . . any more," Kehr, "Only the Style Survives."

"I'm not a sensitive person," RM to Kristi Turnquist, "Russ Meyer: Porno Potentate and Proud of It," *Willamette Valley Observer*, 9/28/79.

"If I wasn't so into tits . . . great filmmaker," RM to Jeff Berry, "Bosom Buddies: Russ and Roger in a Trip Down Mammary Lane," *UCLA Daily Bruin*, 10/5/78.

"This is precisely Meyer's limitation . . . just a goof," David Ansen, "Russ Meyer: Auteur of Sleaze," *The Real Paper*, vol. 4, no. 30, 7/30/75.

"He's a genius . . . in this business," Kitten Natividad to unknown author, "The Ultra-Ultra Girls," *Oui*, vol. 6, no. 12, 12/77.

"The epitome of American fascism," Malcom McLaren quoted by Gary Sperazza (quote originally appeared in *Slash*, date unknown), "Shooting the Sex Pistols: Who Killed the Movie?" *Bomp!* 10–11/78.

"McLaren was sincere . . . in his eyes," RM to Lowry and Black, "Russ Meyer Interviewed."

"A statement of anarchic revolt against the rock millionaires, and the whole British establishment," Roger Ebert, "Anarchy in the U.K.: My Life with Sid Vicious," *Chicago Sun-Times*, 11/2/86.

"A combination of *A Hard Day's Night* and *Beyond the Valley of the Dolls*," RM to Raj Bahadur, "Russ Meyer Revisited," *Scene Update*, 10/23–29, 1980.

"A little nonplussed . . . true to life," Roger Ebert, "Russ Meyer: Ten Years After Beyond," *Film Comment*, vol. 16, no. 4, 8/80.

"After I met Russ Meyer . . . senile old git," John Lydon with Keith and Kent Zimmerman, *Rotten: No Irish, No Blacks, No Dogs*, St. Martin's Press, 1994.

"He was proud . . . run the other way," RM to Scott Morrow, "Adventures in the Skin Trade," *Los Angeles Weekly*, vol. 10, no. 3, 12/11–17/87.

"Rotten definitely had charisma," RM to Cameron Mackay, "The Pneumatic World of Russ Meyer," *Penthouse* (UK edition), 2/81.

"Still be alive," RM to Rose Raidt, "I Couldn't Survive on the Raincoat Brigade," *Up the Creek*, vol. 1, no. 32, 8/17/79.

"Two six-packs of beer and a big can of pork and beans," Roger Ebert, "Anarchy in the U.K.: My Life with Sid Vicious."

Meyer on National Front threats: Harvey Fenton, "Thanks for the Mammaries: Russ Meyer," *Flesh & Blood Compendium*.

"The group broke up largely because of that film," Julien Temple to Todd McCarthy, " 'Rock 'n' Roll Swindle' Emerges as an Early Success at Filmex," *Variety*, vol. 187, no. 2, 3/7/80.

"Names like Wopping . . . that conjured up sexual connotations," Malcolm McLaren in 1988 Jonathan Ross RM documentary (see Filmography).

"Reams of contracts . . . changing his mind," Sandy Lieberson to Craig Bromberg, *The Wicked Ways of Malcolm McLaren*, Harper & Row, 1989.

"What a tragedy . . . a screamer!" RM to Anne Billson, "The mammary millionaire," *Sunday Times Magazine*, 9/13/92 (UK).

"Personally shot a deer with a pistol," Todd McCarthy, " 'Rock 'n' Roll Swindle' Emerges as an Early Success at Filmex," *Daily Variety*, vol. 187, no. 2 3/7/80.

Julien Temple apology: *Screen International*, no. 344, 5/22/82.

"That experience . . . get away from it," RM to Dale Ashmun, "Mondo Russo: Russ Meyer Interview," *Film Threat*, no. 15, 1988.

"The rating board is our censor board . . . won't take advertising," RM to Doug Balding, "Outside of Hollywood," *Arete*, vol. 2, no. 1, 7–8/89.

"To keep the studios . . . business," RM to Jon Lewis, *Hollywood v. Hard Core*.

"It had a bad connotation because of the hardcore people," RM to Beth Accomando, "Russ Meyer: Hellcats for a Modern World," *Hypno*, vol. 4, issue 5, 1995.

"The exhibiting game . . . half a million dollars," RM to Doug Balding, "Outside of Hollywood," *Arete*, vol. 2, no. 1, 7–8/89.

"The days of Vixen are gone," RM to Steve Fugett, Pat Holmes, Douglas "DK" Holm, "Interview with Russ Meyer," *Cinemonkey*, Spring 1979.

"We fight . . . seems to work," Kitten Natividad to Bill Jones, "King Leer of Movies Retains Softcore Throne," *Phoenix Gazette*, 12/8/79.

"I'm glad . . . head off," Kitten Natividad to Bob Hicks, "For King of the Soft Cores, It's Lust and Profit," *Oregon Journal*, 4/26/79 989.

15. Mondo Meyer

JM interviews: Paul Fishbein, Roger Ebert, Garth Pillsbury, Jacqueline Mayo, David Friedman, Kitten Natividad, "Colonel" Rob Shaffner, Dave Ewing, Brent Bowman, Gary Adelman, Haji, Fred Beiersdorf, Jim Ryan, John Waters, David K. Frasier, John McCormick, Paula Parker, Bill Margold, Jane Hower.

"They must be cantilevered . . . buckle at the knees," RM to Nathan Rabin, 1995 interview, *The Tenacity of the Cockroach*.

"Dozens and dozens . . . the California sun," Louis Black, "Faster, Pussycat! Kill! Kill! Staying Abreast With Russ Meyer," *Austin Chronicle*, 6/9/95.

"Like an old hot rod . . . American Classic," Alan Platt, "Uncle Dirty" *Soho Weekly News*, 5/24/79.

"I don't care about . . . the urge," RM to Mike Snider, "Good Morning and Goodbye to Russ Meyer," *Bang!* 1988.

"Going to swell my ego even more," RM to Diana Loevy, "Son of Beyond the Valley of the Dolls," *Home Video*, vol. 2, no. 6, 5/81.

"Russ Meyer invented . . . twenty-five years ago," Roger Ebert, " 'Wild at Heart' Is Full of Woe," *Chicago Sun-Times*, 5/27/90.

"The film is unrelenting . . . you nightmares," RM to Paul Sherman, "Some of My Breast Kept Secrets: An Interview with Russ Meyer," *Filmfax*, no. 28, 8–9/91.

"You've heard of *Berlin Alexanderplatz?* Well, this is *Meyerplatz,*" RM to Lee Server, "Russ Meyer," *Genesis*, 1985, exact date/issue unknown.

"In a very abstract . . . tough shit," RM to Dale Ashmun, "Mondo Russo: Russ Meyer Interview," *Film Threat*, no. 15, 1988.

"It's a tone poem," RM to Sherman, "Some of My Breast Kept Secrets: An Interview with Russ Meyer."

"It will be my song," RM to Ashmun, "Mondo Russo: Russ Meyer Interview."

"All the others obsolete," RM to Jan Golab, "Return from Beyond the Valley of the Dolls," *Los Angeles*, vol. 31, no. 12, 12/86.

"We are going to be intimate . . . the deal," RM to Ron Chepesiuk, RM to Ron Chepesiuk, "Hollywood or Bust," *Gallery*, 3/91.

"With all his makeup . . . the Catskills," RM to Patrick Goldstein, "Into the Valley of the Video Vixens," *Los Angeles Times Calendar*, 8/23/87.

Waters Polaroid: Veronica Vera, "Veronica Vera's New York," *Adam*, vol. 31, no. 12, date unknown.

"Libelous," RM to Richard Von Busack, "The Breast of the Story," Metro section, *Santa Clara Valley Weekly*, 3/22–28/90.

"Fuck and tell book," RM to Cynthia Littlejohn, "The Legendary Russ Meyer: Thanks for the Mammaries," *BAM*, no. 479, 3/8/96.

"The most important . . . purged myself," RM to Jan Golab, "Return from Beyond the Valley of the Dolls," *Los Angeles*, vol. 31, no. 12, 12/86.

16. Janice and the Handyman

JM interviews: David K. Frasier. Eleanor Bucci, MM sister, Jane Hower, Delores Fox, Richard Brummer, Charles Napier, Jim Ryan, Roger Ebert, John Mc-Cormick, George King Carll, Larry Christiani, Morgan "Tex" Hagen, Pandora Peaks, Letha Weapons, Charlie Sumners, Floyce Sumners, Kitten Natividad, Mike Thomas, Haji, Raven De La Croix, Michael Ziton, "Colonel" Rob Schaffner, George Costello, Paula Parker, Jean-Pierre Jackson, Erica Gavin, Tura Satana, Lori Williams, John Waters, Chris Schaffner. Janice Cowart and Julio Dottavio responded to my questions via e-mail on March 1, 2005. Cowart was compelled to note that she felt only three of Meyer's actresses were accurate sources, as "many of the 'girls' make things up to gain attention and have a tendency to embellish the facts. I would have to say this is not true of Lori Williams, Uschi Digard, and Rena Horton [*sic*], who seem to actually be fair and honest when speaking about Russ."

"I am chauvinistic . . . the film game," RM to David Frasier, *DFA*.

Opening description of battered RM: Paul Fishburn testimony.

"She was emitting an odor . . . slightly slurred," Officer Eric Miller testimony, p. 155.

"Wobble to her walk," ibid.

"She was frightened . . . arrest me,' " Donna Fishburn testimony, p. 105.

"She was greedy for penis, very greedy," RM to Michael Holden, "Russ Meyer," *Loaded*, no. 4, 1994.

"You can dig . . . foreign substance," Cory Turczyn, "T&A Q&A," Pop Cult Internet interview, 2002 (interview done 1995).

"To get some sort of heir . . . bless her soul," RM to Arv Miller, "Russ Meyer: Between the Valleys of My Ultravixens," Part Three, *Fling*, vol. 32, no. 2, issue 161, 9/90.

"It was totally unmanageable . . . it," RM to Richard von Busack, "The Breast of the Story," Metro section, *Santa Clara Valley Weekly*, vol. 6, no. 3, 3/22–28/1990.

"I turn to God . . . who need help." RM to Philip Thomas, "Russ Meyer: How Much Is a Pint of Milk?" *Empire*, no. 70, 4/95.

"I don't care for it . . . shithouse," RM, *Playboy's Voluptuous Vixens* (see Filmography).

"If you're going to do . . . a limo," RM to John McCormick, "Sex-Crazed Cinema: Five Hours with Russ Meyer," *Crave,* 9/15/99.

Much information for this chapter was gleaned from court testimony, specifically, *The People of the State of California vs. Debra Angela Masson,* # 9HL017715, 7/20–22/99.

"A loaded gun by a cool drink," lawyer Karine T. Philips during Debra Angela Masson testimony, vol II, p. 268.

"One time I went to get my shoe from under the bed, I pulled a gun out. It went off this close to my head," Debra Angela Masson testimony, vol II, p. 268.

"Melissa shot this hole through the wall in a fit of rage," lawyer Karine T. Philips quoting MM's wall grafitti during Debra Angela Masson testimony, vol II, p. 268.

"She [Mounds] was upset . . . with a rock," Janice Cowart testimony, 7/22/99, pp. 18, 21.

Cowart on length of time with Meyer: 7/20–21/99, p. 45: "I've worked for him ten years."

"Living in the office atmosphere all the time, nothing is private. We weren't getting along," Debra Angela Masson testimony, p. 200.

"And when Janice came we discussed it with her. There were no problems," ibid.

"There was ongoing arguing pretty much the whole day," Jesse Bryner testimony, p. 31, 7/22/99.

"He seemed somewhat intimidated and fearful," Janice Cowart testimony, 7/20–21/99, vol I, p. 51.

"Smelled like alcohol," ibid., p. 54.

"She was very agitated . . . have to give her money . . ." ibid., p. 51.

"She was saying her life was going nowhere," ibid., p. 54.

"She started to berate . . . he was pathetic," ibid., p. 55.

"I thought she was going to hit me," ibid., p. 56.

"She was just sort of saying . . . the way it is,' " ibid., p. 61.

"Russ was missing and I was worried . . . he took off down the street," Debra Angela Masson testimony, pp. 241–242.

"I asked him to please lay off the gin," ibid., p. 205.

"He got a beer . . . spike it up," ibid., p. 205.

"He doesn't like . . . whatever I want,' " ibid., p. 206.

"He pushed me . . . hit him once," ibid., pp. 207–213.

"I did not belittle . . . that to him," Debra Angela Masson (Melissa Mounds) testimony, 7/22/99, p. 48.

"Well, it's a natural feeling on the part of people that don't have as much money, they'd like to get some," Russ Meyer testimony, p. 38.

"I can recall . . . felt severely injured . . ." ibid., p. 8.

"I was being struck . . . a strong woman," ibid., p. 15.

"He gets confused. He doesn't know what day it is . . ." Janice Cowart testimony, p. 46.

"He doesn't like to address it," ibid., p. 47.

"She has manipulating . . . coaching him," Debra Angela Masson testimony, p. 223.

"She has been a very close confidante and honest lady," Russ Meyer testimony, p. 25.

"Probably as a direct result," Janice Cowart testimony, p. 92.

June 19, 2000, conservatorship: Russell A. Meyer Conservatorship, Case BP 062075, Superior Court of California.

"These films are my legacy, they are my children," RM to Veronica Vera, "Veronica Vera's New York," *Adam,* vol. 31, no. 12, circa 1980s (March 3, 2003, Dottavio e-mail: confidential source).

Faster, Pussycat! Kill! Kill! $500 screening: Janice Cowart.

DVD complaints: numerous online posts at the Mobius Home Video forum.

Meyer Keating quote epitaph: countless interviews, also *The Incredibly Strange Film Book,* Jonathan Ross.

"Everybody gets off . . . satisfied," "a treadmill . . . in futility," Howard Hampton, "The Green Door in the Floor," *Village Voice,* 3/21/05.

"Sex today . . . little profit centers," Erica Jong to Laura M. Holson, "The Long View on 'Deep Throat,' " *New York Times,* 9/5/04.

Tarantino on FPKK screenplay, "Screenwriters Are (Obsessive, Creative, Neurotic) People, Too," Lynn Hirschberg, *New York Times Sunday Magazine,* 11/9/03.

"Give up five years of my life," Quentin Tarantino to Mary Kaye Schilling, "The Second Coming," *Entertainment Weekly,* 4/24/01.

"For a while, he was . . . we all want," Gene Mustain and Jerry Capeci, *Mob Star: The Story of John Gotti,* Alpha/Penguin, 2002.

Epilogue: Smell of Female

The Friend is actually a composite of two of RM's friends, both of whom shall remain nameless.

Filmography

Many thanks to Dave Frasier's astute research. Running times are approximations as I haven't checked them against the films.

The central way to obtain DVD/VHS Russ Meyer product is from RM Films, International at http://www.rmfilms.com. Or write to RM Films, PO Box 3748, Hollywood, CA, 90078. Buying from RM Films is not cheap: DVDs run $39.95, VHS $59.95. They don't accept credit cards. Some discount DVD houses (easy to search out via the Internet) offer RM product at better prices.

Nearly all of Meyer femme fatales have websites that can be easily searched out: Kitten Natividad, Haji, Tura Satana, Erica Gavin, Raven De La Croix, Pandora Peaks among them. Tell 'em Jimmy sent you.

166th Training Films

Bivouac in the Ozarks, 1944. Meyer shot this 16 mm training film; there may be others.

Industrial Films

During the late forties and early to mid-fifties, Meyer worked for the industrial film outfit Gene Walker Films. Two titles he contributed to were Southern Pacific's *This Is My Railroad* and Standard Oil's *Safe Every Second!* Meyer has also mentioned working on the films *How to Be a Proper Salesman* and *Dipstick*.

During the mid- to late fifties Meyer also churned out numerous loops of his then-wife Eve (distributed in the 8 mm format and sold by mail order) strutting around in skimpy outfits, but never fully topless. These turn up on Internet auctions from time to time. In 1953 RM shot some never-released 16 mm footage of a rape scenario starring Eve and Franklin Bolger that Meyer considered a predecessor of 1964's *Lorna.*

The French Peep Show (approx. 1952) Producer: Pete DeCenzie. Director, cinematographer: Russ Meyer. Sound, editor: Carl G. Sheldon (Chuck Schelling). Starring: Tempest Storm, "Torrid" Terry Lane, Suzy, Tangerine, Shalimar, Marie Voe, Lilly La Mont, Roberta, Chester P. Floodback III, Ginger Du Val, Yvonne DeCenzie, the El Rey Girls. Out of circulation since theatrical release. Presumed lost.

The Desperate Women (approx. 1954–55) Produced by Samuel Newman, Lou Appleton. Director: Louis Appleton, Screenplay: Samuel Newman. Cinematographer: Russ Meyer. Editor: Albert Shaff. Music: Melvin Lenard. Cast: Anne Appleton, Douglas Howard, Virgina Leon, Eve Meyer. Out of circulation since theatrical release. An "educational" book was sold during the picture's run entitled *Sex: Happiness or Tragedy?*

The Immoral Mr. Teas (1959), aka *Mr. Teas and his Playthings* (UK) aka *L'immoral M. Teas* (Canada).* A Pad-Ram Enterprises release. Producer: Pete DeCenzie. Director, cinematography, screenplay, editor: Russ Meyer. Narration and music: Edward Lasko. Narrator (uncredited): Irving Blum. Assistant editor (uncredited): Igo Kantor. Assistant editor: John F. Link. Assistant director: Ken Parker. Cast: W. Ellis (Bill) Teas, Marilyn Wesley, Ann Peters, Michele Roberts, Dawn Danielle, June Wilkinson, Pete DeCenzie, Eric "Mick" Nathanson, Don Couch, Earl Leaf, Russ Meyer. Color, 63 min. Available on VHS from RM Films.

Short: *This Is My Body* (1959). Ten-minute short starring Diane Webber. Narration written by Mick Nathanson. Out of circulation since theatrical release.

Note: Meyer may have shot footage for *Operation Dames*, a low-budget 1959 war picture directed by Lou Stoumen and starring Eve Meyer. The fabulous production cheesecake stills of Eve done for the movie must've been taken by Meyer.

---

* Various authors have erroneously listed an early-sixties picture called *Steam Heat* either as an alternate title for *Teas* or as a "lost" Meyer film. RM had nothing to do with *Steam Heat*, which I believe was alternately known as *Mr. Teas' Magic Spectacles*. Little is known about the picture other than the fact Bill Teas starred in it (along with Brandy Long and one Enrico Banducci) and at some point Pete DeCenzie distributed it. The pressbook lists no production credits.

Eve and the Handyman (1960), aka *Eve et Son Homme a Tout Faire* (Canada). An Eve Productions release. Producer, director, cinematography, screenplay, editor: Russ Meyer. Art director: Mel Fowler. Narration: Lee Merrin. Costumes by Herberte. Cast: Eve Meyer, Anthony James Ryan, Frank Bolger, Florence Moore, Francesca Leslie, Jackie Stephens, Mildred Knezevich, Iris Bristol, Gigi Frost, Rita Day, Lyle Tolefson, Charles Vaughn, James Evanoff, Ken Parker. Color, 65 min. Available on VHS from RM Films.

Short: *The Naked Camera* (1960). A ten-minute color short directed, written, and shot by Meyer, and starring Mikki France. Co-feature of *Eve and the Handyman.*

Erotica (1961), aka *Eroticon.* A Pad-Ram Enterprises release. Producers: Pete DeCenzie and Russ Meyer. Director, cinematography, screenplay, editor: Russ Meyer. Narration written by Jack Moran. Narrator: Joe Cranston. Music: David Chudnow, Tommy Morgan. Cast: Donna Townsend, Peggy Martin, Sherry Knight, Werner Otto Kirsch, Charles G. Schelling, Pete DeCenzie, Althea Currier, Lana Young, Denise Daniels, Elaine Jones, Russ Meyer. This film is comprised of six segments, titled "Naked Innocence," "Beauties, Bubbles, and H_2O," "The Bear and the Bare," "Nudists on the High Seas," "The Nymphs," and "The Bikini Busters." Color, 65–68 min. Out of circulation since theatrical release.

Wild Gals of the Naked West (1962), aka *The Immoral West — and How It Was Lost* aka *The Naked West — and How It Was Lost,* aka *The Immoral West,* aka *The Immoral Girls of the Naked West,* aka *Naked Gals of the Golden West.* A Pad-Ram Enterprises release, distributed by Films Pacifica, Inc. Producers: Pete DeCenzie and Russ Meyer. Director, cinematography, editor: Russ Meyer. Screenplay by Jack Moran. Music: Marlin Skiles. Art director: Mel Fowler. Cast: Sammy Gilbert, Julie Williams, Jack Moran, Teri Taylor (aka Goldie Nuggets), Donna Scott (aka Donna X), Frank Bolger, Ken Parker, Anthony James Ryan, Pete DeCenzie, Paul Fox, Princess Livingston, Charles G. Schelling, Topanga Gulch Players, Russ Meyer. Color, 62 min. Available on VHS from RM Films.

Heavenly Bodies (1963), aka *Heavenly Assignment.* An Eve Productions release. Producer, director, cinematography, screenplay, editor: Russ Meyer. Cast: Ken Parker, Gaby Martine, Marian Milford, Don Cochran,

Werner Otto Kirsch, Fred Owens, Billy Newhouse, Orville Hallberg, Bill Cummings, Althea Currier, Monica Liljistrand, Yvonne Cortell, Paulette Firestone, Maria Andre, Princess Livingston, F. E. Falconer, Robert J. Ewald, William Knowles, Rochelle Kennedy, Charles Schelling, Nancy Andre, Don Goodwin, Ivana Nolte, Amber Morgan, Binkie Stewart, Russ Meyer. Color, 62 min. Out of circulation since theatrical release.

Short: *Skyscrapers and Brassieres* (1963). A ten-minute color short directed, written, and shot by Meyer, and featuring Rochelle Kennedy. Co-feature of *Heavenly Bodies*. Out of circulation since theatrical release.

Europe in the Raw! (1963). An Eve Productions release. Producer, director, cinematography, screenplay, editor: Russ Meyer. Narrators: Franklin L. Thistle, Vic Perrin, Lynn Held. Cast: Denise Du Vall, Heidi Richter, Yvette Le Grand, Greta Thorwald, Abundavita, Gigi La Touche, Veronique Gabriel, Fred Owens. Color, 72 min. Out of circulation since theatrical release.

Lorna (1964), aka *Lorna, L'incarnation du desir* (France), aka *Lorna-Zuviel fur Einen Mann* (Germany). An Eve Productions release. Producer, director, cinematography, editor: Russ Meyer. Associate producer: Eve Meyer. Screenplay: James Griffith. Original story: Russ Meyer. Sound: Charles G. Schelling. Gaffer: Bill Maley. Sound editor: Jim Nelson. Camera operator: Walter Schenk. Music uncredited. Music coordinators: Hal Hopper, James Griffith. Dialog director: James Griffith. Production manager: Fred Owens. The song "Lorna" written by Hal Hopper, sung by Bob Grabeau. Cast: Lorna Maitland, Mark Bradley, James Rucker, Hal Hopper, Doc Scortt, James Griffith, Althea Currier, F. Rufus Owens, Frank Bolger, Kenneth H. Parker. B/W, 79 min. Available on DVD/VHS from RM Films.

Fanny Hill: Memoirs of a Woman of Pleasure (1964). A Favorite Films release of Famous Players Corporation/CCC Filmkunst GMBH production. Producer: Albert Zugsmith. Director: Russ Meyer. Screenplay by Robert Hill from the John Cleland novel. Director of photography: Heinz Hilscher. Assistant director: Elfie Tillack. Editor: Alfred Srp. Music: Erwin Halletz. Cast: Miriam Hopkins, Letitia Roman, Walter Giller, Alex D'Arcy, Helmut Weiss, Chris Howland, Ulli Lommel, Cara Garnett, Karin Evans, Syra Marty, Albert Zugsmith, Christiane Schmidtmer, Heide Hansen, Erica/Veronica Ericson, Patricia Houston, Marshall

Raynor, Hilda Sessack, Billy Frick, Jürgen Nesbach, Herbert Knippen-
berg, Susanne Hsiao, Renate Hutte (aka Rena Horten), Ellen Velero.
B/W, 104 min. Meyer took his name off the picture for its initial theatrical release. Released in VHS by Paragon Video in the eighties; out of
print.

Mudhoney (1965), aka *Mudhoney . . . Leaves a Taste of Evil!*, aka *Rope
of Flesh*, aka *La Fille du ruisseau, Le Desir dans les tripes* (France), aka
Im Garten der Lust (Germany), aka *Esclave de ses passions* (Belgium). A
Delta Films release. Producers: Russ Meyer, George Costello. Director,
editor: Russ Meyer. Associate producer: Eve Meyer. Screenplay: Ray-
mond Friday Locke and William E. Sprague (from Locke's novel *Streets
Paved with Gold*). Assistant director: George Costello. Sound editor:
Charles G. Schelling. Cinematographer: Walter Schenk. Production
manager: Fred Owens. Gaffer: Bill Maley. Music: Henri Price (Andre
Brummer). Cast: Hal Hopper, Lorna Maitland, Antoinette Cristiani,
John Furlong, Stu Lancaster, Rena Horten, Princess Livingston, Sam
Hanna, Nick Wolcuff, Frank Bolger, Lee Ballard, Mickey Foxx, F. Rufus
Owens, Gil Haimson, William Maley, Wilfred Kues, Peter Cunningham,
Clarence Lowe, Donald Hansen, Milard Ferla, Bill Gunter, Russ Meyer.
B/W, 92 min. Available on DVD/VHS from RM Films.

Motorpsycho (1965), aka *Motor Mods and Rockers*, aka *Les Enrages de
la Moto* (Canada), aka *Le Gang sauvage* (Belgium), aka *Motor-
Psycho—wie Wilde Hengste* (Germany). Working title: *Rio Vengeance*.
An Eve Productions release. Producer, director, cinematography,
screenplay: Russ Meyer. Assosciate producer: Eve Meyer. Screenplay:
William E. Sprague. Original story: Russ Meyer, James Griffith, Hal
Hopper. Assistant director: George Costello. Production manager: Fred
Owens. Production assistant: Richard Brummer. Editor: Charles G.
Schelling. Music: Igo Kantor. Theme song: Paul Sawtell, Bert Shefter.
Sound: Carl G. Sheldon (aka Charles G. Schelling). Cast: Stephen
Oliver, Haji, Alex Rocco, Holle K. Winters, Joseph Cellini, Thomas Scott,
Coleman Francis, Sharon Lee, Steve Masters, Arshalouis Aivazian, F. Ru-
fus Owens, George Costello, Richard Brummer, Fred Owens, E. E.
(Russ) Meyer. B/W, 74 min. Available on VHS from RM Films.

Faster, Pussycat! Kill! Kill! (1966), aka *Pussycat*, aka *The Mankillers*
(UK), aka *Leather Girls* (UK), aka *Plus vite mes chattes, tuez! tuez!*
(Canada), *Die Satansweiber von Tittfield* (Germany). An Eve Produc-
tions release. Producers: Russ and Eve Meyer. Director, editor: Russ

Meyer. Associate producers: Fred Owens, George Costello. Screenplay: Jack Moran. Original story by Russ Meyer. Assistant director: George Costello. Cinematography: Walter Schenk. Second unit camera: William E. Tomko. Assistant cameraman: Gil Haimson. Sound: Charles Schelling. Sound editor: Richard Serly Brummer. Music coordination: Igor Kantor. Theme by Paul Sawtelle, Bert Shefter, and Rick Jarrard, performed by the Bostweeds. Opening narrator: John Furlong. Cast: Tura Satana, Haji, Lori Williams, Susan Bernard, Stuart Lancaster, Paul Trinka, Dennis Busch, Ray Barlow, Mickey Foxx, Russ Meyer. B/W, 84 min. Available on VHS from RM Films.

Mondo Topless (1966), aka *Mondo Girls,* aka *Mondo Top,* aka *La Fête du nu* (Belgium). An Eve Productions release. Producer, director, cinematographer, editor: Russ Meyer, Associate producer: Eve Meyer. Production assistants: Fred Owens, Bill Newhouse, Richard Serly Brummer. Sound mixer (uncredited): Don Minkler. Music performed by the Aladdins (uncredited). Cast: Babette Bardot, Sin Lenee, Diane Young, Donna X (Donna Scott), Pat Barringer, Darla Paris, Darlene Grey, Lorna Maitland, Veronique Gabriel, Greta Thorwald, Denise Duval, Gigi La Touche, Abundavita, Heidi Richter, Yvette Le Grand, John Furlong (narrator), Incorporates footage from *Europe in the Raw.* Color, 61 min. Available on DVD/VHS from RM Films.

Common-Law Cabin (1967), aka *How Much Loving Does a Normal Couple Need,* aka *Conjugal Cabin* (UK), aka *Cette soif d'amour* (Canada), aka *Combien de fois faut-il faire l'amour pour être un couple normal?* (France). An Eve Productions release. Producer, director, screenplay (uncredited), cinematographer (uncredited), editor: Russ Meyer. Producer: Eve Meyer. Screenplay: John E. Moran. Photography: Wady Medawar, Jack Lucas. Sound: Richard Serly Brummer, Irwin Cadden. Sound mixer: Don Minkler (uncredited). Music coordinator: Igo Kantor. Cast: Ken Swofford, Alaina Capri, Jack Moran, Adele Rein, Andrew Hagara, Frank Bolger, Babette Bardot, John Furlong, George Costello. Color, 70 min. Available on VHS from RM Films.

Good Morning . . . and Goodbye! (1967), aka *The Lust Seekers* (UK), aka *Bonjour et adieu* (Canada), aka *Bonjour et au revoir* (Belgium). An Eve Productions release. Producer, director, cinematographer: Russ Meyer. Associate producer: Eve Meyer. Screenplay: John E. Moran. Assistant director: George Costello. Cameraman: Fred Owens. Editors: Russ Meyer, Richard Serly Brummer. Assistant cameramen: Jack Lucas,

Wady Medawar. Sound: Richard Brummer and John E. Moran. Music co-ordinator: Igo Kantor. Narrator: Joe Perrin. Costumes by Herberte. Cast: Alaina Capri, Stuart Lancaster, Patrick Wright, Haji, Karen Ciral, Don Johnson, Tom Howland, Megan Timothy, Toby Adler, Sylvia Tedemar, Carol Peters. Color, 78min. Available on VHS from RM Films.

Finders Keepers, Lovers Weepers! (1968), aka *Null Null Sex* (Australia), aka *Qui s'y frotte s'y pique* (Canada), aka *Viltar Astridur* (Spain). An Eve Productions release. Producer, director, cinematographer, editor: Russ Meyer. Executive producer: Eve Meyer. Associate producer: Anthony James Ryan. Associate director: George Costello. Screenplay: Richard Zachary (aka Rick Husky). Original story: Russ Meyer. Editor and sound: Richard Serly Brummer. Camera operator: Wady Medawar. Music coor-dinator: Igo Kantor. Theme by Melvin Elling with the Casuals on the Square. Costumes by Herberte. Cast: Anne Chapman, Paul Lockwood, Gordon Wescourt, Duncan McLeod, Robert Rudelson, Lavelle Roby, Jan Sinclair, Joey DuPrez, Nick Wolcuff, Pam Collins, Michelle Roberts, Vicki Richards, George K. Carll, Barney Caliendo, Louis Innerarity, Robert Pergament, Walter Cummings, Orville Hallberg, George Cole, Robert Massaroli, Harvey Pergament, Robert Mumm, Anthony James Ryan, John Furlong, Russ Meyer. Color, 73 min. Available on VHS from RM Films.

Vixen! (1968), aka *Russ Meyer's Vixen*, aka *Vixen la Renarde* (Canada), aka *Ohne Gnade, Schatzen* (Germany). An Eve Production presented by Coldstream Films. Producer, director, cinematography, editor: Russ Meyer. Associate producers: Eve Meyer, Anthony James Ryan, Richard Serly Brummer, George Costello. Assistant director: George Costello. Screenplay: Robert Rudelson. Original story: Russ Meyer, Anthony James Ryan. Editor: Richard Serly Brummer. Assistant cameramen: An-thony James Ryan, John Koester (uncredited). Editor and sound: Richard Serly Brummer. Sound mixer: Don Minkler (uncredited). Mu-sic coordinators: Igo Kantor, William Loose. Narrator: Vic Perrin. Cast: Erica Gavin, Harrison Page, Garth Pillsbury, Michael O'Donnell, Vincene Wallace, Robert Aiken, Jon Evans, Peter Carpenter, Jackie Ill-man, John Furlong, Jim Ryan, George Costello, Russ Meyer. Color, 71 min. Rated X. Available on DVD/VHS from RM Films.

Cherry, Harry, and Raquel! (1969), aka *Russ Meyer's Cherry, Harry, and Raquel*, aka *Three Ways to Love* (UK), aka *Les Stimulatrices* (France), aka *Menage a Trois* (France). Presented by Eve Productions and Pana-mint Films. Producer, director, cinematographer, editor: Russ Meyer.

Assistant producers: Eve Meyer, Anthony James Ryan, Thomas J. McGowan. Screenwriters: Tom Wolfe (aka Thomas J. McGowan). Original story: Russ Meyer. Editor: Richard Serly Brummer. Assitant editor: Robert Pergament. Sound: Richard Brummer. Assistant camera: John Koester. Music: William Loose. Music coordinator: Igo Kantor. Theme by Byron Cole, James East, and Stu Phillips, performed by the Jacks and Balls. Cast: Larissa Ely, Linda Ashton, Charles Napier, Bert Santos, Franklin H. Bolger, Astrid Lillimor (aka Uschi Digard), Michele Grand, John Milo, Robert Aiken, Michaelani, John Koester, Daniel Roberts, Russ Meyer. Color, 71 min. Available on DVD/VHS from RM Films.

Beyond the Valley of the Dolls (1970), aka *La Vallée des plaisirs* (France), aka *Hollywood Vixens* (France), aka *Orgissimo* (France), aka *La Vallée des débauches* (Belgium), aka *Blumen Ohne Duft* (Germany), aka *Lungo la valle delle bambole* (Italy). A Twentieth Century Fox release. Producer, director, screenwriter, editor (uncredited): Russ Meyer. Assistant producers: Red Hershon, Eve Meyer. Assistant directors: David Hall, C. E. Dismukes. Screenwriter: Roger Ebert. Uncredited additional script work: Manny Diez. Director of photography: Fred J. Koenekamp. Editors: Dann Cahn, Dick Wormel. Sound: Richard Overton, Don Minkler. Music: Stu Phillips, Igor Kantor, William Loose. Songs performed by Lynn Carey, the Strawberry Alarm Clock, the Sandpipers. Art directors: Jack Martin Smith, Arthur Lonergan. Set directors: Walter M. Scott, Stuart A. Reiss. Cast: Dolly Read, Cynthia Meyers, Marcia McBroom, John LaZar, Michael Blodgett, David Gurian, Edy Williams, Erica Gavin, Phyllis Davis, Harrison Page, Duncan McLeod, Lavelle Roby, Jim Iglehart, Charles Napier, Henry Rowland, Haji, Pam Grier, Garth Pillsbury, Princess Livingston, Veronica Erickson, Stan Ross, Angel Ray, Karen Smith, Sebastian Brock, Bruce V. McBroom, Ian Sander, Koko Tani, Samantha Scott, Tea Crawford, Heath Jobes, John Logan, Susan Reed, Robin Bach, Ceil Cabot, Mary Carroll, Joseph Cellini, Jackie Cole, Cissy Colpitts, Frank Corsentino, Mibb Curry, Coleman Francis, Charles Fox, T. J. Halligan, Rick Holmes, Marshall Kent, Michael Kriss, Tim Laurie, Bebe Louie, Lillian Martin, Ashley Phillips, "Big Jack" Provan, Joyce Rees, Chris Riordian, Bert Santos, George Stratton. Color, 109 min. Rated X. Currently unavailable on DVD in the United States. Released in pan and scan versions by Magnetic Video in 1980 and Fox in 1993. A special edition for which Roger Ebert has already recorded a commentary is said to be imminent, as of 2005. Available in several other countries on DVD.

The Seven Minutes (1971), aka *7 minuti che contano* (Italy), *Los siete minutos* (Mexico). A Twentieth Century Fox release. Producer, director: Russ Meyer. Associate producers: Red Hershon, Eve Meyer. Assistant director: David Hall. Screenwriter: Richard Warren Lewis. Based upon the Irving Wallace novel. Director of photography: Fred "Fritz" Mandl. Camera operator: Orville Hallburg. Editor: Dick Wormel. Sound: Don J. Bassman, Theodore Soderberg. Music: Stu Phillips. Songs by B. B. King, Don Reed, Merryweather and Carey. Art director: Rodger Maus. Set Directors: Walter M. Scott, Raphael Bretton. Cast: Wayne Maunder, Marianne McAndrew, Philip Carey, Jay C. Flippen, Edy Williams, Lyle Bettger, Jackie Gayle, Ron Randell, Charles Drake, John Carradine, Harold J. Stone, John Sarno, Billy Durkin, Robert Moloney, Berry Kroeger, Olan Soule, Stanley Adams, Tom Selleck, Alex D'Arcy, David Brian, Yvonne De Carlo, James Iglehart, Stanley Adams, Yvonne D'Angers, Jan Shutan, Berry Kroeger, Ralph Story, Charles Napier, Kay Peters, Richard Angarola, Shawn "Baby Doll" Devereaux, Regis J. Cordic, John Lawrence, Mora Gray, Stu Lancaster, Henry Rowland, Barry Coe, Calvin Bartlett, Wolfman Jack, Ken Jones, Bill Baldwin, Vince Williams, Robin Hughes, Jim Bacon, John Gruber, Chris Marks, Peter Shrayder, Lynn Hamilton, Patrick Wright, Lillian Lehman, Judy Baldwin, Paul Stader, George De Normand, Jeffrey Sayre, Barry Coe, Russ Meyer. Color, 115 min. Rated R. Out of circulation since theatrical release. Has been broadcast on TV in both uncut and cut versions: fairly easy to find via the Internet.

Blacksnake (1973), aka *Dutchess of Doom,* aka *Sweet Suzy,* aka *Slaves* (UK), aka *Le Serpent noir* (France), aka *Carne cruda* (Italy), *La serpiente negre* (Mexico). Presented by Trident Films. Producer, director, screenplay, second unit cinematography: Russ Meyer. Associate producer: Anthony James Ryan. Screenplay: Len Neubauer. Original story: Russ Meyer, Anthony James Ryan, based upon a script by Manny Diez, *The White Witch of Rose Hall* (uncredited). Director of photography: Arthur Ornitz. Production manager: Fred Owens. Editor: Fred Baratta, A.C.E. Art direction: Rick Heatherly. Sound: Richard Serly Brummer. Music: William Loose. Cast: Anouska Hempel, David Warbeck, Percy Herbert, Milton McCollin, Thomas Baptiste, Bernard Boston, Vikki Richards, Dave Prowse, Bob Minor, Bloke Modisane, Anthony Sharpe, Robert Lee, Carl Corbin, Eggie Clark, Sydney A. Harris, Donna Young, Lawanda Moore, Wendell Williams, Bruce Richard, Don Dandridge. Color, 85 min. Rated R. Available on VHS from RM Films.

Supervixens (1975), aka *Russ Meyer's Supervixens,* aka *Vixens* (Canada), aka *Les Superbes renardes* (Canada), aka *Supervixens Eruption* (Germany). A September 19 Production presented by RM Films International Inc. Producer, director, screenplay, cinematography, editor: Russ Meyer. Uncredited work on script: Jim Ryan, Roger Ebert, Charles Napier. Associate producers: Wilfred Kues, Charles Napier, Fred Owens, James Parsons. Executive producer: Anthony James Ryan. Camera operator: Douglas Knapp. Assistant cameraman: Tom Neuwirth. Art director: Michael Levesque. Sound/sound editor: Richard Serly Brummer. Production manager: Fred Owens. Grip: Stanley Berkowitz. Assistant to the producer: Les Barnum. Makeup: Barbarello Catton, aka Haji. Music: Bill Loose. Song by Daniel Dean Darst. Cast: Shari Eubanks, Charles Napier, Uschi Digard, Charles Pitts, Henry Rowland, Christy Hartburg, Sharon Kelly, Deborah McGuire, Glenn Dixon, John LaZar, Stu Lancaster, Haji, "Big Jack" Provan, Garth Pillsbury, Ann Marie, Ron Sheridan, John Lawrence, Paul Fox, F. Rufus Owens, John Furlong, Russ Meyer. Color, 105 min. Rated X. Available on DVD/VHS from RM Films.

Up! (1976). A RM Films International, Inc. Production. Producer, director, cinematographer, editor: Russ Meyer. Associate producers: Fred Owens, Uschi Digard, George K. Carll. Screenwriters: B. Callum (aka Russ Meyer), Reinhold Timme (aka Roger Ebert, Kitten's narration only). Original story by Russ Meyer, Jim Ryan, Reinhold Timme. Camera operators: Pat Lennef, E. E. Meyer (aka Russ Meyer), Tom Hammel. Second unit cameraman: Master Sergeant (aka Fred "Fritz" Mandl). Art direction: Michele Levesque. Sound: Dan Holland, Richard Anderson, Fred Owens. Music: Bill Loose, Paul Ruhland. Ichthyologist: Charles E. Sumners. Costumes: Maureen of Hollywood. Cast: Raven De La Croix, Robert McLane, Edward Schaaf, Mary Gavin (aka Candy Samples), Elaine Collins, Su Ling, Janet Wood, Linda Sue Ragsdale, Harry, Monte Bane, Larry Dean, Marianne Marks, Bob Schott, Foxy Lae, Fred Owens, Wilburn Kluck, Ray Reinhardt, Francesca "Kitten" Natividad, Russ Meyer. Color, 80 min. Rated X. Available on DVD/VHS from RM Films.

Beneath the Valley of the Ultravixens (1979), aka *Russ Meyer's Beneath the Valley of the Ultravixens,* aka *Imtienfen tal ser Superhexen* (Germany). A RM Films International Inc. release. Producer, director, cinematography, editor: Russ Meyer. Associate producers: Fred Owens, Richard Serly Brummer, Uschi Digard (uncredited). Screenplay: R. Hyde (aka Roger Ebert), B. Callum (aka Russ Meyer). Original story: Russ Meyer. Art director: Michele Levesque. Sound: Fred Owens. Assistant to the producer: Les Barnum. Crew: Uschi Digard, Don Ouellete, Bruce Pastarnack, Mitch Browne, Frank Scarpitto. Music: William Tasker. Sound editor: Richard Serly Brummer. Cast: Francesca "Kitten" Natividad, Anne Marie, Ken Kerr, June Mack, Pat Wright, Michael Finn (aka Mickey Foxx), Steve Tracy, Sharon Hill, Henry Rowland, Robert E. Pearson, De Forest Covan, Don Scarbrough, Aram Katcher, Uschi Digard, Candy Samples (aka Mary Gavin), Stuart Lancaster, Russ Meyer. Color, 93 min. Rated X. Available on DVD/VHS from RM Films.

Pandora Peaks (2001). Producer, director, cinematography, screenplay, and editor: Russ Meyer. Associate producer and sound recorder: Anthony James Ryan. Cinematography: Joe Longo. Sound editing and final postproduction: Richard Brummer. Music: Ron Di Iulio. Wardrobe and makeup: Haji. Narration: Russ Meyer, Uschi Digard, others. Cast: Pandora Peaks, Tundi, Leosha, Candy Samples, Anthony James Ryan, Charles Sumners, Russ Meyer. Color, 72 min. Home video VHS release only. Incorporates some footage from the abandoned *The Breast of Russ Meyer.*

Laser Discs

All the following were released in the United States in the mid-nineties by Image Entertainment/RM Films.

The Immoral Mr. Teas with *Mondo Topless; Eve and the Handyman, Wild Gals of the Naked West!* with *Common Law Cabin; Lorna* with *Mudhoney; Faster, Pussycat! Kill! Kill!* (with Meyer commentary) with *Motorpsycho!; Cherry, Harry and Raquel* and *Up!; Blacksnake!; Vixen, Supervixens,* and *Beneath the Valley of the Ultravixens* (the last three with Meyer commentaries).

A wide-screen *Beyond the Valley of the Dolls* laser disc was released in the nineties.

In 2003–04 an elaborate "Vixen Box" of eight Meyer DVDs saw release in Japan; the transfers are said to be of better quality, but still not from the negatives. Due to Japanese censorship, pubic hair is reportedly fogged out on these releases. A set of new Meyer DVDs were to be released in the UK by Arrow Films starting in March 2005. Sporting a raft of extras, these look to be the definitive Meyer DVD releases thus far, but while the transfers are supposed to be an improvement over U.S. DVD/VHS releases, information suggests they have not been struck from the original negatives.

Music Videos

"Don't Change That Song." Faster, Pussycat. 1987.

"Soultwister!" Jean Park. Germany. 1991.

Vinyl Soundtracks

Vinyl 33⅓ soundtracks for *Vixen* and *Cherry, Harry and Raquel* were released on Beverly Hills Records.

Soundtracks for *Beyond the Valley of the Dolls* (with Lynn Carey vocals replaced by Ami Rushes; see text) and *The Seven Minutes* were released by 20th Century Fox.

Various promotional-only 45 rpm vinyl radio spots for Meyer's films were recorded and turn up on eBay from time to time.

CD Soundtracks

Russ Meyer's *Mudhoney/Finders Keepers, Lovers Weepers/Motorpsycho*. QDK Media CD 011. Germany (all of these German releases feature elaborate color gatefolds with booklets containing stills). 1995. Also released on vinyl.

Russ Meyer's *Lorna/Vixen/Faster, Pussycat! Kill! Kill!* Qdk Media CD 008. Germany. 1995. Also released on vinyl.

Russ Meyer's *Good Morning . . . and Goodbye!/Cherry, Harry and Raquel/Mondo Topless*. QDK Media CD 014. Germany. 1995. Also released on vinyl.

Russ Meyer's *Up!/Mega-Vixens* (aka *Supervixens*)/*Beneath the Valley of the Ultra Vixens*. QDK Media CD 009. Germany. 1995. Also released on vinyl.

Russ Meyer's *The Immoral Mr. Teas/Eve and the Handyman/Wild Gals of the Naked West!* QDK Media CD 020. Germany. 1995. Also released on vinyl.

Beyond the Valley of the Dolls original soundtrack (for the first time with Lynn Carey's original vocals). UK. 2003. Harkit Records, HRKCD 8032. U.S. release, 2004, Soundtrack Classics.

Vixen, Delta 12922. USA.

Cherry, Harry and Raquel, Delta 12919. USA.

Unfinished Productions

Who Killed Bambi? (1977). Script by Meyer, Roger Ebert, Rene Daalder.

The Breast of Russ Meyer

Melissa Mounds 1990s "documentary" said to be completely finished except for the Melissa Mounds narration.

Mondo Topless, Too 1980s/1990s "documentary" starring Eva "Tundi" Horvath, Tami Roche, Shawn "Baby Doll" Devereaux, and Kristine Mills.

Unproduced Scripts

The Eleven (circa 1971). Script by Manny Diez, Jim Ryan.

Foxy aka *Viva Foxy!* (1972–73). Script by Roger Ebert.

Beyond Beyond (1972)

Up the Valley of the Beyond (1990). Proposed "sequels" (co-written by Roger Ebert) to *Beyond the Valley of the Dolls.* May be two different names for the same script.

Choice Cuts (circa 1971–72). Script by (playwright) Jim Ryan.

The Final Steal (circa 1971). Script by Manny Diez.

Blitzen, Vixen and Harry (1982)

Kill! Kill! Pussycat, Faster! (1990s)

The Jaws of Vixen aka *The Jaws of Lorna*

The Bra of God (1990s). Script by John McCormick.

In 1974, Rene Daalder and the architect Rem Koolhaas wrote a script for RM entitled *Hollywood Tower.*

Documentaries

"Russ Meyer." *Incredibly Strange Picture Show,* season 1, episode 5, 1988. 40 minutes. Hosted by Jonathan Ross.

"Russ Meyer." *E! True Hollywood Story,* 1999. Ethan Prochnik, David Schiff, producers. Ashley Adams, segment producer.

"Big Bosoms and Square Jaws." Canada.

"Russ Meyer, King of Sexploitation." 2004 (UK). Jon-Barrie Waddell, director.

Significant Meyer Appearances

Amazon Women on the Moon. 1987 anthology comedy. John Landis directed the segment during which RM appears briefly.

At Risk: Combat Camera. Robert Kirk, director. Produced by Greystone Communications, Inc. 1991.

Shooting War. Richard Corliss, producer/director. Doug Freeman, co-producer. Steven Spielberg, executive producer. Tom Hanks, host and narrator. 2000.

Playboy's Voluptuous Vixens, Playboy Home Video, PBV 0820, 1997.

Playboy's Voluptuous Vixens II, Playboy Home Video, PBV 0820, 1997.

RM contributed still shots to *The James Dean Story,* a 1957 documentary co-directed by Robert Altman.

For the record: All titles with exclamation marks appear above the way they are shown in the actual title sequence in the film itself (in the case of the long-unseen *Erotica, Europe in the Raw!,* and *Heavenly Bodies,* I went by pressbook material). Curiously, while the title sequences for both *Vixen!* and *Cherry, Harry and Raquel!* sport exclamation points, the ad campaigns don't, and with *Blacksnake* it's the opposite case. In Meyer's filmography for *A Clean Breast,* he lists the following titles with exclamation points, although some of these films carried no such punctuation in either the movie itself or the ad campaigns: *Wild Gals of the Naked West!; Heavenly Bodies!; Motorpsycho!; Faster, Pussycat! Kill! Kill!; Good Morning . . . and Goodbye!; Finders Keepers, Lovers Weepers!; Blacksnake!;* and *Up!* Other than *Faster, Pussycat! Kill! Kill!* and *Up!,* which seems to demand an exclamation mark, I have avoided the exclamation mark brouhaha in the text of the book.

Acknowledgments

First things first: Had it not been for an extremely fortuitous, spur-of-the-moment call to author David K. Frasier a few years back, this book might never have been attempted. Mr. Frasier not only encouraged me to go forward with the project, he opened his archives, shared unpublished interviews, and donated his formidable research expertise as well. I highly recommend all his books. During the recent John Waters picture, *A Dirty Shame,* no less than David Hasselhoff can been seen perusing the pages of Frasier's most recent masterwork, *Suicide in the Entertainment Industry.*

Gordon Lish to my Raymond Carver (apologies to RC), Charlie Beesley once again had a hand in many drafts of the manuscript. Hopefully the final results don't smell too bad, Charlie.

Having David McCormick as a literary agent is like having Cus D'Amato in your corner of the ring. You're ready to start punching, even if it's only on a keyboard. The guy is incredible. Thanks also to Leslie Falk, who expedited every detail.

An ace editor, Carrie Thornton, challenged me to do better at every turn. What a dame. She did a tremendous job on this book. I expect to make a return visit to the Island of Dr. Moreau, Thornton. Thanks also to Doug Pepper, my original editor at Crown and the source of a great deal of enthusiasm. And one must not forget Orly "The Unicorn" Treiber.

Amelia Zalcman entered the picture at the last minute, aiding me in making *Big Bosoms* a much more complete work. Glad we're on the same side of the chessboard, Amelia. Thanks to Mark McCauslin for his eagle-eye diligence.

Thanks to Carol O' Connor for the legal research. Many others offered research assistance, among them Eric Caidin, Mike Trombetta, Mike Mariano, Jeffrey South, Dean Harris, Nathaniel Thompson, David

Kalat, Robert Bentley, Ann Sumners, Mike Carroll, Patrick McGilligan, and Marty *Supervixens* Traynor. Thanks to J. Scott Wynn for the great photograph. For helping with interviews, thanks to Souixzan Perry, Teri Thomerson, and Kristen Fischer. Last-minute legal research: Jeffrey C. Graf and Sarah Heldman. German translations: Bettina Briggs. Always a partner in crime, Johnny Legend has a very funny story concerning himself, Leslie Nielsen, and Russ Meyer. Ask him to tell it. The Great Rudolph Grey did much to assist this project. My eternal gratitude to Leo Trombetta, who not only put me at his house on research trips and bailed me out upon occasion, but provided me with a gangbusters ending as well.

Thanks to John Waters, a swell guy. Dolores Fox did everything she could to assist me in my journey. Roger Ebert was a very good sport. Jim Ryan and Tom McGowan were always ready to help. Both "Colonel" Rob and Chris Schaffner were invaluable resources, and a lot of laughs. Thanks to all the rest of the interviewees who are listed in the Source Notes. As always, a tip of the Jimmy top hat to Lux Interior and Ivy Rorschach.

One cannot write about the women of Russ Meyer without acknowledging the work of author Steve Sullivan. He interviewed many of them in-depth for the first time, creating a body of impeccable research to draw upon. So many writers covered the Meyer beat, and this book has benefited greatly from their legwork: Kenneth Turan, Stephen Zito, Arv Miller, Paul Sherman, Burton H. Wolfe, Dan Scapperotti, Dale Ashmun, Kent Beyda, Tony Crawley, Stan Berkowitz, David Lees, Jonathan Ross, Ethan Prochnik, David Schiff, Ellen Goosenberg, Tony Rayns, Richard Corliss, Harvey Fenton, R. Allen Leider, Roger Turrell, Sergei Hasenecz, Charles Schneider, Kris Gilpin, John Donnelly, Phyliss Braden-Lowe, Nathan Rabin, Gene Ross, Jim Morton, Lewis Black, Kristi Turnquist, Nathaniel Thompson, and hundreds of others I've left out. Special thanks to John McCormick for his two excellent Meyer pieces.

Thanks as well to Brian O'Hara, Eliza Paley, Bruce Kitzmeyer, Neva Friedenn, Craig Leibner, Kim Morgan, Brooke Viviano, Richard Meltzer, Isaako Si'uleo, Poncho Sampedro, Liz Main, Sarah Heldman, Bill Bentley, and Eliza Wimberly, wherever you are. Bulletin to Graeme Bowen: Mr. Depp is awaiting your book, G.B. Special thanks to John McDonough, George Hedges, and the future king of the honky-tonks, John Kopf. Inspiration: the fabulous Demolition Doll Rods—Danny,

Margaret, and Christine, aka Thumper. Too bad Meyer never saw these three in action—he might've stuck 'em in a movie or two.

Hair by Jerry Ripley, Portland Tonsorial Parlor.

A very special thank you to Lucy Fur, Anna Hinterkopf, Yumi Atteberry, Jess Kreutter, Kat Heldman, Jessica Wainman, Mara Stevenson, Sarah Heldman, Jessica Winn, and Andrea Viviano. They know why.

Russ Meyer had Eve. For me it's Natalia Wisdom, and I'll never let her go.

Index

A

Abrams, Gene, 252
Accomando, Mike, 239–240
Adelman, Gary, 341
Aivazian, Arshalouis, 153
Albee, Edward, 278
Ali, Muhammad, 258
Alperstein, Glenn, 377
Anderson, Andy, 182
Andre, Maria, 130, 131
Ansen, David, 9, 307, 319
Antz, Bob, 58, 67
Ashmun, Dale, 58
Ashton, Linda, 241, 245

B

Babb, Kroger, 65, 117
Bacon, James, 302
Bane, Monte, 308
Bardot, Babette, 180, 181, 183–184, 186, 187, 188, 189, 191, 192, 195, 205, 240
Barlow, Ray, 165, 169
Barnum, Les, 302, 320n, 332–333
Barringer, Pat, 181, 183
Beiersdorf, Fred, 22, 139, 140, 147, 151, 247, 309, 329, 341
Bell, Virginia "Ding Dong," 81–82
Berens, Jessica, 311
Berkowitz, Stan, 18, 115, 195, 290n, 293, 297, 298, 305
Berliner, Oliver, 185, 186
Bernard, Ruth "Brandy," 165, 170–171
Bernard, Susan, 165, 170–172, 173
Bethune, Ivy, 149, 329
Beyond the Valley of the Dolls, 8, 21, 176, 234, 236, 247, 278
  abortionist character, 88
  absurd personal touches in, 271
  box-office business, 272

casting of, 261, 268
critical reaction, 267, 272–274
as cult classic, 274
Diez's casting-couch incident, 269–270
editing of, 270
emptiness of, 272
inauthenticity of, 258–259
masquerade orgy scene, 266–267
Meyer's assessment of, 274
Meyer's control of production, 259–260
Meyer's hiring for, 249
music for, 260–261
screenplay for, 254–256, 257–258, 259
shooting of, 262–265, 268–269
X rating, 271–272
Z-Man and Ashley St. Ives characters, 265–266
Bibo, Walter, 97
Binstein, Michael, 232, 234
Bixby, Bill, 264n
Black, Louis, 175, 298, 334
Blackman, Lee, 367
Bloch, Charlie, 82
Blodgett, Michael, 262, 265
Blum, Irving, 76, 92, 98, 104
Bolger, Franklin J., 72, 149, 188, 190–191, 241, 244
Bowden, Charles, 232, 234
Bowen, Henrye, 60
Bowers, James, 226
Bowers, John, 61
Bowman, Brent, 339, 340
Brandt, Bingo, 119–120
Brauner, Artur, 143, 144, 145
Breckenridge, Paul G., 302, 303
Brien, Alan, 4
Briggs, Joe Bob, 175

Bromberg, Craig, 325
Brotman, Oscar, 225
Brown, David, 248, 250, 259, 260, 278,
    279, 281, 282
Brummer, Andre, 154
Brummer, Richard, 7, 14, 23, 46, 113,
    169, 170, 171, 173, 174, 182, 188,
    190, 191, 201–202, 215, 216, 217,
    220–221, 243, 244, 245, 258, 276,
    284, 293, 305, 317, 318, 341, 351,
    361–362, 364, 389–390
  Meyer's relationship with, 154–155
Bryner, Jesse, 370, 371
Bucci, Eleanor, 350–351, 360
Burn, Gordon, 18
Burton, Tim, 337
Busch, Dennis, 165
Butler, Jack A., 227
Butterfield, Ralph, 38, 42, 59
Buxton, Janet (Miss Mattress), 128,
    129, 137, 276

C

Canby, Vincent, 205, 273
Capri, Alaina, 54–55, 185–187, 192,
    196, 198, 200, 202, 255, 394
Carey, Lynn, 260–261, 279
Carey, Philip, 280
Carll, George King, 30, 142, 353,
    354–355, 379, 397
Carradine, John, 280
Carroll, Mike, 397
Cash, Johnny, 278
Cellini, Joe, 261
Chambers, John, 267
Champlin, Charles, 272–273
Chapman, Anne, 203–204
Christiani, Larry, 353–354, 355
Ciral, Karen, 196, 198, 199
Citizens for Decent Literature, 229, 231
Cocks, Jay, 281
Cohen, Mickey, 303
Collins, Joan, 81, 82–83
Cook, Paul, 323
Cooperman, Phil, 364, 377, 397
Corliss, Richard, 13, 158
Coshow, Bill, 74
Costello, George, 28, 30, 31, 114, 143,
    144, 148, 149, 153, 154, 165, 169,
    170, 172, 173, 191–192, 193–194,
    195, 199, 200, 201, 203, 204–205,
    209, 213, 217, 218–220, 224, 364
  break with Meyer, 221–223

Couch, Don, 100, 102
Cowart, Janice, 371, 372, 373, 374, 389,
    396–397
  Dottavio and, 385, 386–387, 388
  involvement in Meyer's life, 364–369,
    375–384
  Meyer's death and funeral, 394, 395,
    396
  personal qualities, 364
Cramps, the, 5, 177–178, 339
Crawley, Tony, 268
Cresse, Bob, 117, 121

D

Daalder, Rene, 321–322, 324–325, 326
D'Arcy, Alex, 145
Dean, James, 91
DeCarlo, Yvonne, 280
DeCenzie, Pete, 64–66, 67, 68–69, 88,
    122, 123, 124
  break with Meyer, 125–126
  The Immoral Mr. Teas, 90–91, 93, 94,
    99, 100, 104, 105–6, 107
DeCenzie, Yvonne, 65, 68, 69, 126
De La Croix, Raven, 9, 10, 31,
    304–305, 307, 308–310, 363,
    368–369, 382, 391n, 393, 394,
    395
DeMoss, George, 313, 320–321
Denielle, Dawn, 99
De Vere, Ed, 68
Devereaux, Shawn "Baby Doll," 161,
    280
Dewey, Thomas, 73n
Didion, Joan, 257
Diez, Manny, 21, 254, 263, 265, 268,
    269–270, 275, 278, 279, 280n, 283,
    361
Digard, Uschi, 239–240, 251, 252, 276,
    280, 308, 309, 311, 316, 331, 389
  break with Meyer, 320n
  Cherry, Harry and Raquel, 246, 247
  Supervixens, 292, 297
Disney, Walt, 99
Divine, 177, 341–342
Donnelly, John, 202
Dottavio, Julio, 369, 381, 384–387, 388,
    389, 394, 395, 396, 397
Downard, Harry, 36, 37, 44
Downe, Taime, 340
Duran, Jean, 113
Durgnat, Raymond, 146
Duvall, Denise, 181, 183

E

Ebert, Roger, 7, 8, 12, 16, 53, 109,
115–116, 134, 138, 147, 162, 182,
203, 211 n, 221, 225, 242, 248n,
268, 285, 300, 303, 313, 314, 332,
335, 337, 343, 344, 347, 352, 357,
360, 361, 363, 366–367, 388, 393,
395
  background of, 251
  Beneath the Valley of the Ultra-Vixens,
  316, 317
  Beyond the Valley of the Dolls,
  254–255, 256, 257, 260, 261, 262,
  271, 273–274
  Film Comment article on Meyer, 186,
  251
  The Immoral Mr. Teas, 251
  on meaning of Meyer's films, 18
  on Meyer's historical significance, 6
  Meyer's relationship with, 250–254
  musical preferences, 258
  sexual proclivities, 252–253
  Supervixens, 293, 295
  Up!, 310
  Who Killed Bambi? project, 322,
  323–324, 325, 326
Eden, Barbara, 83
Ekberg, Anita, 83, 86
Ely, Larissa, 242
Emerson, Ken, 301
Erickson, Veronica, 127, 146, 261
Escalera, Rudy, 118
Eubank, Shari, 152, 294–295, 298,
299, 300, 310, 313
Evans, Dixie, 33–34, 57, 72, 73n
Ewing, Dave, 339, 340
Exploitation picture business, 94–97

F

Faithfull, Marianne, 324
Fassbinder, R. W., 143
Faster, Pussycat (band), 339, 340
Faster, Pussycat! Kill! Kill!, 12, 16, 134,
154, 162, 181 n, 206, 323, 339, 343,
388, 392
  box-office failure, 176
  casting of, 165–168
  critical reaction, 175–176
  editing of, 173–174
  feminist perspective on, 10–11
  music for, 174–175
  opening minutes, 2–3
  popularity over time, 177–179

rerelease in 1995, 358–359
shooting of, 168–173
storyline of, 163–164
title for, 174
Varla character, 158, 163, 176
Waters's championing of, 175–177
Fenton, Harvey, 17
Fiedler, Leslie, 106, 273
Fields, W. C., 115
Filipovitch, Darlene, 30
Filipovitch, Lou, 14–15, 25, 26–27, 30,
33
Filipovitch, Martha, 26
Filipovitch, Pete, 25, 26, 27, 31, 32–33,
34
Firestone, Paulette, 84–85
Fishbein, Paul, 335, 344, 347
Fishburn, Paul and Donna, 349–350
Fleischer, Richard, 278
Flippen, J. C., 280
Floodbank, Chester, 115
Flynt, Jimmy, 233n
Flynt, Larry, 229, 231, 232–233
Ford, Luke, 303
Fore, Jet, 256, 269, 270
Fox, Dolores, 22–23, 29, 60, 77, 128,
141, 142, 351
Fox, Fred "F.F.," 42
Fox, Paul, 36, 37, 51, 92
Foxx, Mickey, 148, 165, 172
France, Mikki, 99
Frasier, David K., 7, 15, 17, 24, 31, 52,
53, 97, 108, 109, 114, 122, 129, 134,
136, 146, 175, 197, 198, 262, 270,
277, 344, 350, 351, 352, 353, 354,
355, 355n, 362n, 370n, 374–375,
379, 386, 388, 389, 393, 397, 398
Friedan, Betty, 225
Friedlander, Marvin, 120, 248n
Friedman, Bruce Jay, 62
Friedman, Carol, 120n
Friedman, David F., 17, 82, 95, 120n,
121–122, 126, 138, 140–141, 146,
148, 233, 276, 336, 345, 367, 368
  sexploitation career, 116–119
Fromer, Jill, 144
Furlong, John, 31, 124–125, 148, 149,
150, 154, 183n, 187, 188, 190, 191,
192, 193, 194, 216, 329

G

Gabriel, Veronique, 126, 181–182
Gaffney, Glenn, 227

Gall, Pete, 227, 230, 232
Gardner, Ava, 82
Gaspar, James, 397
Gavin, Erica, 7, 28, 32, 38, 152, 161,
    162, 251, 253, 274, 306, 350, 368,
    383, 384, 387, 394
  background of, 213–214
  Beyond the Valley of the Dolls, 261,
    263–264, 265, 269
  Costello and, 221–223
  Meyer's relationship with, 210–211,
    216, 219, 223, 235–236
  physical appearance, 207–208
  post-*Vixen* life, 234–238
  Vixen, 12, 207–209, 213, 214–215,
    216, 217–220, 224, 225
Gebhard, Paul, 79
Gertz, Elmer, 230, 231–232
Glendale, Miss, 123–124
Goebbels, Joseph, 50
Goldstein, Al, 281
Goosenberg, Ellen, 206
Grant, Ray, 74, 99
Grass, Clancy, III, 132
Gray, Darlene, 182
Gray, Mora, 280
Green, Doyle, 5
Greenspun, Roger, 247–248
Gregory, James, 227
Grey, Rudolph, 139
Grier, Pam, 261
Griffith, James, 130, 131

H
Hagara, Andrew, 188, 190
Hagen, Morgan "Tex," 355
Haimson, Gil, 167–168, 170, 174
Haji, 10, 83, 161–162, 166n, 209, 214,
    222–223, 261, 264, 270, 294, 299,
    312–313, 314, 341, 360, 366, 368,
    369, 376, 378–379, 380, 381, 382,
    383, 391n, 394, 395
  background and personal qualities,
    152–153
  Faster, Pussycat! Kill! Kill!, 166, 167,
    170, 171, 178
  Good Morning ... and Goodbye!, 197,
    198, 199–200
  Motorpsycho, 153, 155–156
Hall, Buck, 275
Hall, Ed, 286
Hannah, Sam, 149
Harding, Warren, 22, 43, 45–46, 397

Harmetz, Aljean, 248
Harry (wolf-dog), 242, 344–345,
    357–358
Hartburg, Christy, 291, 299
Hatch, Kristen, 7
Hathaway, Henry, 115
Haywood, Howard, 2, 25, 56, 60
Haywood, Lucinda, 25, 35, 56, 60, 333,
    358, 386, 395
  death and funeral, 369–370
  mental illness, 2, 27–30
Haywood, Lydia Meyer, 34, 56, 58, 60,
    70, 77, 137, 277, 395
  bust size, 21n
  final years, 331–332
  Lucinda Haywood and, 28
  malice of, 26–27
  marriage to Haywood, 25
  marriage to William Meyer, 24
  mental illness, 21–22, 36
  Meyer's childhood, 25, 26, 32
  Meyer's relationship with, 2, 22–23,
    30–32, 332
  Meyer's visits to grave of, 1
  physical appearance, 23
  serial matrimony, 23–24
  sexuality of, 27, 28
Hedrick, Betsy, 251
Heffner, Richard, 328n
Hefner, Hugh, 3, 7, 78–79, 84, 109,
    261, 275, 391
  Meyer's relationship with, 80
Hemingway, Ernest, 48
Hempel, Anouska, 283, 284
Hitchcock, Alfred, 300
Hitler, Adolf, 50
Hively, Kay, 52
Holm, D. K., 14
Hopkins, Miriam, 145
Hopper, Hal, 137, 149, 150
Horten, Rena, 146, 150, 153, 280n
  Meyer's relationship with, 145,
    151–152
Hower, Jane, 345–348, 351
Hunt, Lillian, 63, 64
Hurrell, George, 86
Huse, Emery, 36, 58

I
Immoral Mr. Teas, The, 4, 16, 83
  box-office business, 105, 106
  casting of, 94, 99–100
  censorship problems, 105–106, 120

cost of, 104
critical reaction, 105, 106
cultural context, 94–97
Ebert's assessment of, 251
editing of, 102–103
historical significance, 108–109
music for, 103–104
narration for, 104
origins of, 88–89, 90–91, 93, 97–98
shooting of, 98–99, 100–102, 111
storyline of, 98
Teas's payment, 107–108
title for, 94
Interior, Lux, 5, 17

J
Jackson, Jean-Pierre, 25, 54, 114, 115,
    306, 367, 383, 389
Jarrard, Rick, 175
Jeremy, Ron, 303
Johnson, Don, 196
Jones, Steve, 323, 325, 326
Jong, Erica, 391

K
Kahrl, William, 343, 355n
Kantor, Igo, 102, 203, 260
Kauffman, Stanley, 272
Keating, Charles, Jr., 273, 279, 390
    anti-pornography crusade, 228–229
    downfall of, 233–234
    Flynt and, 232–233
    Vixen censorship case, 227–228,
    229–232
Kehr, Dave, 301, 318, 319
Keisha, 339
Kelly, Grace, 326
Kerr, Ken, 316, 320n
Kilpin, Kris, 202
Kilty, Jerome, 278, 281
Klaw, Irving, 69
Klawans, Stuart, 259
Knight, Arthur, 301
Knight, Sherri, 124
Koenekamp, Fred, 260
Kramer, Stanley, 53, 195
Kubrick, Stanley, 115
Kues, Wilfred "Bud," 131, 134, 208

L
Lakso, Edward J., 103–104
Lamar, Trena (Donna X), 124, 125, 181
Lamb, John, 212

La Mont, Lilly, 68, 72, 73, 73n, 318
Lancaster, Stuart, 148–149, 150, 165,
    169, 196, 198, 200, 202, 280, 292,
    316–317, 337
Lansing, Joi, 83
La Touche, Gigi, 181, 183
Law, John, 226
La Zar, John, 262, 263n, 264–267
Leaf, Earl, 99
Lean, David, 115
Lee, Ruta, 83
Leighton, Ava, 120
Leis, Simon, Jr., 230–231, 232, 233
Leis, Simon, Sr., 230, 231
Lewis, Herschell Gordon, 117, 138
Lewis, Jon, 327
Lieberson, Sandy, 325
Linee, Sin, 181
Link, John, 102
Livingston, Princess, 124–125,
    149–150, 261
Lloyd, Arthur, 43
Lloyd, Harold, 159–160
Lockwood, Paul, 203, 204
Lollobrigida, Gina, 83
Lommel, Ulli, 143–145
London, John, 275
Longo, Joe, 38, 41
Loose, Bill, 260
Louie, Bebe, 161, 264
Louise, Tina, 82
Lovelady, Steven M., 248
Lucas, Jack, 187n, 189, 201, 202

M
Mack, June, 253, 316, 317
Mahar, Ted, 312
Maitland, Lorna, 130–132, 133–134,
    136, 149, 150–151
Mandell, Sheldon, 226
Mandl, Fred "Fritz," 44
Mansfield, Irving, 255n
Mansfield, Jayne, 83
Margold, Bill, 345
Marie, Ann, 316, 318
Marli, Ysobel, 72
Marshall, Thurgood, 232n
Marx Brothers, 115
Maunder, Wayne, 280
Mayo, Jacqueline, 220, 335
McBroom, Marcia, 255, 261, 263
McCalla, Irish, 75
McCarthy, Todd, 326

McCormick, John, 1, 113, 114, 151–152, 344, 345, 352, 359–360

McDonald, Jeff, 5

McGovern, Kevin, 34

McGowan, Tom, 27–28, 29, 37, 43, 241

McGuire, Deborah, 292

McLaren, Malcolm, 321–322, 323, 324, 325

McLeod, Duncan, 261

McLeod, Gordon, 203

Medowar, Wady, 201

Meisel, Myron, 175, 273, 319

Metzger, Radley, 120–121

Meyer, Betty Valdovinos (first wife), 23, 28, 59–60, 69–70, 93

Meyer, Eve Turner (second wife), 62, 82n, 88, 90, 92, 100, 103, 108, 111, 120, 126, 127, 130, 132, 145, 156, 165, 181n, 221, 225, 280n
  background of, 76
  business acumen, 75, 107
  children, desire for, 128
  death of, 147
  divorce from Meyer, 141–143, 146, 147
  drinking problem, 141–142
  Eve and the Handyman, 111, 122–123
  first encounter with Meyer, 74–75
  marriage to Meyer, 76–77
  Meyer's love for, 87, 147
  Meyer's photographic career, involvement in, 80–81
  Meyer's sexual relationship with, 76, 77n
  modeling career, 75–76, 77–78, 79–80
  physical appearance, 74
  women, attraction to, 142

Meyer, Lydia Howe (mother). *See* Haywood, Lydia Meyer

Meyer, Russ
  American culture, influence on, 3, 6
  assault incident in 1999, 349–350, 371–374
  auto accident, 47
  birth of, 23
  bowel function, obsession with, 32, 340
  as caricature of himself in 1980s, 334, 341
  cartooning by, 33
  childhood years, 22, 23, 24–26, 28, 32, 38

child of, 129
children, attitude toward, 128
A Clean Breast (autobiography), 16, 24, 25, 45, 49, 54, 57, 58, 60, 73, 78, 142, 147, 234, 235, 250, 282, 286, 314, 336; description of, 390; writing of, 343–344, 353–355, 374–375
critics, relations with, 205–206
death and funeral, 393–396
dementia, fear of developing, 21–23, 30
dementia of, 30, 361–364, 368, 373–378, 380, 381, 382–384, 393, 399–400
depressions of, 327
"Dirty Dozen" incident, 49–50
drinking problem, 360–361, 369, 372
end days, 393
generosity of, 26, 359–360
gun ownership, 371
hard-core pornography, distaste for, 12, 211
hipness, lack of, 257–258
Hitler-Goebbels incident, 50
house in Coldwater Canyon, 275–276
house on Arrowhead Drive, 315, 334–335
late-life changes under Cowart's influence, 364–369, 375–384
libel case, 326
loneliness of, 332
male friendships, 114–115
male role model in childhood, lack of, 2
mammary obsession, 6–7, 33, 34, 334, 338, 400
marriages. *See* Meyer, Betty Valdovinos; Meyer, Eve Turner; Williams, Edy
McDonough's attraction to, 19–20
military buddies, post-war contacts with, 51–52, 357
military career, 13, 35–38, 39–51, 53–54
musical preferences, 258
paranoia of, 22
physical appearance, 92
politics of, 52–53
posterity, concern about, 16
religious beliefs, 358
self-mythologizing by, 73

self-revelation, avoidance of, 16–17, 22

sentimentalism of, 54–55, 352

sex life, 32–34, 48–49, 71, 72, 110, 128, 137, 145, 148n, 180, 195, 201, 208, 240, 276, 312, 314, 315, 320, 338, 346, 347

sexuality of, 306–307, 309–310

stinginess of, 8, 104n

Thissen's biography of, 343

tombstone preference, 390, 396

unusualness of, 14–15

video appearances, 362–363

will left by, 396–398

women, attitude toward, 11, 28, 31, 141, 146–147, 263, 307

women's attitude toward, 10

"working class American" persona, 12–13

See also Meyer, Russ, filmmaking career of; Meyer, Russ, photographic career of; specific persons

Meyer, Russ, filmmaking career of
accolades in 1980s, 337

appeal of Meyer's sexual message, 110–111

auteur status, 8

Beneath the Valley of the Ultra-Vixens, 73, 253, 295, 315–321, 327, 329

Blacksnake, 283–285, 287

blinking eyes, editing of, 247

Blitzen, Vixen and Harry project, 242

breaks with long-time collaborators, 125–126, 201–203, 221–223, 320n

The Breast of Russ Meyer project, 337–338, 352

car imagery in films, 197–198

cast members, treatment of, 132–133, 191–192

censorship problems, 105–106, 120, 140–141, 225–228, 229–232

Cherry, Harry and Raquel, 43, 104, 239, 240–248, 260

Choice Cuts project, 281

Common Law Cabin, 162, 180, 186–195, 205, 206

coverage, approach to, 43

criticism, reaction to, 106–107, 205–206

decision on, 51

The Desperate Women, 87–88

DVD versions of films, 388

The Eleven project, 283

energy of untamed youth, 5–6

Erotica, 122, 123–124

Europe in the Raw!, 122, 126–127, 146, 181, 389

Eve and the Handyman, 111, 113, 122–123

Eve Productions, 74, 181n, 221

Everything in the Garden project, 278

Fanny Hill, 143–146, 151

feminist perspective on, 10–11

The Final Steal project, 278

Finders Keepers, Lovers Weepers, 203–206

"floor's-eye-view of sexual congress" image, 224

The French Peep Show, 67n, 68, 69, 90

Good Morning ... and Goodbye!, 104, 135n, 162, 186, 196–202, 203

Heavenly Bodies, 54, 122, 127, 129, 130

historical significance, 6, 8–9, 108–109, 391–392

humor in films, 7

industrial films, 58–59

influences on, 33, 115–116, 136

limitation as filmmaker, 319

Lorna, 6, 43n, 130–132, 133, 134–137, 138, 139–140, 141, 145, 229

loss of interest in filmmaking, 336

male characters, 114, 137–138

"meaning of films" issue, 17–18

Meyer's on-set sexual activity, 195

Meyer's relationship with mother and, 31–32

military experience's impact on commercial films, 53–54

military filmmaking, 35–37, 38, 39–47

Mondo Topless, 6, 126, 181–184

montage style, 174

Motorpsycho, 30–31, 153–156

Mudhoney, 6, 124–125, 137, 140n, 146, 148, 149–150, 151, 155, 205, 206

musicality of films, 5

music videos, 339–341

Nazi characters, source of, 25

overview of, 4

PAD-RAM Enterprises, 93

Pandora Peaks, 113, 116, 352n, 356, 361, 362, 389–390

post-war disappointments, 56

pregnant actresses, use of, 83

Meyer, Russ, filmmaking career
of (cont.)
recognition as filmmaker, desire for,
282
retrospective showings, 277, 278
The Seven Minutes, 202, 278–281
sexual combat in films, 12, 14
six periods of, 116
status of Meyer catalogue today,
387–389
Storm film, 67–68
tastelessness of films, 4
technological innovations, 99
teenage filmmaking, 34–35
This Is My Body, 83
three-picture deal with 20th Century
Fox, 277–278
training in filmmaking, 36–37, 43,
44, 58–59
universe depicted in films, 6–7, 14
unpretentious approach, 8
Up!, 110n, 295n, 299, 305–310, 315
video versions of films, 336–337, 345
violence in films, 307
Viva Foxy project, 285, 286
Waters's assessment of, 184–185
Who Killed Bambi? project, 321–326
Wild Gals of the Naked West, 124,
125–126
women's portrayal, 9–10, 11–12, 198n
X ratings problem, 224, 271–272,
327–329
*See also Beyond the Valley of the Dolls;
Faster, Pussycat! Kill! Kill!; Immoral
Mr. Teas, The; Supervixens; Vixen*
Meyer, Russ, photographic career of,
19–20, 36
bosoms, focus on, 81
"female explosion" pictures, 81–82
first session with undressed woman,
57–58
freelance decision, 80–81
genius for capturing female form, 66
The Glamour Camera of Russ Meyer,
77–78
glamour photography, 61, 62
Eve Meyer photos, 77–78, 79–80
mistreatment of models, 78
movie star photos, 82–83, 91
photo essays, 84–85
Playboy centerfolds, 79–80
self-portraits, 73
shooting techniques, 85–87

Storm photos, 65–66
TV stills, 91
Webber photos, 83
Wilkinson photos, 84–85, 86
Meyer, William Arthur (father), 2,
24–25
Mikels, Ted V., 157, 160
Miller, Arv, 17, 61–62, 67n, 212n
Milo, John, 244
Mishkin, William, 120
Miss St. Louis, 72
Mondo films, 126
Monroe, Marilyn, 79
Monsour, Samantha, 304
Moore, Cleo, 83
Moore, Lt. Gene, 45, 46, 47, 48, 49
Moran, John E. "Jack," 116
break with Meyer, 203
Common Law Cabin, 186–187
Faster, Pussycat! Kill! Kill!, 163, 175
personal qualities, 162–163
Wild Gals of the Naked West, 124, 125
Morton, Jim, 167
Mosser, Adrian, 99
Mounds, Melissa, 340, 356, 390, 396
assault on Meyer, 349–350, 371–374
background of, 350–351
Meyer's relationship with, 351–352,
360–361, 369–371
MPAA ratings system, 224, 271,
327–329
Musto, Michael, 267
Myers, Cynthia, 255, 259, 261, 264,
266, 269
Myers, Mike, 274

N

Napier, Charles, 10, 12, 15, 23, 30, 54,
112, 153, 154, 261, 262, 265, 267n,
280, 282, 301n, 317, 331–332, 344,
351, 357–358, 363
Cherry, Harry and Raquel, 241–245
Meyer's relationship with, 242, 290n
Supervixens, 289–290, 293–294, 295,
296, 299, 300–301
Napier, Dee, 301n
Nathanson, E. M. "Mick," 49–50, 79,
92, 98, 100, 101, 102, 147
Natividad, Kitten, 25, 29–30, 32, 112,
161, 295, 326, 327, 332, 338, 339,
341, 342, 352n, 358, 363, 364, 368,
369, 381, 382, 383, 387n, 391n, 392,
394

Beneath the Valley of the Ultra-Vixens,
   316, 317, 318, 319–321, 329
breast augmentation, 314–315
care for dementia-afflicted Meyer, 376
Meyer's relationship with, 312–315,
   319–321, 329–331, 365–366
personal qualities, 311–313
Up!, 310, 315
Newhouse, Bill, 397
Newman, Lionel, 260, 279
Nudist films, 90–91, 97

O

O'Donnell, Michael Donovan, 216
Oliver, Steve, 154
Ornitz, Don, 37–38, 61
Owens, Fred, 37, 173, 201–202, 251,
   325, 335, 397

P

Page, Betty, 69, 75
Page, Harrison, 216, 218, 219, 225, 251,
   261
Paglia, Camille, 10
Paris, Darla, 181
Park, Jean, 340
Parker, Ken, 37, 92, 100–101, 102
Parker, Paula, 8, 22, 30, 100, 345, 357,
   364–365, 366, 367, 368, 373–374,
   376, 382, 384, 397
Parkins, Barbara, 255
Pasternack, Bruce, 315*n*
Patrick, Robert, 79
Patton, Gen. George S., 42, 50
Paul, Arthur, 80
Peaks, Pandora, 355–356, 362–363,
   389, 390
Peche, Ollie, 168
Peckinpah, Sam, 115
Pergament, Robert, 247
Peters, Ann, 99, 101
Philips, Stu, 259, 260, 261, 262, 276
Pillsbury, Garth, 216, 218, 220, 261, 335
Pitt, Charles, 293, 296–297
Prelutsky, Burt, 267
Preminger, Otto, 132–133
Presley, Elvis, 161, 261*n*
Prowse, David, 115, 283, 284–285, 325

R

Rayns, Tony, 318
Read, Dolly, 255, 259, 261, 261*n*,
   262–263, 265, 271*n*

Rein, Adele, 187, 191
Rich, B. Ruby, 10
Richards, Vikki, 284
Ritt, Martin, 115
Roberts, Michelle, 99
Roby, Lavelle, 203, 261
Rocco, Alex, 155–156
Rocco, Ben, 151
Roche, Tami, 352*n*
Roman, Leticia, 144
Rooney, Pete, 161, 214
Ross, Gene, 134
Ross, Jonathan, 352*n*
Rotsler, William, 138
Rotten, Johnny, 323–324, 325
"Roughie" sex films, 138–139
Rowland, Henry, 261, 280, 290,
   307–308, 357
Royko, Mike, 273
Rudelson, Robert, 212
Rushes, Ami, 261
Ruttenberg, Joseph, 37
Ryan, Jacqueline, 114
Ryan, Jim, 23, 26, 28, 29, 31, 37, 53,
   58, 60, 69, 122, 127, 142, 145,
   151, 204*n*, 211, 212, 222, 241,
   243, 276–277, 281–282, 283, 285,
   286, 287, 293, 296, 299, 302, 306,
   325, 326, 329, 331, 341, 352, 364,
   367, 368, 374, 377, 378, 379,
   383–384, 389, 393, 395, 396,
   397–398
Meyer's relationship with, 113–115
personal qualities, 112–113

S

Sabrina, 83
St. Cyr, Lili, 63–64, 69, 83
St. John, Jill, 83
St. Pierre, William, 103–104
Sanders, Doris, 99
Sandman, Henry, 229, 230
Santos, Bert, 244, 261
Sarris, Andrew, 301
Satana, Tura, 5, 10, 11, 22, 23, 26, 64,
   65, 152, 166*n*, 192, 214, 323, 340,
   381, 392–393, 394
background of, 158–162
Faster, Pussycat! Kill! Kill!, 12, 158,
   165, 166–168, 169, 170–173,
   178–179
Meyer's relationship with, 167–168,
   178–179

Satana, Tura (*cont.*)
  personal qualities, 157–158
  snake incident, 57*n*
Sawtell, Paul, 174
Scapperotti, Dan, 240
Schaaf, Ed, 307
Schaefer, Eric, 108
Schaffner, Rob, 129, 237, 338, 364,
  367–368, 373, 381, 388, 394
Schelling, Charles G. "Chuck," 59, 68,
  173, 174
Schenk, Walter, 173
Schickel, Richard, 277
Schmidtmer, Christiane, 142, 145
Sex Pistols, 321–326
Sexploitation films, 97, 116–121
Shefter, Bert, 174
Sherman, Paul, 337
Siegel, Don, 115
Simon, John, 12–13, 272, 273
Sinclair, Jan, 204
Siskel, Gene, 225, 273, 274, 318
Slater, Electus and Pete, 226
Smith, Paul Morton, 99
Snider, Burr, 108
Sonney, Dan, 117, 118, 336
Spain, Fay, 83
Spector, Phil, 258
Sprague, Bill, 155
Starling, Carlos, 226
Stevens, George, 91
Storm, Tempest (Blanche Banks),
  62–64, 391, 394
  Meyer's films and photos featuring,
    65–66, 67–68
  Meyer's relationship with, 69,
    70–71
Stringer, Julian, 168, 175
Sullivan, Margaret, 33–34
Sullivan, Steve, 214
Sumners, Charlie "Slick," 23, 29, 35,
  38, 39, 40, 42, 44, 45–47, 48, 49,
  50, 51, 54, 85, 128, 129, 147, 241,
  306, 313, 357, 358, 360, 361, 364,
  379–380, 386, 389, 397
Sumners, Floyce, 45, 75, 128, 147, 313,
  379, 380, 382, 386, 394
Supervixens, 240, 286, 307
  bathtub murder scene, 298–299,
    300, 301
  box-office business, 299–300
  critical reaction, 301
  Eubank's involvement, 294–295

  Harry Sledge character, 289,
    297–299
  hostile energy of, 292–293
  location hunting for, 289–290
  Meyer's idea for, 289
  Pitt's involvement, 296–297
  shooting of, 293–294
  storyline of, 290–292
  as technical tour de force, 292
Susann, Jacqueline, 249, 255–256
Swofford, Ken, 187, 188, 189, 190, 191,
  192–196, 205

T

Talese, Gay, 79, 83
Tarantino, Quentin, 6, 392
Tati, Jacques, 98
Taylor, Elizabeth, 82
Teas, William Ellis "Bill," 38, 72, 357,
  368
  The Immoral Mr. Teas, 94, 100,
    101–102, 107–108
  Meyer's relationship with, 108
  personal qualities, 92–93
Temple, Julien, 325, 326
Thissen, Rolf, 16, 23, 129, 343
Thomas, Kevin, 273, 275, 281, 301, 312
Thomas, Mike, 358–359
Thompson, Nathaniel, 54, 134
Thomson, David, 20
Thurber, James, 98
Thyssen, Greta, 83
Timony, Megan, 198
Tomko, Bill, 52, 174
Trinka, Paul, 165
Tundi, 338, 389
Turan, Kenneth, 94, 225, 233
Turnquist, Kristi, 252
20th Century Fox, 210, 248, 255*n*,
  277–278, 281, 325–326

V

Valenti, Jack, 224, 327, 328*n*
Van Doren, Mamie, 83
Van Schmus, Al, 271*n*
Vicious, Sid, 324, 325
Vickers, Yvette, 80, 83
Vixen, 12, 251–252
  box-office business, 210, 224–225
  brother-sister shower scene, 29
  casting of, 213, 216
  censorship problems, 225–228,
    229–232

critical reaction, 225
editing of, 220–221
fish scene, 217
"floor's-eye-view of sexual congress"
  image, 224
girl-on-girl scene, 208–209, 224
origins of, 211–212
shooting of, 208–209, 214–215,
  216–220
storyline of, 215–216
Vixen character, 207, 210
X rating, 224

W

Walker, Gene K., 58, 67, 80, 93
Wallace, Irving, 278, 279, 281
Wallace, Mike, 206
Wallace, Vincene, 208, 216, 224
Wall Street Journal, 248
Warbeck, David, 284
Waters, John, 6, 156, 165, 257–258,
  390
  on Faster, Pussycat! Kill! Kill!, 175–177
  Gavin and, 235
  on Meyer's film career, 184–185
  Meyer's relationship with, 177,
    341–343
  on Natividad, 312
  on Up!, 306
  on women in Meyer's films, 198n
Wayne, Carol, 166n
Weapons, Letha, 356–357, 390
Webber, Diane, 75, 79–80, 83
Weintraub, Murray, 166
Welles, Orson, 315n
Wesley, Marilyn, 99, 102, 111
West, Evelyn "Treasure Chest," 57
West, Mae, 115
Wilde, Oscar, 150

Wilkinson, June, 19, 75, 83, 84–85, 86,
  87, 100, 394
Williams, Edy, 118, 273, 276, 278,
  285–286, 391
  background and personal qualities,
    267–268
  Beyond the Valley of the Dolls, 259,
    265–266, 268–269
  divorce from Meyer, 286, 302–303
  first encounters with Meyer,
    268–269
  marriage to Meyer, 274–277
  Meyer's anger at, 290
  post-Meyer life, 303
  The Seven Minutes, 280
  Supervixens, 290, 293, 295, 296, 299
Williams, Julie, 124
Williams, Lori, 165, 166, 169, 171, 172,
  178, 380, 381
Williams, Robin, 337
Witney, William, 54
Wohlman, Harry, 293
Wolcuff, Nick, 205
Wolfe, Burton H., 211n
Wood, Ed, Jr., 89, 118
Wright, Patrick, 196–197, 198, 316

Y

Young, Diane, 181
Young, Peter, 160, 161

Z

Zanuck, Darryl F., 248n, 281
Zanuck, Richard, 248, 249, 250, 259,
  268, 271, 272, 273, 277–278, 281,
  282
Zito, Stephen F., 233
Ziton, Michael, 363, 368, 369
Zugsmith, Albert, 143–144, 145